# A History of Algeria

Drawing on substantial new scholarship and over a decade of research, this book explores the dramatic modern history of Africa's largest country. James McDougall places Algerian society at the centre of the story, tracing the continuities and the resilience of Algeria's people and their cultures through the changes and crises that have marked the country, from the arrival of the Ottomans in the sixteenth century to the aftermath of the 2011 Arab Uprisings.

James McDougall is an Associate Professor of Modern History at Trinity College, Oxford. He previously taught at Princeton and SOAS. He has been a member of the editorial advisory boards of the *Journal of African History* and the *International Journal of Middle East Studies*. His publications include *History and the Culture of Nationalism in Algeria* (Cambridge, 2006), *Saharan Frontiers: Space and Mobility in Northwest Africa*, ed. with Judith Scheele (2012), and *Global and Local in Algeria and Morocco: The World, the State and the Village*, ed. with Robert P. Parks (2015).

# A History of Algeria

James McDougall

*University of Oxford*

 CAMBRIDGE
UNIVERSITY PRESS

# CAMBRIDGE
## UNIVERSITY PRESS

University Printing House, Cambridge CB2 8BS, United Kingdom

One Liberty Plaza, 20th Floor, New York, NY 10006, USA

477 Williamstown Road, Port Melbourne, VIC 3207, Australia

314-321, 3rd Floor, Plot 3, Splendor Forum, Jasola District Centre, New Delhi-110025, India

79 Anson Road, #06-04/06, Singapore 079906

Cambridge University Press is part of the University of Cambridge.

It furthers the University's mission by disseminating knowledge in the pursuit of education, learning and research at the highest international levels of excellence.

www.cambridge.org
Information on this title: www.cambridge.org/9780521617307
DOI: 10.1017/9781139029230

First published 2017

*A catalogue record for this publication is available from the British Library*

ISBN 978-0-521-85164-0 Hardback
ISBN 978-0-521-61730-7 Paperback

*For my friends who let me discover their country:*
*Tewfiq and Huda, and their sons, in Oran*
*Mohand Akli and Nadia, and their daughter, in Tizi Ouzou*
*Jean-Paul and Marie-France, in Algiers, and their family*
*Medjid, Zeyneb and Meriem, in Constantine*
*Omar and Rahmouna, and their family, in Paris*
*and for*
*Fanny Colonna*
*qui dort fi bledha.*
*kulluhum jaza'iriyyin*

*Imezwura iban-asen*
*Ineggura iban-asen*
*Ahlil ay ilemmasen*

*(For the people of the past the way was clear*
*For those of tomorrow it will be so again*
*Have compassion for those of the times in between.)*

Saying of shaykh Mohand Ou Lhocine (d. 1901)

# Contents

# Figures

# Maps

# Acknowledgements

Earlier versions of some of the material in Chapter 7 and the Afterword appear in 'After the war: Algeria's transition to uncertainty', *Middle East Report* 245 (Winter 2007), reprinted by permission of the Middle East Research and Information Project, Washington DC, and in 'In the shadow of revolution', in Patrick Crowley (ed.), *Algeria: Nation, Culture and Transnationalism, 1988–2015*, reprinted by permission of Liverpool University Press.

# Note on Transliteration

All translations from French, Arabic or other languages, unless otherwise credited, are my own. Transliterating from Maghribi Arabic poses particular problems; for simplicity and to aid the reader in finding names elsewhere in the (especially French-language) literature, in this book I have adopted a very simplified transliteration without macrons on long vowels or diacritics on emphatic consonants (except in notes, when citing Arabic sources, where the *International Journal of Middle East Studies* system is used). *Hamza* is marked with a closing apostrophe (') only when it occurs mid-word (*qa'id*); *'ayn* is marked with an opening apostrophe (') when word-initial or mid-word (*'ulama, shari'a*). For vernacular terms from Arabic or Tamazight, wherever possible I reproduce Algerian pronunciation as reasonably as I can rather than trying to give accurate 'standard' or classical transliteration. Algerian proper names are given in as precise an Arabic or Berber transliteration as is possible from the sources for the period before 1900, after which the French *état civil* became more widely established. In later chapters, I give proper names in the form most commonly encountered elsewhere in the literature, which usually follow conventional Gallicised transliterations: thus, I refer to the saint Sidi Shu'ayb Abu Madyan, not Sidi Choaïb Boumediene; the amir Abd al-Qadir, not the emir Abdelkader, but to Abdelaziz Bouteflika, not Abd al-Aziz Bu Tafliqa; Houari Boumediene, not Huwari Bu Madyan; Chérif Belkacem, not Sharif Abu 'l-Qasim. Overall, I have tried to make it easy for readers to recognise names and terms found elsewhere, rather than giving technically correct but uncommon renderings; so for Kabyle patronyms I use the conventional *Aït* rather than the more correct *Ath*, for Arabic equivalents *Beni* rather than *Banu* (but *Awlad* rather than the Gallicised *Ouled*). Ottoman Turkish terms are given in a simplified and Arabised transliteration for ease of reading and cross-referencing with other works on Ottoman North Africa, so the Regency's janissary force is the *ojaq* not *ocak*, its founder is Aruj not Oruc, the minister responsible for its diplomacy is the *wakil kharaj* not the *vekil haraci*. For place names, established forms that readers will find on maps and, again, elsewhere in the literature have been retained in preference to giving strict transliterations: Tlemcen (for Tilimsān), Bejaïa (Bijāya or Bgayeth), Oran (Wahrān), Constantine (Qsantīna), Timimoun (Tīmīmūn), Laghouat (al-Aghwāt), Cherchell (Sharshāl), Relizane (Ighil Izān), Djebel Amour (Jabal 'Amur), Aurès (Awrās), Touat (Tuwāt). For populations, however, a slightly stricter, though still simplified, transliteration is used, so I refer e.g. to the mountains of the Ouled Naïl in the Saharan Atlas, but to the men and women of the Awlad Na'il. When referring to the colonial period, place names follow contemporary usage, so Orléansville (later al-Asnam, then Chlef), Philippeville (Skikda), Bône (Annaba), Fort National (Larbaa N'Ait Irathen), Palestro (Lakhdaria), Perrégaux (Mohammedia), Aumale (Sour el-Ghozlane), etc.; I have usually given the Algerian (or post-independence) name in brackets after the first occurrence of a French place name in Chapters 2–5 and vice versa, where necessary, in Chapters 6 and 7. Usually, googling a place name will now enable the reader to find both geographical location and pre- and post-independence variants online.

# Abbreviations and Acronyms

| | |
|---|---|
| AAN | *Annuaire de l'Afrique du Nord* |
| AEMAN | Association des étudiants musulmans d'Afrique du nord |
| ALN | Armée de libération nationale |
| AML | Amis du manifeste et de la liberté |
| ANP | Armée nationale populaire |
| ANR | Alliance nationale républicaine |
| APC | Assemblée populaire communale |
| APN | Assemblée populaire nationale |
| APW | Assemblée populaire de wilaya |
| AQIM | Al-Qa'ida in the Islamic Maghrib |
| AUMA | Association des 'ulama musulmans algériens |
| BMPJ | Brigades mobiles de la police judicaire |
| CADC | Coordination des aarouch, daïras et communes |
| CGT | Confédération générale du travail |
| CGTU | Confédération générale du travail unitaire |
| CIG | Comité interministériel de guerre |
| CNC | Conseil national consultatif |
| CNCD | Coordination nationale pour le changement et la démocratie |
| CNRA | Comité national de la révolution algérienne |
| COM | Comité opérationnel militaire |
| CRA | Centre de renseignement et d'action |
| CRUA | Comité révolutionnaire d'unité et d'action |
| CTT | Centre de tri et de transit |
| DCSA | Direction centrale de la sécurité de l'armée |
| DGDS | Délégation générale à la documentation et la sécurité (formerly DGPS) |
| DGPS | Délégation générale à la prévention et la sécurité |
| DGSN | Direction générale de la sûreté nationale |
| DRS | Département du renseignement et de la sécurité (formerly SM) |

xiv

| | |
|---|---|
| DZ/CANA | Algeria, Centre des archives nationales, Birkhadem, Algiers |
| EMG | État major-général (ALN General Staff) |
| ENA | Étoile nord-africaine |
| FADRL | Front algérien pour la défense et le respect de la liberté |
| FFFLN | Fédération de France du Front de libération nationale |
| FFS | Front des forces socialistes |
| FIS | Front islamique du salut |
| FLN | Front de libération nationale |
| FR/ANOM | France, Archives nationales d'outre mer, Aix-en-Provence |
| FR/CADN | France, Centre des archives diplomatiques, Nantes |
| FR/SHD | France, Service historique de la défense, Château de Vincennes |
| FRUS | *Foreign Relations of the United States* |
| GIA | Groupe(s) islamique(s) armé(s) |
| GLD | Groupes de légitime défense |
| GPRA | Gouvernement provisoire de la République algérienne |
| GSPC | Groupe salafiste pour la prédication et le combat |
| HAMAS | Haraka li-mujtama' islami; from 1997, Harakat mujtama' al-silm (or, MSP, Mouvement de Société pour la Paix) |
| JORA | *Journal officiel de la République algérienne* |
| JORF | *Journal officiel de la République française* |
| LADDH | Ligue algérienne de la défense des droits de l'homme |
| MAK | Mouvement pour l'autonomie de la Kabylie |
| MALG | Ministère des armements et des liaisons générales |
| MCB | Mouvement culturel berbère |
| MDA | Mouvement pour la démocratie en Algérie |
| MDRA | Mouvement démocratique pour le renouveau algérien |
| MDS | Mouvement démocratique et social (formerly PAGS) |
| MEI | Mouvement pour l'état islamique |
| MIA | Mouvement islamique armé |
| MMSH | Maison méditerranéenne des sciences de l'homme, Aix-en-Provence |
| MNA | Mouvement national algérien |

| | |
|---|---|
| MNI | Mouvement de la nahda islamique (later MN, Mouvement Ennahda) |
| MRN | Mouvement pour le renouveau national (or Islah) |
| MTLD | Mouvement pour le triomphe des libertés démocratiques |
| OAS | Organisation de l'armée secrète |
| OCFLN | Organisation civile du FLN (cf. OPA) |
| ONEC | Organisation nationale des enfants de chouhada |
| ONEM | Organisation nationale des enfants de mujahidin |
| ONM | Organisation nationale des mujahidin |
| OPA | Organisation politico-administrative |
| ORP | Organisation de la résistance populaire |
| OS | Organisation spéciale (paramilitary wing of the PPA/MTLD, 1947–50) |
| PAGS | Partie de l'avant-garde socialiste (formerly PCA) |
| PCA | Parti communiste algérien |
| PCF | Parti communiste français |
| PPA | Parti du peuple Algérien |
| PRA | Parti du renouveau algérien |
| PRS | Parti de la révolution socialiste |
| PT | Parti des travailleurs |
| RCD | Rassemblement pour la culture et la démocratie |
| RND | Rassemblement national démocratique |
| SAS | Sections administratives spécialisées |
| SFIO | Section française de l'Internationale ouvrière |
| SIT | Syndicat islamique du travail |
| SM | Sécurité militaire |
| SMA | Scouts musulmans algériens (Algerian Boy Scouts' federation) |
| SONATRACH | Société nationale pour la recherche, la production, le transport, la transformation, et la commercialisation des hydrocarbures |
| TEFA | *Tableau des établissements français dans l'Algérie* |
| UDMA | Union démocratique du manifeste algérien |
| UGEMA | Union générale des étudiants musulmans algériens |
| UGTA | Union générale des travailleurs algériens |
| UNFA | Union nationale des femmes algériennes |
| UNJA | Union nationale de la jeunesse algérienne |
| UNPA | Union nationale des paysans algériens |
| ZAA | Zone autonome d'Alger |

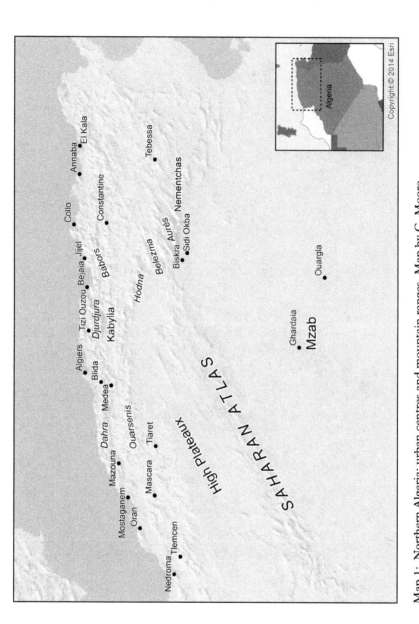

Map 1: Northern Algeria: urban centres and mountain ranges. Map by C. Moore.

# Introduction

Beni Saf is a fishing port on the steep cliffs of the Algerian coastline that climbs north-eastwards from the Moroccan border: a collage of multi-coloured, cubed houses – blue, ochre and yellow – superimposed upon each other against a green hillside above the bay. The local deposits of iron ore that for a century provided employment in mining have been exhausted since the mid-1980s, and the port's famous sardines are becoming rarer and more expensive, but in midsummer the town attracts families and groups of friends who rent houses and spend their short holidays by the sea. A little under a hundred kilometres to the west, at Marsa Ben Mehidi, are beaches where conservative families take their vacations, where women in loose clothes and headscarves swim during the day and take in concerts by rap artists on the boardwalk by night. At a similar distance further east, the coast turns a corner and comes in sight of the long, red Mujurjo mountain that towers over the city of Oran and the dizzying sheer walls of Santa Cruz, the sixteenth-century Spanish fortress that stands on the peak of the mountain above the sea. Here, the Thursday evening weekend road from Les Andalouses to Aïn al-Turk, where men wear shorts, girls bathe in bikinis and young couples hold hands, is packed with cars moving along the uninterrupted chain of grills, barbeques and hotels. One of them sports its name, 'Beach House', the English words spelled out in Arabic script, juxtaposed to the respectable designation *aparthotel familial*. Further east, beyond the lively sprawl of Oran and its rapidly rising apartment and office towers, the twisting road along the corniche reaches the village of Kristel, perched in an inlet on the face of the cliffs running down to the sea. The village's fruit and vegetable gardens, watered from a spring permanently surrounded by children, are said to have supplied Phoenician trading vessels in antiquity, when the site was first inhabited. Above the gardens, a building carries the inscription *École communale 1897*. Above the school, on a promontory of rock over the road, a whitewashed stone cube surmounted by a dome marks the resting place of a *wali*, a Muslim saint. At Kristel the road turns inland before passing by the immense pipeline terminal at Arzew, the site of the world's first liquefied natural gas plant and the country's main crude oil port, where at night the gas flares light up the sky in a bright amber arc. A little further east is the city of Mostaghanem, with its busy street market under the trees and the colonial architecture of the bustling, traffic-packed town centre. On a wall by the railway station, someone has painted a laconic slogan: *tahya firansa – vissa* ('Long live France – visa!'), the first two words in Arabic script, the last in an approximate French. The quiet, crumbling pre-colonial city overlooks the Mediterranean from its cliffs that rise on either side of a ravine filled with trees and birdsong, its empty, narrow streets of coloured houses sprinkled with satellite dishes, and its old mosques from which the call to prayer at noon rises like a sudden cloud of sound.[1]

The landscape is striking; the way people live in it, mark it and move through it, build upon it, name it and make a living from it displays both the diversity of contemporary life and the depth of historical time against which contemporary life is played out. Algeria's modern history has not generally been approached through descriptions of a beautiful and fasci-nating country, or a diverse and creative society going about its daily life. The history of Algeria, since the Ottoman period – three centuries of history hardly known outside specialist circles and still sometimes thought of in antiquated stereotypes of piracy, 'white slavery' and despotism[2] – through 132 years of French colonial occupation (1830–1962) and seven years of 'savage' colonial war (the war of inde-pendence, 1954–1962),[3] up to the more recent terrors of Islamist and state violence since 1992, has often been written about only in terms of upheaval, rupture, violence and trauma. That these have existed in over-abundance in Algeria is not to be doubted, and the pages that follow will seek to account for them in their place. But the history of Algeria as a series of familiar clichés – heroism and horror, triumph and tragedy, anger and agony – is only part of what has made this country what it is, and does not begin to account adequately for the ways Algerians them-selves have lived their lives, understood their country and their place in the world, have made, and continually make day by day, their own futures with the materials their past has given them.

No single study can give an adequate account of the complexity, the suppressed possibilities and unintended outcomes, the many and incom-mensurable aspects of the modern history of such a richly varied land and such a diverse society with so tumultuous a past. Nonetheless, the aim of this book is to explore, as far, as critically and as carefully as possible within the constraints of historical research – which necessarily differ from those of other disciplines, sociology, anthropology or political science, as well as from investigative journalism, while being informed by all of them to a greater or lesser extent – what the reality of Algerian history has been for the people who have lived through it, what its motive forces have been and how these have been understood. Above all, I hope that the reader might gain some sense, not only of Algeria's history 'as it really happened' but of Algeria as a really existing place, rather than as a 'model' or a case study of Third World suffering or heroic revolution gone wrong, and of Algerians as the real people who live there, rather than as abstract actors in a tragic tale. It perhaps ought to be said, too, that this does not involve idealising or airbrushing any aspect of Algeria's history or contemporary social reality: the very least that the outside observer trying to make sense of this country owes its people, beyond an empathy with them and their history, is to look both it and them honestly in the face.

This book has two main, interrelated themes. The first is political and concerns the ways in which those who have most directly formed and shaped structures of sovereign power – Ottoman governors, French colonial settlers and administrators and Algerian nationalist leaders, bureaucrats and generals – have sought to construct institutions of state to rule over Algerian society, extract and profit from the country's resources and the labour of its inhabitants and provide mechanisms for regulating and directing social life.

At first sight, Algeria seems to illustrate to a very high degree the power of the modern state to control and transform social life, through both the dislocations and repression of the colonial period and the ambitious projects that followed independence. Again, this is certainly an important part of the story, and the 'fierce' aspects of the state, as well as its developmental ambitions, will often be referred to. But I will also be suggesting that the formation and exercise of state power in Algeria has never been a straightforward process, that Algeria's state structures have often impinged only tangentially on the lives of many of its inhabitants and that even the most ferociously assertive actions of state apparatuses have generally incorporated the country's people only incompletely into their orbit. They have often done so, too, with little or no understanding, and very inaccurate expectations, of what the consequences would be either for the state itself or for the people it made the subjects of its rule. The sometimes ferocious strength of a succession of states, and their simultaneous fragility and limitations, is thus a first recurring theme. In successive periods of the country's history, the balance between the extent and strength of the state, on the one hand, and its limits and fragility, on the other, has of course varied, but there is no story here of the progressive incorporation of all areas of life into the gradually encroaching power of a model 'nation-state'. Rather, a crucial question concerns the extent to which the transition from the domination of a colonial state imposed by conquest to a national state created in a popular and revolutionary war of liberation, the fulcrum of Algeria's twentieth-century history and the process that drew upon it the attention and often the admiration of the world, has constituted a radical break in the country's history, or a transition in which longer-established power relationships between elements of society and the central, governing and distributing power of the state were able to reconstitute themselves, in new forms perhaps, but with some degree of continuity. The strength and fragility of the state, and the limits and absences as well as the possibilities and ambitions of its projects for governing and transforming society, will be seen as ongoing issues in post-independence Algeria.

Related to this theme is a second one, concerning the history of Algerian society. In a colonial cliché first expressed by Governor General Jules Cambon in 1894 and repeated by Charles de Gaulle in 1959, Algerian society was seen as nothing but a *poussière d'hommes* ('human dust'), disaggregated and anarchic,[4] incapable of generating the social ties and institutions that might constitute the bases of its own self-government, and united in unyielding resistance to the 'civilising' efforts of foreign occupation only by innate violence and the xenophobic 'fanaticism' of Islam. While the colonial prejudices can be dispensed with easily enough, many discussions of Algeria have retained this idea of a weak, fragmented society reduced to helpless prostration before the ravages of colonialism and the depredations of authoritarianism. Discussion has often focused on politics and the state to the exclusion of serious attention to Algerian society, its means of persistence and survival and the ways in which its history has been lived and understood 'from below'. This book argues that just as we need to nuance our understanding of the strengths and limits of state formation in Algeria, so we need to pay more attention to the making and sustaining of what in fact has historically been an extraordinarily robust, resilient society. Not only have social institutions often set limits to, and imposed themselves as interlocutors with, the state, they have also often filled the vacuum left by the absence, uncertainty or incompetence of the state. This is not to be read as a celebration of the autonomy of free social forces. Very frequently such institutions have themselves been oppressive or have worked to benefit a few at the expense of many; they have often filled gaps left vacant by the jurisdiction of the state and its lack of a guaranteed rule of law, but they have rarely themselves provided models of rule-bound, equitable and accountable arbitration. Nonetheless, enduring social solidarities and an extraordinary degree of social energy have continuously characterised Algerian society, and in accounting both for the hardships its people have experienced and for the ways they have survived them, attention to these (and to their damaging as well as enabling effects, their capacity to produce inequalities and conflicts as well as to alleviate and negotiate them) will be seen to be essential.

In this respect, this book argues for a view of Algerian history that emphasises continuities as well as, sometimes more than, ruptures. This is not an argument for 'invariables' ('national constants' as official Algerian rhetoric put it in the 1970s) but for attention to the forms of social capital and solidarity, worldviews, codes of behaviour and self-understanding that govern the constitution of social relations, and their bases in the everyday material realities of social life, as they are changed or remade by different generations in new circumstances across time. The primary focus, then, is Algerian society and the continuous responses, innovations and strategies of people faced with the conditions of life dictated by their environment and inheritance, or imposed upon them by those who would rule them. Both the ferocity and the limits of politics are best understood, from this perspective, not through high policy and palace intrigue, nor by measurement against prescriptive (and in fact mythical) schemes of 'national awakening', developmental modernisation, 'Western-style' free-market democracy or the 'Islamic republic', but in terms of the constant interplay of social forces with the institutions of state, in which the former have often been more robust, the latter less coherent, than has frequently been appreciated.

These themes are explored here over three periods, and the organisation of the book reflects my attempt to explore long-term themes and continuities through the episodic unfolding of events and the disruptions they have often most obviously caused. The first chapter offers a synopsis of the Ottoman period, considering the broad outlines of social and cultural life and the relation of Algerians and their diverse places of habitation to the *beylik* (state) and the wider worlds beyond it. The colonial period is discussed through Chapters 2 to 4, which run in parallel as well as in sequence. Chapter 2 sees the long process of conquest, its effects and Algerians' varied responses to it, as far as possible from the perspective of Algerian society up to the eve of the First World War. Chapter 3 changes the angle of view, looking at the century-long construction of a 'French Algeria', a European-dominated colonial society, and the institutions through which it created what, by the 1940s, seemed a permanent settler state on North African soil but within the body politic of the French republic. Chapter 4 takes up where Chapter 2 left off, to explore the rapidly developing changes in Algerian society and its demands on and contests with the French state from 1912 to 1942. These three chapters reflect a conviction that the 'Algerian' and the 'French' histories of Algeria from 1830 to ca. 1940 need to be seen as both distinct and intertwined; neither aspect can properly be understood without the other, and neither is sufficient as a 'true' record without the other, but these are the histories of parallel, occasionally intersecting, colliding or overlapping societies, not a single common narrative. Indeed, much of the bitterness of the war of independence and of its continuing reverberations in more recent times can only be explained by the peculiar way in which Algerian and French histories of Algeria are both interdependent and incommensurable. Chapter 5 considers the origins and unfolding of the war of independence, its multiple meanings and the diverse ways in which it was experienced, from 1942 up to the independence of the Algerian republic in 1962. Chapters 6 and 7 follow a more straightforward political chronology that also, in these years, falls in with major patterns of social and economic life, as Algeria experienced first the years of revolutionary state consolidation in the 1960s and 1970s, the mounting crisis of the system in the 1980s up to the dramatic events of 1988–92 and the terrible violence and uneasy 'normalisation' of the 1990s and the first decade of the twenty-first century.

Algeria today is an important as well as a 'difficult' country. Little known to most people in most of the English-speaking world, known often in confused and conflicting ways in Europe, especially in France, familiar to most only from news items about terrorism or illegal migration, it is (in surface area) Africa's largest country, a major source and supplier of oil and gas to Europe, a significant actor in the international relations of the Mediterranean region and a focus of attention (however undesired) for all those concerned with 'war on terror', European security and economic relations, immigration and Islamism, as well as for students of colonialism and anti-colonialism, insurrection and counter-insurgency, Third Worldism, 'socialist' development and transitions towards more liberal markets and (perhaps) democratisation, the legacies of imperialism in the postcolonial world and the making of 'the West' in its modern encounter with 'Islam' and 'the Orient'. If some of those readers whose interest in Algeria stems from any of these many reasons why we should pay attention to this country, its people and their historical experiences, find in these pages some clues about how Algerian history has also been lived by those whom it has first, and most of all, concerned, then this book will have served its purpose.

Researching and writing this book has taken far longer than I initially (naïvely) imagined. It would not have been possible without the support of several institutions, and many friends and colleagues. Marigold Acland first proposed that I take it on, when I was a Junior Research Fellow at the Middle East Centre, St Antony's College, Oxford; I have her patience and enthusiasm, and Eugene Rogan's encouragement, to thank for making me think I could do it at all. The project was subsequently supported at Princeton by the history department, the Princeton Institute for International and Regional Studies and the University Committee on Research in the Humanities and Social Sciences; at SOAS, by the University of London's Central Research Fund; and at Oxford again by the History Faculty's research committee, the John Fell Fund and my beautiful academic home since 2009, Trinity College. I was able to finish writing thanks to the Leverhulme Trust, truly the most supportive and enabling of funders. Maria Marsh, Cassi Roberts and Matt Sweeney at CUP brought a long overdue ship into port not only with good grace but with great energy and efficiency. Christine Moore provided essential expertise in map-making at the last moment. Thanks are due to Claire Marynower, Tawfiq Ibrahim, Marie Chominot and Mme Kouaci, Eléonore Bakhtadze, Karim Bouayad and Saïd Abdeddaïm for locating and/or giving permission for use of illustrations.

Research in Algeria was possible only thanks to Daho Djerbal, Joseph Rivat, and especially Bob Parks and Karim Ouaras, and to the opening and flourishing while I was working on this book of CEMA, the Algerian research centre of the American Institute for Maghrib Studies (AIMS) in Oran, with which it has been an honour and a pleasure to be associated. In Algeria, I especially have to thank all those who consented to be interviewed, or who spoke to me off the record or in informal conversations, particularly for questions relating to Chapters 5, 6 and 7. Those who did not wish to remain anonymous are listed in the bibliography: I am immensely grateful to all, named and anonymous alike. I also owe particular thanks to Tewfik Sahraoui, both for conversations and hospitality over several years and for sharing with me a memorable 2,544 km road trip from Oran to Biskra and back in June 2008, and to Nacer and Laïd who guided us through the Aurès. Research in France was greatly facilitated by the welcome afforded by staff and colleagues at the MMSH in Aix-en-Provence, and by archivists and librarians in Aix, Paris and Nantes.

Successive delays in finishing the book brought the advantage of my being able to learn from a new generation of research on Algeria, some of which I have had the honour of supervising or examining. I am grateful in particular to Jennifer Johnson, Brock Cutler, Tom de Georges, Jacob Mundy, Marie Chominot, Jan Jansen, Jeff Byrne, Lakhdar Guettas, Natalya Vince, Hannah-Louise Clark, Julien Fromage, Claire Marynower, Linda Amiri, Afaf Zekkour, Muriam Haleh-Davis, Ed McAllister, Nadjib Sidi Moussa, Nadjib Achour, Annick Lacroix, Augustin Jomier, Arthur Asseraf and Charlotte Courreye for discussing and sharing their work.

For conversations, comments and critical readings I have to thank Omar Carlier, Gilbert Meynier, Mohamed Harbi, Sylvie Thénault, Raphaëlle Branche, Emmanuel Blanchard, Sara Abrevaya Stein, Susan Miller, Susan Slyomovics, Lahouari Addi, Julia Clancy-Smith, Isabelle Grangaud, Francis Ghilès, Abderrahmane Hadj Nacer, Fatma Oussedik, Jean-Paul and Marie-France Grangaud, Mohammed Ghrib, Natalya Vince, Walid Benkhaled, Judith Scheele, Karima Dirèche, Hugh Roberts, Michael Willis, Mohamed Hachemaoui, Neil MacMaster, Jim House, Ben Brower, Marie Colonna, Christian Phéline, Ouarda Tengour, Didier Guignard, Jennifer Sessions, Fatma Zohra Guechi, Mohand Akli Hadibi, Mustafa Haddab, Fouad Soufi, Hassan Remaoun, Amira Bennison, Adlène Meddi and Aidan Lewis. My beloved comrades, Bob Parks and Malika Rahal, generously read each of the chapters as I wrote them; their advice and encouragement have been essential. That some of these friends and colleagues disagree with each other on many points will be apparent to anyone who knows the literature. I have learned from all of them, but none of them might agree with everything, or anything, that I have written here, especially concerning the events of more recent decades. Algeria's recent past is especially contentious: I have tried to present the evidence available to me in such a way as to allow readers to draw their own conclusions. My interpretations, and any errors, are my own responsibility. The book is dedicated to Algerian friends without whom I could never have got to know, let alone understand, anything of their country: it was written with them in mind, in the hope that this version of their story might be one they recognise – or at least, one that does them no injustice.

My greatest debts as ever are to Anna, my partner in love and life, and now also to our wonderful daughter Kate, whose arrival caused only one of the many delays to the completion of this work, but by far the most joyful one.

# 1    Ecologies, Societies, Cultures and the State, 1516–1830

In the late autumn of 1519, the leading citizens of Algiers composed a letter from 'the whole populace of the city' to Sultan Selim I, ruler of the Ottoman Empire who, only two years previously, had swept from Anatolia through Syria and Egypt, conquering the historic heartlands of the Arab and Muslim worlds. 'We had fallen', they wrote, 'in these troubled times from difficulty into difficulty', 'in an unhappy situation of weakness on the edge of misfortune', before the arrival of the man who was now at the head of their state, Khayr al-Din 'Barbarossa'. He, and with him the notables and populace of the city, now declared his 'devotion and faithfulness' to the victorious Ottoman ruler; all placed themselves in his service.[1]

## Ottoman Algeria

At the beginning of the sixteenth century, the central Maghrib – the broad swathe of North Africa between the domains of the Wattasid dynasty of Fez to the west and the Hafsids of Tunis to the east – was caught in a vast geopolitical crisis. The collapse of the late medieval Muslim kingdoms of Andalus in the face of the Spanish Catholic *reconquista* had culminated, in January 1492, with the fall of Granada. The Spanish advance across the Mediterranean, into fortified enclaves on the coasts of North Africa, accelerated the fragmentation of the dynastic states that had ruled the Maghrib in succession to the great unified medieval empires that had passed away in the thirteenth century. The central Maghrib that would become Algeria was not yet conceived of by any of its inhabitants as a single territory, much less one ruled from the port city of al-Jaza'ir Beni Mezghenna (*Alger* to the French, *Algiers* to the English), 'the islands of the Beni Mezghenna', an ancient but modest harbour built against the steep relief of the hillsides facing a small group of islets off the coast, an unsheltered anchorage at the western end of a broad bay. Political sovereignty over the plains and mountains of the central Maghrib and their inhabitants was contested between the Zayyanid dynasty, ruling from the

9

princely trading and textile-manufacturing city of Tlemcen, inland in the west of the country, the Zayyanids' rivals in Fez further west, and the opposing force of the Hafsids of Tunis in the east, who ruled over the learned port city of Bejaïa at the mouth of the Soummam river, 200 kilometres east of Algiers. Continuous regional warfare between them was now combined with the destabilising local effects of a Mediterranean superpower struggle: the Ottoman Empire, in the ascendant since the capture of Constantinople (Istanbul) in 1453, contended with the Habsburgs, embarking on their own 'golden age' with the establishment and pillaging of a New World empire in the Americas. After the fall of Granada, the Spanish 'crusade' encroached on the central Maghribi coastline. Mers el Kebir, the great natural harbour just west of Oran, was taken in 1505, Tenes in 1508, Oran itself and Bejaïa in 1509. Two years later, Dellys, Cherchell and Mostaghanem were obliged to pay tribute to the Spaniards. All the principal coastal towns of the central Maghrib, east as far as the Hafsid domains, had fallen under Spanish control. In 1510, the notables of Algiers too sued for peace, and were obliged to cede possession of the offshore islands commanding their harbour, on which the Spanish commander, Don Pedro Navarro, built a fortress, the *peñon*, with a garrison two hundred strong.[2]

It was in this context that the notables, the chief citizens, of Algiers first called on outside aid, requesting help from an Ottoman adventurer recently arrived in the region – Aruj Bey, who along with his three brothers became better known in history and legend under the surname 'Barbarossa', meaning 'red beard'. Aruj, a Muslim soldier and seaman from the Aegean island of Mytilene, had his first successes as a corsair (privateer) operating from the island of Djerba off the southern coast of Tunisia. Private naval entrepreneurs acting for their own profit but within the context of Ottoman operations against the Spanish were already a feature of warfare in the region, as they were in the Atlantic and Caribbean, where English privateers harassed the Spanish fleet. In the 1490s, the Turkish privateer Kemal Reis, later appointed to command an Ottoman squadron charged with suppressing piracy in the Aegean, had led a corsair fleet against Spanish shipping off the Maghribi coasts.[3] The careers of the elder Barbarossa brothers, Aruj and Khayr al-Din, were especially successful examples of this wider trend. Having created his own fleet, Aruj was called upon to reinforce the attempt to retake Bejaïa from the Spanish. He tried, and failed, to do so twice, from his base at Jijel, but from there, as a leading anti-Spanish war captain, he began to carve out an independent political power of his own. In 1516, he was solicited by the population of Algiers to come to their aid.

But however important the regional context, this was no straightforwardly 'civilisational' war, with clear and simple battle lines between
Muslims and Christians. Local struggles were more complex.
Aruj, installed with his soldiers in Algiers, was unable to destroy the
*peñon*, but threatened the position of the ruling faction in the city and its
leader, Salim al-Tumi, who sought Spanish assistance to remove the
Ottomans. Aruj suppressed this budding 'revolt', allegedly murdering
Salim in his bath; Salim's son sought refuge with the Spanish and
hoped to avenge his father with their aid.[4] A year later, when an anti-
Spanish faction in Tlemcen invited Aruj to extend his rule and evict
Spanish influence from the west, a rival group around the reigning
Zayyanid sultan, Abu Hammu, opposed annexation from Algiers. With
Spanish soldiers, Abu Hammu's supporters laid siege to Aruj in Tlemcen
and massacred troops commanded by his brother Ishaq at the nearby
stronghold of Qala'at Beni Rashid. Aruj resorted to extreme repression
against suspected opponents in Tlemcen, murdering some seventy
Zayyanid princes, according to some sources (and the local historical
tradition of the city), before being killed himself while fleeing from
Tlemcen in 1518. In Tlemcen as elsewhere, different aspirants to sovereignty 'disputed power among themselves, some seeking support from the
Spanish, others from the Ottomans, and changing allies as circumstances
dictated'.[5]

Out of this complex local power struggle, Aruj and his brothers had
succeeded by 1518 in establishing the makings of a military state, supported by factions of the local urban elites opposed to the Spaniards and
backed by their small force of ships, Turkish musketeers and artillery.
After the death of Aruj, his brother Khayr al-Din became 'sultan of
Algiers'. In August 1519, his combined army of local, Andalusi and
Turkish troops repelled an attack by some five thousand Spanish soldiers
and later that same year he offered the sovereignty of his precarious
kingdom to Selim I, conqueror of Damascus and Cairo. In 1529 Khayr al-
Din succeeded in ousting the Spaniards from the *peñon* and by 1533,
when he became *kapudan pasha*, Grand Admiral of the Ottoman fleet of
Sultan Suleyman I 'Qanuni' ('the Lawgiver', known in Europe as 'the
Magnificent'), a new state had come into being in the central Maghrib,
centred on a new capital city: the Ottoman Regency of Algiers. In 1541,
when storms and tenacious resistance defeated the assault on Algiers led
by Charles V, the Holy Roman Emperor, with 516 ships and 22,000 men,
this new state no longer seemed precarious; it began to be called
invincible.

The epic, often romanticised, tale of the Barbarossas and the founding
of the Regency provides in succinct summary the material for many of the

misperceptions that continue to surround the three centuries' history of Ottoman Algeria. Interpretations of the Ottoman period have tended to fall into one of two broad camps, both very much defined by anachronistic suppositions about 'national' development. For some, the Regency was the foundation of an Algerian national state, as yet incompletely integrated, but nonetheless establishing durable frontiers with its neighbours, exercising sovereign foreign relations from a permanently established capital and illustrating a 'glorious' history of warfare and resistance against Christian imperialist aggression.[6] For others, and in contrast to the more positive models of Egypt or Tunisia, the Turkish 'occupation' of Algeria failed to see the emergence of an indigenised ruling elite in command of an emergent national entity. In this latter view, the ruling minority remained a foreign military clique, dependent on the revenues of the 'piracy' by which Aruj had begun his rise to fame and which his successors would pursue for three hundred years, and detached from local society, which it ruled as a 'colony of exploitation',[7] using ruthless taxation and brute force to suppress the country's capacities for development and oppress its populace to such an extent that the Ottomans are said to have 'developed an incapacity to resist [. . .] and objectively prepared the ground for French colonisation'.[8]

It is easy enough to see that both of these positions were defined by twentieth-century preoccupations. Algerian publicists addressing the international community during the later stages of the war of independence relied on arguments about the internally functional and internationally recognised legal status of the Regency to establish precedence for their own juridical claim to represent a legally sovereign state. The French government conversely insisted on its own, nineteenth-century, sovereignty by right of annexation over a territory whose people, occupied by the 'despotic' Turks before the 'civilising' French, had supposedly never achieved political autonomy and were still in need of paternal guidance towards modern development.

Understanding of the Ottoman period has also often been obscured by the very scale and colour of the Regency's early modern history. Salim al-Tumi strangled in his bath, the massacre of the princes at Tlemcen, the exotic figures of the Barbarossas, the plots and assassinations of Algiers palace politics and above all fantastic and sexualised images of the depredations of corsair 'piracy', the enslavement of European men and women and graphic imaginings of the violence and licentiousness to which they were supposedly exposed, all contributed to typecast and self-reproducing images of Algiers. It was the 'scourge of the Christian world ... terror of Europe ... haven of pirates, theatre of every kind of cruelty', in the words of a French churchman in 1619; 'this nest of wasps, this den of thieves', as an English commentator raved in 1728.[9] Colonial-era writers both revelled in the barbarously romantic 'Barbary legend' of the larger-than-life Barbarossas and their heirs, and produced durable stereotypes about Algeria as anarchic, licentious and violent. Algerian nationalists both celebrated the heroic exploits of the *ghuzat al-bahr*, the sea-roving 'combattants of the faith', and deplored the failure of the Ottoman state to indigenise itself and beat back the French invasion. Understood in terms of its own time, and in the increasing light of contemporary sources and their critical interpretation, another assessment of the Regency is possible, one that can take account of the nature of the state and of the disparate social groups and territories it sought to govern.

## Living on the Land

Ottoman Algeria was an overwhelmingly rural society. Throughout this period, some 90 per cent of the population lived on the land, and the greater part of the wealth that the country generated, and whose surplus enabled the functioning of the state, was derived from agricultural production. The land itself, the productive environments it provided and the ecologies (that is, the relationships between human populations and their physical environment) produced by the interaction of human settlement with the resources of the land and climate were highly diverse. The territory that came under the nominal, and variably effective, political sovereignty of the Regency extended from the Mediterranean coast to the principal settlements of the north-central Sahara, traversing four main topographic zones.

From north to south, the first of these is a chain of coastal mountain ranges, rising to around 1,000 metres, of which the most notable are the Dahra, north of the river Cheliff, maritime Kabylia, north of the Sebaou valley, the mountains of Lesser Kabylia from Bejaïa to Collo and the Edough massif west of Annaba. These ranges close off the interior of the country from the sea and give long reaches of the Algerian coast-line – the Dahra and Kabyle 'corniches' – the spectacular aspect of a wall of mountains with their heads in the clouds and their feet in the sea. They are, nonetheless, broken up by river valleys and low-lying coastal plains, especially the broad, flat plains extending westwards from the Cheliff valley to the south and west of Oran, the Mitidja plain south and east of Algiers, the immediate hinterland of Bejaïa and the plain of Annaba. A second zone is defined by the Tellian Atlas, a broader, deeper swathe of mountain chains extending in a shallow arc across the country: from west to east the mountains of Tlemcen, the Ouarsenis facing the coastal

Dahra across the Cheliff valley, the Atlas of Blida defining the southern edge of the Mitidja, the Biban or 'Iron Gates', separating the region of Algiers from the upland country to the east, and the Hodna mountains, which turn south-eastward, away from the coast, dividing the rolling uplands of the Constantine region from the steppe to the south and west.

The southern edge of the Tellian Atlas marks the transition between the littoral region of 'Mediterranean' climate and vegetation and a third zone, the steppe of the High Plateaux. The broad, flat plateaux, narrowing to the east until they meet the barrier of the Belezma and Aurès mountains, change rapidly along their northern edge, and from north to south, between dry-farming agricultural grassland, scrubby, semi-arid pasture and arid, rocky tracts that merge into desert. South of the plateaux, a third series of mountains, the Saharan Atlas, rises to between 1,000 and 2,000 metres: from west to east, the Ksour mountains, Djebel Amour, the mountains of the Ouled Naïl and of the Zab, the Aurès and the mountains of the Nementchas. These divide the agricultural and pastoral lands of northern Algeria from the vast – and also very diverse – Sahara itself.

Each of these broadly defined zones, too, could be further subdivided. The other major topographic division important to understanding Algeria's relief and ecology, however, cuts across these transversal bands from the southeast to the northwest and divides a generally drier, more pastoral west – with lower relief, less rainfall and fewer areas of fertile alluvial soils – from a higher, colder, more agricultural east – with soils rich in potassium and phosphates, more marked relief and higher average rainfall. The hills and plains of the west were the lands of nomadic, Arabic-speaking pastoralists, moving between the northern 'Tell' and the Plateaux in regular, seasonal migrations.

To the east, the mountains break up into smaller chains descending towards the Tunisian frontier, and open up into areas of rolling hills and the 'high plains', suited to wheat and barley growing, around the town of Setif north of the Hodna mountains. The cereal culture supported by the soils and rainfall of this eastern region, along with intensive agriculture in the well-watered mountains, has historically supported higher population levels – up to half the country's total population – and a greater agricultural surplus than other areas.

A clearer idea of both the diversity and the salient common features of these different productive environments, the foundation of Algerian society in the Ottoman period and for long afterwards, can be gained from more detailed consideration of a few specific locales within these broad topographic zones.

Figure 1.1 Hills and plains in western Algeria, from Qalaat Beni Salama, near Tiaret. It was in a cave near this spot that the celebrated historian Ibn Khaldun is said to have begun the *Muqaddima* (Introduction) to his universal history, while in hiding in the 1370s (Author's photograph).

The Sahara itself presents a great diversity of land forms, resources and possibilities for human settlement.[10] At the furthest reaches of Ottoman claims to sovereignty lay the Gourara[11] (from *tigurarin*, 'encampments'), a string of oasis settlements on the southern edge of the Great Western Erg (*reg*, a vast ensemble of high dunes), almost 750 kilometres south of the coast. In medieval times, the Gourara had been a node in the north–south and east–west roads across the northern Sahara. In the sixteenth century, it became relatively isolated, less frequented and only occasionally – at the moment of Ottoman and Moroccan expeditions in 1579 and 1581, respectively – subject to rival regional sovereignties.[12] Inhabited since antiquity, first by the autochthonous ancestors of a part of the black population later identified, as *haratin* (Berber, *isemghan*), with enslaved sub-Saharan Africans and their descendants, the oases were successively settled by ancient Berber-speaking migrants from the north, by Jewish and judaised berberophone arrivals in the second and seventh centuries AD and by nomadic Arabic speakers in the thirteenth and fourteenth centuries.[13] The primary language of the region was *tazenatit* (Zenati), a Berber dialect associated with immigrants of pastoral origin who would become the principal inhabitants of the area.

Historian Lucette Valensi remarks of early modern North Africa that 'the harsher the climate and the more irregular the resources, the more minute was the management of daily life'.[14] Meticulous social regulation as well as technical ingenuity characterised life in the Sahara. Agricultural production – in small familial vegetable gardens and sometimes vast, as at Timimoun in the Gourara, date-palm groves – was made possible by the extraordinarily labour-intensive construction of underground canals (*foggaras*, or *ifeli* in Zenati), an ancient technique of tapping the water table and using natural declivities to channel the stream towards the oasis, where a system of allocation was controlled by carefully calibrated comb-like filters under the supervision of the *kiyal al-ma*, the water-measurer. Extended family groups, associated by lineage (*lqawm*), were historically recognised by their rights to cultivable plots and water allocations, by their possession of a communal, fortified habitation doubling as a secure granary and storehouse (*agham*) and later by their residence in distinct quarters of agglomerations of houses (*ksur*, singular *ksar*), set apart from their groves and gardens.

Figure 1.2 View over rooftops of a *ksar* in the Gourara, near Timimoun (T. Sahrawi).

The labour required to create and maintain irrigation systems and palm groves was largely provided by the servile *haratin*, although the people identified as such in the Gourara today claim a free labouring origin, if one of secondary status to that of their 'white', landowning berberophone neighbours, the *hrar* (free men). Strictly hierarchical social differentiation, on the basis of the successive migrations making up the population, was marked in descent or ethnicity, occupation and place of habitation, with *haratin/isemghan* (free labourers on others' land) and *ijemjan* (slaves brought from West Africa south of the Sahara and their descendants) at the bottom of the scale and authoritative religious specialists, *shurafa* (families claiming descent from the prophet Muhammad) and *mrabtin* (descendants of ancestors locally recognised as saints), at the top.

A different ecological situation, and a different social system, existed to the north and east. In the high plains of the Constantinois (the region whose historic centre is the city of Constantine), as the eighteenth-century English scholar Thomas Shaw remarked, 'they have a great command of water during the whole summer'[15] – at least, in good years. Average rainfall in most of this region is between 400 and 700 millimetres per annum (400 mm being the minimum for cereal growing without irrigation), but as André Nouschi pointed out in his detailed history of rural life in the region, 'levels of rainfall in Algeria can vary by up to one hundred per cent from one year to the next, such that the notion of "average" rainfall loses much of its relevance'.[16] Drought or, equally disastrous, storms, heavy rain and flash floods – especially at the wrong time of year – were constant threats to the livelihood of the peasantry who constituted the great majority of the population. Hailstorms from December to March, and the dry sirocco wind from May to September, could destroy entire crops in the fields. So could locusts, as the French naturalist Jean-André Peyssonnel described during his journey with the Ottoman authorities of Constantine in June 1725:

For nine years now ... these insects have devoured all the seed of this country. They come from the deserts of the Sahara, and in one or two days they eat all the grain of a countryside, where they then rest. They lay their eggs, and afterwards die in the same spot ... We have seen in Algiers how they devoured the olive trees and every fruit-tree, even the pines ... I was mortified one day to see them arrive in a field that they devoured in under twelve hours ... In vain does one run at them, shout to chase them; nothing can turn them away.[17]

Added to the instability of climate was the fragility of the soil's fertility. Though naturally rich in phosphoric acid and potassium, without the addition of more fertilisers it usually needed to be rested to regenerate

Figure 1.3 The Aurès. The Rhoufi gorge, in the southern Oued El Abiod. Traditional houses on the cliff side above the palm grove (on the right of the picture) have been abandoned for the newer settlement by the main road higher up (Author's photograph).

between crop cycles. The region's optimum ecology therefore relied on extensive agriculture with a light plough on large, open fields – where they were available – combined with livestock-raising, with flocks or herds being moved seasonally by populations who often combined settled agriculture with a degree of mobile pastoralism. This combination of lifestyles was especially marked in another principally berberophone society of the east, the *shawi*-speaking people of the Aurès mountains that divide the plains of the Constantinois from the Sahara. The Aurès, a compact mass of mountains and valleys running south-west to northeast, marks a sharp ecological frontier, with the northern and central reaches of the massif supporting cereals and orchards in valleys and on the lower hillsides as well as pastoralism on the higher slopes, while the southern face abruptly presents an arid, Saharan aspect, with valley floors dominated by the date-palm.

In the southern reaches of the Oued el-Abiod, one of the massif's three principal valleys, the population divided the year between fruit- and date-growing in the valleys, with pasturing of flocks on the slopes, and removal of the whole community to the northern Sahara for winter pasture between October and March, leaving behind only a guard over the *teklert*, or communal granary and storehouse, access to which was usually controlled by the community's elder women.

However fragile, though, in 1830 the cereal-growing east probably supported between two-fifths and a half of Algeria's total population of between 3 and 5 million people.[18] These mainly Arabic-speaking peasant producers occupied a variety of positions in a threefold land tenure system. Land belonged to the state (*beylik*), or could be held by communal groups (later referred to as '*arsh* land, associated with '*arush*, tribes) or private owners (*milk*, 'possessed' property).[19]

Much of the best land, on the plains and in permanently farmed estates near major towns, was owned by the *bey*, the Ottoman 'viceroy' of one of Algeria's three provinces, either through purchase or through confiscation. Towards the end of the Ottoman period in the east, a stable system for farming such land, disposed of by the beylik as '*azl* ('grant') land, had developed. '*Azl* lands belonging directly to the beylik were frequently worked as '*azl khammas*, share-cropped land, for which workers were recruited from among the local tribes by an agent or steward (*wakil*). The peasants provided their labour while the state provided the other four factors of production – land, work animals (oxen, mules or horses), implements and seed – and the produce was divided accordingly, with the workers receiving one-fifth of the harvest (hence the term for share-croppers, *khammas*, 'one-fifth'). An account of the system produced shortly after the French conquest of the region observed that:

> *Khammas* were recruited in every tribe, and so many people solicited the favour [of being chosen] that the *wakil* would require ... a certain sum paid in advance before according it. The *khammas* gained the advantage of having excellent land to cultivate, well-fed animals in good health from which more work could be demanded, and finally, an assurance of protection for the harvest.

Given the risks to peasant livelihood in general, farming good state lands was by no means an undesirable option. The same source estimated that for the sharecropper, in a good year, ninety days of work on a well-favoured '*azl* produced 'enough to provide for his family for a year, and he could dispose of the remaining 275 days for his own profit'.[20] '*Azl* could also be let to independent tenant farmers as '*azl jabri*, in which case families cultivated the land with their own resources and at their own risk. The beylik took a set proportion of the harvest (*jabri*, the 'mandatory' payment, also a term for the principal tax on produce on the region), such that in good years, both parties benefited, but in poor years only the state –

which was due its fixed amount of produce whatever the weather – gained from the arrangement.[21] In some cases, however, 'the contract was so desirable that the bey's farmers would let their concessions to sub-contracted cultivators, in return for the [jabri], plus a supplementary advance'.[22] Finally, 'azl azib, 'estate 'azls', were allocated to state functionaries in lieu of salary, and farmed by them as they saw fit.

Peasants were free to move, leave an estate between seasons and quit an employer, but 'azl land could also be occupied over long periods by generations of the same population. Where settlement was stable, the right to live on and work the land was understood to be heritable to the male and female children of tenants, and only in the case of a tenant dying without heirs (either offspring or collateral kin) did the attribution of the land in question revert to the state. The crucial legal principle was that rights to land tenure and use were recognised through the labour by which land was fructified.

This was also the principle at work in a second main category of land tenure, later codified by the French as 'arsh, or 'tribal' land. Often misunderstood as 'collective' property, what came to be known as 'arsh lands were tracts of cultivable or pasture lands to which access was recognised as hereditary in given lineage groups, within which each family also had inherited rights to given plots (though these were never physically enclosed). The land was worked communally, but held individually, to the benefit of each individual family group. How much land a family could access – and correspondingly, how much of its produce they would receive – depended on their capacity to work the land, measured by the number of male labourers they could deploy: this notwithstanding the essential contribution of female labour to the group's agricultural and domestic economy. The right to land was actually, therefore, a 'right to labour', which could not, in the case of 'arsh land, be inherited by women, 'who cannot hold the plough'.[23] A gender division of labour rights thus played a crucial part in the fortunes of family groups, where an absence of male children could mean the reduction of a household to dependence.

Just as a degree of individualised family property rights entered into the 'communal' 'arsh system, conversely, a degree of communal rights attached to the third type of land tenure, milk or 'possessed' land, usually translated somewhat misleadingly as 'private' property. Again, the principle in most of the region – aside from the milk properties of notable landowning families – was that the degree of labour applied by the individual or family group determined the degree of individual rights as against community obligations in owning and disposing of property. Milk property, delimited by physical walls or hedges, was recognised as the 'private' property of families, who either held actual notarial titles to them or (just as legitimately) were said to hold titles derived from land grants made to vaguely recalled ancestors by undetermined past sovereigns. But while, for example, fruit trees planted and maintained by the family, land cleared and planted entirely by them or a house constructed by them could, in theory, be freely sold, cereal crop-lands or old olive trees, maintained at least in part by communal labour, could not. All members of the extended family, the lineage group and the locally defined community – including its members who might happen to be absent at the time, and for however long a time – exercised a right of pre-emption (*shuf'a*) over any such sale, preventing the intrusion of outsiders and holding members of the community to account for the management of their supposedly 'private' holdings. 'The power of [communal] association and of a community of interests',[24] based in these fundamental ecological relations of land, labour and social reproduction, was thus extremely great, a kind of 'tyranny of the community' that created both durable ties of social solidarity and meticulously policed codes of behaviour and responsibility.

Nowhere, perhaps, was this truer than in Kabylia, the area where *milk* property was most common. Conventionally divided into 'Greater' and 'Lesser', or 'upper' and 'lower' regions, Kabylia (*bled al-qaba'il*, the 'land of the tribes', as seen from the point of view of town-dwelling lowlanders in Algiers and Constantine) is defined by mountain regions of the coast, from Algiers to Bejaïa and then eastwards to Jijel and Collo, and of the interior – the Djurdjura massif, whose highest peak, Lalla Khadidja, reaches 2,308 metres, and the Biban and Babors. 'Greater' Kabylia, on either side of the Sebaou valley, between the coast and the south face of the Djurdjura, is bounded to the south and east by the deep valley of the Soummam, which flows east and north to the sea at Bejaïa. Beyond this line to the south and east, the Biban and Babors make up the more extensive, but topographically less imposing, 'Lesser Kabylia'.

Here, an especially densely settled population speaking the Berber *thaqvaylith* dialect built tightly packed villages on the hilltops and cultivated the well-watered slopes (between 700 and 1,000 mm of rainfall annually on the highest peaks) and valleys below them.

Cereals were grown in the river valleys and on small parcels of land flat enough for ploughing, but as in the Aurès, in Kabylia the peasantry invested especially in arboriculture and combined cultivation with shepherding. Olive oil and beeswax were regional exports. Artisanal production, too, in ironwork and jewellery as well as ceramics and textiles for domestic use, was an important part of the local economy, which, however, was frequently unable to absorb the energies of the whole population. Already in Ottoman times, Kabylia exported part of its

Figure 1.4 Kabylia. Foothills of the Djurdjura, looking south in the Sebaou valley near Tizi Ouzou. Note the clusters of housing on hilltops (Author's photograph).

male workforce as seasonal emigrants to the plains and cities. A densely populated area of fragile resources, Kabylia illustrates perhaps most famously the extent to which daily life, in such circumstances, can be bound around with densely elaborate symbolic codes governing land rights and the gender relations that underwrite family and lineage ties, procreation and the maintenance of a family's access to resources and livelihood.[25]

A final area to consider is the coastal plain, especially Algiers' immediate hinterland, the Mitidja. An alluvial depression between the Atlas and the Algiers Sahel (the range of hills from which the Ottoman city faced the sea), the Mitidja formed a major part of the *dar al-sultan*, 'the sultan's estate', a district governed and taxed directly from the capital. An enduring colonial myth held that on the arrival of the French, the Mitidja was nothing but a malarial swamp, and indeed, many early colonists died in its low-lying and badly drained western and eastern extremities.[26] It seems clear that the economic and political crisis of the Regency in the early nineteenth century had a deleterious effect on the

area, which William Shaler, the American consul, described as having
become 'a perfect desert, without inhabitants or culture' at the end of the
Ottoman period. Shaler's description is clearly an exaggeration for literary effect, framed as an indictment of the Regency's 'barbarous despotism' – he also considered the Mitidja to be 'probably one of the most
valuable expanses of territory, its climate, position, and the fertility of its
soil considered, that exists on our globe'.[27] A French reconnaissance
mission in the plain, immediately after the fall of Algiers, reported that
while part of the land was 'arid and little farmed', elsewhere it seemed
'charming, well-cultivated and displaying extraordinary vegetation . . .
The site . . . is one of the most beautiful one could see . . . a place of true
delight'.[28] A century earlier, Thomas Shaw had described the plain as

> rich and delightful . . . watered in every part by a variety of springs and rivulets.
> The many country seats and . . . farms of the principal inhabitants of Algiers, are
> taken out of these plains, and it is chiefly from them that the metropolis is supplied
> with provisions. Flax, al-henna, roots, pot-herbs, rice, fruit, and grain of all kinds,
> are produced here to such perfection, that the Mettijiah may be justly reckoned
> the garden of the whole kingdom.[29]

For most of the Ottoman period, the Mitidja was intensively cultivated
and highly desirable land; private gardens, orchards and country estates
here grew fruits, vegetables, cereals and tobacco, pulses, herbs, maize,
potatoes, chickpeas, melons, squashes, aubergines, cucumbers, peppers,
tomatoes and grapes. The wine of Algiers, according to Shaw, could well
compete with those of Spain and Portugal.[30] Enclosed estates (*hawsh*) or
'gardens' (*jnan*), either state-owned and let to tenants or privately held by
the Regency's elite, were worked by servile labourers, by immigrant
workers from Kabylia and by the local Arab populations, who also held
their own *'arsh* lands in the region recognised as *watan*s ('homelands').
While many such holdings were relatively modest, there were also great
estates: Jnan al-Dey, a property of the last ruler of Algiers, Husayn Dey,
comprised almost 30,000 square metres of orchards, vegetable gardens
and vineyards.[31]

Across the country, the division of land tenure and access to it supported a heavily stratified society. Within the landowning category,
holdings varied from parcels of less than one hectare up to groups of
estates held by a single great family totalling more than a thousand
hectares. Patrician, urban notable (*beldi* or *hadri*) families owned me-
dium to large estates; the rurally based 'lay' aristocracy (*jawad*) and
religious leaders (*mrabtin*) often owned more; the Regency's governing
elite, in their own right or through the distributive powers of the state,
occupied the top of the pyramid. But while supporting a highly

differentiated social hierarchy, the ecological balance of Ottoman Algeria seems generally to have provided the peasantry with a 'decent' standard of living; most people laboured freely and did not usually starve. Even the life of the lowest on the scale of free labourers, the proletarian, landless sharecropper or shepherd, was 'less miserable than has often been supposed, precarious only in times of crisis'. Furthermore, 'they do not appear to be very numerous relative to other cultivators', that is, the independent tenant farmers and semi-nomadic, semi-sedentary occupiers of *'azl* or *'arsh* lands.[32]

But as we have seen, the equilibrium of careful land use with climate and resources was fragile, and 'times of crisis' could be frequent, as could natural disasters like the earthquakes that struck Algiers in 1632, 1676, 1716 and 1755, wrecked Oran in 1790 and destroyed the town of Blida in 1825. After the regional demographic disaster of the Black Death in 1348, plague had returned frequently to Algeria. In 1654–57 it reportedly killed one-third of the population of Algiers.[33] In 1660–65, and again at the end of the seventeenth century, it combined with drought and locust invasion. It broke out again in 1739–42, 1752–53, 1756, 1784–87 and in the early nineteenth century. Drought or storms, producing poor harvests, especially when combined with locusts or increased taxation to fund regional wars (fought against both Fez and Tunis in the eighteenth century), or the stockpiling of grain for export by the authorities and their merchant intermediaries, resulted in frequent periods of famine.[34] An eighteenth-century French consul at Algiers wrote of a country suffering 'all at once, plague, earthquake, and war'.[35] Life on the land was not wildly anarchic, nor despotically crushed, nor was it always precarious; for many, it was secure and sufficient, for some it was highly profitable. But it was often fragile, usually hard, and almost always frugal: 'a home-oriented economy, to which the social unit turned for the satisfaction of its vital needs ... Clothes were plain and food was simple, with coffee and tea considered luxuries.'[36] The systems of shared responsibility, recognised rights and common interests that provided for social cohesion and resilience in the face of frequent hardship came with sharp divisions of privilege and distinctions of status – by wealth, ethnic or religious affiliation, age and gender – and sometimes high degrees of dependence and exploitation.

## 'Islamic' Cities

A major factor of social distinction and a major element in the control and exploitation of the countryside, of course, was the town. Only a tiny

minority of the overall population lived in urban centres – at the end of the
Ottoman period, Algiers had perhaps 50,000 inhabitants: Constantine,
capital of the east, 25,000, and Tlemcen, historic centre of the west
though never the seat of Ottoman government there, 20,000.
The regional government centres of Medea and Mascara were 'very small
towns'.[37] Nonetheless, for a variety of reasons urban life was considered
'normative'. For an older school of scholarship, much of it founded on
colonial-era writings about French North Africa, this 'normativity' of
urban life was based on essentialist ideas about 'the Islamic city', an
ahistorical notion of the centrality and defining features of urban living
in a reified conception of 'Islamic civilisation'.[38] City-dwellers in
Ottoman Algeria certainly considered themselves, by definition, as more
'civilised', their learning and practice of Islam more orthodox, their lifestyles and economic activities more noble, than those of *jabaylis*, 'mountain folk', as the arabophone citizens of the caravan entrepôt, garrison
town and vast palm-growing oasis of Biskra referred to *shawi*-speaking
peasants from the Aurès to their north, or *berranis*, as rural people from
the interior 'open land' were known in Algiers.

But this 'civic ideology'[39] of distinction, though important for understanding the culture of city life and durable attitudes towards 'the countryside', should not mislead us into thinking that the city had an especially
distinct kind of history.[40] The functions of cities, as concentrated centres
of artisanal production, market exchange, legal arbitration, learning,
political and religious authority, all existed in the countryside too, in
locales of specialised handicrafts, at weekly markets, in customary delib-
erative assemblies of adult males (*jama'as*, or *tajma'ats* in berberophone
areas), the person of the *hakem* or *qa'id* (district or local governor), the
shaykh of a tribal fraction or the custodian (*muqaddam*) of a saint's shrine.
Population size is also no guide; parts of mountainous Kabylia could be
so densely populated as to qualify as 'urban' areas,[41] while some self-
regarding 'cities' of the Ottoman period were dismissed by European
observers as hardly more than villages. What was important about cities,
as Lucette Valensi pointed out in trying to distinguish 'cities' from
'towns', was the *perception* of their distinctiveness: 'Life-style – urbanity
or rusticity – established the boundary ... more than did the function of
each entity'.[42] Or rather, *beliefs* about 'urbanity' and 'rurality', defining
perceptions of both, framed the ways in which people behaved and saw
themselves, in a social as well as spatial hierarchy, disguising the fact that
'city' and 'country' were really only points of greater or lesser intensity on
a continuum of social and economic functions. The distinctiveness of the
city was more symbolic and ideological than practical and functional.
If we understand this, it becomes easier to grasp the significance of the

Figure 1.5 Tlemcen, interior of the great mosque (eleventh–twelfth centuries) (K. Bouayad).

'mere villages' that were many of Ottoman Algeria's urban centres, and to see the relation between city and countryside as one of overlap and interdependence rather than – as city-dwelling writers often expressed it – in terms of vulnerable citadels of civilisation surrounded by seas of tribal ignorance and hostility.

The practical as well as symbolic functions of cities were, of course, important, as intensive market centres, and as bases of the state's coercive power and the dispensation of its law. The central government and that of Algeria's three provinces (beyliks – also a term used for 'the state' in general) were based on regional urban centres. Algiers, as the Regency's capital, developed an entirely new significance on the basis of its ancient foundations, as did Constantine, the ancient capital of Numidia in Roman times that became centre of the beylik of the east.[43] The smaller, central beylik of Titteri, south of Algiers, was centred on the town of Medea perched in the Atlas, and the capital of the beylik of the west moved from Mazouna to Mascara before the re-conquest of Oran from the Spanish in 1791.[44]

But urban-centred power was impotent without effective means of transmission to the countryside through rurally based intermediaries.

*Hakem*s, *qa'id*s and *shaykh*s kept local order and represented local interests to distant authorities. Auxiliary tribal groups, so-called *makhzen*
(government, literally 'treasury') tribes, furnished cavalry to the beylik
in exchange for exemption from the taxes they helped raise from their
*ra'aya* (literally 'flock' or 'subject') neighbours. Men of the *zwawa* (an
Arabic term from the Berber *igawawen*) population of upper Kabylia were
recruited to the militia of Algiers and Constantine. Great power also lay
with regional aristocrats like the Muqrani family. From the sixteenth
century, the Muqranis were de facto rulers in the Medjana, an area of
the high plains between Kabylia, the Biban and the Hodna mountains in
the western Constantinois. They raised taxes and administered the region
'as they saw fit', in exchange for an annual tribute to Algiers and the
guarantee of passage through their fiefdom for the Regency's soldiers.[45]
Conversely, some centres of state power, like Tizi Ouzou in the Sebaou
valley, where the Ottomans established a *burj* (fort) which became the
nucleus of an administrative settlement, or even Blida (*bulayda*, the 'little
city') founded by the beylik at the southern limit of the Mitidja in 1535,
hardly qualified as 'cities' in the eyes of patrician, *hadri* inhabitants of
longer-established, more distinguished settlements, whether substantial
commercial and princely towns like Bejaïa and Tlemcen, or smaller
agglomerations like Mazouna, Nedroma or Ghardaïa. These apparently
insubstantial places were steeped in a sense of urbane dignity and historical longevity that constituted a powerful civic ideology: the three last-
named towns provide good examples to illustrate the point.

Mazouna, a market and textile-manufacturing town at the lower south-
western edge of the Dahra mountains, an area of rich land farmed since
antiquity and a point of exchange between the uplands, the coast and the
Cheliff river valley, was described by the geographer al-Idrissi in the mid-
twelfth century:

[It] possesses rivers, fields sown with grain, orchards, markets well-stocked with
merchandise and fine houses. The market is held on a fixed day and the Berbers of
the surrounding area come with various fruits, milk and butter. Honey is abundant. It is a lovely country, very rich and very fertile.[46]

Agriculture, weaving and trade made the town live; what made it a city
was not only its role as a centre for manufacture or the cultivation and
exchange of produce but its self-perception as a centre of 'civilisation',
founded particularly on its medieval *madrasa* (school of Islamic jurisprudence), 'a high seat of culture and justice' esteemed throughout the region
and whose buildings were restored by the Ottoman authorities.[47] It was
here that the great scholar Muhammad ibn Ali al-Sanusi, born in nearby
Mostaghanem in 1791, and later founder of the Sanusiyya brotherhood

that would become a major organisational force of Islam in North and West Africa before providing the first rulers of independent Libya, studied before travelling to Mecca and Medina.

Further west, Nedroma, nestled in the Traras mountains eighteen kilometres south of the coast and thirty kilometres east of the present Moroccan border, had a population in the early colonial period of only about 3,000 people, of whom 15 per cent were Jewish. The town (as the Berber 'Falousen', the almond trees) was mentioned by the geographer al-Ya'qubi in the ninth century. Its mosque was built by the Almoravid dynasty in ca. 1090, forty years before that of Tlemcen. Contested between the rulers of Fez and Tlemcen since the thirteenth century, and between Morocco and the Ottomans from the mid-sixteenth century, the city was garrisoned from Algiers only in 1791, its internal politics being divided, meanwhile, between pro-Ottoman and pro-Moroccan factions. Its well-watered agricultural lands, livestock and grain markets, cotton-spinning, wool and pottery industries, its trading links to Fez and Tangier, its *qasba* (citadel), discreetly elegant courtyard houses and four-way division into distinct quarters were all important features of the town. But what made it a city was its citizens' perception of their own historic dignity: the town's internal government by a *jama'a* assembling representatives of the principal notable families, whose president was invested as *qa'id* in command of the local militia; the endogamy of the elite families and careful preservation of their social capital through the education of their sons and placing them advantageously in commerce; an accent and dialect of Arabic distinctive to the town; the cultivation of the tradition of Arab-Andalusian music, with locally specific techniques of interpreting certain pieces of the repertoire.[48]

Almost 600 kilometres south of Algiers and 200 beyond the Saharan Atlas, in the *shebka* ('net'), a rock plateau in the desert crosscut with deep ravines, fenced off by a jealously guarded independence from the effective projection of coercion or arbitration by the Ottoman state, but forging a carefully negotiated relationship with it, was another group of cities based on an even stronger sense of historically distinctive community. The urbanity of the Mzab, a cluster of five cities in a valley of the same name whose river flowed only once every two or three years, was defined more by its particular religious and scholarly civilisation than by the exceptionally fragile local ecology, and the far-flung commercial activity, that gave the towns physical life. After the destruction in 909 of the Rustamid imamate at Tahert on the southern edge of the Tell, the Mzab was a refuge for its Berber-speaking Ibadi Muslims, adherents of a strict sect considering themselves true believers but denounced as heretics by the ruling Fatimid (Shi'i) caliphs of the tenth century, and also considered such by the Sunni jurists of the Maliki school who later became dominant in North Africa. The principal town of the Mzab, Ghardaïa, was founded in 1053.[49] Date-palm cultivation was possible by irrigating the town's gardens from wells, dug by hand down to the water table, and by a system of channels and basins designed to capture and distribute the occasional waters of the river, but life in the Mzab 'depended on an influx of resources from the exterior'.[50]

As a major Saharan market, Ghardaïa and its neighbours lived primarily from the profits of long-distance trade southward across the desert, with Mzabis organising and financing caravans manned and managed by Arabic-speaking nomadic Shaamba people. Increasingly, from the early modern period, Mzabi men also created an industrious diaspora of commerce and trades in the cities of the north. The constant preoccupation of the cities' leaders and the goal of their economic activity was preservation of the community, identified from its origins as a threatened community of the truly faithful, bound by Ibadi doctrine – whose specificity lay more in community and political regulation than in theological doctrine or ritual practice[51] – and sheltering in a true *dar al-islam* ('domain of Islam') from a world of corruption and unbelief (*kufr*). Institutions of Islamic learning and jurisprudence were central to community life. In the absence, since the destruction of Tahert, of a regularly invested imam, the cities were governed by *jama'as*, councils of representatives of the city's major lineage fractions (*ashiras*) who must be married and fathers, with established social positions and material fortune, presided over by the shaykh of the principal mosque and by the *halqa* ('circle') of *'azzaba*, the community's ascetic religious scholars. All aspects of community life were governed by 'agreements' (*ittifiqat*), decreed by the shaykhs and *'azzaba* in consensus (*ijma*), which was considered binding on the entire community. Matters concerning women were regulated and policed by a group of women, the *thimsirriden*, consulted on such matters by the *'azzaba*. Their particular power derived from their responsibility for the ritual washing of bodies after death, a function they could refuse to perform for those considered as having transgressed the norms of accepted behaviour.[52] A crucial element of community preservation lay in the strict ruling against women, and children up to a certain age, leaving the Mzab. Men frequently travelled north to work for long periods, remitting money to their city of origin for investment in trade and in date-palm groves (the latter, again, a symbolic commitment to the community). But throughout the Ottoman and colonial periods, women were forbidden to leave the valley. The community's particularity was maintained, too, by the use of its Berber dialect as the maternal and domestic language, with

Arabic (on mastery of which great value was placed) taught only from the time a child began to learn the Qur'an, ritual and religious sciences.

Mzabis who came north to the Regency's capital entered a highly stratified but also mobile, diverse and polyglot society to which they were only one of several groups of immigrants. Indeed, the defining feature of Ottoman Algiers was perhaps the significance of its immigrants, who may have constituted a majority of the total population in the period 1580–1640: first their success as distinctly visible groups and then their absorption into the city, which combined their diverse origins into its own cosmopolitan identity.[53] From the late sixteenth century to the end of the seventeenth century, the 'golden age' of the privateer economy, Algiers' wealthy elite was dominated by Andalusis and *'uluj* (singular *'ilj*: in Algiers, a term denoting a Christian captive converted to Islam, the 'renegades' of contemporary European writers).[54] Of a sample of forty-two inventories of the largest inheritances surviving from the period examined by the Algerian historian Lemnouar Merouche, sixteen are of *'uluj* and fifteen of Andalusi origin.

The Andalusis, refugees from the collapse of Muslim Spain who were often referred to in European sources as 'Moors', were an important and distinctive group of the Algerine elite. They are especially present in surviving sources as *mu'allim*s (master-craftsmen) and architects, merchants and manufacturers of silks and other textiles. The wealthiest combined the symbolic capital of religious learning as *'ulama* (singular *'alim*, a scholar of Islamic law and doctrine) with the practical enrichment of commerce, or took to the sea as privateer captains. From the sixteenth century, leading Andalusi families combined with existing Arab *beldi* lineages in marriage alliances, practising 'a kind of caste endogamy, relaxed only occasionally, and reluctantly, and then only for the ruling individuals of the day'.[55]

*'Uluj* came from very different origins to these patrician elites, but their social promotion, after conversion and assimilation into the ruling society – not infrequently by adoption or marriage into the family of a former master – could be astonishing. Most of the superintendents of the treasury in the mid-sixteenth to mid-seventeenth centuries were converts. Ramdan ben 'Abdallah, a convert and soldier in the Ottoman garrison, the freed slave and son-in-law of his former master, died in 1649 leaving in his will 'a large estate, a magnificent house and four Christian slaves' of his own.[56] The Regency's governor during a succession crisis in 1556 was Hasan 'Corso', a Corsican convert, one of whose principal lieutenants was Ali 'Sardo', a Sardinian convert. In the crisis' endgame, Hasan was executed on the orders of a pasha sent from Istanbul, who in turn was murdered by Hasan's friend and ally, the

governor of Tlemcen, Qa'id Yusuf, himself a convert originally from Calabria in southern Italy.[57] Another Calabrese, 'Ilj Ali ('Euldj Ali' in contemporary European sources), captured in the 1530s, rose after his conversion from enslaved oarsman on an Algerine galley to privateer captain, Ottoman pasha of Tripoli in Libya, ruler of Algiers from 1568 to 1571, and Grand Admiral of the Ottoman fleet from 1571 to his death in 1587.[58] Less spectacular but perhaps more extraordinary was the family history of 'the very learned mufti of Islam, Sidi Muhammad ben Sidi Ramdan ben Yusuf al-'Ilj' who in the 1630s was the Hanafi *mufti* (one of two chief judges and religious officials[59]) in Algiers – the son of a senior *'alim* and grandson of a convert.[60] These are exceptional cases; more common was a degree of social and political promotion acquired through professional competence and personal ambition in a society that was largely meritocratic and where the fortunes of the volatile and complex early modern Mediterranean world brought together enterprising spirits from different horizons, capable of negotiating personal and familial destinies across the frontiers of social, political and religious divides.[61] Marriage alliances were also contracted between wealthy and successful *'uluj* and families of Andalusi origin.

The Ottoman elite – as internally diverse as the empire itself, with the addition of *'uluj* from northern as well as southern Europe and the Mediterranean islands – monopolised political and military power, to which no 'autochtonous' Algerine *beldi* Arab or Berber family ever acceded directly. Many of them, particularly the *ra'is* (privateer captains), and the families of the *dey*s (governors) themselves, amassed spectacular fortunes. The largest single inheritance attested from the Ottoman period is that of a daughter of one of the last Ottoman governors, Aisha bint Hasan Pasha, whose pearls and jewellery alone were valued at 730,428 pataques (97,390 Spanish piasters, SP); second in line comes the fortune of the last reigning dey, Husayn Pasha, at 591,159 pataques (78,821 SP).[62] By comparison, the fortunes of leading merchants and high state officials registered at the same time, in the 1820s, generally fall in the range of 3,000–9,000 SP. Merchants in the Arab *beldi* elite sometimes joined their commercial fortunes to political as well as to more locally rooted, symbolic forms of power: Abd al-Rahman al-Barbri, an international merchant, came from a family whose marriage ties connected them both to the household of an Ottoman governor and to the descendants of Sidi Abd al-Rahman al-Tha'alibi, a revered fourteenth-century scholar who had become Algiers' principal patron saint.[63]

At the other end of the scale were the city's least willing immigrants: European Christian captives taken by privateers and Africans from south of the Sahara traded north by slave caravans. While those Christians who converted could enjoy rapid social promotion, there was also a significant differentiation in living standards within the enslaved population. European men, depending on their own background and the likelihood of raising substantial sums at home for their release, were more often held for ransom than enslaved for life. Women were very rarely ransomed, but however dependent as wives, concubines or domestic servants of their owners, their material position was often favourable compared to that of other captives, and their domestic position may have compared favourably to that which they could expect in their countries of origin. Indeed, many converted to Islam and married male converts, frequently from the same region of origin as themselves, creating a kind of expatriate community[64] – one in which women's legal rights were better than those they would have enjoyed in early modern Europe. The conditions of captivity for Europeans, often dramatised in European accounts and particularly by the French and Spanish *rédemptoristes*, 'redeeming' religious orders like the Trinitarians devoted to raising funds and support for their missions to ransom Christians from the hands of 'the Turk', can hardly have been easy. But they cannot reasonably be compared to the mass chattel slavery endured by Africans in the Atlantic trade.

For one thing, 'white slavery' in North Africa was part of a long pattern of Mediterranean social and economic history in which people, like other resources, had been aggressively pursued and moved around the region since antiquity.[65] The Mediterranean slave economy was as much a part of life in Toulon and Naples as it was in Algiers, and eighteenth-century consular records, to take only a few examples, illustrate the extent to which, on both sides of the sea, those who had the misfortune to fall captive played parts in mutually understood diplomatic relations. Muslim slaves on French ships in Toulon were able to send a petition to Algiers to complain that they had 'nowhere to perform their prayers in peace, and that their cemetery was not kept in proper order'. When reports reached Algiers of ill-treatment suffered by Algerian slaves in Naples, the dey in retaliation had the priests and officers of two captured Neapolitan galleys put to work in a chain-gang alongside 'the murderers and criminals' of their crews. On another occasion, the Neapolitans reassured the dey that their own Algerian galley-slaves were treated according to the rules – officers receiving particular consideration – and added, as from one rather superior sovereign to another, that 'one should not be taken in' by the complaints of 'these sorts of people' (on both sides). The king of Sicily on one occasion in 1756 declared himself uninterested in exchanging Algerian captives against his Neapolitan subjects held in Algiers, 'but is still most vexed at the lack of vigilance of the latter, for

allowing themselves to be captured'. After two French slaves escaped
from Algiers aboard a French ship in 1776, the navy minister at
Versailles warned the French consul that although the king approved
the 'wise conduct' of the captain who had allowed them to go free on
arrival in France, 'you must ensure that such a thing does not happen
again; His Majesty will even have the captain punished if the Dey
demands it'. The consul was to reimburse the dey for his loss if
required. Later the same year, a slave who had taken refuge on
a French frigate was actually returned to the Algerians.[66]

Some participants in this forced Mediterranean mobility were in fact
not captives at all, but gave themselves up into servitude in Algiers as
a preferable alternative to the rigours of their home countries' military
service or criminal justice. Spanish soldiers fled the grim *presidio* at Oran
and sometimes ended up as janissaries at Algiers; professional people-
traffickers assisted fugitive Europeans to cross from Italy and Sicily to
North Africa as well as making the reverse journey.[67] In 1776, the French
consul counted 'some 180 fugitives from Oran and from different countries' arriving in Algiers, against 131 captives brought in by sea.[68]
In popular culture, rather than the abomination denounced by the
redemptorists, Mediterranean captivity, however hard, was also simply
one of life's misfortunes, the stuff of adventure tales and love songs: as
a seventeenth-century English lyricist put it, 'In the midst of my sorrows,
whilst others do mourn; 'Tis the want of my Love that doth make me
forlorn: ... No torment like mine was, when I was a Slave: For the want of
my *Betty* was worse than a Grave.'[69]

Secondly, captives' life chances varied enormously. Galley-slaves, like
the Muslim prisoners and forced-labour convicts on European ships,
endured much hardship:

I was constrained either to labor or else to lose my head ... I was in a marvelous
weakness, what with continual labor, with beating, and with sickness ... being in
a most miserable estate without all succor, seeing no man to pity my misery,
having no nourishment but only bread and water and that but small quantity, no
apparel on me but a thin shirt and a pair of linen breeches, and lodged in a stable
on the cold ground ... in sickness and extreme slavery.[70]

The massive defensive works and harbour construction undertaken in
sixteenth-century Algiers were also largely accomplished by slave labour.
But from the seventeenth century onwards, once the fortifications were
complete and the oared galley finally lost its pre-eminence in
Mediterranean navies, the frequency of such experiences diminished.
Other captives, as an English report of 1675 explained, were

better treated than any slaves in all the grand Signors [the Ottoman sultan's] Dominions, haveing the benefitt to Keep shopps, Tauerns, to worke upon their hand craft trade . . . Many thousand Captiues obtayned their liberty by theer own Industry. They haue alsoe liberty to say & and [sic] hear mass . . . The protestants haue alsoe a place to preach & pray . . .[71]

It was customary in the eighteenth century for the French consul to provide bread, meat and wine to 'the poor Christians, slaves at Algiers' at Christmas.[72] At the same time, European consuls, unable to hire reliable domestic servants from home, also routinely employed Christian slaves, affordably leased to them by the Regency, in their own households; though answerable to the discipline of the dey's office, they came and went, exercised their professions, played cards, drank and got into fights as they might anywhere.[73] William Shaler, the American consul not generally inclined to mildness in his judgments of Ottoman 'despotism', reckoned in the 1820s that while slaves must certainly have endured the 'occasional cruelty and hardship . . . inseparable from the unprotected situation of captives of any description', on the whole

their condition here was not generally worse than that of prisoners of war in many civilized, Christian countries . . . and generally all who were industriously disposed easily found the means of profiting by it . . . In short, there were slaves who left Algiers with regret.[74]

Some, indeed, did not leave, though free to do so. Baba Ali, dey from 1754 to 1766, had as his valet before his election a Sicilian boy whom he freed on acceding to the throne. Having initially intended to embark 'for a Christian land', the freedman instead opted to convert a few days after his manumission and remained in his old master's service, having been promised an advantageous post in the administration. 'The young man is very sensible', commented the French consul, 'and was able, while in the dey's service, to obtain the freedom of several poor Neapolitan slaves who sought his help'.[75] Both women and men belonging to important officials are recorded as having left substantial sums in property – between 1,500 and 5,300 pataques – held in their own right at their deaths. A slave might be sold, at around the same time, for 250–400 pataques. In general, women captives seem to have held larger personal fortunes of this kind than their male counterparts.

By far the greater part of the servile and freed population, however, were among the poorest in society, as reckoned by the records of inventories of property at death: most left fewer than 100 pataques. The smallest such property we know of was that of a black slave whose worldly belongings were valued at three-quarters of a pataque. Black African slaves, frequently Muslims or at least nominally converted to

Islam en route across the Sahara, could gain their liberty neither by conversion nor by ransom, though manumission was frequent, giving rise to a generally poor, low-status, free black urban population. Such freed African slaves tended to remain tied in close relations of dependence to their former masters' families.[76] Black African Muslim captives were often no better off, and must generally have been in considerably worse positions, than their white Christian European counterparts.[77]

Between the patrician elite at the top of the scale and the poorest slaves at the bottom, Algiers' society displayed a wide spectrum of wealth and poverty, with a high degree of social mobility in both directions and many people exercising several professions in succession or at once. The ruling political class itself was highly volatile, with positions dependent on patronage, and offices, including the highest, changing hands frequently. An Ottoman *ra'is* could become rich and influential, be appointed to high office, fall from grace and find himself all but destitute, then experience a reversal of fortunes with a change of regime. Religious scholars holding positions as secretaries, imams (prayer-leaders) or court clerks could also be silk-merchants, bookbinders, saddlers or drapers; janissaries and minor privateer captains earned additional income as barbers, black-smiths, shoemakers or owners of coffee shops.[78] Women, on the other hand, worked outside the domestic economy in only a few areas. Aside from the few women of saintly descent who could become guardians of mausoleums and recipients of substantial revenues from pilgrims or pious endowments (*habus*[79]), women worked as midwives, food-stall holders, owners or employees of bathhouses, makers and sellers of candles or as prostitutes. The latter category, again, illustrates a diversity of fortunes. At the death of one woman registered as a prostitute, her property amounted to only 121 pataques. Another – the concubine of the *mizwar*, the agent responsible for policing and taxing prostitution in the city – left a sizeable fortune of 6,342 pataques.

The Jewish population – small overall, but ancient and significant especially in certain towns (perhaps 10 per cent of the populace, or 5,000 people, in Algiers at the end of the Ottoman period) – was itself stratified between a large, modest artisan class and a small elite of inter-nationally connected merchant families. The latter, recently arrived associates of great trading houses based in Gibraltar, France, Livorno (Leghorn) and the eastern Mediterranean, were sometimes able to gain positions of considerable commercial and political importance close to the state elite – whose treasury lent *to* them, exploiting its own preconcep-tions, at 3 per cent interest.[80] The former, the great majority of the community, were descendants of immigrants who had come to North Africa in the ancient diaspora, of Berbers who had adopted Judaism in late antiquity or of fifteenth- and sixteenth-century Andalusi refugees. Long established in communities across the region, from the coast to the Sahara, and in the major nodal towns of trade, culture and manufacture from Ghardaia to Constantine and Nedroma, most continued long into the nineteenth and early twentieth centuries to occupy working-class positions, as couriers, porters or tailors' assistants. Though sometimes living in distinct quarters and governed in civil matters by their own rabbinical authorities, there was often little to mark out the Jewish population from their Muslim neighbours: residential areas were not usually exclusive, and in many aspects of language, culture and profession they were indistinguishable from the other poorer classes of society.

Some immigrant groups, on the other hand, specialised in niche occupations which they dominated (without having a legally recognised monopoly[81]): Jijelis were bakers, Mzabis bath-house managers, Biskris porters and couriers. These groups of *barrani*s, immigrants from the interior, were organised along with other professional groups in *jama'a*s ('corporations', known as *ta'ifa*s in the Mashriq) under the authority of an appointed *amin* or head of the corporation, responsible for the quality of work in each trade, for taxation and levying fines. The chief *amin*, or *amin al-umana*, a hereditary post from the second half of the seventeenth century, met with the *muhtasib* (market inspector and censor), the *qadi* (judge) of the town and an appointed *shaykh al-bled* (chief of the municipality) in a kind of municipal council for the regulation of local and commercial affairs.

This mobile and cosmopolitan urban society gradually coalesced over the course of the eighteenth century, with the absorption of the descendants of immigrant groups – Turks and their children, referred to as *kuluglis*,[82] Andalusis and *'uluj* – into a local urban elite within which foreign 'ethnic' identifications were no longer differentiated,[83] and the rise to prominence of *barrani*s in the city's craft and labour market. As slavery became, first, a state monopoly, and then marginal – with at most 500 captives in Algiers at the end of the 1780s – the role of the converts, pre-eminent in the sixteenth century, disappeared. Incomers from the countryside joined the *ojaq* (the corps of janissaries)[84] and became master-craftsmen and heads of corporations, roles earlier dominated by immigrants from Andalus or elsewhere.[85] In the final flourish of corsairing, during the Napoleonic wars in Europe, the chance of quick enrichment was opened up to *barrani*s and their offspring: Ra'is Hamidu, the legendary admiral of the Algerian fleet killed in battle against the American navy in 1815, was the son of an Algiers artisan. While most migrants from the interior to the city remained poorly paid manual labourers, and some gained respectable positions in commerce, trades or crafts that carried with them the dignity of *beldi* status, a few managed to realise in fact the ideological image of the city as the place which, above all, could give access to riches, power and fame.

## The Beylik and the World Beyond

Supported by rural production and capped by the division of power and privilege in the cities, the societies of Ottoman Algeria were shaped, beyond their local environments, by relationships to the state, to the larger community of Islam and to the wider worlds of Africa and the Atlantic, the Mediterranean and Europe. Algerians imagined and acted out their place in these overlapping contexts through origin stories that explained their ancestry, in the local landscape of sacred space and the practices of ritual and learning that symbolised the rootedness as well as the universality of Islam, and by their engagement in far-flung networks of exchange and mobility.

We have seen how the Regency came into being through a coalition of local urban politics and adventurous regional entrepreneurism in the context of Ottoman expansion; reference has also been made to the volatility and periodic crises of its government.[86] The unstable conjuncture of circumstances that saw its birth, and the frequent tumult of its high politics, however, should not disguise the basic continuities of Ottoman rule that gave the state substance over the three centuries of its existence. The synergy of local and immigrant interests that brought the state into being continued to enable it to function on various levels, from the security of land tenure and local markets that provided both production and taxation to the consolidation of notable family fortunes by marriage to high administrators or convert corsairs. The balance between local autonomy and recognition of imperial paramountcy varied over time, but both elements remained important to the end of the period. Khayr al-Din and his immediate successors ruled as semi-independent *beylerbeys*, governors general of North Africa, representing Ottoman power on the front line of its war with the Habsburgs which came to a stuttering end after the temporary destruction of the Ottoman fleet at Lepanto in 1571 and (conversely) the Ottoman recapture of Tunis in 1574. From the mid-1580s, pashas were named to govern Algiers for three-year terms, signalling more direct, but less durable, control by the Sublime Porte (the central Ottoman government). At the same time, privateering, though no longer a front in the early modern 'world war', entered a phase of massive expansion, increasing the power of the *ta'ifat al-ra'is*, the corporation of corsair captains, and the *ojaq*, who in 1659 overthrew the appointed pasha and attempted to establish their own military republic. The chronic instability of this system led in 1671 to the assumption of power, in turn, by the *ra'is*, who installed one of their own number as ruler, with the title of *dey* (from the Turkish *deyi*, 'uncle').

The rule of the deys, elected from among the *divan* or governing council that formed the city's ruling oligarchy and confirmed in their positions by the Ottoman government in Istanbul, continued until the overthrow of the Regency in 1830. Algiers' effective autonomy from the Porte was thus greatly increased, but the symbols of rulership in the deys' Regency bore the marks both of locally legitimised and internationally recognised sovereignty and of attachment to the distant imperial centre. The dey was a recognised power in his own right in diplomatic terms: the treaty of peace with Britain signed in 1816 was formally 'between His Majesty the King of the United Kingdom of Great Britain and Ireland, and His Most Serene Highness . . . Dey and Governor of the Warlike City and Kingdom of Algiers'.[87] But from 1520 until 1830, coins struck in Algiers consistently bore the name of the reigning Ottoman sultan and his title, 'Lord of the Two Shores and Sovereign of the Two Seas', marking the place of Algeria at the edge of a Eurasian empire that stretched from the Indian Ocean shores of Arabia through the Balkans to the western Mediterranean. The notion of belonging to the wider world of Ottoman sovereignty remained important, particularly for the Turkish-speaking military and political elite, but not only for them.[88] Into the middle of the twentieth century, Friday sermons in mosques in rural districts of eastern Algeria were still being said in the name of the last reigning Ottoman sultan.[89]

At the local level, the due forms of sovereignty are clearly captured in an account of the investiture of a new dey by the military, political, scholarly and religious elites of Algiers in 1766. The chief officials, or *nadi wuzara* ('circle of ministers'), 'met and entrusted Mehmed Osman Pasha with rulership', and the following day

the *agha* [commander] of the soldiers, with his deputy, the whole council and the two *mufti*s, the judges, the *naqib al-ashraf*,[90] and the notables of the people, gathered at the residence of the sovereign.[91] Mehmed Pasha sat down on the throne of the ruler, and the *'ulama* first gave him the *bay'a* [oath of investiture], followed by the *naqib al-ashraf*, the ministers, the whole council and all the people, and he put on the robe of office. Then the cannon were fired and the procession set out, and he went up to his house with his escort . . . and he appointed to office those who merited appointment, and dismissed those who merited dismissal.[92]

The political history of the Regency has often been reduced to one of factional struggles within Algiers, between *ra'is* and *ojaq*, or 'pure Turks' and *kuluglis*, in which the 'autochtonous' population – whether *beldi* elite or peasant mass – plays no discernible role except to furnish extorted taxes. As we have seen, however, social dividing lines were not as clear, especially over the long term, as such views suppose, and the account quoted above, from an Algiers notable of a local Arab sharifian lineage, suggests the need to relativise the division between a 'foreign' ruling clique and the indigenous population. Other, more complex, hierarchical divisions were more significant. The beylik's rule was never a matter of a few thousand 'foreign' janissaries holding millions of 'natives' in permanent subjection.

The effective limits of the state, and the extent to which its rule was recognised, varied over both time and space. When threatened by a hostile incursion from the Moroccan Tafilelt region in 1578, the people of the Gourara and neighbouring oases had no hesitation in seeking protection from the Ottomans in Algiers.[93] The inhabitants of the Mzab, on the other hand, 'do not suffer their towns to be garrisoned, and the government of Algiers has never been able to make them submit'[94] according to a well-informed late eighteenth-century observer, but their trading privileges and freedom of worship were well established and recognised by the beylik, on whose stability their commercial prosperity and community survival depended. The Kabyles, depicted as almost perennially in revolt in the nineteenth-century account of De Grammont, certainly resisted effective Ottoman rule in the mountains and the upper Sebaou valley, where in the sixteenth century an autonomous statelet, the 'kingdom of Kouko', existed, founded by the Aït l-Qadi lineage whose regional influence continued long after their state submitted to the Regency in 1542.[95] A chain of forts in the Sebaou and Soummam valleys did little more than attempt to control communications in the region and enable some limited tax-raising. But equally, the bey of Constantine largely depended on *zwawa* recruits, from the *igawawen* tribes of the high central Djurdjura, for his army, and Kabyle labourers worked the estates and gardens of the Ottoman elite in Algiers and the Mitidja. The only massive, widespread rural revolts against the Regency's government came in the first years of the nineteenth century, in a context of unprecedented general crisis.

The variable parameters of the state's sovereignty are visible in economic and fiscal terms as well as in the extent of control over territory and population. Local and sectional interests within the elite frequently carried the day over any putative central sovereignty of the state. Control of foreign trade was sometimes considered a 'state monopoly' in contemporary outside sources.[96] In fact, it was a multi-tiered system of intermediary influence in which state officials, from the most modest tribal shaykh or local *qa'id* up to the *khaznaji* (treasurer), *wakil kharaj* (minister of naval and foreign affairs) or dey himself at Algiers, acted in his own as well as his administrative office's interest.[97] In 1817, during an extreme crisis in Algiers brought on by widespread famine, the bey of Constantine was stockpiling grain 'up to the ceilings' of his warehouses at Bône, in anticipation of a high price for export.[98] The variability of both currency and taxation also illustrates the unevenness of integration under the Regency's rule. From the early eighteenth century, the French *Compagnie royale d'Afrique*, which made substantial purchases of grain from Algeria throughout the century, used a specially clipped currency, by agreement with Algiers, in its transactions with Algerian partners, each coin being legal tender exclusively in the port or market for which it was intended – thus Collo, Bône (Annaba), La Calle (El Kala) and Constantine each had its own specially 'adjusted' piaster. Taxation too varied: *hukr* (groundrent) and *'ashur, zakat* or *jabri* (property taxes assessed on livestock or land under cultivation) were collected from areas, like the Dar al-Sultan around Algiers or the plains of Constantine, easily controlled from the city, but the authorities satisfied themselves with the more flexible *lezma* or *gharama* (head tax or 'fine') on less easily assessed populations, nomads or villagers in the mountains. The effectiveness of tax-raising declined with the friction of topography as well as that of distance from the centres of government, although into the mid-twentieth century, folk memories in areas like the Atlas mountains above Blida remembered the violence of Ottoman fiscal expeditions and still referred to lowlanders only half-jokingly as 'Turks'.[99] The primacy of Algiers over the provinces, too, was symbolised by the *dannush*, a twice-yearly remittance of taxes from each of the three regions to the capital, and by the correlative confirmation of beys in post by the dey, but each province enjoyed a considerable degree of relative autonomy. Salah Bey, who remains a legendary ruler of Constantine in local historical memory, even attempted to assert the independence of his, most fertile and wealthy, province from the suzerainty of Algiers at the end of the eighteenth century.[100]

As the state functioned between claims to imperial sovereignty and negotiations with local power and interests, so the cultural worlds of Algeria's populations were defined by both universalist codes of meaning and belonging, and local hierarchical divisions. Most of the country's people were Arabic-speaking Muslims who were ultimately descended from the Berber-speaking populations who had lived in North Africa since remote antiquity. Their own understandings of their ancestry and place in the world were governed by genealogical affiliations, from the extended family up to a tribal group of associated lineages, claiming descent from a single ancestor as *aït . . .*, *awlad . . .* or *beni . . .* ('the children of . . . '). Often, such associations were inherited by place of habitation rather than by actual descent, with successive migrations of new groups adhering to established lineages either by absorption or in degrees of dependence and clientship, but the genealogical idiom of shared ancestry served to anchor social solidarity in an imagined commonality of blood ties. Origin stories, preserved in oral and written literature, expressed the populations' own histories on the basis of memories or myths of descent from 'prestigious' ancestors. The Arabic-speaking, pastoralist Awlad Na'il of the steppe and mountains in the Hodna region, for example, preserved the history of their ancestors in fragments of the epic of the Beni Hilal, Arab nomads whose migration to North Africa in the eleventh century became the basis for one of Arabic literature's greatest romances.[101] Stories of migration to, or of the founding of, settlements attributed their origins to early heroes of the Islamic conquests – as at Sidi Okba, founded at the desert's edge south of the Aurès around the tomb of Uqba ibn Nafi, a companion of the Prophet and the first Muslim conqueror of the Maghrib – to virtuous warriors in the service of medieval caliphs, as at Nedroma, supposedly founded on the site of the tomb of one such martyr, or to Muslim saints (*awliya*, singular *wali*, literally one 'near' to God), as in the Gourara, where the foundation of *ksur* and the original irrigation of oasis gardens was frequently attributed to saints.[102]

The saints, often termed *mrabtin*[103] ('marabouts') and their descendants, who inherited the *baraka* (charismatic power of 'blessing') of a saintly ancestor, provided the local infrastructure of Islamic learning and practice across the country, in towns as well as in the countryside. The tombs of such saints were often considered sanctuaries and repositories of spiritual power.

A mosque and centre of learning, sometimes with a library and hospice for students and pilgrims, might be attached to the mausoleum, the whole complex being termed a *zawiya* (plural *zawaya*). The most famous saints – Sidi al-Hawari (Lhouari) in Oran, Sidi Bu Madyan at Tlemcen, Sidi Abd al-Rahman al-Tha'alibi in Algiers[104] – became, and remain, local patrons of the cities where their tombs were situated as well as regional scholarly or miracle-working celebrities to whose shrines pilgrims would come from far afield to pray, study or seek aid and intercession with God. Other, lesser saints' shrines, domed and whitewashed *qubba*s over tombs or *maqam*s marking a stopping place, were scattered across the countryside. They indicated the passing or the resting places of *rjal al-bled*, the 'men of the land', anchor points for

Figure 1.6 Sanctity in the Sahara: the *qubba* of a saint, said to be Sidi
Lhouari, near Timimoun (T. Sahrawi).

the universalism of Islam and of learning in the local fabric of landscape
and society. In the late eighteenth century, Husayn ibn Muhammad al-
Warthilani, a scholar from eastern Kabylia, composed a massive *rihla*
(travelogue) detailing his travels in search of the world's 'deserts and
settled places, parched watering-holes and luxuriant gardens, cultivated
villages and fortresses; the virtuous, distinguished and cultivated men of
learning of all places; the shaykhs to whom knowledge has been given
and the brothers who seek after truth ... from West to East'. He
describes the great mosques of Cairo in the same vein as his visit to the
little coastal Kabyle town of Dellys, where he went 'to make a *ziyara*
[ritual visit] to [the tomb of] the shaykh, the pious *wali*, Sidi Ahmad ibn
Umar, of whom I had heard in my childhood that he was among those to
whom God had granted sanctity ... '[105] In this worldview, at once
expansive and localised, there was no conflict between rural and
urban, blessed saints and scholars of the law, the particular and the
universal. From Kabyle *awliya* to the centres of learning and piety in
Egypt and the Hijaz, the *umma* (community of the faithful) was rooted in
the everyday.[106]

From the late eighteenth century especially, the custodian families of
many local shrines and *zawiya*s became affiliated to one of the several Sufi

(mystical) orders, or brotherhoods, of Islam whose networks spanned the Muslim world from West Africa to Southeast Asia, the most important in Algeria being the Rahmaniyya, Qadiriyya, Tijaniyya and Derqawa.[107] The orders, in Arabic *tariqas* (plural *turuq*) or 'ways', represented institutionalised hierarchies of learning and spiritual initiation, from disciple to shaykh, giving access to specific practices of communal and individual devotion. As well as memorising the Qur'an and studying the law, students (*tolba*) learned to recite the *dhikr* ('remembrance' of God) and the *wird*, a liturgy specific to the order, recited by permission of the shaykh. Such special learning, sometimes combined with esoteric or ecstatic practices leading to trance-states, sought attainment of *haqiqa*, the inner truth of things and especially of God, beyond (never instead of) fulfilment of *shari'a*, the outward laws of religious observance. Both the immediacy and the universality of Islam were thus present and accessible across a whole spectrum of religious sophistication, from the everyday rationality of the 'ordinary religion' and cosmology of peasants to the rarefied gnosis of saintly shaykhs and their itinerant students. Abd al-Qadir ibn Muhyi al-Din, the great Algerian state-builder and leader of resistance to colonial conquest in the nineteenth century, who would in later life become one of the greatest ever mystical commentators on the Qur'an, drew his faith and his profound spiritual and philosophical learning from a succession of Sufi initiations and discipleships, beginning with his family's affiliation to the Qadiriyya order, and proceeding through initiation into the Naqshbandiyya *tariqa* in Damascus while on pilgrimage in the 1820s, to affiliation with the Shadhiliyya way through his last master in Mecca in the 1860s.

This rich mix of linguistic and cultural diversity did not, of course, simply make a melting pot without friction and exclusion. But social divisions were not drawn straightforwardly along religious, cultural or linguistic lines, between clearly separate Muslims and Jews, foreigners and natives or Arabs and Berbers. Muslims and Jews living in cities like Nedroma or Constantine might see themselves as closer to each other than either was to their respective co-religionist in the countryside. Conversely, the distinction between groups of Arab or Berber ancestry was often elided in their shared belonging to Sunni Islam, the Maliki school of Islamic law and saint-mediated everyday religious practice. And, by contrast, Berber-speaking, sedentary Kabyle peasants, whose Islam was Sunni and Maliki and structured by *mrabtin* and *tariqa*s, were as 'foreign' as nomadic Arabic-speaking pastoralists to Mzabi Muslims of the Ibadi rite, who were also Berbers, but who unlike the majority

Sunni community recognised neither *tariqa*s nor *zawaya* (although the Mzab had its share of saints and a densely sacred landscape of Ibadi cemeteries). Arabs and Berbers were less strictly defined ethnic groups than they were language communities, and language practice was often multilingual in contact zones between mountains and plains, at markets or in cities. It also shifted across generations, as Berber-speakers assimilated to Arabic-speaking society and (particularly in the Aurès) vice versa. Such processes were greatly accelerated with the population movements of the colonial period and have continued to the present.

Social status and belonging were codified by wealth and by local conceptions of race as well as by language and religion. Such hierarchical divisions within broader language and religious communities were at least as important as divisions between them. Social ranking by precedence of family – with whom it might be acceptable to exchange women by marriage, with whom it would be unthinkable – were most important. Arabic-speaking, nomadic tribal groups on the western plains and plateaux might be privileged *makhzen* soldiers, 'aristocratic' *sharif*s claiming descent from the Prophet or 'subject' *ra'aya*. Berber-speakers in the Gourara were divided between *isemghan*, lower-status, darker-complexioned inhabitants of autochthonous or imported slave origin, and their lighter-skinned social superiors who supposedly originated in migrations of pastoralists from the north. In Kabylia, groups in certain settlements, or living near valley floors as workers on the agricultural lands of notables, were identified as 'the descendants of slaves' (*eklan*) and culturally coded as 'black' in distinction to 'white' *imazighen* or 'free people'. The word *imazighen* became generalised to denote all 'Berbers' only in the second half of the twentieth century. The pale-complexioned Arab *hadri* (urban, urbane) elite of Tlemcen recalled their Andalusi origin against the darker-skinned Arab pastoralist inhabitants of the surrounding countryside. Such distinctions persist today. Arabic-speaking *gnawa* ('people of Guinea'), black Africans originating in or south of the Sahara, were an identifiable professional and ethnic group in the cities of the north, often occupationally specialised and producing the distinctive style of music named after them. At Nedroma, where the *gnawa* community was very small, its members formed the nucleus of a specific *tariqa* which specialised in healing rituals and was called upon in need by the other communities.[108] In a country so strongly shaped by the intersection, crossing and re-crossing of intercontinental religious, cultural and political frontiers, the community ties of inclusion, and the boundaries marking exclusion, could for that very reason be both very localised and very sharp.

## The Crisis, Recovery and End of the Regency

The Regency of Algiers was an early modern tributary state, broadly comparable in the nature of its prerogatives, and its ability to have them respected, to other such states elsewhere.[109] Privateering, which in contemporary polemics, colonial myth and some subsequent scholarship supposedly defined the exceptional nature of the state and provided its most crucial revenue, was marginal after the seventeenth century, replaced as a source of wealth by tribute payments, guaranteeing treaties of peace, from other seafaring states, customs and taxation, increased agricultural production, and trade, especially exports of wheat to Europe. Trading relations had existed, interrupted occasionally by famine and rural unrest, since the foundation of the Regency: French coral fishing and export rights were first established in 1547. In what Merouche has termed the 'century of wheat' after 1680, and particularly the second half of the eighteenth century up to the 1790s, the Regency enjoyed unprecedented general prosperity and stability, a period of which the quarter-century reign of Baba Mehmed Osman Pasha (1766–91) is emblematic.

The authorities in Algiers repeatedly claimed, in answer to instructions from Istanbul that the practice be definitively discontinued, that corsairing was essential to guarantee the salary of the *ojaq* and thus political stability, but this was no longer true in the eighteenth century. The scale and the profits of privateering, as well as the personal status and prestige of the *ra'is*, had declined. While the state took over from individual entrepreneurs as principal financier for expeditions, their importance in the revenues of the state and its elite was no more than 'highly variable and uncertain'.[110] The importance of corsairing, in which the Regency's elite continued to invest, was rhetorical and symbolic, part of the regime's ideology, an attachment to its origins and character as a 'corsair state' – like Malta[111] – in the seventeenth century's 'golden age' of privateering, and to the image of 'Algiers the Most Warlike' as *dar al-jihad*, the 'bastion of holy war' – even when it was in fact at peace and profitably trading with most of the nations of Europe.[112] French ships in particular traded between Algiers, Marseille and other Mediterranean ports, carried Algerian pilgrims to Alexandria en route to Mecca and transported high officers of the Regency with their customary gifts between Algiers and Istanbul.[113] Relations with France in the later eighteenth century were so cordial that in October 1777, Louis XVI personally ordered French naval vessels to assist in the salvage of an Algerian corsair shipwrecked near Perpignan. The officers and crew were received by the king's lieutenant general in the province and returned to Algiers aboard a French ship carrying a certificate of their good treatment.[114]

But commercial dependence on Europeans and their fleets posed longer-term problems. From 1793, when Britain entered the European war against revolutionary France, and through the Napoleonic invasions of Spain, Italy and Egypt that followed, the Regency re-entered a period of geopolitical crisis on a scale not unlike that which had given it birth almost three centuries earlier. Now, however, the global distribution of power was radically changing, and the rules of the relationship between north and south, 'the West' and the states of Asia and Africa, were being rapidly rewritten.

Internally, too, the long period of stability up to 1791 was followed by several crises. From 1791 to 1817, eight deys ruled, their reigns begun and ended in a series of putsches – one, Muhammad Khaznaji, ruled for only fifteen days in 1815. Behind this political turmoil were economic and social stresses. Landowners and intermediaries had been greatly enriched by grain exports, a prosperity shared by the lower classes in the preceding years, but when food shortages returned and elites attempted to maintain high volumes of exports, unrest broke out in the countryside.

The worst crises came in the early nineteenth century. From 1803 to 1805 harvests failed and wheat prices increased tenfold, reaching a record at Algiers that meant fifty-six days' labour were required for a construction worker to buy a measure of grain.[115] Riots broke out in Algiers in June 1805. A prominent Jewish merchant, Naptali Busnac, seen as close to the dey and held responsible for shortages due to his involvement in the grain trade, was assassinated, and Ottoman Algiers' first and only anti-Jewish pogrom killed perhaps one hundred people.[116] In September, a revolt overthrew the dey. The crisis abated, but returned in 1814 when locusts devoured the harvest and was aggravated through the following five years: food shortages and plague, falling population and decreased agricultural production created a vicious cycle producing popular discontent and revolts that became widespread across the country, organised and legitimised by rurally based religious figures associated with the *tariqa*s. In 1804, the Derqawa raised an anti-Ottoman insurrection in the west. Forces rallying to the Tijaniyya *zawiya* at Aïn Madhi resisted a siege by the beylik in 1820 and themselves besieged Mascara in 1827. Ferocious reprisals against rebels failed to stamp out revolt and increased the force of religious leaders' denunciations of a corrupt and unjust government. A pattern of rural rebellion that would be repeated over the rest of the century against the French was already taking shape in the final years of the Regency.

So was the beylik in inevitable decline, its history doomed to end in unavoidable European conquest? Things were not so simple, and the Ottoman period cannot be seen merely as a 'pre-colonial' prelude to French rule. Not only would many of the foundations of society visible in this period endure long after 1830, structuring deep continuities in Algerian society that remain relevant today. A limited recovery of the state was even possible in 1817, when a new dey, Ali Khoja, came to power determined to break the cycle of instability at the summit of the state and its faltering control over the country. The memoirs of Ahmad Sharif al-Zahhar, *naqib al-ashraf* ('syndic' of the descendants of the Prophet, a notable dignitary) of Algiers, describe how, once properly invested, the new ruler dismissed his ministers, sparing some and executing or exiling others, and appointed in their place either the irrelevant and powerless or the exceptionally able, thus concentrating power in his own hands and those of trusted allies. 'For the benefit of all the people and so that the dissensions created every day by the soldiers in the city should cease', he secretly removed the treasury and his own residence from the Janina palace to the *qasba* (citadel) above the town. Leading mutineers among the janissaries were executed and 'the fires of *fitna* (dissension) were extinguished'. A subsequent attempt by the *ojaq* to march on Algiers from the east was defeated by troops loyal to the dey. In a campaign of moralising zeal, attendance at communal prayer was to be enforced, 'the suppression of fornication and of alcohol' ordered and *shari'a* penalties strictly applied in cases of contravention.[117] This 'revolution', symbolised in Zahhar's account by what to him were no doubt the properly puritanical strictures of good governance, was more practically an attempt to re-centre power in the state around the office of the dey, against the entrenched interests of the *ojaq* and with support from the marketplace, the urban elites and the Kabyle *zwawa* and *kulugli* elements of the army.

Ali Khoja's attempted re-foundation of the beylik came shortly after the suppression of the janissaries in Tunis and Mehmed Ali's massacre of the mamluks in Cairo in 1811, and anticipated the so-called Auspicious Event that broke the janissaries' power in Istanbul in 1826. Such radical moves in these cases led to periods of sweeping reforms and the strengthening of the state. If Ali Khoja had such a revolutionary project, however, he did not live to see it through – reigning for less than a year, he died of plague in March 1818. A limited stabilisation continued under his chosen successor, Husayn Pasha, 'a man of reason and piety, who respected the *'ulama*, the *sharif*s and the saints',[118] but he was unable either to contain revolt in the countryside or to strengthen the state against newly hostile outsiders. Internal troubles and commercial dependency coincided with a changing view of the Regency – and of the Arab and Muslim worlds generally – in post-Napoleonic Europe.

The restored European order that emerged from the French revolutionary wars and the Congress of Vienna saw itself as advancing in universal peace, rational government and 'civilisation', containing revolution with rationed doses of liberalism and preaching 'liberty' as its own watchword. It saw 'piratical' Algiers, where corsairing had briefly flourished again during the disruption of trade brought on by the European conflict, as a barbarous relic of a previous age.[119] In April 1816, the English Lord Exmouth negotiated terms of peace with Algiers on behalf of Sardinia and Naples that included the free release, as British subjects, of Gibraltarian and Maltese captives, and indemnities to be paid by the Italian states for the release of Sardinians and Sicilians. This was still recognisable diplomacy in the old style, but European public opinion was unimpressed, and in August Exmouth returned, bombarded Algiers and demanded the abolition of 'slavery', the restitution of all Christian captives and the repayment of the indemnities – a properly firm action, to European eyes, on behalf of 'civilised' nations against a refractory 'outlaw' state. This, quite suddenly and without forewarning, was a new world, one to which the Regency's elite was ill-suited, and to which they had neither the time nor the resources to adapt. Fourteen years later, a French army would descend with crushing weight of numbers and firepower upon Algiers 'the Most Warlike', Husayn Pasha would be sent into exile and Ottoman rule in Algeria was brought abruptly to an end.

# 2    Conquest, Resistance and Accommodation, 1830–1911

To Gustave Mercier, a lawyer, politician and official commissioner for the celebrations marking the centenary of French Algeria in 1930, the French army's landing at Sidi Fredj, a beachhead west of Algiers, on 14 June 1830 had 'truly marked the beginning of a new era'. 'Like the discovery of the New World', he wrote, this new age had brought 'a new continent . . . into the orbit of civilisation' and led to the creation of 'a Great France, peopled by seventy million inhabitants, whose frontiers are the Rhine and the Congo'. For Mercier, this had been 'the capital event of the past century'.[1] Nothing so grandiose could have been imagined at the time. As historian Charles-André Julien, whose own work towards a more liberal history of Algeria had already begun in the 1920s, later observed, the beginnings of the French conquest of Algeria in fact lay in 'a shady business deal . . . an incident provoked by a suspect diplomat . . . the mediocre expedition of a discredited general . . . [and] a victory viewed with indifference or hostility by public opinion and followed by the fall of the dynasty that won it'.[2]

For Ahmad Sharif Zahhar, notable and chronicler of Algiers' old regime and an eyewitness to the conquest, on the other hand, the French invasion marked a cataclysm: it signalled 'the dominion of war' over the city,

and the departure of its people into the open desert, seeking aid for themselves against the enemy, until they came to beg among the tents of the [nomadic] Arabs, and they tasted suffering, and hunger, and fear, and the signs of their city were obliterated and its symbols struck out . . . Its notables perished, its scholars dwindled away, its poets fell silent. Its writers and public speakers were struck dumb.

For Zahhar, this tribulation nonetheless fit within a divinely sanctioned and predictable universal order: 'And such is the way with countries, when the course of their civilisation is run, and thus they come to a halt, according to the will of God most high, and they retreat, falling into decline.'[3] Popular poetry, inflected with the spirit of religious revolt against the Ottoman regime, told a yet more dramatic story:

The end of time has come; Henceforth no more rest. The day of battle has shone, Grief to the living, Happiness to the dead ... I am grieved, O world, about Algiers! ... These miseries, it is God who brought them! ... After her days of glory, [Algiers] was dishonoured. Tyranny and injustice were the cause of her fall; Wine was honoured and debauchery tolerated. The God of creatures is every-where, sees and never sleeps ... The days, O brothers, see fortunes change ...[4]

The end of time or beginning of an age; the judgment of God in a cycle of rise and decline; a cataclysm, a new dawn: however understood, the fall of Algiers to French invasion marked a momentous shift in North Africa's history. As the nineteenth century unfolded, to many Algerians the conquest would indeed seem like an act of divine judgment, an apocalypse, while to some in France it would appear, after the loss of the Bourbon monarchy's empire overseas and the defeat of Napoleon's empire in Europe, as a crucial milestone in a long recovery of national 'greatness'. But at the same time, the events of 1830 were the ill-planned result of an accidental accumulation of undistinguished events. It was not the begin-ning of a grandly designed French 'New World' in Africa, and although it decapitated the Algerian state, it did not suddenly transform the deeper patterns of Algerian society. Despite the immense upheaval and terrible mortality that ensued, the occupation of Algiers and the long struggle that followed it resulted neither from the single-minded pursuit of an expan-sionist policy (not a great-hearted project of civilisation, nor a genocidal one of extermination[5]) by the French, nor from a continuous and undif-ferentiated 'century-long resistance'[6] by the Algerians. Beyond such myths, the story is more complex, less clear-cut. An interplay of uncer-tainty and ambition, opportunity and pragmatism, self-sacrificing resolve and ruthless determination, messianic revolt and resigned practicality, combined to extend and consolidate an initially hesitant, unpopular and ill-conceived conquest in response to both the acts of resistance and the attempts at accommodation with which, almost from the outset, the invaders were met.

### The Fall of Algiers and the 'Restricted Occupation'

The 'shady deal' that became the backdrop for the conquest of Algeria began in the 1790s, when the Livorno-based Jewish merchant houses Busnac and Bacri, backed by a group of creditors including the Algerian dey's treasury, furnished revolutionary France and its armies with Algerian grain supplies. Liquidation of the French state's debts to Bacri, which remained a subject of litigation into the 1820s, systematically ignored the claims of the Algerian state on sums due to Bacri but which Bacri himself owed the dey. In a famous altercation in April 1827, Husayn

Dey, 'unable to bear an affront that exceeded all acceptable limits' on the part of the French consul, Pierre Deval, over the French refusal to respond to Algiers' repeated demands on Bacri's debt (and for the removal of Deval himself, a discredited 'schemer'), struck Deval with his fly-whisk and ordered him out of the audience chamber.[7] Deval and his superiors decided to make a diplomatic incident of this 'horrid and scandalous outrage',[8] demanding that the Regency's highest officers go aboard a French ship to make excuses to the consul, and that the French flag be flown from 'the most visible place' of the qasba (citadel) and port and honoured with a one-hundred gun salute. When the dey refused these deliberately insulting conditions, war was declared by both sides and French ships blockaded Algiers. The blockade would be maintained, ineffectively, for three years.

The incident of the *coup d'éventail* (the 'blow with the fly-whisk') would become legendary in French imagery and schoolbook narratives that described an indignant nation justly punishing a 'Barbary prince' and stamping out his 'piratical' state, leading as if by design to the construction of France's massive African empire. But the decision to resolve this absurd war with a military expedition to overthrow the Regency was in fact the last meagre throw of a different, and abortive, grand strategy. The government of the restored Bourbon king, Charles X, had hoped for an alliance with Russia to counter British naval preponderance in the Mediterranean, to dismember the Ottoman empire and to redraw the political map of Europe. With the collapse of these schemes – especially the rejection by Mehmed Ali, the ruler of Egypt, of a proposed Franco-Egyptian campaign that would have aimed to bring Tripoli, Tunis and Algiers under French and Egyptian control – the assault on Algiers remained as the last attempt of a wildly unpopular government to gain international prestige, shore up its domestic support, and silence the opposition's demands for limits on royal power. Six hundred and seventy-five ships carrying 37,000 men sailed from Toulon, observed by enthusiastic day-trippers. An additional benefit of the expedition, and perhaps a secondary motivation for it, was the pillaging of Algiers' treasury. By 10 August, just over a month after the city's capture, five shipments had carried off over 43 million francs in gold and silver from the qasba, after the army's own expenses were met, and larger sums disappeared from the official accounts: in France the personal enrichment of senior officers by ill-concealed looting quickly became a public scandal. A fevered search for 'hidden treasure' in Algiers continued into September.[9] The swift success of the invasion, however, had done nothing to save the Restoration regime. The dey capitulated to the French on 5 July, but three weeks later a revolution in Paris overthrew Charles

X and put Louis-Philippe, Duke of Orléans, on the French throne. The new French government inherited the occupation of Algiers without any agreed idea of what to do with it.

On the Algerian side, the failure of the Regency's combined forces, about 50,000 strong (though the 'regular' janissary corps numbered only about 7,000 men), to prevent the French landing, and the disarray that followed initial French success, illustrated the state's fragility and the divisions within it. The landings at Sidi Fredj were virtually unopposed: supported by naval fire, the disembarking soldiers met 'only very weak resistance' and faced no regular troops.[10] The first large-scale attack on the French lines was attempted on 19 June, five days later. When the Algerians' attack was beaten back, the French moved on to capture the camp at Staouëli (Ousta Wali) and further attempts to prevent the invaders reaching the hilltops inland of Algiers failed despite French confusion over the lie of the land. On 4 July French artillery bombarded the city's main landward fortification, Borj Mawlay Hasan (known to the French as Fort l'Empereur). Panic gripped Algiers' population, and the *beldi* merchant notability, considering the fight lost and opposing a call for a mass popular rising whose consequences might be anarchic, pressed the dey to sue for peace. Husayn, 'calm but sad',[11] acceded. He and his entourage went into exile in Naples; shortly afterwards, the rest of the city's Ottoman establishment and many of the janissaries were deported to Izmir.

This sudden decapitation of the state left Algiers itself in a disorder compounded by the abuses of an ill-disciplined army against persons and property (despite the official proclamation by Bourmont, the commander-in-chief, that the inhabitants' rights of religion, property, commerce and industry would be respected), and the Regency's territories in a disarray exacerbated by the fragmentation of political authority. Hajj Ahmad, bey of Constantine, refusing to submit to any authority but that of the Ottoman sultan, returned from the defence of Algiers to re-fortify Constantine and put down, with his Kabyle troops, an incipient revolt against his rule by the janissaries. The bey of Titteri, Mustafa Bu Mezrag, threw in his lot with the victors and agreed to submit to French suzerainty, until the requisitioning of private houses and billeting of troops in the mosques of Algiers demonstrated the vacuity of Bourmont's promises, provoking Bu Mezrag into open resistance. The elderly governor of the west, Hassan Bey, whose authority had already crumbled against the anti-Ottoman revolts of the Derqawa and Tijaniyya, gave up Mers el Kebir and the redoubtable forts of Oran to the French without firing a shot, and shortly afterwards sailed to Alexandria.

Leading notables in Algiers, on the other hand, sought to manage the French and protect their interests with a mixture of opportunism and pragmatic far-sightedness. Jacob Bacri, installed as head of the Jewish community, quickly earned the animosity of his fellow Jews, who accused him of appropriating the community's welfare funds for his own cronies. Hamdan Amin Sekka, a merchant appointed by Bourmont to the post of 'Agha of the Arabs' (an Ottoman office supervising the *dar al-sultan* and its inhabitants) and then dismissed, pleaded with the Minister of War, 'I have been unjustly sacrificed ... I have too much confidence in the French government to believe that it would abandon so devoted and faithful a servant.' Ahmad Bu Darba, a merchant with links to Marseille and a French wife, sought to establish a new tributary state run by the Arab notability under French suzerainty. In 1831, he proposed a municipal government for Algiers composed of 'the principal inhabitants' drawn proportionally from the Arabs, *kuluğli*s and Jews, and a 'grand council' of twenty notables including the *qadi*s who would receive deputies from the interior tribes and themselves send an annual deputy to Paris. By such means, he claimed, 'the entire Regency, within a year, might make submission, without expense or the shedding of blood'. He also proposed printing a newspaper in French and Arabic, and sending the children of 'leading families' to French schools.[12] An associate of Bu Darba and the son of a high Regency official, Hamdan ben Uthman Khoja, travelled to Paris and sought in a widely read pamphlet, published there in October 1833, to convince the occupiers that

French authority [in Algiers] has acted in a way entirely opposed to the liberal principles and benefits that we justly hoped for ... It would be worthy of the King of the French to emancipate the Algerians, re-establishing harmony between our two peoples, and reviving trade and agriculture ... The Algerians, too, have the right to enjoy freedom and every advantage enjoyed by the nations of Europe.[13]

These would-be peacemakers, despite their appeal to the very ideas of liberal civilisation supposedly ascendant in Europe, were disappointed. Bu Darba, who was ready to declare France his 'new fatherland' and who was for a while a member of Algiers' municipal council under the military, soon fell under suspicion of being 'the instigator of every resistance and head of [the] opposition'. Hamdan's correspondence from Paris was judged by the French military 'unfavourable to our cause'. Both were eventually arrested and exiled. Bu Darba settled in Marseille and continued his business affairs; Hamdan retired to Istanbul. 'Oppression reigns in Algiers', he wrote from exile, 'more hideous certainly than it was under the Turks'.[14]

Assemblies of the interior tribes also attempted to negotiate an accommodation with the new rulers, this time in terms that recalled the old order. The people of Bu Agab in the Mitidja, for example, having joined the local insurrection and deserted the markets which the French controlled, but on which the occupation army also depended, wrote to the general-in-chief, 'sultan of the city of Algiers and lord of its province':

> You tell us, Come freely to buy and sell, as you did before. You say that we should return to our lands and our city, and we shall have safe passage . . . We shall not so return, nor buy and sell, unless you write to us confirming a truce for twelve months . . . And you should grant us privileges, and a rank of consequence, for we desire only dignity . . . If you act for us as we have said, we will secure the roads for you against all the brigands, and supplies will come to you from the whole country.[15]

Patterns of cupidity and pragmatic compromise, self-promotion and dependence, liberal visions and their frustration, the grand pronouncements of the regime and its abandonment of those who believed in them can all be seen here in the first months and years after the conquest. Such patterns would recur for many years afterwards. Some, like Bacri, would secure office for their own advancement through the exploitation of their own community. Hamdan and Bu Darba, neither the sell-outs nor the proto-nationalists that different accounts have tried to make them, would not be the last to seek a liberal, negotiated settlement and find themselves labelled as 'agitators'. Neither would Hamdan Amin Sekka be the last to cast himself in the role of 'faithful servant' of France, only to be compromised and abandoned. Bu Darba claimed that Louis-Philippe himself had assured him, 'You and your compatriots now belong to the great family of France, of which I am the father'.[16] The same hollow, patronising idea would be echoed as late as 1958.

And yet, as a series of French commanders succeeded each other, the occupation remained uncertain and its future unclear. After seizing the ports of Oran and Bône – which were abandoned on news of the July revolution in France, and then re-occupied – and barely able to secure the immediate hinterland of Algiers against an insurgent rural population, the French at first attempted to reconstitute the tributary Regency with themselves as the new Turks and Tunisian subordinates as vassal beys of Oran and Constantine. The attempt – by the new commander-in-chief, Clauzel, unsanctioned by his superiors in Paris – to establish such a system by treaty with the Husaynid rulers of Tunis soon collapsed. Tunisian troops landed in Oran in February 1831 but were evacuated in August. Clauzel's duplicitous treaty negotiations and the opposition met by the Tunisian contingent, merely 500 strong, made the affair another early 'scandal' of the French administration. Clauzel's other enthusiastic experiment, a model farm in the Mitidja which would be a first outpost of agricultural colonisation, was also a failure. General Berthezène, who followed Clauzel briefly as governor, was opposed to schemes of colonisation for which financial and material means were unavailable, and restricted activity to the city itself. His successor, the overbearing General Savary, duke of Rovigo, by contrast, was the first to push the line of military occupation inland to the vicinity of Algiers, constructing a series of blockhouses linked by a perimeter road from a point northwest of the 'valley gate', Bab el-Oued, to another at the mouth of the little Harrach river that drained into the sea from the Mitidja to the city's southeast. Rovigo was also responsible for three events that marked the beginning of the real terror of the conquest for Algerians, and that proved dark harbingers of things to come.

To open up roads in the congested lower city of Algiers, Rovigo's engineers cut straight lines through two cemeteries, destroying tombs as they went and shovelling human skeletal remains along with broken tombstones into the road fill. A lurid rumour that human bones had even been exported to France where they were used to make bone char for sugar refining may, in the atmosphere of unprincipled and uncontrolled speculation and profiteering that followed immediately on the heels of the conquest, have been more than the horrific fantasy it seems.[17] With similar, and similarly alarming, disregard for Algerians' religious and moral dignity, it was Rovigo who ordered the confiscation of one of the Ottoman city's most splendid mosques and its consecration as a cathedral church. Several hundred Algerians protesting this violation of Bourmont's guarantees were evicted at bayonet-point from the Ketshawa mosque, at the centre of the lower city near the old palace of the dey, in December 1831. The building, its distinctive twin octagonal minarets surmounted by crosses, was consecrated as the cathedral of Saint-Philippe on Christmas Day, 1832. Having acquired a reputation for expeditious violence and inquisitorial methods as Napoleon's Minister of Police twenty years previously, Rovigo was hardly a governor to inspire confidence in the new regime's justice. A third dark precedent was set in spring 1832, when he ordered the extermination of a small tribe, the Ouffias, and the seizure of their livestock in retribution for a theft – committed by others – against a deputation visiting Algiers from Ferhat ben Said, a south Constantinois notable seeking alliance with the French against Ahmad Bey. Pellissier de Reynaud, an army officer and early chronicler of the conquest, described how the whole tribe was killed 'without even attempting to defend themselves. Everyone alive was condemned to die, and everything that could be taken was seized; there were no distinctions of age or sex. Only the humanity of a few officers saved some of the women and children.'[18] 'May God preserve us', Hamdan Khoja would later write, 'from the justice of the French'.[19]

These actions, by an ageing and especially tempestuous military governor, in one sense merely illustrate the extent to which individual temperament and decisions taken on initiative and without either appeal or oversight were the order of the day in the chaotic first months after the conquest. General Pierre Boyer, on taking command as the military governor of Oran in September 1831, similarly held that 'the law they need is that of the sword', and made a policy of expeditious public executions.[20] On the other hand, such acts can also be taken as illustrative of a system with a logic of its own, beyond individual temperaments or conscious design, that was already developing in France's new colony: Algeria was a 'French possession', and nothing was sacred in the property or persons of its inhabitants; 'order' would be kept by means of institutionalised extra-legal coercion, with occasional resort to unstinting and indiscriminate violence when it was deemed necessary.

To French observers at the time, however, little could be discerned of the future shape of French Algeria. In the summer of 1833, one senior officer of the occupation army wrote that 'the French government's lack of resolve in the matter of the conquest of Algiers astonishes and depresses everyone. The result is that the generals, left as it were to their own devices, dare undertake nothing, are without influence on the country they are supposed to govern, and in three years colonisation has made only meagre progress.' Military operations in the hinterland of Algiers were restricted, too, by the impossibility of camping in the Mitidja in summer; even the line of fortified posts established by Rovigo had to be regularly abandoned in July, when sickness sent 'up to a hundred men a day to the hospital'.[21]

At the same time, stormy debates in the Paris parliament between proponents of colonisation and sceptics resulted in a two-stage commission of inquiry, instituted in July and December 1833, to report on the state of the occupation, its conduct to date and the recommendations to be made for its future, in respect of 'the advantages that [...] France can propose to gain for herself from the possession of Algiers', whether 'political, military, administrative, commercial, industrial, agricultural [or] financial'. All of the competing options propounded by the various metropolitan lobbies were declared open to consideration, including 'the violent expulsion of the natives, the [...] occupation of the territory and the immediate substitution of a European population for that which now exists'. But although this was a course which 'has been seriously proposed', it was raised in the commission's instructions 'only so that no

aspect of this great question should be excluded from examination'.
The War Ministry itself clearly had doubts

as to what extent it might be practicable, and whether, should it be admitted that the civilisation of our time could consent to such a course of action, the subjugation of the Regency by [...] this system would not demand a deployment of forces and a profusion of expenses out of proportion to both the result and the means which France ought to devote to the enterprise.[22]

More serious was the question of what kind of colonisation – military or civilian – to undertake, how to secure the development of a settler society that would have to live alongside the 'warlike' Arab population and to what extent the territory of the Regency inland of the occupied ports should be incorporated into the area under French control. Withdrawal, though still championed by some in the Chamber of Deputies, was not a serious possibility. Political pressure, strategic concerns, commercial lobbies (especially that of the city of Marseille) and a generalised sense of the importance of recovering a French influence that had been dissipated on the world stage since 1815 combined in favour of pursuing the conquest, however undecided its real purposes, let alone the means of achieving them. In its two reports, both published in 1834, the commission duly recommended the permanent occupation of the Regency and its development by a settler population of agricultural smallholders.[23] But the first report also presented an excoriating denunciation of the abuse that military government had already brought upon those subject to its rule, 'in contempt of the simplest and most natural rights of peoples':

We have sent to the gallows, on the merest suspicion and without trial, people whose guilt has remained more than doubtful, and whose heirs have since been despoiled of their goods; we have killed people carrying promises of safe-conduct, massacred on suspicion whole populations who were afterwards proven innocent; we have dragged before tribunals men who are venerated and considered in the country to be saints because they had courage enough to [...] intercede with us for their unfortunate compatriots. [...] In a word, we have outdone in barbarism the barbarians whom we came to civilise and we complain of not having been able to succeed in civilising them![24]

All the tensions that were to plague French (mis)understandings of their 'mission' in Algeria, and which would, as a result and much more severely, plague the lives and cause the deaths of Algerians for over a hundred years, can be read here in embryo: unaccountable acts of atrocity denounced as such by a government unable to prevent them, and whose own avowed policies made them possible; conversely, a sincere and humanist liberalism unable to extricate itself from a conception of 'civilisation' whose territorial expansion by European agency among 'backward' peoples would provide the warrant for every act of expropriation and brutality. Finally, and perhaps most importantly, came the creation of a legal-administrative state of exception. At exactly the time when the ascendant European bourgeoisie's own developing liberalism was tending to restrict the unaccountable power of its rulers and build up the rule of law against the abuse of authority for the protection of 'the simplest and most natural rights of peoples',[25] such rights, and the rule of a law that would protect them, were to be systematically denied to the liberal power's newly conquered subjects. The outcome of this 'period of uncertainty', to adopt the phrase of Charles-André Julien, in which the 'restricted occupation' of Algeria was less a matter of policy than of an absence of policy, was the ordinance of 22 July 1834, regulating the government of 'the French possessions in North Africa (formerly the Regency of Algiers)' by the power of royal decree delegated to a military governor general, who would be answerable to the Ministry of War, administering both military and civil spheres as he saw fit. The ability to rule by decree, bypassing parliamentary accountability and legal recourse to appeal, gave the colonial government a blank cheque that, though constitutionally illegal, would remain valid until after the Second World War.

## Abd al-Qadir's Islamic Sovereignty

This confused combination of uncertainty, brutality and contorted logic that characterised the French occupation was of course only one dimension of the developing situation after 1830, and perhaps not the most significant. In the vast interior of plains and mountains, Algerian society had its own dynamics and internal tensions; these played out, in the new situation brought about by the conquest, according to their own logic as much as in response to the actions of the invaders. French invasion, indeed, was in a sense simply the 'external shock' that broke the fragile internal equilibrium of Algerian society, accelerating the movement of underlying social and economic forces that had already been slowly in motion since the end of the eighteenth century.[26] The collapse of the Regency's central authority meant not only political anarchy but the disruption of trade and communications, and the destabilisation of established local and regional hierarchies. As we have seen, while the invaders' ultimate intentions could only be guessed at, spontaneous popular insurrection in the countryside went hand in hand with attempts at conciliation and accommodation, and the pattern of revolt itself was shaped by local circumstances, rivalries and aspirations. In the west, the generalised uprising of the tribes south and east of Oran was a continuation of the

earlier anti-Ottoman revolts, pitting the former *ra'aya* (subject) population against the erstwhile *makhzen* tribes that had enjoyed fiscal
exemptions in exchange for service as auxiliaries of the beylik.
In Tlemcen, the armed *kuluğli* population, all that remained of the
Ottoman establishment, barricaded themselves in the city's *meshwar*
(the fortified enclosure containing the seat of local government), trained
their artillery on the town and resisted all attempts to dislodge them until
the arrival of French troops, with whom they allied themselves, in
January 1836.[27] In Constantine, and in the teeth of a cholera epidemic,
Ahmad Bey attempted to re-establish Ottoman sovereignty, convening
a *diwan* (council) of the city's notables, striking his own currency in the
name of Sultan Mahmud II, and corresponding directly with Istanbul to
gain support for his autonomy against the threat of the French, the
instability of local revolts and the bey of Tunis's apparent ambition to
annex his province.[28]

It is in this context that we need to place the sudden rise to prominence
and remarkable career of the young Abd al-Qadir ibn Muhyi al-Din al-
Hasani, who as 'the emir Abdelkader' would become famous as the
principal organiser of resistance to the French up to his eventual surrender in 1847, and later, after his exile to Damascus, as a prominent
nineteenth-century celebrity. With the collapse of the Regency in the
west, the notables of Tlemcen called upon the Moroccan sultan,
Mawlay Abd al-Rahman (r. 1822–59), to assert his sovereignty over the
region, but his intervention, like that of the Tunisians, was short-lived.
A *khalifa* (deputy), the sultan's young cousin Mawlay Ali, was posted to
Tlemcen at the head of a small force of Moroccan troops; he was succeeded by the more able *sharif* Muhammad Belhamri, but diplomatic
pressure from France, backed up by the threat of gunboats, obliged the
sultan to recall Belhamri in March 1832, and to renounce any claim to
sovereignty over the territory of the former Regency.

The departing *khalifa* left in his place, as vice-regent in the name of the
sultan, the regional leader of the Qadiriyya tariqa, Sidi Muhyi al-Din ben
Mustafa. A *sharif*, tracing his ancestry back through Idriss, the founder of
Fez, to Hasan, son of Ali ibn Abi Talib and Fatima, daughter of the
Prophet, and the head of an influential family within the powerful Beni
Hashem tribe, the elderly Muhyi al-Din enjoyed an immense social
prestige coupled with great spiritual authority in western Algeria.
The family's *zawiya*, at Guetna ta' Oued al-Hammam in the Gharis
plain near Mascara, had become a regional centre of learning, and
Muhyi al-Din was sufficiently influential to have been held briefly under
house arrest by the embattled Ottoman administration in the west before
removing himself from the regional fray by embarking on pilgrimage to

Mecca and Medina in 1826. But although he led repeated attacks on the French positions at Oran in the summer and autumn of 1832, he was unable to federate a generalised resistance among the disparate interests of the region. On 22 November 1832, the 75-year-old Muhyi al-Din acceded to the demands of the most influential regional tribes, the Beni Hashem and Beni Amir – and, so it was reported, to the instructions vouchsafed him in a dream by the great saint Sidi Abd al-Qadir al-Jilani of Baghdad – and led the assembled tribal leaders and *mrabtin* of the region in investing his second son, Abd al-Qadir, then aged 24, as *amir al-mu'minin*, commander of the faithful, and leader of the effort to re-establish order against internal anarchy and foreign incursion.[29]

Abd al-Qadir, a *sharif* and a leading member of a saintly lineage, was already considered suitably learned and devout. He had accompanied his father on the pilgrimage to Mecca and Medina, and had seen something of the great cities of the Ottoman east and of the state-building experiments of Mehmed Ali in Egypt before distinguishing himself as a valiant horseman and war captain in his father's raids on Oran. He was nonetheless a young man, one among a number of claimants to some kind of sovereignty in the confused aftermath of the Regency's fall, and of those neither immediately the most likely nor the most powerful. Local governors ensconced in the ports of Arzew and Mostaghanem, and tribal leaders formerly allied to the Ottoman state in the south or in the environs of Oran ignored or rejected Abd al-Qadir's investiture as *amir* (prince) and his claim to be *sultan* (ruler, the title adopted for him in ordinary correspondence by his subordinates). The urban elite of Tlemcen expected Abd al-Qadir to declare his own loyalty to Mawlay Abd al-Rahman, the sultan of Morocco, while the latter initially considered Abd al-Qadir as little more than 'a petty chief trying to carve a niche for himself'.[30] When, much later, Abd al-Qadir's claim to sovereignty was extended into the distant beylik of the east, it meant little there except as a means of advancing more local claims to pre-eminence in the Medjana and the Constantinois pre-Sahara.[31] But by means of a consistent appeal to the unity of the Muslim community under a properly invested ruler, and energetic military and diplomatic activity aimed at realising in fact the formal titles that had been accorded him, by early 1834, just over a year after the first *bay'a* (oath of allegiance) was sworn to him at Mascara, Abd al-Qadir had established a fledgling state in western Algeria that would survive, through successive attempts to secure peace and intermittent recourse to war, for a decade.

The terms in which Abd al-Qadir laid claim to his newly declared leadership were clear and unambiguous. On entering Mascara, having received its allegiance and taken possession of the old beylical capital, he attended noonday prayer along with the inhabitants at the town's principal mosque and then 'preached a long inaugural sermon (*khutba*), comprising exhortation, vows, and warnings, and commands [to do good] and prohibitions [against wrongdoing], and he urged jihad'.[32] Shortly thereafter, Abd al-Qadir convened a council of *'ulama*, which on his behalf issued a proclamation to the chiefs of the region's tribes calling for their recognition of his leadership in similarly canonical terms:

> To the communities of the Arabs and Berbers: Know that the affairs of Islamic princely authority and of the upholding of the religious duties of the Muhammadan community have now passed into the hands of the Protector of Religion, the Lord Abd al-Qadir ibn Muhy al-Din. And the declaration of allegiance has been made to him in recognition thereof, by the *'ulama*, the *sharif*s, and the notables at Mascara. And he has become our *amir* and guarantor of the upholding of the bounds of God's law. He does not follow in the footsteps of any other, nor imitate their example. He does not take a surplus of riches for his own share, as others may have done. He does not burden his subjects in anything save that in which he is commanded by the immaculate *shari'a*, and he disposes of nothing save in the proper manner. And he has unfurled the banner of jihad, and bared his forearm to the task, for the welfare of the servants of God, and the prosperity of the land.[33]

A few months later, the newly declared *amir* wrote to Qa'id Ibrahim, an Ottoman officer originally from Selanik (Thessalonika) who had established himself as governor in Mostaghanem: 'It is my duty to rally you to my banner, for only unity means power, division produces weakness. Let us therefore efface all the racial differences among the true Muslims. Let us see Arabs, Turks, *kuluğli*s, and Moors live as brothers, all worshipping the true God, and let us all together have one armed hand raised against the enemy'.[34]

It would later be claimed, both by and on behalf of Abd al-Qadir, that his government replaced the 'aristocratic', tribal system of the Ottomans with 'maraboutic', more strictly Islamic rule, pursuing social equality by effacing the distinction between *makhzen* and subject tribes, and abolishing non-Quran'ic taxation.[35] Conversely, it has also been argued that the language of religious legitimacy in which Abd al-Qadir's rule was framed was 'merely' ideological and instrumental, and that in his actual practice of state-building, 'abstract religious principles usually gave way to considerations of state'.[36] Neither argument is actually very helpful to understanding Abd al-Qadir's state. The dichotomy between religious sincerity and political pragmatism sometimes imagined by historians, along with the more obviously reductive images of Abd al-Qadir as either a 'fanatic' or a 'nationalist', are preconceptions without meaning for the situation they try to describe. For Abd al-Qadir, there was clearly nothing abstract about Islamic principle, and there was no contradiction between the claim to establish a unified sovereignty on the basis of 'the pure law of God' and the recourse to the practical means available for its enforcement. His vision of state-building combined an emphasis on properly legitimate sovereignty over a unified Muslim community with the recognition that such sovereignty would be meaningless without the effective force needed to assert it, both internally and against the threat of the invader. This is reflected in his pragmatic appointment of former officials or allies of the *makhzen* where their administrative experience was needed, and his replacement of old *makhzen* tribes with new trusted auxiliary groups that were accorded fiscal privileges similar to those enjoyed by the allies of the former Ottoman regime. His recourse to the non-Qur'anic *ma'una* (assistance) tax as an additional levy to support the army, supplementing the more canonical alms (*zakat*) assessed on manufactures, property and livestock, and tithes (*'ushr*) collected on produce in grain, reflects the same principles.[37]

Abd al-Qadir's bid for sovereignty, then, was made in opposition to the remnants and the recent popular memory of the Ottoman beylik but also in succession to it. His promise to establish justice and equity echoed the recent regional tradition of tribally based and religiously legitimated opposition to the injustice and 'corruption' (*fasad*) imputed to the Ottoman regime by the revolts of previous decades, but he sought to rally former servants of the Ottoman regime to his cause and to reinstitute, on a more effective basis, the capacity to project power and assert fiscal extraction across the countryside. His model of himself as commander of the faithful drew on the long-standing sense of western Algeria as a sphere of influence of the Moroccan sultanate, where the sharifian prestige of the Alawi dynasty, combined with a model of political leadership as properly incarnated in ascetic, saintly and upright *mrabtin* capable of upholding the rule of law and beating back foreign invasion, went back to the sixteenth century.[38] His demand for allegiance rested on a claim to enforce and preserve the unity and integrity of the community under the proper regulation of the law as judged by himself and as guaranteed by the *'ulama*.

For a while, Abd al-Qadir was able to establish a new, autonomous sovereignty in these terms, the first time since the establishment of the Regency that an independent Algerian emirate had existed between Morocco to the west and the limits of Ottoman sovereignty to the east. But while he declared himself an independent sovereign by virtue of the recognition of the people and their leaders in the *bay'a* given him as upholder of justice in his own realm, Abd al-Qadir also depended on a triangular relationship with more powerful neighbours. He was careful both in the management of his necessary recognition by, and alliance with, Mawlay Abd al-Rahman, and in deriving every possible advantage that could be gained from his recognition by, as well as his opposition to, the French. Both of these relationships would ultimately come undone under the pressure of the irreconcilable interests of each party, and when they did, Abd al-Qadir's sovereignty, too, unravelled.

In the initial establishment and extension of Abd al-Qadir's power base, both his effective action against the French, and recognition of him by the French as their principal interlocutor in the interior of western Algeria, were crucial. Unable to rally sufficient force to carry an assault on Oran itself, he instead declared and enforced a blockade, obliging the French to resupply their garrison by sea. Abd al-Qadir forcibly asserted his authority over the former *makhzen* tribes of the Duwa'ir and Zmala who occupied the land surrounding the city, but who also held substantial properties in Mascara that they were afraid to lose.[39] He entered Tlemcen, though he could not evict the *kuluğli*s from their fortress, thus bringing both of the major interior towns of the west under his sway; he attacked the French at Mostaghanem, and captured the *qadi* of Arzew, Sidi Ahmad ben Tahar, who had refused to recognise Abd al-Qadir and had instead conducted a profitable trade with Oran in defiance of the blockade.[40] By the autumn of 1833, Abd al-Qadir's credentials as a *mujahid*, a fighter for the faith, defending the integrity of the Muslim community and its territory, were thus established.

At the same time, internal opposition persisted, and could not be overcome without an agreement with the French that would suspend hostilities and enable the amir to gain ascendency over his rivals. Such an agreement was reached in February 1834, with General Desmichels, who since April 1833 had commanded the French forces at Oran. Desmichels, limited in his own capacity to extend effective French control inland but anxious to demonstrate to his superiors that his province was subdued, believed that Abd al-Qadir's emergence as the principal Arab leader in the west gave him an important opportunity to reach an agreement that might end hostilities and provide France with an effective ally in the interior. Reaching official agreement with Abd al-Qadir's representatives on 26 February, Desmichels telegraphed to Paris announcing 'the submission of the province of Oran, the most important and the most warlike of the Regency'.[41]

The six articles of the treaty provided for a ceasefire, an exchange of prisoners and the establishment of consular representation for the French at Mascara and for Abd al-Qadir at Oran, Mostaghanem and Arzew, the protection of Muslims' religion and customs, and freedom of commerce. In addition, extradition of deserters and criminals was guaranteed by both parties, and safe passage 'throughout the country' was guaranteed to any European (in the Arabic text, 'any individual Christian') carrying a visa approved by the amir's consul and by the general, 'governor of the city'. This treaty, ratified by the French government, far from signalling the 'submission' of the region, amounted to a remarkable recognition of Abd al-Qadir's sovereignty. Desmichels' instructions were to secure 'recognition of French sovereignty by Abd al-Qadir, who will pledge faith and homage to the King of the French, [in exchange for] recognition of Abd al-Qadir by France as *bey* of a certain number of tribes, invested as such by the King'.[42] By creatively interpreting the French text of article 1, which promised the 'union and friendship that must exist between two peoples whom God has destined to live under the same dominion', Desmichels could claim to have gained an implicit recognition of French rule over the former Regency. The terms of the Arabic text of the treaty, in which Abd al-Qadir is established as *amir al-mu'minin* and his interlocutor as merely 'the general, governor of the French armies in the city of Oran', leave no doubt as to the meaning of the phrase 'two peoples for whom it has been decreed by God that they shall live under one rule' as Abd al-Qadir must have understood it. His prerogative as guarantor of safe conduct for Christians 'throughout the country' was a perfectly classical expression of the proper responsibility of a Muslim ruler.[43]

As if this were not enough, a secret convention appended to the treaty and ratified by Desmichels (though not by the French government) shortly afterwards modified article 4 of the agreement on freedom of commerce, stipulating both that the French were to guarantee the amir free access to trade in arms and munitions and that all foreign trade from the region was to be under Abd al-Qadir's control, 'as it was [in the hands of the state] in the time of the former rulers', with exports to be made exclusively from the port of Arzew: 'As for Mostaghanem and Oran, nothing is to enter there save what is sufficient for their inhabitants, and no-one shall engage in [foreign] trade there; indeed anyone wishing to charge cargo shall go to the port [of Arzew] to load his vessel'.[44] Taken together, the official and the secret articles, all of which were, as far as Abd al-Qadir was concerned, elements of a single agreement, gave the amir grounds for considering his jurisdiction established, not only over the interior of the region but over its external relations.[45]

Desmichels, considered to have exceeded his orders, was replaced a year later, in February 1835. But in the meantime, the treaty bought Abd al-Qadir not only time, but resources in arms, ammunition and technical assistance. At the suggestion, apparently, of Abdallah 'd'Asbonne', a Palestinian 'mamluk' veteran of Napoleon's army in Egypt who was dispatched as consul to Mascara, Abd al-Qadir began to build his own, regular *nizam jadid* (new order) army along the lines adopted already further east in Egypt and the Ottoman empire, and later developed in Morocco. Infantry battalions were equipped with French rifles and drilled by French instructors, and a small force of artillery was supplied with French field guns; at the same time, arms shipments also came to the amir from Europe via Morocco.[46] With this force at his disposal, Abd al-Qadir was able to suppress the dissent of tribes recalcitrant to taxation or displeased by peace with the French, and put down a rival attempt to raise jihad, led by the Derqawa *tariqa* in the environs of Medea, capital of the old beylik of Titteri south-west of Algiers. By the summer of 1835, Abd al-Qadir had secured his preeminence over rivals and dissidents in the west, had crossed the Cheliff river to the east and entered Medea, extending his power tentatively eastwards towards the old centre of the Regency.

Peace with the French, however, did not outlast the effective establishment of Abd al-Qadir's rule. In the spring of 1835, the former *makhzen* tribes of the Dawa'ir and Zmala near Oran sought protection from the new French commander, General Trézel. His granting of support to them, as significant military allies, broke relations with Abd al-Qadir, and hostilities ensued. On 28 June, the amir's troops, though suffering heavy casualties themselves, routed a French column caught at the Maqta, a narrow defile between a line of low hills and the swampy outlet of the river Habra east of Arzew. The 'disaster' of the Maqta caused outcry in France, prompting the recall of the governor general, Drouet d'Erlon, and his replacement by the pro-colonist Marshal Clauzel, whose troops took Mascara in December and entered Tlemcen in January 1836. Abd al-Qadir's avoidance of a direct engagement with the French, along with Clauzel's failure to follow up his successes and his alienating of his own potential allies (notably the population of Tlemcen, on whom an immense indemnity was assessed), spared the amir from disaster. By the summer of 1836 he had pinned down French troops in the region, and a pitched battle, fought on 6 July 1836 at the Sikkak river, where a French army destroyed Abd al-Qadir's combined regular and tribal force of almost ten thousand men, was not followed by any more decisive French occupation inland. The isolated garrison of Tlemcen remained the only French force in the interior. Concentrating his efforts on the beylik of the east, Clauzel attempted to take Constantine in November 1836, but was beaten back by the weather and Ahmad Bey; the politicians in Paris called for a policy of 'restricted, progressive and peaceful' occupation, focusing on the coastal enclaves and their hinterlands, and leaving the interior to vassal chiefs who might accept French sovereignty – as they imagined Abd al-Qadir would do.[47]

To this end, General Thomas-Robert Bugeaud, the victor of the Sikkak, was charged with negotiating a renewed peace agreement with Abd al-Qadir that would give the French time to prepare a second expedition against Constantine; from Abd al-Qadir's perspective, it would relieve pressure on his own, still precarious position. Bugeaud, an earthy and taciturn veteran of Napoleon's campaigns in Spain and more recently a parliamentary deputy inclined to privilege his own 'parish pump electoral politics'[48] over grander designs, hastened to conclude a treaty that could only become a cause of further conflict. Instructed to re-establish France's recognition of the amir as a 'great vassal of France'[49] (Bugeaud's own expression) in exchange for an annual tribute, the general in fact quickly dropped the issue of tribute, extracting instead a series of largely meaningless concessions from Abd al-Qadir in exchange for the effective acceptance of the amir's rule over most of the interior of Algeria. Agreed on 30 May 1837, the treaty of the Tafna did stipulate, in contrast to the engagements accepted by Desmichels, that foreign trade must be conducted from French-occupied ports, but both Abd al-Qadir and French shipping ignored this provision. Freedom of movement and free trade internally were also envisaged in the treaty, but were limited in practice by Abd al-Qadir's ability to control and tax trade and to forbid Muslims from settling in French-held areas. The territorial delimitations laid out in the treaty contained the French presence in the hinterlands of the major ports of Oran, Mostaghanem, Arzew and Algiers, evacuating French forces from Tlemcen and giving Abd al-Qadir the right to rule (in the Arabic text) or to 'administer' (in the French text) the remainder of the former beyliks of Oran, Titteri and Algiers.

As with the Desmichels treaty, crucial ambiguities allowed Bugeaud to present this agreement as a submission to French force of arms. The first article of the French text declared that Abd al-Qadir 'recognised the sovereignty of France in Africa', but the Arabic text merely noted that the amir 'is aware of the rule of French power (*ya'rifu hukm saltanat firansa*) in Africa'. What Abd al-Qadir himself made of this phrase we can only infer from his own correspondence with Bugeaud before the treaty negotiations: 'You boast of your power. Are we here under your orders that you should send us such a letter? . . . You have spoken to us of your power, for our part we have courageous men and we shall die Muslims'; 'I have understood your power and all the means at your disposal. We do not doubt it and I well know what harm can be done. Power is in the strength of God who created us all and who protects the weakest ... If power lay in numbers, how many times would you have destroyed us?'[50] Abd al-Qadir could hardly be unaware of French power; in the Tafna treaty he believed himself to be containing it to manageable proportions on the edge of his own, much vaster sovereign territory.

The limits of that territory, beyond which, again according to the Arabic text, he might not aspire to 'rule' (the French text more robustly claimed that he might not 'penetrate' beyond it), were clear enough in the west and centre of the country. France held the immediate environs of the western ports, the Mitidja and its environs south of Algiers as far as Blida and the first foothills of the Atlas, effectively the old *dar al-sultan*. To the east, however, a deliberately ambiguous phrase referred to French territory in the province of Algiers 'as far as the Oued Kaddara and beyond (*et au-delà*)' in the French text, 'to the boundary of the Wadi Khadra onward (*ila quddam*)' in the Arabic. The river in question, flowing north to the coast at a point east of the bay of Algiers, just west of today's Boumerdès, and known as Oued Boudouaou towards its outlet, was taken by Abd al-Qadir to mark the eastern limit of French territory; the words *ila quddam* or *au-delà*, which were to seem so obscure to later historians, to him most likely implied simply 'downstream'.[51] Bugeaud, however, intended by this clumsy formulation to preserve French freedom of action in the whole of eastern Algeria. These divergent implications of the agreement already prepared the ground for its collapse.

Defeated militarily, but by an enemy unable to press his advantage, Abd al-Qadir had nonetheless twice triumphed over the French diplomatically. In addition to the formal provisions of the Tafna treaty, secret agreements made with Bugeaud assured the amir that he would obtain army rifles, ammunition, the relocation away from Oran of the secessionist Dawa'ir and Zmala tribes, and the exile of their chiefs in exchange for a cash payment, which was spent by Bugeaud to further his electoral cause through road-mending in his constituency. French policy in Algeria was still, in mid-1837, a matter of shady deals and personal profit. In the aftermath of the Tafna treaty, however, from Abd al-Qadir's point of view it seemed that a durable basis of accommodation had been reached. He began to establish a new and more secure capital, far inland at Tagdempt, and put his government on a firmer footing with the aid of a substantial *fatwa* (juridical opinion) from Ali al-Tasuli, a leading *'alim* of Fez. This affirmed the view that the imam (leader of the community) or his deputy – as Abd al-Qadir was considered the deputy of the Moroccan sultan – had the right to determine when to declare jihad, that dissidence against the state and refusal to pay taxes were 'crimes against the *umma*' (the Muslim community as a whole), and that emigration (*hijra*) from 'the land of corruption' under non-Muslim rule was a religious duty.[52]

With his administration relayed by *khalifas* (deputies) in each province from Tlemcen in the west to the Medjana in the east, Abd al-Qadir's jurisdiction after 1837 extended over some two-thirds of Algeria. Still, his position was not entirely assured nor universally respected. At the moment of his greatest security vis-à-vis the French, Mawlay Abd al-Rahman in Morocco urged resumption of the jihad, and the amir's writ ran neither in the mountains of Kabylia nor among the followers of other *tariqa*s, foremost among these being the Tijaniyya, whose forces had themselves recently besieged Mascara when it was an Ottoman capital and who now, in the person of the head of the order, Sidi Muhammad al-Tijani, refused to recognise Abd al-Qadir's sovereignty. Fortified in the great *zawiya* at Aïn Madhi on the edge of the Sahara, the Tijaniyya asserted their autonomy. Abd al-Qadir's attempt to force them into submission went spectacularly awry when his expedition, in July 1838, was unable to enter the town by force and instead became embroiled in an inconclusive siege, at the end of which, in December 1838, Sidi al-Tijani agreed to go into exile rather than submit.

By this time, relations with the French were once more becoming frayed. A second assault on Constantine, in October 1837, had taken the city, from which Ahmad Bey and his immediate circle withdrew to pursue their resistance, and quell local dissent, from the southern Aurès mountains. For the first time, a secure French presence was established inland. The 'restricted occupation' was coming to an end. Although some 4,000 Europeans left Algeria in 1839, 6,881 immigrants arrived; by the end of the 1830s, Algiers and its vicinity, where the greater part of the new colonists lived, already had over 14,000 European inhabitants, against some 12,000 Muslims and 6,000 Jews.[53] Pressure to maintain and extend the conquest was growing steadily. In July 1839 Marshal Soult, then serving as Prime Minister, wrote to Governor General Valée that his policy should be one of 'advancing slowly and never drawing back'; the latter had himself written in February 1838 that 'the sole aim' to be achieved should be 'to establish French domination from Morocco to Tunis, and from the Mediterranean to the desert'.[54] In October 1838, a settlement was founded on the site of ancient Rusicadae (Skikda) on the north Constantinois coast and named Philippeville in honour of the French king. The agricultural centre of Boufarik in the Mitidja, despite being 'less a village than a cemetery where, in 1839, they buried one fifth of the population', received a continuous influx of new inhabitants.[55] On 14 October 1839, the Minister of War officialised the new-found French confidence in their possession, writing that 'the country occupied by the French in North Africa will henceforward be referred to as Algeria (*Algérie*)'.[56]

At the end of that same month, Valée and the Crown Prince, the Duke of Orléans, led 4,000 soldiers on a march through the Biban ('Iron Gates') pass between the Medjana and the upper Soummam valley, arriving in Algiers on 2 November and thus linking up the newly conquered ex-beylik of Constantine with the centre of French territory, passing through the territory in the eastern Algérois that Abd al-Qadir had consistently considered to be under his sovereignty. Abd al-Qadir had written directly to King Louis-Philippe in March that such a contravention of the Tafna treaty would be considered an act of war, warning that 'the Arabs ... no longer have any confidence in, nor desire for, negotiation with you. We have no aversion to peace, but the opinion of my counsellors and notables [which inclines to war] will carry the day.'[57]

The war that followed, and that lasted eight years, until Abd al-Qadir's surrender on 21 December 1847, was the undoing of Abd al-Qadir's state and the beginning of the more profound dislocation of Algerian society. On 20 November 1839, Abd al-Qadir's forces attacked French army posts and farms in the Mitidja, taking no prisoners and sweeping the small colonial population away in panic to Algiers. Although the French army was able to occupy the Algerian-held towns – Cherchell on the coast, then Medea and Miliana – one after the other, Marshal Valée's strategy of garrisoning these fixed points dispersed his 60,000 troops, and Abd al-Qadir, again avoiding frontal confrontations that he could not hope to win, harried the French lines and isolated garrisons. At the end of 1841, Valée was recalled, and replaced as governor general by Bugeaud.

Bugeaud had opposed the continued occupation of Algeria, 'a disastrous legacy' of the Restoration regime.[58] As an agriculturalist who took pride in his upbringing close to the peasants of his home estate, he declared that the Regency was 'not cultivable'; as a general he declared the war in North Africa useless for training troops 'because they all die there [of disease]'.[59] Now he declared that 'absolute domination, the absolute conquest of the country' was necessary 'by force of circumstance', since 'every lost engagement demands revenge' and an occupation restricted to the coast was strategically untenable. In a remarkable access of frankness, he told the French parliament: 'Great nations ... must make their mistakes with greatness (*grandeur*). Yes, in my view, the possession of Algiers is a mistake; but since you wish to make it, since it is impossible not to make it, you must make it entirely (*grandement*); it is the only way to derive any gain from it'.[60] More ostensibly liberal opinion agreed. Alexis de Tocqueville, returning from a visit to Algiers in the summer of 1841, wrote that France could not quit Algeria since 'abandonment ... would be the surest announcement of our decadence to the eyes of the world'. To ensure the security of colonisation, he went on, the war against Abd al-Qadir must be total:

I have often heard, in France, men whom I respect but with whom I cannot agree, express their disapproval of our burning crops, emptying grain stores and taking prisoner unarmed men, women and children. Such methods, in my view, are unfortunate, but anyone wishing to make war on the Arabs will be obliged to adopt them ... We shall destroy the power of Abd al-Qadir only by making the situation of the tribes who support him so unbearable that they will abandon him ... I believe that every means should be employed to devastate the[se] tribes, save only those that common humanity and the law of nations reject.[61]

De Tocqueville's flimsy limitation counted for little, and the implications of total commitment to the war were calamitous. By 1842, Bugeaud had 83,000 men in the field; by 1846, his troops numbered 108,000. He set up a line of fortified positions deep inland, on the northern fringe of the high plateaux, and deployed flying columns, unencumbered by baggage or artillery, that set about the systematic occupation and devastation of the countryside. Declaring that 'in Africa ... there is only one target that can be attacked: agriculture',[62] Bugeaud aimed at destroying Abd al-Qadir's state by laying waste the ecological basis of Algerian society. Livestock was seized or destroyed, crops burned, grain stores ruined, tress cut down. In every locality, negotiations were refused, complete surrender demanded. One of Bugeaud's officers, Saint-Arnaud, whose rapid promotion from battalion commander to general exemplified the careers to be made in this 'African war', had no qualms describing the campaign in letters to his brother:

The country [in the Dahra mountains inland from Cherchell] is magnificent, one of the richest I have seen in Africa. The villages and houses are packed close together. We have burned and destroyed everything ... Such a lot of women and children, seeking shelter in the snows of the Atlas, have died of cold and misery! [...] The night was terrible for those out of doors, though good for us [encamped in the houses of a captured village]. Next day, the sun came up on two feet of snow, no road, nothing but snow ... Piles of corpses, pressed one against another and frozen to death in the night! This was the unfortunate population ... whose villages and huts I had burned, and whom I had caused to flee before me. [...] Decidedly, they are sick of fighting, and no wonder! What ravages! What destruction![63]

By 1843 all of Algeria's urban centres were in French hands. Their populations, fleeing, swelled the numbers of the harried and homeless in the ravaged countryside. Abd al-Qadir conducted a rapid war of movement from his mobile capital, the *zmala* (encampment), a tent city 30,000 strong, but this was surprised and destroyed on the steppe south of Tiaret by cavalry under Prince Henri d'Orléans, the Duke of Aumale, on 16 May 1843. In December, Abd al-Qadir was forced to seek refuge in Morocco. With widespread support among the population for the pursuit of jihad – and fearing the popularity of Abd al-Qadir as its most energetic proponent – Mawlay Abd al-Rahman and the Moroccan *makhzen* now threw their full weight behind war with the French, but the Moroccan army was destroyed in a pitched battle on the border at Wadi Isly near Oujda on 14 August 1844, and French gunboats shelled the ports of Essaouira and Tangier. The Moroccans sued for peace, and declared Abd al-Qadir, who pursued the war in cross-border raids, a 'corrupter' (*mufsid*) rather than a fighter for the faith (*mujahid*). One leading shaykh of the Tayyibiyya *tariqa*, which had affiliates throughout Morocco and Algeria, warned against 'devils who set themselves up as fighters of the holy war, under the pretext of religion, and mislead those ... who listen to their lying words, and then draw them into danger and abandon them'.[64]

Between 1844 and 1847, relations between Abd al-Qadir and his increasingly reluctant Moroccan hosts degenerated into a civil war for control of the Rif in northern Morocco, where Abd al-Qadir's struggle was now based. To Mawlay Abd al-Rahman, the Algerians' state-within-a-state on his territory, and the popularity of Abd al-Qadir among his subjects, was a threat to his dynasty. Combined with the increased pressure of the French, it was a threat to the whole sultanate.[65] Faced with an ultimatum that he either retire to Fez or quit the territory of the sultanate via the Sahara, and with Moroccan troops sent against him, Abd al-Qadir crossed the Muluwiyya river and, finding the French cordon too tight to penetrate with his entourage, negotiated terms of surrender. 'I have fulfilled my duty towards God', he reportedly told the area's tribal leaders; 'Now that I find myself powerless ... I wish to rest from the weariness of war.'[66] On 20 December 1847, he wrote to General Lamoricière, requesting the safe return or sale of slaves, camels and horses belonging to his retinue and held by neighbouring tribes, the release of Bu Hamedi, his envoy to Mawlay Abd al-Rahman who had been imprisoned in Fez, and the safe passage of any of his entourage who wished to follow him into exile: 'We wish you to send us word ... that can be neither diminished nor altered, to guarantee us that you will transport us to Alexandria or Acre, and nowhere else'. Lamoricière replied that:

I have orders ... to grant you the safe conduct that you have requested, and to give you passage ... to Alexandria or Acre; you will surely not be taken elsewhere. Come as may be convenient, by day or night, and have no doubt

Figure 2.1  The amir Abd al-Qadir, photographed in exile in the 1860s. An international celebrity after saving Christians from massacre during the 1860 Damascus riots, the amir is portrayed wearing European decorations including the *grand cordon* of the Légion d'Honneur over his *burnus*. This image would serve contemporary French accounts which 'domesticated' Abd al-Qadir within a narrative of 'progress', one that obscured both his state-building and his spiritual-intellectual career (Library of Congress).

of this word, which is definite ... You may be sure that you will be treated as befits your rank.[67]

Abd al-Qadir surrendered three days later; he would spend the next five years as a prisoner in France.

## *Mahdi*s, Millennialism and 'Total' Conquest

After the fall of Constantine in 1837 and the resumption of war in the west in 1839, the repercussions of the seizure of Algiers began to be felt in earnest throughout the territories of the former Regency and across its porous borders with Tunisia and Morocco. Ahmad Bey, having led a separate and rival struggle in the east of the country to that of Abd al-Qadir further west, surrendered six months after the amir, in June 1848. Both had sought to recompose a centralising sovereignty in their respective domains. Ahmad, having failed to keep the French out of Constantine, sought a negotiated settlement that would leave him autonomous governor of his province, which he refused to quit.[68] Abd al-Qadir's state-building venture had been a spirited attempt to accommodate the French by containing them, as a tolerated minority occupying the coastal cities from which they could not (yet) be removed, while establishing a unified religio-political authority throughout the interior of Algeria, and aspiring to at least nominal jurisdiction over the Muslim population in the territory around the occupied ports from a capital inland. After 1839, these unifying attempts could not be revived.

Instead, claims to guidance from God and to leadership of the community fragmented and proliferated. Revolt took the form of locally rooted millenarian insurrection, sparked by dramatic ecological crisis or by rumours and anxieties of impending catastrophe, and illuminated by apocalyptic cultural codes in which the *mahdi* (the 'rightly guided one') or *mawl al-sa'a* (the 'lord of the hour') were anticipated as messianic heralds of the end of earthly tribulation and the dawn of a 'realm of justice'.[69] For the next forty years, apparently sporadic and desperate uprisings would punctuate what the French began to call the 'pacification' of Algeria. As the invaders moved from merely declaring their sovereignty over the former Regency to implementing the actual occupation of the land, the gradual extension of their presence and its effects came increasingly to seem like a cataclysm. But in seeking, by sudden and divinely inspired action, to overturn the increasingly inflexible hold of the invaders over the land and its inhabitants, insurgents one after another unwittingly drew French forces further and further into the interior, as the perimeter of security for expanding colonial settlement was threatened from ever deeper south into the desert, ever higher up into the mountains.[70] Once the maintenance of the occupation was decided and settlement – however disorderly – begun, brute facts on the ground dictated their own logic.

The millenarian dimension of rural insurrection emerged in the latter stages of the war against Abd al-Qadir, just as the French believed themselves to have gained a firm grip on the populations and territories formerly under his control. In early 1845, in the Dahra mountains north-east of Bugeaud's new strategic centre of Orléansville (today's Chlef) in the Cheliff valley, and apparently 'in the midst of the deepest peace',[71] a young ascetic, claiming to be a *sharif* and known locally as Bu Ma'za ('the man with the goat'), took the name of Muhammad ibn Abdallah – the name of the Prophet, popularly associated with the expected *mahdi* – and raised an insurrectionary movement. Bu Ma'za's jihad spread rapidly in the spring and summer of 1845 through the Dahra and Ouarsenis, and ultimately across the country 'from the banks of the Muluwiyya to the peaks of the Aurès'[72] before his capture in April 1847. The repression was merciless: tribes that submitted but could not pay tax arrears saw their property destroyed; whole populations, including women and children, like the Awlad Riyah who took shelter in caves in the Dahra, were asphyxiated, burned to death or buried alive in their refuges. Following the principle that the general population and their means of subsistence must be the target of 'pacification', indiscriminate looting, rape and murder became the norm.[73]

A similar dynamic occurred on the edge of the Sahara two years later, when in the summer of 1849 a man known as Bu Ziyan, whose hand was said to have turned green from contact with the Prophet Muhammad in dreams, declared himself to be the *mahdi* and led a revolt centred on the oasis of Za'atsha in the Ziban, west of Biskra. Rallying local *tariqa* affiliates to his cause, Bu Ziyan's rising spread to the Aurès and Hodna. At Za'atsha, he and his followers withstood a fifty-two-day siege in which French forces lost some 1,500 men, before the oasis was taken and destroyed, its defenders massacred. Many of the survivors of the repression subsequently perished in a cholera epidemic that killed up to three-quarters of the population of the neighbouring oases.[74]

In 1850–51, resistance to the beginnings of French encroachments in Kabylia and the Babors found expression in the figure of another *sharif*, Bu Baghla, 'the man with the mule', who precipitated an uprising of the hitherto relatively autonomous and un-threatened population in the Djurdjura. Punitive expeditions here cut down trees and burned whole villages: the region of Ouzellaguen, along the northern edge of the Soummam valley, wrote the official *Moniteur algérien*, was systematically 'pillaged and burned. The lesson was so severe that, as our troops returned to camp, not a single rifle shot was aimed at the rearguard. But they left the villages in flames, on paths strewn with the corpses of killed enemy men and horses.'[75] After Bu Baghla's death in battle in Kabylia in 1854, resistance in the mountains continued under the leadership of a female marabout, Lalla Fatima N'Soumer. But repeated French incursions into the region gradually opened strategic roads through the mountains until, in a forty-five-day campaign between May and July 1857, troops under Marshal Randon captured strongpoints along the ridge of the Djurdjura. They established a fort (Fort-Napoléon, later Fort-National) at L'Arba'a N'Aït Iraten, subduing the *igawawen* Aït Yenni and Aït Menguellat confederations, took their fortress at Ichiridden, 1,065 metres above sea level, and captured Lalla Fatima.

The conquest of Kabylia in 1857 seemed to mark the end of the long campaign of 'total conquest', but in fact neither the conquest nor resistance to it was yet over; in fact, the dynamic interplay of incursion and response would continue for at least another thirty years. Revolts broke out again in the Aurès in 1860 and 1879, among the Awlad Sidi Shaykh in the south-west in 1864–65, in the Ziban in 1876 and along the ill-defined Saharan border with Morocco in 1881. The most serious of all revolts in the period of 'pacification' broke out in Kabylia in 1871 and spread across the east and centre of the country. The distant fastnesses of the Sahara would not be incorporated into France's Algerian empire until the 1890s; the Berber-speaking Tuareg people of the central Saharan Ahaggar mountains were not 'pacified' until 1902. The mid-century subjugation of the Kabyle mountains did, though, mark something of a watershed. French troops had by now arrived at the edge of the Sahara, taking Laghouat in 1852 with a terrible carnage – after which, it was said, vultures and crows circled the town 'as if over a slaughterhouse'[76] – imposing a protectorate over the Mzab in 1853[77] and occupying the Wadi Righ and Suf oases in the Saharan southeast, near the Tunisian border, at the end of 1854. In the latter areas, as in Kabylia and the Ouarsenis, revolts inspired by a sharifian *mahdi* figure and relayed by *tariqa*s, the followings of local notables, and tribal populations threatened in their autonomy or subsistence, had drawn the French far into the interior before being overcome by superior firepower and the exhaustion of their own resources.[78] There were now few areas left in the former territories of the Regency beyond the at least nominal control of the new rulers or their appointed auxiliaries; future revolts would emerge from the breakdown of relations between these, or from exacerbated pressures on the balance of survival reached at the end of the wars of conquest, rather than from outright initial resistance to invasion.

The consequences of the immense destruction of the war waged from 1839 onwards reverberated through the end of the 1860s, and reached well beyond the more obvious political and military spheres. Ecological factors, as well as religio-cultural codes and stimuli to action from encroaching troops, tax-collectors and colonists, had played a major part in the patterning of revolt. The crop cycle and the seasonal transhumance of pastoralists between mountain, steppe and desert affected the availability of manpower for insurrectionary movements in the plains or oases. Access to markets to offset only partial self-sufficiency among mountain-dwellers or nomads, and the reliability of control over supply and rates of exchange in the market for town-dwellers, landlords and peasants, were crucial components of the fragile ecological equilibrium upon which all sectors of society depended. Threats to this balance could make the difference between opting for quiescence and breaking into revolt.[79] But natural disaster also added its own force to the pressures now bearing down on the Algerian population. In 1867–68, when the older threats to survival returned – earthquake, locusts, drought then flood, and crop failure – the social systems and patterns of land use that previously mitigated their impact had been laid waste. They were joined, too, by typhus and cholera, the latter a new import from Europe. The resulting famine and epidemic may have killed upwards of 800,000 Algerians, and half of all Algerian-owned livestock, in the course of a few months.[80] In the centre, and especially on the plains of the west of the country, whose inhabitants had already lost the most land to colonisation and were reeling from the repression of the 1864–65 insurrection, mortality was especially high. Half of the Algerian population of the province of Oran may have died. In one village near Mascara, of 150 inhabitants, at least 115 died.[81]

Those worst hit were the inhabitants of the open countryside, the plains and steppe now designated as 'military territory' by the French, beyond the perimeter of 'civil territory' encroaching from the coast along the valleys, where settled colonisation and municipal government were established.[82] From the ravaged west, refugees fled far into the colonial centres: a census of 'vagabonds' arrested in Koléa, near the coast west of Algiers, listed large numbers of families that had come from Oran and Mostaghanem.[83] Ragged, starving and ill, thousands of Algerian men, women and children dragged themselves into the civil territories where they begged for aid, lived on roots or stole whatever they could, to the consternation of settlers. The effects were starkly described by local administrators in the newly French provincial towns: 'The misery among the natives is extreme. As a result, the number of beggars swarming in the streets has grown even greater, to the point that within the town of Miliana, one could see nothing but starving people covered in rags, holding out their hands to passersby.'[84] In Mouzaiaville, a colonial village established in 1846 in the Mitidja west of Blida, 'in civil territory, in the centre of the commune', 'three hundred persons, all strangers to the district, were camped in ravines, living on acorns and, whenever the opportunity arose, taking from our own laborious native workers [whatever they could], a goat, a sheep or some poultry'. The mayor wrote that from one locality

> I picked up 130 of them . . . and left at least 100 more for lack of anywhere to lodge them until a convoy should arrive [to take them away]; these people, including women and children, have been living in huts under palm leaves, and it is in these disease-ridden shacks, giving off fetid vapours that turn one's stomach, that one realises the misery that has struck these poor people. We have sent to Miliana or Blida . . . 150 of them, at least as many remain and the number grows every day. The presence of this population among us is not only an expense but a scourge.[85]

Administrators and the police scrambled to deal with the 'invasion', to arrest and 'repatriate' the 'beggars' and 'vagrants' from the outskirts of colonial settlements and Europeanised towns or to isolate them in *dépôts de mendicité* (almshouses), which became incubators of typhus.[86] Another expedient solution was to make the victims of the catastrophe into a labour force. In Miliana, the municipality put refugees to work cleaning streets and breaking rocks, in exchange for a bread ration, 'by which means, the town is purged of beggars, who gain their food by making themselves useful. Several of the [European] inhabitants have also taken on some of them [to work] under the same conditions, which has lessened the expense incumbent on the commune.'[87] The municipal council in Algiers had to give up on a plan to put the 'vagrants' to forced labour building roads only because of the threat it was feared they would pose to public health. [88]

The European population was largely sheltered from the storm, though among the poorest and most vulnerable of them, the effects of the epidemic and shortages also made themselves felt, with hospital expenditures for paupers in the department of Algiers increasing by almost a third in the course of a year.[89] The areas least affected – the coast and the mountains of Kabylia – were those whose ecologies were least fragile, or least disrupted by the thirty years' progress of the conquest. The extraordinary carnage caused by these 'natural' catastrophes illustrates the extent of the havoc wrought on the rural economy and social system by the dislocations and dispossessions of the war and colonisation, and the taxation and territorial regulation of the new regime. As historian and demographer Kamel Kateb notes drily, 'social and military factors amplified the effects of [these] natural calamities'.[90] The real cost of the conquest, and the limits of the possible accommodation of French rule to Algerian realities, are more starkly visible than anywhere in these few months' whirlwind of calamities.

The last great attempt to throw off colonial over-rule was a desperate gamble in these desperate times. In the northwest Constantinois and lower Kabylia, Muhammad al-Hajj al-Muqrani had succeeded in 1853 to the hereditary position that his family had long held, but which, after passing in his father's time successively from allegiance to the Ottoman bey through alliance with Abd al-Qadir, was now maintained by Muhammad's investiture as *bash-agha* by the French. Al-Muqrani had seen his prerogatives increasingly eroded, his position (despite his spectacularly large income) as a great aristocratic chief diminished to that of a subordinate to lowly French administrative officials, and his resources depleted by the aid he dispensed – at the cost of contracting substantial debts – to the tribes of the region during the famine. He saw in the precipitate French defeat at the hands of the Prussians, in September 1870, both a threat (that of a new civilian government that would not honour his position) and an opportunity to re-establish the dignity of his fiefdom in the Medjana, to remove his local (and familial) rivals, and to reassert himself as a privileged interlocutor with the French rather than as their mere functionary. On 16 March 1871, his troops attacked and pillaged the town of Bordj-Bou-Arreridj, a strategic centre on the road across the Medjana from Algiers to Setif and Constantine.

As historians have long recognised, this was neither a millenarian attempt to throw the French into the sea nor a sudden recrudescence of 'primary' resistance to invasion; it was, rather, a defence of interests and of an established system of social relations that had thus far been able, however uneasily, to come to terms with the new conquerors.[91] French 'native policy', especially in the as-yet largely un-colonised Constantinois, had remained up to 1870 largely 'a protectorate of feudal grandees' run by the Arab affairs experts of the colonial army.[92] Military aristocrats like al-Muqrani, and his brother Bu Mezrag who assumed the leadership of the revolt after al-Muqrani was killed on 5 May 1871, sought, like the notables of Algiers in 1830, to accommodate the French, or at least those among them with whom they felt they could deal on acceptable terms. As Bu Mezrag told the assize court of Constantine before which he was judged in March 1873, it was the plebeian citizenry 'whose pretension is to govern Algeria' that they saw as the threat and the enemy: 'I fought against the [government of the] civilians, not against France, nor for holy war'.[93] Al-Muqrani hoped to force the French to negotiate; it was when his offer of negotiations in April 1871 was refused that it became apparent that the gamble was lost.

Already, though, his revolt had been overtaken by events, submerged in a more radical and popular insurrection. Al-Muqrani was obliged by the limitations of his own forces to call for the sanction and alliance of the most influential religious leader of the region, shaykh al-Haddad, an elderly Kabyle *murabit* living in saintly isolation in the Soummam valley whose popularity had increased with the affiliations of many Kabyle peasants to the Rahmaniyya tariqa, of which he was a *muqaddam* (dignitary). On 8 April, he issued a call to jihad. Inflamed by promises of deliverance from a France apparently vanquished and in turmoil (the Paris Commune was at its height; in Algiers, settler republicans had set up their own Committee of Public Safety), and seizing in every locality on particular grievances against the encroachments of settlement, taxation and French-appointed local administrators, thousands of Algerians rose in revolt and stormed French outposts and villages. Within a month, the insurrection spread towards Algiers and across the east, as far as Ouargla and Touggourt in the Sahara, but reinforcements from France crushed the rising in the second half of the year. In May, shaykh al-Haddad and his son, Si Aziz, capitulated; Bu Mezrag was captured, almost dead from exhaustion, in January 1872.

The course of the war reflected the new distribution of forces in Algeria. The army was not the only actor in the repression: civilian settler 'self-defence' militias were responsible for indiscriminate extrajudicial killings. In Batna, a new French garrison town on the northern edge of the Aurès, the official commission of inquiry into the insurrection found that 'absolutely innocent' Arabs had been murdered by police and militia, and similar events occurred elsewhere. The death tolls were also, of course, heavily unbalanced: of the very precise number of Europeans (2,686) known to have been killed during the conflict, half died of disease.[94] No estimate could be made of the deaths among Algerians.

But it was the aftermath of 1871 that was particularly terrible. Leaders of the revolt were executed or deported to New Caledonia. Massive confiscations of land and an enormous indemnity of 36.5 million francs imposed on the insurgent tribes reduced to absolute penury areas that had hitherto been spared the worst ravages of conquest and demographic collapse. In parts of Kabylia, peasants were reduced, after losing most of their land, to selling their fruit trees and ploughs – their only means of subsistence – and their clothing.[95] The effects on livelihood and social order, unmeasurable even through the archives of sequestration and taxation that show an Algerian society and economy bled white for the benefit of colonisation, echo in the popular poetry of the time. The great Kabyle poet Si Mohand Ou Mohand Aït Hmadouch had been born around 1845 into a landowning and clerical family at Icheraiouen in the Djurdjura, which in 1857 became the site of the French strongpoint, Fort-Napoléon; the old village was razed and its people forced to move down the mountainside. After 1871, his father was executed and his uncle deported, other family members fled into exile in Tunis and the family's lands were confiscated.

> Here I am, wounded eagle
> Lost in the mist
> Left to tears and cries of grief.
> In the days when my wings spread forth
> I was first to take flight
> To soar across the seas.
> O saints who apportion merit and blame
> I find no joy in pleasures
> Since now the beaks of cockerels tear at falcons. [...]
> From east to west,
> The land is shattered [...]
> The world for all is torn apart [...]
> Men born to milk and honey
> Wander naked in the forests,
> Without even a shirt of wool.
> Thus has God willed this century
> Where, limed in anxiety
> We stumble at every step.[96]

## Making 'Peace'

The losses suffered by the 1870s, in land and lives, were and remain incalculable. Hundreds of thousands of hectares, including much of the country's best agricultural land, had already passed into colonial hands. Algerian direct 'combat deaths', sustained in the field and subsequently of wounds, numbered perhaps 650,000, perhaps 825,000, between 1830 and 1875. Famine and disease killed at least as many, very possibly many more.[97]

And yet, Algerian society and culture were very far from being crushed to dust. From the 1850s onwards, the rule of the *rumiyyin* (Christians, French) was manifestly an established fact. Prophecies and folktales circulated to explain the catastrophe as well as, or instead of, predicting its imminent end, and ordinary people as well as religious and aristocratic notables set about finding ways to minimise its impact, preserve their remaining margins of autonomy and work the system to their least disadvantage.[98] Resistance as well as accommodation now meant finding ways of incorporating an understanding of the cataclysm that had befallen the cities and the countryside within Algerians' cultural and spiritual imaginaries. From local historians in Constantine to popular folktales in the Mitidja, accounts of the conquest as a judgment of God attempted to put order back into the apparent chaos of the world:

A servant of [the saint] Ibn Reqqa was one day taken prisoner by the French during a revolt. He was to be taken before the military tribunal in Algiers. He called out to his master, 'Save me, O my lord!' And when he appeared before the members of the tribunal, he saw his master there, sitting there among them, and presiding over the council in the uniform of a French general, and he was acquitted. Without divine secrets, and had the saints not wished it, the Europeans would never have been able to conquer our lands.[99]

It also meant living with the realities of defeat and dispossession, reconstructing whatever could be salvaged from the wreck, and getting on with life in the hope of better days to come. Service to the beylik had always meant something of a compromise between local autonomy, personal advancement and familial security. In 1855 the Prefect of Constantine could observe that if 'ten years ago an Arab and a good Muslim had only disdain for a native who sold his services to France, calling him a "Turco"', the return in December that year of a battalion of Algerian infantry (*tirailleurs*) from the Crimea was celebrated enthusiastically by notables and common folk alike.[100] From 1830 onwards, attempts at accommodation – from petitions through offers of alliance to acceptance of subordination in the hope of preserving property and status, or merely of staying alive – patterned Algerian responses to the unpredictable, halting and unwieldy progress of the conquest in parallel to movements of organised or spontaneous armed resistance, prophecies of catastrophe or deliverance, or silent and anxious adaptation to terrible times. From mid-century, heads of *zawiya*s and leaders of *tariqa*s concluded uneasy pacts of coexistence with the new order of things. Leading landowning or *makhzen* families with a history of state service adapted to the new rulers and found acceptable justifications for doing so. Ordinary people did what they could or had to.[101]

Colonial records indicate the variety of people who thus sought to 'make peace' with the conquest. At the end of the ruinous wars in which Algerians from all walks of life had hedged their bets or found themselves in unexpected positions, the French state paid out pensions or relief payments to granddaughters of a former Ottoman bey of Oran, to the descendants of long-dead deys of Algiers, to the surviving womenfolk of a governor of Medea hanged by Abd al-Qadir as well as to Abd al-Qadir himself and his family in exile in Syria, and to a very few of the very many who had lost something: to Belkacem ben Ahmed Chennoufi, a *tirailleur* 'amputated of the left arm from a wound received in Kabylia', and to Djouher bent Lounis al-Kari, the widow of an Algerian 'killed in the service of France during the insurrection of 1871'.[102] Some of the Ottoman-era aristocracy managed to negotiate their survival, especially under the relatively *indigénophile* and hierarchically minded Second

Empire (1852–70) but even to some, albeit declining, degree as *grandes familles* thereafter. The Ben Siam family of Miliana, established among the *makhzen* notability and animated by dynastic politics in opposition to Abd al-Qadir, kept office, sent their sons into French administrative and military service, and became substantial landowners in the Algiers suburbs, pillars of the colonial establishment. Ahmad Sharif Zahhar, the *naqib al-ashraf* of Algiers whose chronicles of the late Regency we met earlier, served Abd al-Qadir in the 1840s before being imprisoned by the French on the island of Sainte-Marguerite, but then returned to Algiers where he resumed his (formal) title and a substantial social prestige. His youngest son, Ali, captured as a child when French troops overran Abd al-Qadir's *zmala*, was schooled in France and became a military interpreter, then an army officer and a naturalised French citizen. Si al-Hashemi, a younger son of Abd al-Qadir who grew up in captivity and exile, returned to Algeria in 1892 to die peacefully at Bou Saada on the Sahara's edge. His two surviving sons entered the French officer corps: the 'emir' Mustafa, who would die in service, and the 'emir' Khaled, born in Damascus in 1875 but educated in Paris and at the Saint-Cyr military academy, who would become a cavalry captain and serve at the front during the First World War.[103]

These were not merely cynical moves into enemy ranks: to maintain their positions, and their usefulness to the state, such families had also to retain at least some degree of influence among their own communities. Si Sliman Ben Siam, celebrated by *indigénophile* writers for his family's early 'loyalty' to France, was 'politically very astute, manoeuvring constantly between the French and the Arabs so as to be well regarded by both'.[104] The Emir Khaled, as he became known, once invalided out of the army, would emerge into a new kind of political activity in Algiers in 1919.[105] The romantic picture of Algeria's 'francophile' Arab notables, celebrated as evidence of French moral progress among a valiantly aristocratic people, regularly paraded at official occasions in their white turbans, red cloaks and decorations of the *légion d'honneur*, became a misleading trope of colonial imagery. No more useful is the corresponding, later, image of all such careers as those simply of *beni-oui-oui*: 'yes-men', traitors and collaborators. As Peter von Sivers' studies of landowning and rural auxiliary administrators' families demonstrated, the common image of Algerian society as having been 'decapitated' along with its state, its existing elite replaced with supine nonentities, is misleading. Instead, despite everything, there remained 'a strong historical continuity of the leading segments of Algerian rural society from Turkish times to the early twentieth century'. If the French sought to control the Algerian elite, that elite in turn 'successfully manipulated the French by renewing itself continuously in ways that were beyond the latter's control and by maintaining its monopoly of local power'.[106]

Some families that thus maintained themselves through the end of the century ended up fading into obscurity and poverty thereafter, but others would survive to see their descendants after 1914 take new roles in a re-emerging public sphere. Up to the first decades of the twentieth century, Algerian society thus proved astonishingly resilient, capable of recovery from the demographic near-collapse of the conquest and its conse-quences, and of reconstituting its spiritual, cultural – even, in some cases, its political and economic – capital, and, in the countryside, main-taining reduced but still important margins of self-direction. Local jama'as deliberated and registered decisions over questions of local boundaries and resources. Even when appointed by local administrators, who imagined them as the nuclei of a 'civic education' to be dispensed by France rather than as long-standing forms of locally rooted self-government, such assemblies could, on occasion, be capable of negotiat-ing, reducing and even outright refusing the administration's demands on their land.[107]

Resistance, ever more fragmented, could still find expression in dis-creet sedition, popular preaching and storytelling, and in circulating rumours and echoes of events, sometimes from far away, expressing millenarian hopes for an end to the daily grind of oppression, as well as pragmatic adaptation or despair for the present. During the Greco-Turkish war of 1897, for example, a Kabyle murabit affiliated to the Rahmaniyya order, an insurgent of 1870 who had been imprisoned on Sainte-Marguerite, was amnestied in 1885, and then settled in the Algiers suburb of Mustafa, reportedly held regular hadras (prayer sessions) at the mausoleum of the saint Sidi Abd al-Qadir Bu Qabrayn, at which he exhorted his disciples to keep their children away from Christian educa-tion, and foretold the imminent salvation of Algeria thanks to the victor-ious armies of the Ottoman Sultan Abdülhamid II. A few months later, his own nephew entered service with the Algiers municipal police. At the same time, Khayra bint Abd al-Qadir, a woman from the countryside around Berrouaghia south of Algiers, was arrested in Médéa. Claiming to be from a maraboutic family, she had come into the area after being divorced by her husband, left 'without resources' and reduced to prosti-tution; in her suffering, she had taken to preaching against the French in public. Lahouari ben Halima, a discharged spahi (cavalryman), carried forged letters purporting to come from Bu Amama, leader of the long-running insurrection on the Moroccan frontier, to tribes near Sidi Bel-Abbès, where they caused a minor sensation. But he then presented the letters to the French authorities in Oran, perhaps hoping for some

Figure 2.2 A street in Sidi Okba, 1890s. On the edge of the colonial economy, pre-Saharan oasis towns like Biskra and Sidi Okba became 'living tableaux' for European imaginations of a 'changeless' Arab-Muslim social and cultural life (Library of Congress).

reprieve, if not reward: 'When I left the service . . . despite my good record I received nothing . . . You are my family, whom I have served, and I wish to serve no-one else . . . I am worn out with walking and sick from fatigue.' He was sent to prison.[108]

Moments of overt revolt or refusal continued to break out where the demands of the new order became gradually intolerable, or conditions suddenly threatened to tip over the balance of survival. Thus a tax revolt broke out among the Nememcha tribes on the bleak southern flank of the mountains south of Tebessa in 1897, when rumours of the imminent arrival of the Sultan with a Turkish army combined with a poor harvest and seven months of uninterrupted locust invasion. 'Had the year been good', one witness averred, 'we should not have listened to such stories'.[109]

In 1901, slow but inexorable dispossession culminated in insurrection at Margueritte, a colonial farming community near Miliana, where the peasants, by killing five Europeans, threw settler society into a panic at what it could only understand as a recrudescence of religious 'fanaticism'.[110] And yet, in 1892, the same peasants had told a visiting Parisian delegation of the injustices they suffered at the hands of their European neighbours, saying that 'when we have paid all our taxes, we have nothing left, and if we wish to complain, no-one listens ... The administrator pays no attention to us. The *indigènes* do not count.'[111] In 1911, hundreds of families from Tlemcen emigrated to Morocco, and thence to Syria, in response both to the slow degradation of their city's ancient dignity and to the immediate threat of the conscription of Algerians into the French army, then being debated in Paris.[112]

At the same time, such movements overlapped with new forms of expression and the formulation of new demands. From around 1904, the first independent Arabic newspapers and periodicals began to emerge. In 1912 the so-called *jeunes Algériens* ('Young Algerians', derisively nicknamed by their detractors in reference to the 'Young Turk' and 'Young Tunisian' movements) presented their manifesto to Paris. Algerians, these French-educated, professionally mobile sons of notables now declared, would enthusiastically discharge their patriotic duty in paying the 'blood tax' of conscription in exchange for expanded civic rights and a beginning of real 'assimilation' to the promises of French liberty and citizenship.[113]

The long continuities observable in these patterns of resistance and accommodation persisted, then, up to the eve of the First World War. What the French called 'pacification' was for Algerians a long struggle to retain, in the face of the conquest and the colonial settlement that came in its wake, a measure of control over the terms of a minimally secure and peaceful existence. No straightforward division between heroism and compromise is possible or desirable in accounting for the way these events reflect Algerian society in these tumultuous years. More is explained by the political ecology of armed struggle, negotiation and quiescence that made certain possibilities, certain avenues of agency, open or close at different times in different places across the long chronology of total conquest. But 'pacification' never meant peace. On the contrary, the 'law and order' that followed, and with which Algerians thereafter had to contend, remained, as we shall now see, a life lived under conditions of continuous, low-intensity warfare.

# 3    The Means of Domination, 1830–1944

'We will pay, sooner or later, for the errors we are making.'[1] So, in September 1883, wrote Thomas-Ismaïl Urbain, an interpreter and official in the French War Ministry, great-grandson of a slave in French Guiana, sometime advisor on Algerian affairs to the Emperor Napoleon III, and Saint-Simonian social reformer who had converted to Islam while in Egypt and married an Algerian woman from Constantine.[2] The history of Algeria over the previous fifty years had been one of hesitation and inadvertence, ruthlessness and catastrophe, of struggles for survival and ascendency, and of the tumult of nineteenth-century politics, both Maghribi and French: state-building jihad, millennial revolt; imperial glory-seeking, industrious citizenship. The next sixty years would see the apparent stabilisation of 'French' Algeria, a settler society and a colonial state within the republican body politic that had emerged, after 1871, from the uneasy settlement of France's own eighty years of post-revolutionary ferment. As Urbain was writing, the battery of legal provisions set in place under the nascent Third Republic (1870–1940) was finally breaking the last grasp of Algerians on their land, and establishing a new colonial regime dominated, as the settlers had argued since the 1840s it should be, by the European civilian and citizen population and its interests, expressed by its elected representatives in civil and democratic institutions.

Urbain and other *indigénophiles*, particularly those Saint-Simonians in the army and the administration who, like him, had been active in the 1850s and 1860s in attempting to create an alternative model of state and society in Algeria, were equally committed to the ascendency and durability of French imperial dominion in North Africa. They had argued, though, that Algeria was not only a European colony but also an 'Arab kingdom', and that the former should preserve and 'improve', rather than destroy and replace, the latter. This was an idea congenial to conservative, aristocratic and hierarchically minded army officers who, since the 1830s, had seen Algeria as their special domain, as well as to the imperial and authoritarian regime of Napoleon III (r.1852–70). For them, older

Figure 3.1 The *Place du gouvernement*, Algiers, 1890. The equestrian statue of the Duc d'Orléans, to the French a hero of the war of conquest in the 1840s, stands in front of the Ottoman *jami'a jadid* ('New Mosque') near the waterfront. Until the eastward relocation of the city centre between 1910 (when the central post office was built at the eastern end of the rue d'Isly) and the 1930s (when the new Government General building was completed), this was the political and symbolic centre of colonial Algiers (A. Beglet. FR ANOM 8Fi431/2).

notions of noble, equestrian Arabs as worthy opponents and possible 'vassals', and of Algeria as a vast, as yet untamed and adventurous land of conquest, an open stage for the demonstration of martial valour and virtue, held a special attraction.

Such ideas were anathema to the settlers. In the ascendant after 1870, they saw their own place within the free and equal republic of citizens as viable only by the complete subordination of Algerian territory and its resources – including, crucially, its inhabitants' cheaply exploitable labour – to their economic and political control. They saw their security of livelihood, home and person as dependent on the continued subjugation of the Algerians, the 'native peril' whom they saw through a confused combination of racial and religious stereotypes, exotic fantasies, imagined paternal benevolence and, from time to time, hysterical terror. In their view, the army was in Africa to protect the settlers, their families, their land and their labour from 'these savages with a human face', as one European deputy exclaimed after the Margueritte revolt,[3] not to protect the 'natives' from the march of progress and the market, and certainly not to rule 'despotically' over hard-working and tax-paying French citizens, as before 1870, when Algeria was governed through the Ministry of War, it was seen to have done.

If the secure place of Algeria and its European population within the French polity was constantly reaffirmed under the changing colours of the Second Republic (1848–51), the Second Empire (1852–70) and the Third Republic (1870–1940), and, indeed, those of Vichy and Liberation from 1940 to 1944, the anxieties, resentments and insecurities that marked relations between the settler population and their government were nonetheless persistent.[4] They would reach their climax in the final agonies of the war of independence, with the 'revolution of 13 May' in 1958, the OAS and its reign of terror in 1961–62.[5] But whatever their intensity, such tensions were fought out within the French polity, and within its politics of citizenship, progress and the protection of persons and property, from an equal part in which by far the greater part of Algeria's inhabitants, disinherited in their own land, were excluded. It was through these conflicts, indeed, more than by design, that French Algeria took on its particular, and particularly perverse and intractable, shape.

France's Algeria was neither the contemporary American West of extermination and reservation, nor the later South Africa of apartheid, though both would be invoked in Algeria as examples at different times and to different purposes. There was – despite the arguments of some virulent pamphleteers – no deliberate near-extermination, or a legally enforced spatial segregation, of the subordinate population. But – despite the proclamations of colonial theorists about 'assimilation' – nor was there any serious attempt by the colonial state to make 'Algerians into Frenchmen'. And despite frequent daily contacts between poor working-class or small peasant-proprietor French Algerians and their equally poor and laborious Algerian neighbours, or between lycée-educated professional Algerians and their French counterparts, nor could there be a cross-community, multi-confessional social harmony that could blot out the fundamental political character of a colonial society.[6] The great, if obvious, irony of colonial Algeria's peculiar position within the French polity was that it was citizenship and democracy, the liberal-revolutionary gains of the European nineteenth century enjoyed by the settler society of French Algeria, that sealed the subjection of Algerian Algeria, once 'pacified', to a fate of exclusion, dispossession, denigration and impoverishment. The means by which this subjugation was achieved, while all the time its proponents spoke the language of improvement, progress, liberty and civilisation, were hardly less disastrous than the wars that had gone before. What is remarkable – as we shall see in the next chapter – is the way in which Algerians not only survived the effects of this enormous paradox, but worked to turn it to their own purposes.

## By Sword and Plough

Swiftly in the wake of the uncertain and brutal conquest came specula-tors, settlers and heated arguments over what kind of colony Algeria was to be. Just as the war of conquest was largely a matter of intention and policy attempting to catch up with and control, rather than initiating and directing, the logic of events on the ground, so European settlement, at first, was a disorderly business compounded by disputes over what form it ought to take and who, above all, ought to make it. The colonial state that ultimately emerged from the combined and conflicting actions of Algeria's military and civilian conquerors reflected all the tumultuous tensions of France's metropolitan politics in the years between the over-throw of the Restoration monarchy in 1830 and the crisis of the Third Republic a century later. But as with the devastation wrought by the immediate effects of war and the repression of insurrections, so a century of disputed colonial politics, however muddled, contradictory and bitter, had the overwhelming effect of dispossessing and demeaning Algerians, subjugating them to the rule of an especially punitive and authoritarian law, confining them in a legal no-man's-land that subjected them to all the obligations of membership of the French body politic while granting them none of its freedoms or protection, and reducing the great majority of them to pauperisation and penury.

When Algiers fell, there were a few hundred Europeans in the territory of the former Regency. The diplomatic crisis with France had led some of those previously established in Algeria – Mediterranean migrants of an older type such as Lazarist missionaries who occasionally functioned as French consuls, and whose presence had been tolerated since 1646 – to leave after 1827.[7] By 1834, Europeans numbered almost 10,000, and four years later, more than 20,000, a number that doubled again in 1842. By 1848 there were over 100,000 Europeans in Algeria; between 1854 and 1856, their birth rate for the first time exceeded their mortality; and in 1872 the European population stood at 244,600. In addition, 34,574 Algerian Jews living in civilian territory, without yet being considered 'European', had also become French citizens. Immigration to Algeria, though much less dramatic than the currents of 'explosive' colonisation transforming the Americas and Australasia, expanded at the end of the century, but the European population that had taken root in Algeria began, from the 1890s, to outnumber incomers. In 1901, for 340,000 Europeans who had migrated to the colony from France or elsewhere in Europe, there were 355,000 (plus 65,000 French citizens of Algerian Jewish origin) who had been born in the territory. The 1911 census counted 752,043 French Algerians. Thereafter, with the end of large-scale immigration, the population stabilised; in 1936, it stood at 946,000 and in 1954, at 984,000.[8]

This growing population, initially, neither grew as rapidly nor followed the patterns desired by the politicians and publicists who, in the colony's formative years under the July Monarchy (1830–48), sought to shape and direct it. Colonial settlement was intended to be agricultural; to provide French markets with 'exotic' and tropical goods; to have a moralising and fortifying effect on the poor labourers who would undertake it, and a purgative effect on the too-rapidly growing metropolitan towns and cities from which they were drawn. For some, its 'contact' with Algerians and the example of diligent, scientific and purposeful labour it would provide, in a market of 'free competition' that would stimulate productivity and prove, ultimately, to be universally beneficial, would even serve to 'regenerate' the conquered society and bring Algerians, by material interest, ever closer to their conquerors.[9] But early settlers were concentrated overwhelmingly in Algiers and its immediate vicinity, as far south only as Boufarik in the Mitidja, and in the other coastal towns, Oran, Philippeville and Bône. Only in the 1850s did the proportion of Europeans living in rural areas reach 50 per cent, and this proportion declined thereafter. From the 1920s onwards, the absolute number of Europeans in the countryside was progressively reduced. Between 1936 and 1954, the rural population came to account for fewer than 200,000 of Algeria's almost 1 million 'French' inhabitants.[10]

Moreover, as model agricultural colonisers, the first settlers were a great disappointment. In 1832, the government later complained, they had been given 'rations, tools, seeds, and draught animals. But these penniless men opened bars [cabarets], carted goods, and did precious little farming.'[11] Of the 109,400 Europeans counted by the administration in Algeria in 1846, only 16,422 were engaged in agriculture, while an alarming 1,500 of them sold tobacco or alcohol for a living. Already in 1837, there had been one alcohol vendor for every twenty-six Europeans in the colony, proportionally almost four times as many as in Paris (which had more cafés or public houses per head of population than any other European city). Instead of the 'true colonisation' founded on virtuous free labour, fructifying investment, moral hygiene and the public interest imagined by the theoreticians and advocates of colonisation, 'bad colonists' – speculators, innkeepers, 'loose women' – risked the ruin of the enterprise.[12]

The administration congratulated itself in 1840 that its population figures, showing a ratio of women and children to men of two to three, along with 'a real progression in the number of women', demonstrated that 'the family is gaining ground in Algeria, that the population is becoming stronger and attaching itself to the soil'.[13] But at the same time, like other frontier societies, in the eyes of the bourgeois social reformers and conservative administrators of the mid-1800s, colonial Algeria suffered from a propensity to moral degradation especially apparent in its alarming gender imbalance, with between 1.5 and 3 adult European men to every European woman in the colony from 1833 to 1847, and the large numbers of women (more than one in a hundred, or proportionally between five and fifteen times as many as in Paris) working as prostitutes.

Regulating prostitution – in order to control sexually transmitted diseases, and with soldiers', rather than women's, health most in mind – was one of the first acts of the colonial government, in August 1830. In 1838, officials reckoned that although 227 *filles publiques* were registered in Algiers, the total number was probably between 350 and 400 (in mid-1845 they would count 381), 'which means one prostitute for every fifteen inhabitants: in Paris the ratio is one to 225'. In 1857, the authorities registered 375 *filles inscrites*, but emphasised 'the terrible influence, much worse yet' of clandestine prostitution, whose practitioners were thought to be at least twice as numerous. Worries about public hygiene and 'moral health' extended to the Algerian population: indeed, over time concerns about hygiene and morality in colonial society came to be concerned less with European women than with Algerian prostitution. The Civil Intendant's office noted delicately in 1838 that in addition to the presence of large numbers of troops, it was especially the 'constantly increasing *malaise*' of the dispossessed 'Moorish' and Jewish inhabitants of Algiers that 'throws the young women of these two communities into vice', and that had contributed to the alarming rate of prostitution. At the same time, among these most vulnerable and disadvantaged of women workers, one registered *fille mauresque* in five (40 of 213) was being treated for illness (presumably, mainly syphilis), a 'frightful result' compared to the Parisian figure of one in twenty-one. In 1836 and 1837, between 2 and 3.5 times as many Algerian as European women were found to need treatment at the special dispensary set up for prostitutes in Algiers.[14]

While the colonial authorities themselves already recognised that it was the *malaise* into which the subjugated populace had been thrown that was responsible for this situation, the durable image covering the exploitative reality of colonial prostitution would portray it as an inherent part of Algeria's simultaneously alluring and degenerate 'native' landscape for a century to come, from the generically captioned, semi-nude *femmes Ouled Naïls* or *danseuses* in Jean Geiser's (d.1923) photographs that were frequently reproduced on postcards, to the 'girls of all nations' mentioned in the opening sequence of Julien Duvivier's much-admired 1937 film *Pépé le Moko*.[15] Here, as in other respects, important patterns are discernible from the very beginning of the occupation: colonial society was not what colonial theorists envisaged; if its effects produced moral anxieties among the elite, they were catastrophic for the most vulnerable; and the conditions into which indigenous society was thrown by the force of conquest came over time to be imagined as its 'natural' state.

Denounced in its early stages as 'anarchic', colonisation was only gradually brought under control, officially sponsored and regulated, over the course of the 1840s. 'Official' colonisation, moreover, which recruited emigrants, provided them with assisted passage to Algeria, and furnished them with land concessions or access to a locally organised labour exchange once there, was far from being a straightforward business of state control. As early as 1831, local authorities in Paris and the provinces sought 'to sponsor the emigration of beggars, criminals, and other troublemakers' to alleviate social tension and prevent 'Disorderly Riot', as the Parisian Prefect of Police put it, but troublesome and indigent immigrants were unwelcome to the army's government in Algiers, and by 1834 the first organised immigrants from Paris were being sent home.

After restricting emigration as far as possible to more desirable and self-sufficient workers and their families, the first wave of official colonisation began in 1838, followed by a larger-scale program in 1848. Workers applying for passports had to furnish certificates of morality and of physical aptitude as well as demonstrating their suitability to a trade required in the colony (although matching the demand for manual labour or artisan trades to the availability of suitable immigrants proved exceedingly difficult to manage), such that colonial settlement should be restricted to 'workers whose capacity and morality give them a right to the government's benevolence', in the words of the mayor of Nantes. Other local officials nonetheless continued to see Algeria as an outlet for 'an excess of Proletarians', and colonisation as a means 'to create a future for them, and above all to rid the country of them'.

For their own part, would-be emigrants petitioned the authorities as deserving fathers, mothers, sons or daughters, respectable folk thrown into necessity and anxious to fulfil their duties, not to some imperial ideal, but to their families and, as historian Jennifer Sessions observes, to a 'conception of working-class honour defined by skilled labour and economic independence', especially for men, and by the need to find 'honourable' work for women. While the government sought to rid French provincial towns of 'dangerous elements' or to mobilise a 'deserving poor', workers themselves saw in colonial emigration an opportunity to improve their lot and even, in the official schemes promoting it, the chance of asserting claims on the state to an 'incipient right to labour'. For the agricultural colonists of 1848, free transport, rations, land, housing, tools and seed, work on public projects in the off season and the promise of a secure property title after three years of fruitful labour held out a prospect of betterment that matched the inclusive aspirations of citizens of the new Second Republic. 'I take the liberty, Citizen Minister', wrote one inquirer from Amiens, of asking how he might go about benefitting from 'the advantages that the State is according to all French citizens'. Five fathers from Cuvilly, north of Paris, awaiting the departure of the convoy in which they were due to travel to Algeria (and listing under each of their names the number of their dependent children), petitioned the 'citizen representatives' of the National Assembly, expressing 'the impatience we feel that this hope should be realised as soon as possible, because of the absence of work that makes our situation ever more miserable; we earnestly desire to see arrive the painful, perhaps, but happy moment when . . . we shall be able to find in that other homeland the means of existence that we lack'.[16]

Bugeaud had envisaged the colonisation of Algeria by soldiers: the veteran, married, settled in a disciplined agricultural community, drilled against the threat of Arab insurrection, would 'never let his rifle rust'. Rejecting the distinction between 'civil' and 'military' colonisation, he maintained that the only viable settlement in Algeria was a necessarily militarised one: 'the sword and the plough', in his phrase, were to work together. Projects for such soldier colonies, proposed or experimented between 1842 and 1847, uniformly failed.[17] Other projects for 'ideal' colonies proliferated, some in surprisingly similar form though inspired by entirely different political visions. Prosper Enfantin, the 'father' of Saint-Simonian social reform, argued in his 1843 brochure *Colonisation de l'Algérie* that Algeria could provide the ground for a new 'association' of settler and indigenous interests that, by regenerating society through communal labour, would ultimately re-'civilise' France itself, overcoming the social ills of industrial capitalism and urbanisation, and ensuring a more peaceful future of progress for all. Enfantin was an energetic proponent of civil government, as opposed to military rule, but the communities of his model colonies were imagined along highly disciplined lines, with uniformed colonists organised in groups of families, three families to each section, twenty-four to a company, with a hierarchy of officer-engineers to supervise them.[18] At the other extreme, by the 1860s, large-scale investment by private capital, organised in joint-stock companies that acquired vast estates, was increasingly turned to in preference to the generally failing agricultural smallholders who had originally been imagined as the ideal colonial population. Ironically, European settlement was actually reduced in those areas, such as the great wheat fields near Setif, where such *grande colonisation*, like that of the Compagnie Génévoise, had its intensive, market-oriented farms. The cheaper labour of dispossessed Algerians, now working as tenants or agricultural wage-labourers on what had been their own lands, replaced that of the *petits colons*, and enabled correspondingly greater profits, 'spectacular fortunes' that settler commentators would denounce as contrary to the national interest.[19]

All such schemes, however, had in common one preoccupation: the constitution of private property as the essential foundation on which colonial society must be built. This meant the transfer of land, on as large a scale as possible, from Algerian to French hands. The sack of existing urban property rights had proceeded apace in Algiers, where speculative frenzy, demolition and remodelling, and new imperatives to document and map urban space had 'dismantled the very logic of the city' in a few years after the conquest.[20] Dispossessing the greater mass of Algerians of their rural property was more complex, and took more time. The process began almost immediately, with a decree of 8 September 1830, by which the properties of the defunct Ottoman state, including all properties held personally by officials of the Regency as well as all *beylik* lands, were taken over by the state domain.[21] *Habus* properties were added by a decree of 7 December; later, a royal order of 21 August 1839 allowed for the disposal of *habus* and other domain properties equally, and all remaining *habus* properties not already on the registers were merged with the state domain in March 1843.

Given the absence, destruction or disappearance of records, and the uncontrolled property transfers that were already taking place, however, it proved impossible to identify, reconstitute and seize the domains of the state as they had actually existed prior to the invasion, and the decrees on *habus*, whose location, value and status were equally difficult to establish, were only very partially applied. Nonetheless, in both practical and symbolic terms the impact of this first land grab was very great. In addition to insurgent tribes whose lands were summarily sequestered, peasants who had enjoyed recognised use rights to *beylik* land, as well as notable families connected to the Ottoman establishment, found themselves dispossessed. More seriously, although confiscated *habus* properties made up only

4.5 per cent of the land turned over by the state domain to colonisation by 1852,[22] the violation of the religious principle that they represented, and the despoiling of the educational and benevolent infrastructure that had depended on them, was a grievous affront to Muslims. While the state formally became merely the 'guardian' of these endowments, and undertook to support the mosques, schools and almsgiving to which they had been dedicated, this commitment was paper-thin. As far as Algerians could see, the French had stolen property made over in dutifulness to God and the community, and given it away to Christian settlers.[23] Regaining control of *habus* would be a central, and popular, demand of the *'ulama* into the 1940s.

The acquisition and disposal of Algerian land by French law, the French state and France's settler population now proceeded through two major series of measures which would accelerate colonial settlement through the end of the nineteenth century. Firstly, royal orders of 1 October 1844 and 21 July 1846 set aside Islamic law in respect of prior property transactions, ruled that perpetual leases or those without fixed terms (which had been common in early transactions between Algerian owners and European speculators) constituted a 'definite and irrevocable transmission' of ownership, and that uncultivated land, or land without verifiable title, in areas designated for colonisation would be annexed to the state domain. By 1852, a total of 364,341 hectares of the land acquired by the state had been allocated to colonisation, the greater part having been classed as former *beylik* property or acquired through the application of the laws of 1844 and 1846. Another 249,000 hectares would be seized during the 1850s. Although the administration spent great pains in justifying its various measures, in the circumstances there was little difference between legal expropriation for public utility (for which owners would supposedly be indemnified, although often, in the absence of prior valuation, they were not) and summary confiscation.[24] Algerians living closest to the cities, or who had entered into property transactions with Europeans, were worst affected. Many populations were dispossessed of their best lands for want of a 'verifiable' title acceptable to commissioners of inquiry, and the evidence of customary recognition of rights of access and use, which as we saw were more central to the old Algerian property regime than formal titles of ownership, was of no avail.

The general effect of these operations was the *cantonnement*, or restriction, of Algerian populations within reduced areas of their previously customary landholdings, following the widespread and energetically promoted belief that Algerians' extensive agriculture and mixed patterns of peasant-pastoral land use were 'wasteful'. *Cantonnement*, an army staff officer explained in 1859, 'has two purposes, one of which consists in creating resources for European colonisation, the other in giving to the natives the land necessary for their existence'.[25] Algerians, colonial observers believed, obviously had more land than they could possibly need. They were generally allowed to retain less than they could possibly live on. In the Mitidja, the Beni Khelil were left with 12.5 hectares on average per family; the Beni Moussa were reduced to 6.5 hectares per family. Near Jemmapes, one of the agricultural colonies created in 1848 southeast of Philippeville, Algerian peasants lost two-thirds of their land, retaining only 15 hectares per family, of which less than half was cultivable: as a native affairs officer noted drily, 'this is recognised as being insufficient'.[26] Peasants were pushed by these inadequate resources into wage labour for incoming colonists; in bad years, or when usurious debts mounted up, they were frequently further obliged to sell much of what land they had retained. Losing their resources in land and increasingly reduced to dependence, such populations also saw their internal social relations, which had been based, as we saw in Chapter 1, on collective ecological and economic interests, coming under strain.

These pressures, already felt by the 1850s, would be intensified thereafter. The second series of measures began with the land law of 16 June 1851, which established the state's 'private' rights of property (*domaine d'Etat*) distinct from those of the public domain (*domaine public*), and both confirmed the immunity of titles previously acquired by Europeans against invalidation under Islamic law, and recognised, without defining them, Muslim property rights existing prior to the conquest. But the most important instrument was the Sénatus-Consulte of 22 April 1863. This law was inspired by a combination of the desire to extend to Algeria the ongoing extinction of common-land property, and its replacement by *partages*, 'parcelling out' into individual private ownership, in rural France, and, in place of the disastrous practice of *cantonnement*, to apply the Saint-Simonian notions of protection, improvement and 'association' of Algerian society alongside the progress of European settlement. 'We must convince the Arabs', wrote Napoleon III in a famous letter to Marshal Pélissier, his governor general in Algeria,

that we have not come ... to oppress and despoil them, but to bring them the benefits of civilisation ... The land of Africa is sufficiently vast ... that each should be able to find his place there and let his activities freely flourish, each according to his nature, his customs and his needs ... The natives like the colonists have an equal right to my protection; I am the Emperor of the Arabs just as much as I am Emperor of the French.

The 'tribes of Algeria' were declared to be 'proprietors of the territories of which, under whatever title, they have permanent and traditional use'.[27] Algerian property was to be set on a legally secure footing by surveying these 'territories'; classifying *beylik* and forest lands that reverted to the state, communal land (as *'arsh*) and private property (as *milk*); delivering titles to the latter and preparing the way for the eventual conversion of collective properties into individual ones by subdividing tribes into territorially fixed *douars-communes* (from *duwar*, the traditional term for 'circles' of tents, now inscribed into French law as a geographical unit of administration) whose assembly (*djemaa*, from the existing *jama'a* of rural self-government, which it ostensibly revived) would manage communal lands. Ultimately, undivided family land rights and collectively held cultivable land would be parcelled out among the 'proprietors' thus identified, their ownership certified by legal title – and ready to enter the market.

If the intentions were mixed, the effect was dramatic. Although very incompletely enacted, by 1870, 372 tribes, or half the total Algerian population counted in 1872, were covered by the provisions of the Sénatus-Consulte. The Domains administration acquired just over 1 million hectares, or 14.9 per cent of the land surveyed.[28] Rural social organisation was heavily, although unevenly, impacted; some areas, notably in Kabylia, escaped the 'parcelling out' of tribal groups and their lands, while others, like the Ouarsenis along the course of the Cheliff river, felt its full force. But the Sénatus-Consulte was important less for its immediate effects than for what it subsequently enabled: the private acquisition of Algerian property by Europeans on a large scale. Napoleon III and his Saint-Simonian advisors would be swept from the scene by the Prussian victory over France's Second Empire in 1870, and the settlers – to whom the notion of Algeria as an 'Arab Kingdom' had been insufferable, and the idea of protecting 'Arab' property an absurdity – lost no time in benefitting from the possibilities henceforward open to them.

First came the massive sequestration of 446,406 hectares inflicted on Algerians after the 1871 insurrection, and the resumption of official colonisation (only in part to benefit displaced French citizens of Alsace-Lorraine whose former homes were now in German territory). The 'Warnier law' (named for Dr Auguste Warnier, ex-Saint-Simonian and now a vocal advocate of settler interests) of 26 July 1873 placed all property transactions involving Europeans, and those between Algerians for property already surveyed or registered in any way by the state, entirely under French law, and the 1887 land law completed the legal arsenal by giving Europeans the means to force the sale of undivided Algerian property.[29] The 1851 land law had already annexed forests and water-courses to state ownership; the introduction of a forest protection law in 1874 criminalised traditional practices of grazing, gathering, seasonal brush-clearing and planting in woodlands, on which, as they were pushed off more fertile lands in valley floors, Algerian populations were increasingly reliant.[30]

These measures all acted in concert. Between 1871 and 1885, more than half a million hectares passed into European hands. From 1881 to 1890, another 227,500 hectares were bought up in private transactions alone, and if the pace of expansion slowed in the 1890s, it recovered after 1900: every year up to 1919, European landholding grew by an average of 23,445 hectares.[31] 'Official' smallholding colonisation gave way to private investment and the accumulation of lands into larger, more efficient and more profitable estates. While, fed by credit and vulnerable to market downturns, fortunes made in the 1880s could be lost again by 1900, and then recover by 1914, in general, and with political support that included, for example, a favourable tax regime for European landed property, the colonial economy became able to withstand the fluctuations both of market prices and of yields and rainfall. Algerians, on the other hand, suffered disproportionately both from global slumps and from the local vicissitudes against which they had increasingly reduced margins of manoeuvre. Special taxes, known as the *impôt arabe*, and still classified by Ottoman-era terminology as *hukr*, *ashur* and *zakat*, were increasingly payable in cash and at fixed rates, instead of being proportional to any year's agricultural return. Tax receipts that rose rapidly, from less than 300,000 francs in 1840 to above 4 million by 1845, then to 22 million annually in the 1860s and almost 41 million in 1890, demonstrated the expanded reach and acquisitiveness of the state, not an increasing prosperity among Algerian farmers.[32] After several years of drought, from 1876 to 1881, and while colonial agriculture was expanding and shifting from wheat to more profitable wine, even Algerian populations that had lost little or no land, as in the south Constantinois, saw their flocks and herds halved or decimated, and their harvests collapse.[33]

In total, by the First World War, Algerian peasants had lost the ownership or use of almost 11.6 million hectares of farm, pasture and other land, including some 2.5 million hectares of forest, 2,317,447 hectares of which were in private European hands. The latter figure would rise more modestly to 2,614,798 hectares in 1944 and 2,706,130 hectares in 1950.[34] In 1944, Algerian-owned agricultural property was reckoned in total at 7,577,099 hectares.[35] But aside from both the obviously unbalanced ratio of land to population (in 1944, 23 per cent of Algeria's total

agricultural property was in the hands of 1.7 per cent of the rural population), and the fact that the European-owned sector constituted most of
the country's best agricultural land, the overall extent of landholdings was
also intensely unevenly distributed. In 1944, almost 2 million of the 7.6
million hectares of Algerian-owned land was in lots smaller than a bare-
subsistence 10 hectares, and another 3 million was in parcels of 10–50
hectares. A smaller number of owners held 1.3 million hectares in farms
of between 50 and 100 hectares, and another 1.1 million hectares in farms
between 100 and 500 hectares in extent. By contrast, almost 2.1 million
of the 2.6 million hectares in European hands were concentrated into
larger farms of over 100 hectares. Almost a quarter of this was in estates
larger than 1,000 hectares. Figures for population density in 1936, correspondingly, calculated that the rural population numbered seventy-nine
Algerians per square kilometre of arable land, and five Europeans.
Moreover, peasant proprietors who owned some land accounted, by the
1940s, for barely half of the Algerian rural population: landless share-
croppers (*khammès*) and agricultural labourers made up the rest.[36]

The colonial land regime and the market pressures it brought to bear
resulted, then, on the one hand, in the fragmentation, diminishing size
and reduced returns of Algerian landholdings (while the Algerian rural
population, after the 1880s, steadily increased), growing mainly the
Algerian food staples of hard wheat and barley, and on the other, in the
concentration, increasing mechanisation, and increasing profitability of
those that belonged to (relatively ever fewer) Europeans, growing hard
and soft wheat but also citrus fruits and, from the late 1880s especially,
vines for winemaking. The Bank of Algeria, created in 1851, provided
accessible credit to Europeans while Algerians were forced into short-
term, high-interest loans, and hence into near-permanent indebtedness
that became a widespread rural condition by the 1930s. In 1937, after two
years of declining harvests, an administrator at Souk Ahras, near the
Tunisian border, reported that:

the native working class that forms the greater part of the population is at the
present time in extreme distress. Every calamity has come down upon it . . .:
ferocious usury, acute unemployment, depressed wages, a total absence of public
works . . . The nerve-centre of the situation lies in the agonising contrast between,
on one hand, the marvellous prosperity of colonisation whose abundant production finds no buyers, and on the other, the extreme, unspeakable misery, to which
there is no end of sight, of an entire underfed population . . . The supply of labour
may be plentiful, but it can hardly justify famine wages, which, truth be told, are
profiteering from poverty.[37]

If, indeed, by the 1880s the threat of the 'disappearance' of Algerians
through war, expropriation, starvation, and *refoulement* ('driving away'

onto marginal lands) had receded from view – if Algerians had narrowly escaped 'the sad fate of the redskins', as a future leader of Algerian nationalism would later put it – and if this fact was not uncongenial to the European society that now dominated the towns and countryside, this was above all because the colonial economy had come to rely very substantially on Algerian labour.[38] Although wages varied across and within regions, and were briefly higher during the First World War, by the 1920s, agricultural workers earned three or four francs for a twelve-hour day, workers in rudimentary rural industries like processing palm fibres, which employed women and children as well as men, between two and a half and four and a half francs for a slightly shorter day. The state paid Algerians between three and five francs per eight-hour day (and European supervisors between six and eight francs) on public works projects to soak up unemployment. In 1929, women were paid between five and twelve francs for agricultural or industrial work (e.g. canning, match-making, tobacco processing) in the Algérois, although the largest numbers of identifiable wage-earning women were employed as domestics at thirty-five to forty centimes an hour. In 1910, the equivalent wage for Algerian women in Algiers had been only ten to sixteen centimes per hour; but in 1910, European maids in the city were already being paid twenty-five centimes hourly.

Europeans, indeed, were consistently paid more for the same work: in 1934, European farm workers could expect wages of between fifteen and twenty-four francs per day, while for corresponding labour, Algerians earned between six and fourteen francs. The diet and living standards of poor Algerian peasants and even poorer agricultural day-labourers were therefore basic in the extreme: barley bread twice a day, some vegetables and potatoes, meat once a week and couscous on feast days if one was relatively fortunate. At the end of the colonial period, a European agricultural worker's income was up to one hundred times that of an Algerian.[39] As historian Charles-Robert Ageron observed, 'If "free competition" between the strong and the weak in economic terms is in any case a charade, all the more is it so between the master and his subject'.[40]

## From the 'Rule of the Sabre' to a Colonial Democracy

An 'eternal supplicant, an obstinate demander of his due, rather than the free pioneer of legend', in the words of Ageron, the settler who had become 'the master' in Algeria was nonetheless a 'perpetual complainant' who, 'in revolt at every opportunity against the power of the state', was 'concerned more to profit from his agitation than to seek a proud independence'.[41]

The political culture of French Algeria made much of the 'legend' of the settler pioneer, the hardships endured by the colonists of the 'heroic' early period and the independent spirit of the new 'Algerian people' that they generated. 'Wild beasts, still numerous, attacked their livestock even in the villages; parasites ravaged them and the cholera epidemic, which killed 250 people at [the colonial village of] Mondovi in 1849, did worse; the natives committed ever more numerous thefts and their insurrections claimed victims in several villages ... '[42] Albert Camus, who was born in Mondovi, a small settlement at the edge of the plain south of Bône, in 1913, left among the notes for his unfinished and semi-autobiographical last novel, *Le premier homme*, an image of the pioneer drawn starkly from his own research on the early colonists: 'At Boufarik, they work with rifles on their shoulders and quinine in their pockets. [They would say, of someone looking sickly, that] "He has a Boufarik face." ... Quinine is sold in cafés, like a drink.'[43]

But, as we have seen, while colonial farming came to dominate the countryside, with the extension of European landholding came its consolidation, and throughout the colonial period, Algeria's European society was primarily urban, concentrated in the coastal cities and in the larger interior towns. Most of these people were not, in their own estimation, *colons*, wealthy and exploitative 'colonists' in the image of the mid-nineteenth-century, aristocratic *colons en gants jaunes*, 'yellow-gloved colonists' with their great estates, but simply poor, self-reliant migrants who, by dint of hard work and tenacity, had gained a measure of rights and prosperity. Early on, the term *colon* was used in Algeria specifically to denote agricultural settlers, and especially, by the late 1800s, large landowners;[44] much the greater part of Algeria's Europeans were urban small proprietors, artisans and workers, generally of modest origins and modest means. The gains they made, in property and politics, as a colonial population living in legal privilege over the majority of the country's inhabitants, were defended with all the more determination. Prosper Enfantin, the Saint-Simonian visionary, had declared in 1843 that 'no-one thinks ... to govern the settlers of Algeria as if they were in France'.[45] But this was precisely what the settlers expected.

From almost the first days of the occupation, tensions emerged between the civil and military imperatives of governing Algeria. Bugeaud, the authoritarian paternalist and social conservative, was convinced that only he could make Algerian policy, and bridled at taking orders from mere Ministers of State (even when the minister was Soult, a soldier since 1785 whom Napoleon had made Marshal in 1804). He saw security as the foremost concern, and military freedom of action as the foremost principle of a government necessary to ensure it. In time, he

thought, Algeria's settlers would have 'civil interests' for which municipal organisation and civil law would provide, but in the meantime, at
least, the only government appropriate to the colony was a military
government. Other military governors whose own politics were not
necessarily aligned with Bugeaud's nonetheless adhered continuously
to this fundamental belief. General Eugène Cavaignac, who from the
office of governor general went in 1848 to that of Minister of War, and
was responsible for the repression of the Parisian workers' insurrection
in June that year, but who in the revolution of 1830 had been a declared
republican, considered from his early experience in Algeria that 'security
can only be the result of ... war, which we consider indispensable.
However one views the question of Africa, ... war is necessary, not to
destroy nor to drive out the Arabs, but to contain and subdue them.'[46]
Marshal Patrice de Mac Mahon, governor general from 1864 to 1870
and commander in 1871 of the troops that liquidated the Paris
Commune, an avowed conservative and monarchist who nonetheless
respected democratic legality as President (1873–79) of the Third
Republic, liked to remind Paris that Algeria 'has been subdued, but
has not submitted'.[47]

Other advocates of France's colonial 'mission', equally desirous of
'order' at home as overseas, nonetheless denounced the army's 'rule of
the sabre' and insisted that liberty, as well as security, was necessary
for the success of 'true colonisation' in the new, liberal, post-slavery,
entrepreneurial and capitalist world of the nineteenth century. Alexis
de Tocqueville, in his lengthy 1841 work on Algeria, denounced
military government as 'violent, arbitrary, and tyrannical, and at the
same time ... weak and powerless' to make real progress in the work
that colonisation required. What colonisation required was the rule of
law as well as force, and the liberation of 'all the energy of the passions
to which private property gives birth', 'to allow the settler as much
freedom of action as possible, and to open to his hopes as vast a field
of action as possible'. As Tocqueville had observed in his work on
America, the promotion of civil liberties and private interests, asso-
ciating individuals in local self-government, was the surest way to
promote a successful colony, but in Algeria 'the very principle of
municipal life [had] been destroyed'.[48] 'You forget that we are your
brothers!' a petition in the name of the colonists exclaimed to their
metropolitan compatriots in 1846:

We have the same love for the *patrie* and her laws; we are as jealous of her
liberties and as proud of her glory [as you are] ... And yet for fifteen years
you have abandoned us to oppression ... We wish only to obey your laws, to

enjoy your rights, and share them with all men, whatever their country or race, who are worthy of adoption by our generous and liberal nation. [But] ... we are condemned ... to be governed by subalterns, and administered by soldiers.

French settlers in Algeria, declared another petition the following year, 'were citizens like you; they have the right to that title when they return to French soil, they do not wish to lose it in a land that has become French. ... Give us laws, the laws of France ... as law-givers for Algeria, you will be the first among colonisers.'[49]

From the 1840s, therefore, although the same outcome – the perpetuation and preponderance of the colonial presence – was agreed by all, the principal dynamic of French Algerian policy was an ongoing tussle between different means of achieving it. The conflict was resolved after 1870 to the benefit of the settlers' demand for civil government and the juridical 'assimilation' of Algerian institutions to those of the metropole. Along the way, it had produced arguments that by the 1880s routinely and rhetorically evoked 'assimilation' as a more general principle of colonial government, espoused by republicans and imbued with the democratic, post-revolutionary universalism that they saw themselves as carrying over from the inheritance of 1789. 'Assimilation' thus conceived was opposed to 'association', a more cautious and yet more expansive view that, borrowing from the Saint-Simonians' notion of 'protecting' indigenous institutions against capitalist rapacity, as well as from the army officers' instinctive social conservatism and dislike of democracy, had emerged simultaneously as the principle that colonial territories, with their specificities of population and culture, could not be ruled simply as extensions of the metropole. The latter view, briefly ascendant in Algeria during the 1860s under the influence of Urbain and his colleagues, gained ground again in arguments over the 'new imperialism' of the 1880s and would go on to inform colonial doctrine in the expanding French empire at the turn of the century and over the following twenty years. Algeria, with its long history of uncertainty and insurgency, would often serve in these arguments (especially over Morocco) as a counter-model.[50] But by then, the Algerian settler community had established its hold over both the geographical and the political space of the country – its vineyards and wheat fields, its municipal councils and parliamentary representation – and had begun to celebrate its triumph, and the principle of 'assimilation', as France's 'great colonial work'.

In an outburst of republican enthusiasm following the February revolution of 1848, a decree of 4 March declared Algeria to be 'an integral part of French territory'; in November, the constitution of the Second

Republic created three *départements*, of Oran, Algiers and Constantine, in place of the three royal provinces, and in the image of the post-revolutionary administrative organisation of metropolitan France.[51] Each *département* would be administered by a Prefect, answerable initially to ministers in Paris and then, from 1870, to the governor general, with an elected *conseil général* (first constituted in 1858) to deliberate on matters of civil government. In 'civil territory', where 'pacification' was assured and European population centres were established, settlers were afforded self-government in 'full' municipalities (*communes de plein exercice*), with mayors and municipal councils: there were 96 such communes in 1871, 196 in 1882 and 276 in 1921. Supposedly just as French as their homologues in Burgundy or Bordeaux, Algeria's European municipalities were often ten times the size of their metropolitan equivalents, their territory – and, crucially, their income – swollen by the annexation of neighbouring Algerian *douars* whose tax receipts were spent, inevitably, by and for the Europeans. In 1881, for example, Tizi Ouzou had 236 French citizens on the electoral roll; their chosen representatives controlled the revenue raised from 22,537 Kabyle tax-payers. Algerians laconically expressed nostalgia for 'the time of the military' before the depredations of 'the government of the mayors'.[52] The Federation of Mayors, collectively articulating the most local-level expression of this settler politics, became the most vocal and intransigent defender of European preponderance.

At the opposite end of the political scale, in Paris, Algerian affairs were also addressed by elected representatives: from 1881, two deputies (increased to three in 1928) were elected from each *département*, joined after 1884 by one senator per *département*.[53] Some of these, around the turn of the century, would dominate Algerian politics for decades. Emile Morinaud, the lawyer son of landowning *colons* from Philippeville first elected on an anti-Semitic ticket in 1898, held office in the National Assembly continuously from 1919 until 1942, and at local level until 1947. Gaston Thomson, a left-wing republican journalist and defender of Dreyfus, born in Oran in 1848, was re-elected continuously for Constantine from 1877 to 1932. Eugène Etienne, four years Thomson's senior and the leading spokesman of the 'colonial party' in the National Assembly, was continuously deputy and then senator for Oran from 1881 to 1921. While often enjoying successful political careers in Paris (Morinaud, Thomson and Etienne all held ministerial posts), Algeria's elected representatives made themselves first of all the spokesmen of settler interests, and not infrequently ensured their constituencies by promising land allocations to voters: 'The influence of an Algerian parliamentarian', in Ageron's judgment, 'was measured especially by the number of hectares distributed to his clientèle'.[54]

Local political office was equally, if not more, important than seats in Paris, and was often combined with national-level mandates – or extra-parliamentary influence. Morinaud was Constantine's mayor as well as its deputy. Henri Borgeaud, proprietor of an immense winemaking estate near Algiers and of a large portfolio of industrial and commercial interests, from banking and automobiles to cigarettes and cement, was mayor of Chéragas, in the Algiers suburbs, from 1930 to 1962, *conseiller général* from 1933 to 1960 and senator for Algiers from 1946 to 1959. Jacques Duroux, an industrialist and landowner of modest origins who in the interwar period became the richest man in Algeria, was a *délégué financier* for only a year in 1920, and senator relatively briefly, from 1921 until 1939. But thanks to his wealth and contacts, he was probably the colony's most politically influential figure. Added to these men's economic and political influence was their weight in informing and shaping opinion: Duroux owned *L'Echo d'Alger*, the colony's most widely circulated newspaper, Borgeaud, the *Dépêche quotidienne*.

The military maintained a residual grip on Algeria in the first years of the Third Republic, as Admiral Louis de Gueydon and General Alfred Chanzy governed the colony, but from 1879 onwards, with the appointment of Albert Grévy, the first 'civil' governor general with a non-military background (a lawyer and politician, he was the brother of a president of the Republic), the Governorship-General, responsible to the Ministry of the Interior, became one of the highest offices in the republican bureaucracy. Algeria's military forces were placed constitutionally under civilian control, and the settlers' 'republican' colony gained its durable hold over the country. 'Civil' territory grew rapidly, from just over 12,000 square kilometres in 1869 to over 100,000 square kilometres, or practically the whole of northern Algeria, by the end of 1881. The area under military rule, the *territoires de commandement*, correspondingly shrank, until in 1902 Algeria's three *départements* were delimited to the south, with the army's authority remaining intact only over the vast *Territoires du Sud* in the Sahara.[55]

By a law of 13 April 1900, the colony's self-government was reinforced with budgetary autonomy, exercised by an elected assembly sitting in Algiers, the *Délégations financières*. Created in 1898 to provide for Algeria's 'social and economic self-government', the *Délégations* comprised forty-eight Europeans – twenty-four elected by *colons*, i.e. rural proprietors or managers, and twenty-four by the much more numerous *non-colons*, urban rate-payers – and, initially, twenty-one (from 1937, twenty-four) Algerians. The latter were divided into Arab and Kabyle sections, ostensibly to recognise different tax systems, but doubtless also to split the 'Muslim' vote and over-represent Kabylia, where European influence was (wrongly) believed to be more welcome. A 'colonial parliament' dominated by European agricultural interests, the *Délégations* became, especially from the mid-1920s, a body sufficiently powerful to impose its views on the governor general's office.[56] Finally, a *Conseil supérieur du gouvernement* (Higher Government Council) convened since 1860 to advise the governor general, and presided over by him, brought together thirty-one indirectly elected members chosen from the *conseils généraux* and *Délégations* with the Government-General's twenty-two heads of department and seven appointed 'notables', four of whom were Algerians. Essentially unreformed until 1945, the *Conseil supérieur* and *Délégations financières* were replaced, in the Statute of Algeria of 20 September 1947, by an *Assemblée algérienne*, elected in April 1948.[57]

Together, over the century from the revolution of 1848, these different levels of representative government entrenched the minority rule of the European population. But it is important to appreciate that the construction of this system followed no pre-determined plan. On the contrary, it was improvised in response to the tensions, as we have seen, of military and civilian rule, and also out of the conflicts that arose within the politics of the settler community itself. From coalescing in the 1880s and 1890s into a self-defining, fractious and turbulent 'Algerian' or 'Franco-Algerian' people, in their own and contemporary observers' terms, the Europeans came to see themselves by the 1940s as all the more decidedly French in that their Frenchness was recent and, it seemed, only reluctantly accepted by the metropolitan *Français de France*. Correspondingly, they were all the more ferociously attached to their distinctiveness and their rootedness in Algeria in that their hard-won rights and freedoms had, in their own eyes, been carved out from the poverty and marginality of their penniless migrant origins, in a land they had made their own for 'civilisation' in the face of malarial fever and Muslim 'fanaticism', and under a government that as often despised as supported them. 'Public officials disdain us', wrote an Algerian-born European lawyer in Bône in 1900, 'newcomer schoolteachers treat our children as incapable ... Yes, the French treat us as pariahs.'[58] Algeria's Europeans were 'animated by the desire to be French', wrote a sympathetic historian in 1967, 'combined with the feeling of being such in very particular conditions, which they would not disavow for anything in the world and of which they [were], indeed, very proud'.[59]

The desire to be French, in fact, developed very slowly and as a function of social and economic necessity, as well as of political opportunity. Non-French immigrants and their offspring outnumbered French citizens in Algeria until the 1850s. Despite official colonisation's efforts to implant a solidly French colony, 'foreigners' – mainly Spanish, Italian, Maltese and Balearic islanders known as Mahonnais – continued to account for almost half of Algeria's Europeans, and in the 1870s the balance again began to tilt slightly in their favour. Although naturalisation was available, there was initially no drive to acquire French nationality among non-French settlers; indeed, there was sometimes little desire to settle permanently in Algeria as part of an orchestrated European, let alone French, presence. Instead, at least into the 1880s and to a degree thereafter, older types of Mediterranean mobility persisted. Coral fishers and construction workers migrated seasonally, in winter, from southern Italy and Sicily, returning home in the summer. Agricultural workers from southern Spain, derisively considered *des traîne-savates andalous*, 'Andalusi foot-draggers', little better than vagabonds, and nicknamed *escargots* (snails), carried their tools and belongings on their backs around French-owned farms. Even after coral fishing, for example, was closed to non-French workers in 1885, and Italians rushed to be naturalised (a thousand of them almost immediately, compared to fewer than 2,000 over the preceding twenty years), many continued to return to Italy after the season, just as they had always done. Other Europeans continued to supply a mobile and relatively cheap workforce in the towns and countryside until the First World War. In 1911, in addition to the almost half a million French citizens in Algeria, the census found 137,746 Spaniards and 36,795 Italians.[60]

To absorb and settle non-French immigrants, the nationality law of 26 June 1889 automatically naturalised as French citizens all children born in Algeria to foreign fathers, marking a decisive step in bringing Algeria's heterogeneous non-Muslim population within the fold of the Republic, and in welding that population into a single community that would become *les Français d'Algérie*, 'Algerian French', and who would eventually become more generally known as *pieds noirs*. The 'fusion of the races', as this was called, between Europeans of different origins, was largely achieved by the 1920s in both political and cultural terms. And, as the divisions between communities and individuals of different European origins became blurred and tended to dissipate, so the line demarcating Europeans en bloc from Algerians, with the latter ethno-religiously defined as 'Muslims', became harder, remaining as the primary focus of social and political antagonism.[61]

But this was not immediately apparent, and while much celebrated in colonial literature, the 'fusion of the races' was neither rapid nor uncomplicated. Indeed, in the 1890s, the central conflict of settler politics was articulated around European 'racial' tensions. On one side was a 'French

Figure 3.2 A coffee house (*kahoua; café maure*) in Algiers, ca. 1890. In both urban and rural areas, cafés were vital and multifunctional spaces of Algerian male sociability, both preserving social ties and exclusions, and, from the early 1900s, incubating a new 'civil society' where work, music, news, football and politics were all organised and expressed (Library of Congress).

party', whose press denounced the 'foreign threat' (*le peril étranger*) that the newly naturalised 'neo-French' (*les néos*) as well as the still numerous non-French Europeans supposedly posed to French sovereignty in the colony. On the other was a so-called 'Algerian party', loosely imagined as expressing both the resentful pride and the conquering self-confidence of the 'European people of Algeria' in aspirations to autonomy or even separation from the metropole. In 1895, Felix Dessoliers, a law professor who had been a left-republican deputy for Oran in the 1880s, published 'an economic study of Algeria' under the inflammatory title *L'Algérie libre*, 'Free Algeria', which, on the basis of a comparison with the British dominions, proposed a financial and commercial autonomy to be governed by an elected 'colonial council' in Algiers with budgetary powers independent of Paris. His younger readers went further, declaring that 'Tomorrow, or the day after, Algeria will be simply Algerian'; 'The *patrie* will be Algeria.'[62]

Figure 3.3 The Europeans' city: Algiers harbour, the Marine quarter and waterfront seen looking inland from the lighthouse, with the casbah on the hillside beyond, ca. 1899 (Library of Congress).

Such ideas, envisioning more complete settler self-determination in a 'Canadian', a 'South African' or even a 'Cuban' Algeria, were especially welcome against the background of widespread anxieties over a multifaceted 'crisis' in the colony at the turn of the century. The effects of economic downturn, fears of insecurity and the *péril étranger* were all amplified by a particularly virulent press, whose free expression, since the application to Algeria of the liberal French press law of 1881, was eagerly seized by local politicians and journalists in a frenzy of competitive rumour-milling, recrimination and incitement. Into this boiling pot, in March 1891, came a Senatorial commission of inquiry under the patronage of Jules Ferry, the former prime minister of the Republic and champion of colonialism's 'civilising mission' whose government had established the French protectorate over Tunisia in 1881 before being unseated in 1885 by the failure of the Tonkin expedition in northern Vietnam, and who was now a leading figure in the Senate. The scandalous state of the colony, its corrupt local politics, embezzling mayors and rampant oppression of the indigenous population had affronted liberal Parisian opinion. The subsequent purge of mayors, disciplining of bureaucrats and threats to entrenched interests alarmed the colony's 'French' party. Its interests now joined with the ambition of local radical republicans and socialists, Ferry's political opponents, in the 'Algerian' party, to wrest power from the moderate 'opportunist' republicans who had been the dominant political current in Algeria, as in the metropole, since 1870.

The dominance of the 'opportunists' in France was a function of the weight of pragmatic republican opinion, led by Léon Gambetta and then by Ferry, seeking gradual social reform against both right (monarchist and Bonapartist) and left (radical socialist) oppositions. In Algeria, radicals and 'autonomists', seeing themselves as the authentic expression of the settler *petit peuple* against disdainful officialdom, identified 'opportunist' electoral advantage with the bloc vote of Algerian Jews living in civil territory. Northern Algeria's Jews had been naturalised as French citizens by decree in 1870, but were reviled among their new fellow-citizens by a poisonous anti-Semitism that was as strong among Algeria's Europeans, in the years around the Dreyfus affair, as in metropolitan France and elsewhere. In elections between 1896 and 1898, candidates combining the defence of settler self-determination against metropolitan meddling with a politicised anti-Semitism, and proclaiming themselves both *Algériens* and *antijuifs*, won control of municipalities in the major towns, majorities in the *conseils généraux*, and four of the colony's six seats in the National Assembly. Edouard Drumont, the ringleader of French anti-Semitic nationalism whose propaganda sheet, *La libre parole*, created in 1892, had stoked the campaign, was elected as deputy for Algiers. Organised attacks on Jews and Jewish property intended to intimidate the community into abstention had the desired effect, and anti-Semitic rioting, having begun already in Tlemcen in 1881 and in Algiers in 1884, became a prominent feature of Algerian political life. In the mid-1890s anti-Jewish electoral 'leagues' flourished; rioters attacked Jewish shops and homes in Oran and Mostaghanem in May 1895. In January 1898, a crowd led by a student activist, Maximilien Milano, known as Max Régis, the son of an Italian immigrant and 'political director' of *L'antijuif algérien*, mouthpiece of the Algiers Anti-Jewish League that had begun publication the previous year, burned and pillaged for five days in central Algiers, killing two people, destroying the synagogue and several homes, and ransacking eighty-seven businesses. The same crowd enthusiastically fêted Drumont when he visited Algiers, elected him alongside local anti-Semite Charles Marchal in May and voted Régis into office as Mayor of Algiers in November.[63]

Régis' *Antijuif*, whose columns in January 1898 carried overt calls for extermination in the form of popular patriotic songs, echoed Drumont's metropolitan anti-Semitism in its slogan of 'France for the French', and proclaimed a decidedly assimilationist French nationalism aimed at the colonial working class: 'We've been too long stuck in poverty/Kick out the foreigners/That'll make work/A better wage is what we need ... '.[64] At the same time, the popular movement of which Régis was briefly the darling flirted ostentatiously with the idea of autonomy, claiming to represent the true voice of an 'Algerian' people belittled and downtrodden by the *Français de race* and promising to wrest 'freedom' from the metropole, seizing on the vocabulary and imagery of revolutionary France – the Third Estate, the *doléances*, the 'tree of liberty' which, said Régis, they would 'water ... with Jewish blood' – to do so.[65] The politics of autonomy were short-lived: the electoral alliance between 'French' and 'Algerian' parties that had made it briefly powerful was bought off by a new governor general, Laferrière, who arrived in Algiers in August 1898 and announced the creation of the *Délégations financières* alongside other conciliatory measures. Alarmed by settler unrest, the Paris politicians conveniently lost interest in Algeria's 'scandals', and stopped trying to reform the colony's local politics. The 'crisis' dissipated, leaving the would-be revolutionaries without an audience and, soon afterward, out of office. Their vision of the settlers' 'proud independence' was the expression of a popular politics without a real separatist agenda. Anti-Semitism, like autonomism, drew on underlying social prejudices and frictions, but became a political force and a popular movement only in particular circumstances, in the alignments of electoral politics, amplified by a feverish press and manipulated by ambitious politicians for short-term gain.[66]

But the conjoined 'anti-Jewish crisis' and 'autonomist moment' of 1898 were a fulcrum, a watershed in the emergence of popular settler politics and the coalescing of French Algerian society, its self-image and its political culture that would become entrenched over subsequent decades. The assertive popular 'street' of European Algeria, imbued with a sense of its own heteroclite 'Latinity', its distinctiveness from the metropole and its no-nonsense tenacity rooted in the hard graft of workers who had earned their right to respect, nonetheless expressed itself, even when threatening secession, within the legal spaces – the free press, the electoral lists, the right to assembly – and the symbolic politics of the French Republic.

Nowhere was this cultural and social self-view more vividly expressed than in the popular literary character of Cagayous, the swaggering, foul-mouthed, mischievous, comic Artful Dodger of the Bab el Oued street invented by an Algiers-born minor civil servant and journalist, Auguste Robinet (writing as 'Musette'), whose adventures were first published in 1895 in the satirical journal *Le Turco*, and remained popular into the 1930s and beyond. Portrayed at Algiers' fishing port quayside, his hat askew, in striped jersey, checked trousers and short jacket, his exploits narrated in the first person and a comically exaggerated rendering of the *pataouète* ('potato-eater') dialect of the Algiers working class, Cagayous was the hero of the European *petit peuple*. At the height of his popularity, the ten-centime *feuilletons* carrying Musette's stories regularly sold out from newsstands within a few hours of publication; anisette distillers and men's tailors sought the character's endorsement to advertise their brands.[67] It can be no accident that, while the character would subsequently be remembered with fond nostalgia for less virulent expressions of 'Algerianist' sentiment, Cagayous' popularity was established in the years around 1898. In the 'crisis' of that year, Musette published *Cagayous antijuif*, in which his protagonist rails against 'the Jews' with all the racial hatred of contemporary anti-Semitism, declaims, 'Down, down with the Jews, that's my opinion, my own ... We'll kick them into the sea off the soles of our shoes!', and boldly greets Drumont on his arrival in Algiers.[68]

For all his distinctiveness, his famous riposte *Êtes-vous Français? – Algériens nous sommes!* ('Are you French?' – 'Algerians we are!'), the *nous autres*, 'we others' for whom Cagayous speaks and who, as his reading mass public, identified themselves in him, were increasingly and self-consciously *French* Algerians, their language increasingly French, and no longer Spanish, Italian or the *pataouète* that never became an autonomous creole, but remained a French dialect peculiar to Algeria. This dialect, moreover, increasingly gave way to the French learned by the settlers' children in the republican primary schools that were provided free of charge, and at which attendance was compulsory, after Jules Ferry's landmark public education laws began to be applied to Algeria in 1883. By 1901, 84 per cent of European children were in these schools.[69] Before the First World War, Cagayous' popularity was already an expression of nostalgia for a cultural particularism that was passing away. Its importance would remain in its fusion with the assertive, demanding posture towards the metropole that the politics of settler citizenship had always required. Cagayous' last adventure, serialised in *L'Écho d'Alger* in 1919 and published separately in 1920, was, fittingly enough, *Cagayous poilu*, in which the Algiers street-fighting man shoulders his part of the greater burden as a soldier of the Republic.[70]

After 1900, fears of the 'foreign threat' receded, the settler population stabilised and reproduced; schooling, marriage patterns, work and

settlement in the vivacious working-class districts of Algiers, Oran and
Bône, or in colonial villages like Rio Salado (El Maleh), Boutlelis or
Hammam Bou Hadjar, near Oran – which a century later would retain
their characteristic, straight main streets of two-storey, whitewashed,
shuttered buildings lined with clipped trees, municipal buildings in
a central square, and lower-status housing at their edges – produced
a common culture and an attachment to common interests.[71] Some
22,000 Europeans from Algeria, of 115,000 who saw action, were killed
on the battlefields of the metropolitan *patrie* in 1914–18, and this common service and sacrifice, abundantly memorialised across Algeria as in
the metropole during the 1920s, solidified a vocal French nationalism
combined with a persistent 'Algerian' particularism. Together, they created a myth of French Algeria as 'saviour of the republic'. This idea,
already expressed in 1848, when the settlement of Algeria was thought
a sovereign remedy against workers' uprisings in the metropole, was
enhanced in the 1940s, when an Algerian resistance, albeit a very small
minority within the settler population, assisted the Allied landings in
North Africa, and the Republic's Provisional Government under
Charles de Gaulle established itself in Algiers before the liberation of
the *mère-patrie*. A belief in Algeria as France's bastion and saviour, and
identification with a tradition of popular colonial politics as resistance
against 'tyranny', would resurface, with disastrous effect, in 1958–62.

   This pattern of a relatively rapid, if uncomfortable and at times violent,
transition from older Mediterranean and Maghribi patterns of movement, settlement, economy and community to republican incorporation
would also be followed, though with very different implications and in
a diametrically opposed way, by those very Algerian Jews against whose
inclusion in the body politic settler anti-Semitism had reacted, and
against whom settler self-identity had in large part coalesced. In the first
years after 1830, Jewish entrepreneurs and intermediaries had inventively
negotiated their way through the unstable circumstances of the conquest.
David Duran, from a leading rabbinic and merchant family established in
Algiers since the fourteenth century, served as emissary between the
French and Abd al-Qadir (and was accused, on occasion, of supporting
the latter rather than representing the former). Jacob Lasry, a merchant
born in Morocco, based in Oran, and a British subject with family connections in London and Gibraltar, consolidated his social position by his
death in 1869 as a pillar of French 'civilising' in Algeria generally and
among Algeria's Jews in particular. But as Joshua Schreier has shown,
Lasry's activities during the 1830s, when he advanced finances for the
first French expedition against Constantine and was involved in collect-
ing the indemnity assessed on the population of Tlemcen, while hedging

his position between British consuls, French generals and the beylical court in Tunis, demonstrate much less adherence to a new colonial reality than a continuity of older Mediterranean business practices on which the ill-resourced French army was sometimes obliged to depend, and which 'both underwrote and undermined' the chaotic French advance.[72]

A tenacious pattern in North African Jewish historiography has tended to reiterate liberal colonial images of previously downtrodden Algerian Jews being emancipated and uplifted by the civilising influence of French law and education, but, as other historians have argued, the true picture is, once again, much more complex.[73] The cases of Duran and Lasry illustrate how notable members of the Jewish community, like their counterparts among their Muslim neighbours, tentatively sought for opportunity and tested the limits of the unpredictable new order that they, as well as the equally uncertain French, thereby shaped. A language of improvement and 'regeneration' was systematically directed at Algeria's Jews through the Jewish consistories, governing councils of the community, that were established in Algiers, Oran and Constantine in 1845, extending to Algeria the institutions for 'enlightening' Jews and incorporating them into the citizenry that had existed in France since 1808. The same mission would be embraced by the Alliance Israélite Universelle after its creation in 1860.

But Algerian Jews, unsurprisingly, did not consider themselves in need of 'regenerating'. They both resisted the reformers' policies, and adopted their language and institutions to their own ends, seeking to protect and preserve the continuity of their own religious, educational and familial practices that were marked out by the government and by metropolitan Jewish liberals as obstacles to their becoming properly 'civilised'. In 1848, Jewish protestors in Oran and Mostaghanem echoed the revolutionary language of democracy and universal suffrage to oppose the imposition of consistorial authority and to recover 'the liberty to govern themselves' as they had 'during the times of the Regency'. In the 1850s and 1860s, locally prominent figures used the internal politics of the consistories to fight local battles over rabbinical authority, to preserve local practice against norms imposed from outside or, conversely, to press for the abolition of rituals now considered too close to 'Arab' (Muslim) ones, and to keep their own *midrashim* (religious schools), private synagogues and marriage practices. Attitudes to citizenship were not straightforward; as a man named Sasportès explained before the assize court of Oran in 1875, 'We all want to be French for business, ... so foreigners no longer abuse us. But for all that concerns marriage and repudiation, we want to remain Jews.'

Sasportès, who had contracted a second marriage, was on trial for bigamy, which was illegal under French civil law. He, along with all the Jewish inhabitants born in 'the *départements* of Algeria' (excluding those in military-ruled Saharan territory), had become a French citizen by decree on 24 October 1870, and Jewish civil law, regulating matrimony, divorce and inheritance, was held no longer to apply to him. Sasportès did not see it that way, as he declared on the stand, 'French law cannot change my religious law ... I never asked to become French ... I am Jewish. I want to remain Jewish. That's all there is to it.' Sasportès had seemingly, nonetheless, taken the precaution of backdating his bigamous marriage contract to 1869, before his acquisition of citizenship: his protestations of ignorance of the law were disingenuous. But his case demonstrates the extent to which Algerian Jews after 1870 'accepted citizenship but nonetheless quietly refused to accept French jurisdiction' over their personal lives and domestic affairs. It was precisely these areas that French law and liberal 'regenerators' wished to 'civilise'.[74]

The decree of October 1870 became known as the 'Crémieux decree' after its sponsor, Isaac Adolphe Crémieux, a distinguished republican lawyer and parliamentarian who found himself interim Minister of the Interior and of War in the government of national defence at Tours while Prussian armies besieged Paris. Rather than a worked-out policy of colonial emancipation, it was thus a radical measure issued at an opportune moment of national emergency in the first weeks of the embattled Third Republic, and when 'normality' returned it would be savagely attacked by opponents of Jewish emancipation. Settler opinion wrongly attributed the insurrection of Muqrani and shaykh al-Haddad, which broke out five months later, to Muslim outrage at the social betterment of the Jews. The decree's application to Algerian Jews in the Sahara, notably in the Mzab, would be resisted until they were finally and abruptly accorded citizenship in 1961.[75] At the same time, the decree was a decisive resolution of the protracted wrangles over a 'civilising mission' towards the Jews of Algeria that had gone on for almost forty years, since 1833, when Crémieux himself and other members of the Paris consistory had first pressed for the inclusion of Algerian Jews in France's enlightening project. The language of these arguments both presaged the later ideological rhetoric of the Third Republic and set up, as we shall see, legal structures that were intended to prepare the entry of 'backward' colonial populations into citizenship, but that served to exclude them durably from it. Northern Algeria's Jews, who uniquely escaped this trap by virtue of Crémieux's astutely peremptory decree, were the exception that proved the rule.

After 1870, as the Sasportès case illustrates, there was no sudden embrace of 'civilising' norms imposed from above. But there was, over the following generations, a slow but steady transition of the Jewish community from its rootedness in the 'indigenous', Arabic- and Berber-speaking population, to identification with European, French Algeria – much to the horror of the Europeans. In 1872, identifying Crémieux with a program of separating church and state, secularising education, progressively assimilating Algeria to the metropole and guaranteeing a 'truly civil' administration, radical republicans in Algiers voted him into the National Assembly as their representative.[76] But for the same constituency, soon afterwards, the prospect of Algerian Jews' political and cultural proximity to their own privileged status breached the racialised boundary beyond which they saw only the threatening and polluting 'native'. As Emmanuel Sivan pointed out, the settler anti-Semitism in Algeria that was largely responsible for 'the birth of modern anti-Semitism as a mass movement' in France was a 'hatred of the Jew *as an Arab*'. As a former prefect of Oran wrote in 1871, Jews remained 'outside of Western civilisation'. Their morals, language and clothing marked them as 'Oriental'; they were 'Arabs of the Jewish faith'. The stereotypical features of 'Arabs' (meaning Muslims) in colonial popular culture – 'savagery, poverty, dirtiness, dishonesty, lasciviousness' – were also those attributed to Jews, all the more so as Jews increasingly secularised their lifestyles, adopted the French language and European dress, and became socially mobile.[77]

Anti-Semitism continued to be a feature of Algerian politics, although its expression shifted, from the 1890s to the interwar period, from being an expression of radical and socialist republicanism to being more firmly associated with the racialised nationalism and fascism of the right. Increasing again in tone in the 1920s and 1930s, anti-Semitic agitation was central to local politics in Oran, where Dr Jules Molle, the founder of the *Unions Latines*, an anti-Semitic popular movement, became mayor in 1925 and deputy in 1928, and the abbé Gabriel Lambert, who flirted with fascism and denounced the left's 'Jewish imperialism', became mayor in 1934. In Constantine, the left-leaning but ferociously anti-communist deputy and mayor Morinaud's alliance with local Jewish councillors in the early 1920s did not prevent him from returning to anti-Semitic tirades in the 1930s. Local newspapers in both cities – *La Tribune* in Constantine and *Le Petit Oranais* – made anti-Jewish propaganda their stock in trade. In 1934, European anti-Semitic agitators and local political divisions between Jewish and Muslim electorates in Constantine combined to inflame community tensions, resulting for the first time in anti-Jewish violence by an Algerian crowd in the city. In rioting on 3–5 August that year, twenty-five Jews and three Muslims were killed, and Jewish property was ransacked.[78]

Settler anti-Semitism thus provided a propitious environment for the Vichy regime and the application in Algeria of its anti-Jewish statutes after the fall of the Republic in 1940. Many Europeans (including Morinaud) who argued against collaboration and wished to pursue the war with Germany were nonetheless enthusiastic when, on 7 October 1940, a law named for Vichy's interior minister Marcel Peyrouton abrogated the Crémieux decree and stripped Algeria's Jews of their citizenship. This measure was rescinded three years later, as de Gaulle consolidated his position at the head of the Comité français de libération nationale.[79] By 1940, Algeria's Jews had come to see themselves as fully and loyally French: the community's leadership protested against the Peyrouton law to Pétain, the Vichy head of state, that 'this undeserved measure ... exacerbates, for us, the present distress of the *patrie* ... Hitherto French citizens, we remain entirely French at heart. Long live France! Long live French Algeria!'[80] Just as the *néos* had come to cling all the more strongly to a visceral nationalism because of its newness and fragility, so, and even more so, did most of Algeria's Jews come to feel themselves both particularly Algerian and 'desperately French'.[81]

Conversely, until the First World War, it was possible for isolated Europeans, brought by the hazards of life into the deep interior of Algeria, to form strong attachments in local society. Some of these *âmes-frontières* were thoroughly exceptional. The writer and adventuress Isabelle Eberhardt, daughter of a Russian anarchist father and aristocrat mother, dressed as a man, married an Algerian *spahi* sergeant, considered herself to have been born Muslim and embraced Sufism and the Sahara before dying in a flash flood at Aïn Sefra in 1904.[82] Aurélie Picard, a seamstress from a modest background, married Ahmad Ammar al-Tijani, grandson of the founder of the Tijaniyya brotherhood, whom she met at Bordeaux, in 1871, and lived at the grand house she built at Kourdane near Aïn Madhi until her death in 1933, a figure of fascination to romantically inclined Europeans and a dutiful and godly benefactress in the eyes of the Tijaniyya.[83] Other, more modest but no less extraordinary lives crossed the colonial lines and forged links that endured even through the turmoil to follow. Baptiste Capeletti, born to Italian immigrant parents near Constantine in 1875, settled in the Aurès where he became a miller, and was successively married to two local, Shawi Muslim women, with one of whom he had a son named Chérif. Well regarded in the region, he discovered an important prehistoric archaeological site and was close friends with the region's most celebrated social bandit, Mas'ud Ben Zelmat: he remained in the Aurès through war and revolution, until his second wife, Hmama, died in 1975. Baptiste himself lived on, eventually in the care of Catholic nuns at Annaba, until 1978.[84]

Exceptional in his longevity, Baptiste was no less so in having left traces for historians to find: in the countryside around 1900, there must certainly have been many other such individual life stories, isolated and perhaps 'eccentric', escaping from the norms of colonial society and colonial government, but nonetheless part of colonialism's everyday life.[85] Such lives lived on the edge of the colonial order no doubt became rarer after the First World War. There were still Muslim, Jewish and European families living alongside one another, even sometimes in the same shared houses, in towns like Setif, into the 1950s.[86] But among the overwhelmingly urban European population, by 1950, less than 2 per cent spoke any Arabic. In the countryside, as the nationalist leader Ferhat Abbas later remembered, there remained 'French people [who] lived among us, were our neighbours and often our friends and the friends of our peasants'.[87] Such surviving *petits colons* spoke Arabic, laboured in the fields and lived 'sometimes on the edge of poverty'; here, everyday life, friendships and solidarities still blurred and crossed community lines. But these were small margins: such colonial smallholders, by the 1950s, accounted for one-third of all European rural proprietors, but owned between them less than 1 per cent of all rural property in European hands (even in the Mitidja, the figure was only 2 per cent).[88] So although the lines that divided the European and Algerian, the citizen and subject populations of colonial society could in places be blurred, and in others, crossed, over time they grew more clearly defined and less easily traversed, and in some respects – in civil rights, in the administration of taxation and 'justice', in access to social mobility – they were sharp and inflexible. Increasingly, as the colonial regime stabilised after 1900, Algerians would begin to 'work' this system, which had developed to keep them down and out of the settlers' politics of citizenship, to articulate their own aspirations and demands, moving into the social and political spaces, and adopting the languages of dignity and rights, from which settlement and *cantonnement* had sought to exclude them. But to do so, even within the terms set by the system itself, they had a formidable machinery of repression to contend with.

### The *Bureaux Arabes* and the *Indigénat*

Algeria's European 'masters' fought vigorously to achieve and maintain their political as well as their economic dominance. Arguing against proposals, in the 1880s, for elected representation for Algerians on the departmental *conseils généraux*, one Constantine newspaper insisted,

'It would be a good thing if we stopped assimilating the vanquished to the victors, and reminded the former that we are, once and for all, the masters; that we wish to take care of our own affairs, and even of their interests, without their having any say in the matter.'[89] 'The day will come, no doubt', wrote Algiers' senior lawyer in 1860, 'when, emancipated, Algeria will be nothing more than a French province, when every law passed at the seat of government in the metropole will run with equal force up to the edge of the Sahara and into its oases. Then, there will no longer be any question of exceptional laws ... or administration.'[90] This, however, remained a far-off prospect, and the mechanisms of colonial rule established to ensure the 'maintenance of order' and the settlers' management of 'their own affairs' in the meantime ensured that it would never come to pass.

As a general, and as governor general, Bugeaud had believed unswervingly in the primacy of armed force: 'You have made them submit by force of arms, you will maintain their submission only by force of arms', he wrote in 1842. 'Do you believe', he rhetorically asked his liberal critics, 'that this people, so proud, so warlike, so quick to revolt, which knows no government but military rule ... can be contained and conducted by your administrators and [their] code of law?' For the same essential reason of ensuring the security of settlement, he also wrote that 'after the conquest, the first duty and the principal interest of the conqueror lies in the good government of the conquered: he is commanded in this both by policy and by humanity'.[91] What 'good government' meant in this context can only be understood, in an inversion of Clausewitz's adage, as the pursuit of war by other means. 'The King, your master and ours', Bugeaud announced to Algerians under French rule in 1845,

wishes that his Arab and Kabyle subjects should be as well governed and as happy as the French are ... The first means to make good the evils of war and to be happy is to remain loyal to the promise of submission that you have made ... You must frankly accept the decree of God by which we have come to govern this country. You know what ills have befallen those tribes who have risen in revolt against us and against the will of God. The second means is to engage yourselves, with activity and intelligence, in agriculture and trade ... We love you as brothers, and it pains us each time that you oblige us to do you harm.[92]

As his subordinate and successor Cavaignac had already written, Algeria was to be ruled, not by wiping out Algerians, but by 'containing' them. And while the settlers and their vociferous deputies had trumpeted their demands for liberty and denounced the 'tyranny' of military rule, they and the civilian government set up in their interests fully adopted, and further developed, the colonial state fashioned by the army as an

Figure 3.4  The *bureau arabe* of Oran, 1856. L-R, Muhammad ibn al-Hajj
Hassan (the *khodja*, secretary and interpreter), Qaddur ibn Khadra,
a tribal *shaykh*, Mouin and Olivier, the *adjoint* and *chef de bureau*,
respectively, Mustafa wuld al-Hajj Mustafa Bey, *shaykh* of the '*village
nègre*' (the new Algerian quarter, inland of the old city, known to Algerians
as *mdina jdida*, the 'new town'), Salim ben Jafar (*chaouch*, from Arabic
*shawush*, sergeant-at-arms) (F. Moulin. FR ANOM 8Fi429/4).

instrument for the containment of Algerians and the restriction of their
liberties. Hemmed in spatially and economically by *cantonnement* and the
1863 Sénatus-Consulte, Algerians were also subjected to a constant
regime of both euphemised and overt violence, by legal text and administrative practice, whose basic pattern was set in 1844 with the establishment of the *bureaux arabes*, the military 'Arab bureaux' tasked with
governance of the countryside and its populations, and which endured
for a century thereafter. Only in 1944 would France's government of
Algerians begin to be 'normalised', moving away from exceptional

'native' statutes and towards a politics of citizenship – and then, as we shall see, the consequences were far from peaceful.

The *bureaux arabes*, run on a shoestring budget by army officers and their minuscule local staffs, exercised largely unregulated and unrestricted authority over Algerians in the countryside in the wake of the conquest. Sometimes celebrated in the literature as benevolent, 'enlightened despots', armed with an intimate knowledge of the territories and an instinctive sympathy for the people under their jurisdiction, as well as with a youthful dynamism, dash and *élan*, some of them were certainly animated by Saint-Simonian ideas of progress and improvement.[93] But as we have seen, such ideas were more usually the conjoined twin, not the antithesis, of repression and dispossession, and the bureaux's officers remained generally as dismissive of civil liberties and liberal law as Bugeaud had been. Summary executions of suspects and 'exemplary' punishment were the norm. 'I had no formal power of life and death', one former officer wrote, 'but I could have exercised it without anyone causing a stir'.[94]

Initially, from the 1840s, administration in the countryside was calqued on the system established by Abd al-Qadir's state, with French territorial divisions and jurisdictions replicating the *aghaliks* and *khalifaliks* through which the amir had exercised authority. Local 'chiefs', conservative figures invested with 'aristocratic' authority, were sought as the natural allies of the new, conservative and sometimes equally aristocratic, rulers. Settlers and liberal opinion denounced the 'feudalism' and arbitrariness of the bureaux, and in the 1850s their 'despotism' was attacked in press campaigns and even in judicial proceedings. Except in the south, where the bureaux system remained in place in the Saharan regions under military rule, after 1870 local administration even in military areas was subordinated to the civilian bureaucracy, and, as we have seen, 'civil' territory absorbed most of the army's rural *territoires de commandement*. The 'chiefly' system with its Ottoman nomenclature of *aghas, bashaghas* and *khalifas* was reduced in stature and in attributions, leaving the 'native adjutant', the *adjoint indigène* or *qa'id* ('caïd'), an essentially clerical functionary, as the sole, and sorrily denigrated, interlocutor between Algerians and the administration. Old families thus saw their standing, and sometimes their self-respect, reduced; and yet, as we saw in the previous chapter, they often endured.[95] In 1798, Mahfuz ibn Abi Zayd ibn Salem, the head of a saintly family living at the southern edge of the Atlas southeast of Algiers, had been presented with a certificate exempting his family from taxation under the Ottomans. His son, Muhammad Ben Salem, was agha of the Beni Ja'd *makhzen* at the end of the Regency. One son of Muhammad Ben Salem, Ahmad Tayyib, was invested as bey of this strategic corridor, towards the south-western edge of Kabylia, by the amir Abd al-Qadir; another, his brother Omar, was made bashagha by Bugeaud. Omar's two sons became *qa'ids*; two of Ahmad Tayyib's sons went into exile in Syria, but his eldest son, Muhammad, remained in possession of the family estate and in office under the French. By 1910, Muhammad's son Aomar Bensalem, the great-great-grandson of Sidi Mahfuz, aged 28, 'literate in Arabic, of a gentle character ... with a good education' and holding himself aloof from the local Europeans, had inherited the office of caïd from his father and held the family's 300 hectares together with his two younger brothers.[96]

The rule of the army, attacked by the settlers as well as by metropolitan reformers for its unaccountability and violence, was civilianised rather than reformed after the 1860s.[97] Military rule, however 'well intentioned' and progressive in purpose, had never been a beneficent despotism; its guiding principle had remained the expeditious discipline by which disorderly 'natives' had to be kept in line. Government by law now sought to codify and regulate the colonial state already established under government by the sword.

The crucial legal measure that now came to define the position of Algerians within the colonial order was a second Sénatus-Consulte, that of 14 July 1865, on personal status (*statut personnel*) and naturalisation. As with the 1863 measure on landownership, the 1865 law was imagined as a normalising, liberalising step away from the wars of conquest, towards the incorporation of Algerians under the French empire's improving 'Arab kingdom'. Louis-Hugues Flandin, the lawyer-parliamentarian who presented the bill to the Senate, declared that 'There are two ways to pacify a country; the first ... is the subjugation or destruction of the conquered people. The second, which alone accords with the traditions and morality of France, is that which has begun ... It consists in a patient and continuous work of assimilation, of progressive initiation into the benefits of civilisation.' 'The Muslim native is French', declared article 1 of the statute; 'Nonetheless, he will continue to be governed by Muslim law.' An Algerian Muslim man (since the law considered legal agency as open only to men) could serve in the army or navy, could (theoretically) hold public office – and could, at his request, be admitted to the plenitude of rights afforded the French citizen, in which case he would henceforward be governed by French civil and political law. Article 2 defined the legal status of Algerian Jews in the same way; a subsequent article opened French citizenship to (European) foreigners who had resided in Algeria for three years.[98]

This brief statute would be the keystone of Algeria's political architecture for the next eighty years. Declared a French national, but not a French citizen, Algerian Muslims (and, until 1870, Algerian Jews) as a whole were legislated into a false promise of emancipation that in fact created the legal space of their oppression. Once again, the system emerged gradually, in response to practical difficulties faced by administrators and the courts – in this case, questions of adjudicating family law, especially regarding polygamy, and access to the liberal professions – rather than by design. But the effect was to produce a durable, intractable regime that, even given a political will to reform it, proved unreformable.[99]

The logic of personal status law, on the one hand, defined Algerians as *indigènes* (natives) trapped – for the present – in a debilitating *indigénat* (the condition of being a native, 'native status'). This, to republican lawmakers, was a matter of social norms, behaviours and religious beliefs that, like immaturity in adolescents or irrationality in women, were incompatible with the full exercise of citizenship. The Sénatus-Consulte also enshrined the principle that Algerians were legally French, and that their full admission into the *cité*, the political community of citizens, was a matter of time, of individual or familial social promotion and of more general social 'evolution'. In the meantime their religious and customary practices in matters of civil law (marriage, inheritance, divorce) would be respected – and, thereby, sharply differentiated from the properly 'civilised' norms expected of citizens, especially in matrimonial and sexual matters. But, at some future time, thanks to cultural 'contact', economic and social 'uplift', moral and material 'civilisation', Algerians might be expected to escape or to 'abdicate their *indigénat*', as administrators liked to put it. The colonial situation – the political dominance of the minority community – was thus posited as a transitional state, awaiting the effects of the 'patient and continuous work' of civilisation.

This did more than provide a seemingly practical solution to the immediate difficulties of regulating the rights and duties of persons. It opened a liberal horizon of 'improvement' that would serve for decades to structure the public discourse of a humane and generous 'civilising mission'. It combined the preserving principles of 'association' with the universalist aspiration of 'assimilation' in a powerfully reassuring idea of colonisation as progress, while in fact it made 'progress', towards the resolution of the colonial situation in the ultimate emancipation it affected to imagine, impossible.

For on the other hand, the legislation that gave practical, institutional form to *indigénat* ensured that this 'transitional' state would be perennial. What colonial lawmakers thought of as a debilitating and temporary condition coincided, for Algerians, with the one remaining domain of Islamic law over their lives. In matters of criminal, commercial and

Figure 3.5 Women in an Algiers interior, 1890s. A relatively sympathetic version of a common theme, this photograph avoids the exoticisation of the 'harem interior' fantasy common in European portrayals of feminine domesticity. From the moment the Romantic painter Eugène Delacroix unveiled his celebrated *Femmes d'Alger dans leur appartement* in 1834, the 'secret life' of Algerian women was a subject of eroticised fascination for European artists and their public, and unvarnished erotic photography became a staple of colonial popular culture and postcards. Anxiety over the seclusion and 'protection' of women became all the more important to Algerian society, and women's education and emancipation from paternal or fraternal discipline, and from the rigours of the domestic or rural economy, was made correspondingly more difficult (Library of Congress).

property law, Islamic law had already been set aside in the 1840s; in criminal law, the *indigène musulman* was already by 1865 subject to both French common law and to the particular repressive measures meted out by the officers of the *bureaux arabes* and, from 1860, their disciplinary commissions. The colonial state's 'respect' for what it called 'Muslim law' in civil matters defined a residual jurisdiction of *shari‘a* that would become correspondingly all the more central to the community's self-definition, as a space of solidarity and self-preservation, voluntary abdication of which, for most Algerians, was equated with apostasy. Algerian community leaders vigorously opposed proposals by radical reformers in France, beginning in the 1880s, for the abolition of discriminatory 'personal status' and the collective conferment of citizenship, following Crémieux's example, on Muslims. And, until it was too late and had become meaningless, the mass acquisition of citizenship for Algerians *dans le statut*, without renunciation or abolition of Muslim personal status, was not a practical proposition – although, as we shall see in the next chapter, it would nonetheless become central to Algerian politics. Unlike northern Algeria's Jews, sufficiently few to be 'emancipated' (with, as we have seen, conflictual consequences), and unlike the small, and largely Muslim, electorates of the French 'Four Communes' of Senegal whose citizenship had been granted in 1848, the majority community of Algeria's Muslims had to be contained in the *indigénat* and excluded from citizenship.[100] The colony's minority rule, which for the settlers was coextensive with French sovereignty, depended upon it; the settlers and their elected representatives, from the mayors of the Algerian communes upward, insisted upon it. Algerians' containment in the trap of *indigénat*, and their concomitant exclusion from the *cité*, indeed, was the primary concern and the necessary condition of the settler republic's fragile stability. As we shall see, when this delicate and brutal mechanism began to cease to function, after 1944, the intrinsic, legal violence that it embodied began, correspondingly, to erupt in overt, physical form.

In the meantime, as *indigènes* Algerians were subject to an especially coercive system of government. Administered from 1844 to 1870 by the army's Arab bureaux, from the 1870s they fell under 'the government of the mayors' in European municipalities, or that of civil administrators in the rural *communes mixtes*, 'mixed communes' with too few Europeans for full municipal government, where, up to the 1950s, most Algerians lived. Imagined, as we have seen, as 'protection' and preservation, 'regeneration' and reform, colonial rule for Algerians effectively meant a disciplinary regime diametrically opposed to the expansive democratic freedoms demanded, and increasingly enjoyed, by Algeria's Europeans. The latitude of the army's discretionary powers of repression, the 'despotism of the sabre', was preserved by the Republican governments' *régime de l'indigénat*, or 'native-status' regulations.

Rather than a body of law, despite being often referred to as a *code*, the *indigénat* in this sense was a hazily defined set of repressive practices whose common features were a lack of due process and the fact that only non-citizens, *indigènes*, were subject to them. Seeking to regulate its practices more firmly, the colonial government enacted a series of laws to codify aspects of the '*indigénat* regime', most prominently in the law of

28 June 1881 that enabled *commune mixte* administrators to inflict fines or imprisonment for infractions, proven or suspected, 'particular to the *indigénat*', that is, committed by non-citizen Algerians. Higher officials retained existing powers to order individual internment, house arrest or exile, and collective fines or seizure of property, and no single legal text ever formalised the full extent of the repressive system. But the local administrators' disciplinary powers under the 1881 law came to sum up and symbolise the *indigénat* for those subjected to it.[101]

Many of the 'infractions' subject to punishment under this system were neither clearly defined nor, in many cases, ordinarily punishable under French criminal law: acts of disorder in markets and public places, delayed payment of taxes, departure from place of residence without authorisation, departure on pilgrimage without authorisation, lack of respect for authority, refusal to comply with requisitioning orders, refusal to provide information to the authorities, seditious speech, 'acts hostile to French sovereignty'. The procedures required were minimal; sentences could be multiplied, and when handed down by the governor general could be of indefinite duration. Justified as emergency powers in a context of insecurity, and initially supposed to expire after seven years, the repressive provisions of the law of 1881 in fact codified existing practice, and would be repeatedly renewed until their final abolition in 1944. In addition, from 1902 to 1931, Algerians accused of committing common crimes were tried by special 'repressive tribunals', with expedited procedures and minimal provision for appeal, instead of by the regular courts. Special criminal courts were also set up in 1902 to try cases with Muslim defendants, who since the introduction in 1870 of trial by jury – juries being composed exclusively of citizens, and therefore of Europeans – had, to liberal alarm, suffered disproportionately in the assize courts. But these special courts, without juries, where cases were tried by three French judges assisted by two Muslim assessors, were not noticeably kinder to Algerians than the settler juries of the assize courts. They remained in place until 1942.[102]

The logic of the *indigénat*, following the principle that anything escaping the administration's control was potentially a danger to its security, and must therefore be regulated, was to criminalise almost anything Algerians might do, or omit to do, from failing to show respect for the government's local auxiliaries through concealment of potentially taxable goods to moving around the country without a permit. Most aspects of the everyday behaviour of dominated peasant populations, in other words, that fell far short of ordinary criminality, let alone insurrection, became punishable on the spot and without appeal.[103] After a peak in 1883, when 30,837 punishments were recorded, sentencing rates under the *indigénat* generally fell, and after 1914 became much lower, but from 1892 to 1913, administrators in *communes mixtes* handed out between 17,000 and 27,000 punishments every year. In the first ten years of the *indigénat*, almost 1.7 million francs were levied in fines, and Algerians served over 700,000 days in prison. From 1897, fines or imprisonment could be transmuted into sentences to forced labour: by 1910, 600,000 days' work had been thus exacted from Algerians in penalties.[104] In 1883, with the exercise of disciplinary powers under the *indigénat* added to convictions in all the regular courts combined, some forty-two Algerians per thousand of the total population faced judicial or administrative sanctions, compared to seventeen in every thousand inhabitants of metropolitan France. At the more frequent level of 'petty crime', Algerians were at least three times more likely to face conviction than were inhabitants of the metropole.[105]

But the arbitrary iniquities that administrators' powers could inflict on Algerians' daily lives go beyond what statistics alone make visible. The women of the Tablat *commune mixte*, in the Atlas south of Algiers, were restricted in January 1892 to washing their laundry between sunrise and 5 pm on Saturdays only, so as not to inconvenience the local European women; the decree was still in force in 1904. The Algerian families of the colonial village of Renault, near Mostaghanem, were obliged in December 1893 to obtain a written permit to live within the 'European' town limits, and threatened with expulsion from their homes within forty-eight hours if they failed to receive one. Three men – Moulay Ali ben Ahmad, Ahmad ben Muhammad Lagab and Muhammad ben Ali Kerbib – agricultural workers from coastal Kabylia probably reliant on itinerant, seasonal employment – were placed under surveillance and denied travel permits for six months in July 1901, on nothing more than suspicion of involvement in a theft from a farm at Birkhadem in the Algiers suburbs. Thus, and in thousands of similar cases, at the height of the *indigénat*, the petty despotism of the administration fenced Algerians round with decree after onerous, and sometimes illegal, decree.[106]

Colonial rule, imagined as a patient work of peaceful progress, was thus in fact a routinised infliction of low-intensity warfare: criminalisation, collective punishment, denial of due process and of an effective right of appeal, the slow, continual erosion of property and the grinding effects of impoverishment, the arbitrary and stingingly disproportionate exercise of everyday 'ordinary violence' characterised Algerians' experience of their subjection to the state up to 1944. The eventual abolition, in that year, of the *indigénat* statutes and the promised opening, at the same time, of access to citizenship for all Algeria's inhabitants, finally opened to Algerians the formal public space that had been shaped a century earlier by the politics of colonisation. But it did so in the midst of a global conflict in which the meaning and the future of colonialism everywhere was radically at stake, and in the context, within Algeria, of increasing community tension and violence. And at the same time, as we shall now see, Algerians had already and increasingly moved uninvited into the colony's public sphere, into the public spaces of its 'French' towns and cities, and into the symbolic politics of the Republic, all of which the settlers intended to keep to themselves.

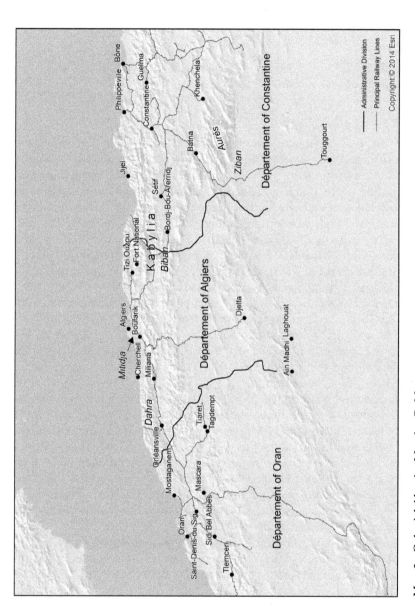

Map 2:  Colonial Algeria.  Map by C. Moore.

# 4　The Politics of Loyalty and Dissent, 1912–1942

In 1914, Chérif Benhabylès published a reform-minded book, *L'Algérie française vue par un indigène*, 'French Algeria as seen by a native.' A son of a great Constantinois aristocratic family that had 'rallied' to the French in the course of the nineteenth century, Benhabylès had been educated in French schools and was both a judge in Islamic law and a doctor of French law. While still considering himself a properly believing Muslim, he had been 'naturalised' as a French citizen under the terms of the 1865 Sénatus-Consulte. In 1939, Albert Camus published a series of harrowing reports on social conditions in Kabylia for the leftist newspaper *Alger républicain*. A young journalist from a working-class Algiers family, born in Mondovi (Dréan), one of the pioneer colonial settlements founded in 1848, Camus had lost his father to the war in France in 1914, and had gained his social promotion through the republican school system. He had gone to impoverished Kabylia to document the life of the countryside while awaiting the appearance of his first major literary work, *Noces*, which was about to be printed.

Benhabylès' work attacked, in particular, the prevailing fear, resentment and aversion in colonial society to the emerging Algerian elite of the early 1900s, the so-called *évolués* who, having gained a French education and become active in journalism, politics and the professions, sometimes took the difficult decision (as he had) to divest themselves of Muslim 'personal status' and become 'naturalised' French citizens, with their personal affairs regulated under French civil law. This was a step equated by most Algerians with apostasy, and *naturalisés* found themselves shunned and labelled *m'turni*s, 'turncoats', by friends and family, as well as being attacked by the colonial press and settler society as dangerous and pretentious upstarts. There was no room in either community for the careful arguments about the differences between statute, *shari'a* and belief, political rights and cultural belonging, that Benhabylès wished to make. 'It is therefore essential', he wrote,

to welcome with open arms every young Algerian who, with a sometimes sublime
tenacity, succeeds in breaking through these barriers; he is a hero in his own way,
especially when he belongs to what one is accustomed to call a 'great family'. Who
can tell of the internal struggles some have gone through in their heart of hearts?
Who can describe [their] hesitations and feelings of anguish?[1]

Focusing, in contrast, on the miseries afflicting the poorest Algerians,
Camus' articles expressed a different anguish. In Kabylia, he wrote:

an entire people is suffering from hunger and three quarters of them are living on
the charity of the local administration. These men, who have lived under the law
of a democracy more perfect than our own, are living out their days in a material
impoverishment that slaves never knew. ... I cannot forget the welcome I was
given at Maillot by thirteen Kabyle children who asked us for food, their fleshless
hands held out through their rags. I cannot forget the inhabitant of the native
quarter at Bordj Menaïel who showed me the touching face of his little daughter, a
ragged skeleton, and who said to me: 'Don't you think that this little girl, if I could
dress her properly, keep her clean and feed her, would be as beautiful as any
French girl?' And how will I forget him, since I felt in myself a consciousness of
guilt that I should not be alone in feeling. But to feel it, one needs to have seen ...
the swarms of children up to their ankles in the mud of the gutters, the schoolchildren whose teachers told me that they fainted from hunger in their classes, the
exhausted old women walking miles to fetch a few measures of grain given out as
charity in distant towns, the beggars displaying their cracked ribs through the
holes of their garments. Such sights are not forgotten except when one wishes to
forget them.[2]

## Worlds in Contact

In their starkly different ways, both Benhabylès and Camus pointed to
the disjuncture between the two worlds in contact of colonial Algeria, the
acute sharpness of the boundaries between them, the necessity but the
difficulty of bridging them politically, socially, even perceptually, their
close yet incommensurable coexistence.

In the years that elapsed between these striking depictions of Algeria by
these very different men, the country was transformed. The First World
War, the emergence of a new Algerian electorate and of mass politics,
economic crisis, large-scale labour migration to France, the rapid spread
of the Arabic-language press and the appearance of radio, the creation of
new forms and spaces of sociability – of sports clubs and theatres, cultural
societies and new religious schools, labour unions and mass meetings –
dramatically altered the social, cultural and political landscape. Old,
influential Algerian families were finally eclipsed, or else reinvented
their standing by investing in new forms of education, professional
employment and political activity; emerging, 'middling' peasant families

and small business owners, modest entrepreneurs and skilled workers began to exercise influence of their own. Among Algeria's Europeans, the tensions felt in Paris, Rome and Madrid ran high too in Algiers, Constantine and Oran as the Republic struggled to contain the countervailing pull of fascist and communist mobilisation. Spain's civil war reverberated among the large Spanish-speaking population of Oran, while Constantine's Jews found themselves facing both growing resentment from the newly vocal politics of their Muslim neighbours and inflammatory anti-Semitism from their European fellow-citizens. Among Algerians, inspiration and anxiety alike came from news of the war of independence and the end of the Ottoman caliphate in Turkey, the Wahhabi conquest of the holy places in Hijaz and the founding of Saudi Arabia, the Rif war against France and Spain in Morocco, the ferocious suppression of revolt against Italians in Libya, revolution against the British and at least nominal independence in Egypt, occupation and insurgency in Iraq and Syria, and, increasingly, the conflict over Palestine. Algerians also followed dramatic events elsewhere, in Ireland, India and Russia. In Paris and Lyon, Algerian workers rubbed shoulders with socialist and communist labour organisers. In Tunis and Cairo, Algerian students of Arabic and the Islamic sciences joined discussions about the Arab *nahda* (revival), Arab nationalism and Muslim solidarity.

At the same time, between Benhabylès' book and Camus' columns, the fundamental, intractable problem did not budge: the rapidly growing Algerian population remained contained, for the most part, within the confines of the *indigénat* and closeted, almost entirely, in a segregated political space of at best second-class citizenship. The aspiring elite, now more numerous, more self-assured and more vocal, still faced a wall of rejection from settler society and its politics of preponderance, which only grew harder the more easily they expressed, in dress and manner and speech, their identification as loyally French and the more ably they dissented from the colonial status quo by articulating French freedom and equality as demands for themselves and their compatriots. The mass of peasants and labourers, much more numerous, and both more hard-pressed and better able to invent new ways of ameliorating their distress than in the preceding decades, remained dispossessed and disenfranchised in their own land. For many of them, *al-bulitiq*, 'politics', meant something dangerous, irresponsible or self-serving. Neither merely quiescent nor 'lacking consciousness', they continued to make their way, and to protect their homes and families, as best they could, loyal to a more immediate sense of community with kin and co-religionist, obedient as far as necessary to established authority. But among a rapidly growing number of Algerians, dissenting demands expanded, loyalty began to attach to a new and larger sense of community, the patience even of the most cautious wore thin, and it became clear to almost all, by 1940, that France's Algeria would never be theirs.

A refrain of reform, improvement, stability and cautious but necessary liberalisation emanated from Paris and from the Government General, animated by anxieties over the durability and security of France's imperial position, to which Algeria had become central. But the settlers and their politicians countered with perceptions of a 'Parisian threat' to their hard-won security, animated by anxieties of their own that were grounded in the fragility of their hold on recognised rights to citizenship and property, which for many were barely a generation old. This combined with their perpetual fear, the 'native threat', which grew with their uneasy awareness of Algerian demography. The European population, in these years, grew only very slightly; having established their political and economic dominance, they now saw Algerians outnumbering them ever more visibly in the countryside, and crowding in on them in the cities. The triumphalism of their celebrations of 'the centenary of Algeria' in 1930 barely disguised their fretful insecurity; in the summer of 1945, it would be exorcised in a savage and deliberate slaughter, which the newly liberated and re-consolidated French Republic would support in full force.

And yet, it was primarily within the spaces, and often with the symbols, created by that Republic that Algerians in these years reconstituted and asserted their social, cultural and political life. As settlers of diverse origin were gradually aggregated into a sense of community as *Français d'Algérie*, so Algerians from the Mzab to Kabylia, from Tebessa to Tlemcen, recognised their own shared condition and found ways to contest it. This process of political community-formation, however, was by no means straightforwardly integrative, and neither was it in any sense complete by 1945, or by 1954. It was driven by disagreement and pushed individuals and families in different directions; the war of independence, after 1954, was itself not the result but a part of this process, which it would violently accelerate and bring to a climax. Within the institutional and physical spaces of colonial Algeria, its single public sphere, these two parallel, unequal, sometimes colliding and uneasily overlapping societies ran their historical course in tension together.[3]

At these two societies' overlapping, frictional edges was what has been called the *monde du contact*, a fragile 'contact zone' between preponderant and subjugated communities that was nonetheless 'capable of creating real relations' between them.[4] Among intellectuals and professionals, journalists, schoolteachers and social reformers, in schools and at university; in cafés, political parties and freemasons' lodges; in rural medical clinics, markets and post offices; and at particular, brief moments, especially in the enthusiastic mobilisations around the Popular Front in 1936, Algerians of all confessions and languages, citizens and non-citizens, met, disputed and agreed, worked together and across the divisions of colonial society. Beyond such small spaces and moments, broader forces of government and market brought the 'interpenetration' of France and Algeria to bear more widely: even 'peripheral' areas like the Kabyle mountains became peripheral relative to new centres – not only Algiers but the factories of France – in dependent relation to which, as Camus graphically portrayed, local life was now lived. Expanding school provision and increasing urbanisation among Algerians in the late 1940s produced an everyday urban coexistence that later, nostalgic *pieds noirs*' memories would see as a normal 'fraternity' that was to be brutally destroyed by 'the events' after 1954.[5] 'Arkhoun and Benmiloud, Navarro and Sanchez, Martin and Leteunegger, Salama and Hazan, as the teacher read out the list . . . was a natural world', but, as André Akoun, born in a Jewish family in Oran, observes of his childhood in the early 1940s, 'there was, in these years, a sort of social somnambulism about Algeria's colonial situation'. Recalling the sight of young Algerians filling Oran's streets in 1963, he records his astonishment 'at seeing them, so many of them . . . Where did all these boys and girls . . ., whom [I'd] never met, come from? . . . Where had they been hidden? But [I] knew, deep down, that the real change was less in their presence than in the fact that it had become visible . . . '[6] The overriding characteristic of the colonial situation was not Algerians' 'contact' with Europeans but their invisibility; as Benhabylès and Camus had both, differently, observed, and as Jean-Paul Grangaud, born in Algiers in 1938, would point out years later, Algeria's European society was 'organised so as not to be aware of certain things'.[7]

## The Resilience and Re-composition of Algerian Society

What Algeria's Europeans avoided awareness of was the objective fact of their relation to Algerian society. But they increasingly, uneasily discerned the dynamic re-composition of that society. On its base arose a new Algerian politics which they could not avoid noticing, and which, however moderate, they battled furiously to suppress. The Algerian population had first recovered, after 1881, from a half-century of catastrophes, and then grew rapidly, from just over 4 million people in 1906 to 4.5 million in 1926, and just over 5.5 million in 1936. It would reach 9 million by 1954.

This rate of growth quickly outstripped the diminishing resources of the colonised countryside, and after the First World War, rural overpopulation and its corollary, unmanageable migration to towns, became a systemic problem. The first signs of peri-urban overpopulation in the unpaved, unlit and unsanitary so-called *villages nègres* of Oran, Constantine, Tlemcen and Mostaganem were becoming visible in 1914, and the ever more densely populated Casbah of Algiers was already becoming home principally to migrants from Kabylia.[8] By the 1930s, the old city's urban fabric, equally romanticised and denigrated, was falling into decay; its inhabitants, according to official estimates, suffered from overall mortality rates double, and infant mortality three times higher, than those of the rest of the city. The Casbah could not accommodate new arrivals. By 1941, when the Vichy authorities discovered the problem, shantytowns, newly named *bidonvilles*, had sprung up. The *bidonvilles* spread out north and south of the city: to the north, on the hillside around the el-Kettar cemetery west of the old Ottoman citadel, in nearby quarries, and to the south, on the hillside between the villa Sésini, a neo-mauresque mansion built in the 1920s by an Algiers lawyer, and the Fort des Arcades on the heights above the European district of Clos Salembier.

In 1941, the Algiers prefecture counted 1,259 families, totalling 4,805 people, already living in the shantytowns. Most were paying monthly rent of between thirty and fifty francs for their jerry-built housing, on irregular daily wages of between ten and twenty francs for men who were mostly day labourers – the lowest wages recorded were for girls and women working as domestics, at two to four francs. Some were, very relatively, comfortable: Hachemi Gherbi had come from Biskra in 1929, had a regular job in road-mending and lived with his two wives Haizia and Fatmou, four sons, three daughters and a son-in-law in a house which he owned himself in the Mahieddine shantytown, on the hillside directly above the European working-class district of Belcourt. Two other families – one a widow, Aisha, and her two children – also shared the house, bringing in fifty-five francs' monthly rent. At the other extreme was the family of Said Bouafna: originally from Tadmaït, on the road to Tizi Ouzou, he had moved to Algiers in 1931 and into the el-Kettar shantytown five years later. His wife Fatma and daughter Ourdia, one of their six children, together earned four and a half francs daily as cleaners, which combined with the three francs he earned selling cloths to meet their monthly rent of thirty-five francs, and their family's other needs. At the same time, monthly rent for social housing in Algiers, provided by the municipal 'HBM' office (Public Office of Affordable Housing), would cost a family 140–160 francs, well beyond the means of the poorest. The large-scale remodelling of Algiers imagined in the 1930s had been abandoned; rehousing projects drawn up in 1941 to absorb the *bidonvilles* would not be completed until the early 1950s. By then, the shantytowns had grown enormously: in 1950, the 'cité Mahieddine' alone housed some 10,000 people. A young medical student, Sadek Hadjerès, who would soon join the Algerian Communist Party, wrote that year of the shantytown's inhabitants: 'Here you meet people from every region of Algeria, driven from their own lands by hunger and misrule ... Here is something of our villages and tribes, transported into the middle of Algiers. But the look in the eyes of each tells of the arid, painful road of exile that has brought these families here.'[9]

Such migration was one part of a much broader, new pattern of movement. The 'Tlemcen exodus' of 1911, when hundreds of that city's families emigrated across the Moroccan frontier, was the last major manifestation of migration as an expression of avoidance and refusal of the colonial state – in 1912, France declared a protectorate over Morocco and after 1919, with the collapse of the Ottoman empire and the subsequent French occupation of Syria, there was simply nowhere left to go. Migration, especially for study and pilgrimage, to Fez, Damascus, the Hijaz and more particularly to Tunis and Cairo remained important throughout the interwar years, but rather than leaving Algeria behind, such movements now maintained and reinvigorated contacts between localities in Algeria and centres of ideas, political organisation and cultural production elsewhere, especially through the increasing circulation of the Arabic periodical press and, in the 1930s, cinema. The expanding opportunities of the colonial economy, as roads and railways connected markets and investment opportunities not only across Algeria but throughout 'French' North Africa, facilitated such networks in new ways, with profound social and cultural consequences. Ibadi entrepreneurs engaged in commercial transport began to move their wives and children north to live with them, provoking a crisis of religious and social authority in the Mzab. Ideas about the reform and regeneration of Islam spread with newspapers, preachers and teachers travelling along the colonial railway. Young men from the villages and oases travelled to Constantine, Tunis and Cairo rather than to rural *zawiya*s to study, and in the cities they joined students' associations, wrote articles in journals and began to dress differently. More began to attend French primary schools, and a very few went on to the *lycée* and, in Algiers, Montpellier and Paris, to university.[10]

Between 1914 and 1918, some 173,000 Algerians served in the French army, on the Western Front and at Gallipoli, of whom 86,519 were volunteers; another 119,000 or so Algerian workers were recruited by the administration or, before 1916, travelled freely to provide labour for the war effort.[11] After the war, while agricultural labourers continued to move seasonally within the Maghrib (notably, for example, between northern Morocco and the wine-growing Oranais countryside), from 1920 onwards large numbers of Algerian workers began to move across the Mediterranean to factories and construction sites in France. Drawn especially from Kabylia, a region that had always exported its manpower and from where embarkation for the metropole was rapid through the nearby ports of Algiers and Bejaïa, emigrant workers – male and single – became a lynchpin of the local economy in the countryside, sustaining its precarious and increasingly inadequate agriculture with the wages they sent home. At the same time, they formed a new urban proletariat in cities stretching from Marseille and Lyon to Paris and Lille. Departures peaked at 71,000 in 1924 before dropping during the economic crisis of the early 1930s, rising again to 46,500 in 1937, and taking off after the Second World War: 80,000 workers left Algeria for France in 1948, 142,000 in 1951. By 1954, it was reckoned that there were some 300,000 Algerians in the metropole.[12] Conditions for these migrant workers were often atrocious: during the First World War, the workforce, including boys under 15 years old, was generally housed in unsanitary barracks or in factory spaces, worked ten-hour shifts and was wracked by overwork and illness. Death rates among French war workers were half, sometimes less than one-third of those that afflicted Algerians.[13] These were especially terrible times, but housing and health were not much better for subsequent migrants, particularly in the shantytowns like those of Nanterre which, from the 1950s into the 1970s, housed later Algerian migrants and refugees from the war of independence. The sadness of *el-ghorba*, the 'exile' of labour emigration, would be captured by the great *sha'bi* ('popular') singer Dahmane el-Harrachi in his famous song *Ya Rayah*:

> You who leave, where are you going, growing weary, going onward?
> How much did they regret, the unwary ones who went before you
>   and me?
> How many crowded cities have I seen, and emptied countrysides?
> You who are absent, in the land of others, how you'll grow weary . . .

The consequences of this new pattern of migration, above all, would be revolutionary in more ways than one.

At the same time, in Algiers, Constantine and elsewhere, older urban inhabitants, the *beldi* families that had known how to hold on and adapt, were re-emerging in the associational, cultural and political spaces that proliferated from the early 1900s onwards. Many such families had for decades after the conquest chosen avoidance of the colonial state as the best path to preservation of their moral as well as their social standing, but this began to change in the years around the First World War: here again the 'Tlemcen exodus' of 1911 marks a watershed. Other families had long since learned to combine preservation of their cultural capital and dignity with careful, strategic accommodation, seeking both to protect their patrimony and to engage the authorities to improve the condition of their compatriots. Just northwest of Tlemcen, in Nedroma, the distinguished jurist Hamza Ben Rahal served as local judge and administrator for the amir Abd al-Qadir and then under the French; his sixth son M'hamed Ben Rahal, born in 1858, was educated in both French and Arabic. Succeeding his father as *qa'id* of Nedroma in 1878, he resigned the office only six years later, its status having declined after Nedroma was made a *commune mixte* under a French administrator. In the 1890s he testified before Jules Ferry's senatorial commission of inquiry, propounding legal reforms and parliamentary representation for Algerians, and was central to ambitious plans to reorganise and expand the education offered by the so-called *médersas* (*madrasas*), the official schools in Tlemcen, Algiers and Constantine that had been set up in 1851 to train bilingual functionaries for the civil courts and the administration. In 1897, in a lecture on 'The Future of Islam' given to the eleventh International Congress of Orientalists in Paris, he deplored the negative vision of his faith common in Europe, and predicted that Islam's renaissance would be forged 'under the guns of Christianity'. Retiring to Nedroma in 1900, he devoted himself to the spiritual life through his affiliation to the Darqawa *tariqa*, but later returned to politics as a *conseiller général* in 1904, and was elected to the *délégations financières* between 1920 and 1925, where he stood out as the principal spokesman of the small Algerian delegation and several times, to no avail, addressed his vision of education and emancipation for Algerians alongside the preservation and renewal of their Islamic law and culture to the authorities in Paris and Algiers. Warning that colonial policy must change 'quickly, if any reconciliation is not to become impossible', Ben Rahal died in Nedroma in 1928. His family retained their prominence throughout the subsequent decades: his great-nephew, Abdellatif, born in 1922, trained as a schoolteacher and taught mathematics before, in 1963, becoming independent Algeria's first ambassador to France, and in the 1970s, his country's representative to the United Nations.[14]

The Ben Badis family of Constantine, descendants of an ancient, originally Berber dynasty that had produced the Zirid princes of Ifriqiya (Tunisia) in the tenth century, had similarly maintained much of their standing after 1837, by judicious investments in both older and newer avenues of education and activity. Si al-Mekki ben Badis (d. 1889) continued to serve as *qadi* under the French, sat on municipal commissions and on the colony's Council on Public Education, and was decorated with the *légion d'honneur* by Napoleon III in 1864. His son, Muhammad Mustafa, born in 1868 and educated in French and Arabic, was in 1914 a mere *adjoint indigène* for El-Khroub, a circumscription just outside the city. But he maintained and improved the family's agricultural estates, became a municipal councillor and, in 1921, a member of the Constantine *Conseil général*. He was elected to the *Délegations financières* in 1923, in due course receiving the grand cross of the *légion d'honneur* in recognition of his influence and loyalism. In a telling division of labour, Si Mustafa's second son, Mouloud, received a French education, passed the *baccalauréat*, became Constantine's first Algerian lawyer and in the 1930s directed a francophone newspaper; his elder brother Abd al-Hamid, born in 1889 (and who would later affect an inability to speak French), studied Arabic and the classical Islamic sciences, first in Constantine and then at the Zaytuna mosque-university in Tunis. On completing his studies in 1912, Abd al-Hamid made the pilgrimage to Mecca and Medina, where he met his former teacher, shaykh Hamdan al-Wanisi, who had emigrated to the Hijaz in 1904, and who advised the young man neither to accept employment under the French, nor to use his learning to seek it. Instead, in 1914 the young shaykh began teaching independently in a small mosque buried deep among the markets of the old city in Constantine, the *jami' al-akhdar* (Green Mosque, sometimes called Sidi Lakhdar); when he entered journalism in the 1920s, he would write only in Arabic.[15]

Another Constantine family related by marriage to the Ben Badis, the Bendjellouls had been among the wealthiest in the city at the end of the Ottoman period and, though their material fortune had declined, were still substantial citizens in the 1920s. In the 1880s M'hamed Bendjelloul was a schoolteacher who recovered the family's fortunes by marrying into the old beylical family of Constantine; his son, Muhammad-Salah Bendjelloul, was afforded both a Qur'anic education in Arabic and – unusually among the *beldi* families of Constantine before 1914 – secondary schooling in French at the Constantine *lycée*, then medical school in Algiers. In 1924, the 31-year-old Dr Bendjelloul was appointed *médecin de colonisation* (a state-employed rural physician) for the Aurès.[16]

In Algiers, two grandsons of Ahmad Bu Darba, the merchant who had fruitlessly attempted to negotiate a liberal compromise with the city's occupiers in 1831, maintained their family's standing and a position as would-be interlocutors on behalf of their compatriots. Their father, Ismaïl Bouderba, the son born to Ahmad and his French wife in Marseille in 1823, had been educated at one of Paris's most prestigious schools, the Louis-le-Grand *lycée*, had joined the French army's interpreters' service in 1853 and by his death in 1878 was celebrated in the colonial academy for his contributions to France's 'scientific exploration' of the Sahara. In 1914, Ismaïl's son Omar was a wealthy businessman in Algiers while his elder brother Ahmad was one of only three Algerian lawyers in the city. Their cousin Ali was a medical doctor and a municipal councillor. Omar was, with another medical doctor, the ophthalmologist Belkacem Benthami, a leading member of the so-called Young Algerians, the reform-minded group of notables like Chérif Benhabylès who embraced the French vision of 'civilisation' and sought to harness it to emancipate Algerians.[17]

By the 1920s, there were a few hundred such individuals, connected by family to modest fortunes and administrative positions, educated in French and either commercially successful – in manufacturing tobacco, cooking oil, soft drinks – or professionally trained as schoolteachers, pharmacists, dentists, doctors or lawyers. Their numbers increased only very slowly: in 1938, there were still only seventy Algerian lawyers, forty-one medical doctors, twenty-two pharmacists, nine dentists and three engineers. Before 1945, on average only one hundred Algerians emerged from secondary education each year with the coveted *baccalauréat*.[18] These, then, were elite families, but others, smaller in fortune, had similarly picked their way through the years of dispossession and famine, to re-emerge in the years after 1914 with a capacity to invest in new educational and economic opportunities, and to develop at least local influence. It was they who would provide the broader social base of the politics that re-emerging elites would begin to espouse.

In the countryside, too, despite the frequent misery, and though frayed by the terrible pressures colonisation had brought to bear, ties of social solidarity and patterns of continuity proved resilient. The basic building block of many rural populations, the *firqa* or tribal 'fraction' that grouped several extended families in a long-established local political geography, maintained its cohesion, especially in the mountains. This was so, despite the administrative disaggregation of tribes into *douars-communes* (which was not always as complete in practice as legal texts might lead one to believe) and the attempted instrumentalisation of an 'official' *jama'a* in each *douar* under the local administrator. The *firqa* and its established *jama'a*, which often operated as a 'clandestine', or real, council below the 'official', legal body appointed by the authorities, were too small and too nimble to be captured in the thinly stretched net of colonial administration, and throughout the colonial period they continued to provide the basis of social organisation and political deliberation in villages across the country. The *jama'a* was the locally rooted institution of peasant political life, often invisible to the administration and regulated by the mountain communities' habitual silence and secrecy towards outsiders as much as by their highly codified, masculine and patriarchal relations between themselves. It survived and adapted as the society represented in it did, regulating feuds, bargaining with boundary surveyors and administrators, maintaining – above all – a united front against the world outside.[19]

Anti-conscription revolts that broke out during the First World War, and persistent 'social banditry' in the mountains into the 1920s, were signs as much of this vital, sustained rural social solidarity as they were of the under-administration of the countryside in which the writ of the state still ran very unevenly. Already in October 1914, the Awlad Shaykh of the Sidi Daho tribe, a locally influential saintly family, orchestrated a revolt against conscription among the Beni Chougrane in the mountains north of Mascara by binding families to an oath not to deliver their sons to the French, and the local administrator was kept ignorant of the scale of the resistance for a week after the first abstentions from the recruiters' roll calls.[20] Resistance to conscription was widespread, reaching its peak in the winter of 1916–17 in the district of Batna, where at least 14,000 soldiers (one for every four inhabitants of the area) were deployed to repress an anti-conscription movement that grew into an insurrection.[21]

Army deserters and escaped draftees took to the forests where criminal gangs were rarely distinguishable, for the authorities, from social protestors; during the war, concerns about 'insecurity' were rife. In Kabylia and the Aurès, local and family networks generated and sustained such 'insecurity', as well as suffering from it. For local populations, bandits could be both protected and protectors. Omar Kezzouli, from Illula Umalu high in the Djurdjura southeast of Tizi Ouzou, was first identified as a bandit in 1895, but was never denounced or caught. In 1915, one of Omar's sons, Hocine, had deserted from the army and joined his cousin, Ahmad, in a gang thought to be promising security in the vicinity in exchange for protection against the authorities.[22] Mas'ud Ben Zelmat (or Ugzelmad) became an outlaw in the northern Aurès in 1917, apparently to avenge the death of his brother, himself a fugitive from the law who had been denounced and killed, and evaded the authorities until he was tracked down and shot on Ahmar Khaddou, the arid mountain plateau in the south of the massif, in 1921. In the meantime he had become a local legend, romanticised in poetry sung by women in the mountains as a peasant righter of wrongs, demanding due pay for workers and striking down exploiters and oppressors:

> Messaoud Ug-Zelmad, with his shoes on his feet
> Has climbed up the ravine,
> He has put on his woollen belt . . .
> He wears a bandolier, and veils across his face
> Messaoud is a sharpshooter
> One bullet is enough

He is his mother's beloved son . . .
He is known from one side of the mountain to the other.[23]

Rural insecurity had already worried official circles in the 1890s, when they began to fret that the peasantry was sliding into a 'poverty dangerous to public safety'. Under laws designed to favour the colonial property market, Algerians could now obtain title to their land and sell it on to Europeans, and had done so in unexpectedly large numbers, a tendency encouraged by taxation, immiseration and indebtedness but which officials put down to 'the natural lack of foresight (*imprévoyance*) of the Arab character'. By 1898, perversely, a commission was instituted to consider whether new limits on land sales were needed to stop Europeans so easily acquiring Algerians' means of livelihood.[24] At the same time, the failure of small colonial farms and the drift of Europeans away from the countryside, the tendency to consolidate landholdings into larger and more profitable estates, and the rise of a recovering middle stratum of Algerian peasant landowners, combined to begin a slow recon-solidation of rural property by some Algerians. From 1898 to 1920, Algerian peasants still sold more land to Europeans than they bought back from them, and transactions between Algerians benefitted a middle-landowning class and, especially, a small fringe of great landowners, at the expense of small peasant proprietors. From 1928, the application of a new land law liquidated collective rights to *'arsh* lands, parcelling out tiny plots that were sold by those who could not live on them to those able to buy. The increasingly overworked marginal land onto which Algerian agricul-ture had been pushed provided ever-diminishing returns; cereal produc-tion fell and herds shrank dramatically in size. In 1920, a severe famine added to the miseries of typhus and Spanish flu. Malnourishment was endemic; in 1928, 64 per cent of Algerian men called up for military service were found to be medically unfit for duty. But perhaps between a fifth and a quarter of all Algerian proprietors, with landholdings of between 10 and 50 hectares, managed to maintain themselves and even to increase both in number and in their overall share of rural property between the First World War and the early 1950s. Rural Algerian society was thus extremely unequal, and the inequalities between the dispos-sessed and proletarised, the rich becoming wealthier, and those in between who had held on and were now, after 1919, at least a little more secure, became sharper as time went on.[25]

While social solidarities, then, persisted, social tensions were exacer-bated too. And at the same time, beginning shortly before the First World War and re-emerging more strongly in its aftermath, associative life both in small towns and in the cities began to foster the social base of new political and cultural movements in which both solidarities and tensions could be played out. Legalised by the 1901 French law on civil society associations, spaces for sociability multiplied. The periodical press, administratively suspect and restricted despite the liberal press law of 1881 (which, guaranteeing free expression to citizens, thus withheld it from Algerians), also proliferated in both French and Arabic. Cafés, musical societies, the theatre, sports clubs, the press, religious groups, trades unions and political parties all blossomed from the first decade of the twentieth century and grew in the interwar period. A new urban working and lower-middle class of small business owners and shopkeepers, investing in transportation and retail, and skilled workers – bus, tram and railway workers, post office and hospital employees – appeared in the towns. Algiers' tramway workers, for example, joined unions, read the press and mobilised for political demonstrations, creating a base both for a new urban popular politics and for a new urban popular culture. In Algiers and other towns, athletic clubs, especially for boxing and soccer, emerged.[26] Popular musical forms, quintessentially Algiers' *sha'abi* (*chaabi*), were not only consumed but produced in this milieu: the singer Dahmane al-Harrachi, born in Algiers in 1926, was a tramway worker before leaving for France in 1949, as was Allalou, the first Algerian actor to write for the stage in local Arabic dialect. The 'creator' of *sha'abi* music, Hajj Muhammad al-Anka, found the public for it, a vernacular form of the more classical Andalusi music in which he began his career, among the ordinary working people of the dockside and the Casbah, where he himself had been born to migrants from Kabylia in 1907.

In the 1930s, this new public – composed of both men and women – in the cities and provincial towns watched Egyptian films at the cinema, attended performances by the children of independently run, Arabic-teaching community schools, read (or listened to others reading out) newspapers in homes and (for men) cafés, where musical ensembles also rehearsed and performed, and turned out in their thousands for the regular tours of Algeria's leading theatrical troupe, Al-Mutribiyya, led by the singer, playwright and impresario Mahieddine Bachetarzi. Born in 1899, the descendant of an Ottoman Algiers family, Bachetarzi began his career in Qur'an recitation at the *jami' jadid*, the seventeenth-century 'new mosque' at the edge of the Place du Gouvernement on the Algiers waterfront which the French called the *mosquée de la Pêcherie*, but in the 1920s he began recording for Gramophone and switched from sacred to secular music. His shows mixed melodrama with social satire and comedy of manners, and his songs were periodically banned by the administration as subversive, although he also taught at the Algiers conservatoire and, in

Figure 4.1 Musical patrimony: the *jawq* (classical orchestra) of shaykh Larbi ben Sari in Tlemcen, ca. 1930. Shaykh Larbi sits third from left, his son shaykh Redouane (later a celebrated singer and pianist in his own right) third from right with the violin. The other instruments are the *qanun* (zither, centre-left), *tar* (a type of tambourine, at left), *kouitra* (long-necked lute, held by shaykh al-Qarmuni behind the tambourine), *rebab* (held by shaykh Larbi), *oud* (second from right) and *darbouka* (FR ANOM GGA 9H37).

1926, took part in the inauguration of the decade's headline project of official imperial culture, the Paris Mosque.[27] The Mutribiyya company included Algerian actresses and female singers as well as European actors who played 'French' roles.

Bachetarzi's recording career was patronised by his teacher and mentor Edmond Yafil, the Jewish performer and scholar of classical Andalusi music who founded al-Mutribiyya in 1912, and whose 1904 publication of Andalusi song texts, collated from earlier manuscripts, brought this high art form to a mass public for the first time and launched its modern 'revival'. Yafil's work, and the frequent centrality of Jewish musicians to Andalusi and, later, *cha'bi* performance, was both an echo of an older, pre-colonial and cross-confessional urban culture, and an indication of the extent to which cultural spaces could still exist at the overlapping margins of colonial society. In Constantine, the later career of 'shaykh' Raymond Leyris, the adopted son of a poor Jewish family born in 1912, who in the 1950s became one of the leading exponents of Constantine's *ma'luf* repertoire, and who was assassinated in 1961, illustrates both the persistence and the fragility of such spaces. In the early 1900s, Europeans in Arab dress (who like Algerian *naturalisés* were labelled *m'turnis*) could still be found enjoying Andalusi music in 'Moorish' cafés around the lower Casbah, alongside Jewish and Muslim musicians and aficionados. The vitality of this tradition as the expression of a sophisticated, virtuoso Algerian culture was rooted deeply in the older urban societies of Constantine, Algiers, Nedroma and Tlemcen, where it was passed down and reshaped in the hands of masters and ensemble (*jawq*) leaders like Yafil's own teacher Muhammad ben Ali Sfinja in Algiers (d.1908), Ahmad Bustanji (d. 1946) in Constantine, and Shaykh Larbi ben Sari of Tlemcen who, born in 1867, lived into his nineties, and who represented Algeria at the Congress of Arab Music in Cairo in 1932.[28]

Social and political protest as well as coexistence could also find its voice in sport and culture. Most of the 2,000 Algerians (two-thirds of the reported audience) who turned out in Algiers in November 1937 to see local boxing star Omar Kouidri defeat the metropolitan contender Paul Rebel in twelve rounds for the national middleweight title were apparently more interested in boxing than in turning the event into a political protest, but several spectators were heard shouting encouragement to 'put Rebel out, like we should put all the French out!'[29] The crowds of boys – the ubiquitous so-called *yaouleds* or *petits cireurs*, the 'bootblacks' of colonial towns – who enthusiastically filled the front rows of cinemas in the late 1930s clapped and cheered when the hero made stirring speeches about Swiss independence in *William Tell*, when the Foreign Legionnaire heroes in *Les hommes sans nom* ('The Men With No Name') were shot by Moroccan insurgents in the desert, and when 'indigenous' troops – or, in 1938, more worryingly, German ones – marched across the newsreels.[30] In Algiers, the poet Muhammad al-Aid, who was for several years director of the independent, reformist *madrasat al-shabiba 'l-islamiyya* (School for Islamic Youth) founded in 1922, from 1924 published openly nationalist verse in the Arabic-language press. Ahmad Reda Huhu, the son of a notable family from Sidi Okba who had both Arabic and French primary education and worked briefly for the postal service before his family's emigration to the Hijaz in 1934, returned to settle in Constantine in 1945, where he too taught. In 1947, he published the first Algerian novella in Arabic, *Ghadat umm al-qura* ('The Young Woman of Mecca'), and went on to found a successful theatre company that produced both his own original work and adaptations of French plays, before he was assassinated in March 1956.[31] If Huhu was to become a nationalist martyr, even Bachetarzi's work, picking its way cautiously through intense police scrutiny and censorship, had a critically reflective edge: as well as adapting French classics like Molière's *L'Avare* (*Al-Mushahha*, 'The Miser'), his plays in the 1930s pitted trickster folk heroes against social parasites (*Djeha and the Usurer*), championed educated and aspirational reformers against their corrupt and jealous rivals (*Al-Khadda'in*, 'The Traitors'), and played out generational tensions and moral dilemmas between the young and honest and their unscrupulous, uneducated and dishonourable elders (*Beni Oui Oui*).[32]

The stages, in towns throughout the country, where these plays acted out their themes – social inequalities, the pressing need for education to overcome ignorance and exploitation, changing norms of gender and generation within the family, the emergence of electoral politics – combined with the associations of doctors, medical auxiliaries and schoolteachers, with the press, religious circles and independent primary schools to amplify expression and debate of Algeria's social problems.[33] And as ideas of colonial reform and development grew along with the more general expansion of the state and its remit, especially from the 1930s, the reach of the state – its hospitals and schools as well as its police and its bureaucracy – began to extend, albeit very reluctantly and at a pace far outstripped by demography, a little further into Algerian society. Education remained very limited, especially for girls: most girls' classes that did exist were workrooms teaching domesticity and handicrafts, and by 1938 less than 5 per cent of Algerian girls received any kind of education.[34] Free and compulsory public instruction would not be extended to them until 1958. Still, although as a proportion of the primary school-age population their number remained minuscule – under 2 per cent in 1890, not quite 6 per cent in 1918, almost 9 per cent in 1944 and nearly 13 per cent in 1954 – the absolute numbers of Algerian schoolchildren (overwhelmingly boys) rose steadily over the same years: 10,577 in 1890, 49,071 in 1918, 108,00 in 1944 and 306,737 in 1954.[35]

Simultaneously, around the First World War and increasingly in the interwar period, refusal and avoidance of the colonial state among Algerians gave way to ever more assertive demands on it. The 'loyalism' of Algerian soldiers fighting on metropolitan French soil during the First World War was attested and celebrated by the authorities; it was in recognition of this that the government began, in 1919, to acknowledge the necessity of a politics of 'reform' in Algeria. But as Gilbert Meynier observes, 'if Algerians fought, and fought better than well, it was because [...] life in the army seemed to them on the whole more egalitarian than life in the colony'. Paternalist and mobilising military discipline 'reinforced the myth of a "true" France which, in Algeria, was contradicted by her wayward servants'. Tellingly, those most fiercely resisting conscription, at the same time, expressed their autonomy in the same language: before killing the sub-prefect and burning his archives, the leaders of the Batna insurrection, in November 1916, began their uprising by proclaiming *al-bublik*, 'the Republic'.[36]

## The Rights of Being 'French', the Meanings of Being 'Muslim'

The Republic, indeed, was now the principal horizon of reference for Algerian social and political aspirations. In 1892, Jules Ferry had noted the emergence of a *parti des Jeunes* in the person of Dr Tayyeb Morsly, a frock-coated physician from Oran who had become a municipal councillor in Constantine, and in 1893 a short-lived periodical, *El Hack*, was published in Bône, first in French and then in both French and Arabic, proclaiming itself 'For God, Homeland (*patrie*), and Equity!' Its title announced 'The Truth', but *al-haqq* equally conveyed the sense of a moral or legal 'right'. Small societies, like the 'Young Algerian Circle' in Tlemcen and the 'Salah Bey Circle' in Constantine, both founded in 1907, provided discussion space, adult education and lending libraries, and became centres of activism promoting education and 'moral hygiene'. At the *cercle Salah Bey*, which Chérif Benhabylès attended, the jurist (and later mufti of Constantine) Mawlud Ben Mawhub waged 'war on ignorance' in public lectures, while other groups denounced gambling and alcohol, and opposed child marriage, polygamy and inequality in divorce. Social improvement, for these young activists, meant above all access to the education which they, exceptionally, had gained in French schools; political emancipation, correspondingly, was envisaged through the ideals of reason, progress and civilisation, which, their schoolmasters had taught them, were embodied above all in the Republic. If France in Algeria did not live up to the ideals of the 'true' France of Republican liberty and progress, what Algeria needed was a more perfect legal, institutional and even – for some – cultural assimilation to the idealised metropolitan model. The entry to the *cité* of citizenship that Algeria's heterogeneous Europeans had gained over the course of the nineteenth century was now imagined as the solution to the colonial predicament of Algerians in the twentieth.

An idiom of social and political reform thus emerged, carried from one ephemeral journal to another, and summed up in the tag-line of one of them, *El Misbah* ('The Torch'), published in Oran in 1904: 'For France by the Arabs, for the Arabs by France.' Other titles would evoke the *trait d'union* ('hyphen') or the *entente* ('understanding', coexistence) between 'races' that the tiny, emerging francophone elite saw itself as representing. The nickname 'Young Algerians', affixed to them by their detractors in mocking reference to the Young Turks who, in the 1890s, were radical exiles in Paris, was a loose appellation for a heterogeneous group, less a movement or 'party' than a social status group, united more by their 'Europeanised' lifestyle and improving aspirations than by any political program. They wore European dress, usually with the *tarbush* or fez, as their *effendi* equivalents in Egypt did, they spoke French and in accordance with prevailing ideas of social and cultural hierarchy, they sought to be, as abusive colonial parlance put it, *évolués*, 'evolved' above the miserable status of their compatriots. They enthusiastically appropriated the idioms of France's 'civilising mission' – a mission supposedly shared by the Republican school and the colonial empire – in a long-term vision of a fraternal 'union of the races' between all of Algeria's inhabitants, to be achieved by the slow, progressive societal betterment of 'the ignorant masses' of their compatriots, and the more immediate protection of their own material interests and prospects. For some, such 'progress' was inexorably on the march, as Ismaël Hamet, an army interpreter and author in 1906 of a celebratory book on the achievements of those Algerians who had embraced France's civilising influence, maintained. Arabs and Berbers, he wrote, could hardly be untouched by their 'permanent contact' with the *fusion des races* among Algeria's Europeans. Given modern education, they could acquire an 'aptitude for social equality and moral assimilation' with Europeans. The long history of the Maghrib showed successive waves of invaders combining with the indigenous inhabitants, but while in the past, religion had been the greatest force for the unification of different populations (as Islam had been for Berbers and Arabs), under the material progress of modern civilisation, religion was in retreat, 'giving way to the play of economic and sociological laws'. It was these, unfettered, that would bring progress to Algeria.[37]

Others made more limited and immediate claims: at a meeting attended by more than a thousand Algerians in Bône in December 1909, and in a reform program published in the journal *L'Islam* in 1911, the demands were equalisation of taxation, suppression of the 'exceptional' jurisdiction of the *indigénat* and repressive tribunals, and application of equality before the criminal law for all, electoral reform that would give greater representation to the educated elites (in place of the administration's own agents, *qa'id*s and handpicked *beni oui oui*), and the right of Algerian municipal councillors to take part in mayoral elections. For some, the aim was a 'progressive assimilation of the Algerian élite ... to the French bloc ...', when and insofar as its education shall render it suitable', in the words of Ben Ali Fekar, a Tlemceni lawyer who taught Arabic in Lyon while studying there for his doctorate, who had opted for 'naturalisation', and who with his schoolteacher brother had co-founded *El Misbah*.[38] And certainly, central to their agenda was access to the vote, to eligibility and to administrative office for those whose education, by the lights of Republican meritocracy, entitled them to it. But their appeals for legal equality, the extension of education, liberalisation of forest laws, oversight to guard against administrative abuses and protection against usury (on which Fekar wrote his thesis, distinguishing between interest on capital, which alone could enable Muslims to compete economically, and usury, which kept them in dependence) went well beyond the narrow, elitist self-interest of which the 'Young Algerians' were accused at the time by the settler press, and for which they would subsequently be reproached by historians.[39]

The overriding issue of the day before the First World War, however, was conscription. Alternately opposed and endured in the countryside from 1908 onwards, the nomination and incorporation of young Algerian men into the French army was seized on by the Young Algerians as a means of both demonstrating loyalty to the Republic, and exacting reforms from it.[40] Two delegations from Algiers went to Paris to oppose conscription without the concomitant extension of civil and political rights: the first, led by Omar Bouderba, was received by the President of the Council of Ministers, Clemenceau, in October 1908, and a second, led by Dr Benthami, met his successor Poincaré in June 1912. Benthami's delegation submitted a petition, which would become known as the 'Young Algerian manifesto', demanding equal terms of military service for Algerians alongside French citizens, extended electoral representation, including representation for Algerians in the French parliament, the ineligibility of *qa'id*s for elected office, reform of the *indigénat* and of taxation, a more equitable distribution of public funds between European and Algerian communities,[41] and the right for Algerians, having discharged their military service, to opt for full French citizenship by simple declaration (thus eliminating the bureaucratic and often obstructionist application process existing under the Sénatus-Consulte). A third delegation of more traditionally dressed notables, sent a few months later from Nedroma and Nemours (Ghazawat) and led by M'hamed Ben Rahal, intended to restate their unconditional opposition to conscription, but realised that the government would not budge and, for lack of an alternative, added their names to Benthami's manifesto.[42]

What thereby became a joint statement, authored – too optimistically – by the *redingote*-wearing eye doctor and endorsed – somewhat reluctantly – by the sage Sufi in his white wool *burnus*, marked the beginning of a long struggle to represent Algerians' civil and political futures. In the differences between these two groups lay tensions over leadership and legitimacy, as to who could claim to represent Algerians, and over the shape of their visions of Algeria as it was and should be: what it meant to be Muslim, what it might mean to be French. But they also had much in common, more than the labels used at the time by colonial commentators to distinguish traditionalist *vieux turbans*, 'old turban-wearers' like Ben Rahal, from *jeunes Algériens* like the Bouderba brothers, suggest. Ahmad Bouderba, like Ben Rahal, had spoken before Jules Ferry' 1892 commission of inquiry and like him had argued for reform and improvement of the official *médersas*. Animated by positivist enthusiasm and Republican anticlericalism, a few of the francophone elite, like Omar Bouderba, would rail against Islamic law and its *'ulama*, and call as loudly as the most vocal colonial ideologues for Algerians to 'emancipate themselves from religious influences that impede their free economic development'.[43] In the 1930s, the journal *La Voix indigène*, run by the schoolteacher Rabah Zenati, similarly identified 'Muslim clericalism' as an obstacle to progress which, for the benefit of the 'masses, still too ignorant to discern their own interests', Algerian elites should disavow.[44]

A very few Algerians, perhaps a few thousand by 1920, did so, through conversion to Christianity. For many such Christians, especially in Kabylia where the Society of Missionaries of Africa ('White Fathers' and 'White Sisters', the order founded by Cardinal Lavigerie, Archbishop of Algiers, in 1868) was most active, however, their baptism was a 'conversion out of misery'. Most early converts were the most marginal people in a desperately poor society – widows, orphans, ill or handicapped children – and if later baptisms were sometimes the result of families' strategies of social promotion through the excellent schooling the missionaries provided, more were the result of gratitude for medical care or charity. If, as was often the case, missionary schooling led to exceptional social promotion and mobility (usually meaning migration to Tunis or to France), most converts nonetheless remained both strongly attached to their Kabyle (and Muslim) culture and, however professionally successful, 'condemned to "social suicide" in Algeria'. Conversion often – though not always, and by no means directly – led on to 'naturalisation', but rarely to acceptance. As Fadhma Amrouche, an illegitimate child educated by White Sisters who herself safeguarded an important part of Algeria's cultural patrimony by passing on a great store of Kabyle folk poetry to her son, the writer Jean el-Mouhoub, and her daughter, the singer Taos Amrouche, wrote of her family's experience in Kabylia in the 1950s: 'For the Kabyles, we were *roumi*s, renegades; for the army, we were *bicots* ("niggers") like the rest.'[45]

Conversion was – and converts were – always very marginal, held in suspicion as much by colonial administrators as by their Muslim neighbours, and few among the francophone 'intelligentsia' shared the anti-clerical views of Omar Bouderba or Rabah Zenati. One of the early reformist newspapers, *El-Hack (Le jeune égyptien)*, published in Oran by Nedromi notables, and which organised Ben Rahal's delegation to Paris, expressed its suspicion of the coat-and-fez-wearing *naturalisés*, and instead emphasised the defence of Muslim 'personal status', the last bastion of Islamic law, as the kernel of community cohesion. Some *naturalisés*, like Chérif Benhabylès, did not consider themselves to have abjured Islam – whatever their 'ignorant' compatriots might think – in removing themselves from the jurisdiction of what in any case was a colonial codification of a mere remnant of the *shariʿa*. Ahmad Bouderba, a *naturalisé* who, as he told Ferry, nonetheless fasted during Ramadan, also pleaded before the Ferry commission for access to equal citizenship without loss of Muslim personal status:

We reconcile the Muslim religion and our status as French citizens [...] Most *indigènes* do not want naturalisation, because they see in this an abandonment of the Muslim religion. In our view, we could remove such scruples by facilitating access [to citizenship]. It would be enough to leave personal status untouched: there is no economic reason why an *indigène* may not marry in his own way, according to his law.[45]

This position – citizenship *dans le statut*, without change of personal status – would be the central plank in reformist politics for decades to come. Certainly, like anxious social elites elsewhere, such reformists stopped short of advocating immediate, full citizenship and the franchise for all, fearing that the poor, uneducated and impressionable 'masses' would be bought, cajoled or bullied into voting for other people's vested interests rather than for the common good. Again, it was the extension of education, and the linking of political rights and social advancement to educational achievement, that was crucial. And, for the settler press and their representatives the mayors and *Délégués financiers*, it was equally crucial to oppose such 'useless' education, which, they proclaimed, would only encourage pretension and 'agitation' among the 'natives' while reducing the pool of agricultural labour; they resolutely prevented increased educational provision until they were over-ruled in 1944. They resisted equal citizenship for longer – until, indeed, it no longer meant anything.

The maintenance of the *statut personnel* alongside the extension of schooling and political rights, the desire, after 1905, fully to apply the principle of the separation of the state from the management of religious affairs, the extension of the franchise and the reform or abrogation of the *indigénat*, and, increasingly, the extension of basic freedoms of assembly and expression in Arabic as well as in French thus formed the basis of a gradualist, reformist politics that fez-wearing, French-educated professionals and turbaned or *chechia*-capped Islamic scholars draped in the *burnus* could comfortably share. Above all, they championed education – in French and Arabic, for boys and girls, at all levels – and opposed administrative iniquity, popular ignorance and 'superstition', and the entrenched interests of the *bachaghas, qa'ids* and elected exploiters who were satirised in the character of 'Ali al-Ummi' (Illiterate Ali), the *Délégué financier* and oppressive father in Mahieddine's play *Beni Oui Oui.*

This gradualist, reformist politics greatly expanded in significance after 1919. The 'Jonnart law' of 4 February 1919, named for the liberal Governor General Charles Jonnart, did not grant citizenship *dans le statut* – in fact, it added a list of conditions to be met by applicants for 'naturalisation', and gave the administration a veto in 'undesirable' cases. Algerian women were unable even to apply for citizenship until a new law in 1929 extended existing provisions to them.[47] But it did greatly extend the franchise for Algerians without citizenship, giving the right to vote in municipal council and *jama'a* elections to 425,000 Algerian men, some 43 per cent of the male population over 25 years of age. Electors in *communes de plein exercice* and *jama'a* members in the *communes mixtes* could also vote for a larger number of Algerian *conseillers généraux* and *Délégués financiers*. From 930 seats on municipal councils, Algerians now had 1,540; the proportion of non-citizen councillors was still fixed at a threshold that guaranteed European minority control, but was raised from one-quarter to one-third of the total, and Algerian councillors could now take part in the election of the mayor, from which they had been excluded since 1884. Algerian *conseillers généraux* and *Délégués financiers*, hitherto chosen by only 5,090 electors, would now be selected by 103,149 voters. The posts of administrative agents – from rural constables to *qa'ids* and *bachaghas* – were ruled incompatible with elected office, instituting the possibility of a separation of powers. At the same time, non-citizen Algerians were declared admissible to most public offices.[48]

This was a small reform in some ways – it did not enlarge access to citizenship, did not give Algerians representation in Paris and did not touch the *indigénat*, although significantly it did take members of the new electorate out of its jurisdiction. But it meant the advent of mass politics, of institutionalised electoral politics at the level of the 'official' *jama'a* throughout the countryside, and the emergence of new urban patterns of political mobilisation. By the mid-1920s, it brought the beginning of 'professional' politics, a plural and competitive political field, and a new generation of political actors who built on existing practices of petition and protest, but who used the languages both of the Republic and of the 'Muslim personality' to appeal to a much wider swathe of society than the older notable elites or the pre-war 'Young Algerians' ever had.

The first personality to seize on these opportunities was none other than Abd al-Qadir's grandson, the Emir Khaled. Already briefly involved in Algiers politics in 1913, in support of a 'Young Algerian' candidate for the *Délégation financières*, Khaled had pursued a career in the army, serving in Morocco in 1907–09 and being promoted captain in 1908.[49] He went to the front with a cavalry unit in 1914, but spent most of the war under varying degrees of suspicion (especially after his uncle, Abd al-Malik, began a pro-Ottoman campaign in the Spanish zone of northern Morocco in 1915) and languished behind the lines as a staff officer until he was evacuated, diagnosed with tuberculosis, in 1916. Recovering in Algiers, he hoped to rejoin the army and did so briefly in 1918, but was refused a command. In May, he secretly wrote to Woodrow Wilson, laying out the impoverishment and oppression of Algeria, where 'under a so-called Republican regime, the greater part of the population is ruled by exceptional laws which would make barbarians ashamed', and requesting that freely elected Algerian delegates should present their case before the League of Nations. The President's fourteen points, he maintained, should mean 'the liberation of all small, oppressed peoples, without distinction of race or religion'.[50]

Khaled retired from the army in September 1919. Two months later, his list of candidates won the 'Muslim' (non-citizen) vote at the municipal elections in Algiers in a landslide against Dr Benthami, most of whose candidates were *naturalisés* and who argued for an expansion of 'naturalisation' under the terms of the Jonnart law (with abandonment of Muslim personal status) as the only way to increase Algerian political representation. Most of Khaled's positions – against the *indigénat*, for equality before the law and parliamentary representation, for the expansion of education and public works, against social ills like poverty, alcohol and gambling – were shared with Benthami, with whom, in 1920, he agreed to work again. But his platform, crucially, gave greater prominence to the defence of Muslim community against selective and individual naturalisation which, he argued, far from being a means of gradual emancipation, could only erode the community and sharpen tensions within it. In 1910, Khaled had refused to make the application for citizenship that would have allowed him further promotion in the army, adopting the colonial codification of the *statut personnel* as emblematic of a vital, 'inassimilable' Muslim identity and declaring his attachment to it. Now he adopted the principle of citizenship *dans le statut* in opposition to the *naturalisés*, denouncing the Jonnart reform as an 'illusion' and mobilising popular hostility to *m'turni*s to build a mass constituency for a more assertive style of politics that would demand Republican liberties for all, irrespective of 'race or religion'.

In February 1920, the administration annulled the election results, but Khaled continued to speak at public rallies, to promote his platform in the newspaper *L'Ikdam*, and to mobilise support, and went on to win more elections for municipalities, the *conseil général* and the *Délégations financières* in 1920, 1921 and 1922. Constantly attacked in the press and by the administration, which accused him of 'fermenting Islamic nationalism', he repeatedly resigned his seats in protest at the bureaucracy's flagrant meddling in elections, only to win them again, before in August 1923 he was harassed by the authorities out of Algeria, travelling first to Alexandria and then to Damascus, his birthplace, where he died in January 1936.[51]

Khaled's political 'moment' was brief but intense, and laid the ground for subsequent contests. From the mid-1920s, social movements and political activity accelerated in tandem. The Rif war from 1921 to 1926, the celebrations of colonial Algeria's 'centenary' in 1930, then the global economic crisis, the Popular Front that came to power in the summer of 1936, increasing international and domestic tension from 1938, and the sudden collapse of the Third Republic in 1940 formed a tumultuous backdrop to equally turbulent events in Algeria. In 1924, while keeping a rhetorical distance from the French Communist Party (PCF), Khaled nonetheless spoke in Paris at its invitation to an audience of North African migrant workers, and later that year the communists organised a Maghribi workers' congress in Paris. In July 1925, Abd al-Hamid Ben Badis, emerging as the leader of a group of Islamic scholars and teachers whose concerns combined social improvement and political liberties with Arabic education and the reform (*islah*) and revival, or renewal (*tajdid*), of Islam, published his first periodical, the weekly *Al-Muntaqid* ('The Censor'), in Constantine. It was followed that October by a monthly review, *Al-Shihab* ('The Meteor'), which would run without interruption until 1939. In March 1926, a group of migrant workers and communist deputies meeting in Paris created the *Etoile nord-africaine* ('North African Star') (ENA) association, predominantly grouping Algerians in a movement covertly supported by the PCF. In June, the group held its first formal, public meeting in Belleville. A 28-year-old migrant worker from Tlemcen, Ahmad Mesli, known as Messali Hadj, was elected its Secretary General. In February 1927, Messali went to Brussels as the association's spokesman at the Congress of the Peoples of the East being held there under the auspices of the communist Third International. Also in 1927, with support from the centre-left socialist Governor General Maurice Viollette, the independent elected representatives who had emerged from the new political competition within Algeria created the *Fédération des élus musulmans* ('Federation of Muslim Elected Representatives'), which in 1930 split into three autonomous federations, one in each *département*.

These developments indicated a shift in the political centres of gravity. Where in 1914, the arena of protest and negotiation had been in the small elite circles of Algiers, by 1930 the cafés and factory-floors of Paris, and the municipal theatres and mosques of the Constantinois, were more important, and the audience was Algerian workers, ex-soldiers, *jama'a* members, postmen, shopkeepers, small farmers and office clerks. Women, too, though still few and discreet in public life, attended meetings, sent congratulations to the families of victorious anti-establishment election candidates, and, wherever they could, sent their daughters to independent Arabic-teaching schools. It was especially in the Constantinois that the *Fédération des élus* became a major political force, under the leadership of Dr Mohamed-Salah Bendjelloul, who assumed its leadership in June 1932 and who for a decade was the best-known figure of Algerian politics. Bendjelloul, who had been at medical school in Algiers from 1914 to 1922, and so witnessed Khaled's career, scored an anti-establishment coup by defeating Mustafa Ben Badis, shaykh Abd al-Hamid's father, in the Constantine *conseil général* election of 1931, and in 1934 he also took Ben Badis' seat at the *Délégations financières*.

With his colleague Ferhat Abbas, a pharmacist from Setif who had begun his political career as a student journalist and association leader at university in Algiers, Bendjelloul inherited the reformist vision of the earlier 'Young Algerians', their belief in the emancipatory potential of education, 'civilisation' and entry for Algerians into citizenship *dans le statut*. But the new *élus* saw the generation of Benthami and Bouderba as out of touch with Algerian society, especially in the countryside, and as having directed their efforts – as indeed they had – much more towards the French than towards their own people. And they had no sympathy with parsimonious 'naturalisation' that could only cut the French-educated and upwardly mobile off from their mass constituency. Abbas wrote scathingly of the policy that created 'a "class of naturalisés", thus exacerbating social anarchy and division', and asked rhetorically, 'Do you want to raise this country to a higher level, or do you want to divide and rule?'[52] Following Khaled, their politics both appealed to the idealised Republic, proclaiming their loyalty to the 'true' France of which French Algeria was as yet a very deformed imitation, and identified with the community of culture and social solidarity that colonial law had circumscribed in the *statut personnel*. As Abbas wrote in 1926, 'Islam has remained ... our spiritual homeland (*notre patrie spirituelle*); Muslim personal status is our real country (*notre pays réel*).'[53]

Abbas, unlike the *beldi* patrician Bendjelloul, was from a dispossessed peasant family and had grown up in the lower Kabyle countryside where his father had become an *agha*. He was a scholarship student at the boys' *lycée* in Constantine when the Batna insurrection of 1916 broke out just after his seventeenth birthday, and a 21-year-old completing his military service at Bône during the famine of 1920. One of his first articles, in 1924, was a denunciation of conditions in the countryside. In 1931, in riposte to the centenary celebrations that he found insulting, 'an exhibition of the wealth of some before the poverty of others', Abbas, then completing his pharmacology course in Algiers, published a collection of essays entitled *De la colonie vers la province: Le jeune Algérien*.[54] If he thus took up the 'Young Algerian' ticket, Abbas' vision was not that of a narrow, urban elite; if Algerians' spiritual home was found in Islam, the countryside too was their *pays réel*. Instead of 'creaming off' educated Algerians into the Republic, Abbas wanted France to bring her Republic to the village:

> We glimpse a day ... when, thanks to a better policy, our mountains will be covered by white houses, by metalled roads, by fountains running clear water. The *gourbi* ('native hut') will fall into ruin, never to rise again. In the distant *douars*, in the centre of the village of mud, a stone is laid ... The houses multiply. Here is the school, the municipal *jama'a*, the hospital, the post office, the police station. Here there is hygiene, medical assistance, security ... The Algerian village is created. The plough is forged, the mind is cultivated and disciplined, the hand becomes dexterous. And under the golden sun of Africa, the cult of Labour and Peace enters every heart.[55]

Only seven years after its creation, the Constantine *Fédération des élus* was able to claim the adherence of some two-thirds of elected Algerian office-holders in the *département*; when in July 1937 Bendjelloul called for a mass resignation of *élus* to put pressure on the new government in Paris,[56] between one-third and almost one-half of them followed his appeal. Many of these were members of *jama'as* in the *communes mixtes*; while the leadership of the Federation may have been predominantly urban and French-educated, the social base of its politics was much broader, including shopkeepers, artisans and small farmers and reaching, through its network of affiliated local clubs (*nawadi*, 'circles'), much further into the rural population than ever before. Bendjelloul was a popular icon, celebrated for protesting the living standards of the local peasants at Aïn M'lila in 1937 by throwing a handful of roots and black bread at the feet of a local administrator and his *qa'id*s in front of visiting Parisian parliamentarians. Popular songs extolled him as the *fahl* ('stallion', an approving epithet for a virile leader) and declared, fists raised and to the tune of the communist anthem *L'Internationale*, that 'there's no-one else like Bendjelloul, from here as far as Istanbul'.[57]

The *élus* thus sought to constitute a 'loyal opposition', not only recognising but actively appropriating French sovereignty in Algeria, and articulating their demands on it through a vigorous and sometimes spectacularly populist politics of protest. At the same time, they adopted the cause of Muslim community solidarity as both a symbolic language of mobilisation and as a central part of their agenda. Bendjelloul and his supporters drove to their mass meetings in cars flying green (for Islam) flags, were met by members of their 'Green Youth' (*Jeunesse verte*) youth wing and, at the same time, preceded their speeches by laying wreaths, in a gesture shared with European politicians, at the municipal war memorial.[58] In April 1939, in the largest display of Algerian popular mobilisation yet seen, the Federation's nascent political party, the *Union Populaire Algérienne* (UPA), created by Abbas in 1938, whose symbol was the French Revolution's liberty cap encircled by the crescent, brought out between 170,000 and 200,000 demonstrators in the Oranais and the Constantinois to protest, in solidarity with their fellow-Muslims, against the Italian invasion of Albania.[59]

The politics of the *élus*, then, combined the legalist, gradualist reformism of their 'Young Algerian' forebears, centred on obtaining increasing access to citizenship, with a resolutely new, more open and more vociferous, mass politics oriented towards and in defence of the Algerian Muslim community. After 1920, more united than divided this new generation of 'Young Algerians' and the simultaneously emerging current of modernist Islamic scholars and teachers whose educational itinerary had gone through the Qur'anic school and Tunis, Damascus, Cairo or Medina rather than the *école communale*, the *lycée* and the faculties of the University of Algiers. They would periodically compete, through the late 1930s and 1940s, as to which of them were truly the best-authorised spokesmen for Algerians, and their disputes were occasionally sharp. This was most notably demonstrated in February 1936, just a month after the widely mourned death of the Emir Khaled, when Ferhat Abbas countered attacks against him in the French press by titling an article *Aux marges du nationalisme: La France c'est moi!* ('On the edge of nationalism: I am France!'). Denounced, as Khaled had been, as an anti-French 'nationalist', Abbas disavowed the term:

If I had discovered the 'Algerian nation' (*la patrie algérienne*), I would be a nationalist and I would not blush at that as if it were a crime. Men who have died for the national ideal are daily honoured and respected. My life is not worth more than theirs. But I will not make this sacrifice. The Algerian *patrie* is a myth. I have not found it. I have questioned history, I have questioned the living and the dead, I have visited the cemeteries – no-one has spoken to me of it.

The Islamic and Arab empires which his opponents feigned to see him wishing to revive, he wrote, were things of the past. The future for Algerians was irrevocably tied 'to that of the work of France in this land':

Six million Muslims live in this land which has been French for a hundred years, living in shacks, barefoot, without clothing and without bread. Of this famished multitude, we want to make a modern society through the school, the defence of [the rights of] man, that this society should be French. ... Without the emancipation of the *indigènes*, French Algeria cannot endure. *La France, c'est moi* because I am the multitude, the soldier, the worker, the artisan, the consumer. To refuse my cooperation, my welfare and my contribution to the common effort is a gross heresy.[60]

In reply, two months later Abd al-Hamid Ben Badis' *Al-Shihab* published a 'frank statement' from the *'ulama*:

No, gentlemen! We speak in the name of a great part of the nation (*al-umma*). Indeed, we claim to speak in the name of the majority of the nation ... For our part, we have consulted the pages of history, and we have consulted present circumstances, and we have found the Algerian Muslim nation (*al-umma 'l-jaza'iriyya 'l-muslima*) existing just as the other nations of the world have been formed and exist. This nation has its history, filled with great deeds, it has its religious and linguistic unity, its particular culture, its customs, its moral character ... Furthermore, this Algerian Muslim nation is not France. It cannot become France. It does not want to become France. It could not become France even if it wanted to. On the contrary, this nation is distanced in every respect from France, in its language, its moral character and its religion.[61]

But this famous exchange of views should not mislead. The difference was a matter of emphasis and of competition over authority in the emerging public space of the press, the meeting and the street, not over principles or policy. Abbas had always defended Islam against its colonial detractors; in the 1920s, like many across the Arab world he had identified Ibn Saud, the Wahhabi conqueror of Hijaz, and Mustafa Kemal, the hero of Turkish independence, both of whom he immensely admired, equally as heroes of Islam. The *'ulama*, who supported education in French as well as in Arabic[62] and whose own journals were published in both languages, did not (as yet) contest Abbas's basic assumption that working through a reformed French sovereignty provided the only imaginable way towards the social improvement and emancipation that they

Figure 4.2 The delegation of the Muslim Congress outside the Finance Ministry, Paris, 1936. Shaykh Tayyib al-'Uqbi is seen in profile at the far left of the picture; the two figures also in white on the steps behind him are Bashir Ibrahimi (second from left) and Abd al-Hamid Ben Badis (third from left). Second and third from right in the front row, in suits and tarbushes, holding gloves, are Ferhat Abbas and Mohamed-Salah Bendjelloul (Getty/AFP).

all sought. Abbas insisted that 'there is nothing in our Holy Book to prevent a Muslim Algerian from being "nationally" French ..., "loyal at heart", conscious of national solidarity; nothing prevents this except colonisation itself'; Ben Badis, a year after the exchange over *La France c'est moi*, elaborated on the distinction between an 'ethnic nationality' (*jinsiyya qawmiyya*), which was historically deep, defined by language and religion, and 'political nationality' (*jinsiyya siyasiyya*), which changed with the tide of events, in much the same terms as those of the Muslim *pays réel* and the Republican *pays légal* that Abbas had adapted from French Catholic nationalism.[63]

The same people, in clubs, societies and local associations across the country, especially in eastern Algeria, were often supporters both of the *élus* and of the *'ulama*; in the small circles of Constantine and its provincial towns, *élus* and *'ulama* knew each other well and worked together frequently. They could not always read the press in both languages, but between them, the same social circles certainly read and discussed news and comment both in Arabic and in French. While Abbas' text spoke ostensibly to his French detractors, and *Al-Shihab*'s to the *élus* who, it claimed, mistook their own speech for that of 'the nation', both articles addressed themselves to this same broader public. Abbas and the *'ulama* certainly differed, at least implicitly, as to the relative importance, and desirability, of Republican liberties and Islamic law in making Algeria's future, and as to where, in that future, social, moral and political authority should lie, how society might be governed and what shape it should take. But on the more pressing, immediate concerns of the improvement and emancipation – from ignorance, impoverishment and the *indigénat* – of their community, defined by its being Muslim, they were agreed.

But if the *élus* hoped to gain the rights to which Algerians could supposedly aspire as 'French', it was the *'ulama* who had the means to define what it meant for them to be Muslim. Already in 1887, Abd al-Hamid's grandfather Si al-Mekki had been among the organisers of opposition in Constantine to a proposal, floated by two radical left Parisian deputies, for the collective naturalisation of all Algerians (a proposal that was also, of course, attacked by the settler lobby and buried without further ado in parliament). One thousand seven hundred Constantine notables put their names to a petition opposing 'naturalisation' as implying 'the complete suppression of our law', although the proposed bill was undecided as to whether the *statut personnel* must be abandoned or should be maintained.[64] By the 1930s the politics of reform had come to centre on the question of extending the rights as well as accepting the duties of Algerians' French nationality while rallying the community around its Muslim 'personality'. The significance of that 'personality' itself, however, was also undergoing profound changes.

For colonial lawyers, the Muslim *statut personnel* was simply a means of 'preserving' the jurisdiction of Islamic family law, dispensed by a subordinate branch of the judiciary according to a colonial codification of Maliki jurisprudence, in matters of marriage, inheritance and divorce.[65] But as we have seen, by defining the legal space of Algerians' exclusion from citizenship and their subjection to the repressive apparatus of colonial rule, it also came to define Algerians as a political community. The limits of community belonging, in the face of the settlers and the administration, were vigilantly policed by public opinion; individual 'naturalisation', irrespective of the individual's beliefs or propriety of practice in fasting, prayer, or almsgiving, was taken as renunciation of the community. It was in this sense that *m'turni*s were seen as apostates, as having betrayed 'their people' by removing themselves from the jurisdiction of the law that God had laid down for them. As in Tunisia at the same time, in the 1920s and 1930s *naturalisés* were refused burial in Muslim cemeteries. The son of a *naturalisé* could receive proper burial, ruled Ben Badis, only if he disavowed before death the act that had made his father a citizen.[66] Defence of the 'Muslim personality', ironically centred on the colonial codification of 'personal status' more than on any other aspect of Islamic practice or belief, came to mean defence of all that defined Algerian religion, culture, language and history – and history, language, culture and religion thus became battlegrounds.

The context of these struggles over the meanings of Arab-ness and Islam, of course, was much wider than Algeria. Across the Muslim world, from the 1880s into the 1940s, new forms of education, communication, sociability and politics amplified new ideas about Arab history and the Arabic language, and about the meaning, the proper practice and the future of Islam. Movements of revival or reform drew on long-established Islamic idioms of periodic religious renewal but also on new European ideas of evolution, civilisation, decadence and decline. In turn-of-the-century Algiers, the scholars Abu 'l-Qasim al-Hafnawi, M'hand Said Ibnou Zekri and Muhammad Bencheneb had already experimented with reformist ideas about Islamic education and practice, as had the Tlemceni shaykh Abd al-Qadir al-Majjawi in Constantine in the 1870s, before the visit to Algiers of the famous modernist mufti of Egypt, Muhammad Abduh, in 1903.[67]

By the 1930s, the language of 'reform' (*islah*) and defence of the truly orthodox 'way' (*sunna*) of Islam (or, for Ibadis, defence of their truly orthodox *madhhab*, or school of law) had become more polemical than doctrinal, an idiom of contest 'mobilised by religious actors in competition for leadership'.[68] This contest centred on questions of orthopraxy, rather than of doctrine, in other words on how Islam was 'performed', particularly in public space – streets, schools, cemeteries, mosques – where it could be observed (and criticised by Europeans as 'fanatical' and 'backward') and on control over such spaces and what people did there.[69] At the same time, the reformists sought to bring traditionally private, or familial, religious practices 'out' into public space as expressions of the whole community under their own, properly qualified leadership. Disputes thus focused on the propriety of processions, ritual meetings and wedding parties, on the public recitation of poems in honour of the Prophet or music and dancing during celebrations, on giving lavish private receptions for returning pilgrims or instead marking their return by pious public meetings, and above all on the practice of pious visits (*ziyaras*) to the tombs of ancestors and saintly 'pious ones' (*salihin*) of the past, where intercession with God was sometimes sought. Practices involving cemeteries in particular were widespread, especially in the countryside and among women. Seasonal festivities, sometimes seen by reformists (as by Orientalist scholars) as pre-Islamic survivals of paganism rather than as the properly Muslim 'everyday religion' that their celebrants understood, were equally denounced as illicit *bid'a* ('innovation'). Veneration of the saints (*awliya*) and devotion to the particular rites and founding figures of the great *tariqa*s were now said to be no different to the central heresy of *shirk*, the association of partners with God that denied the cardinal Islamic principle of His irreducible unicity (*tawhid*).

In the 1920s, the broader movement of Islamic revival included leading figures of the Sufi brotherhoods, like shaykh Ahmad Ben Aliwa of Mostaghanem, who created a successful new *tariqa*, the Alawiyya, in 1920 and who, like Abd al-Hamid Ben Badis, took a fierce line on individual naturalisation. But in the 1930s, the self-proclaimed reformists (*muslihin*) increasingly defined themselves against the *tariqa*s, whose leaders largely left the Association of Algerian Muslim *'ulama* (*jam'iyat al-'ulama al-muslimin al-jaza'iriyyin* or *Association des ulama musulmans algériens*, AUMA) that had been set up under the Presidency of Ben Badis in Algiers in 1931 to coordinate the reformist mission. The *tariqa*s would find themselves increasingly stigmatised as proponents not of Islam but of *confrérisme* or *maraboutisme*, judged doubly illicit by virtue of promoting 'heretical' practices that exploited peasant 'superstition' as well as serving to divide the community between alternative centres of religious authority. The AUMA's doctrinal principles, eventually crystallised in 1937, attacked the *tariqa*s as illicit innovations 'that our pious forebears never knew', which promoted 'sectarian partisanship' and led to 'stultification and moral degradation'.[70]

The beginnings of a struggle over religion as a discernibly distinct space of social authority had begun around 1907, when the French law of 1905 on the separation of the state and religious affairs was applied, in truncated form, to Algeria, setting up local and regional 'religious associations' (*cultuelles*) for the management of mosques which, supposedly devolved from the administration, rapidly became foyers of local politics, patronage and competition.[71] After 1931, while working tirelessly, above all, for what it saw as the necessary 'union' of all Muslims in a collective revival of the community and its culture, the AUMA became engaged in an increasingly intense – and divisive – struggle over the authority to define what that culture was, espousing education and modernism and fulminating against 'backwardness' and 'ignorance', by which they meant not merely illiteracy but *jahiliyya*, the ignorance of God that preceded the revelation to the Prophet. These were strongly loaded terms. In some regions, accusations of abiding *jahiliyya* came to 'cover, more or less, the religion and daily life of the peasants' in their entirety, their very means 'of celebrating life and death'.[72]

'Reform' to the *'ulama* thus meant more than the morally and socially improving agenda that they, too, inherited from the pre-1914 reformers and that they shared with the 'Young Algerians': against alcohol, gambling, child marriage and abusive divorce, and in favour of religious and literary revival, education for girls, symbolic dowries to make marriage more affordable. It meant redefining Islam as many Algerian Muslims knew it. The control of the spaces in which Islam as the central code of community life was defined and practised – schools and mosques as well as local community associations, theatrical groups, study circles and clubs (*nawadi*, sing. *nadi*) – thus became a central point of contention. In 1933, attempting to contain the reformists' 'agitation', the administration forbade imams or preachers other than those salaried by the state from speaking in 'official' mosques (i.e. the historic buildings supposedly maintained by the colony's budget since its confiscation of their *habus* endowments, and since 1907 formally managed by the *cultuelles*). Independent, community-funded 'free schools' (*médersas libres*) and mosques independent of the administration and what now became known as its 'official clergy' proliferated. The leading centres of reformist activity, the Progress Club (*Cercle du Progrès, nadi al-taraqqi*) on the Place du Gouvernement in Algiers, the *shabiba islamiyya* and *tarbiyya wa 'l-ta'lim* primary schools in Algiers and Constantine, respectively, the *Dar al-Hadith* madrasa inaugurated in 1937 in Tlemcen, the Ben Badis Institute in Constantine, and the Association of Algerian Students of the Zaytuna, which was officially recognised in 1934, were joined by hundreds of more modest spaces in small towns across the country.

Throughout the 1930s and 1940s, local political battles were played out by the reformists and their political allies for control of *cultuelles* and schools from Bejaia to Batna and Aïn Beida, and in the Mzab, over control of the *halqas* of the Ibadi cities of Guerrara and Berriane (which the reformists won), Ghardaia and Beni Isguen (which they lost).[73] In Paris, in 1936, the *'ulama* established a *nadi al-tahdhib* ('Education Club'), to minister to the emigrant workers who, for want of qualified men of religion, as the *nadi*'s patron and leading Kabyle reformist Fadil al-Wartilani put it, were 'straying further and further from the precepts of the Qur'an'.[74] In addition to the 'missions' of reformist teachers sent to establish schools, clubs and mosques, the message of *islah* found voice in the press. *Al-Shihab* serialised Ben Badis' *tafsir* (Qur'an commentary) and printed essays on social and political questions, literature, religious matters and juridical opinions; the weekly paper *Al-Basa'ir* became the reformists' news-sheet and polemical platform, while *La Défense* and, from

1952, *Le jeune Musulman*, run by the rising generation of reformist-trained students, gave the movement outlets in French. The small but active Mzabi community, which, through its traditional investments in education and commerce and its diaspora networks across northern Algeria, in Tunis and Cairo, was widely represented among both intellectuals and businessmen, played a leading role in printing and publication. Its own reformist journals, *Wadi Mizab* and *Al-Umma*, circulated across the country.[75]

The leading personalities of the AUMA became major public figures, increasingly influential in their communities and obsessively watched by the colonial police: Ben Badis in Constantine, where he benefitted, to a degree, from the protection of his family but also, especially after his father's electoral drubbing by Bendjelloul, was often at odds with them; Tayyib al-'Uqbi, the powerful orator who presided over the *nadi al-tarraqi* in Algiers, and who was falsely implicated, almost certainly by the police, in the murder of the mufti of Algiers, Mahmud Ben Dali 'al-Kahhul', in 1938; Bashir al-Ibrahimi, who moved to Tlemcen in 1933 and taught in a supporter's shop there before assuming the direction of Dar al-Hadith. Other shaykhs became dominant figures in smaller localities: the leading intellectuals, preachers and organisers al-Arabi (Larbi) al-Tebessi and Mubarak al-Mili in their respective eastern home towns of Tebessa and Mila, Muhammad Khayr al-Din in Biskra, Ibrahim Bayyud in the Mzab. Abbas Ben Shaykh al-Husayn (Bencheikh Hocine), who quarrelled with his own saintly family over his adoption of reformist ideas, set up schools and taught in places as far apart as Beni Saf, Bône and Constantine. Others still were active less as scholars and teachers than as professional journalists, writers and publicists, like the Mzabi journalist entrepreneurs Ibrahim Abu 'l-Yaqzan and Abu Ishaq Attfiyash whose careers took them to Algiers, Tunis and Cairo, Lamine Lamoudi, the bilingual editor of *La Défense* who was close to the Communist Party, or the dapper, suit-and-tarbush-wearing *littérateur* Ahmad Tawfiq al-Madani, whose *Kitab al-Jaza'ir*, an encyclopaedia of Algerian history and geography published in 1932, carried on its frontispiece the lapidary formula, 'Islam is our religion, Algeria our homeland (*watanuna*), Arabic our language'. Born for the most part between 1889 and the years around the turn of the century, their educational trajectories almost all involved a period of emigration from Algeria and intense engagement with the intellectual and political ferment of the Mashriq. Within Algeria, between the foundation of their Association in May 1931 and the premature death of Ben Badis in April 1940, as evidenced by the thousands of mourners who filled the streets of Constantine for his funeral and brought the city to a standstill, reformism had gained an immense social and cultural authority – as well as bringing about a 'war of ideas' that animated a vigorous and sometimes violent cultural politics in towns and villages across the country, and that sometimes 'set the members of families against each other'.[76]

For all their vehemence in opposition to 'maraboutism' and *jahiliyya*, nonetheless, the reformist *'ulama* before 1940 generally espoused a cautious political gradualism that, like that of the *élus*, meant working with and through the French colonial regime, in the name of a certain idea of France. The first number of Ben Badis' journal *al-Muntaqid*, in 1925, flagged the loyalist limits to its dissenting posture as clearly as it could:

> We are a people (*qawm*) of Algerian Muslims within the colonial domain of the French Republic ... To safeguard our religious traditions is to safeguard the elements of our peoplehood (*muqawwamat qawmiyyatina*) and the greatest cause of our felicity and wellbeing; for we know that people cannot resolve to live without religion, that religion is a powerful force not to be disdained, and that a government that ignores the religion of the people errs in its policy and brings harm and censure upon itself. Indeed, it may cause disturbances and civil strife ... We love whomever loves our homeland (*watanana*) and serves it, and we hate whomever hates and oppresses it, and we shall strive our utmost in the service of our Algerian homeland ... As colonial subjects of the French Republic, we shall strive to tie bonds of friendship between ourselves and the French nation, and to improve the links between our two nations, tied by common interests on both sides ... The Algerian nation (*umma*) is a weak and backward nation, and recognises that it needs, to sustain its life, to be under the wing of a strong, just, and civilised nation to lead it up to civility and civilisation.[77]

The administration closed *al-Muntaqid* down anyway after four months and eighteen editions. But at least until 1937, Ben Badis continued to declare in public (whatever he might have thought in private) that despite France's 'many promises, none of them kept', Algerians should 'prove to France that if, during the war, you arose as one to defend her, you are equally able in time of peace to arise as one against those egoists [i.e. the settler lobby] who are just as dangerous for France as her enemies are'.[78] Tayyib al-'Uqbi, whose relations with the AUMA soured after he was framed for the Kahhul murder, complained about the Association's increasing politicisation and, while he maintained cordial relations with some leading AUMA figures, publicly broke with the group and into the 1950s carried on his own, independent reformist mission in Algiers, through his newspaper *al-Islah*, teaching and patronage of a benevolent society.

But, beginning in 1933 when 'official' mosques were closed to them, and more markedly in 1938 when the administration began to prosecute teachers at unlicensed independent schools, the reformists were pushed towards confrontation. In April 1940, Bashir al-Ibrahimi, soon to be Ben Badis' successor as President of the Association of *'ulama*, was arrested and placed in internal exile in the small town of Aflou, 1,400 metres up in the Saharan Atlas north of Aïn Madhi, having refused to make a radio broadcast endorsing the French war effort. Under his leadership, and that of his Vice-President Larbi Tebessi, from the 1940s the *'ulama* sought to position themselves above rival political movements as those who 'alone are qualified to guide the people', as Tebessi put it in 1944.[79] By then, though, the political landscape had changed, and reformism, in religion or in politics, was no longer at the leading edge of the competing tendencies that were, rapidly but by no means straightforwardly, resolving themselves into an Algerian nationalist movement.

## Revolutionary Populism and the Illusion of Reform

What the *élus* and the *'ulama* shared above all in their struggle to improve and emancipate their community – and what they had in common, despite their other differences, with the earlier *jeunes Algériens* – was a belief in their own necessarily leading role as the community's elite, as properly qualified by education and standing to speak for it, to envisage and to shape its future. And this above all, despite other things that they shared – a deep loyalty to the community defined by its 'Muslim personality' and a political culture heavily coloured by the French Republic – was what divided *élus* and *'ulama* from the militants of the movement that by the mid-1940s would become Algeria's most popular and most radical political force. The radical, populist nationalism that became embodied in the Algerian People's Party (*Hizb al-sha'b al-jaza'iri, Parti du peuple algérien*, PPA), which in March 1937 succeeded the banned *Étoile nord-africaine*,[80] and in its iconic leader, Messali Hadj, was influenced by, but quite distinct from, the political visions of the *élus* and the *'ulama*, and saw itself as such. The labour migrants, dockers and railway workers, emerging small businessmen and shopkeepers on the fringes of interior towns, who increasingly obtained just enough formal education to obtain the *certificat d'études* (primary school certificate) but who would rarely become schoolteachers, doctors, or pharmacists, preachers or commentators on the Qur'an, themselves produced their own political leadership. By 1940, PPA militants were the main rivals, emerging 'from below', to the leadership of those who saw themselves as guiding the people from above. And their political vision was not one of gradual, legalist reform, but of social and political revolution. While they too moved into the spaces – the streets, the press, the elections, the public meetings and demonstrations, the combative partisan ambiance – of the French

Republic, they never sought its citizenship. Instead, their view of the French Republic, both idealised and suitably modified, was as a model for their own, Algerian one.

Messali was a near-contemporary of Abbas and Ben Badis; born in 1898, he was seven years younger than the latter, 17 months older than the former. But his itinerary was quite different. Mobilised in 1918, he was in training at Bordeaux at the armistice and was promoted sergeant in 1919. Messali would later recall that he had been more concerned at the fate of Turkey than rejoicing in victory at the end of the war, more inspired by the strikes of railway workers and by the left-wing anti-colonialism of French communists like the deputy Paul Vaillant-Couturier, who visited Tlemcen in 1922, than by the electoral campaigns of the Emir Khaled during the shortages and famine of 1919 and 1920. One evening in the winter of 1920, when Tlemcen was full of news about the Turkish war of independence, during a concert by Larbi Ben Sari's orchestra in which 'almost every song asked for by the audience alluded to the Greco-Turkish war', Messali made his first political statement by standing on a table and shouting 'Long live Mustafa Kemal Pasha!'[81] The gesture was characteristic of a man whom rivals would consider a 'turbulent demagogue', and whom even other leading members of the PPA would find alarmingly 'given to spontaneous, sometimes crude, emotional ... improvisation ..., lacking modesty and any political sense of the situation'.[82] It was also emblematic of the beginnings of a more assertive, vocal and physical politics of the occupation of public space.

Aged 25, in October 1923 Messali went to find work in Paris. There he sold bonnets and Tlemceni handicrafts door to door, and met and married his French wife, Emilie Busquant, a worker revolutionary's daughter three years his junior, with whom he would have two children and who would stand by him throughout his later life of militancy, imprisonment and exile. (In 1946, Abbas, too, would marry a Frenchwoman, Marcelle Stoetzel, the widow of a doctor and daughter of a family of Alsaciens who had emigrated to Algeria at the turn of the century.) Messali was in Paris when the first meetings of Maghribi workers there were organised by the communist *Union Intercoloniale*, calling for the independence of all colonies, and as heated debates took place over the Rif war and the revolt in Syria. His friend Abdelkader Hadj Ali, a member of the PCF's colonial commission, recruited him to the party in 1925. In Brussels in 1927, Messali outlined the ENA's immediate demands – abolition of the *indigénat* and amnesty for all those convicted under it; freedom of movement, the press, association and assembly, and to form trades unions; education for all, at all levels, in Arabic as well as in French; the application of labour and social welfare legislation to Algeria; and representation for all in municipal councils and in an Algerian parliament to be elected by universal suffrage. The tone was clearly different to anything being openly demanded in Algeria, but the longer-term political program was even more direct: it called explicitly for the total independence of Algeria, the evacuation of occupying troops, the constitution of a national army, the confiscation of large estates and their redistribution to the peasantry. The more detailed political program adopted by the ENA in Paris in May 1933 added more thoroughgoing short-term demands – suppression of the *communes mixtes* and of military rule in the Sahara, compulsory education in Arabic, open and equal access to all public posts for all – and spelled out its vision of a 'revolutionary national government' which would take control of land, forests, banks, railways, mines and public services; confiscate and redistribute large agricultural properties; recognise the right to strike and immediately implement a program of economic assistance to the peasantry.[83]

Despite its significance as a 'founding moment', it was perhaps less the headline demand for independence that was novel in Messali's Brussels speech – this had been called for before, most recently by an 'Algerian-Tunisian committee' of Ottoman-allied propagandists, some of them of Algerian descent, meeting in Lausanne in 1919, and Messali's short speech in Brussels had, at the time, hardly more impact than their declarations.[84] More significant was the content given to independence, the program for a revolutionary and redistributive state in the service of the people that was a commonplace image in the workers' cafés of Paris and of a piece with the anti-imperialist line of the Third International, but utterly different to anything then being envisaged in the towns and villages of Algeria. The social base and political culture, and the political geography, too, of this new, revolutionary populism were quite different to those of the *élus* or the *'ulama*. Emerging in the radical atmosphere of the CGTU and the PCF shortly after the split within the French labour movement that had given birth to rival Socialist (SFIO) and Communist parties, the movement of which Messali became the spokesman was just as influenced by the French political landscape as Bendjelloul and Abbas were. But it was soldered together not by the ideals of the Republican school but by the basic mutual assistance and self-help spirit of poor migrant labourers, small shopkeepers and industrial factory-hands. It found a revivalist force in religion, but was permeated by a popular Islam of moral conduct and community belonging shaped more by the intimate fraternity of the rural or small-town *zawiya* than by the austere moralism of *islah* (although that, in due course, would play a role too). Messali would later admit that, even while a member of the Communist Party, he did not 'always really understand what its ideology was'.[85] But for proletarised peasants whose families had been dispossessed by the colonists' *grands domaines*, the restitution of the alienated products of their labour by means of a revolutionary seizure of the means of production made sense enough without their needing to develop a 'class consciousness'. In October 1930, Messali wrote in the first edition of the ENA's journal, *El Ouma*, that 'Our brothers must organise themselves to seize by force their social rights and shake off the yoke of slavery'. From a nucleus of communist militants, the association had grown by 1929 to number perhaps 4,000 members.[86]

Still, the ENA was a movement of, albeit temporary, exiles, and it would take a decade after its founding to begin to spread within Algeria itself. Other Algerians found the means of political expression more directly within the turbulent politics of the late Third Republic: the French socialist and communist parties provided platforms for reformist or social-revolutionary anti-colonialism shared with Europeans, and reformist *'ulama* in particular often found both physical and political common ground with Europeans in the programs and the social spaces of the SFIO and the PCF. Secularist schoolteachers, too, were sometimes affiliated to the *Ligue des droits de l'homme*, and to the freemasons' lodges that were such a powerful network of contacts and influence within the French political establishment in Algeria as in the metropole.[87] All the European parties, from the PCF to the far-right 'Leagues', thought they could harness the 'mass' of *indigènes* in a merely passive role to support their competitive occupation of the street and of symbolic politics, from the right-wing European mayors who tried to enforce participation in *Rassemblement national* parades with fascist salutes, to the Algerian socialist who told his compatriots that they should have confidence in the government and be good 'passive citizens'.

But this was to underestimate Algerians' capacity to seize on the forms and spaces of the Republic's politics for their own use.[88] The tone and the workings of Messali's own political movement were clearly influenced by his own, albeit brief, immersion in the PCF. Ferhat Abbas's short-lived 'mass' party the UPA, whose slogan was to be 'by the people and for the people',[89] cannot be understood without the prior experience of party politics that some, at least, of its founders had gained in the SFIO. In October 1936, the Algerian region of the PCF was re-founded as the Algerian Communist Party. By then, the party claimed several thousand members, and undertook an active campaign to 'Arabise' its militant base, printing bilingual tracts that declared the communists to be 'the worthy successors of the Algerian national heroes Abd al-Qadir, Muqrani, and Khaled'. In 1937, there was an Algerian *nadi* called the 'Emir Khaled Club' run by PCA militants in the Lamur suburb of Oran.[90]

Figure 4.3 Algerian and European comrades side by side: CGT demonstration in support of the Popular Front, Saint-Denis-du-Sig, 1936 (FR ANOM 92 5I 151).

Up to the 1950s, the PCA would provide a major forum in which ordinary European and Algerian militants could work side by side with a common political aim.

By the time the ENA was reconstituted after its first dissolution by the authorities in May 1933, relations with the PCF had deteriorated, but its members nonetheless participated in the general strike and anti-fascist demonstrations called in Paris on 12 February 1934 by the socialist and communist trade unions in opposition to the right-wing nationalist riots of 6 February. On 14 July, Bastille Day, 1936, thousands of Maghribi workers joined the popular march in Paris behind the ENA's flag, and across Algeria, thousands of Algerians took to the streets, in some places outnumbering European participants.[91] Addressing international opinion fifteen years later, Messali would emphasise, as evidence of Algerian nationalism's democratic credentials, how the ENA had 'joined the ranks of the democrats to lead the struggle alongside the people of Paris [...] against the first demonstrations of fascism'.[92] The mid-1930s saw the high point of alliance-building both between Algerian movements and between them and the French left. The anti-fascist Popular Front, supported by mass mobilisation of Algerians alongside French socialists, communists and trade-unionists, raised expectations on coming to power in April–May 1936 that reform through legal means might at last come about.

To press for such reform, the communists, *élus* and *'ulama* united in an Algerian Muslim Congress, which met in Algiers in June and sent a delegation to Paris at the end of July, to present a program of reforms to the government of Léon Blum and his Minister of State, the anti-com-munist and liberal colonialist former Governor General Maurice Viollette. Viollette, who had been forced out of Algeria in 1927 by the colonial lobby that labelled him *Viollette L'Arbi*, 'Viollette the Arab', for his reformist views, had subsequently written a manifesto for change in the colony, *L'Algérie vivra-t-elle?*, adopting the views of the earlier Young Algerians – selective citizenship for Algerian *évolués* – as the only means of safeguarding the future of France's African empire.[93]

When Viollette's proposals were presented as a draft law, in what would become known as the Blum-Viollette bill, in December 1936, they alarmed legal opinion in France and panicked Algeria's Europeans, who mobilised at once to bury the project, but in fact they were already well behind the times. The proposal was merely an updated version of the Jonnart reforms, in that it proposed to extend the franchise to adult male Algerians meeting a new list of qualifications, on the same terms as for French citizens and without renunciation of the *statut personnel*, in parlia-mentary as well as municipal and regional elections. To the usual cate-gories of 'notables' (*qa'id*s, *bachagha*s, holders of the *Légion d'honneur*) were added some larger groups, including all those with secondary edu-cation, all decorated ex-soldiers, and all holders of elected office, which since 1919 included presidents of *jama'a*s and the expanded numbers of Algerian municipal councillors. All in all, at the next legislative elections scheduled for 1940, an additional 30,546 Algerians (in a population of 5.5 million) were expected to be entitled to vote.

The Congress platform had already gone considerably further. The 'Charter of demands of the Muslim Algerian People' agreed by the Congress's committee on 7 June 1936 included particular demands of the *'ulama* for the full application of the separation of the state from religious affairs, restitution to the Muslim community of all religious buildings and *habus* revenues, and freedom of expression and education in Arabic, as well as the suppression of the *indigénat* and implementation of a raft of social development measures including a single education system open to all, expanded healthcare and unemployment assistance. It also called for the suppression of all Algeria's existing political institu-tions – the *communes mixtes, Délégations financières* and Government

General – and the 'pure and simple attachment (*rattachement*)', instead, of Algeria's institutions to those of metropolitan France, with amnesty for all political prisoners, parliamentary representation and universal suffrage in a single electoral college with the maintenance of Algerians' Muslim personal status.[94] The Congress thus envisaged nothing less than the complete institutional integration of Algeria and all its inhabitants within the Republican *cité*. Meeting again in a 'second Congress', in July 1937, to keep the movement alive, its proponents insisted that implementation of the Charter was an 'indispensable minimum'.[95]

Blum-Viollette was a long way from this. Nonetheless, the bill held out a real possibility of rebalancing Algeria's parliamentary representation, and in particular its municipal politics, where the European mayors had long held a stranglehold over local life and local budgets. It thus threatened to break the grip that the settlers had fought so long to gain and maintain over their France in Algeria. To the *élus*, socialists and communists this seemed to be the beginning of a move in the right direction, providing greater access to power-sharing *dans le statut* and enfranchising enough new voters to counterbalance the swing of settler politics to the right. (In 1936, the *Parti social français*, the openly fascist *Parti populaire français*, and the *Croix de feu* as well as the communists had all gained ground among Algeria's Europeans over the previously dominant radical socialists.[96]) The *'ulama* could see in the bill the beginnings of a policy that would recognise Algerians' right to the autonomous management of their religious, cultural and educational affairs. On the return of part of the Congress delegation to Algiers, Tayyib al-'Uqbi told the crowd of 3,000 people that had gathered on the Place du Gouvernement to meet the delegates that they would soon 'be treated on an equal footing with their French brothers of the metropole', since all, 'without distinction, are sons of the same *patrie* which is France'.[97] To this end, Blum-Viollette seemed worth supporting.

The ENA, on the other hand, rejected the proposals outright. In June 1936, with Messali just returned from Geneva where had met the pan-Islamic activist and nationalist Shakib Arslan, and a month before the arrival of the Congress delegation in Paris, the ENA submitted its own, toned-down 'Register of demands' to the Ministry of the Interior, focused on equality of social rights and freedoms for Algerian workers in France. But at the same time, Messali reiterated in *El-Ouma* the demand for a freely elected Algerian parliament, declaring that only by such a measure 'will we be able to say that justice has been done ... that the democratic France of [17]89, of [18]48, will have achieved a civilising work, by emancipating the Algerian people from exploitation ... '[98] While 'the democratic France of '89' was still looked to by others, Messali roundly condemned the Congress' vision of Algerian emancipation through parliamentary representation in Paris.

On 2 August 1936, the Congress organised a mass meeting at the Algiers municipal stadium to report on their Charter and its reception in Paris. They had every reason to be sure of their welcome: thousands had turned out early in the morning only days before to see them arrive. But Messali, unscheduled to speak but allowed three minutes 'as a courtesy' to greet the audience as a representative of the emigrant community in France, upstaged the Congress in a dramatic denunciation of its policy, which *El Ouma* triumphantly took up in the following weeks:

Indeed, we approve the immediate demands of the Charter . . ., which are modest and legitimate . . . But we say categorically, . . . that we disapprove of the [demands for the] attachment of our country to France and parliamentary representation . . . We are for the suppression of the *Délégation financière* and the Government General, and for the creation of an Algerian parliament, elected by universal suffrage without distinction of race or religion. This Algerian national parliament, once established, will work under the direct control of the people and for the people. We believe, for our part, that this is the only way for the Algerian people to express itself freely and frankly, safe from all oppression . . .[99]

Messali's speech was cheered uproariously; he himself was taken from the stage on the shoulders of his supporters. He would later remember this as 'one of the most beautiful days of my life', and considered that it 'marked the beginning of Algerian nationalism and the first stirrings of national consciousness'.[100] It certainly marked the beginning of the implantation of the ENA in Algeria as a mass movement, and as the key competitor to the other movements that sought to articulate Algerians' political aspirations.

In March 1937, two months after the ENA was dissolved a second time, it was succeeded by the PPA, whose statutes as a political party were registered at the Prefecture of the Seine in April. Quickly spreading in Algeria following Messali's Algiers speech and his subsequent three-month propaganda tour, by December 1936 the ENA had some twenty local sections in Algeria, almost as many as in France. By 1939, there were thirty-eight sections with a total of some 2,500 members in Algeria, according to the police (whose estimates may be well below the real figure), in addition to the 1,500 militants in France.[101] On 14 July 1937, the party was able to show its strength with a massive, separate cortège of perhaps 25,000 Algerians in the Algiers Bastille Day parade. Marching at the end of the demonstration, behind a green flag and to slogans of 'Freedom for all', 'The land to the peasants', 'Respect for Islam' and 'An Algerian Parliament', the PPA virtually occupied the

Place du Gouvernement, the end point of the march, to the alarm of the settler press.[102]

On 20 November that year, in response to the repression that had begun to strike the movement – Messali and four other PPA leaders were arrested for threatening the security of the state in August – a one-hour strike was organised. Closing down the Algiers waterfront and the Casbah, the strike was at least partially observed as far away as Dellys and Constantine. In October, the party had cannily put up all its imprisoned leaders as candidates in the *conseil général* elections, winning at least a few votes everywhere but spectacularly coming first in Algiers, where Messali stood *in absentia*. In the re-run Algiers *conseil général* elections of April 1939, the PPA candidate Muhammad Douar, an Algiers tramway worker who (having a uniform and a salary) was a very respectable member of the urban working class but hitherto a political unknown, saw off PCA, Congress and UPA candidates and won by a clear margin in the second round, demonstrating the party's potential to take on all the other Algerian parties and 'administration' candidates and win.[103] Around the same time, the funeral of Arezki Kehal, the PPA's interim president after Messali's arrest, who died in prison in April 1939 and thus became the party's first 'martyr', was observed by a crowd that, *El Ouma* claimed, numbered 15,000.[104]

By the time Messali was convicted of threatening the integrity of national territory by a Vichy military tribunal in March 1941, his image as *za'im*, the charismatic popular leader, and martyr to his people's cause embodied in the movement he led, was well established. He was sentenced to sixteen years' hard labour and twenty years' proscription from residing in Algeria, and sent to the notorious penitentiary of Lambèse (Tazoult) on the northern edge on the Aurès, where he would spend the next two years in atrocious conditions. His imprisonment, and that of his co-defendants, enhanced his prestige. On 11 May 1941, the feast day of Joan of Arc, PPA militants in Algiers covered the walls of the Casbah and Bab el-Oued with the slogans 'Long live the PPA', 'Free Messali' and 'Algeria for the Algerians'.[105]

From 1937 to 1939, despite the repression that began to fall on the movement, an important nuance had entered the PPA's tone: the party declared itself for 'the total emancipation of Algeria, without thereby separating ourselves from France', specifying that this meant full internal autonomy on a British 'dominion' model, with a sovereign Algerian parliament expressing majority rule, which would be 'freely integrated into the French system of collective security in the Mediterranean'. 'I am anti-imperialist, not anti-French', Messali explained; he repeated this position at his trial.[106] After 1938, when Blum-Viollette was shelved

Figure 4.4  Messali Hadj in exile at Belle-Isle-en-Mer, 1956 (P. Jamet).

without having been debated in Paris, some of the *élus* were moving towards this position too – a multi-confessional, sovereign and democratic Algeria with equal rights for all, under a reformed French aegis. The PPA's new paper in May 1939 was entitled *Le Parlement algérien*; in 1946 Ferhat Abbas would launch *La République algérienne*. Up to 1940 then the PPA too, its long-term revolutionary vision notwithstanding, framed its immediate agenda as well as acting out its politics through the symbolic and institutional spaces of French public life.

But the PPA, with its radical, grassroots political culture of open confrontation, its symbolic politics of mass mobilisation – the crowds of young men in the street who marched to nationalist anthems, index finger raised aloft in a sign of Muslim solidarity – also reflected something else about what that public life had by now become. It could not avoid becoming a part of the increasingly febrile, 'communitarian' politics taking shape within the deeply divided and violent public sphere of the late Third Republic. Communists and socialists identified the PPA with the French right, especially with Jacques Doriot's fascist *Parti populaire français* (PPF),[107] and saw it as objectively aligned with the interests of the Federation of Mayors (which was also vitriolic about Blum-Viollette) and their landowner masters. Such perceptions would last beyond 1945. Lamine Lamoudi and other *'ulama* as well as Bendjelloul, speaking for the Congress, criticised the PPA's irresponsibility, its 'pseudo-nationalism' and its extremism that would allow the French, by labelling all 'nationalists' alike, to throw out their carefully crafted politics of negotiation and 'legitimate demands'. In reply, the PPA was not above accusing the Congress of being in thrall to atheistic Stalinism, and the PCA of being 'judeo-communists'. Far from 'converging' in these years into a single 'national movement', Algerian politics was riven by fractious rivalries and prone, as the Republic was, to violence in the streets. The administration, too, was beginning more frequently to exercise violence against its own legal processes: the victory of the *traminot* Douar was annulled on a pretext by the Algiers Prefecture, the friendly *notable* Mahieddine Zerrouk declared elected in his place. Douar lodged a legal appeal. On 8 June 1940 he was stripped of his mandate by decree and sent to a 'special native disciplinary section' of the army at Reggane, deep in the Sahara, the hardship of whose punitive regime eventually killed him.[108]

In 1939, the PCF's leader Maurice Thorez made a much-discussed speech in Algiers in which he declared, in keeping with the party line that now favoured anti-fascist union over anti-colonial nationalism, that Algeria was a 'nation in formation', an emerging political community that would eventually unite Arab, Berber and European in a 'new race', but which had not yet reached 'maturity'. Thorez was politically wrong: there was no possible single political future for Algerians in equality alongside Algeria's Europeans, because despite individual exceptions, especially among communists, liberals, left-wing Jews, Protestants and social Catholics, Algeria's European society as a whole was constitutionally incapable of accepting it. Despite individually personable relations, as a whole they feared and despised Algerians, and could not conceive of an Algeria under a reformed French sovereignty that would open France's democracy to Algerians while also guaranteeing their own future. Most spokesmen for Algerians, in these years, on the other hand, believed such a future to be the only possible solution to their predicament. They were not wrong: the only alternative would be bloody civil war, which all political tendencies in these years feared, and to which they all pointed as a threat they sought to avoid.

But, in a way he did not suspect, Thorez was historically correct. An Algerian nation was indeed being imagined and practised into being by the politics that were transforming the Algerian Muslim community from a community of culture, excluded by that criterion from political rights, trapped in the expectation of an 'evolution' that the colonial situation itself rendered impossible, into a political community in its own right, seeing itself as already existing in its own history, language and religion, and as having a right to self-determination as such. It was not that colonialism was unable to break Algerian social solidarity by 'assimilating' Algerians into itself – within the logic of the colonial system, there was never any such possibility, and nor did colonial 'policy', such as it was, have any intention of doing so, except in an imagined distant future which the system itself made unrealisable. Instead, the system had made the key symbol of Algerian social solidarity, the *statut personnel*, the organising principle of the subjection of Algerians en bloc. And Algerians had rallied around that symbol, re-appropriated it and invested it with new and powerful meaning to give dignity and self-direction back to their people. At the same time, they sought a peaceful, negotiated resolution of the colonial situation by working within what they still hoped were the possibilities of a 'truer' France. Even the PPA, at its most practical, envisaged a re-negotiation of Algeria's relationship with France rather than outright separatism.

But rather than the 'lost opportunity' that historians would later see as having been embodied in the hopelessly inadequate Blum-Viollette pro-posals, the promise of reform proved to be an illusion.[109] It was an illusion that much of Algerian opinion would nonetheless bravely cling to, but whose realisation, in the terms of the idealised Republic of liberty, frater-nity and democracy for all, irrespective of race or religion, was stymied by the hard realities of the actually existing Republic: the settlers' Republic of tacitly racialised citizenship and a regime of property and prosperity reliant on minority rule; the metropolitan Republic that was not in fact what its best-schooled students believed it to be.[110] Reform in these years that would resolve the colonial situation was not a missed opportunity but a structural impossibility. Little wonder that Mahieddine Bachetarzi, one of whose star turns had been to render the *Marseillaise* into Arabic, sang to his compatriots in 1937 that *Ma a'rifnash 'ash min trig na'khudhu*, 'We know not what road to take':

We know not what road to take/Should we part company or shall we still wait?
   Or rest our hope in God, the One/May he provide us solace.
   For one hundred years they have taken care/That the Arab should be an ass, that we should not understand,

And now the time comes that we desire understanding/They by force would keep us in blindness.

If you tell him 'I love you', he says it's a lie/If you reason he treats you as stupid.

We have become, O people, on this earth/As strangers, within our own country . . .

For more than a year have we waited, expectantly/Our enemies still say 'Wait: Or by God, you will bend, you will fall into line/All will be under our boot!' [111]

The song was banned. In the summer of 1940 the Republic collapsed, and the Vichy boot came down hard on Algerian Jews and on Algerian Muslim nationalists. There would be only one road to take.

The end of the war in Europe in May 1945 brought little relief to Algeria. On Labour Day, 1 May, Algerian nationalist militants organised peaceful marches in their own, separate cortèges behind those of the communist and trade union movements to participate, as they had before the war, in demonstrations of anti-fascist unity. Across the country, demonstrations passed mostly without incident, but Messali Hadj, who had briefly been freed two years before, had been deported to Brazzaville in the Congo on 23 April, and PPA supporters marched under Algerian flags to slogans of 'Free Messali, free all political prisoners' and 'Independence!'[1] In Algiers, police fired on protestors, killing between two and seven, injuring twenty-three; in Oran, one demonstrator was killed and fifteen injured. Still envisaging their politics as a contest over opinion in open public space, while also beginning to consider the possibilities of armed struggle, the PPA's leadership aimed for a peaceful show of strength in the victory marches anticipated the following week. Instead, there was a bloodbath.

On the morning of 8 May, PPA organisers in Setif prepared a separate demonstration to mark their numbers out against the European parties, ordered that weapons be removed from demonstrators and stocked securely, and that the slogans should be 'Free Messali' and 'Long live free and independent Algeria.' They hoped to show the Algerian flag alongside those of the Allied powers, and to lay a wreath alongside the other parties at the municipal war memorial. As the marchers, between 7,000 and 8,000 of them led by the town's Muslim Scout troop, processed from the mosque east of the European town centre through the Porte de Constantine and along Avenue Clemenceau, Algerian flags and slogans on placards appeared. The police were ordered to seize them, and set up a barricade on the corner of Avenue Clemenceau and Rue Saint Augustin, outside the Café de France.[2] Sometime between 9 am and 9.25 am, when demonstrators reached the barricade, there were scuffles. Shots were fired. The demonstrators retreated; it seemed that order was maintained, and at 10 am 3,000 to 4,000 reassembled demonstrators placed their wreath at the war memorial, honouring the tens of thousands of

North Africans who had been killed or wounded serving in French uniform over the past five years.[3] But in the meantime, panic and murder had
spread in the streets. Peasants in town for the market were caught up in
the demonstration and the shootings, and began attacking Europeans at
random, killing twenty and injuring forty-eight. Police and gendarmes
shot at Algerian crowds. Eyewitnesses later spoke of bodies lying everywhere in the streets. A tense calm returned in Setif by 11 am, but a curfew
was imposed, police powers were handed over by civilian authorities to
the army and by evening, armoured cars of Foreign Legion and West
African soldiers were said to be patrolling the streets and shooting
Algerians on sight. Martial law was declared and arms distributed to
Europeans. Known nationalist militants and sympathisers, and in some
places all adult and adolescent males, were arrested. In Guelma, 180 km
east of Setif, where a small demonstration was held outside the town at
5 pm and broke up an hour later, having been prevented by police from
entering the European centre, the curfew and roundup were followed by
summary mass executions organised by local militia under the former
*résistant* sub-Prefect, André Achiary.

As news spread of the killings in Setif, from the afternoon of 8 May and
for the next three days, a spontaneous peasant insurrection spread in the
north Constantinois countryside; isolated farms were attacked, colonial
villages besieged. In all, 102 Europeans were killed, more injured, and
several women were raped: couples caught on the road, low-level representatives of authority, inhabitants of small, isolated rural farms, the
targets of improvised, unpremeditated violence. By the time the PPA,
belatedly responding, called on 18 May for a general insurrection to begin
on 23 (only to countermand the order shortly afterwards), it was already
over, and had entirely escaped the nationalists' control. The repression,
first by settler militia, then by regular troops and artillery, aerial bombing
and strafing of villages, and naval bombardment of populations in the
coastal Kabyle mountains, lasted until 22 May; ferocious, spectacular and
utterly indiscriminate, it may have killed between 6,000 and 8,000
Algerians. Many more were imprisoned and beaten. The PPA would at
first claim 30,000, then 45,000, martyrs.[4]

Ferhat Abbas was outside the governor general's office in Algiers,
waiting to offer formal congratulations on VE day, when he heard the
news and was arrested. During the eleven months he spent in prison
without trial, he thought of giving up politics and composed a 'Political
testament'. Warning, in the wake of the terrible repression, that 'the use
of violence is a crime against the people', he wrote of armed insurrection as pushing 'poor peasants into a collective suicide'. Horrified by the
communal violence of which, among others, the 'honest' postal worker

Albert Denier, the Setif PCA secretary, was a victim (Abbas' friend Edouard Deluca, the socialist mayor of Setif, may in fact have been shot by a European), he penned a call to young Algerians both French and Muslim, published a year later, to renounce racial and religious hatred, and embrace an inter-confessional, democratic future without 'assimilation, nor new masters, nor separatism'.[5] Kateb Yacine was a 15-year-old budding poet from a village near Setif who attended the town's secondary school, took part in the demonstration and saw the violence at first hand. Arrested and imprisoned along with thousands of other Algerian men, he would later speak of the 'brutal realisation' he experienced when 'I saw the people (*les gens du peuple*) for the first time, close up, between four walls ...; their lives were charged with poetry ... ' It was 'these people ... whom until then I had not seen, the out-of-work, the day-labourer, the peasant' who suddenly incarnated for him 'the fact of being Algerian, what that means'.[6] Mohamed Mechati, born to a family of impoverished shoemakers in the old city of Constantine, was a 24-year-old army radio operator. Influenced in his youth by an Arabic-speaking French communist technical-school teacher and by older boys' clandestine PPA meetings, he had joined the army before the war for lack of other work. Promoted sergeant after Monte Cassino, he was on his way back to Algeria with his regiment from the liberation of Italy and France, and was in a French army barracks at La Ciotat near Marseille when he learned of what that army had done in his home region. His reaction, he would remember, was 'shock, fear, incomprehension'. On returning to Constantine and hearing the full extent of the massacre, he became a partisan of immediate armed struggle.[7]

Abbas continued to believe – and, years later, would reiterate his view that most Algerians long afterwards still believed – in a solution imposed by the metropole, the 'true' France whose real interests were betrayed by the short-sighted racism and violence of the colony.[8] For Kateb, it was clear, as he would tell an audience in Paris in 1947, that Algeria was 'an African nation that has found its way and its meaning in a Muslim moral unity', and which was still fighting 'the fight for independence begun by Abd al-Qadir'.[9] He called on progressive French friends to associate themselves with the struggle. Mechati, who had served out his term of engagement in the army, immersed himself completely in clandestine politics. He joined the underground PPA; by 1948, he was a member of its paramilitary 'Special Organisation' (*Organisation spéciale*, OS) preparing an armed struggle for independence.[10] A nationalist cult of martyrdom spread in the wake of repression. The boys of Muslim Scout groups would sing, in memory of the victims:

> Mother, why do you weep for me?
> Your son has sacrificed himself for freedom . . .
> My blood I offer
> My life I sacrifice
> I give them for my country.[11]

At Easter 1949, André Mandouze, a left-wing Catholic professor at the University of Algiers later renowned for his work on Saint Augustine, attended the anti-war and anti-nuclear World Congress of the Partisans of Peace in Paris, a meeting inspired both by communist internationalism and by veterans of the wartime French Resistance. There he described colonialism as 'a chronic state of war' and declared that Algeria, like France under the occupation, was 'in a state of resistance'. And he warned that colonialism, already 'an internal state of war, is on the way to becoming an overt and generalised state of war'.[12]

### The Dynamism and Paralysis of Politics

The explosion of 8 May 1945 came from a combination of volatile factors. The PCA denounced a 'fascist plot' and 'provocation' in which, it claimed, the PPA was complicit (a claim also made by the left-leaning diplomat, Governor General Yves Chataigneau[13]); the PPA, for its part, saw a colonialist plot prepared by the army and militia in concert to commit a 'genocide'.[14] In fact, the violence was the result of short-term tensions that revealed deeper factors at work. With cereal production down to 2.4 million quintals in 1945 from 7.6 million in 1944 and 16.9 million in 1939, and hard wheat, the peasants' staple, in the Constantinois down to 0.8 million quintals from 2.1 million in 1944 and 4 million in 1939, the countryside was suffering from a subsistence crisis that exacerbated and amplified anger over the peasants' underlying and long-standing land-hunger.[15] Operation Torch, the Anglo-American landings of November 1942, had precipitated the collapse of Vichy's North African administration and set off a scramble for primacy among French leaders which de Gaulle, with British backing, eventually won in mid-1943. Algeria was occupied by well-fed American soldiers with impressive new equipment which, notably, impressed Algerians in the French army who were re-supplied with it.[16] French prestige, so high in the 1920s but already dented by the defeat of 1940, was lower than ever in Algerian eyes.

Against this background, since 1942, nationalist politics had become rapidly radicalised. The PPA's more modest demand for 'dominion' status that had put Messali and his colleagues in jail was now definitively abandoned in favour of complete independence. In spring 1941, Ferhat

Abbas had written to Pétain proposing a program of Algerian 'renovation' under French sovereignty, but between December 1942 and February 1943 he drafted a more radical statement to the Allied powers, which at the end of March would be presented to the new governor general, former Vichy Interior Minister Marcel Peyrouton, as the 'Manifesto of the Algerian People', calling for the 'condemnation and abolition of colonisation . . . [which] is nothing but a collective form of the individual slavery of medieval times', the recognition of Arabic as an official language alongside French, land reform, the right of self-determination for the Algerian people and an Algerian constitution that would guarantee the 'absolute freedom and equality of all its inhabitants without distinction of race or religion'.[17] Small and less small acts of self-assertion by Algerians – schoolboys likening themselves in class to the slaves of ancient Rome or inscribing acts of rebellion ('I am Algerian, Algeria is my country') in their exercise books, Muslim Scout troops singing songs of the Resistance, a crowd liberating detained nationalist militants and throwing stones at officials[18] – combined to unsettle, indeed to panic European inhabitants and administrators. The public politics of protest inherited from the interwar years now unfolded in a sharpened atmosphere, and when things got out of hand, even the PPA's party politics were incapable of containing the more fundamental revolt of the people on whom they called. Algerians' attempts to claim the public space of European squares and streets, and the police's attempts to keep them out and to keep a colonial conception of 'order', quickly degenerated into violence.[19] The army's apprehensions of disorder (to counter which, its generals were aware, it had insufficient means) joined with the settlers' insecurity and vigilantism.

The Europeans' ferocious anxiety had another wellspring too: their opposition to the new tone of reform emanating, more seriously now than ever before, from the Government General of the liberal social reformer Chataigneau, appointed in September 1944, and from the reconstituted government of liberated France. On 12 December 1943, in Constantine, de Gaulle announced a new expansion of citizenship *dans le statut* and an increased Algerian representation in local government.[20] At the same time, a 'political, social and economic reform' commission was set up to advise on future policy. On the basis of the most conservative proposals emerging from this commission, on 7 March 1944 the provisional government issued an ordinance that finally abolished the repressive *indigénat* system, extended the second-college (non-citizen) franchise to all male Algerians over the age of 21 and gave full French citizenship without change of personal status to some 65,000 more. In May 1946, all Algerians would be declared citizens of the French Union, the re-imagined post-war imperial community, and the constitution of the Fourth Republic, in October, would reaffirm Algerians' French citizenship *de statut local*, that is, with their civil status unchanged.

The 1947 Statute of Algeria, a conservative proposal voted through the new National Assembly in Paris against a boycott by both Algerian and European representatives from Algeria, created an Algerian Assembly of 120 members with parity of representation for the two electoral colleges, such that the 532,000 mostly European electors of the first college maintained their predominance over 1.3 million Algerian voters, confined in the second college, who represented a population eight times larger. Each college would now send fifteen deputies to the National Assembly in Paris. The Statute also provided for a number of further reforms, some of which met pre-war 'immediate demands', including the suppression of the *communes mixtes* and of military rule in the Sahara, the independence of Muslim religious institutions and the teaching of Arabic at all levels of education as well as the extension of the vote (which French women had finally obtained in 1944) to Algerian Muslim women. None of these measures, which were subject to a two-thirds majority in the Algiers assembly, were implemented.

Some saw these reforms as a definitive solution to 'the Algerian problem'. Robert Montagne, a distinguished sociologist and educator of colonial soldiers and administrators, thought that as of 1947, Algeria had found its 'balanced equation', allowing Algerians to gain, little by little, predominance in the internal government of their country's affairs under a safeguarded French sovereignty, as education and 'development' would allow ever more second-college voters to make the transition into the full citizenship of the first.[21] Some of the more moderate *élus* who had signed the Manifesto, including former dissidents like Dr Bendjelloul and loyalists like the erstwhile Young Algerian-turned-administration candidate Mahieddine Zerrouk, welcomed de Gaulle's Blum-Viollette-style reforms as 'the realisation of a dream'.[22] The communists, competing for support with the PPA, welcomed the new electoral landscape that, they thought, would favour them over the conservative settlers and the neo-feudal 'lords of colonisation'.

But such promises were much too little for most Algerians. Now the minimal demands of most of the Algerian parties went beyond piecemeal enlargements of basic liberties that only, for the foreseeable future, preserved minority rule. The *'ulama*, Abbas and his allies, and the PPA, denounced the reforms as hopelessly insufficient and outdated. They united in their opposition to the Statute, calling instead for an 'Algerian republic'. At the same time, the promised opening of political space to Algerians seemed an intolerable threat to settler society, whose spokesmen derided Chataigneau as the 'Grave-digger-General of Algeria'.[23] Opposition by the European deputies in Paris and at the Algiers Assembly guaranteed that even the modest reform agenda proposed by the government would be consistently blocked. Algerian politics remained governed by the containment, within an incrementally increased inclusion, of the expansion of Algerians and their aspirations into French-dominated public space: as in 1919 and in 1936, the reforms offered were at least a decade behind the demands being made. Bashir al-Ibrahimi, now President of the Association of *'ulama*, told the reform commission in Algiers that Algerians 'do not seek the honour of being "elevated" to French citizenship, considering themselves to be sufficiently elevated already by virtue of being Muslims'. He demanded an equal Algerian citizenship for all, and an Algerian government responsible to an Algerian parliament. Messali demanded the same. Slogans on walls now denounced French citizenship, proclaiming instead 'Long live Algerian citizenship for all!'[24]

Nonetheless, the Ordinance and the Statute did effect a broadening and accentuation of mass politics. They created the framework for a new world of party-political competition – not least by giving the parties substantial targets to attack – and opened a 'decade of party politics'[25] that began with the June 1946 Constituent Assembly elections and that would continue until the dissolution of the Algerian parties and their absorption in the *Front de libération nationale* (FLN, *jabhat al-tahrir al-watani*, National Liberation Front) between the spring and summer of 1956. For ten years, militants of the different parties competed, tenaciously, often aggressively, their energy continuously dissipated in ever more acrimonious conflicts and frustrated by the administration's ever more blatant fraud and repression. By 1956, many would see 'politics' itself in this vein – electoralist, legal, parliamentary, plural – as thoroughly discredited, ineffective at best, the deliberately time-wasting and obstructionist business of 'traitors' at worst. The FLN, in an important respect, would in this sense be an anti-political movement of militarised direct action. In the longer term, the consequences of this would be dramatic.

But for these ten years, for the first time, multiparty political competition provided Algerians with differing perspectives, different projects for the country's future. Although the Manifesto itself was a statement of unity across the Algerian nationalist spectrum, divisions in oppositional politics emerged almost immediately. An association of opposition groups, the *Amis du manifeste et de la liberté* (AML, Friends of the Manifesto and Freedom), was formed by Abbas in March 1944 to push for the implementation of the Manifesto, but it was quickly taken over from the inside by the burgeoning PPA (clandestine since its prohibition in 1939 but now rapidly overtaking the other tendencies in grassroots militancy) before being dissolved by the authorities in May 1945. The PCA opposed the AML, arguing instead that for the Algerian Muslim who 'seeks the road to the future', it would be 'the new France ... which will be nothing like that of yesterday' that would bring about 'an Algeria rid of the colonialist regime'.[26] When other attempts at coalition-building with the left-wing French parties failed, in the early summer of 1946 Abbas and his colleagues created the UDMA (*Union démocratique du manifeste algérien*, Democratic Union for the Algerian Manifesto). First participating in elections in June 1946 – officially in the absence of the PPA, which called for a boycott, but benefitting in some localities from the support of PPA militants[27] – the Union won eleven of the thirteen second-college seats, annihilating its principal rival, the PCA. The UDMA's platform sought a negotiated solution, beginning with a project for an Algerian constitution and campaigning, from 1947, for an autonomous Algerian republic within the French Union as the expression of a multi-confessional, democratic Algerian nationalism.

Also in the summer of 1946, Messali was freed. The combined influence of French socialists and of Azzam Pasha, the Secretary General of the new Arab League, along with the UDMA's early success, convinced him of the need to participate in electoral politics to advance the PPA's platform. For the November 1946 legislative elections, PPA candidates were presented on a list entitled *Mouvement pour le triomphe des libertés démocratiques* (MTLD, Movement for the Triumph of Democratic Freedoms); until 1951, when the PPA was finally suppressed by the new party's leadership, the MTLD would serve as the legal, electoralist cover of the clandestine party, demanding above all a sovereign Algerian constituent assembly that would, by negotiation, lead the Algerian people to independence. Over time, despite the fraud and intimidation to which its militants, like those of other parties, were subject, the MTLD's electoralism grew from a tactical participation into an investment in electoral politics itself and, especially at local level – where in 1953, by allying with European liberals, the party was once more able to win seats on municipal councils – some degree of influence over policy. Within the party, nomination for and election to office also became stakes and interests around which internal conflicts coalesced. Clandestine 'activists' refusing electoral participation on principle were 'stupid leftists' to their critics, while those increasingly preoccupied with legal activity were criticised as weak and ineffectual 'moderates', 'reformists' avoiding the real issue of colonial power relations.[28]

Competition with other parties on the streets was even more vehement, with meetings often broken up by rival 'shock troops' and proposals for 'national union' consistently undermined by an exclusivity of vision, especially on the part of the more radical members of the PPA-MTLD, who denounced the UDMA as 'bourgeois' reformers and decried the PCA's doctrine of an Algerian 'nation in formation' that would achieve its autonomy alongside a democratic and socialist France.[29] 'In Setif', one PPA militant recalled, 'we were very sectarian towards the UDMA. There were fights, blood was spilled.'[30] At the same time, at least during moments of cooperation in 1951–53, militants of different parties were able to share platforms and worked together distributing tracts and organising meetings.[31] Party lines were drawn within neighbourhoods and even within families. In Oran, shaykh Tayyib al-Mehadji, a distinguished Islamic scholar, founded the first independent *madrasa* in the city, and left the AUMA in protest at its attacks on the *zawaya* while maintaining respectful relations with its leadership. His younger son, Brahim Zeddour, was an UDMA member, his elder son Bilqasim (known as Kacem) a PPA militant who would be one of the first martyrs of the revolution.[32] Ahmed Boumendjel, the son of a Kabyle schoolteacher, was a PPA sympathiser and Messali's defence lawyer in 1939 before joining Abbas to found the UDMA in 1946; his younger brother Ali, also a lawyer, was a liberal-minded UDMA militant whose closest friends since his school days included leading PPA activists.[33] Mouloud Hamrouche was born in 1943 to a family that, like many others, had migrated from the countryside to the city and settled in a popular quarter of Constantine. His grandfather and brother were members of the AUMA (which in Constantine was especially close to the UDMA), one of his uncles was a PCA militant, his father was in the PPA and his sister Malika, who would be an urban guerilla organiser herself, married a member of the PPA's paramilitary wing.[34] If the conflicts between these currents could be sharp, the commonalities and exchanges between them, too, animated a plural political life that ran more deeply than ever through Algerian society.

But while the UDMA, the PCA and an electoralist current within the MTLD argued for a gradualist politics to challenge the colonial status quo through the ballot box, and all three parties stood for election, their success – especially when the MTLD took a third of the seats, and virtually the whole second-college vote in major towns, in the 1947 municipal elections – scared the administration into subverting its own democratic institutions through electoral fraud. The new governor general appointed in February 1948, Marcel-Edmond Naegelen, a socialist former education minister of working-class Alsatian origin, a hero of Verdun in the First World War and an anti-fascist resister in the Second, saw the Algerian opposition as akin to the pro-German autonomists of Alsace, and (like the PCA) identified the PPA-MTLD with fascism.[35] In the April 1948 and February 1951 Algerian Assembly elections, MTLD candidates and supporters were arrested and beaten up, ballot boxes stuffed with votes for 'administration' candidates, Muslim districts conspicuously patrolled by soldiers. The UDMA and MTLD saw their representation reduced, from 18 and 33 per cent respectively of the seats won at the municipal elections of October 1947, to only eight and nine seats respectively in April 1948 (against forty-one 'independent', administration-backed candidates), and to seven and five seats (against forty-eight *administratifs*) in February 1951. Protests against such obvious fraud in France and internationally obliged Naegelen to resign in March 1951, but the same procedures wiped out UDMA and MTLD candidates at the national legislative election of June 1951 and the Algerian Assembly election of February 1954.[36]

In August 1951, the PCA, MTLD, UDMA and *'ulama* put aside their differences to form a common protest platform in the *Front algérien pour la défense et le respect de la liberté* (FADRL, Algerian Front for the Defence and Respect of Liberty), which was active until May 1952 and survived formally until the municipal elections of May 1953. But this attempt at creating a legal, non-violent 'union for national independence'[37] was deprived of meaningful electoral opportunity by the administration and undermined by disagreements among the parties. While the PCA's organisations – the newspapers *Liberté* and *Alger républicain*, the CGT and the Union of Algerian Women – boosted the Front, the MTLD-dominated Algerian Muslim Scouts (SMA) and Association of North African Muslim Students (AEMAN, which in the 1920s had been led by Ferhat Abbas) kept their distance.[38] The dynamism of electoral competition and the vehemence of street-level politics in meetings, cafés and neighbourhoods were stifled by suppression. As its ostensible policies of political reform and socio-economic development – expanded school places, welfare provision, jobs, the extension of irrigation and reforestation, agricultural improvement projects and the beginnings of an industrialisation program[39] – began to address Algerians' social conditions, the administration simultaneously sought to continue, as ever, to contain the majority population and their political aspirations within the unreformable colonial order of minority rule. The dynamism of legal, political opposition turned to paralysis.

The parties' own internal conflicts, too, led by the early 1950s to immobility, especially in the PPA-MTLD. Within the UDMA, too, more militant local sections contested the leadership's positions.[40] But

it was division within the PPA-MTLD that catalysed the abandonment of legal politics and the resort to arms. United in their aim of
pursuing independence through radical, populist politics, convinced
that they alone truly represented the Algerian people, the members of
the PPA nonetheless differed vehemently over strategy, and especially
over influence and internal politics within the party. Messali, 'Si el-
Hadj' – the great orator, given to theatricality, a popular icon sanctified by his suffering in prison and exile – was more charismatic
a personality than ever on his return from Brazzaville. Always
a patriarchal, 'prophetic' figure, with his long beard, tall *tarboush*,
flowing gown and cane he looked like a modern, political saint.
Denied residence in Algiers by the authorities, he settled in
Bouzaréah, a suburb on the mountain northwest of the city, and the
crowds of well-wishers who flocked up the long, steep road to visit
him looked to some suspiciously like pilgrims. Before long, Messali
faced accusations that he was practising a 'political maraboutism',
a dangerous personality cult that threatened not only the internal
democracy of the party but also its discipline and order. By force of
personality and personal authority, Messali was able to convince the
party's February 1947 congress to establish the MTLD and to engage
in electoral competition, against the opposition of some of its best
political talents who favoured popular mobilisation through the PPA's
existing networks. Foremost among these was Dr Lamine Debaghine,
a 30-year-old medical doctor from Cherchell who as leader of the
clandestine party since 1942 had brought a wave of young, radical
militants into its ranks. Increasingly riven by tension between Messali,
who sought to gain a greater hold over the party, members of the
central committee who increasingly saw Messali as a problem to be
managed, and 'activists' who saw the party drifting into dead ends of
electoralism and personality politics when its vocation was to lead the
people to arms, the MTLD became tense and authoritarian.

These tensions began to play out in ways that prefigured later and deeper
divisions. In 1948, at the annual fundraising gala of the PPA-dominated
students' association (AEMAN) in Algiers, participants were outraged to
discover just before the curtain rose that the popular nationalist song in
Kabyle dialect, *Ekker a miss U-Mazigh* ('Stand, Amazigh son'), written by
Idir Aït Amrane at the Ben Aknoun *lycée* in 1945, had been peremptorily
removed from the program by 'someone' acting for the party's central
leadership. They sang it anyway but the apparently trivial incident pointed
to something weightier. 'Until then', remembered Sadek Hadjerès, one of
the student organisers, 'we had paid only little attention to the diversity of
our maternal languages and regions of origin, but we would certainly never

have opposed them to one another so stupidly ... In the name of a small-minded idea of unity, division was created.'[41]

The PPA's political culture and ideology had always been minimal – the unity of the community defined by its being 'Arab' and 'Muslim', the demand for independence. Insistence on 'unity' was all the more intolerant the more factional the party became. There was no room for deeper discussions about what content to give to 'independence', what kind of polity should be created and – beyond a notional socialism – what project for society it would seek to implement. Centralising and 'purified' definitions of Arabic, Arabism and Islam, the cultural nationalism of the *'ulama* that resonated with the less lettered, communitarian politics that the PPA had radicalised in the wake of the Emir Khaled, became synonymous with unity, while recognition of Algerians' greater cultural, linguistic and religious diversity was condemned as expressing divisive, particularistic 'regionalism'. Those who failed to follow the party's directives – at one moment to vote, at another to boycott voting, without explanation as to the change of tactics – were roundly condemned as *kuffar*, 'unbelievers'. Leadership was imposed by force of personality, not by agreement on vision; the party's rallying cries had no deeper content.[42]

This minimal tolerance for cultural diversity and democratic discussion was less an ideology in itself than a function of pride in the party's radical and 'plebeian' character, its origins in the hard world of ex-peasant labourers, sharpened in polemics against the UDMA's 'bourgeois' professional liberals and the PCA's theoretically articulate cadres. This exacerbated a grassroots anti-intellectualism that created frictions as the party drew in a new generation of young, educated militants, many of them from modest backgrounds as sons of schoolteachers from Kabylia. Thanks in part to colonial ethnographic misconceptions that held berberophone Kabyles (though not other Berber groups) to be irreducibly distinct from and opposed to Arabs, and simultaneously more 'Mediterranean', closer to European civilisation, and thus more receptive to French tutelage, than other Algerians, schools had opened earlier and in greater numbers in Kabylia than elsewhere.[43] Because Kabylia was also an early and heavy exporter of labour, the earliest ENA and PPA in France had also drawn very substantially on the large proportion of Kabyles in the emigrant community.

In these circumstances, and in the absence of a culture of internal debate in the party, political divergences and personal resentments were easily expressed in the poisonous terms of ethno-cultural antagonism. Already in 1936, Messali's proposal for an Algerian parliament and cooperation with the Popular Front was opposed by Amar Imache, an emigrant mineworker and the ENA's General Secretary, who insisted on

the primacy of independence and argued that Algeria's own institutions –
collective landholding and the *jama'a* – already provided the basis of
a future social democratic polity. Imache, who drew on the image of an
archaic Kabyle village republicanism dear to colonial ethnography as it
was to Camus, was supported by fellow-Kabyles, while militants from
other regions backed Messali.[44] The accusation of 'Berberism' was born.
In 1948, a small group of student progressives within the party held
a seminar in Kabylia to develop a more substantial and inclusive conception of the PPA's program, which they expressed the following year in the
brochure *Vive l'Algérie*.[45] Signed 'Idir el-Watani' ('Idir the Patriot'), the
text was authored by Hadjerès, the lawyer Mabrouk Belhocine and Yahya
Henine, all young PPA militants originally from Kabylia. In implicit
contrast to the authoritarianism and cultural reductivism of the party's
dominant line, it called for 'nationalism, revolutionism and democracy' in
equal measure, celebrated a 'rich popular culture' of maternal languages,
Arabic and Berber, as well as the centrality of a popular Muslim morality,
and envisaged the integration of the European minority within the
Algerian nation as achievable through the liquidation of the colonial
regime.[46] Passages authored by Belhocine on Algeria's pre-Islamic
Berber history had already been expunged from Messali's 1949 brochure
for the UN, *Le problème algérien*,[47] a censorship that raised hackles in Paris
among the Kabyle-dominated leadership of the MTLD's Fédération de
France and its newspaper *L'Étoile algérienne*, whose editors included the
young intellectuals Mostefa Lacheraf and Abdelmalek Benhabylès
(Chérif Benhabylès' nephew). Already suspect as *mushawishshin*, 'troublemakers' refractory to the party line, the young progressives were now
attacked as 'Berbero-materialists' or 'Berbero-Marxists' for their conception of an historically evolving, culturally plural community that recalled
the PCA's 'nation in formation'. While they never denied the importance
of Arabic or Islam – quite the reverse – their 'Algerian Algeria' became
rhetorically opposed to an 'Arab-Muslim Algeria'. The unfounded accusation that they were preparing a Kabyle secessionism within the party
was given wide credence. In April 1949, the party's leadership dissolved
the Fédération de France, expelling militants and occupying its offices by
force. In Algiers, this move was an internal *coup* against Debaghine, who
was accused of protecting the so-called Berberists, to the benefit of his
electoralist rivals and Messali's personal loyalists. The cultural issue was
significant in itself, but its political instrumentalisation in the name of
authority and factional interest, the valorisation of homogeneity against
pluralism and the purge of intellectuals were alarms of other things to
come. Messali wrote of 'the Berberists' as a 'virus' and later claimed that
they constituted 'a colonialist creation' intended 'to destroy Arabism'.[48]

Thoughtful young militants committed to a democratic future Algeria left the party; leftists like Hadjerès, Abdelhamid Benzine and Yahya Henine joined the PCA, progressive liberals like Belhocine and purged leaders like Debaghine provisionally quit politics altogether.[49]

Another tension in the PPA's personnel and political culture, less acute at the time but as weighty if not more so in its significance for the future, was that between the 'military' and the 'political'. In 1947, only a few months after sending its first deputies to the Paris parliament, the MTLD created the *Organisation spéciale* (OS), a paramilitary wing tasked with preparing an armed insurrection, under the direction first of Mohamed Belouizdad and then of Hocine Aït Ahmed, a 21-year-old militant from Michelet (Aïn el Hammam) high in the Djurdjura, who had joined the PPA in 1943 while at secondary school. In April 1949, OS commandos held up the central post office in Oran, and in October, the group unsuccessfully attempted to dynamite the new monument to the memory of Abd al-Qadir (which sought to memorialise the emir as a 'friend of France'), at Cacherou (Sidi Kada) southeast of Mascara, a few days before its official inauguration by Naegelen.[50] Around the same time, the group eliminated a militia of Algerian mercenaries in Lower Kabylia that, under a local *bashagha* and with the complicity of the administration, was held responsible for several murders of known nationalists. Already, in the wake of May 1945 and especially in Kabylia and the Constantinois, the nationalist struggle had escalated into violence between Algerians, partly disguised by the older idiom of the local vendetta but partly following its logic, and mobilising the tradition of social banditry in the mountains where, ever since 1945, armed young activists had been in hiding. Inflexible discipline, internal suspicion and recourse to force within the movement, too, were already making themselves felt. OS militants signed up for unlimited service – once in, there was no getting out – and when the pressure of underground activity became too much for some, they fell under suspicion.

In March 1950, following the botched kidnapping in Tebessa of one such militant who was suspected (perhaps wrongly) of passing informa- tion to the authorities and who subsequently fled to the police, several OS members were arrested. Their confessions, extracted under torture, led to the discovery and dismantling of the group.[51] Officially disavowed by the MTLD, which sought with some success to portray the OS affair as a police smear campaign against the party, the network's remaining militants were kept in hiding, sent on gruelling underground conscious- ness-raising tours of remote rural areas or smuggled out of the country. Ahmed Ben Bella, a former soldier and in 1947 an MTLD municipal councillor in his hometown of Marnia on the Moroccan border, who in

1949, aged 31, had succeeded Aït Ahmed at the head of the OS, was sentenced to seven years' imprisonment. After his arrest, he refused the party's instructions to deny any connection between the OS and the MTLD. Other militants followed the party line but remained just as bitter about their treatment by those whom they increasingly saw as unworthy leaders.

Within the party, militants selected for service in the OS had gained enormous prestige. A certain cult of armed struggle, with roots in an almost mythical sense of popular resistance, elevated them above the rest. 'Legal' and 'clandestine' militants lived differently, 'worked differently' and increasingly saw things differently.[52] Political and military functions in the movement became attached to persons and to positions in a competitive hierarchy of prestige, rather than being seen as complementary aspects of a single strategy, relating respectively to ends and means. Later, the attempt to assert the primacy of politics and of 'civil' political direction over the military command of the revolution would be considered not as a constitutional principle of subordinating 'the military' to 'the political', but as an attempt to impose the rule of politicians (*les politiques*) over the militants-in-arms (*les militaires*) who had accustomed themselves to taking precedence. This cleavage of political from military that originated in the PPA's political culture became 'constant': in the minds of the FLN's activists and the institutions they created, 'it followed the itinerary of the revolution all the way to independence',[53] and beyond.

In March 1952, Ben Bella escaped from prison and fled to Cairo, whither Aït Ahmed had already gone. There he also joined Mohamed Khider, six years his senior and an early ENA militant from an impoverished background in Biskra who had been sentenced along with Messali in 1941 before becoming one of the MTLD's deputies to Paris in 1946. A partisan of armed struggle nonetheless, Khider too quarrelled with the party over the OS (which had used his car, without his knowledge, to transport the money stolen in the Oran post office raid). Another leader of the group, Mohamed Boudiaf, a son of a 'great family' from the Hodna, born in 1919, who had been in charge of the OS in the east, also escaped the dragnet and remained underground in France.

Tensions were running high between the MTLD central committee and Messali. In April–May 1952, the *za'im* undertook a propaganda tour in Algeria, opposed by the committee, which ended with the police firing on crowds at Orléansville and Messali's confinement to house arrest in Niort, in the rural west of France. The April 1953 MTLD congress strengthened the party's legalist wing against Messali's supporters, warning against the risks of populist 'provocation'. Between January and March 1954, the conflict came to a head, with Messali calling for a 'Committee of Public Safety' to rescue the party from the 'bureaucracy' that had abandoned revolutionary principles and become 'compromised'.[54] Rival congresses were held in the summer of 1954 by the central committee in Algiers in August and, against those now labelled 'centralists', by the 'Messalists' at Hornu in Belgium in July, where they declared Messali the party's President for life. The centralists, borrowing from Soviet political language, denounced Messali's 'personality cult'. Militants fought each other in meetings and in the streets, issued death threats against each other. The party had collapsed.

In March, while Messali was calling on the MTLD's base to revolt against the rest of its leadership, Boudiaf met with the party's General Secretary and veteran central committee member, Hocine Lahouel, and other committee members including Mustafa Ben Boulaïd. Lahouel was an early ENA and PPA member; one of the party's first organisers in Algiers in 1936 and editor of its paper *El Ouma*, he had been imprisoned for his militancy already in the 1930s before becoming an adversary of Messali a decade later. Ben Boulaïd, an ex-OS militant from the Aurès, where he had been stockpiling weapons, had been a trade unionist in France in 1937 and a soldier during the war before acquiring a modest business running buses between Batna and the little town of Arris in the valley of the Oued el Abiod; he had joined the MTLD in 1946 and was close to Messali. At Lahouel's instigation, they created the Revolutionary Committee for Unity and Action (CRUA), attempting to reunite the party as the precondition for armed struggle. They failed; the ex-OS activists' alliance with the centralists had fallen apart by the summer, and they were equally unable to bring Messali into dialogue with his opponents. In July, the CRUA too ceased to exist.[55] In place of a political agreement to create unity and enable the armed struggle, the armed struggle would have to create unity, by force. And politics would have to wait.

By the autumn of 1954, the political impasse had created a deceptive sense of calm in Algeria, which colonial observers contrasted with the violence that for two years already had engulfed neighbouring Morocco and Tunisia. The alarming news was of the earthquake that struck Orléansville, killing over a thousand people, early in the morning of 9 September. During his highly publicised official tour of Algeria in late October, François Mitterrand, Minister of the Interior in the government that had just ended the war in Indochina and recognised internal autonomy for Tunisia, told mayors assembled in Oran that 'the French presence will be maintained in this country . . . We have no intention of taking a leap into the unknown.'[56] But others knew otherwise. 'For twenty-five years', Ferhat Abbas had written in 1945, 'I have struggled with all my heart against the forces that oppress us. My heart is worn out; one must ... make room for new men, for the rising generation ... We are atop a volcano.'[57]

## The Choice and Necessity of Violence

The crisis of 1953–54 that destroyed the largest and most radical of the Algerian parties also, and more importantly, short-circuited the larger systemic impasse of Algerian politics. In June 1954, faced with the implosion of the party and the failure of the CRUA to prevent it, Mohamed Boudiaf convened a meeting of twenty-one (often mistakenly referred to as the 'committee of 22'[58]) ex-OS members in Algiers. There, in what was in a sense already a *coup d'état* of the military against the political',[59] bypassing Lahouel and imposing his own choice of leaders, Boudiaf proposed to transcend the schism in the party by the immediate recourse to arms and the creation of a new Council of the Revolution to direct it. The twenty-one agreed that the armed struggle for which they had been working for nine years should begin immediately and last indefinitely, until the achievement of independence. Leadership was vested in a 'committee of six' mostly former OS militants. In addition to Boudiaf and Ben Boulaid, they were Larbi Ben M'hidi, who had grown up in Biskra and Batna, had been imprisoned in May 1945 and had been on the run since his release; Mourad Didouche, the son of Kabyle emigrants to Algiers whose family had risen to own a bakery and a bathhouse; Rabah Bitat, a minor militant and former employee of a tobacco factory in Constantine; and Krim Belkacem, who joined the committee shortly afterwards. The son of a rural constable from Kabylia, Krim was not an OS member but had been in the maquis since 1947 following a local feud that was both familial and political. Ben Bella, Aït Ahmed and Khider, already in Cairo, joined them as the Council's external delegation, making up the 'nine historical leaders' of the revolution. All except Didouche were of rural origin; all were young men who had become militants even younger; in 1954 they were aged between 27 (Didouche) and 42 (Khider), their average age was 33, and except for party veteran Khider, who along with Krim had not been part of the OS, all had joined the PPA–MTLD since 1942.

Despairing of the factionalism of their party and the futility of legal opposition, Boudiaf and his colleagues were also spurred by the armed struggles in Morocco and Tunisia, encouraged by the tone of revolutionary nationalism across the Arab world in the wake of the July 1952 Free Officers' coup in Egypt, and inspired by the victory, at Dien Bien Phu

Figure 5.1 The 'committee of six', October 1954; a studio portrait taken in Algiers the week before the launch of the revolution. Standing, L-R: Rabah Bitat, Mostefa Ben Boulaïd, Mourad Didouche, Mohamed Boudiaf; seated, L-R, Belkacem Krim, Larbi Ben M'hidi (Print from a private collection, courtesy of Saïd Abdeddaïm and the family of Zoubir Bouadjadj).

in May 1954, of the revolutionary Vietnamese people's army against the French expeditionary force in Indochina, which seemed to prove that the French empire could be broken by a peasant guerilla force such as the Algerians themselves might create. Meeting on 22–24 October, the six divided regional commands among themselves: five loosely defined zones, later more formally organised as *wilaya*s (military-political governorates) were demarcated in the Aurès (later *wilaya* 1, under Ben Boulaïd), the North Constantinois (W2, Didouche), Kabylia (W3, Krim), the Algérois (W4, Bitat) and the Oranais (W5, Ben M'hidi).[60] Boudiaf assumed overall responsibility for coordination and rearmament, to be organised from the Moroccan frontier. They fixed the beginning of their insurrection, to be undertaken in the new name of the FLN-ALN, distinguishing the political movement from its armed wing (the *Armée de libération nationale, jaysh tahrir al-watani*, National Liberation Army), for the night of Sunday, 31 October–Monday, 1 November, 1954. On November 1, as they celebrated All Saint's Day by visiting the cemeteries in which they had laid their loved ones, Algeria's Europeans began to hear news of thirty terrorist attacks, mounted all across the country, in which eight people had been killed.[61]

The 'rising generation' of whom Abbas had written were products of their time and of their experiences. Formed in the Second World War, in the relentless discipline of the OS and the rigours of life in the maquis, their strategy of revolutionary popular struggle drew on international inspiration but even more on internal conviction. They faced an extreme penury of means but an inexhaustible self-confidence: 'We began with absolutely nothing at all, it's unimaginable', one of the '21' would recall, 'except that we had the supreme weapon, the conviction that we were going to win'.[62] Ex-OS militants, mostly men from Algiers and the east like Didouche, Ben M'hidi, Mechati, Benabdelmalek Ramdane (who would be killed in the first days of November) and Abdelhafid Boussouf (who would survive the war), had spent the years since the organisation's dissolution especially in the rural Oranais. Doing political work on the ground all the way from the Mediterranean to the Sahara, living in hiding and close to the rural population, they could gauge their sympathies and state of mind. Conscious of increasingly brutal police repression, 'people were afraid ... people avoided us', but 'they were ready ... the will was there'; 'our certainty came from the people'. A phrase later made famous by Ben M'hidi, 'We have only to throw the revolution into the street, it will be carried by the people', already before 1 November expressed the common belief of the activists who would launch the FLN.[63] Mouloud Hamrouche, aged only 11 on the outbreak of hostilities, growing up among urban politics but from a family tied to the realities of the countryside, would later consider that 'repression was such that people were ready to die'; for his generation, there was no questioning the struggle for independence, only 'the time and the price': when, and at what cost, it would come.[64] The MTLD's politicians – with some notable exceptions, especially Lahouel – on the other hand considered armed struggle ill-advised and premature. Paradoxically, they reasoned, as Abd al-Hamid Mehri, then a 28-year-old central committee member himself, later observed, 'like soldiers', assessing the hopeless military balance. The impatient paramilitaries of the ex-OS, conversely, took an 'eminently political' decision, seeing colonial politics as an unresolvable deadlock, and the broader colonial situation as an unbearable tension, both of which could only be broken by armed action which, once begun, would grow to command the support of the millions still denied their political voice.[65]

The FLN's revolution, then, began as the radical gesture of a militant minority. Despite its title, the FLN renounced the political union that had proven elusive since 1936. It would not be a 'front' of combined, existing political movements. Instead, its leaders demanded the dissolution of all existing political parties and the adherence of all patriotic Algerians, individually, to the new movement of national liberation. The FLN's proclamation, dated 1 November and mimeographed at Ighil Imoula in the mountains south of Tizi Ouzou, was a blunt statement of war aims preceded by a denunciation of the personal and factional disputes that had undermined the national movement as well as of 'imperialism and its agents, administration yes-men and other worm-eaten politickers'. By political and military action within Algeria and the simultaneous internationalisation of 'the Algerian problem', the Front declared itself dedicated to 'national independence by (1) the restoration of the sovereign, democratic and social Algerian State within the framework of Islamic principles, [and] (2) the respect of all basic freedoms without distinction of race or religion'. 'All the uncorrupted forces (*énergies saines*) of the Algerian people' were to be assembled and organised 'for the liquidation of the colonial system'. The struggle was envisioned as being long, but victory certain; to limit the loss of life, the Front presented its 'honourable platform for discussions' with the French authorities on the basis of the latter's recognition of a 'single and indivisible Algerian sovereignty'.[66] Conceived as breaking the colonial legal regime within which effective opposition was impossible, and as putting an end to the increasingly bitter and violent conflicts between the nationalists themselves, the creation of the FLN was a politically astute gamble on the depth of latent popular support and at the same time a negation of politics. But it would be unable to escape the political struggle that gave it birth. Born out of the crisis of the MTLD, one aspect of its war was bound to remain the pursuit of factional struggles between rival Algerian nationalists; its own internal politics would generate even more, and more deadly, such struggles. Yet its ambition was to incarnate 'the people in arms'. The choice of violence to pursue the former, and the necessity of violence to make the latter a reality, would shape the war the FLN was to fight.

In its first few months, the FLN consisted of only a few hundred men under arms, active mainly in the mountains of the centre and east of the country. Guerilla groups had gone into action on 1 November everywhere from the police station at Biskra and the barracks at Khenchela to the gasworks, radio station and oil depôts in Algiers; gendarmeries across Kabylia; an arms depôt at Boufarik; farms in the Dahra and the railway at Rio Salado south-west of Oran. But several operations misfired; some were aborted. Many were carried out by a handful of men with few and unserviceable weapons. The most successful and therefore most noticed actions were in Kabylia and the Aurès. Initial French military 'operations to maintain order' were concentrated in the Aurès, where the first attack to gain press attention – because of the unintended killing of a young schoolteacher, Guy Monnerot, and the wounding of his wife, victims of a botched attack on the local *qa'id* – had taken place in the Tighenamine gorge, in the Oued el Abiod south of Arris.[67] European opinion was convinced that a criminal band of 'rebels' had imported terrorism from neighbouring Tunisia, where so-called *fellaghas* ('bandits'), in fact armed partisans of the Neo-Destour, had been prosecuting their own armed struggle. The FLN's sudden emergence did not, indeed, provoke a mass rising, but nor was it expected to. The insurgency had to overcome, not what French psychological warfare officers would assume to be the inert neutrality and *attentisme* ('waiting-game') of the masses, and even less any widespread loyalty to France, but rather 'hesitation and incredulity towards an enterprise that seemed too reckless to succeed'.[68] Memories of 1945 and fear of repression, an aversion to *bulitiq* ('politicking') and to troublemakers from outside, suspicion and, no doubt, self-protection made many unwilling to aid the insurgents: at Cassaigne (Sidi Ali), northeast of Mostaghanem, in November 1954, local peasants themselves turned in FLN commandos to the gendarmes.[69] Mass adherence to the FLN and to the national independence it promised would come slowly, accelerated over the next six years in spasms of violence.

Individual militants and sympathisers of various parties nonetheless quickly rallied to the armed struggle and in some areas, especially in the mountains of Kabylia and the Aurès, whole rural populations did so almost at once. Communists in Algiers contacted by Ben M'hidi provided medical personnel, and others in the Aurès agreed, in the first weeks after the beginning of the insurgency, to provide material aid to the FLN.[70]

Ferhat Abbas and other UDMA leaders were also in touch with the FLN in the spring of 1955, promising material (especially medical) aid while maintaining, for the moment, their independence of action and of political vision.[71] The *'ulama* preached support for the families of *mujahidin* and sanctified the armed struggle in their own terms, while insisting, too, on their own mission and autonomy.[72] Mobilising enough spontaneous popular support to survive its first punishing winter in 1954–55 was the movement's first crucial victory, especially in areas like the Oranais, where the operations of 1 November had been resounding failures in military terms, and in others like the Aurès and north Constantinois, where repression was intense and losses – including, in January 1955, Didouche – were heavy.

Also, and as the FLN's leaders knew it would, the deliberate ramping up of revolutionary violence and the consequent punitive actions of the French 'forces of order' worked together to generalize Algerian popular support for the armed struggle. The conflict's first major turning point, marking its escalation from an insurgency of small, isolated armed groups to a full-scale war, came in August 1955. It was the second anniversary of the deposition, in 1953, by the French administration in Morocco of the popular Sultan Sidi Muhammad Ben Yusuf, opposition to which had mobilised nationalists across the Maghrib. Zighout Youssef, Didouche's successor as commander in the north Constantinois, found himself under pressure and isolated, despite increasing his forces to between 200 and 300 men (from only a few dozen in January) and keeping up a rate of action such that the new governor general, Jacques Soustelle, a distinguished ethnographer and anti-fascist intellectual who had been appointed in January with a mandate to accelerate socio-economic and political reform, wrote in May of a 'psychosis of fear' in the region.[73] In April 1955, a state of emergency and martial law had been declared, but at the same time, Soustelle freed many of the MTLD activists who had been arrested in November, had met Abbas to try to find a political compromise and was holding talks with members of the UDMA, ex-MTLD centralists and *'ulama*. In a special edition of *Alger républicain* for 1 May, the historian and editor of the AUMA paper *al-Basa'ir*, Tawfiq al-Madani, wrote that 'force will never resolve anything' and that 'the new Algeria' must be created out of 'a free and frank discussion between the French government and the authentic representatives of the Algerian people (without distinction of origin or religion)'. Abbas wrote on the same page that the 'events' of 1 November announced a widespread crisis of 'popular discontent' with the colonial situation, and warned that 'force should no longer have any place in relations between France and Algeria, even less in relations between French people and Muslims'. He insisted,

as he always had, that a political solution was possible that would 'peacefully reconcile two worlds, the Arab and the European ... that will live
together in reciprocal respect and in a real equality and fraternity.
The time we lose each day is one chance fewer for constructive
solutions.'[74]

Zighout, and the FLN more broadly, saw such calls to conciliation as
warnings that the administration and the 'moderate' leaders in Algiers
might broker a political solution that would undercut the armed struggle
and lose the FLN radicals their self-proclaimed primacy as leaders of the
people before they were able really to assert it. He sought, therefore, to
radicalise and extend the conflict, to accentuate it from attacks on administration and economic targets, symbols of the colonial regime, to communal violence targeting the European population itself. There were also
tactical considerations: to relieve the relentless pressure of repression on
the Aurès, to breathe new life into the maquis, and on a larger plane, to
gain recognition for a revolutionary Algerian struggle that was struggling
to gain momentum at the very moment when Moroccan and Tunisian
nationalists were moving towards negotiated independence and winding
down their own armed movements. Intent on repressing the guerillas by
'brutal action', and faced with a 'conspiracy of silence' from the peasantry, the French army had by May 1955, with Soustelle's assent, enforced
a 'vigorously' applied doctrine of collective responsibility, holding the
Algerian population as a whole responsible for 'rebel' activity in their
areas – and thereby generating popular support for the FLN where it
might have been absent.[75] Zighout, conversely, had already experimented
with attacks involving local people, armed or unarmed, alongside the
*junud* (soldiers) of the ALN. Now he decided to call the population of
the north Constantinois, whose especially vivid memories of May 1945
generated more desire for vengeance than fear of reprisal, into the war's
first mass rising.

On 20 August, Zighout launched a major offensive against the town
of Philippeville (Skikda) and its environs, sending the local peasantry,
men, women and children, armed with knives, hatchets and agricultural tools, combined with ALN maquisards against police stations,
farms, army camps and urban centres. In the attack on a military camp
at El Khroub, nineteen Algerian women and eleven children as well as
eleven civilian men were killed alongside twelve *junud* in uniform; at El
Halia, an iron ore mine near the coast east of Philippeville, insurgents
consisting largely of workers and former workers at the mine killed
thirty-four Europeans, including ten children. The spectacular violence
of the insurrection – 123 killed (71 European and 21 Algerian civilians,
31 members of the security forces), the murders of women and

children and the mutilation of corpses – provoked ferocious repression. In Skikda, several hundred Algerians were rounded up in the stadium and shot. When the army arrived at El Halia in the aftermath of the attack there, eighty Algerians were summarily executed. In the country-side, whole villages were destroyed. Unlike May 1945, there was no organised settler militia, and the army had sole charge of the repression. Europeans' anger was vented on the government and on Algerians at large in the towns, especially at the mass funeral of victims in Philippeville where officials' wreaths were trampled, and which was followed by a spontaneous lynching spree in which seven Algerians were murdered. Such so-called *ratonnades*, 'little rat-hunts', the name itself breathing racist violence, became increasingly common, especially following the funerals of the victims of ALN terrorism. Officially, 1,273 insurgents were killed; the FLN claimed a figure ten times higher and other sources suggest between 2,000 and 5,000 deaths. Whatever the precise death toll, and despite the subsequent criticism of Zighout's 'suicide mission' by his superiors, the effect was clear. The yawning gulf that objectively separated the preponderant and dominated communities in the colonial situation, that in daily contact on a local level and in the rhetoric of progress and good intentions could still, some-times, be believed bridgeable, had been materialised in a ditch full of blood dug between Algerians and Europeans.[76] 'There would be no bridge between the communities any more'; Algerians would have to choose, 'to be with their own community or to leave with the others'.[77]

As 1955 wore on, the insurrection slowly gained ground, both geographically and politically. Acting in concert with the Moroccan 'Maghrib Liberation Army', ALN officers and arms had been arriving in northern Morocco since the spring; one of them was a 23-year-old from Constantine, Mohamed Boukharouba, a young man with no previous political affiliations who had been studying in Cairo. Perhaps to disguise his Constantinois origins, he adopted a nom de guerre with Oranais connotations: Houari Boumediene. The ALN was also joined by former UDMA and *ulama* militants, by Algerian soldiers who began to desert from the French army, and by politically unaffiliated young men out of work. In the autumn, the guerilla spread to the mountains of Tlemcen and the Traras around Nedroma in the west, and contact was established between the Aurès, the north Constantinois, and Kabylia. The state of emergency, hitherto limited to particular districts, was extended through-out Algeria. By the end of 1955, the ALN had some 6,000 men under arms and was beginning to operate more like a regular army.

Slowly, Algeria's political movements too slid into the war. In the aftermath of 20 August, on 26 September sixty-one second-college

Algerian deputies sitting in the Algerian and metropolitan assemblies, including the UDMA *élus* Ferhat Abbas, Ahmed Francis and Ahmed Boumendjel, but also figures like Dr Bendjelloul and Chérif Benhabylès and a long list of habitually 'pro-administration' notable family names, signed a protest (the 'Motion of the 61') against repression. There was now 'immense majority' support for 'the Algerian national idea', they wrote; politics within its existing limits had been left behind.[78] The scale of repression had radicalised even the most 'loyal' of the administration's Algerian interlocutors. (The FLN's leadership, unimpressed, commented acidly that 'the "61" are the same bastards they always were, they fell into line because they're afraid they'll be shot. That's all.'[79]) On 5 October, Algiers' mayor, Jacques Chevallier, protested against the repression policy in *Le Monde*, declaring that Soustelle's plan of effecting the juridical and institutional 'integration' of Algeria to the metropole – the 'pure and simple attachment' demanded by the Muslim Congress back in 1936 – was now 'practically inapplicable'.

Algerian personalities of what the FLN now called the 'former political class', notably Allaoua Abbas, Ferhat Abbas' nephew, like his uncle a pharmacist and UDMA *élu*, and shaykh Abbas Ben Shaykh al-Husayn (the latter in fact now one of the more radical leaders of the AUMA), were targeted too on 20 August – Allaoua Abbas was killed. Shaykh Ibrahimi, who had been in Cairo since 1952, raising the profile of the *'ulama* as representatives of Algeria in the wider Muslim world, had refused to support the FLN publicly by broadcasting a call to jihad, and instead, in a speech aired by *Sawt al-'arab* (Cairo radio's famous 'Voice of the Arabs') in June 1955 reminded the *mujahidin* of the Islamic rules of war, warning against burning crops and attacking civilians.[80] In October, Ben Shaykh al-Husayn was in Cairo, trying to convince Ibrahimi to join the Front. In December, the remaining UDMA deputies, regional and municipal councillors resigned their seats en masse. Between January and April 1956, the *'ulama* and leaders of the UDMA publicly rallied to the FLN. Many of the older notable families, or at least their younger members – Bouderba, Ben Siam, Ben Gana, Hadj Hamou, Benhabylès – had also given their support.[81] The Front's desire for a monopoly of representation was unambiguous, and beginning to be successful, although its leaders' view of the older 'notable' personalities was as sectarian as ever: writing of Ibrahimi, Khider, in Cairo, told his colleagues in Algiers that 'we would've been quite happy [had he not been inclined to join us], since with these old turban-wearers (*ces vieux enturbannés*) you never know when they'll betray you'.[82]

Similar feelings prevailed about the PPA's old rivals and sometime enemies, the PCA. Unwilling to remain inactive after the outbreak of the insurrection but also reluctant to dissolve themselves into an as yet largely unknown and probably (as indeed proved to be the case) anti-communist FLN, the communists created their own guerilla group, the *Combattants de la libération* (CL), in early 1955. Widely condemned in European opinion as complicit with the FLN, the PCA was banned on 21 September 1955, by which time many of the party's militants, Algerians and Europeans alike, were underground. Active mainly in urban centres but also in the Ouarsenis, the CL was responsible for a major coup in April 1956 when Henri Maillot, a soldier and PCA militant born in Algiers, followed the party's call to support the armed struggle and deserted with a truckload of arms and ammunition, much of which was passed to the FLN. Maillot's own unit, including another European, Maurice Laban, a veteran of the International Brigades in Spain, was ambushed by the French army in June, and Maillot and Laban were both killed. The following month, the CL's leaders, Hadjerès and Bashir Hadj Ali, the latter a poet, former post office technician, and PCA militant since 1945, negotiated the group's integration into the ALN.

On the French side of the ditch, too, European opinion in Algeria and the government in Paris pushed inexorably towards an escalation of the conflict. Jacques Soustelle's desire for a liberal compromise did not survive the sight of the mutilated corpses at El Halia.[83] After the funerals at Philippeville, he told Algiers' liberal Mayor Chevallier: 'Now it's a war. We have to fight it.'[84] In January 1956, Albert Camus and Ferhat Abbas appeared together at the Cercle du Progrès in Algiers, supported by European and Algerian figures including shaykh Tayyib al-'Uqbi and the communist leader Amar Ouzegane, the writer Emmanuel Roblès and the architect Roland Simounet, to call for a 'civil truce', in a last attempt to stop the spiral of communal violence. A European crowd met them with shouts of *Camus au poteau!* ('Camus to the stake!'). On 6 February, the new socialist Prime Minister Guy Mollet, elected on a platform promising 'Peace in Algeria' with a large left-wing coalition, was met by a furious mob at the war memorial in central Algiers. In front of the Government General building, European demonstrators jeered and pelted him with earth and objects (most famously, though perhaps apocryphally, tomatoes). Mollet's nominee to succeed Soustelle, General Georges Catroux, the ageing colonial soldier who as de Gaulle's governor in 1944 had refused to discuss the Manifesto but whose Ordinance had abolished the *indigénat*, and who was identified by Algeria's Europeans as the man who had announced independence for Syria and Lebanon, was withdrawn and replaced by a new governor general, renamed

'Resident Minister' in Algeria, the socialist and resistance veteran Robert Lacoste.

Wrongly seeing Catroux's nomination as a signal that the government would *brader*, 'sell out', Algeria, the Europeans believed they had forced the head of the government to reverse sail. In fact, Mollet's belief in the possibility of 'saving' French Algeria by 're-establishing order' and promoting reforms was a continuation, only sharpened by the outbreak of the insurgency, of every Parisian government's policy since 1944. On 12 March 1956, the National Assembly voted sweeping 'special powers' to the government and by delegation to Lacoste, who gained a free hand to reform Algeria's government and suppress the 'rebellion' by 'all exceptional measures' that might be thought necessary. While for the FLN, pursuit of a military solution had come despite and against the reluctance of Algerian politicians, the French escalation of the conflict, putting ever greater and unchecked powers into the hands of the army, was the fully conscious decision of elected politicians.[85] On 12 April, the Algerian Assembly was dissolved by decree, its responsibilities assumed by the Government General. The colonial self-government that the Europeans had long

Figure 5.2 French army patrol in Kabylia, May 1956 (AP).

held dear was over. Now they demanded, instead, that their *Algérie française* be protected by the full and unrestricted weight of repression against *les hors la loi* ('the outlaws') and the fullest extension yet of direct French sovereignty. The deployment of the army was rapidly ramped up. In March 1956, there were around 200,000 French soldiers in Algeria. By July, there were almost twice that number.[86]

By the summer of 1956, political alternatives were at an end, the war was raging, and the FLN was in the ascendant, both in Algeria and internationally. In April 1955, while the ALN within Algeria was struggling, the Front's participation alongside Moroccan and Tunisian delegates at the Bandung Conference of non-aligned states in Indonesia, where the right of all three Maghribi nations to independence was affirmed, had also marked the beginning of a diplomatic offensive that would prove crucial to winning the war on the world stage.[87] In November, the situation in Algeria was tabled for the first time in the UN General Assembly (the French delegation walked out in protest against unwarranted interference in France's 'internal' affairs). From the gamble of a radical minority within Algeria's own nationalist movement, the FLN's struggle was becoming a symbol for revolutionary struggles across the Arab world and Africa, and for anti-imperialist movements throughout the emerging Third World.

### Algeria's National Counter-state, France's Colonial Re-conquest

In August 1956, the FLN leadership inside Algeria met in the mountains on the left bank of the Soummam valley in Kabylia to institutionalise the revolutionary movement and its army, and decide the governing principles of the war. The meeting was convened by Abbane Ramdane, an ex-MTLD militant from Kabylia who, although not an OS member, had been imprisoned after the OS trials of 1950 and had rallied to the FLN immediately after his release in January 1955. Ascetic and demanding, Abbane had resisted torture in detention and endured a protracted hunger strike in jail. Quickly rising to a coordinating and directing role among the informal leadership of the Front in Algiers, he became the principal contact for the ex-MTLD centralists who, arrested in late 1954, were freed in the spring of 1955 and passed over to the FLN. He also facilitated the other political parties' rallying to the Front. Despite his own impeccably militant credentials, Abbane's association with these 'politicals' and 'late-comers',[88] as well as his lack of interest in the populist, Arabist and Islamically infused nationalism that the PPA had promoted and for which Ben Bella, notably, had a romantic enthusiasm, his personal hardness and impatience that gained few friends while making enemies easily, suspicion of his austere intellectual calibre and irritation at his being a Kabyle with a dominating personality would all soon tell against him. But at this crucial moment in the insurgency, it was Abbane above all who articulated the form and content that would be given to the FLN as the political counterpart to the Army of Liberation.

The FLN, he wrote, was not a party, but 'the projection on the political plane of the Algerian people in its struggle for independence'.[89] The Front's significance lay in its being the only legitimate interlocutor that could stand for the ALN, and it was up to the political leaders to earn the right to the army's recognition. Refuting the notion that negotiations with Messali, Abbas or the ex-centralists might end the insurrection, he insisted in June 1955 that 'the Army . . . accords no-one the right to speak in its name. Only the leadership of the FLN . . . can speak for the army. Anyone else who wishes to share in this honour needs to roll up their sleeves and get their hands dirty. It is on this condition . . . only that the army might perhaps listen to them.'[90] The force of the FLN's political struggle was thus recognised as relying on the ALN and its insurgency. But at the same time, Abbane reminded his colleagues that the armed struggle was the military means to a political end, and that its coordination and strategic orientation required political direction. Mass 'civil' organisations were needed, too, to link the Front to every section of society: thus the students' union (UGEMA), trades union (UGTA) and shopkeepers' union (UGCA) were created between July 1955 and September 1956.[91] Abbane also insisted that overall leadership must rest with those on the ground within Algeria. In March 1956, he had vituperated the external delegation's diplomatic efforts and prioritising of North African union over the practical need for 'arms, arms, arms' which was the interior ALN's 'sole concern'. A few months earlier he had reacted with characteristic bluntness to a tract received from Cairo, which the FLN in Algiers refused to distribute, 'signed [by] Ahmed Ben Bella [as] representative in Cairo of the Army of Liberation': 'While we're in the shit up to our necks and risking our lives every day *Monsieur* . . . already takes himself for Gamal Abd al-Nasser . . . Ben Bella is not the representative of the National Liberation Army . . . You are patriots who have emigrated east, the FLN and ALN have charged you with a mission to the exterior, nothing more.' 'If one day we should constitute a provisional government', he wrote, again in 1956, 'it will be in Algeria and nowhere else. If by misfortune you should play at putting together a government outside [the country] we shall be obliged to denounce you publicly.'[92]

At the Soummam Congress, therefore, and against the reticence of some of the field commanders, especially Zighout and Amar Ouamrane, the chief of the Algérois maquis (W3), the primacy of political over military considerations, and of the 'interior' leadership over the 'exterior' delegation in exile, were adopted. The congress also decided on the military-political organisation of the six *wilaya*s and an Algiers Autonomous Zone (ZAA, entrusted to Ben M'hidi), and on a system of unit structure, ranks (of which Colonel would be the highest) and internal discipline within the ALN that sought to turn the guerillas into a regular, uniformed, rule-bound army: tribunals, not individual officers of whatever rank, would pronounce death sentences; throat-slitting was banned, as was mutilation of corpses; prisoners of war were not to be executed; recruits should have medical inspections, individual records, fixed salaries, family allowances and leave. And as Algeria's national army took shape, so did the state it was meant to serve. Popular sovereignty was vested in a National Council of the Algerian Revolution (CNRA) of thirty-four members, which should meet annually and would ultimately have the responsibility for engaging negotiations and declaring a ceasefire. Executive power rested with the FLN's Coordination and Execution Committee (CCE) of five – Abbane, with two of the 'six', Larbi Ben M'hidi and Belkacem Krim, and two ex-MTLD centralists, Saad Dahlab and Benyoussef Benkhedda – which took overall control of both military and political affairs.[93] There was no single head of government. Instead, the principle of collegial leadership was adopted in opposition to any return to the 'cult of personality'. Individual pre-eminence had become suspect in itself, and accusations against Abbane, ironically, would soon focus on the 'dictatorial' ambitions imputed to him.

The Soummam platform marked a decisive moment for the FLN, both because it laid the bases of an Algerian counter-state that would build its sovereignty against the French campaign to re-conquer and (at last) 'integrate' its Algerian *départements*, and because of the conflicts it provoked, which in turn would shape and colour Algerian politics for decades afterwards. The external delegation had not been able to send a representative – Ben Bella would claim he had been excluded – the Fédération de France and the South (W6) were also absent, and the Aurès, whose historic chief Mustafa ben Boulaïd had been killed in March by a booby-trapped radio planted by the French secret services, was without a clear leader and also went unrepresented. Of the 'exterior' leaders, only Aït Ahmed approved the Congress's decisions – and others accused him of doing so only out of 'Kabyle' solidarity with Abbane and Krim. Ben Bella, outraged at the prominence allowed to the rallied 'politicals', wrote that the Soummam's decisions risked 'wringing [the revolution's] neck'.[94] The 'constitutional' principles of the primacy of political over military (understood, whether Abbane intended it or not, as raising politicians above soldiers) and of the interior over the exterior would be comprehensively undermined within eighteen months both by design and by the brutal unfolding of the war.

First came the loss of much of the interior leadership: the deaths of founding guerilla leaders like Ben Boulaïd, Zighout (killed in action only a month after the Congress), Ben M'hidi (murdered in custody in Algiers in March 1957) and their successors, Colonels Amirouche, the famously ferocious chief of *wilaya* 3, and Si Haouès (W6), caught in an ambush laid for them on their way to a reckoning with the 'exterior' on 29 March 1959, and Colonel Lotfi, chief of *wilaya* 5, killed in action a year later. Abbane himself was condemned for 'fomenting dissent' (*travail fractionnel*) and murdered in Morocco in December 1957 by the FLN's secret services set up there by Ben M'hidi's successor in command of *wilaya* 5, Abdelhafid Boussouf.[95] The CCE would itself be obliged to flee the country on 27 February 1957, during the 'great repression' of the so-called Battle of Algiers; from then on, the revolution's leadership would be abroad, in Cairo and Tunis, and at the headquarters of two 'Operational Military Committees' (COM) established in spring 1958 in Ghardimaou (*COM-Est*) and Oujda (*COM-Ouest*) on the Tunisian and Moroccan frontiers, respectively. The massive French deployment and progressive re-conquest of the countryside and the completion in late 1957 of electrified barrages along the Moroccan and Tunisian frontiers tightened the noose around the interior ALN and, from early 1958, cut it off almost entirely from resupply.

At the same time, the 'exterior' leadership became embroiled in factional rivalries and sometimes vicious personal struggles for ascendancy. In the world's first incident of 'aerial piracy', in October 1956 the outside leadership, Ben Bella, Boudiaf (who, based in Morocco after 1 November, had not subsequently returned to Algeria), Aït Ahmed and Khider, accompanied by Mostefa Lacheraf, travelling on a Moroccan jet between Rabat and Tunis, were hijacked. The plane's French crew landed in Algiers and the five were interned, first at the Santé prison, later at the chateau d'Aulnoy, an eighteenth-century country house southeast of Paris, where they would be joined in 1961 by Rabah Bitat, who had been in French hands since March 1955. For the remainder of the war, although named as 'honorary' members of the CCE in August 1957 and as ministers in the Provisional Government in September 1958, the detainees would be cut out of decision making and the political manoeuvring that went with it. The CNRA, meeting for the first time in Cairo in August 1957, declared that since 'all those who

participate in the liberation struggle, in or out of uniform, are equal ...
there is no primacy of the political over the military, nor difference
between interior and exterior'.[96] In the guise of reaffirming fraternal
equality, this was a coup by the military chiefs against Abbane, who
abstained from the vote, and against the ex-centralist 'politicians'
Dahlab and Benkhedda, who were evinced from the CCE. Although
a major step in gaining international visibility and legitimacy, the
announcement of a Provisional Government of the Algerian Republic
(GPRA) in September 1958 did not give civilian politicians the government of the revolution. No institutionalised political structure would be
allowed to subordinate the army to itself. The builders of the new state
were concerned with establishing clientelist fiefdoms more than
a constitutional future; after the Soummam as before, in reality 'the
FLN had no existence of its own distinct from the ALN' and by the end
of 1957, at the head of the movement 'there were no longer any political
tendencies, only factions (des clans)'.[97]

The patrons of these factions in the army and security services built on
the frontiers increasingly became the dominant centres of power. From
mid-1957, Boussouf, 'the man in dark glasses', successor to Ben M'hidi at
the head of wilaya 5, and his fellow-ALN colonels, Lakhdar Ben Tobbal
(Zighout's deputy then successor in wilaya 2) and Belkacem Krim,
known as the 'three Bs', came to constitute the main power centre of
the FLN. Krim was responsible for the army in the CCE, then as Minister
for Armed Forces and Vice-President of the GPRA; Boussouf, responsible for 'liaison and communication' in the CCE and then chief of the
MALG (Ministry of Armaments and General Liaison), set up the FLN's
secret services, tasked not only with monitoring French communications
and countering infiltration but, perhaps more crucially, with counter-
espionage and 'vigilance' aimed at the FLN's own militants and at
Algerian society more generally. Until 1960, the '3 Bs' held power within
the FLN, and held each other in suspicion.

Within Algeria too, it proved impossible to create durable political
institutions that could govern the conduct of the war. Often out of
touch with each other and with the leadership across the borders, increasingly prone to fear of conspiracy and betrayal, and occasionally taking
political matters into their own hands in revolts against their superiors,
individual ALN chiefs prosecuted the war in the countryside and gained
the support of local populations by variable combinations of consent and
coercion. There can be little doubt that in the mountains, especially, local
adherence to the FLN was gained by young militants' overcoming the
reticence of older members of the jama'as, and systematically building on
these deep-rooted village institutions as well as invoking basic codes of

communal solidarity, often expressed in terms of a popular religious morality, to solidify support for the *jaysh*, which was recognised as being the people's own army.[98] In some 'liberated zones', or in parallel to the French administration, 'people's assemblies', elected five-man committees, briefly emerged. The basis of a civil government – dispensing justice and education as well as extracting taxation and enforcing discipline – was laid by political officers of the FLN's *nizam* ('organisation', in French the *Organisation civile du FLN*, OCFLN), which the French army referred to as the 'OPA' ('political-administrative organisation') and ruthlessly targeted. In late 1956 and early 1957, French intelligence identified the emergence of people's assemblies in Kabylia and all across the Oranais, but by September 1957 the 'unrelenting struggle against this category of persons', as a French army bulletin put it, led FLN directives in *wilaya*s 4 and 5 to suspend them, and by the end of 1959 French 'Instructions for Pacification' noted that the insurgency's 'administrative function has completely disappeared'.[99]

In areas hitherto barely touched by a bureaucratic state, and often still ruled by rural notables who now either threw in their lot with the Front or found themselves its targets, the FLN's tax-collectors and judicial tribunals were a truly revolutionary force. But while popular assemblies became untenable, the *nizam*, especially as a fiscal and disciplinary apparatus, survived and spread: the result, inevitably, was that the FLN in the countryside became an authoritarian and militarised 'neo-*beylik*',[100] controlled by personal loyalties and run more by force than by deliberation. Relations between FLN leaders were 'not transparent political relations, but traditional [family, regional] relations expressed in a modern political language', acted out like those of 'one mafia boss to another'. At the same time, 'the FLN thought of itself . . . as a state that contains society within itself . . . Political vision was tied to disciplinary practice.'[101] If FLN instructions to boycott some colonial institutions – elections, law courts, taxation – were widely followed (boycotts of schools[102] and medical facilities were less successful), the more community-focused disciplines of giving up tobacco and alcohol, avoiding bars and cinemas, not wearing berets, etc., were also sometimes ruthlessly enforced. Although formal regulations prescribed fines and imprisonment for contraventions, punishments were often more summary. Persistent smokers' noses could be cut off; the 'morally lax', from habitual smokers to women condemned as 'prostitutes', were sometimes murdered. Bashir Chihani, an early guerilla chief in *wilaya* 1, was accused of homosexuality and 'executed' as such by his fellow-*mujahidin* in October 1955. 'Traitors', however defined, were killed without further ado.[103]

The building of the Front's counter-state in this sense, to different degrees in different localities, meant the forcible capture of society by the military-bureaucratic apparatus of the ALN. But this only worked where there was a reciprocal capture of the state apparatus by local individuals and social groups. Far from imposing itself everywhere merely by terror, as the French authorities claimed, nor simply through the 'awakening' and political 'nationalising' of the population as its militants thought, the FLN came to function through logics of incorporation, discipline, clientelism and interests, mobilised around local, sectional, familial and class tensions that the escalating violence greatly exacerbated. As the Kabyle schoolteacher and novelist Mouloud Feraoun, a friend of Camus, wrote in his diary, communal solidarity among Algerians certainly reached new and self-sacrificial levels: 'There is an unshakeable enthusiasm ... an unbreakable determination, an absolute belief in a better future. The idea of dying for this future scares no-one any more, and everyone accepts ... the certainty that the sacrifice of those who die will ensure the happiness of generations to come.' But communities were at the same time being torn asunder, along with the fragile fabric of colonial society:

People tell themselves too that the moment is come to avenge our ancestors ... A century of life in common is deliberately forgotten ... Yes, enthusiasm is great, determination ferocious. The game is, who can be more patriotic than his neighbour or comrade-in-arms. Everyone thinks he can order, command ... Brutal executions, arbitrary ransoms, the arrogance of a newfound, short-sighted and disdainful authority, all this will by and by come to seem a yoke much less bearable than the one that's supposedly being thrown off ... It has become fashionable not to mourn 'traitors' when one hears of their deaths, to say, 'May they go to hell', and to cover their memory with a retrospective hatred that makes other people think well of you, without necessarily preventing you from ending up shamefully dead yourself. Fear now occupies a great deal of space among us; all that space that used to be taken up by pity ...[104]

And in some places, the FLN's grip was resisted. One group of villages in the lower Soummam valley wrote in February 1956 to their notable *élu*, who a few months earlier had signed the 'motion of the 61' but whose family had refused pressure to join the FLN, to request protection, either by French troops or by arming them directly, against 'the continuous and bloody troubles, of fratricidal murder and savage destruction ... so many execrable horrors that our religion reproves and that humanity rejects ... '[105] The 'red night' (13–14 April 1956) massacre of the entire population of the village of Ifraten, in the lower Soummam valley, in reprisal for the villagers having accepted French protection, was subsequently condemned at the Soummam congress. But the ALN in Kabylia later ordered all such villages to be burned and their adult men killed.[106] Feraoun wrote of 'the blind authority of the [French] army that tramples, dishonours, beats and kills, the vindictive and tyrannical authority of the [ALN] terrorists who insult, humiliate and hang'.[107] In the mountains east of Médéa, one son of a declining *qa'id* family would remember, 'folks said there are these people ... whom they called *fellaghas*, people who come from all over the place, they come down the chimney ... you don't know how they get in, then they cut your nose off, or they cut your head off ... folks talked about that everywhere ... ' When his father, the head of a *firqa* (tribal fraction) was falsely denounced as an FLN organiser, the army burned down the family farm. But then the FLN in turn put pressure on this minor local notable and 'one day he'd had enough, he went to see the [French army] ... he told them, I want to come to the [colonial] village, to protect myself, and there's my son ... and my brother ... and we'll take arms against the FLN ... and that's how it was'.[108]

From early 1955, Soustelle's administration created 'Special Administrative Sections', army units tasked with establishing a 'civil' presence in the under-administered countryside and in Algerian urban and peri-urban neighbourhoods.[109] They both ran schools where there had never been any and collected intelligence, seeking to extend the reach of the French state as never before and to recapture Algerian society from FLN influence. They mobilised *harka*s ('mobile units', whose members were called *harkis*), and home guards, archaically labelled *makhzen*s (with participants referred to as *moghazni*s) as auxiliary self-defence units to defend both colonial settlements and Algerian villages. These Algerian auxiliary (*supplétif*) recruits into French uniform, along with career and conscript soldiers, would be celebrated as proof of a pro-French 'silent majority': there were perhaps between 103,000 and 220,000 of them, all told, between 1958 and 1961, and still almost 117,000 (68,000 of whom were auxiliaries) in March 1962, many more (at most in a ratio of six to one) than the ALN ever mustered under arms at one time.[110] French wartime propaganda made much of this figure.[111] But a conscious and uncoerced pro-French 'choice' can have been taken by very few of them. Many may have come from family traditions of military service or some level of association with the colonial state – as rural constables, *qa'id*s or local *élus* – and have thus been in vulnerable positions, pressurised both by the administration and the nascent FLN, as the war spread. Some retaliated for FLN attacks, or fell in with the administration against the FLN along the existing fracture lines of local social and political influences, in which paternal or patriarchal authority held sway. In the Ouarsenis, the *bashagha* Saïd Boualam, a career soldier and Second World War veteran from a family of *qa'id*s, deputy in the National Assembly from 1958 to 1962, mobilised the Beni Boudouane behind his own decision to oppose the FLN and affirm his loyalty to France.[112] Bitter local conflicts resulted, in which villages and families hedged their bets – oscillating between the FLN and the French, or sending some sons to one side and their brothers or cousins to the other – to survive as best they could. Others simply responded to the incomprehensible violence engulfing their society by seeking aid and protection from the nearest and most seemingly reliable source:

> We were between two fires ... on one side there's the French army that does you no harm, then if there are people [i.e. the FLN] at your place they [the army] shoot at you ... then there are the others who take everything you have and threaten to kill you ... you had to choose ... you risk being killed by one or the other, and us, we chose France and so, well, that's that ... My father, his idea ... was that Algeria would never be a country ... in his head ... he's always said they'll never be ..., you know, a state ...[113]

The FLN's military effort gained ground through 1956 and 1957, with perhaps 20,000 armed *mujahidin* organised into units of the ALN in the maquis, and as many urban guerillas (*fida'iyyin*), auxiliaries and liaison agents (*musabilin*) by mid-1958. Operations became more ambitious. Some, like the ambush and annihilation of a French infantry unit near Palestro (Lakhdaria) on the edge of Kabylia in May 1956, became sensational stories in the French media.[114] Alongside the rural insurgency, the FLN aimed further to radicalise the struggle by targeting the European civilian population in the cities. The urban guerilla, most famously the 'Battle of Algiers' (September 1956–October 1957), was, on the military front, defeated by a ruthless campaign of repression. An eight days' general strike, called for 28 January 1957 to coincide with the UN General Assembly debate on Algeria, was broken by the 8,000 soldiers stationed in the capital. Given police powers in Algiers to halt the FLN's campaign of bombings and assassinations, the 10th Parachute Division under General Jacques Massu systematised roundups and the torture of suspects, eventually dismantling the urban guerilla organisation, murdering Ben M'hidi in custody, capturing the ZAA's military chief, Saadi Yacef, alongside the *fida'iyya* Zohra Drif, and killing the *fida'iyyin* Ali 'la Pointe' Amara, Hassiba Bent Bouali, Mahmoud Bouhamidi and the 12-year-old liaison agent 'Petit' Omar Yacef by blowing up the house in the rue des Abderames, in the Casbah, where they were hiding. The FLN in Algiers would be reconstituted only very partially before the end of the war.

Torture, ostensibly 'necessary' for intelligence gathering and 'justified' by the terrorism that had, for the first time, struck ordinary men and women in the European districts of Algiers, had in fact been common in

Figure 5.3 Larbi Ben M'hidi in 1956. This striking portrait was drawn from a photograph taken shortly before Ben M'hidi's death (Private collection, courtesy of Tawfiq Ibrahim).

Algerian police stations at least since the growing political repression of 1945–50. Henceforward, it became widespread and systematic. As early as February 1955, Roger Wuillaume, a government Inspector General investigating the detention of Algerians arrested after 1 November, reported that all the police services were using methods of torture during interrogations; he recommended that 'the veil of hypocrisy' be lifted and the practice regularised and restricted to the judicial police.[115] By 1957, torture – by beatings, water, electricity, rape – was routinely practised by soldiers, gendarmes and police in official or secret 'sorting and transit centres' (CTT) and from 1958 in 'intelligence and action centres' (CRA), some of which, like the villa Sésini above Clos Salembier in Algiers, or the Ameziane farm outside Constantine, became notorious. In such centres, detainees were held in an extrajudicial limbo of 'disappearance' (covered, from 11 April 1957 onwards, by the legal fiction that they were under house arrest (*assignés à résidence*)), before being delivered to prison. Torture came to serve less as a last resort to obtain information than as a generalised practice of asserting an arbitrary and absolute authority over prisoners, 'to panic, to paralyse the victim, proving his powerlessness' as Colette Grégoire (aka Anna Greki), a European-Algerian militant and poet, herself arrested and tortured in 1957, expressed it.[116]

Such routinised use of torture to terrorise, intimidate and extract false confessions as well as to gather intelligence was most famously demonstrated by the case of Djamila Boupacha, brought to public attention by Gisèle Halimi, a Tunisian Jewish lawyer and feminist activist. An FLN liaison agent, Boupacha was arrested in February 1960 and tortured until she confessed to a bombing she had not perpetrated. Thousands of others, in the cities and countryside across Algeria, FLN militants, European progressives or ordinary suspects, were subjected to the same brutalities, sometimes tortured to death or murdered in custody. Ben M'hidi was hanged in his cell on 6 March 1957 by French paratroopers, his death crudely camouflaged as a suicide in which no-one believed. Two weeks later, on 23 March, a similar fate befell Ali Boumendjel, the lawyer and former UDMA militant close to the leadership of the FLN in Algiers, who had been tortured in custody by parachutists for forty-three days before being thrown to his death from the sixth floor of the then partly constructed building, on avenue Clemenceau in the Algiers suburb of El Biar, where he was being held. His 'suicide' was announced the following day. Maurice Audin, a PCA militant and mathematician, was arrested by soldiers on 11 June and tortured to death. On 12 June, his comrade Henri Alleg, editor of *Alger républicain* (which, along with the PCA, had been suppressed in September 1955), was arrested. He was detained and tortured for a month at El Biar. In the *bled* (countryside), summary executions, often carried out to dispose of tortured suspects, were euphemised as *corvée de bois* ('firewood detail') or as 'shot while trying to escape'.[117]

Boumendjel's case, and then, especially, Audin's, mobilised liberal and leftist opinion in France. A 'Maurice Audin Committee' campaigned for the truth about 'disappearances' in Algeria and from 1960 published *Vérité-Liberté*, in which activists argued that colonialism and the war fought to defend it threatened French democracy. In September 1960, *Vérité-Liberté* carried a statement from 121 leading French cultural and intellectual figures including Jean-Paul Sartre, Simone De Beauvoir, André Breton and Marguerite Duras, supporting Algerian independence and conscripts' refusal to serve in the war. Alleg's terse and harrowing account of his own torture, *La question*, was released in Paris by the militant and *ancien résistant* publisher Éditions du Minuit in mid-February 1958. It went through seven editions before it was banned at the end of March, and sold tens of thousands of clandestine copies thereafter.[118] In France too, though, where the FLN's Fédération de France had by 1958 made the émigré population into the revolution's main tax base, and where, in 1958 and 1961, several police officers were assassinated in FLN attacks, symbolic and physical violence by the police against Algerians was accentuated.[119] In Paris, this violence reached a peak in September–October 1961, when at least 120 Algerians were murdered by police.[120] On the night of 17 October, tens of thousands of Algerian men, women and children, organised by the FFFLN, came out on the streets in a peaceful march (strikingly, without banners or slogans) in an act of civil disobedience in support of the revolution and against the curfew imposed upon them by the Paris Prefect of Police, Maurice Papon. Papon, a former Prefect of Constantine who had been responsible for deporting Jews from Bordeaux under Vichy, saw himself as prosecuting a 'counter-subversive war' against the FLN in the Paris region. On 17 October, demonstrators were shot or beaten to death, some of their bodies thrown into the Seine by policemen with help from métro engineers, firemen and passers-by. At the height of the war, Paris too thus became a site of characteristically colonial – racialised and extrajudicial – violence.[121]

Overt repression was also, however, only one side of a broader war of colonial re-conquest. Successive French governments, convinced that the FLN was merely a terrorist organisation ruling its hapless people by fear and objectively (whether it knew it or not) advancing a global communist threat, and that the loss of Algeria – with, from 1956, its newly discovered hydrocarbon resources in the Sahara – would be catastrophic for France's international standing and economic security, insisted that 'the Algerian problem' was social and economic rather than political. They sought to smash the FLN's nationalism and break its insurrection both by force and by a forced-march development agenda that would in its own way revolutionise the countryside. Beginning under Lacoste in 1957, and with increasing intensity from 1958, the counter-insurgency campaign became a total war engulfing almost the whole Algerian population. Launched by de Gaulle at a speech in Constantine on 3 October 1958, shortly after his return to power, the 'Constantine Plan' for the industrialisation and infrastructural equipment of Algeria was imagined as a counter-insurgent 'revolution' from above, ending the inequalities of colonialism and dragging Algerian living standards up to those of their European 'compatriots'. To preserve 'the close union between Algeria and France', metropolitan planners now announced, Algeria had to 'conquer, by its labor and for all its inhabitants, its full participation in the civilization of the twentieth century' – an immense task of development, as de

Gaulle insisted in Constantine, that only France could undertake.[122] The metropole was thus at last imposing a solution, but as ever, it was a solution to the problems of twenty years earlier.

The imagined 'modernisation' thus suddenly embarked upon was to be pursued through urban regeneration – the demolition of shantytowns and creation of new housing complexes – by rural land reform, investment in the oil and gas sector that would drive new industries (especially a flagship iron and steel works at El Hadjar, near Annaba), by the extension of schooling and by a correspondingly revolutionary legal and political transformation that would make all of Algeria's inhabitants, as de Gaulle announced in Algiers in June 1958, 'fully French, with the same rights and the same duties'.[123] Algeria's salvation, in de Gaulle's words, lay on 'the road of renovation and fraternity' – at last, there would be full and equal citizenship for all, the vote for Algerian women, a single electoral college. But none of this – with the exception of increased numbers of Algerians in administrative office, which in the event prepared a post-independence bureaucracy – much mattered now. At the same time, the war was pursued. The reality of the 'development' drive, to most Algerians, was the massive *regroupement*, or forced resettlement, of the rural population, begun as a security measure in the Aurès in 1955 and subsequently extended across the countryside. Mountainous areas were declared 'forbidden zones', where villages were dynamited to deny cover to the ALN, their inhabitants resettled in camps under military supervision. From late 1959, implementing plans for rural modernisation that had first been drawn up in the mid-1940s, a 'one thousand villages' program sought to turn these resettlements, which often began as mere clusters of huts behind barbed wire, into development centres, with permanent houses and public services, where Algerians would at last 'learn' municipal self-government and, leaving the archaic agriculture of the mountain to which colonisation had in many cases restricted them, 'plunge into the modern economy'. By 1961, some 3 million Algerians were affected by *regroupement*.[124] Some 300,000 more became refugees across the borders and perhaps 700,000 fled to the shantytowns around Algeria's cities whose existing inhabitants the authorities were already struggling to 'absorb'.

As the remaining people of a rural district in the east of the country wrote in 1956, the result was 'atrocities and miseries that fall upon a poor people dying of hunger and without defence ... God cannot permit such injustices'.[125] Eyewitness testimonies and images of the war in the countryside became part of the conflict. The French government promoted images of France's modernising beneficence, as in *Képi bleu*, a 1957 'documentary' film on the work ('of understanding ... tolerance') of the SAS, counterposed to those of FLN 'savagery' like the photographs of

Figure 5.4 Woman and child near a *regroupement* centre, probably ca. 1959 (CANA).

mutilations reproduced in Jacques Soustelle's 1956 manifesto, *Aimée et souffrante Algérie*, and later in General Massu's account of the 'Battle of Algiers'.[126] Conversely, not only the FLN's Information Ministry but sympathisers like the American writers Richard and Joan Brace, or *engagés* photo-journalists Dominique Darbois and Philippe Vigneau, produced accounts and photographs, especially from visits to refugee camps on the Tunisian frontier, that not only illustrated the effects of bombing and napalm, and the penury and suffering of Algerians, especially women and children (alongside the increasingly professionalised military look of their menfolk in the frontier ALN), but, by publishing children's drawings and stories, gave voice to their aspirations – to learn to read, to play football, to become a teacher, a nurse, a policeman, a barber, to buy an aeroplane, to go home . . . – and experiences.[127] 'We were busy when France invaded our house', wrote Rabia, an 11-year-old girl on the Tunisian border:

They asked us what [the FLN] brought here. We said 'I don't know.' So they hit my sister and started laughing, for three days they never left us in peace. And my father, after they hit him, he didn't last a month and then he died. And that was it. And even afterwards, they hit the donkey, and they put my mother in another room and we were very scared.[128]

Women and children both participated in the war differently to men and suffered from its violence, especially its sexualised violence – although that was inflicted on men too – in different ways. Like their men, Algeria's women were torn between engagement in the struggle for liberation, seeking safety for their families from the reciprocal violences of revolution and counter-insurgency, and struggling to get by in a country ruined by war. At the same time, women themselves became a particular stake and a battleground in the conflict. Part of the moribund reform agenda since 1943, after 1954 women's 'emancipation' suddenly gained the administration's attention. There were projects for new legal measures on women's status and for the extension of education. Social change that made polygamy increasingly rare, women increasingly educated and patriarchal authority at least in urban areas less unquestioned was seen to be preparing the ground for 'the notion of the rights and duties of the individual' to be extended to Algerian women. Officials concluded that 'the civilising mission of France is needed more than ever ... its humanism, its sense of moral values are needed to build a community in which citizens will enjoy the same rights without distinction of sex, race or religion'.[129] Public demonstrations of unveiling and the burning of *haïks* (the traditional, calf-length white wrap of Algiers' women) during orchestrated shows of 'fraternisation' at the Government General in Algiers in May 1958 ostensibly announced the 'liberation' of Muslim women.[130] Conversely, as the Martiniquais psychiatrist Frantz Fanon, writing for the FLN in Tunis, observed, the theatre of veil-burnings had the unintended effect of provoking symbolic resistance: 'Spontaneously, ... women who had long ago ceased wearing the veil put on the *haïk*, to show that it is not true that women liberate themselves at the invitation of France and General de Gaulle.'[131]

In fact, in some urban areas, educated Algerian women had begun to cease wearing the veil long before the war: the daughters of the Hadjères and Boumendjel families, in Larbaa south of Algiers, whose fathers were schoolteachers – both secularly minded themselves and actively involved in the local *nadi al-islah* (Reform Circle) for the revival of Arabic and Muslim culture alongside the local *'ulama* – went unveiled in the 1940s, as did the daughters of local notables and small businessmen.[132] If the war had an accelerating effect on the 'desacralisation' of the status that women had held in rural society, it was very ambivalent:

Women care for the wounded, carry them on their backs . . ., bury the dead, collect funds, keep watch. The maquisards mobilise women and the soldiers . . . arrest and torture them. Maybe a new world is being built on the ruins, where women will wear the trousers, literally and metaphorically, where the remains of the old traditions of the inviolability, physically and metaphorically, of women will be swept away . . . All in all, women take the weight of the war hard, they get hit like men, tortured, killed, put in prison. After all that, de Gaulle's decrees . . . can still propose reforms, it's over, there's nothing left to reform.[133]

Uncountable numbers of women were raped by French soldiers during the 'pacification' of the countryside; there was also, undeniably, violence against women by the ALN.[134]

While Djamila Bouhired, Zohra Drif, Samia Lakhdari, Baya Hocine and Hassiba Bent Bouali, the young FLN operatives who planted bombs in the European districts of Algiers, unusually played major roles within the guerilla organisation and became iconic heroines, views on women's role in the struggle within the FLN more broadly were much more ambiguous. While the insurgency could never have survived without the shelter, food and care offered by rural women from the outset of the war, for ALN commanders it was the proper role of women, as 'precious *auxiliaries* of the forces of national liberation', to cook food, wash clothes and ask no questions.[135] Women were often active in urban *fida'i* groups, but except on photographs intended for external consumption, women only very exceptionally bore arms in the maquis; essential as they were as nurses, and more often as cooks and laundresses, Algerian women who went into the maquis, especially after the 1956 student strike, were not always welcome. 'I remind you one last time that without authorisation from the Zone it is forbidden to recruit *jundiyyat* (women soldiers) and nurses', wrote a zone commander in the Tlemcen mountains to his subordinate: 'In independent Algeria the freedom of the Muslim woman will stop on the threshold of her house. Women will never be equal to men.' The same instruction transmitted orders to find and execute specific women in the maquis.[136] In the north Constantinois, it was 'strictly forbidden to all women to join our ranks' and any who tried were to be sent back, even if the French were to capture them.[137] ALN commanders, prone to a degree of moral panic, were intent on keeping women and men separate, avoiding unregulated relationships, and poli-cing sexual propriety: men and women in the maquis could marry, but only if their request were approved by their commanders. The FLN announced, and many Algerian men as well as women doubtless believed, that the armed struggle was a revolutionary one that would 'open for the Algerian woman radiant horizons of fulfilment and emancipation in harmony with our epoch', but at the same time the FLN was itself a patriarchal authority that enforced as strongly as ever a rigidly gendered and conservative code of social and sexual morality.[138]

Although its social authority among Algerians became ever stronger, from mid-1958, the interior FLN's military strength and position vis-à-vis the French army continuously declined. In 1959, a series of French offensives masterminded by General Maurice Challe systematically combed the maquis from west to east. ALN units, harried by concentrated air and ground forces, by rapid-deployment *commandos de chasse* and helicopters, were forced to break up into small bands and seek refuge where they could. Denied supplies and cover, deprived of close contact with the population by *regroupement* and cut off from the outside, the *wilaya*s began to asphyxiate. In December 1958, Colonel Amirouche and three other interior commanders condemned the GPRA's apparent inaction on the frontiers as 'treason' and 'sabotage'. Six months later, under the 'steamroller' of Challe's operations 'Pierres précieuses' ('Gemstones') and 'Jumelles' ('Binoculars'), ALN officers in Kabylia asked themselves 'what the hell [the "exterior"] was doing'.[139]

Outside Algeria, though, the tide ran in favour of the revolution. The independence in 1956 of Morocco and Tunisia had provided rear bases and diplomatic support for the FLN. The ALN's 'army of the frontiers' and its general staff (*État-major général*, EMG), created to unify the eastern and western COMs in December 1959–January 1960 under the command of Boussouf's protégé and deputy, Colonel Boumediene, began to constitute a powerful armed force. And beyond the region, crucially, the FLN's international standing and political credibility gained strength. The GPRA, created in Cairo in September 1958, was moved to Tunis two months later, after the discovery of a conspiracy of colonels (the 'Lamouri plot') to overthrow it with the backing of the Egyptian secret services.[140] In Tunis the GPRA put a public face on the FLN's claim to sovereign statehood, with talented young professional cadres staffing ministries led by representatives of the pre-1956 parties. Ferhat Abbas was the GPRA's first President, the AUMA's rhetoricians became ambassadors to the Arab states; ex-MTLD activists became political counsellors and planners. The GPRA's Ministry of Foreign Affairs, led by Lamine Debaghine and then (after rivals ousted him from the Armed Forces Ministry) by Krim, built a professional and effective diplomatic corps. Official visits to China, Vietnam and Latin America raised the profile of the Algerian struggle. ALN officers were trained in Iraq, and their troops supplied with equipment from Czechoslovakia; students received bursaries for East German universities, and an Algerian mission led by another ex-centralist, M'hammed Yazid, lobbied the UN in New York and the US government in

Figure 5.5 The frontier army: ALN troops training in Tunisia (M. Kouaci).

Washington. From 1958, the FLN had a touring artistic company of musicians and actors, and a professional football team.

Gradually, this independent state-in-arms, though exiled and embattled on the ground within Algeria, secured the mass support of a population over whom colonial sovereignty had never been more tangibly asserted. While in August 1955 the ALN had deepened the insurgency by enlisting civilians alongside *junud* in taking arms, it was ordinary Algerians' own initiative, in the cities and shantytowns, that produced the mass demonstrations of 10–12 December 1960. Beginning as spontaneous local opposition to colonial demonstrations and attacks on them by Europeans, and without central FLN coordination, tens of thousands of Algerians took to the streets of Algiers, Oran and other towns, where since 1957 the 'rebellion' had been thought quelled and 'law and order' re-established. Over one hundred Algerians were killed when soldiers fired into the crowds, but by proving massive public support for independence and the FLN, the demonstrations made visible a decisive shift that had already occurred militarily, the ALN within Algeria was in crisis, but politically, its war was already won.

## Revolution, Civil War and the Political Solution

If, by 1961, the FLN could legitimately stand as the political expression of
the Algerian people, this position had been achieved by popular adhesion
more than by the Front's coercion. Nonetheless, its struggle was a civil
war as well as a revolutionary one. Not only had the hand of the *jaysh* in
rural Algeria often been heavy, the FLN-ALN had also had to impose
itself, both in Algeria and among Algerians in France, against other
Algerian nationalists who had not accepted its hegemony. In late 1954
and early 1955, many militants of the ex-MTLD still identified nationalist
leadership with Messali – including, especially, much of the party's base
in Kabylia and the Constantinois and most of its grassroots membership
in France. Many who did so hesitated to accept the FLN as the nationalist
vanguard that they thought they themselves and their historic leader
represented. The creation of the Front had been intended to stop in-
fighting between 'centralists' and 'Messalists'. Instead, it brought it to
a fratricidal crescendo.

In December 1954, partisans of Messali created a parallel organisation,
the *Mouvement national algérien* (MNA, Algerian National Movement),
which fought for four years against the FLN in Algeria and among the
emigrant community in France. It was especially in France, where until
1958 the war of independence appeared mainly as continuous, bloody
score-settling within the Algerian community, and in Kabylia that this
'most tragic episode in the history of Algerian nationalism' unfolded.[141]
Although less costly in life than the earlier 'red night' killings, the so-
called Melouza massacre at Mechta Kasba, a hamlet in the *douar* of Beni
Ilmane on the edge of the Hodna mountains at the southern fringe of
*wilaya* 3, on 29 May 1957, became the most highly mediatised FLN
atrocity against Algerian civilians refractory to its control and considered
loyal to Messali. 'Melouza' (the name of a nearby settlement which in fact
was pro-FLN) was publicised by the French as evidence that 'the Algerian
rebellion is in fact . . . a totalitarian movement [which employs] the most
inhuman methods, the massive extermination of those who oppose its
designs'.[142] The men of the village, and boys aged over 15, were killed by
order of the *wilaya* 3 chief, Mohammedi Saïd, for refusing to rally to the
ALN, and declaring that 'Messali was their leader'. But in this transitional
zone between mountain and plain, where the colonial state had never
been visible and political socialisation was minimal, where berberophone
Kabyle *junud* were unwelcome among Arabic-speaking locals and 'low-
level ALN cadres behaved as if they were in conquered territory', the
violence indicated more the local complexities and confusions of the war
than clear political divergence.[143] Even within the ALN in Kabylia, it was

not until 1956 that rank-and-file militants became aware of the depth of the crisis issuing from the MTLD's split, and heard with shock for the first time that Messali was to be considered 'a traitor'.[144]

In other areas, the MNA formed guerilla groups. The movement also sought political recognition abroad as the legitimate representatives of Algerian nationalism, and a Messalist trade union, the USTA, was created in February 1956, ten days before the announcement of the FLN's UGTA. From May 1957 to July 1958 there was even a military 'third force', the 'National Army of the Algerian People' 2,000 to 3,000 strong, in the south Algérois under Muhammad Bellounis, a Second World War veteran, PPA activist and former MTLD municipal councillor, who convinced the French that he had created a 'counter-maquis' and fought the ALN with their assistance, vainly hoping to impose an alternative nationalist platform for negotiations. But the MNA lacked the FLN's traction and momentum. The MNA's representatives in Cairo, PPA veterans Ahmed Mezerna and Chadli Mekki, were arrested by the Egyptian authorities at the FLN's behest in July 1955. From being beaten up by their adversaries in 1955, the Front's organisers in France had won the battle on the streets and in the cafés by the end of 1957. By September 1959, when the FLN attempted to assassinate le père, 'the Father', as his supporters still called him, Messali's separate movement had been broken.[145]

Within the Front, too, at the same time as it was strangled by French military pressure, the interior ALN fatally weakened itself, killing thousands of its own in internal struggles and purges of real or supposed 'traitors'. Particularly in wilaya 3 under Colonel Amirouche in the summer of 1958, fears of infiltration by French agents – fears that the French assiduously fed – led to an epidemic of torture, show trials and executions within the maquis. Recruits from Algiers, following the eight days' strike, former 'Messalists', and especially French-speaking 'intellectuals' with any level of post-primary education, such as those who had rallied the Front after the students' strike, were particularly suspect. Amirouche's bleuite (fear of a plot by les bleus, militants in blue workmen's jackets 'turned' in detention and sent back by French intelligence to 'poison' the maquis) was the most spectacular, but purges affected the whole interior ALN, spreading suspicion, sapping morale and killing perhaps between 3,000 and 7,000 militants between 1958 and 1961.[146] In his memoirs, Ferhat Abbas recalled writing to Krim Belkacem before the murder of Abbane: 'If armed militants today turn their guns on other militants, we may as well say that tomorrow they will turn them on the people and on their freedom. And in that case, what nation and what homeland shall we have, if those with arms can impose their will on the people?'[147] As always, his pessimism was prescient.

As Algeria was increasingly, irrevocably riven along communal lines, and as Algerian society was torn by internal violence as well as bearing the weight of repression, the French polity too began to buckle under the strain. And while in Algeria, the French army's 'pacification' unceasingly worked to produce its own political defeat, correspondingly, within the French state the military situation was overtaken by political crisis. French bombing ostensibly directed at FLN positions in Sakiet Sidi Youssef on the Tunisian border on 7 February 1958 killed and injured at least 200 people, including women and children. The bombing was widely covered in the international press, and Tunisia's President Bourguiba denounced French aggression at the UN. While international opinion tilted further against France, and US President Eisenhower insisted the French government accept American 'good offices' to open negotiations and end the war, Algeria's Europeans and bristling patriotic opinion in the metropole and, especially, in the army, revolted. On 15 April, the French government fell on a vote of confidence. France was without a government for thirty-seven days. The constitutional order of the Fourth Republic itself was seen by many as unequal to the situation.

On 13 May, insurgent Europeans in Algiers seized the Government General. In alliance with an eclectic group of European militants including Alain de Sérigny, editor of the *Echo d'Alger*, and Pierre Lagaillarde, a law student and militant organiser at Algiers University, General Massu and his superior Raoul Salan, commander-in-chief of France's armed forces in Algeria, joined by Jacques Soustelle, formed a revolutionary 'Committee of Public Safety' in Algiers and called on Charles de Gaulle, who had been in retirement for over a decade, to return to power to save the Republic. For more than a hundred years after 1830, Algeria's Europeans had practised a politics that combined assertive opposition to the metropole with demands for its recognition and support; now they saw themselves as the tenacious last bastion of France's *grandeur* in the world, and the preservation of 'French Algeria' as saving France itself. They had imposed their will, they thought, on Mollet in 1956. Now their 'revolution of hope' would impose a new and more determined order on the state, to bring about a 'national unity' of the metropole and its Algerian 'province' that had never previously existed – and that they had never previously desired. 'Conscious of the union that exists between all the communities living in Algeria and the Sahara', the Committee of Public Safety claimed, '[we] affirm before the world that henceforward nothing can weaken this unity, and unanimously declare that all citizens of this Province are fully French (*des Français à part entière*)'.[148]

Facing, and also playing on, the very real threat of a military coup d'état, de Gaulle came to power on 1 June and three days later arrived in Algiers to delirious acclaim – cheered along the streets in a rain of confetti, standing in an open-topped car, arms outstretched. By December, as President of the new Fifth Republic he had escalated both the development drive and the military campaign in Algeria, appointing Challe commander-in-chief and an economist, Paul Delouvrier, as civil Delegate General to oversee the reform of civil administration and socio-economic conditions. With customary paternalism, in October he offered a *paix des braves* ('warriors' peace') to the ALN, declaring that a 'white flag' would be accepted and that combatants might 'return without humiliation to their families and their work'.[149] Near to their lowest ebb, many in the maquis took the offer seriously, which increased internal suspicion and renewed purges. The *paix des braves*, which was nothing but a demand for surrender, was sharply refused by the newly formed GPRA. De Gaulle, like his predecessors, intended that Algeria should remain, one way or another, French. Strategically it was more important than ever: in 1956 work at Mers el-Kébir completed the Mediterranean's only nuclear blast-proof naval base, oil began flowing from the Sahara in early 1958 and in February 1960, the first French nuclear weapon was tested at Reggane.[150] Various schemes of preserving a French Sahara or, ironically enough, a return to the coastal 'restricted occupation' of European enclaves, were entertained. But international circumstances including significant economic pressure from the Americans, the FLN's growing strength abroad and, despite the relentless counter-insurgency, its tenacity within Algeria, and perhaps above all the irreversible disintegration of colonial society in spiralling violence between and within the European and Algerian communities forced de Gaulle to recognise that Algeria was becoming an impediment to, rather than the foundation of, the 'renovated' France he wished to create. In September 1959 he announced the necessity of 'self-determination' for Algeria, promising progress and fraternity if a federal solution (such as Abbas had envisaged fourteen years earlier) could be found, and warning of the chaos and regression that would come with 'secession'. From early 1960 he would be obliged to 'give ground all along the line',[151] speaking in November of a future '*Algérie algérienne* ... an Algerian republic', calling a referendum on self-determination in January 1961 and beginning discussions in view of negotiations with the FLN the following month. Although slow and fitful, talks began in May 1961 at the French Alpine spa town of Évian, near the Swiss border, that would eventually lead to the Évian accords and a ceasefire agreement on 18 March 1962. The accords provided for a referendum on independence; held on 1 July and largely

Figure 5.6 Djamila Bouhired addresses an FLN rally, 27 June 1962 (AP).

boycotted by the Europeans, by almost 6 million votes for to 16,500 against, it finally gave democratic political form to the aspirations of the overwhelming majority of the country's inhabitants, and a political solution to the conflict that military resolve alone, on either side, could not bring to an end.[152]

From 1960, correspondingly, Europeans began to leave, transferring their savings out of Algeria, travelling to a France they and their families had often never known, *pour voir*, 'just to see': to look for apartments, to look for work. The European *ultras*, conversely, dedicated to saving at all costs an *Algérie française* that they now saw de Gaulle betraying, resorted to arms, first to pressurise government and public opinion, and then to resist decolonisation by force. Already in 1956, European terrorists including André Achiary, the man responsible for the Guelma massacres of May 1945, had created a 'French Algeria Resistance Organisation' (ORAF). The ORAF was notably responsible for the most costly single attack of the 'Battle of Algiers', when on 10 August 1956 ORAF militants blew up part of the rue de Thèbes, in the Casbah, with thirty kilograms of plastic explosive, killing sixty, in reprisal for which the first FLN bombings of civilian targets in central Algiers were carried out a month later.[153] A few months afterwards, on 16 January 1957, 'ultras' attempted to assassinate Salan (mistaking him for a 'sell-out' because he had commanded the army in Indochina) by firing a missile into his headquarters in central Algiers. But in May 1958, demonstrators with *Algérie française* placards climbed onto the statue of Bugeaud, in the square that bore his name on the rue d'Isly, to acclaim the same Salan when he appeared alongside Soustelle at the balcony of the same building.

In November 1958 the ORAF was succeeded by the 'French National Front' (FNF), then in 1960 by the 'Front for French Algeria' (FAF). It was an FNF leader, the bar-owner Jo Ortiz, who coined a phrase that became famous when he told a meeting in Algiers in December 1959 that if they gave in to self-determination, the Europeans would have to choose either 'the suitcase or the coffin'. FNF activists led Algiers' Europeans in an attempted insurgency in 'barricades week' (24–29 January 1960), a would-be replay of 13 May which, this time, failed to carry the army with it, and in December 1960, the FAF made several attempts on de Gaulle's life during a visit to Algeria. It was largely in response to FAF ultras' anti-Gaullist demonstrations and attacks on Algerians, in Oran and Algiers on 9 and 10 December 1960, that the massive Algerian popular demonstrations of the following days took place. In early 1961, a small group of ultras including Lagaillarde, now in exile in Madrid, created the Secret Army Organisation (OAS). On 21–25 April, four generals, all veterans of the war in Algeria – Salan, Challe, Zeller and Jouhaud – mounted a putsch in Algiers, in an abortive attempt to overthrow the government that for four days hung a cloud of civil war over France. De Gaulle appealed to the nation and its army on radio and television, and the coup collapsed; but while Challe and Zeller gave themselves up, Salan and Jouhaud went underground, and the OAS of which they became the chiefs emerged as a clandestine armed movement in Algeria.[154]

Commanding widespread support among the European population, the OAS believed, as one of its leaders later wrote, that the FLN's 'rebellion' was already vanquished, that the prospect of Algeria's Muslims being 'thrown out of France' (a France which, for over a century, had in fact never yet included them) originated entirely with de Gaulle, and that the FLN's 'real power was exterior to Algeria, residing especially in a craftily managed propaganda directed from the Eastern bloc'. But now, 'we saw that this power had made itself French, too, and that it came from the highest office of state'.[155] In 1961–62, the war entered a new phase as the OAS targeted liberal Europeans and those suspected of planning to leave, and rained indiscriminate violence on Algerians. On 7 February 1962, an OAS bomb intended for de Gaulle's culture minister, André Malraux, maimed and blinded a four-year-old girl, Delphine Renard, in Paris; on 15 March, OAS commandos machine-gunned education officials at the El Biar Social Centre, killing six, among them Mouloud Feraoun. Plastic explosive, gun and bomb attacks occurred daily in Algiers and began to occur in the metropole, especially against Communist Party and Gaullist targets, where they outraged opinion. The day after the attack intended for Malraux, police repression of a large anti-OAS demonstration in Paris left eight dead and over one hundred injured at the Charonne métro station; half a million people marched in memory of the victims five days later. In late March and early April, OAS commandos and French troops and gendarmes fought a pitched battle for control of Bab el-Oued. In March, as the FLN's war was ending, the OAS called for escalating terrorist actions in Algeria and France, to paralyse the government and national infrastructure, and to create a 'climate of generalised insecurity'.[156] Enacting a 'scorched earth' policy, OAS militants sought to deny the FLN the fruits of France's civilisational work. On 7 June, they burned down Algiers University library. On 25 June, they blew up petroleum reservoirs in Oran. Salan was arrested in Oran on 20 April, leaving a 'National Council of the Resistance' (CNR) under the former Prime Minister and leading wartime Resistance figure – Jean Moulin's successor, in fact, as head of the original CNR in 1943 – Georges Bidault to continue the struggle 'against the abandonment of Algeria, the Gaullist dictatorship and international communism'. Bidault declared of the referendum approving the Évian accords, held in the metropole on 8 April, that the people had been 'consulted on the amputation of a French province. This is illegal, unconstitutional, illegitimate.'[157]

It was a particularly perverse twist of self-perception, and misperception, that brought the ultras – some former *résistants* like Soustelle and Bidault, others right-wing populists like Lagaillarde and Ortiz – to see themselves as defenders of a fraternal, multi-confessional Algeria that had never existed and that they, certainly, could not create. It was no less ironic that those who most desperately resisted the departure of Algeria's Europeans, seeing themselves to the end as imposing conditions on the FLN that would allow the maintenance of a European presence, in the end did most to make it impossible for Europeans, in any significant numbers, to remain in Algeria after independence. If the ALN had begun to accentuate the logic of communal division in August 1955, it was the terror of the OAS in 1961–62, and violent ripostes to it that culminated in a wave of abductions and murders of Europeans in Oran in July 1962, that consummated the rupture. Before 1954, it is worth recalling, no Algerian political movement had envisaged the massive departure of Algeria's Europeans as necessary for the 'liquidation of colonialism' that all sought. Abbas, in 1957, still insisted that the future cohabitation of all in equality was possible.[158] But the logic of the war exacerbated the communitarian tendency inherent in the PPA, of which in a sense the OAS terror was, by 1962, an enlarged mirror image. The FLN's stated position, repeated in tracts circulated by the Front within Algeria as well as in declarations by its government-in-exile, was that Europeans and Jews of goodwill would all have their place in the new and independent state: 'You have been Algerians for millennia', FLN circulars assured the country's Jews, reminding them of the Europeans' anti-Semitism, and a GPRA brochure published in Tunis in 1961 reaffirmed the statement of 1 November 1954, that once colonialism was indeed liquidated, Algeria's people could be *All Algerians*.[159] Instead, there was an exodus. Some 800,000 French citizens were 'repatriated' in 1961–62, to a *patrie* that most had never seen, to which they would feel themselves exiled, and where they would become the *pieds noirs*, their personal histories and sense of community defined by the war, the betrayal of their confidence and their departure, set against the fictionalised background of an idyllic Algeria whose deeper realities they had never been able to apprehend.

For many – perhaps most strikingly the Jewish population of the Mzab, hastily accorded a French citizenship that, as inhabitants of the military-ruled Southern Territories, they had never previously been given, and suddenly flown out of their ancestral home – the experience was of a sudden and confused uprooting. This was above all the case, though, for those Algerians who had, for whatever reason, ended the war in French uniform. Orders were issued against embarking *harki*s and their families, but among the nearly 135,000 'French Muslims' of Algerian origin counted in France in 1968, some tens of thousands belonged to *harki* families who had been evacuated or found their own way out of Algeria. These generally unwelcome and unplanned-for *rapatriés* ('repatriated persons') were 'temporarily' housed in isolated camps in the rural south of France, like Mas Thibert in the Camargue, and left there. Some such camps, notably Larzac in the Aveyron, had previously served as detention camps for Algerian internees during the war, or, as at Rivesaltes near Perpignan, for Spanish republican refugees in 1939–40 and then, under Vichy, for Jews being deported to extermination camps. Some evacuees were later settled as whole communities in forest hamlets where their patterns of housing, routine and employment echoed the *regroupement* camps of the war, or were dispersed in the growing suburban *banlieues* where they faced both metropolitan anti-immigrant racism and their stigmatisation as 'traitors' by other Algerian immigrants.[160] Many of the *harki*s disarmed and left behind in Algeria were rounded up and killed, often, following the ceasefire on 19 March, by a suddenly emerging army of so-called *marsiens* (a play on 'March-ists' and 'Martians'), men who flocked to join the ALN when all was over save the opportunity to flag one's loyalty by exacting revenge on those who were now defenceless. Others were interned in punitive work camps – 'no pity ... only hate, only the whip, only killing ... the work of misery, the food of suffering, and ... the stick, every morning, every evening ... the things they did, you can't tell people ... ' – where they sometimes remained for years before being released.[161]

On 3 July 1962, the French government recognised Algeria's independence and the GPRA arrived in Algiers; on 5 July, Algerian men, women and children took over the streets in cities across their country in celebration. The cost of the conflict to Algeria had been incalculable. In 1959, the FLN's mouthpiece *El Moudjahid* wrote of 1 million Algerians killed, and from 1962 the official death toll was fixed at the entirely symbolic, and demographically impossible, figure of 1.5 million martyrs. It would also be claimed, equally impossibly, that 150,000 *harkis* had been massacred by the FLN at the end of the war. Such figures served, crudely, to capture the otherwise inexpressible depth and intensity of the violence that had ripped colonial Algeria apart. In all, 2,788 European civilians had been killed and 7,541 injured. As in every outbreak of violence since 1830, while the European death toll was precise, it would be impossible to know exactly how many Algerians had been killed: an impossibility of accounting, as well as an unaccountability, that was characteristic of colonial violence. Only in the summer of 1962, when the colonial order had broken down and was not yet replaced, did Europeans 'disappear' in uncertain numbers. The plausible Algerian death toll may have been as high as half a million. The best available – though very approximately calculated – estimates suggest that between 250,000 and 300,000 Algerians lost their lives, of whom perhaps 141,000–145,000 were ALN combat casualties and 6,000 to 7,000 killed in internal purges, another 6,000 or 7,000 *harki*s killed in revenge attacks at independence, perhaps 30,000 Algerians killed by the FLN, and between 40,000 and 65,000 civilian victims of the French war of re-conquest.[162]

The society that re-emerged from the ruins was not the radically transformed 'new personality', demystified and 'discover[ing] the real', that Fanon brilliantly imagined.[163] As Ben M'hidi had expected, Algeria's people had borne the war in both senses, suffering and supporting it, rather than experiencing it as a liberation in itself. The war itself, in its atrocious unfolding, more than any ideology or program of the FLN, had indeed revolutionised Algerian society, mobilising long-standing codes and structures of social solidarity into a new, assertive, militant sense of political community. And the unfolding of the war, its constraints and vicissitudes, had created an Algerian state – an apparatus for rule – nominally 'by the people and for the people' that the people recognised and claimed as their own. But whether the revolution could be made to work for the people, and the state to govern by the people, remained open and unanswered questions. When independence was won, everything, in this sense, remained yet to do.

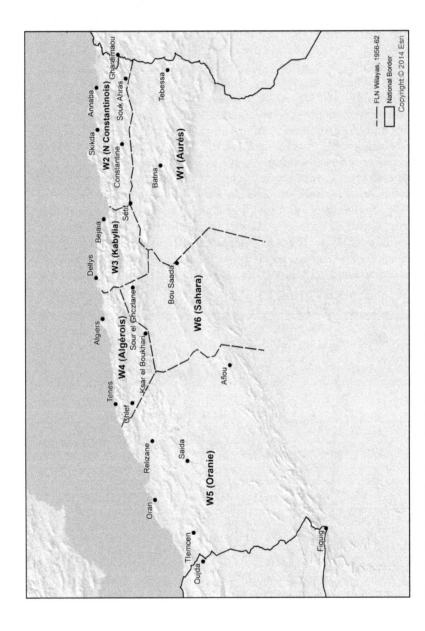

Map 3: Algeria: FLN *wilayas*, 1956–62. Map by C. Moore.

Within the map:

Ghardimaou
Annaba
Skikda
Souk Ahras
W2 (N Constantinois)
Constantine
Tebessa
Batna
W1 (Aurès)
Bejaia
Sétif
Dellys
W3 (Kabylia)
Bou Saada
Algiers
Sour el Ghozlane
W6 (Sahara)
W4 (Algérois)
Tenes
Ksar el Boukhari
Chlef
Aflou
Relizane
Saida
Oran
W5 (Oranie)
Tlemcen
Oujda
Figuig

FLN Wilayas, 1956–62
National Border
Copyright © 2014 Esri

# 6    The Unfinished Revolution, 1962–1992

In July 1962, almost all Algerians could be wholly and spontaneously of one mind about one thing: they and their country were free, independent and overjoyed. The war was over and with it the colonial era. In a report for the news magazine *Jeune Afrique*, journalist Kamal Jawad noted, among the millions of graffiti that covered 'every wall, every telegraph pole, every car and even their tyres', some remarkable examples of anonymous political literacy, 'such as "It is the intervention of popular causes that has created the conditions of a true revolution."' One inscription in particular caught his attention, 'hidden in a narrow street, in the depths of the village, laboriously drawn in Latin script ... "Tahia El Hourria", *vive la liberté*, said in Arabic and written in French; ... this slogan, as it is and where it is, is all of independent Algeria'.[1]

The same popular feeling could be heard as well as read everywhere, in songs that had been broadcast by radio from Cairo and Tunis over the previous four years and, taken up in demonstrations from 1960 onwards, were known to everyone, from the PPA's old martial, militant hymns – *'Min jabalina tala'u sawt al-ahrar/Yunadina ala 'l-istiqlal'* ('From our mountains rises the voice of the free/Calling us to independence') – to more recent and more intimate expressions of love and sacrifice: *Yemma matibkish, jaysh al-khaiba magatlnish* ('Mother, don't cry for me/The army of defeat has not killed me'). Simpler songs were sung with gusto by children in the shantytowns, as the Catholic social worker Marie-Renée Chené found at Bou B'sila, on the eastern outskirts of Algiers near the Oued el-Harrach, in March 1963: 'O brother *mujahid*/They came with their guns/They said, "Don't be scared"/They said, "The harkis have gone"/ ... The *mujahid* with a uniform like the paras'/Isn't like a *harki* dressed in rags/ ... Hey, sell-outs/Why have you sold your religion for two francs?' In a small, but telling, sign, two years later the authorities announced a national competition to choose 'the hymn of Algerian children', to complement the official national songs already devoted to students and workers. Entries, composed of no more than four stanzas of six lines each, and in classical Arabic, were required to 'contain the

Figure 6.1 The eve of independence in downtown Algiers, 2 July 1962
(Marc Riboud/Magnum).

following themes: the past and victory over obscurantist forces; love of the
Nation and the promise to the martyrs; socialist engagement, the duty to
learn and develop one's physical strength; solidarity and international
friendship; the joy of living through socialism'. The accompanying
music was to 'be inspired by the Algerian musical patrimony in conformity with the recommendations of the colloquium on Algerian music'.
Not only popular liberation, but its expression in words and music was
already being bureaucratised.[2]

Algeria's independence marked a critical moment for the history of an
emergent 'Third World', in the optimistic sense that that term carried in
the early 1960s. Across the Arab world, Africa and Asia, popular struggle,
anti-imperialist sovereignty and the forging of a new future for the aspiring, youthful populations of ambitious, new nation-states promised
immense possibilities for a world at last liberated from the dead weight
of colonial rule. Within North Africa, with the exception of the remaining
Spanish enclaves in Morocco and the western Sahara, Algeria's liberation
completed the region's decolonisation, and high hopes for the emergence
of a new, fraternal and prosperous 'Arab Maghrib' within a broader,
progressive Middle Eastern and Afro-Asian world went hand in hand
with the vision of building a revolutionary society at home. The decades

from independence to the end of the twentieth century would be caught between this sense of possibilities, the revolutionary future glimpsed in the victory of national liberation and the domestic as well as international constraints limiting their realisation. Those constraints were imposed partly by regional and global political and economic forces, partly by the not always free choices made by the country's leaders, and partly – perhaps most of all – by the conditions in which liberation itself had been won. The inheritance of the long and costly war in destruction and dislocation, suffering and sacrifice brought with it intense popular mobilisation and the creation of an assertive popular political culture, ready to demand delivery on the immense promises of freedom. It also brought a deeply secretive and factional system of political power based on the close solidarities of the wartime army and security services, rivalries between interior *wilayas* and the frontier ALN (at independence renamed the ANP, National People's Army), between early PPA militants-turned-maquisards and late-coming professional soldiers who had deserted in the course of the war from the French armed forces, between left-wing revolutionaries intent on pursuing the thorough transformation of society and others opposed to radical change and seeking to combine material progress with a stern, socially conservative morality under the banner of religious and cultural 'authenticity'.

The war had torn Algerian society and even Algerian nationalist politics apart; the unifying fiction of unanimous national resistance that it was now necessary to promote, in enshrining the revolution, the war fought by and against the Algerian people, and the 'million martyrs' to independence as the new founding myth the nation required, papered over the rips but could not suture them back together. The history of the war and of the FLN became legends, both drawn upon in a routinised rhetoric to claim legitimacy for those in power and appealed to by those excluded from power, or suffering under it, as a 'confiscated' truth which, if only known in uncensored detail, would reveal the hidden cause behind all the country's subsequent ills. The new political class that came to power was deeply ambivalent about the longer history of the nationalist struggle, few of whose founding figures were still in their ranks, and some of whose leaders they had themselves eliminated along the way. And they were impatient, still, with the practice of law-bound, constitutional and plural politics that they identified with the failed legalism of the years before 1954 and the 'politickers' who had rallied 'late' to the armed struggle. While endorsing the slogan that proclaimed – originally, in Algiers in the summer of 1962, against Ben Bella – 'the people' (in the singular) as the 'sole hero' of the war, the new state's leaders shared a widespread conviction that Algeria's people (in the plural) could not yet manage their own affairs.[3] The state they built was meant to work for the people, but it would not need to include them in exercising the sovereignty it had won.

The tension between radical ambition and the constricting force of authoritarian politics, and the context of the changing world in which they found themselves, meant that, in Algeria as elsewhere in Africa and the Middle East, the revolutionary hope initially embodied in 'the Third World' would give way, over the decades following independence, to a more sombre meaning, connoting poverty, insecurity and the frustration of hopes for the future. This was not, by any means, apparent or inevitable in the halcyon days of Third World optimism in the 1960s and revolutionary state-building and social progress in the 1970s. The dramatic gap between what had seemed possible and what, thirty or forty years later, would be visible would lead many Algerians to believe that they had been betrayed all along: only the occult powers of a neo-colonial fifth column, *hizb fransa*, the 'party of France' serving the malign interests of France by keeping Algeria down, invented by the diabolical genius of de Gaulle and maintained in power through every turn of events since independence, could account for it.[4] But the primacy of factional interests over a commonly deliberated public good hardly needed neo-colonial French orchestration (imagined as operating with a degree of coherence and foresight which the French state had never been able to exercise before 1962) to prosper – although particular cliques and factions taking advantage, in due course, of French political, financial and commercial contacts would undoubtedly prosper disproportionately from the early 1980s onwards. The changed fortunes and mounting pressures that, by 1992, brought the country to a bloody and disastrous new crisis, resulted as ever from more than a single cause: and these causes were to be found within Algeria's unfinished revolution, within Algerian society and in wider, impersonal factors beyond them, more than among those who wished them ill.

### *Pouvoir*, Putsch and the Charismatic State

Algeria's sovereign, independent state came into being out of seven long years of war and from the war's sudden culmination in crisis in the summer of 1962: out of a long and tenacious struggle with colonialism, but also out of internal struggles between Algerians that had durable and debilitating effects. In the later stages of the war, from the beginning of 1960, there was no longer a question of whether the reckless gamble of 1954 would succeed, but of who would take precedence in the new state when it did. The FLN which Algerian crowds in December 1960 acclaimed as what Abbane had intended it should be – the political projection of the people's aspirations to freedom – had never, throughout the war, become distinct from what Abbane had also identified as its legitimate role: merely the authorised interlocutor with the real power of the army.

In December 1959, after four months of deliberation in Tunis by a meeting of a 'committee of ten' chief colonels of the ALN, the CNRA had met in Tripoli and reshuffled the provisional government's cabinet. From then on, power was concentrated in an 'Interministerial War Committee' (CIG) consisting of Krim, Boussouf and Bentobbal, and in the army's new General Staff (EMG) under Boumediene. The latter, based in Ghardimaou on the Tunisian border, reorganised the frontier army into battalions combining men originating from different *wilayas* to counter 'regionalist' tensions and rivalries, and became one of two central institutions in the 'exterior' ALN. The other was the MALG, Boussouf's intelligence service created at Oujda and later based also in Tunis and, from July 1960, at the '*Base Didouche*' ('Camp Didouche'), an abandoned barracks in the desert south of Tripoli in Libya. With its intelligence-gathering expertise, its iron discipline of living and working in complete secrecy and, more crucially, its extensive archive of dossiers on FLN militants and ALN officers as well as on Algerians filed as having 'collaborated' with the French, the MALG was itself a stake in the coming power struggle. Increasingly identified – and themselves often identifying – personally with Boussouf, 'Si Mabrouk',[5] from whose shadow Boumediene had now emerged in his own right, its multi-lingual, administratively efficient and close-knit officers were both an unusually cohesive and a particularly capable group within the ALN. A small number of them, the so-called 'red carpet' group, had already, in the winter of 1961–62, spent time in Moscow for training.[6] In the summer of 1962, EMG troops seized the MALG's archives in Morocco and Libya.[7] Boussouf himself, as Krim and Bentobbal had been, was now eclipsed in the army's hierarchy by Boumediene; after 1962 he would retire from the scene. Many of his former officers, disenchanted or outraged by Boumediene's 'betrayal' of his own former patron, were demobilised from the army and entered civilian life in business or in the offices of the new administration. Others backed Boumediene as chief of the ALN; some remained in the security service of the new army that after independence would become the *Sécurité militaire* (SM), under MALG veteran Abdallah Khalef, known during the war – when all MALG officers went, even among themselves, by assumed names – as 'Merbah', and after 1962 as Kasdi Merbah.

By the time of the ceasefire in March 1962, Boumediene held the real power behind the scenes of the FLN's state, but it was not yet clear who would stand in the spotlight. Since July 1961, when Boumediene and his closest colleagues in the EMG had penned a denunciation, directed at the GPRA, of the 'depth of the cancer that has eaten away at our revolution', the provisional government and its military staff had been at odds.[8] Their confrontation culminated on 30 June 1962, when Ben Youssef Ben Khedda, the GPRA's President since August 1961, alongside one group of the government's ministers that included Boussouf, Boudiaf and Krim, and denounced by another including Ben Bella, Khider and Bitat, sacked the army's high command. As this cleavage showed, the government was also internally split, as were the surviving 'historic leaders' who, imprisoned since October 1956, had joined the Algerian negotiating team in Switzerland the day after the ceasefire. Ben Bella went to Cairo at Nasser's invitation and deliberately annoyed Tunisia's President Bourguiba by proclaiming, on arriving in Tunis on 14 April, 'We are Arabs, we are Arabs, we are Arabs!', a declaration of his own preference for alliance with Egypt and a broad Afro-Asian 'international' against the global north, which also, given the hostility between Nasser and Bourguiba, ran implicitly against closer relations with neighbouring Morocco and Tunisia. This refrain also seemed to confirm the OAS's claims about 'Arab' communalism, further alarming Algeria's Europeans about the reliability of the FLN's guarantees of their future as a minority in Algeria, and exasperating the GPRA. Ben Bella annoyed Aït Ahmed, too, by referring to Algeria's 'Arab revolution', and while supported by Khider, he was opposed, in his presumption of precedence, by Boudiaf as well as by Krim. The GPRA also undermined itself by its disorderly disavowal of the ceasefire agreement with the OAS, announced on 17 June, which had been reached by the power-sharing Provisional Executive that was now installed under the terms of the Évian accords at Rocher Noir (Boumerdès), the new administrative city built east of Algiers in the last years of the war. With Algerian members nominated by the GPRA and led by the former speaker of the Algerian Assembly, Abderrahmane Farès, the Provisional Executive served as Algeria's transitional administration until the formal announcement of independence; it was to this body that de Gaulle formally handed over sovereignty on 3 July.

The CNRA, still constitutionally the revolution's sovereign body to which the GPRA was answerable, met for the last time at Tripoli in Libya between 25 May and 7 June to debate a program for the constitution and policy orientation of the new state, and to plan for a new government, envisaged as being constituted by a reformed FLN under a new Political Bureau. The Tripoli program had been drafted at Hammamet in Tunisia by an able and independently minded group of mostly left-leaning and intellectual FLN cadres including Mostefa Lacheraf, one of those hijacked in October 1956, Redha Malek, the director of *El Moudjahid* who had taken part in the Évian talks, and Mohammed Harbi, a student leader in the FLN's Fédération de France in 1954–58 and subsequently chief of the central office of the GPRA's foreign ministry. Of the group, only Harbi espoused an explicitly Marxist analysis of Algeria's social relations, present challenges and political future. None of them were allied to any of the emergent factions in the FLN's leadership. Ben Bella, who along with the GPRA's Information Minister, M'hammed Yazid, was also a member of the commission, had vetoed a proposal for a formally secular state, and it was the intervention of Ali Haroun, a lawyer representing the Fédération de France at the CNRA, that added a reference to 'socialism', but the text was a radical one nonetheless: Ferhat Abbas disliked its 'ill-digested communism'.[9] The program prioritised agrarian revolution, education, free public healthcare and women's social and political emancipation, and envisaged an assertive anti-imperialist foreign policy. It attacked both the 'neo-colonialism' inherent in the Évian accords, doubting (a preoccupation of Malek's) the capacity of the 'immense majority' of Europeans to play a constructive part in Algeria's future, and, more strikingly (a preoccupation of Lacheraf's) the 'political feudalisms, "chieftainships" and partisan clientèles' within the FLN, which was seen as hamstrung by its 'ideological indigence' and 'the absence of any democratic education among militants and citizens'.[10]

The PPA's old problem – programmatic superficiality, the rule of slogan, faction, and clique, and an absence of open debate – still characterised the FLN, and was never more serious than at the moment when sovereignty was actually to be taken up. There were real differences of substance, orientation and principle, as well as simple rivalries of persons and factions in pursuit of power, dividing the revolution's surviving leaders. They represented a diverse political spectrum from former liberal-professional, progressive but anti-Marxist *UDMistes* Abbas, Ahmad Boumendjel and Ahmad Francis through socialist-inclined intellectuals like Aït Ahmed, the *étatiste* praetorians around Boumediene, and the romantically Arabo-Muslim populist Ben Bella, to the Islamist maquisard Colonel 'Si Nacer', Mohammedi Saïd, who had been responsible for ordering the carnage at 'Melouza'. Nonetheless, signing up to its *marxisant* critique of 'feudalism' and 'petty-bourgeois spirit' and to its program for pursuing, beyond political independence, a social and economic, 'democratic and popular revolution', the CNRA rapidly and unanimously adopted the Tripoli proposals. It fell apart over the more significant business of agreeing on who should be in a position to implement them. The in-fighting over nominations for the new Political Bureau of the FLN produced deadlock. Ben Khedda, by departing unannounced during the night of 6–7 June to resume his post as head of the government-in-waiting in Tunis, exacerbated the crisis rather than transcending it. His departure brought the process to an end without a resolution, and enabled his opponents to charge him with dereliction of duty.

Coalescing around alliances based on interests and grudges more than on shared principles or policy orientation, two camps had emerged in the CNRA: Ben Bella, Khider, and Bitat, supported by Boumediene's EMG, were joined by Abbas, Boumendjel and Francis. Against them were the rest of Ben Khedda's GPRA, along with Aït Ahmed, Krim, and Boudiaf, and a coalition of interior *wilayas* hostile to the incursions of the EMG and the frontier army, which they saw as allowing eleventh-hour 'opportunists' to supplant the true ALN *mujahidin*. Within the ALN in Algeria, *wilayas* 1, 5 and 6 supported the EMG, while *wilayas* 2, 3 and 4 and the reconstituted Algiers Autonomous Zone opposed it. The latter group was joined by representatives of the Fédération de France in an 'inter-*wilaya* committee' at Zemmorah, north of Bordj Bou Arreridj in the east of *wilaya* 3, on 24–25 June. The inter-*wilaya* committee accused emissaries sent from the EMG to drum up support in the interior, especially in *wilaya* 2 and Algiers where armed confrontations had already occurred, of 'fomenting dissidence' (*travail fractionnel*). It denounced the EMG itself for 'rebellion', announced that it would support only a unified government, not one faction among others, and declared a state of emergency in the areas under its control.[11] As the symbolic date of 5 July approached, the power struggle was unfolding rapidly.

Although the struggle would take three years to play out fully, within three months it was effectively all over. When the GPRA arrived in Algiers on 3 July, it came without two of its ministers, Ben Bella and Khider. On 22 July, the latter, with their supporters, unilaterally declared their Political Bureau in Tlemcen, while Ben Khedda claimed legality for the truncated GPRA in Algiers. Inconclusive attempts at negotiation failed to resolve the dispute. On the ground, different units of the ALN, under officers acting for themselves as well as for one or another faction, confronted one another. As EMG and *wilaya* 1 troops approached Algiers from the south, former comrades fired on each other at Ksar Boukhari (Boghari) and Sour el-Ghozlane (Aumale). On 25 July, EMG troops under a veteran *wilaya* 1 maquisard, Larbi Berredjem, occupied Constantine and arrested, among others, GPRA minister Lakhdar Bentobbal, with whom Berredjem had originally taken to the mountains in 1950. Boudiaf and Krim, from Tizi Ouzou, sought to organise resistance to what they saw as Ben Bella's attempt to seize power by force. Aït

Ahmed called for a 'popular congress', a notion for which no-one had any time. An ephemeral 'Council for National Unity and Salvation' formed by 'neutral' militants in Algiers gained no traction.[12] At the end of July, troops of *wilaya* 4, with encouragement from Khider, overran those of the ZAA and took control in Algiers. With de Gaulle's spokesman Alain Peyrefitte threatening intervention to protect French nationals, an agreement was reached on 2 August, and the Political Bureau arrived in Algiers the next day, but at the end of August, fighting broke out again in Kabylia and around Algiers between *wilaya* 3 and 4 guerillas, on one side, and EMG troops on the other. Civilians demonstrated, demanding an end to the fighting with the slogan *saba'a snin, barakat,* 'Seven years, enough!' The confrontations cost several thousand casualties before they ended in early September; by the time Boumediene's troops reached Algiers on 9 September, resistance was over.[13]

The FLN's bitter and bloody fragmentation was produced by long-standing, deep-running fissures and tensions in the movement as well as by the sudden pressure of independence, and the ambitious, pragmatic or opportunistic actions of individuals. The inability of the revolution's formal political institutions to contain and structure rivalries, or to place the crucial questions of the objectives and the content of immediate and future policy above factional interest, and the outweighing of institutional procedure by the balance of armed force on the ground, reflected both the realities of the revolution as they had developed through the course of the war, and the political culture of the movement that had begun the war in the first place. These, in turn, had been shaped by the constraints of pre-war politics, and then by the murderous repression that the war had unleashed. The task of taking in hand the infrastructure of the state inherited from late colonialism's frenetic flurry of both repression and reform – the fifteen administrative *départements* that during the war had replaced the three old ones, with their expanded and partly Algerianised bureaucracies, the raft of new statutes that, combined with the provisions of the Évian accords, had overhauled Algeria's legal system, the projects for agrarian reform and industrialisation announced since 1958 – and consolidating it with the ministries and the army built in Tripoli and Tunis, was immense. Although the Tripoli program formally expressed the ideological orientation and policy priorities of the new regime, there was no clear, practical plan for addressing that task.

The forum for doing so was the National Constituent Assembly, plebiscited on 20 September from a single list of FLN candidates which, in the course of the July–August crisis, had been purged of many of the Political Bureau's opponents, especially those associated with the ex-GPRA and *wilaya* 2.[14] Over the following year, until the ratification by referendum of the constitution on 8 September 1963, and its formal promulgation two days later which created the Democratic and Popular Algerian Republic, and despite genuinely open and vigorous debate among some members of the Assembly, the consolidation of power perpetuated the existing tendencies rather than overcoming them. At the war's end, the CNRA had not become a true 'parliament', deliberating on government policy and holding the government to account, and nor did the Assembly that succeeded it. For Ben Bella, 'the party' of the FLN to which all the Constituent's deputies belonged held primacy over the Assembly, but the FLN had never yet been a party. Indeed, as Abbane and others had insisted, during the war it was precisely *not* 'a party', and it had not been reconstituted as such since the ceasefire. The Tripoli program had called for a 'conscious vanguard' drawn from all segments of the population – peasants, workers, youth and revolutionary intellectuals – to direct the revolution. It also identified these groups with 'the people' as a whole, and whether the FLN was to be a mass party or a revolutionary vanguard remained undecided. In the constitution adopted on 10 September 1963, and in the 'Algiers Charter', including the party's statutes, produced by the FLN's first congress seven months later, the FLN was designated Algeria's 'single vanguard party', responsible for educating and organising the masses, whose 'deep aspirations' it was held to reflect. The FLN was the vehicle through which the revolution was to be achieved and socialism built; it was to define policy, and control both the government and the National Assembly. At the same time, 'the vanguard' of the people was identified, again, with 'the *fellahs*, the labouring masses and the revolutionary intellectuals' in general, and the Republic was oriented 'in conformity with the principles of socialism and the effective exercise of power by the people'.[15]

This was not mere verbiage; independent Algeria's first, most fundamental formal laws were outweighed by but also reflected the realities of its 'real' constitution, the real system of power that Algerians would come to call *le pouvoir*, and that had already taken firm shape behind the nascent institutions of the new state. Unity and unanimity, at least in public, were still essential; divisions and disagreement would be played out offstage. There was to be no separation of powers, no institutionalising of divergent views and programs, neither in a multiplicity of competing parties nor within the FLN's National Assembly, as became clear to the more independently minded and active members of the first Constituent who failed in 1964 to gain re-selection for the second – or who, by then, had resigned or been arrested.[16] The Assembly would be merely a sounding board for decisions made elsewhere, not a sovereign legislature: even the constitution it was convened to draw up was in the end created by FLN militants gathered by Ben Bella elsewhere (as had been customary for large meetings since the 1930s, in an Algiers cinema hall) and imposed on the Assembly. The party, the state and the people as formally conceived were almost indistinguishable; the FLN was held to be the expression of the people en masse, as all 'healthy' elements of the national community, and in this sense, 'the people' imagined as being represented in the FLN was substituted for the real people in the 'effective exercise of power'. At the same time, while the declared intention was that the state should be 'in sum, nothing but the instrument of the Party', it would be truer to say that the FLN was merely 'a façade behind which hides the power of the State'.[17] The party itself, like the wartime FLN before it, would have no autonomy; it merely 'animated', less with ideological spirit or programmatic intention than with the bodies of its personnel, the bureaucratic machinery of the state which its members filled. The power of decision lay with the factional interests above them, behind which lay the army and its political police. Ben Bella, anxious to preserve his independence from the armed force that had brought him to power, would indeed claim that the party was truly all-encompassing, that even 'the ANP only exists within the framework of the FLN', but 'the FLN' here was merely a slogan.[18] In fact the reverse was still true: the FLN existed only as the civilian front of the army.

In late September 1962, as the Assembly was poised to elect Ben Bella President of the Council of Ministers, Boudiaf founded the first of several underground opposition parties, the Socialist Revolutionary Party (*Parti de la révolution socialiste*, PRS), with support from former members of the Fédération de France and *wilaya* 2 officers. Briefly arrested for 'plotting against the state' on 21 June 1963 and then released, he went into exile in Morocco, where he would remain for the next twenty-nine years. On 29 November, the PCA was banned anew. In August 1963, all political associations were banned. Ferhat Abbas resigned his post as President of the Constituent Assembly. Boussouf and Bitat left the country. Rising tensions between Ben Bella and Khider had led to the latter's resignation as Secretary General of the FLN in April 1963; he passed into open opposition in exile in July 1964, when he announced from Switzerland that the FLN's funds deposited there in his name would be made available to those opposing the regime. A dangerous precedent was set on 11 April 1963 when the young and brilliant Minister of Foreign Affairs, Mohamed Khemisti, a 32-year-old former medical student, was shot leaving the National Assembly. He died after two weeks in a coma. Independent Algeria's first major political assassination went unresolved – the 'mentally deranged'[19] lone killer convicted never revealed an explanation for the crime – but it is perfectly likely that, as a promising and potentially influential figure unbeholden to any of the major backstairs cliques, Khemisti was a victim of the covert power politics that, carried over from the war, still underlay the formal re-composition of the state.[20] Khider would be assassinated in Madrid on 4 January 1967. Krim, who later also went into exile and opposition, would meet the same fate in Frankfurt, on 18 October 1970.

At the end of September 1963, Aït Ahmed, after fruitlessly opposing Ben Bella's faction from within the Constituent Assembly, formed his own opposition party, the Socialist Forces Front (*Front des forces socialistes*, FFS). Joining Colonel Mohand Ou El-Haj, a veteran of the Kabyle maquis since 1955 and Amirouche's successor as commander of *wilaya* 3, Aït Ahmed and the FFS maquisards embarked on an armed revolt in Kabylia. In early October, war broke out with Morocco over disputed territory around Figuig and Béchar, and when the fighting intensified later that month, Ou El-Haj called off the insurrection to save national unity against an external enemy. But while Ou El-Haj was re-integrated into the FLN and its Political Bureau, Aït Ahmed, who had expressed his 'determination to destroy the regime', continued the struggle. Warning of 'a politics of faction (*politique des clans*) and new oligarchies', he observed that 'the single party is a fiction. It is the many sub-parties [of personal cliques] that constitute the reality experienced by our compatriots.'[21] The FFS revolt would run on, beyond Aït Ahmed's arrest and imprisonment in October 1964, until June 1965. Aït Ahmed was tried in April and condemned to death, a sentence immediately commuted to imprisonment. He escaped in May 1966, and would live for almost fifty years in exile. The Kabyle maquis was put down by the ANP under Boumediene, now Minister of Defence, with a violence that would live long in the region's memory, such that five decades later women in the mountains could recount, matter-of-factly, that 'after the war with the French, there was the war with the Arabs'.[22]

There was also armed opposition to the regime in the west and south. Having failed to position the 30-year-old *wilaya* 6 chief, Colonel Mohamed Chaabani, one of the Tlemcen group's supporters in July 1962, against Boumediene by appointing him to the general staff in March 1964, Ben Bella removed him from his command on 31 May. When Chaabani refused to accept the order, he was accused of rebellion against the state; arrested in July, he was incarcerated at the military prison in Oran and executed on 3 September. At the same time, Ben Bella's police were engaged in a purge of opponents. Among others, Ferhat Abbas and Abderrahmane Farès were imprisoned – Abbas was interned at Adrar, deep in the Sahara. Ahmed Taleb Ibrahimi, the son of shaykh Bashir Ibrahimi, had been a medical student in France in 1954 and a militant in the UGEMA, the Fédération de France, and prison during the war. Now practising at the Mustafa hospital in Algiers, he had several times refused to work with the new administration, which his father had openly criticised. In July 1964, he was arrested, tortured and held in secret solitary confinement, deprived of daylight for three months, before being transferred to civil prison and released in January 1965 without ever facing charges.[23]

After two and a half tumultuous years, a relative stabilisation seemed to have been achieved by early 1965. And through the tumult, the new regime had projected a vigorous, assertive image of the new Algeria both at home and internationally. To compensate for his lack of reliable support in the fragile and shifting coalitions at the summit of the state, Ben Bella capitalised on his personal popularity, seeking to channel the mass enthusiasm of independence as a counterweight to the army.

Enthused by Frantz Fanon's ideals of redemptive peasant revolution as well as by Nasser's Arab populism, by Cold War anti-imperial

Figure 6.2 Ahmed Ben Bella in January 1964 (AP).

internationalism and by the ongoing African revolution (in Angola, South Africa and Mozambique), Ben Bella cut a handsome figure on a dramatic world stage, meeting Khrushchev in Moscow, welcoming Che Guevara and Yasir Arafat to Algiers, and seeing himself as the equal of Castro or Lumumba.[24] While adherence to 'the principles of Islam' as announced in the 1 November proclamation was always important to him, he conceded no authority to anyone to speak for Islam. He responded furiously to the elderly Bashir Ibrahimi's criticism, published in April 1964, on the anniversary of Ben Badis' death that coincided with the opening of the FLN congress, that 'our people desires . . . that the theoretical bases of our government's action should not be drawn from foreign doctrines but from our Arab-Islamic roots'.[25]

The regime's espousal of socialism, while not enough for Aït Ahmed, and too much for Ibrahimi and the *'ulama*, and despite the concessions made to the latter in the Algiers Charter's formulaic reaffirmation of 'the Arab-Muslim essence of the Algerian nation', took on a markedly leftist orientation. Rather than a premeditated ideological commitment on Ben Bella's part, the radical tone was the work of an 'intellectual minority' of independently minded 'partisans' (*franc-tireurs*), as one of them would later put it, who worked in the openings afforded by Ben Bella's improvisational politics, especially in the preparatory commission for the 1964 FLN congress that drafted the Algiers charter.[26] They themselves derived their radicalism less from sustained Marxist engagement – no such thing had ever existed in the FLN – than from the self-reliant independence of action necessary to survival in the maquis, their youth and idealism, their belief in the emancipatory potential of the popular euphoria following independence and their readings less of Marx than of Mao's writings on revolutionary war. As editor of the FLN periodical *Révolution africaine* and a counsellor to the Presidency, Mohamed Harbi was able to push the regime's language and priorities in a more radical direction. Other figures in the Presidency, notably the Alexandria-born Greek Trotskyist, Michaelis 'Pablo' Raptis, a theorist of workers' self-management who advised on economic reconstruction, drew the ire of more conservative opinion that saw the cosmopolitan radicalism of such so-called *pieds rouges* as corrupting, anti-Muslim influences.

Ben Bella combined his accumulation of popular support with the radicalism of his advisors by announcing the nationalisation of formerly European-owned rural property and legalising their occupation by agricultural workers. As Europeans had precipitately abandoned their homes and lands in the summer of 1962, a spontaneous movement of workers' *autogestion* (self-management) had already occurred, and a series of decrees announced in March 1963 put such 'vacant properties' into the hands of the state, and provided for their management by workers' councils. But while capitalising on popular enthusiasm, Ben Bella also, and more importantly, tended rapidly towards the centralisation of power. The nationalisation of agricultural land still in European hands was ordered by presidential decree and announced by Ben Bella at a public meeting on 1 October 1963, without the notionally legislative Assembly even being informed. Two days later, as the crisis in Kabylia worsened and troops mobilised on the Moroccan border, the President invoked article 59 of the constitution, authorising him to take 'exceptional measures' and rule by decree.[27] While 'self-managed' enterprises were given directors representing the state who rapidly bureaucratised the practice of *autogestion*, at the centre of the state Ben Bella's Presidency began to annex his colleagues' prerogatives. He first assumed Khider's role as Secretary General of the FLN, then in summer 1964 that of Ahmed Medeghri, who had been Boumediene's adjutant in *wilaya* 5, as Interior Minister. In December he added the information and finance briefs to his own office. In May 1965, as Algiers prepared to host the second Afro-Asian summit, a much-anticipated sequel to the 1955 Bandung meeting, Ben Bella told Abdelaziz Bouteflika, who had succeeded Khemisti at the foreign ministry, that foreign affairs too would be incorporated into the Presidency's portfolio.

By both co-opting and repressing real or imagined dissidents, and building on both Algeria's immense international standing and the wave of domestic enthusiasm, Ben Bella's regime survived in a constant and volatile balance of factions. But the play of factions on which he relied, the alienation of support generated by repression, and the concentration of power and prominence in himself as a figurehead all paved the way for his downfall. Another former *wilaya* 5 officer and a close ally of Boumediene, Bouteflika had become Minister for Youth and Sports in September 1962, aged only 25. Born to Algerian parents at Oujda on the Moroccan side of the frontier, Bouteflika was also a prominent member of the so-called Oujda group of former ALN officers who had come to prominence in Boumediene's entourage while, in 1957–59, he commanded *wilaya* 5. The others were Medeghri, Kaïd Ahmed, a former UDMA militant from Tiaret who joined the ALN in *wilaya* 5 in 1955 and had been Minister for Tourism in the first independent government before resigning during the July crisis in 1964; Cherif Belkacem, a UGEMA militant in Morocco who had been chief of the army's headquarters in the West for the EMG; and Mohamed 'Larbi' Tayebi, a Second World War veteran and OS militant who served in *wilaya* 5 before, in 1959, joining the frontier army in Morocco. Ali Mendjli was the only member of this faction, besides Boumediene himself, not born in the Oranais and connected to another region; he had been an MTLD municipal councillor in Azzaba, near Philippeville (Skikda), before joining the maquis in *wilaya* 2 and becoming Boumediene's colleague in the EMG in 1959. These men, who had created Ben Bella's power base at Tlemcen in 1962, saw themselves being edged out. Threats to the army – its formal subordination to the FLN in the Algiers charter, from the elaboration of which they had stayed aloof until the last moment, and Mohamed Harbi's proposal for the creation of popular militias, a clear attempt at creating a parallel armed force to stave off a possible army coup – threatened their own security. On the eve of the 1964 congress, Boumediene, Kaïd Ahmed, Medeghri, Bouteflika and Cherif Belkacem offered their resignations, which Ben Bella refused to accept. But as the Afro-Asian conference approached, they learned – apparently from the army chief of staff and former *wilaya* 1 chief, Colonel Tahar Zbiri – that the President intended to bring the conflict to a head by removing them just as the international meeting got underway.[28]

Ben Bella no doubt sought to remove the last and most serious source of domestic rivalry at the moment when his global prestige would be at its height. The conference was due to open on 22 June. Early in the morning of 19 June, Colonel Zbiri, whom Ben Bella had previously tried to co-opt against Boumediene by naming him chief of the general staff, at the head of a squad of soldiers arrested Ben Bella in his residence, the Villa Joly. A radio announcement by Kaïd Ahmed declared that the 'instability, demagogy, anarchy, lies and improvisation' of Ben Bella's government were over.[29] The leaders of the coup stressed their respect of 'revolutionary legality', the necessity of their 'corrective movement' as ensuring the continuity of the revolution, and the 'normal' functioning of all the state's institutions. But in fact they had already decided that there would be no rapid move towards constitutional legality; the coup would put the revolution to rights, but its pursuit could not be trusted to an open FLN congress or to free elections. A Council of the Revolution, dominated by the army and under the Presidency of Boumediene, was installed as the state's supreme authority, while parliament and the constitution – which had been practically irrelevant since the end of 1963 – were quietly suspended. The principle of collegial leadership was reaffirmed: the 'cult of personality', anathema since the split over Messali's leadership of the PPA, was a convenient and effective accusation against Ben Bella, but more significant were the putschists' resentment of their exclusion from power, and their fear of the policy 'drift' of an administration that was both too disorganised and too 'scientifically', internationally socialist for their liking. They disliked what they saw as Ben Bella's demagogic popular mobilisation, but they resented his centralisation of power even more. And at the same time, Algeria's first president merely reaped what he, among others, had helped sow: the primacy of the army and military security apparatus behind the civil institutions of the state had been well entrenched before 1962, and Ben Bella's overthrow was simply the outcome of a logic begun with the rise of the frontier army and the marginalisation of the FLN's civilian politicians for which Ben Bella himself was partly responsible.

Disdainful of the 'anarchy' of Ben Bella's regime, annoyed by his too-often empty rhetorical flamboyance, unpredictability and lack of discipline, Boumediene was intent on establishing 'order' and propriety through a strong, top-down state. Aged only 32 on 19 June, unlike the FLN's 'historic' leaders themselves Boumediene was a product of the war of independence. Born in a poor peasant family near Guelma, he was 12 in May 1945 and despite studying at the Kettaniyya madrasa in Constantine, an independent Islamic school whose directors were opposed to Ben Badis' reformist *'ulama* and whose students were heavily involved in the PPA, he had been active in none of the pre-war political parties. Indeed he had no political background at all prior to his time as a student in Cairo, where he frequented other Algerian students who were PPA militants. While at al-Azhar, he was involved with a volunteer group organised by the exiled Rifi emir Ibn Abd al-Krim al-Khattabi for a Maghrib Liberation Army, some of whose recruits sailed, as Boumediene did, to northern Morocco in 1955 to join both the Moroccan armed resistance and the ALN. This background – rural, conservative, religiously educated, uninvolved in pre-war urban politics but influenced by the Arab radicalism of early 1950s Egypt, and coming of age through the hard choices of the war – reflected, more closely than did Ben Bella's vanguard Third Worldism, the experience of the popular masses whose aspirations both, rather differently, sought to incarnate. Under Boumediene, there was an immediate toning down of the *marxisant* agenda, a re-emphasis on a 'specific', Algerian and Islamically inspired rather than 'scientific' (and godless) socialism. As Boumediene declared on the third anniversary of independence, a few weeks after the coup, 'socialism is part of our historic patrimony ... It is the expression of the will and aspirations of our people ... Henceforth, rhetorical socialism (*le socialisme verbal*) is dead, the construction of a socialist economy will begin.'[30] Dignity and social justice would be pursued in a register of social morality as well as that of social revolution. The coup was thus applauded by the inheritors of Ben Badis' movement, who had informally reconstituted their network of *'ulama*, and by more conservative opinion generally, but it also resonated with the peasantry whose better interests

Boumediene, while abandoning Ben Bella's romantic Fanon-ism, saw himself as more truly serving.

There were nonetheless strong continuities across the rupture of 19 June, not only in the Council of the Revolution's formal reaffirmation of the goals and policy orientations of the Tripoli program and the Algiers Charter, but in the reality of the distribution of power between factions (*clans*) within the system, and the marginalisation – now overt rather than disguised – of institutional politics or forums for open deliberation by the informal mechanisms of arbitration and influence between 'clans'. When, ten years later, Boumediene began to try to reconstruct the basis of formalised and more open political processes, he would find it more difficult than he had perhaps foreseen.

Within the army and the bureaucracy, Boumediene was able, as Ben Bella had not been, to impose himself as the supreme arbiter over the informal factions and different constituencies who were now brought into the system. In addition to the FLN militants of the exterior and interior, survivors of the war or latecomers at its end, who were now part of the party's local and regional structure, there were francophone technocrats who had entered the expanded bureaucracy during the war or who, pursuing higher studies, had joined the FLN between 1956 and 1960. There were smaller, close-knit groups of old comrades like the 'Oujda' clan itself, whose members would all hold influential positions until the mid-1970s, and the ex-MALG security hierarchs of the *promotion tapis rouge*, the former *wilaya* commanders and their followers, and the so-called DAF (*déserteurs de l'armée française*), who had joined the frontier ALN in the last years of the war. The DAF group, in particular, including the tank battalion commander Slimane Hoffman and the director of Boumediene's private office (*chef de cabinet*) Abdelkader Chabou, were men whose professional military expertise, combined with their lack of pre-war militant credentials (which mirrored his own), and consequent lack of other connections in the wartime FLN, made them especially useful – and close – to Boumediene. There were also small private fiefdoms and backstage but central roles reserved for close confidants, perhaps most notably Messaoud Zghar, an entrepreneurial, anglophone arms dealer, international property tycoon and wartime associate of the MALG in Morocco, when as 'Rachid Casa' he obtained contacts and equipment for Boussouf. Having begun his career dealing with US bases in Morocco, in the 1970s he became the lynchpin of Boumediene's back-channel political and economic diplomacy with America.

While Ben Bella had promoted his own colourful charisma, seeking a base of support through a direct connection with the masses,

Boumediene was colder and more aloof and yet in a sense more truly reflective of, and attuned to, the greater part of the population. For the next fifteen years, a kind of charisma would be embodied more in the image of the state itself, in the revolutionary past it claimed, the general betterment and dignity that it promised and seemed to be delivering, and in Boumediene as the symbol of that state, rather than in the individual leader personally. For two weeks after the coup, Algerians did not even know who the members of the new Council of the Revolution were, and cameras covering Boumediene's first televised speech shot the microphone, not the speaker. The regime moved slowly, over the course of the 1970s, from such highly impersonal to a more 'televisual government', harnessing the mass media and Boumediene's growing confidence in public.[31] Boumediene's Algeria, while grounded in bureaucratic power, was in a sense a charismatic as well as an austere state, especially in regional and international politics. Ditching Ben Bella's 'demagogy', disliking foreign revolutionaries and postponing the Afro-Asian conference did not mean abandoning assertive Third Worldism. This was most clear in Boumediene's striking vision for a 'new world economic order' announced at the United Nations in 1974, after the first energy crisis, when Algeria took the lead among non-aligned states in calling for the producer countries of the global south to recover sovereignty over their natural resources, their processing and pricing, from the world market based on the interests of the minority of developed countries in the north. Within the Maghrib, supporting the POLISARIO Front in its demand for independence from Spain and then from Morocco in the western Sahara, and in the larger region foregrounding solidarity with Palestine, opposing Egypt's separate peace in 1978 and promoting an Arab 'steadfastness front' against Israel, Boumediene's Algeria sought to continue the revolution, as it understood it, both at home and abroad.

## Liberation and Its Limits

Others understood it differently, but found themselves isolated as well as repressed. The 'libertarian euporia', the demonstrations of young people and women, at independence and the belief that the revolutionary potential of the people themselves could check the factions and their armed force inspired an immediate and unplanned movement of resistance to Boumediene's putsch. Leftists in the FLN, notably Hocine Zehouane, a former *wilaya* 3 political officer who, related by family to Belkacem Krim, had been jailed by the French as a youthful PPA militant and was now in the FLN's political bureau, Mohamed Harbi, now in the party's central committee, and a group of communist militants who, despite the banning of the PCA, had relaunched *Alger républicain* – Bashir Hadj Ali, Adelhamid Benzine, and Sadek Hadjerès – together with a group of ex-maquisards, went underground and in July released a call for resistance in the name of the Popular Resistance Organisation-Party of the Vanguard (*Organisation de la résistance populaire-Parti de l'avant-garde*, ORP-PAG). 'Betting on popular hostility' against the definitive militarisation of the state, the ORP's spontaneous opposition, as they would later recognise, while measuring the full weight of the coalition behind Boumediene, misjudged the potential energy of the popular movement that they hoped to animate especially among workers and students.[32] The few demonstrations, mostly by students in central Algiers, were dispersed with tear gas and truncheons.[33] The ORP was rapidly infiltrated by the SM and by the end of September most of its leaders were under arrest and being held, and tortured, in secret prisons. The poet and PCA leader Bashir Hadj Ali, who in 1963 had helped found the Algerian Writers' Union, smuggled out an account of his torture which Éditions du Minuit – the Paris publisher that had publicised the Audin affair and printed Henri Alleg's *La question* – published in 1966 alongside a series of Hadj Ali's 'poems for September nights'. The essay, *L'arbitraire*, an extraordinary mix of acute political sociology and poetic evocation, diagnosed the persistence of torture in Algeria not simply as a legacy of colonialism and the revolution, but as 'the corrupted fruits' of arbitrary, unaccountable rule. Only the democratic liberty of the people charged with its own self-direction could rid Algeria of the unaccountable violence that, as Zehouane wrote in his preface to the book, was 'written into the logic of the system itself': 'When the masses are excluded from political life, the citizen has no guarantee of not being tortured.'[34]

The ORP's leaders remained in secret detention for five years and were then placed in administrative internment outside the major cities. Although their movement was quickly and easily extinguished, both the errors and the accuracy of their assessment of Algeria in these years would turn out to be prescient. They had overestimated the power of popular revolutionary social energy to counter the organised force of the post-war elite factions that had hooked themselves into the bureaucracy and the army, they had underestimated the staying power of the system – and had not, of course, foreseen the fuel and lubrication that rising hydrocarbon revenues would provide to it. On the other hand, they saw the long-term significance of the culmination in Boumediene's regime of the power struggles that had played out in the FLN since 1959. They saw that it represented, and would create, unaccountable vested interests within the state which would endure and reproduce themselves, and saw, perhaps above all, that however much material progress such a regime could achieve, it would be incapable of opening itself to real popular participation and thus to genuine popular enfranchisement – and its violence, remaining above the law, would not soon to give way to the rule of law.

The June coup and the suppression of the ORP closed three years of struggle over the inheritance of the wartime FLN. In January 1966, the surviving ORP leadership, principally former PCA militants, issued a declaration in the name of the 'FLN-ORP', claiming the role of socialist vanguard against what they saw as the reactionary forces of the FLN's right wing and calling for a 'democratic and popular front' to resolve the crisis. Faced with the fragmentation and repression of the opposition, however, the communists shortly afterwards reconstituted the PCA by adopting the other part of the ORP's label and creating a new clandestine Socialist Vanguard Party (*Parti de l'avant-garde socialiste*, PAGS) to keep the party alive and to push for a more thoroughgoing socialism from a regime whose practical and ideological orientation was as yet unclear. The first major nationalisations, in the globally revolutionary summer of 1968, as well as the Soviet refusal to countenance open opposition, encouraged the left to move closer to the regime and prompted a call for the union of progressive and anti-imperialist forces expressed – alongside a denunciation of the continuing arrest and torture of PAGS militants – in a 1968 letter from Hadjerès to Boumediene. While the PAGS, whose small numbers of militants carried on a disproportionately intense activity especially within the UGTA and student bodies, moved towards what would become known as a position of 'critical support' for the regime, the party remained underground, its leaders in hiding and sought by the police. Official Soviet and PCF support for the Algerian regime, and declarations by left-wing observers elsewhere that it had become truly 'socialist' (which on the French left were part of an internal debate over whether Algeria had fulfilled their wartime hopes), were received by Algerian communists at risk of arrest and torture in their own country as expressions of 'treason' and 'blindness'.[35] Other sources of opposition were also eliminated by the end of the 1960s. An attempted coup in December 1967 by dissident army officers, mostly ex-ALN veterans incensed at the rise of the 'DAF' around Boumediene and led by one of the principal co-conspirators of 19 June, Tahar Zbiri, was defeated when aircraft fired on Zbiri's tank column south of Blida. In April 1968, Boumediene himself escaped, unscathed, from an assassination attempt presumed to have been organised by opponents in exile. Belkacem Krim, who through an intermediary had unsuccessfully sought assistance from the US State Department and the CIA against Boumediene and who, in October 1967, had set up an opposition movement, the Democratic

Movement for Algerian Renewal (MDRA), was widely thought to be responsible. Two years later, Krim was found murdered in a Frankfurt hotel room.[36]

Government in Algeria was now managed by a balance of factions of which Boumediene was the architect and arbiter – despite his own assertive personal authority and the accusation by Zbiri and others that he had simply replaced Ben Bella's dictatorship with his own, there was less concentration of personal power. But in the broader terms of state-building, the centralisation begun under Ben Bella was reinforced. While in political terms this meant an austere authoritarianism pervasively policed by Kasdi Merbah's *sécurité militaire*, in the economic sphere it provided an opening for young, able and professional cadres entrusted with long-term projections and planning. For society, the mass organisations envisaged during the war to mobilise Algerians behind the FLN became arms of the bureaucratic state. In January 1971, the arrest of several students associated with the PAGS provided the pretext for the dissolution of the independent National Algerian Students' Union (UNEA), and its replacement with a students' union subordinated to the FLN. Between 1963 and 1975, workers', women's, youth and peasants' organisations were folded into the single-party system.[37] Above all, the new regime saw itself as responsible for creating 'a state capable of outliving particular governments and individual men', as the 19 June proclamation had announced; this came to mean asserting the primacy of bureaucratic institutions, firmly side-lining the FLN party as well as suppressing political opposition, and applying a technocratic developmental agenda from above to the pressing problems of the economy and society.[38]

These were certainly urgent. Perhaps 70 per cent of the adult male workforce were un- or under-employed at independence, the treasury empty, the rural economy shattered by the combined effects of dispossession, demography and war.[39] Much of the population was dependent on food aid from abroad, especially from the United States. The country's managerial and technical expertise, all but monopolised by the Europeans, had fled along with their financial capital. Against the agricultural emphasis of the first years of independence, Boumediene's economic agenda adopted the primacy of *dirigiste* industrialisation that had been promoted by French development planners after 1958. Projects initiated from 1959 as part of the Constantine plan's development drive – an iron and steel complex at El Hadjar near Annaba, the gas terminal and petrochemical installation at Arzew near Oran, fed by a pipeline from the gas wells of Hassi Messaoud in the Sahara, housing projects across the country – had been continued after independence and now became flagships of the new socialist economy. Foreign interests, as well as most local private enterprise, were taken into state ownership. Nationalisation had begun with small firms (cinemas, hotels, restaurants) as well as French-owned properties under Ben Bella, and proceeded apace after 1965: mining, banking and insurance were nationalised in 1966, and, much more significantly, engineering and construction, petrol and gas distribution, and food distribution in 1968.

Having consolidated itself in power, in January 1970 the regime launched its first four-year development plan. The following year saw the dramatic conclusion to protracted negotiations with France over hydrocarbon resources, when in February 1971 the Algerian state nationalised oil and gas installations and took a controlling stake in French oil companies operating in the country. That November, the agrarian revolution was begun, and edicts on the socialist management of enterprises announced. These moves signalled the launch of the Boumediene regime's central development initiatives: hydrocarbon-driven, capital-intensive, heavy industrialisation, along with land redistribution, welfare measures, and infrastructure spending funded by oil and gas revenues and loans raised on international capital markets would permit the building of a socialist economy under the aegis of the state for the benefit of a collectivist, revolutionary society. National companies under 'socialist management', especially the national oil company, SONATRACH (*Société nationale pour la recherche, la production, le transport, la transformation et la commercialisation des hydrocarbures*), created in 1963, became the principal vehicles for investment and the building of 'economic independence' through a series of development plans. The 'pre-plan' of 1967–69 was succeeded by the first and second four-year plans (1970–73 and 1974–77); two five-year plans (1980–84 and 1985–89) were envisaged to follow. Income from oil and gas exports provided more than half of the state's income throughout the decade, and boosted by the oil price hikes of 1973 and 1979 this seemed easily to compensate, alongside foreign loans, contracted on favourable terms in an era of seemingly abundant global credit, for the limits of domestic capital formation. The Tripoli program, which had prioritised a slower build-up of capital accumulation and foresaw industrialisation only in the long term, had already warned against economic over-reach. Between 1972 and 1976, sovereign debt grew from 18 to 40 per cent of gross national income; it reached 50 per cent in 1978. By 1979, disbursed and outstanding foreign loans amounted to 15.3 billion US dollars (23.2 billion including undisbursed funds). In 1978 alone, Algerian borrowing on international capital markets and from the World Bank totalled at least 1,385 million dollars. The gamble was that the projects financed by such investment would in due course build true economic independence, and the oil price spike that increased export receipts by 53 per cent between 1978 and 1979 made the borrowing affordable.[40] But in anticipation of socialist independence, Algeria had become a hostage to the fortune of oil prices and interest rates in the capitalist world economy.

The results were mixed. High growth rates (an overall annual average of 7.2 per cent, and up to 13 per cent in basic industries between 1967 and 1978) brought rising living standards, but the economy was wildly unbalanced: industry expanded, but agriculture stagnated or regressed. Much of the investment planned for agriculture was never applied. Mechanisation of farms actually decreased: there were fewer tractors in Algeria in 1977 than there had been in 1967.[41] From a net exporter of foodstuffs in 1966, Algeria became a net importer of food in 1967 and by 1977 was critically dependent on imports.[42] For the first time in its history, Algeria was governed by an elite that had itself come from the people and the peasantry, but life chances for the children of landless agricultural workers remained poor: in 1980, salaried workers' children were fifteen times more likely to enter university than were agricultural workers' children, those of private sector farming families thirty times more likely and those of technical and professional workers 285 times more likely.[43] Disposable incomes rose, while price controls and import restrictions suppressed consumption; prices rose too, by just under 9 per cent per annum in 1974–77, 12 per cent in 1977, 17 per cent in 1978.[44] Falling unemployment, the generalisation of education and the provision of free healthcare came alongside low productivity, under-used capacity and dependence on foreign technical experts in industry, limited commercial possibilities and a lack of consumer goods. Labour migration to France, instead of ceasing with independence, accelerated during and after the war, creating durable and dense, 'bottom-up' social ties between Algeria and the ex-metropole. In 1946, there had been at most 50,000 Algerians in France. In 1962, emigrants numbered perhaps 400,000; by 1975, there were more than twice that number.[45] More highly skilled professionals also began to migrate further afield, to Belgium, Britain, the United States and Canada.

While school attendance figures skyrocketed – from ca. 25 per cent of children aged 6–13 in 1962–63 to 71 per cent in 1977–78 – illiteracy, especially among rural women, remained high. Regional disparities remained marked, unsurprisingly so since in 1966, illiteracy rates in mountain and oasis regions reached 80 per cent. Education was a particular priority: while most ministerial budgets were increased by 3–4 per cent in 1970, spending on education rose by 20 per cent. But just as it exceeded food production, population growth also outran

Figure 6.3 Houari Boumediene (R) with US Secretary of State Henry Kissinger, 14 December 1973. Algerian Foreign Minister Abdelaziz Bouteflika is in the centre of the picture; Kissinger's aide Joseph Sisco is behind him. Kissinger was en route to Cairo; Algeria would resolutely oppose Egypt's eventual separate peace with Israel, but despite frictions Boumediene maintained businesslike relations with the United States (AP).

educational provision: the number of school-age children, for both girls and boys, in primary education more than doubled between 1966 and 1978, but the proportion of the school-age population in class rose by just under 25 per cent. High dropout rates and low exam pass rates meant that in 1979, of one hundred pupils in the expanded primary schools, only four would qualify to enter university.[46] Above all, despite the promises of an 'Agrarian Revolution' launched in 1971, the persistent stagnation of the agricultural sector and the continuing flight of rural people towards the cities constituted a serious challenge. By the mid-1970s the limits of the experiment were beginning to be visible. Those who were supposed to benefit most from the regime's policy choices remained disenfranchised and impoverished. Peasant farmers in state-run cooperatives complained of their inability to supplement their living with a little of their own livestock or poultry production, seeing themselves as having become mere 'sharecroppers of the state' as they had previously been sharecroppers of the *colons*.[47] Workers staged 72 reported – and illegal – strikes in 1969, 521 in 1977.[48]

From 1971, the state's social project also included a cultural revolution, announced by Boumediene on the fifth anniversary of the 19 June coup in a televised speech that was transmitted, for the first time, across the whole of Algerian territory.[49] In November 1965, Algeria's iconic actors Mahieddine Bachetarzi and Rachid Ksentini could still be photographed for the regime's dynamic new francophone cultural newspaper, *Algérie Actualité*, in their roles for an Arabic-language production of Molière's *L'Avare*. The same paper's fashion section advised that a short skirt, sweater, tights and flat shoes made up 'practical fashion for young women who work ... an elegant style', both modern and modest. In its pages, the information minister Bashir Boumaza announced that 'revolution is serious, but not necessarily austere. It has to know how to smile and laugh at itself.'[50] At the same time, the revolution set conceptions of culture, along with education policy and debates over gender and generational relations, history, language and religion within a broader project of cultural decolonisation, aimed at the recovery of 'the components of our national personality and the factors that make up its authenticity', as Boumediene put it in 1972.[51] The cultural revolution came first in the enumeration of the means of building socialism in the 1976 National Charter that, redefining the regime's doctrinal orientation and strategic priorities, aimed at creating 'a new man in a new society'.[52] Just as 'the battle for oil' signalled the 'recuperation of national riches' in the assertion of sovereignty over Algeria's natural resources, the cultural revolution pursued the struggle to 'restore our national culture', to build the future 'by reconnecting with the past and with our ancestors',

as Ahmed Taleb, as Minister of National Education, told students in
Algiers in September 1965.[53]

'The past' and 'our ancestors' were themselves politically sensitive.
The FLN's official version of nationalist history expunged the fraught
internal history of the PPA-MTLD from its memory, along with much
else. 'Messalists' were painted simply as 'traitors'; Abbas and the UDMA
became indistinguishable from bourgeois 'assimilationists'. Ben Badis,
conveniently dead since 1940, would in short order replace the incon-
venient Messali (who died in exile in France in 1974 and was buried,
accompanied by an immense crowd but without official recognition, in
Tlemcen) as the 'father' of a national movement re-imagined and taught
to youngsters as one in which the political struggle for independence was
subsumed in and given meaning by a cultural and religious quest for the
'restoration' as much of a purified community as of a sovereign state. This
was a tendentious misreading of the history of Algerian nationalism, but it
was also one that Algerian nationalism's history itself had produced.[54]
The political culture of the independent state inherited directly from that
of the pre-war PPA, through that of the wartime FLN, its intolerance of
sustained debate and its superficial doctrines of national community as
Arab and Islamic, without much thought being given to the question of
whose Arabic or what Islam was being referred to, let alone to any
recognition of the more complex linguistic and cultural practices both
of ordinary Algerians – arabophone, berberophone or francophone, or all
three at once – and of the institutions of the state itself, whose officials
continued to work primarily in French, and then bilingually, for decades
after independence.

The defence and promotion of Islam had a particular double edge.
Islam was to be *the state's religion*, articulated by state-appointed authorities in support of the goals, and sanctioning the legitimacy, of the
regime; it was also the *religion of the state*, defining 'national personality'
and cultural 'authenticity', a source of legislation and a model of social
morality, providing a language and a terrain that remained, as they had
inevitably been in the colonial period, heavily politicised.[55] In the countryside in the 1930s, left-wing ideas and calls for social justice went along
with popular Islamic morality; the future communist leader Sadek
Hadjerès would recall from his childhood a *kuttab* teacher who cited the
Qur'an alongside sayings of the PCF leader Maurice Thorez.[56]
Immediately after independence, 'there was absolutely no contradiction'
for an intellectual activist like Slimane Chikh, the son of the national poet
Mufdi Zakarya and descendant of a distinguished family of Mzabi *'ulama*,
between an Islam marked by social solidarity and mutual assistance and
the socialist project.[57] Boumediene's regime too sought to combine God

and socialism. Friday sermons, distributed to preachers in state-controlled mosques across the country, broadcast by radio and television, and reprinted in the Ministry of Religious Affairs' periodical, *al-Asala* ('Authenticity'), published from 1971, were written and vetted at the Ministry. They frequently made explicit connection between Islamic social teaching and the socialist revolution, and exhorted the re-moralisation of society as a revolutionary aim and a duty of respect to the martyrs of national liberation.[58]

The regime thus co-opted but also amplified the agenda of those on the religious right who might otherwise be opponents – troubled by the effects of rapid and disorderly urbanisation, alarmed by demographic growth that saw a ballooning and unruly younger generation whose behaviour seemed to portend moral dissipation and social breakdown, offended, above all, by the regime's infringement of property rights in its redistri-butive and industrialising policies. Conservative religious opinion had welcomed Boumediene's seizure of power, but had subsequently suffered in the regime's clampdown on independent centres of political thought and activism, especially after the attempted coup of December 1967. The Islamic Values Society, *Jam'iyat al-qiyam al-islamiyya*, which had drawn attention to itself by publicly protesting the Egyptian regime's execution of the Islamist ideologue Sayyid Qutb in August 1966, was first banned from operating in the *wilaya* (now the term for an adminis-trative governorate, replacing the old *départements*) of Algiers and then, in March 1970, dissolved by the authorities. In their periodical *Humanisme musulman*, the members of *al-Qiyam* had vituperated 'those who ... dare to invite foreigners and enemies of God to Algeria, to this country, home of the only great contemporary revolution made in the name of God';[59] the true historical vocation of the revolution, for them, had been and remained to serve the cause of 'our independence, our freedom, our own personality, and especially our Islam'.[60]

The equation of anti-colonial revolution and the FLN's state-building project with a re-moralising 'war for Islam' under the sovereignty of God was a minority position in the mid-1960s, and remained so until the late 1970s, when the Iranian revolution provided a major boost to such ideas. But already, a current of Algerian 'fundamentalist' opinion existed, influ-enced by the Egyptian Sayyid Qutb, by the Pakistani ideologist Abu A'la Mawdudi, and, at something of a tangent to these Islamist thinkers but sharing some of their preoccupations – with the primacy of reconstructing the sovereignty and integrity of a global Muslim community, and within that community, reasserting Islam as a total ethical system, a code of social solidarity, and a cultural, political and 'civilisational' force – by the Algerian writer and educator Malek Bennabi, who had spent the revolution in exile in Cairo, returned to Algeria in 1963, and was a leading inspiration to members of *al-Qiyam*.[61] Bennabi wrote mainly in French, and had been a nationalist journalist before 1954. His works remained mostly unpublished, except in Arabic translations printed in Cairo or Beirut, but French-language copies were distributed by sympathisers, especially from 1968 onwards through the students' mosque on the campus of Algiers University. Bennabi also wrote for the campus mosque's bulletin, *Que sais-je de l'Islam*.

Over the course of the 1970s, and increasingly as the economic and social ambitions of the revolution ran into difficulties, and then began to stall, the uneasy balance between the state's hegemony over a religio-cultural agenda harnessed to its pragmatic ends, and the pressure of those committed to a 're-Islamising' ideological agenda, tilted, albeit erratically, in favour of the latter. Already in the early 1970s, those responsible for the regime's religio-cultural messages were sensitive to those aspects of state messaging that were less congenial to them. Boumediene's famous speech at the Organisation of the Islamic Conference summit in Lahore in February 1974, in which he stressed the priority of economics and poverty alleviation over religious concerns ('no-one wants to go to Paradise with an empty stomach ... A hungry people does not need to hear verses sung'), and which provoked anti-regime protests in Algeria, was not mentioned in *al-Asala*.[62] Tensions mounted throughout the decade, in particular around central social and policy areas that were both important stakes in their own right, and that, increasingly as social change outran the regime's capacity to manage it, became lightning rods for underlying divergences: demographic change, youth culture, gender relations and family policy, language planning, education and Arabisation.

The first of these was perhaps the overriding challenge to the regime in the decades following independence. Algeria's rate of population growth was one of the world's highest, and despite overall economic performance, it outstripped the country's capacity to house, feed and educate its people. In 1972, the annual rate of demographic growth was reckoned at close to 3.5 per cent (in 1979 it remained at 3.2 per cent).[63] Sixty per cent of the Algerian population – some 8.5 million individuals – was under 20 years of age. Despite the rapid expansion of education, only some 2.5 million were in school, and with the massive rural-urban migration that marked the post-war years, and continued apace through the 1970s, several million young people were already reckoned to be out of school, out of work and on the streets.[64] This was the Algeria of *Omar Gatlato*, Merzak Allouache's 1976 film in which the war of independence is already a distant echo across the tenement blocks of a new, young country, where housing is already in short supply, where young men struggle with the 'virility' (*al-rajula*) expected of them, expressed in slick haircuts and sharp suits, exorcised on the football terraces, frustrated in technicolour visions of courtship by the unconquerable distance across impassable streams of traffic that separate Omar from the girl in the final sequences of the film: *Omar gatlatuh al-rajula*, 'Omar Manliness-Kills-Him'. At the same time, both men and women expressed a simultaneously gritty and emotionally open popular culture in music, especially the *raï* genre that had spread across western Algeria in the interwar years. Discarding both the elaborate instrumentation and the elevated language of more classical forms, *raï* singers like Saadia al-Ghizania, a singer from an impoverished rural background near Relizane who in the 1940s became popular as Cheikha Rimitti (from her ordering *remettez!*, 'another [drink]!'), and who during the war was considered subversive by the French and dissolute by the FLN, had brought songs about drink, sex, love and the tough life of mothers and workingmen to public audiences in cabarets and weddings. In the 1970s and early 1980s, electric instruments and influences from Egyptian, Spanish and European pop music joined with the sensibilities of a younger generation of singers who took stage-names as *cheb* (*shab*, young) for men or, more rarely, *cheba* for women and turned *raï* into both a vehicle of very intimate self-expression and a global commercial style.[65]

Such complex, sensitive images of Algerian urban youth culture, emotion and sexuality contrasted sharply with the stark denunciations that, by the mid-1970s, had become a *leitmotiv* of the cultural revolution. Beginning with a vigorous campaign 'against the degradation of morals' in the autumn of 1970, such views were particularly expressed thereafter in the annual Seminars for the Propagation of Islamic Thought sponsored by the Ministry of Religious Affairs. Originating in three modest meetings organised independently in 1969 by disciples of Bennabi within the ministry, from the fourth seminar in 1970 the seminars were brought within the official program of the ministry's activities and thus both considerably expanded in scope and funding while also being brought under control. The tone had already been set by the *al-Qiyam* group, as Mokhtar Aniba, the director of *Humanisme musulman*, wrote in 1965: 'anti-Islamic ideas have turned a great number of our young people of both sexes, supposedly "educated", into a youth that is immoral, vicious, undisciplined, ... renegades [to Islam] and unconscious of their liberty so dearly bought. ... Our Muslim Algeria must not be contaminated, or serve as a breeding ground, for anti-Muslim ... ways of life.'[66] In 1970, Mouloud Qasim, the Minister of Religious Affairs, echoed the same ideas, attacking 'the wave of ... sexuality, juvenile delinquency, and divorce' threatening the country. The official newspaper *El Moudjahid* denounced the rise of alcoholism, prostitution, suicide and divorce, 'the signs of Western culture, carrying all the degenerate tendencies of that decadent civilisation'.[67] Qasim's keynote speech to the fourth Islamic Thought Seminar, held in Constantine in August, stressed that under colonialism, 'we never ceased to be ourselves, proudly attached to the values of religion, language and tradition which constitute our personality', but since independence Algeria was under threat from a host of internal enemies, corrupted by foreign influences: 'depersonalized persons' (*afrad mamsukhin*, literally, transformed, or deformed individuals), 'renegades', '"liberals" of all kinds'.[68] Such language may not have prompted, but cannot have discouraged, attacks on the more free-thinking revolutionaries still to be found in Algiers, above all perhaps the poet and artist Jean Sénac. The openly homosexual son of a Spanish mother and unknown father, born in Beni Saf in 1926, Sénac supported the FLN's armed struggle, encouraged young Algerian poets and abstract painters, and hosted a poetry program on Radio Algiers – in 1969 he broadcast a series entitled 'We are making the revolution, therefore we exist' – before his murder in Algiers in 1973.

Calls for social re-moralisation framed the cultural revolutionaries' views of society in general and of youth, in particular, in terms of a dissipated masculinity, a threatened femininity, and a generalised moral disorder. Against this background, the regime proved incapable throughout the 1970s of negotiating the most sensitive of all policy areas, that of legislating for gender relations and family policy. Boumediene's personal moral and cultural conservatism – indeed, the austere and 'honourable' masculinist dignity which did so much to strengthen his image as *za'im fhel*, a 'stallion' leader, among Algerian men and women alike – mirrored a society in which family patterns and gender roles remained, with few exceptions, governed by patriarchal norms and codes of behaviour. Boumediene, who undoubtedly wished to see progressive change come, albeit gradually, for women, told *Le Monde* in 1978 that the revolution for women would be made 'in five or ten years' by the millions of girls then entering school and university.[69] A few months earlier, Boumediene's friend and ally Messaoud Zghar had kidnapped his own sister, Dalila Maschino, who had married a non-Muslim man, in Montréal, flown her to Algeria in a privately chartered jet and virtually imprisoned her in their home town of El-Eulma near Sétif. The International Human Rights League appointed a wartime pro-FLN lawyer to press the case alongside the Canadian foreign minister but the

Algerian government told them that Dalila's abduction was a private matter and sent them home.[70]

The Dalila Maschino affair was an unusually headline-grabbing but symptomatic instance of the persistence, among those pursuing ambitious change in other areas, of much older gender norms. Algeria's new civil law code of 1975, which replaced the French statutes inherited at independence, remained without a revised family law until 1984. Work on legal dispositions that would regulate gender relations within the context of rapid, ongoing social change, high expectations among progressives for the realisation of revolutionary aspirations and powerful lobbying from religious conservatives found itself rapidly hamstrung. Draft texts circulated but were shelved in 1964, 1966, 1973 and again in 1979.[71] Rising numbers of girls in school and of women going to university and out to work, and the generalisation, with urbanisation and rising living standards, of what ten years earlier had been lifestyles restricted to a tiny urban elite – women abandoning the *ha'ik* and dressing in a style still called *civilisée*, i.e. 'like Europeans' – generated anxiety among conservatives. The fourth Islamic Thought Seminar resolved that family law should be based exclusively on the prescriptions of Islamic jurisprudence, and in his speech to the delegates, Mouloud Qasim warned that 'the Algerian woman' must not 'abjure her personality and become one of the deformed kind, that is to say, a mosaic and a mixture of diverse elements without homogeneity, thus becoming a curse on her milieu and an evil for her society'.[72] Other speakers in the same forum agreed: as one woman member of the seminar's commission on national education declared, 'Western and Muslim man are two different species ... The division of the world into nationalities and blocs, most of them atheistic ... makes marriage to foreign men or women impossible.'[73]

The same notions of an imagined ideal community under threat flowed into the domain of language policy. When the National Commission for Educational Reform discussed the challenges of Arabisation in April 1970, Boumediene attended the meeting in person, and told the commissioners that this problem 'represents a national imperative and a revolutionary goal. We can make no distinction between Arabisation and the objectives of the revolution in other areas'.[74] At the same time, the regime recognised that practical considerations limited the possible pace of Arabisation. At the third UNESCO/Arab League education ministers' conference in Marrakesh in January 1970, Algerian delegates along with their Moroccan and Tunisian counterparts had insisted, against Syrian and Egyptian protests, on the necessity of Arabising technical education only 'as far as possible', citing the need to 'agree on realities'.[75] Writing in December 1962, Ahmed Taleb Ibrahimi, a future close ally of Boumediene and energetic proponent of Arabisation, had explained that bilingualism would be a 'reality ... for years, even decades to come', since bilingual education was a necessary transitional stage 'between a colonial and an authentically national education'.[76]

But this transitional stage, intended to avoid the perennisation of a 'static' bilingualism in which Arabic would be the language of the street and French that of the elite, proved difficult to transcend. For one thing, throughout the 1970s, the twin objectives of Algerianisation and Arabisation in education proved difficult to reconcile. By 1977, the great majority of *francisants* teachers in both primary and secondary schools were Algerians; most of those who were still hired from abroad taught in Arabic. In higher education, the asymmetry was even more acute: by 1978, francophone university courses had a staff-to-student ratio of 1:7, compared with 1:19 in arabophone classes, and Algerians accounted for 59.9 per cent of the faculty members teaching in French, but only 20.9 per cent of those running courses in Arabic.[77] In these circumstances, the practical, developmental aspects of language planning in education were overtaken by its ideological dimensions.

Disputes over language planning, and what should be the 'national' language of artistic expression and education, initially centred, in addition to the challenges of replacing French with Arabic, on the issue of diglossia, and of how to manage the relation of formal, 'classical' Arabic – read by very few Algerians at the moment of independence, and spoken by fewer – to the distinctive vernaculars that were most arabophone and berberophone Algerians' languages of daily life as well as of local culture. While francophone intellectuals too often lacked understanding of local – especially rural – Arabic or Berber culture and saw them as 'subcultures', the *arabisants* who denounced francophones as 'alienated' were just as likely to lack any 'anchorage' in the depths of the country, its histories and cultures, which they too saw, especially when it came to rural berberophone culture, as unworthy archaisms. Unlike the workers who went to France and maintained tenacious ties with rural landholdings and families left at home, boys from the village who, over the generations since the First World War, had followed the massive migration to the lowland towns and their schools, became urbanised and 'refined', cutting their links to the village and all that it represented. The second generation of lettered Kabyle families whose parents had moved to Algiers before 1914 thought of themselves as fully *Algérois*, and almost never returned to the village.[78]

As in Ottoman times, the city meant distinction, the rural *bled*, backwardness. There was immense, emotional popular appeal in evocations of the deep ancestral culture whose survival was threatened by urbanisation, war and generational change, as was vividly demonstrated in the sensation produced in the mid-1970s by *A vava inouva*. A Kabyle poem by Mohamed Benhamadouche (Ben Mohamed) set to music and sung by Hamid Cheriet, a shepherd's son from Aït Yenni in the high Djurdjura who took the stage name Idir (*ydhir*, 'he will live', a traditional name for a boy born weak), *A vava inouva* depicted a family in winter, gathered around to hear a mother tell a folktale. Produced as a single in Algiers with a sleeve-note by the poet and Berber linguist Mouloud Mammeri before featuring on Idir's first album, cut in Paris in 1976, it was the first Algerian song to be a major international success.[79] But within Algeria, popular culture had no such open recognition. The iconoclastic novelist and playwright Kateb Yacine was almost alone in arguing throughout the 1970s in favour of artistic expression, and especially popular theatre, in Algerian vernacular Arabic (*darija*): 'we must speak the language of the people', he told an interviewer in 1972; 'We should opt systematically for the popular vernacular and struggle vigorously against what they call "literary" [Arabic], which one way or another will mean *embourgeoisement* of our thinking and distancing ourselves from the people.' For others, vernacular dialects were an artificial invention of European Orientalists: *tamazight* meant backwardness, rurality, ignorance and neo-colonialism, while *darija* was merely 'bad Arabic' to be overcome by Arabic speakers themselves who needed to work towards a universal spoken language. Still others, notably Abd al-Hamid Mehri, who in the early 1970s was secretary general at the Ministry of Education, considered that diglossia, though real, was a distraction; 'In reality', he told the periodical *Jeune Afrique*, 'the choice is between [French ] and Arabic ... Refusing Arabisation in the name of vernacular Arabic means resigning oneself to the hegemony of a foreign language.'[80]

But the problems were real, and persistent. In a 1976 study of Algiers secondary schools, the sociolinguist and Arabic professor Khaoula Taleb Ibrahimi (Ahmed Taleb's niece) observed the class differentiation and 'elite closure' already present in the division between well-off students in bilingual classes and the Arabic-language instruction provided to 'the most deprived social groups', concluding that

one of the ironies of the policy of Arabisation has been its transformation into 'an instrument of social selection aiming to exclude from competition [in the job market] all those less favoured individuals who know only Arabic'. ... More and more, one has the impression that Arabisation is nothing but a rhetoric for the masses, one which is affectively gratifying but completely at odds with the facts.[81]

Faced with the impasse of Arabisation, in 1977 Boumediene attempted a change of direction. In a major reshuffle in May 1977, Abdellatif Rahal, the great-nephew of M'hamed Ben Rahal and a veteran nationalist militant who had been chief of staff to Ben Bella and a senior diplomat under Boumediene, was named Minister of Higher Education and Research, while Mostefa Lacheraf became Minister of National Education. Rahal, pointing out the continued difficulties of finding adequately trained Algerian university teachers in Arabic, insisted in November 1978 that 'the rigorous, efficient and modern Arabisation that our policy requires can only be carried out by Algerians themselves ... At the present stage ... we must not sacrifice the quality of education ..., and thereby our students, to a pointless haste.'[82] Lacheraf had already gone considerably further. In a furious exchange of press articles with Abdallah Cheriet, a University of Algiers professor and prominent advocate of thoroughgoing Arabisation, in August–September 1977, Lacheraf castigated the 'mediocrity' and pedagogical 'backwardness' of those tasked with carrying out the Arabisation of education, and denounced the 'hypocrisy' of those ideological Arabisers whose own children were enrolled in Algiers' French *lycée* Descartes. Replying, Cheriet denounced Lacheraf's position as leading Algeria down a 'bourgeois road' and expressing an élitist 'disdain' for Arabic.[83]

Faced with persistent pressure from conservatives, and increasingly vocal dissatisfaction from the often ill-taught, undervalued and underemployed graduates of Arabised school and college curricula, official pronouncements placed ever-increasing insistence on the demand for 'complete' Arabisation, equating Arabisation with a 'true' Algerianisation, including, as had always been implicit in the more fundamentalist arguments, even when written in French, the re-'Algerianisation' of francophone Algerians. Early on, bilinguals – Algeria's best-endowed cultural and intellectual brokers – were marginalised and a mutual 'culture of exclusion' divided French- from Arabic speakers over 'a struggle for power, as to who would have access to posts' in the bureaucracy, in which 'technical competence' and 'authenticity' respectively served as pretexts for sectional self-promotion.[84] The regime's rhetoric contributed to this framing of the language question as one of conflict between 'authentic' and 'inauthentic' cultures, when in fact so-called *francisants* also – of course – spoke (dialectal) Arabic or Tamazight, and many Arabic speakers, most of whom were far from entirely monolingual, themselves had very ambivalent attitudes towards the French language and to norms deriving from French culture.

A sharply conservative turn put an end to the debate without resolving the problem in 1979. Lacheraf was replaced in March by Mohamed Kharroubi, whose support of Arabisation was all the stronger for his being from Kabylia. A resolution of the FLN's central committee on 30 December 1979 demanded the accelerated Arabisation of teacher training and educational administration at all levels, and simultaneously made religious instruction obligatory and an element 'in all examinations'.[85] Abd al-Rahman Chibane, an inspector of Arabic in the Education Ministry known to be close to the fundamentalist current, became Minister of Religious Affairs. At the fourteenth Islamic Thought Seminar in Algiers in 1980, Ahmad Taleb's assertion that Islam was essentially socialist was attacked by a delegate from Saudi Arabia who maintained, instead, that socialism meant 'atheism and heresy'.[86] By 1981, the exposition of Khomeini's doctrine of *vilayet-i faqih* by an Iranian delegate to the fifteenth Seminar was opposed among Algerian participants, not because the state was legitimate on the nationalist and revolutionary grounds of popular sovereignty, but because 'the state corrupts', and the Islamic vocation transcended it.[87] Times were changing.

### 'For a Better Life'?

Boumediene died on 27 December 1978 after six weeks in a coma.[88] The succession to the Presidency was not, of course, to be decided by an open election. Behind-the-scenes negotiations in the military, in which Kasdi Merbah played the central role, initially focused on Bouteflika, a candidate on the right, and Mohamed-Salah Yahyaoui, on the left. A former pupil of Ben Badis' *'ulama* but nonetheless a committed socialist, Yahyaoui had been a schoolteacher, an ALN officer since 1956 and a member of the Council of the Revolution in 1965, then director of the joint forces' officer school at Cherchell. Opting against both rivals, the conclave instead nominated the 50-year-old commander of the second military region (headquartered in Oran), Colonel Chadli Benjedid. Since 1962, the country's population had doubled, from 9 to 18 million, but per capita income had more than trebled and had never been more evenly distributed: a great deal had been achieved.[89] For many Algerians and outside observers, whether or not the 1970s in retrospect seem a 'golden age',[90] an emphasis on personalities and 'palace politics' has often encouraged the view that the crisis that struck Algeria ten years later should be explained by the deliberate abandonment of Boumediene's

project by his successor and those around him, the sudden irruption of
Islamism onto the scene in the early 1980s and the encouragement of the
latter by the former.[91]

The death of Boumediene and the reorientations of personnel, factional preponderance and policy orientation that followed undoubtedly
marked a major shift. But as ever, the break was far from total; on the
contrary, the basic realities of le pouvoir and its tutelary relation to society
established at independence did not change. The change of personalities
undoubtedly mattered: above all, in Algerian popular opinion, the contrast between the personal modesty and discretion of Boumediene and his
wife Anissa and the spectacular self-enrichment of Chadli's family, especially the circle around his second wife Halima, which became a byword
for corruption. But even such spectacles were symptoms of systemic
factors that mattered more. 'There was a change of persons, of style ...
but Chadli tried to play the same politics [as Boumediene had]. His
contribution was to show the limits of that system.'[92] The crises that
came to the surface in the 1980s had developed long before. It was
changing circumstances, more than the passing away or the rise to prominence of individuals, that caused them to erupt; individuals could only
seek to resolve them, or choose to exacerbate them. Chadli's weakness
was his inability to impose himself, as Boumediene had done, as the
recognised arbiter of factional conflict. He was faced by mounting domestic crises in the economy and in society that were coming to a head at
precisely the moment when the change of regime occurred. And these
crises had to be addressed in a rapidly worsening international context,
especially in economic terms. It was the conjuncture of world oil prices
and international credit markets that, by the mid-1980s, would make
them unmanageable.

Initially, at the beginning of the 1980s, the outlook was good, and
Algerians hoped for more freedom. A cautious liberalisation had been in
motion already since 1976, after the regime had moved towards both
broadening its base and returning to the institutional legality interrupted
in 1965. In late 1975, a climate of debate was encouraged for the first time
since independence in popular consultations on a new National Charter,
and new presidential and legislative elections were announced.
Boumediene (the only candidate) became an elected president
in December 1976, and the first election to a new national legislature,
the Popular National Assembly (APN) took place in 1977. These moves
could be seen as bolstering the existing system and its policy orientation –
the National Charter proclaimed from beginning to end the necessity of
building socialism, and the limits of debate were clarified when Ferhat
Abbas, Ben Youssef Ben Khedda and others, who in March 1976

published an appeal for a freely elected constituent assembly, were promptly put under house arrest. From 1977, the need for a political and economic change of course nonetheless became visible to some inside the system. Younger, critical voices within the regime would observe that those only a decade older than themselves 'had only the colonial system in their heads; they'd reproduced it. A closed, brutal system.' 'The major weakness of Boumediene', a pragmatic soldier with no experience of political militancy, 'was that he had only ever been to closed countries. People began to say that we needed to look elsewhere.'[93]

Boumediene himself was widely believed to have recognised the impasse, and to have begun to address it with his 1977 ministerial shake-up; but whatever he might have intended, he did not live to see it. From 1979, under the slogan 'for a better life', adopted for the fourth FLN congress, the party and state promoted an adjustment of priorities, attempting to strike a balance between the maintenance of the system and a modestly reforming agenda, scaling back and reorienting (as Boumediene had perhaps intended) the state's ambitions and letting up (as Boumediene perhaps had not) on the tight discipline that had hitherto reined in both the covetous appetites of factions at the summit of the state and the aspirations of society at large. Restrictions on travel, on the availability of foreign currency and consumer imports, and on the opportunities of middle-class private enterprise were relaxed; political prisoners were released and opposition figures were pardoned and returned from exile.

Ideologically uncommitted and intellectually undistinguished, keener on Italian couture and tennis than on long hours at a desk, Chadli had not sought the Presidency. Good-looking, affable and a keen sportsman where Boumediene had been hollow-cheeked, ascetic and wreathed in cigar smoke, he was certainly less sharp and shrewd than Boumediene had been, and his detractors – of whom there would be many, both on the street and within the system – made great play of his alleged illiteracy and stupidity. Boumediene came off well in jokes told about him after his first few years in power ('There were three Presidents, the Russian, the American, and the Algerian ... '), but in the 1980s jokes at Chadli's expense became something of a national sport. In fact, his background was not unlike Boumediene's: from a Constantinois peasant family, he had no pre-war political ties, and had joined the ALN in 1955, becoming a zone commander in *wilaya* 2.[94] Unlike the 'DAF' who came later, he fought for three years in the maquis; like some of them, in 1959 he was in Boumediene's entourage in the EMG at Ghardimaou. He himself had thought Boumediene a 'visionary',[95] which he was not, and without the advantage of Boumediene's Arabic education, his inept speeches in the early 1980s laid him open to much ridicule. At the same time, observers noted that, unlike his predecessors, 'he speaks only when he has something to say'.[96] Boumediene himself reportedly observed that Chadli 'speaks rarely ... but has a lot of good sense'.[97]

Chadli was not only given to 'a peasant's good sense' and practicality, he had a political astuteness that his initial sponsors had not suspected.[98] He moved rapidly to consolidate his position: many of Boumediene's earlier inner circle were already gone, but the remnants were swiftly removed. Larbi Tayebi, Minister for Agriculture and the Agrarian Revolution since 1970, was discreetly demoted and retired; Bouteflika, the only other survivor of the Oujda group, similarly lost the Foreign Affairs brief in 1979 and in 1981 was removed from the FLN's political bureau. In 1983, he was convicted on corruption charges, and left Algeria for the United Arab Emirates, where he would live until 1987. Boumediene's energy and industry minister and the architect of economic strategy since July 1965, the ex-MTLD centralist Belaïd Abdesselam, had already been demoted to light industry in Boumediene's own 1977 reshuffle. In 1980 he too left the Political Bureau, and like Bouteflika he faced corruption charges in 1982. Messaoud Zghar, Boumediene's backstage fixer who had amassed a colossal personal fortune, was investigated for corruption and jailed in 1983. He died of a heart attack at his home in Madrid in 1987.

In cultural and social matters, as we saw, the attempted change of direction in 1977 had already run into trouble and was abandoned in 1979. In these areas, the attempt to co-opt and contain Islamist pressure was stepped up while the regime also moved to close down some of its more vociferous platforms. The official magazine al-Asala, considered to have become too stridently fundamentalist, was discontinued in 1980, the same year that the FLN's youth union (UNJA) launched a campaign against the Muslim Brotherhood. In late 1981, clauses of the long-awaited family law leaked out, provoking women's demonstrations in central Algiers in which former mujahidat including Zohra Drif, wife of Rabah Bitat who was then the president of the Assembly, participated. When debated in 1982 and finally enacted in 1984, the law was markedly regressive in provisions for women's rights. Women were made legal minors for life; consent to a woman's marriage was the prerogative of her 'guardian' (wali), not her own; women were legally obliged to obey their husbands (who could, in particular, forbid them to go out to work); the male privileges of polygamy and repudiation were upheld and divorce made more difficult for women.[99] The state's claim to champion Islam was materialised in the building (funded in part by public subscription) of the Emir Abd al-Qadir mosque and University of Islamic Sciences in

Constantine, where the prominent Egyptian cleric and ideologue of the Muslim Brothers, Muhammad al-Ghazali, was invited to teach. Cultural and gender issues were perhaps seen as a secondary area in which concessions could be made to relieve pressure on the regime, and where, as in Egypt and elsewhere at the same time, Islamists' support could be bought for use against other opponents. As elsewhere, this would turn out to be a disastrously bad calculation. At the same time, the regime's monopoly was reiterated: at the end of 1982, Chadli reminded Algerians that 'there is no other political philosophy [in Algeria] than that of the FLN and there is one sole language expressing that philosophy'.[100]

But the 'philosophy', such as it was, was increasingly irrelevant and discredited. Chadli both catered to the poorer in society by an 'anti-penury program' that financed the import of a hitherto unimaginable range of consumer goods – from food to electronics to bric-a-brac – sold in state-run supermarkets incongruously named *suq al-fellah* ('Peasant's mart'), and chased impoverished migrants back to the countryside in forced shantytown clearances (*débidonvillisation*). He favoured the emergence of a new middle class – which in practice consisted of the 'new class' of the state's own 'bourgeoisie' – whose conspicuous consumption rapidly rose. As the FLN's revolutionary lustre began to wane, the celebration of the war was monumentalised in the massive concrete palm-fronds of the *Maqam al-shahid*, the Martyr's Memorial, built in 1982 at a cost of some 300 million dollars by a Canadian company on the former Fort des Arcades above the popular el-Madania (ex-Clos Salembier) and Sidi M'hamed (Belcourt) districts.

Towering over the 1950s high-density housing of Diar el-Mahçoul and Diar es-Saada that were built to absorb the shantytowns of the 1940s and that became sites of popular demonstrations in December 1960, and abutting the villa Sésini that had been the 1st Foreign Legion Parachute Regiment's torture centre in 1957, the monument was symbolically as grotesque as it was grandiose. Adding insult to injury as far as Algiers' poor were concerned, in the complex below its stony-faced statues of *mujahidin* and pseudo-Islamic crypt was the *Riyadh al-fath* ('The gardens of victory'), an upscale shopping centre complete with nightclub. Islamists designated the monument *hubal*, the name of a pre-Islamic idol destroyed by the Prophet in Mecca, and spoke scathingly of *riyadh al-fasq* ('the gardens of vice').

From the early 1980s, opposition began to mount. A younger generation, demanding greater freedoms and bridling at the frustrations of authoritarian rule, corruption and unaccountability, a rapidly worsening housing crisis and limited job opportunities came of age in a system which had no means of channelling or negotiating with dissent outside the

Figure 6.4 Monumentalising the revolution: The *maqam shahid* (martyr's memorial) in Algiers (Author's photograph).

regime's own established, informal systems of influence from which the burgeoning younger generation was excluded. At the same time as mono-lingually educated Arabic speakers protested at the unavailability of jobs in a still largely francophone technocracy, demanding more rapid Arabisation of government, education and the professions, other political activists, especially among Kabyles in France, had begun to see the regime's closed and unaccountable politics as of a piece with its cultural authoritarianism. Correspondingly, they saw 'amazigh', Berber, cultural and linguistic freedoms, which had been denied their place in official expressions of national culture, as bound up with and as vehicles for broader demands for change. The regime's emphasis on 'standard' Arabic devalorised *darija* as much as it did Tamazight (Berber) dialects. But while attempting to downplay the 'racial' or ethnic connotations that

Arabisation seemed to some, already, to imply, the regime's dominant line also implied that no distinctively Berber or berberophone culture could be considered legitimately part of an Algerian national patrimony. As Ahmed Taleb told trade union leaders in March 1972, 'When people say that Algeria is made up of Arabs and Berbers, this is false. Algerians are Berbers who have been more or less Arabised. Algerian blood is Arabo-Berber, with a predominance of Berber, whose culture is Arab culture.' Thus, he insisted, Arabic should be 'the only voice in which to express Algerian culture'.[101] In reaction to this doctrinaire line, Kabyle intellectuals, artists and political activists increasingly linked cultural freedom of expression, *taqbaylit* and the ancient *tifinagh* alphabet (which had been preserved only among the Tuareg) with their region's revolutionary and anti-colonial past and with anti-authoritarianism in the present. In 1966, an eclectic group including the PPA veteran, ex-*wilaya* 3 officer and FFS maquisard Mohand-Aarab Bessaoud and the singer Taos Amrouche had created the *Académie Berbère/Agraw Imazighen* in Paris, the first expression of an Algerian Berberist cultural politics. The movement gained some ground before being dissolved by the French authorities, at the Algerian government's behest, in 1978.

On 10 March 1980, the *wali* (governor) of Tizi Ouzou officiously cancelled a lecture on ancient Kabyle poetry due to be given at the city's university by Mouloud Mammeri, whose Berber language courses at Algiers University had been stopped in 1973. The university's students, incensed, demonstrated and petitioned, and a month later, on 7 April, demonstrations were held again at the Place du 1er mai in Algiers and outside the Algerian embassy in Paris; demonstrating students in Algiers, prevented from marching by the police, held a meeting at the central university campus and declared a strike. On 10 April, a counter-demonstration organised by the authorities in Tizi Ouzou and a UNJA declaration condemned 'cultural neo-colonialism' and 'enemies of the revolution', identifying the protests in Kabylia with the 'Parisian salons' of the *Agraw Imazighen* and the FFS, with neither of which the striking students had anything to do. On 15 April, Tizi Ouzou's secondary school and university students who had occupied university buildings in a sit-in protest were joined in a general strike by hospital staff, factory workers and others across Kabylia. Chadli, apparently without irony, condemned 'those who would exploit [Algerian culture] for political ends'. On 19 April, riot police stormed the university. The forcible eviction of the student protestors and their professors – and the detention and torture of activists within university buildings – led to widespread rioting and repression that spread across Kabylia. At one state-owned factory, police and workers fought a pitched battle; medical staff who had constituted a 'vigilance committee' at Tizi Ouzou's hospital were arrested and replaced by army doctors.

The regime subsequently sought to calm tensions and re-establish dialogue, releasing detainees, modestly increasing radio programming in Kabyle, and allowing a cultural seminar to take place, attended by Mammeri and Kateb Yacine, near Azazga in August.[102] But it was the repression that would be remembered. In March the following year, a general strike in Kabylia was widely observed in commemoration. From what would come to be called the 'Berber Spring' (*thafsut ima-zighen*) was born a Berber Cultural Movement, demanding social and political freedoms via the claim to equal recognition of Amazigh cultural and linguistic rights within the nation. Concentrated in Kabylia and in the Kabyle émigré community in France, the Berber movement found little echo, until much later, in other berberophone areas, the Aurès or Mzab (and much less in those, like the Dahra or Tlemcen mountains, where berberophones were far fewer and language boundaries had become very blurred). As a 'Kabyle' movement it picked up on and relayed to a new generation the older regional tensions, expressed once more through cultural differences, that had plagued the PPA and the FLN. While for Kabyle activists this meant seeing themselves in a long line of defeated heroes and betrayed patriots, from Fatma N'Soumer to Abbane Ramdane, their adversaries and the regime accused them, as others had accused the PPA progressives in 1949 and Krim and Aït Ahmed during the war, of fissiparous 'Berberism' or overweening 'Kabyle imperialism', both 'regionalist' threats to national unity and integrity.

At the same time, on the religious right, Islamists became increasingly dissatisfied with the state's control of the country's 'official' religion and began to demonstrate their numbers in mosques and on university campuses. In May 1980, students claiming to defend Arabic and Islam at Bab Ezzouar, a technical university in the eastern Algiers suburbs, attacked their peers who were striking in sympathy with Tizi Ouzou, injuring several dozen. At the same time, Islamists attacked students and professors on the university campus at Annaba with knives and iron bars. Public buildings were attacked in Sidi Bel Abbès and Bejaïa.[103] The influences on this movement were diverse: the Arab-Islamic communalism of Algeria's own nationalism, the 1979 Iranian revolution, the radicalised Egyptian Muslim Brotherhood, the anti-Soviet war in Afghanistan and the Saudi *sahwa* ('revival') movement that exported Wahhabi religious doctrines, a reductive orthopraxy in dress and ritual and a missionary re-moralisation of wider society. Violent incidents between Islamist and leftist students, and attacks by Islamists on 'immodestly' dressed young women, multiplied in Algiers, Constantine and elsewhere: in 1982, students were killed – a leftist at Algiers' Institute of Political Studies and an Islamist at Bab Ezzouar. In November 1982, a tract circulated, calling for 'the establishment of justice among men by the application of *shari'a*' and denouncing pell-mell the influence in Algeria of 'international communism, freemasonry, Jewry and American imperialism [and] ... their agents, propagators of communism, racism and Ba'thism'.[104]

This text was signed by Ahmad Sahnoun and Abd al-Latif Soltani, two elderly shaykhs who had been members of the pre-war Association of *'ulama* and opponents of the regime since independence – in 1974, Soltani had been the author, from exile in Morocco, of a book alleging that 'Mazdaism [Zoroastrianism] is the origin of socialism'[105] – and a 51-year-old educationalist, Abassi Madani. Abassi was a former MTLD militant from Sidi Oqba and one of the group who, with Rabah Bitat, had mounted the abortive attack on Radio Algiers during the night of 31 October–1 November 1954. Arrested two weeks later, he had spent the whole of the war in prison before becoming a teacher, a member of *Jam'iyat al-qiyam* in the 1960s and a professor of the sociology of education at Algiers University where in the early 1980s he preached at the campus mosque. When around a thousand activists identified as 'Muslim Brothers' were arrested in the wake of the tract's release, Abassi, Sahnoun and Soltani were all detained. Soltani died, still under house arrest, in April 1984, and the immense crowd at his funeral (at least several tens of thousands strong) persuaded the regime to release his confederates. In 1985, Mustafa Bouyali, a *wilaya* 4 veteran, began a minor Islamist insurgency in the mountains south of Algiers at the head of an 'Islamic Armed Mouvement' that survived until Bouyali's death in a firefight in January 1987.

Amidst this turbulence, the country's underlying structural weakness was its dependence on hydrocarbon exports, and the unaccountable rentier economy of private predation on the public purse that had grown up around it. Tolerated and instrumentalised for political purposes – to buy off or gain leverage over opponents, to reward allies – under Boumediene, corruption had thoroughly insinuated itself into the system by his death and became epidemic after it. The dangers were increasingly stark as it became apparent that the expensive 'industrialising industries' of the 1970s had failed to stimulate a more self-sustaining and diversified economy, and although until the mid-1980s few of those in a position to profit from the steady flow of state income worried, the problems ran very deep. From the time of the first three-year plan in 1967, one state industry manager would later consider, 'voluntarism [had] trumped economics'. Planning was characterised by 'a kind of bulimia'; large numbers of large-scale projects were privileged over existing smaller-scale enterprise, in particular the artisanal industries of places like Tlemcen, which, already economically embattled, were now disregarded as simple folkloric survivals. The local bases of production and potential entrepreneurship among the old artisan and business class were politically suspect and, if not closed down – the private sector survived and even, especially in agriculture, often did better than the state sector – were delegitimised by a 'demagogic' rhetoric in which even the individual artisan was an 'exploiter'. The policy of importing industrial units wholesale (*clés en main, produits en main*, i.e. with the entire production process pre-planned and 'ready to go' on delivery) brought excessive costs and, ironically for a strategy aimed at securing economic independence, a complete lack of 'in-house' control, with 'everything, including project management, delegated to outside agencies'. The products that resulted were too often too expensive, and obsolete or uncompetitive by the time they emerged.[106]

While from the mid-1970s economic development was thus stymied by politics and the bureaucracy more than it was guided and managed by them, from 1974 the massive influx of hydrocarbon revenues, into a system with limited capacity to productively absorb such wealth, served to cover systemic deficits and, at the same time, nourished the circuits of corruption that had grown up around the state's monopolies and among those – in ministries, the administration, the army and their internal networks – who were well positioned to siphon off and redistribute money, in the form of commissions, or goods and services, among their clients. Such injections of cash came at the worst moments from the point of view of economic planners who were already able to perceive the necessity of changing course rather than keeping the ship afloat on a tide of rent: as one of them would later remark, 'easy money destroys good ideas'.[107] At the same time, the regime, by its success at redistributing wealth and welfare that brought it the approval of popular conceptions of social justice, avoided the development of excessively stark inequalities. But in the 1980s this underlying crisis came to a head, when the long-term inadequacies of the state industrial sector were conjoined, first, with the demographic bulge of the 1970s arriving on the labour market, and then, above all, the balance of payments crisis that would strike in 1986. This, as one insider later judged, was 'the death-knell of the old system'.[108]

Chadli had adopted 'a slow and deliberate approach to change' in the economy, 'tinkering at the margins' to orient policy in overall continuity with preceding trends while introducing some major changes of emphasis.[109] New high-profile projects were initiated at great cost – the redevelopment of the el-Hamma district in Algiers, Algiers' subway system, an urban masterplan for 'Greater Algiers' – while others were reined in. The enormously expensive plan to develop liquefied natural gas

(LNG) for export by tanker to the North American energy market in partnership with the Texas-based El Paso company, which had been a major piece of Boumediene's strategy both of development financing and of Algerian-US relations,[110] collapsed when El Paso walked out of price negotiations in 1981 and priority was given instead to the Transmed pipeline, supplying Italy via Tunisia and Sicily. Further expansion of LNG was halted and a second pipeline to Spain was projected instead.[111] Already, as part of Boumediene's weighing of options in 1977–78, a report had been prepared on 'market socialism', envisaging the restructuring of state-owned enterprises (SOEs) by breaking them up into smaller units to escape from the system's gigantism and to encourage competitiveness and efficiency.[112] This was now applied. State planning and 'socialism' were still the foundation of the system, but large-scale industrial projects that had been plagued by cost overruns and unachievable targets were abandoned; national enterprises seen as too large to function efficiently were broken up. State bank loans were provided to private investors to encourage small local business, especially in construction. But instead of generating discipline and benign competition, in the wake of the second oil price spike in 1979 and a new flood of 'easy money', restructuring created 'sub-monopolies' and the 'democratisation of corruption' among thousands of 'uncontrollable local potentates'.[113]

In 1980, Algeria's creditors were optimistic about the country's prospects. Although the proportion of export revenue required to service Algeria's foreign debt stood at 25 per cent, this was thought manageable, and the World Bank projected that debt service would be reduced to 17 per cent by 1984, and 6 per cent by 1989.[114] In his first years, Chadli actually paid down the debt. But the world oil price crash and the fall in the value of the dollar in 1985–86 precipitated a major crisis. Algeria's hard currency earnings fell by almost half. Imports had to be cut. The economy contracted in 1987; budget deficits, unemployment and inflation rose; consumption fell; shortages of staple foodstuffs, housing and even municipal water supplies became acute. Chadli did not wish to face the problem. Abdelhamid Brahimi, Prime Minister since 1984 (Chadli's former adjutant in *wilaya* 2 and Minister of Planning in 1979), and his Finance Minister Abdelaziz Khellef resorted to short-term borrowing – at high rates of interest and short, two-year or less, maturities – to cover the shortfalls. This rapidly made a severe problem a great deal worse. With revenue slashed, the debt burden mounted; foreign debt rose from 16 billion dollars in 1984 to 26 billion dollars in 1989, and with annual export income then standing at less than 8 billion, by 1988–89 debt service cost not the once hoped-for 6 per cent, but between 50 and 66 per cent or more (according to different estimates) of export earnings. By 1993 this would rise to at least 73 per cent, perhaps 91 per cent. With the unrevealed sums also owing to Russia for military equipment added, the real debt service burden was no doubt in excess of 100 per cent of Algeria's foreign earnings.[115]

Watching this crisis mount was an informal working group of planners who in 1986, under the aegis of the Secretary General to the Presidency, Mouloud Hamrouche, began to develop proposals to breathe new life into the economy by autonomising state-owned enterprises and decentralising their funding. Pressed by the crisis and, from late 1987, with Chadli's acquiescence, their economic reform program gathered pace and began to address every economic sector, public services, landownership and the press. Hamrouche's group was not a *clan*, nor a tendency within the FLN party, nor even a coalition of interests. It was a serendipitous combination of individuals, initially in 1986 a closed working group of a dozen to fifteen people, enlarged in 1987 such that, at one time or another, several thousand cadres – planners, technicians, engineers, statisticians and industry managers – were involved. The core group consisted of technocrats from SOEs and the Ministry of Planning who were united only around their perception of the necessity of some form of major, 'rational' adjustment to the system in order to save it from itself and from the threats to it: the foreign debt that threatened Algeria's sovereignty from outside, the internal wastage, parasitism, bureaucratic corruption and rentierism at the centre of the system that undermined the country from within.

Hamrouche himself was an altogether atypical character within the regime. The 'multiconfessionalism of everyday life'[116] that he remembered from his childhood in Constantine and his family background of politically diverse militancy prior to 1954 were very rare among the cadres of the army and the state in the 1980s. Having joined the *wilaya* 2 maquis aged 16 and trained as an ALN officer in Iraq, he had pursued a discreet career at the military academy in Cherchell, then in the office of the director of protocol at the Presidency, of which he became the head in 1979. The real 'deciders' in *le pouvoir* disregarded him. Thinking him merely 'the President's umbrella-bearer', 'they didn't see him coming'.[117] Hamrouche also lacked any real power in Chadli's Presidency: he had been promoted to the office of Secretary General of the government in January 1984, and to the President's office in February 1986, but real power throughout this period lay with General Larbi Belkheir, the director of Chadli's private office and long-time right hand. Brought with the new President from the HQ of the Oran military region where he had been his chief of staff, Belkheir was a faction-fighting heavyweight among the principal DAF officers who, by the mid-1980s, had risen to commanding heights in the army. He had deserted the French army in the summer of 1958, reaching Tunisia via Switzerland, and was a captain in the frontier army that occupied Constantine in 1962. After staff college in Moscow he rose steadily, becoming indispensable to Chadli in Oran and then Algiers. He now controlled the Presidency's dossiers on foreign affairs, the army, the Interior Ministry and the administrative bureaucracy, in other words all the central fiefdoms of both coercion and patronage, leaving Hamrouche the oversight of education, culture and the technical management of the economy, of whose significance the *militaires* had little appreciation. But this gave Hamrouche space to create something new, which he also had the intelligence and imagination – and, suddenly now, the opportunity – to do.

Hamrouche's reformist group did not begin by fixing on a deliberate policy direction, and even less were they responding to directives from within the regime. They embarked on a 'pragmatic', not an ideological, program and there was, as one of those involved recalled, 'no intrinsic desire to let us get on with the work, but there was a conjunctural possibility when they didn't have any choice'.[118] And they were not aiming at economic 'liberalisation' as understood in the orthodoxy of neoliberal 'transition-from-socialism' theory. For one thing, their problem was not the country's notional commitment to socialism, which had in any case become increasingly vacuous since 1976, but the reality of its dysfunctional state capitalism. Inasmuch as Algerian socialism had been intended to build a sovereign state for the better development of Algeria's human potential and resources, through economic planning in pursuit of a collective social project, they pursued that aim. They hoped to correct the system, and manage its correction, from above; not to dismantle the public sector but to make SOEs competitive and efficient within a state-regulated economy in which central planning would harness and be 'increasingly linked to the working of the market'.[119] They would dynamise the public sector, avoid waste and cost overruns and stimulate competitiveness. They would make risks real, such that, with the exception of the few 'structuring' enterprises in the hydrocarbon and heavy industrial sectors whose management required 'central arbitration',[120] public companies could go bankrupt if they got it wrong; a 'guarantee fund' would provide bailouts where justified to fix short-term problems, but public sector management would become a real responsibility rather than a lucrative sinecure. This would give real impetus to decision making by directors of enterprises who would, crucially, become autonomous managers. Freed from the control of their respective ministries, they would receive no cross-subsidy and would make their own decisions: this separation of powers between the state bureaucracy and the economy would cut all the channels in which cronyism and corruption had become entrenched, making economic logic and the success or failure of enterprises autonomous of the political system, while preserving public ownership.

To the autonomy of enterprises, with which the reformers began, were added three further, crucial proposals. First, the central bank would become independent of the government, with an independent governor who, like judges in the judiciary, should have security of tenure for the duration of his term in office. All foreign direct investment would pass via the bank, which would control foreign loan agreements and the currency. Second, the state's monopoly of foreign trade, which had more than anything else provided a benign environment for corruption through exclusive and overpriced contracts, especially with French partners, managed by well-connected Algerian importers (in food, medicines, machinery, etc.) who earned massive 'commissions', was to end. Foreign trade and investment would be liberalised and regulated; foreign enterprises would gain access to the Algerian market in exchange for obligatory reinvestment in the country. Third, and perhaps most crucially, the finances of state companies would pass through a competitive and independently managed system of eight 'sectoral participation and investment funds', the *fonds de participation*, none of which could hold a majority of shares in any public company, although each would specialise in a particular sector. These investment vehicles, which would control the flow of state money into the public sector, would replace ministerial and bureaucratic tutelage over SOEs and would be, in effect, 'the new centre of power'.[121]

This was not, at first, imagined as a political program: Hamrouche's team were central planners and worked as such, devising projections and previsions, taking a highly technical approach to solving what they nonetheless saw as systemic and ramifying problems. It was Hamrouche himself who raised the prospect of political consequences, asking whether they realised where they were going, and pointing out that 'there can be no economic democracy without political democracy'.[122] While hoping to alleviate, not deepen, the crisis, Hamrouche recognised the political implications of such significant moves to reform the system. For some of his colleagues, the aim was clear: to push for 'an irreversible exit' from the system, producing 'constitutional' change – a thoroughgoing remodelling of Algeria's political economy that was only more or less disguised, initially, as 'technical' modification.[123] For a year, between 1987 and 1988, the reformers worked intensely at projects that even among themselves, one would remember, they had not previously 'dared even to think about'.[124]

The interests they threatened were very powerful ones, and worse still, had little or no understanding of what the reformers were doing. But the autonomy of public enterprise and especially the *fonds de participation* were – accurately – perceived as a direct attack on the sources and circuits of rent. Everyone well placed to benefit from the 'false equilibrium' of factional power-sharing and clientelist redistribution that the system provided – the army high command, security services, party *caciques*, barons of the regional and local bureaucracy, and private business and property networks often composed of former security service and party bosses and their families – saw their interests threatened. Hamrouche and his reformers were an unknown quantity, doing work few others understood, and this amplified suspicions of their intentions among established circles within *le pouvoir* with whom they had little or no communication. Above all, they lacked the time, the powers of persuasion and explanation, and the guarantees that might have broadened their support within the regime: instead, 'by playing too clever', as one of them would self-critically express it, they alienated important interest groups and made themselves the targets of powerful enemies.[125]

At the same time, popular disaffection with the regime was worsening rapidly. Inflation, shortages and unemployment stoked social misery. In November 1986, the brutal repression of student protests had led to rioting in Constantine and Setif. Chadli attempted to shore up his own position in advance of the sixth FLN congress scheduled for December 1988. Having opted for a gamble on the reformers, he made an ill-tempered speech on 19 September 1988 to a meeting of FLN cadres, warning off the 'enemies' of reform within the system. Two weeks later, on 4 October, anti-regime demonstrations, rioting and a carnival of popular protest complete with spontaneous street theatre and the ritual humiliation of authority figures broke out in Algiers and spread rapidly over the next few days to other towns. The National People's Army took to the streets and fired on young protestors with live ammunition, killing hundreds.[126]

## October, June, January

October saw the 'historic' legitimacy of the FLN in power, or whatever remained of it, collapse. To what degree the uprising was an expression of popular frustration, resentment and anger, and to what degree stoked, set alight and manipulated by which faction(s) within the regime, remains impossible to prove. Some saw the riots as manipulated by Chadli to gain ground over his opponents, although the protestors' slogans that attacked the President personally had made him, above all, their target. Others were convinced that the violence was an attempted coup against Chadli, perhaps with a view to bringing Ahmed Taleb, as a crowd-pleasing echo of Boumediene, to the Presidency and Kasdi Merbah, whom Chadli had sidelined, into government. A wave of arrests the previous week had put large numbers of PAGS militants in jail; but whether this was to neutralise leftist opponents of economic liberalisation, or to leave the way clear for others, especially Islamists, to occupy the street, was a matter of speculation.[127]

Merbah did become Prime Minister, while Abdelhamid Brahimi and the FLN's central committee secretary, Mohamed Cherif Messaadia (one of the officers implicated in the Lamouri plot in 1958 and an FLN apparatchik under Boumediene and Chadli) were sacked. Chadli attempted to seize the initiative, declaring a series of sweeping political reforms and reshuffling the army high command. Having first secured his own third presidential term in December, in February 1989 he rushed through a new constitution that opened the way to multiparty politics and elections. This was a flight into the unknown, and accelerated, rather than ameliorating, the crisis. Hamrouche and his team had envisaged a rapid change of institutional structures, but elections only much later. Faced by distrust and in an environment of mounting instability, they knew they lacked time as well as institutional space to develop consensus, seek accommodations where necessary and find allies in the *pouvoir réel*. As one of them remembered, 'there was a great deal of brutality ... in the reforms. ... They required a pedagogy ... for which we hadn't time, because there had to be results quickly.' The reformers were unable to 'explain themselves' either to *décideurs* in the regime or to the (principally French) political allies, financial partners and commercial contacts of the latter. 'We underestimated the resistance', Abd al-Hamid Mehri, the veteran nationalist who succeeded Messaadia at the head of the FLN, would later say, 'of the powers in place'.[128] There was also more widespread resistance to the loss of the 'comfort' offered by the monopolistic system: journalists, for example, presented with the prospect of the removal of the state's monopoly on the press, were initially resistant to being thus cut adrift and obliged to create their own newspapers. The coalition – from ordinary workers through to import barons and army generals – ranged against the reforms was formidable, while their own position was extremely fragile.[129] Despite enjoying an advantage in the correlation of forces within the regime for the time being, in reality they were isolated, if not embattled, within the system. And as part of the system they were isolated from the broader social movements of protest

among the population, which from 1988 onwards were powerfully harnessed, especially, by the ascendant Islamist movement which, in the
'ideological vacuum' left by the erosion of older, nationalist and socialist
imaginaries, 'monopolised religious, oppositional, and moral discourse'
all together.[130] The last things they needed were combative party politics
and a rush to elections.[131]

Merbah came into conflict with Chadli after ten months in power and
left office in September 1989. Hamrouche now became Prime Minister
and several members of his reform group took ministerial portfolios as
well as the direction of the central bank. They hoped to pursue economic
and political reform at separate speeds. Economic reforms that, though
immediately both painful and open to abuse, would attack structural
problems for the long term – liberalising foreign commerce, establishing
the independence of the central bank, removing the bureaucracy from
agriculture – would be pushed through rapidly. But Hamrouche had
hoped to avoid the instability of multiparty politics and instead, alongside
Mehri, he hoped to formalise the existing plurality of ideological 'tendencies' within the FLN. Abandoning the single party and returning to the
formula of 1954, the FLN as a broad front 'of political families', rebuilding the party from the ground up and opening it to real debate, they
would, as Hamrouche expressed it, 'do 1956 in reverse', bringing the
political spectrum that had then been absorbed into the FLN back out of
it in a slow and gradually managed transition towards pluralism.
Hamrouche needed three years, he thought, 'to save stability'.[132]

He got less than two. In defiance of the July 1989 law on political
associations and the constitution, parties based on regional or religious
platforms of competing identity politics – the Islamic Salvation Front (*Al-
jabha al-islamiyya li'l-inqadh, Front islamique du salut*, FIS) and the
Kabyle-based Rally for Culture and Democracy (*Rassemblement pour la
culture et la démocratie*, RCD), an offshoot of the Berber cultural movement led by a medical doctor, Saïd Sadi – had been legalised, along with
the 'old' opposition, Aït Ahmed's FFS and the PAGS, and newly emergent groups, creating a proliferation of parties across the political spectrum from the Islamist right to the Trotskyist left.[133] The crystallisation of
social, regional and cultural conflicts along party lines, especially those
drawn along the fissures of Berberist and Islamist politics that had been
increasingly aggravated since the 1970s, could not have been better
designed to push the country towards instability.

The FIS, in particular, capitalised on the popular unrest, and emerged
victorious from the municipal elections of June 1990. A broad coalition of
Islamist groups that came together in February 1989, the FIS included
internationalist    radicals    calling    for    the    implementation    of

a fundamentalist interpretation of *shari'a* law in a purified 'Islamic republic' alongside so-called 'Jaza'irists' ('Algerianists'), inspired more by the
Islamic dimensions of Algeria's own nationalist and revolutionary history.
Organised around popular, local mosques that provided some of the few
available public spaces for socialisation and politicisation among young
men, driven by a utopian belief in an 'Islamic solution' to their country's
multifaceted crises, and articulated in an accessible language of social
respectability, moral rectitude, economic justice and political accountability to the masses that both drew on existing popular sentiments and
seemed to provide a new avenue out of the impasses of the FLN's system,
the FIS rapidly became the political expression of a broad social movement, and gained the support of many who, while not sharing its agenda,
saw it as an effective means of registering their protest against the FLN
and all it had come to stand for. The US-led Gulf War in 1991, when FIS
demonstrators marched in support of Iraq behind Ali Benhadj, a popular
preacher in a Bab el-Oued mosque who had been born to a refugee family
in Tunisia in 1956 and whose father was a *shahid* (martyr) to independence, heightened its popular appeal further.

Their initial popular momentum led the Islamists to overplay their
hand. In April 1991, the government passed an electoral law intended
to benefit the FLN; in protest, in May, Abassi Madani, the veteran
Islamist activist who had become a founder of the FIS and was now its
principal leader, demanded early presidential elections and called for
a general strike to bring down the regime.

Having previously maintained a conciliatory tone towards the
Presidency and the electoral process, he now denounced Chadli as *mismar
Djeha*, 'Djeha's nail', that had to be pulled out – an allusion to a popular
folktale in which Djeha, the trickster, sells his house but retains the right
to a single nail in the wall, from which he suspends increasingly disgusting
and decomposing items, making the house uninhabitable. Chadli, he
implied, was the source of the nauseous corruption that prevented
Algerians from breathing and that had ruined their country. FIS demonstrations were allowed in Algiers' major public spaces, the Place du 1er
mai (ex-Champ de manoeuvres) and Place des martyrs (formerly the
Place du gouvernement). Approached by other opposition groups with
a view to an electoral alliance, Abbasi had dismissed them as mere
'smurfs' (*sanafir*), of no significance, and hoped his own supporters
would create a mass movement to force Chadli to resign.[134]

The 'unlimited strike', however, had a very limited effect. FIS supporters, demonstrating in large numbers in the streets of central Algiers,
wearing beards and long white 'Afghan' shirts (*qamis*), brandishing the
Qur'an and chanting slogans, made a great visual impact, and there were

Figure 6.5 FIS leader Abbasi Madani greets supporters on his way to a press conference, 13 June 1990, after the party's victory in Algeria's first multiparty municipal elections (AP).

some confrontations with security forces. But by 4 June, when tanks arrived in Algiers, nationally the strike was being followed, according to one account privy to reports from the *Inspection du Travail*, by only 1.5 per cent of workers in the state sector, by virtually no one in the private sector, and in Algiers itself the movement was fading. There had been 'no violence, no destruction anywhere in any state-owned industry', and the FIS's popularity, including in many of the municipalities which they had now governed for a year, was already waning.[135] The party's internal contradictions, between pragmatic *jaza'iristes* and salafi radicals, utopian ambition and political tactics, were driving it apart, and the government and part of the political class, content to manage the Islamists as a political movement rather than as a security problem, expected its momentum to fade. It was at this point that the army, under Generals Khaled Nezzar, the minister of defence who had been in command of ground forces in October 1988, Mohamed Lamari, his successor in that post, and Abdelmalek Guenaizia, the chief of the general staff, intervened, putting troops onto the street and violently dispersing the FIS sit-ins in central Algiers, killing several, and imprisoning the party's leaders. A state of siege was declared. For the reformers, a 'strong signal' had been sent to Chadli that he should 'put a stop to this reform crap' that, the generals thought, 'had brought a lot of trouble'[136] as well as threatening their own pockets and positions. The Hamrouche government, accused of being 'soft' on an 'insurrectionary strike' which had been anything but, fell, and its policies were abandoned or reversed.

The image of the FIS as 'a party of martyrs' persecuted by heavy-handed regime oppression restoked the party's fires. At precisely the moment when it had been 'close to breaking up', the army's intervention 'solidified it'.[137] The Islamists gained popular sympathy for having stood up to le pouvoir in October and faced its tanks in June. With Abbasi and Benhadj in prison, the party named Abdelkader Hachani, a 34-year-old oil engineer from Constantine and a prominent 'Djaza'irist', to lead it; in a rush, a few weeks before elections were due to be held in December 1991, the FIS announced that they would participate. Their candidates were young, anti-establishment and untouched by corruption, with a respectable nationalist demeanour. Despite the febrile political climate, the new government under former SONATRACH head Sid Ahmad Ghozali proceeded to legislative elections anyway, hoping to balance inevitable FLN losses at the polls with heavy gains for independent candidates who could be influenced into supporting the government against the Islamists and other, less significant, leftist opposition groups. This gamble misfired dramatically; the first round of voting, on 26 December 1991, gave the FIS 188 of a total 232 seats with 198 remaining to be contested in a second round, most of which the FIS looked likely to win.[138] On 11 January 1992, faced with an ultimatum from the military décideurs, including those on whom he had long relied, Chadli dissolved parliament and resigned. The following day, the election was annulled and the second round cancelled. An interim 'High State Committee' (HCE) was formed 'to safeguard the republic'. On 9 February, it declared a state of emergency. The first coup d'état against Hamrouche in June had put the army on the streets; the second in January put its generals at the head of the state. The ill-starred attempt to find a way out of the country's crisis was overturned. Instead, Algeria's rulers had chosen to perpetuate the system, and to do so through 'the management of society by violence'.[139]

# 7    The Fragile and Resilient Country, 1992–2012

In his darkly poetic and posthumous novella *The Last Summer of Reason*, Tahar Djaout portrayed the rise of a fascistic theocracy as seen through the eyes of an Algiers bookseller, a man whose youthful hopes of 'a humanity liberated from the fear of death and of eternal punishment' have been drowned by the rise of an ultra-militant Islamism, its 'dream of the purification of society' in 'blood and all-consuming flood.'[1] Born in 1954 in Oulkhou, a village perched in sight of the sea on the Kabyle coastline just east of Azzefoun, Djaout was ten months old when the war of independence began. After university he became a journalist for *Algérie Actualité* and by the late 1980s was one of Algeria's foremost literary talents. In January 1993, he helped launched an independent newspaper, *Ruptures*, which was as critical of the state since Boumediene's coup as it was of the Islamists. On the morning of 26 May 1993, he was shot in a parking lot as he left his home in the west Algiers suburb of Baïnem. After seven days in a coma, he was pronounced dead on 2 June.

## Who? Whom? – And for What?

Officially attributed to an Islamist terror group, Djaout's killing was never transparently investigated. It became one of the first, and perhaps the best known, of many murders, of journalists, intellectuals and artists but also of many thousands more Algerian women, children and men, to become caught in a controversy over the attribution of culpability, whether to some faction of the Islamist insurgency, to some fraction of the state's security services or to some combination of the former manipulated and instrumentalised by the latter. Other murders added to a mounting death toll that became incalculable, and to a horror that seemed incomprehensible: 21-year-old Karima Belhadj, a secretary in a police station, was killed on her way home from work in April 1993, leading sociologist Mohammed Boukhobza, at his home in Algiers in June 1993, beloved *raï* singer Cheb Hasni, outside his parents' apartment in Oran in September 1994, and acerbic journalist Saïd Mekbel, in an Algiers pizzeria in December 1994; the left-wing, feminist architect Nabila Djahnine, in a Tizi Ouzou street in February 1995, the Bishop of Oran Pierre Claverie who, born in Bab el Oued in 1938, had returned to Algeria in 1967 and remained there, in a doorway in Oran in August 1996, and the militant, secularist musician Matoub Lounès, on a road in Kabylia in June 1998; entire families and neighbourhoods in the Algiers suburbs and villages in the Mitidja in 1997–98, and in the districts of Blida, Medéa, Aïn Defla, Chlef, Relizane, from 1994 onwards ...[2] By 2002, a decade of bewildering, horrifying war was said to have taken anything between 100,000 and 200,000 lives, the routine imprecision of the esti-mated death toll expressing both the enormity and the unaccountability of the violence.

From the mid-1990s onwards, gnawing doubt and bitter dispute about *qui tue qui?* (who is killing whom?) troubled the Western media, the online public sphere and the political quadrilles danced around the Algerian crisis by the international community. It exasperated and infuriated many of those in Algeria who themselves were living with constant threats of death and saw their friends and colleagues murdered around them. The West's seeming indulgence of Islamists, as some saw it, during the 1990s, and criticism in European liberal opinion of Algerian opposition to Islamism as indistinguishable from the military regime's 'dirty war', angered those who saw a violent, intolerant and incipiently totalitarian Islamism on their doorsteps as the real threat to their lives, their families and their country. Some of Djaout's former colleagues would be scathing that the same French leftists and liberals who mobilised against fascism in France, when the Front National's Jean-Marie Le Pen reached the second round of presidential elections in 2002, had entertained the prospect of an FIS victory in Algeria ten years earlier. To them, Le Pen was 'a choirboy by comparison' with the Islamists. They were indignant that 'terrorists' were given asylum in France, Britain, Germany and the USA, while 'those who were threatened with terror' were left to face it alone because it was not the government that threatened them. They saw withering irony in the international about-face after al-Qa'ida's attacks on the USA on 11 September 2001, the recasting of Algeria as an early victim of armed Islamism and *avant la lettre* line of defence in a 'global war on terror', which the regime spun skilfully in its favour, along with the mounting Western racism and Islamophobia that they and their compat-riots now faced, irrespective of their own experiences.[3] Others, perhaps equally opposed to Islamism but more inclined to credit the state with a monopoly of violence, decried the naïvely simplistic misrepresentation of the Algerian conflict as a struggle between Islamists and 'republicans', seeing the many irregularities, opacities and unexplained circumstances around the proliferating violence as signs of a deliberate, orchestrated campaign of deception and misinformation as well as assassination and state-sponsored terror by *le pouvoir*.

Within Algeria, and in the intertwined public spheres of media and migration that connected Algeria and France, each side in the argument viewed the other with impatience and incredulity. Some, fleeing for their lives from secret police threats into exile in Europe or North America, alongside European democracy and human rights activists, some of whose engagements with Algeria dated back to the war of independence, saw themselves as unmasking the lies and conspiracies deliberately built up by a regime that had resorted to terrorising its own people on a massive scale. Others, pointing out that they were still in Algeria and perhaps knew more than exiles and outsiders about what was happening to them, pointed to their unenviable choice between 'plague or cholera' and accused the promoters of 'the deleterious question of *qui tue qui*' not only of 'sowing confusion' but, implicitly, of being complicit bystanders in the violence engulfing them.[4] In the global media that multiplied over these years through internet and satellite, Algeria – increasingly isolated as foreigners fled, consulates closed and exit visas became the most sought-after of commodities – became a horrific spectacle, a cautionary tale, a vicarious trauma, anything but 'a country with people in it'.[5]

In these circumstances, and since the 2006 law on 'National Reconciliation' which criminalised in Algeria 'declarations, writings or any other act' bearing on 'the National Tragedy' of the 1990s that might 'cause injury to the institutions [of the state] ... the honour of its agents ... or impugn the image of Algeria on the international stage',[6] the possibility of writing a satisfactory history of what happened in Algeria in the mid-1990s remains slim twenty years later, not because sources are unavailable – testimonies of various kinds as well as intense contemporary media coverage abound – but because, in the context of a fundamentally unresolved conflict, the tools necessary to the indispensable criticism of the sources are lacking. The competing narratives spun out of the crisis and war, each situated within the crisis itself, became aspects of the war, means of seeking understanding and self-location in relation to the violence, more than analyses of it. Recounting the war became indistinguishable from taking a position within it, uncovering 'secret histories' or refuting their accusations, disputes over which tended to become a grotesque rhetorical double, in the ether of the global media, of the war itself, and which became structured by their own narrative economy of political expediency, consumer demand, 'acceptable' opinion and a market for the sensational, the 'secret' and the obscene. Conspiracy theories abounded, seeking to identify a single, hidden rationality behind apparently irrational events that were otherwise beyond comprehension.[7] Individual 'testimonies' or 'revelations' were valued for their supposed ability to uncover 'confiscated truths' more than for their own truth to be confronted with others: in place of the unanimist narratives that fell apart along with much else after 1989, Algeria in the early 2000s had a proliferation of publishing and an immense public interest in its recent past, but Algerians were given '*témoignages* instead of history.'[8]

Narratives of the 1990s within Algeria and outside remain deeply divided and, needless to say, the evidence of the archive or of those, within the apparatus of the state, most centrally implicated is unlikely ever to become available. In addition, the broader frames of reference that structured social-scientific accounts of the crisis as it unfolded have arguably proved actively unhelpful to understanding it. The mounting crisis from 1986 onwards that culminated with the army's intervention and ejection of Chadli in January 1992, and then the war that escalated through the end of the decade and was winding down, unresolved and unaccountable, just as the 'global war on terror' began, coincided with dramatic changes on the world stage: the democratic revolutions in eastern Europe and the fall of the Soviet Union, the end of the Cold War after 1989 and the apparent ascendancy of a unipolar, neoliberal and American-led world order, then, in 2001, the challenge to that order by a utopian and sectarian, millenarian Islamism and, after 2003, its testing to overstretch by its own spectacularly delusional ambition. Then came the global crash of 2008, and the rise of a new global instability and anxiety, combined with both renewed democratic aspiration and a new wave of war across the Arab world.

The academic industries of political and economic 'transition' studies and those of 'conflict management' for 'new wars' that emerged in the briefly triumphal moment after 1989, and then those of 'terrorism and security studies' that succeeded them a decade later, were mostly interested in 'lessons from Algeria' that, often misunderstood, could be (mis) applied to validate highly questionable general models; they themselves proved quite inadequate to understanding Algeria.[9] Between the promised 'new world order' that was supposed to follow the Cold War and the new wave of global fear, proxy war, neo-imperialism, terrorism and unaccountable state violence that spiralled into the twenty-first century, Algeria's murderous decade from 1992 was framed, as it unfolded and as Algerians and others attempted to understand it, by competing narratives and interpretations – of human rights and humanitarianism, democratisation and international law, terror and counter-insurgency, religion and politics, freedom of speech and cultural difference – whose only common feature was their greater propensity to become stakes in the conflict than means of accounting for it, let alone contributing to any resolution of it.

Algeria's history in the 1990s, then, must be seen as one of contradictory stories, of the divergent ways in which Algerians themselves sought to make sense of what was happening to them and to their country. It is perhaps the most terrible chapter of the country's history, but – like not dissimilar stories from Rwanda or Congo, Lebanon or Iraq – it cannot be understood if it is seen simply as a spectacle of carnage. If the logics of violence themselves remain all but impossible to penetrate, and can only be accounted for hypothetically or in multiple ways, the subsequent developments in Algerian state and society, after the turn of the millennium, nonetheless illustrate important underlying dynamics. The fragility of political order, the rapidity with which it came apart and the ruthless brutality with which it was reconstituted to the benefit, once again, of a few and to the effective exclusion of the majority, demonstrated the resilience of the state's core of coercive force despite, or because of, its disconnection from and increasingly predatory relationship to the population supposedly constituted of its citizens. The latter, for their part, would increasingly view their ruling class and its apparent 'contempt' (*hogra*) for them with irony and disgust, deriding the incompetence of *hukumat Mickey* ('Mickey Mouse government') and the self-serving privileges of *tchi-tchi* (chic, cossetted) apparatchiks' families and *mujahidin Taïwan* (fake, 'made-in-Taïwan' claimants to ALN veterans' rights). They would lament the rising rate of teenage suicide and the increase in *harraga*, the clandestine migration to Europe of which, each summer, dozens of young people would become victims by drowning at sea, at the same time as they, just as often, held to a sense of political community marked by a self-image of insubordination, dignity and combative national pride.

And at the same time, while the near-collapse of Algerian society in a maelstrom of blood and terror might be most apparent – the unravelling of social solidarities as neighbours were murdered in their stairwells or sitting rooms by others they'd known as children, the pervasive fear induced by car bombs in city streets and *faux barrages* ('false', insurgent-mounted control points) on country roads – at least as important, in the longer term, would be the underestimated and often unobserved endurance of society relative to both the absence and the ferocity of the 'forces of order', its capacity to sustain and rebuild itself amidst the destruction of insurgency and repression as it had under the ravages of colonialism and in the throes of revolution. And while both state and society thus proved more resilient than might perhaps at first appear, the relations between them too, however torn, were capable of reconstitution.

While the early 1990s saw the disintegration of social bonds as well as of the formal political sphere, and the apparent dislocation both of the state from society, and of society from itself, a formal political sphere was recomposed, from 1997, over the resilient, 'informal' but real core of the state. This, and its uneasy, fragile but tenacious, endurance through the regional upheavals of the 'Arab Spring' that began in Algeria and Tunisia in the winter of 2010, was possible not only because of the unfettered violence so ruthlessly unleashed to win the war – and not, in particular, because of any deep and abiding fear of that violence among the population at large – but rather because of the rebuilt, informal connections between the state's centres of decision, access and patronage and local networks of support, distribution and negotiation. Algeria put itself back together, after the 'dark decade' (*la décennie noire*),[10] through long-established practices of informal politics and even older institutions – *jama'a, ashira* and *zawiya* – as well as through a recomposed, formally pluralistic party-political machinery that often doubled, or was linked to, such institutions at local and regional level. And after the devastations of utopian jihad and cynical *Realpolitik*, Algerians tentatively rebuilt their social space on the basis of a broad consensus of values, within which social and political divisions could be played out without recourse to arms. By 2012, Algeria was neither at peace, nor was it a pathological, traumatised society endemically at war with itself, but one engaged in a slow, episodically overt struggle over its shape and that of its polity, and over the meanings of the values – nation, religion, personal morality and social justice, the inheritance of the past and the means of moving beyond it – that its people generally held in common.

## The Descent into War

The drama of 1989–92 had not, despite appearances and especially despite comparisons with what was happening at the same time in Eastern Europe, been a promising transition to democracy that was suddenly reversed by the army. It was, rather, a case of manipulative crisis management gone awry. The opening of public space to associational life – for everything from clubs for former students of particular schools to proselytising Islamic associations like shaykh Mahfoud Nahnah's *jami'yat al-irshad wa'l-islah* (the Guidance and Reform Society) – a proliferating and remarkably free media, and a massive social mobilisation, especially through near-continuous strike action across all sectors of the economy and the professions, certainly liberated and encouraged an immense out-pouring of social energy and enthusiasm as well as anger and dissent, especially among younger Algerians. Journalist Hocine Belalloufi would remember that Algeria 'was fizzing ... A wind of freedom had begun to blow across the country.'[11] But the conditions for the translation of Algerians' diverse and assertive visions of themselves and their possible futures into a rule-bound, stable and mutually tolerating, substantively democratic politics were by no means in place: in fact, quite the reverse.

What quickly became the largest Islamist movement, embodied after two constitutive meetings at the al-Sunna mosque in Bab el Oued on 18 February 1989, and the Ibn Badis mosque in another Algiers neighbourhood, Kouba, on 10 March, in the FIS, was impatient and utopian, undecided about its tactical position on electoral democracy (but opposed to democracy in principle as unable to distinguish between 'impiety and faith'[12]) and inclined to see its opponents, at best, as deviants who were ignorant of Islam and in need of correction and, at worst, as unbelievers or apostates who had no place in the national community. Its project was one of social moralisation rather than of governance and its militant fringes, while pushing their opponents into the arms of the army, were not above espousing violence themselves.[13]

The FIS drew its inspirations and its slogans from an eclectic range of influences. It claimed a filiation with Ben Badis' pre-war reformism that was quite unjustified in terms of intellectual content or social program but very effective as a claim to the continuity of incorruptible, religiously based opposition to oppression, and more strongly asserted a claim to be the true inheritor of the wartime FLN and its revolution that corrupt apostates had stolen from the people: the FIS was thus allegedly the *fils*, the legitimate son, of the historic FLN. Its adherents had been influenced by the broader movement of *al-sahwa al-islamiyya*, the Islamic 'awakening' that spread in the 1980s from Saudi Arabia, Pakistan and Egypt, the writings of Hassan al-Banna and Sayyid Qutb, ideas of a 'caliphal state' and of a republic based on 'consultation' (*shura*): the duty of each properly instructed believer to exercise his opinion as to the government of the community, guided by the interpretation of *shari'a*, under the sovereignty of God. It brought together ambitious veteran Islamists like Abbasi with younger firebrands like Benhadj alongside Mohammedi Saïd, 'Si Nacer', who had worked for German intelligence during the Second World War and was famous for the German helmet he wore as well as for his rhetoric and incompetence in the maquis, where he was colonel of *wilaya* 3 in 1956. At the same time, there was undeniably 'a real adhesion' among broad swathes of society to the FIS, which more effectively than other, rival Islamist movements tapped into a widespread, 'profound attachment' to religion and captured the enthusiasm of younger people, especially, in the cities and in peripheral neighbourhoods, for a radical vision of morality, dignity and justice.[14] Against them was not only the generals' intense dislike of the threat the FIS posed to the established system and to their own custodial sense of public order, but also a visceral anti-Islamism among other opponents of the regime. This was to be found especially, for example, among members of the PAGS who saw the contest as a life or death struggle against fascism, and the activists of the RCD, whose own political socialisation had been in the fledgling anti-authoritarian human rights movement of the mid-1980s when many of them had been imprisoned, but whose opposition to Islamism trumped their antipathy to the regime. Such divisions, which ramified throughout society, were likely to serve nothing better than the interests of the factions in power.[15]

It has been argued, partly because the FIS was legalised in September 1989 after five months of waiting, because of the FIS's own relatively liberal (though also very abstract) economic program and initial lack of criticism of Hamrouche's economic reforms, that a tacit understanding was reached by Chadli and Hamrouche with the FIS, which they hoped to instrumentalise in the service of economic liberal-isation against an FLN 'old guard' still identified with étatist/socialist policies.[16] Other accounts, by contrast, point to the legal recognition of the FIS, as well as those of the RCD, whose creation was announced by MCB and human rights activists at Tizi Ouzou on 9 and 10 February, and the Trotskyist PT (*Parti des travailleurs*, Workers' Party) as having been decided by Hamrouche's opponents in the regime. As one insider put it, all three parties were 'born in Larbi Belkheir's office'.[17] The FIS's founders were themselves undecided about the form their movement should take. Having originally imagined it as an umbrella organisation for the unification of *da'wa* activities (the proselytising 'call' to what they saw as 'true' Islam), they rushed to adopt the form of a political party when the opportunity arose, under the February 1989 constitution, to translate their implicitly political stance into actual political action.[18] The decision to legalise the party seems to have been made not by Hamrouche's government, but by his predecessor Kasdi Merbah's Interior Minister Abubakr Belkaïd, almost certainly at the behest of Belkheir (and Chadli?), putting Hamrouche, when he took office three days later, before a fait accompli.[19]

In any event, Hamrouche and his government came into a political landscape in ferment, which in the months after October 1988 had already blown away their previously preferred option of a slow and managed political opening. Given the way in which the formal multi-party system was subsequently – from 1995 onwards – recomposed around the *décideurs'* rules of entry into the system, and especially the roles played in that system by the RCD (as a counterweight to the

FFS), the PT (as a notional revolutionary leftist and secularist party, the only one in the Middle East and North Africa to be led by a woman, Louisa Hanoune), and the permanent presence of two, mutually balancing, legal Islamist parties, there is every reason to think that from early on in the 'management' of the crisis of the system in 1989, the factions of the *pouvoir réel* had decided on the creation and instrumentalisation of a multiparty 'shop window' for the regime, with party machines serving as channels both to diffuse dissent and split opposition, and as networks for clientelism and patronage. As one observer put it, 'most of the parties they legalised [in 1989–90] were non-entities (*des partis bidon*)', which, if not vanity projects like Ben Bella's Movement for Democracy in Algeria (MDA), which had existed since 1984 without having any constituency within Algeria, were simple vehicles for distributing influence, their strings pulled by elements of the regime.[20] Algeria's reconstituted party system – put together as a remarkably rapid return to 'constitutional legality' in the midst of the worst of the violence between 1995 and 1997 – would be structured by an unreasonably neat choreography: two 'Kabyle' parties (FFS and RCD), two Islamist parties, a far-left party (the PT) to supplant the PAGS (which imploded in December 1992) and a new regime party, the National Democratic Rally (RND), created almost from nothing for elections in 1997, as well as the FLN (which would be recuperated after a stint in opposition under Mehri between 1992 and 1995), along with a large number of tiny independent parties and a few electorally insignificant groups created as personal vehicles by historic FLN figures.

This suspiciously tidy division of 'seats at the table' (*kursis*), which could be (and from 1997 onwards would be) periodically reshuffled almost at will, would serve the interests of the regime's factional power brokers, not only in lieu of and more effectively than the old single-party façade of the FLN but, more importantly, in place of any more genuinely autonomous and plural political field, whether emerging from the old FLN, from the newer social forces of a younger generation or from a generational reconciliation that might have combined the two. The larger reform project that had been briefly imagined by the team around Hamrouche as the necessary basis for a longer-term, stable liberalisation and democratisation of the system had been destroyed in 1991 before the suspension of the formal electoral process; the latter, even had it been allowed to continue – which in the circumstances was exceedingly unlikely – would not have equated to a substantive democratisation of Algeria's polity. Competitive party pluralism mobilised especially around mutually exclusive identity politics, the pressure of elections, and above all the opportunity of a utopian opposition party to benefit from a massive popular protest vote which, however, was hardly an overwhelming mandate for an Islamic state, all militated against deeper, structural democratic change, and pressed Algeria, instead, headlong into open civil conflict.[21]

Presiding over this sabotage of the country to rescue their entrenched positions from the crisis of the single-party system were the *janviéristes*, the army and security hierarchs who were behind the heavy-handed intervention of June 1991 and the deposition of Chadli in January 1992, who by 1997 would succeed in returning to elections with a new multiparty regime façade more in tune with post–Cold War times, and who by 2002 had maintained themselves in power by prosecuting a vicious war against the Islamist insurgency and anyone else who might threaten them, while actively preventing any negotiated political solution to the crisis that might allow all sides of Algerian society to arbitrate their own future. Whatever else about the war remained opaque and impenetrable, one thing was abundantly clear: while almost everyone else in Algeria had lost by it, they and their associates had won.

The central group of *janviéristes* were all of the same generation and similar backgrounds. Born mostly in the late 1930s, none had been political militants before the revolution, most had been trained in the French army before joining the ALN on the frontiers and all had risen through the ranks as professional military 'technicians' under Boumediene before reaching command positions in the mid-1980s. Khaled Nezzar (b.1937), who had been Chadli's adjutant at the *base de l'est* and one of the first cohort of Algerian officers trained at staff college in Moscow after independence, took overall command of ground forces in 1986, was appointed chief of the General Staff in November 1988 and in July 1990 became Minister of Defence (the first time since 1965 that this post was separated from the prerogatives of the Presidency). Abdelmalek Guenaïzia (b. 1936), who deserted his post as a warrant officer in a French unit stationed in Germany with Nezzar in April 1958, succeeded him in 1990 as Chief of the General Staff. Mohamed Lamari (b. 1939), who would succeed Guenaïzia in turn as Chief of the General Staff in July 1993, was commander-in-chief of ground forces in January 1992. Benabbès Gheziel (b.1931) had been commander-in-chief of the National Gendarmerie (the paramilitary extra-urban police, run from the Ministry of Defence) since 1987. Chadli's long-serving right hand Larbi Belkheir (b. 1938) had become Interior Minister in October 1991, putting him directly at the head of the bureaucracy and police forces as the final act of the crisis approached. Mohamed 'El Moukh' ('the Brain') Touati (b.1936) was an advisor to the General Staff; Ismaïl 'Smaïn' Lamari (b. 1941), a veteran of the *sécurité militaire* (SM), was head of its department of internal security and counter-espionage, and his immediate superior Mohamed 'Tewfik' Mediène (b.1939) had taken charge of the SM, which he renamed DRS (*Département du renseignement et de la sécurité*, Intelligence and Security Department), in 1990.[22]

Most of these men – Nezzar and Belkheir, in particular, but also, indirectly, 'Tewfik', who as a minor SM officer had been brought to Algiers from Oran under Belkheir's wing – owed their ascension to their long-term patronage by Chadli. But some of them, most notably Tewfik, were also allegedly notable within the system for their ascension in opposition to an attempt in the mid-1980s by Chadli and two principal army figures, chief of staff Mustafa Belloucif and SM director Medjoub Lakhal-Ayat, to professionalise and modernise the army and intelligence services and to reduce the influence within them of the old ex-ALN and MALG factions whose networks within and outside the armed forces, entrenched since independence, stood in the way of establishing a more efficient, meritocratic officer corps and intelligence service (and, no doubt, new networks of influence independent of those already in place). An ex-maquisard and career soldier, Belloucif was appointed Secretary General of the Ministry of Defence (effectively the head of the armed forces, answerable only to the President) in July 1980. He was one of the first cohort promoted to the new rank of Major General in October 1984, and the following month became the first man to hold the office of Chief of the General Staff since it was abolished by Boumediene after Zbiri's attempted coup in 1967. He became a proponent, in particular, of diversifying Algeria's military procurement away from dependence on the USSR. Lakhal-Ayat, also a career officer, became director of the SM in 1981 and head of the new General Delegation for Prevention and Security (DGPS) within the SM, which Chadli split from the Central Directorate of Military Security (DCSA) in a reorganisation of the security services in 1987.[23]

Both Belloucif and Lakhal-Ayat encouraged the recruitment of a new intake of university graduates into the army and the SM, but at least some of those who joined came to observe the persistence of parallel structures of solidarity and patronage, organised both by factional loyalty and by region, in particular the importance of officers from the east of the country, the so-called BTS triangle of the region between Batna, Tebessa and Souk Ahras. Less qualified but more pliable recruits with the right connections were seen to benefit from accelerated training and promotion. Tewfik, who 'didn't count for much' on his arrival, is said to have been recruited into the MALG in 1961 in Tunis from the French navy, and to have owed his subsequent career entirely to Belkheir.[24]

In 1986, he was made head of the Department of Defence and Security Affairs, one of Belkheir's apanages in the Presidency, and when DCSA chief Mohamed Betchine, an ex-ALN maquisard who was also an army moderniser, was promoted to succeed Lakhal-Ayat as head of the DGPS after the bloodshed of October 1988, Tewfik took over from Betchine as head of military security. When Betchine subsequently resigned, in 1990, it was Tewfik who took over command of both departments of the SM, reorganising and greatly expanding the service under the new title of DRS. When January came, it was he who presided over the extensive powers of the secret services; and he owed his position to manoeuvres that already indicated a dangerous degree of factionalism even within them.

While undoubtedly serving their own interests and those of the system as they saw it, it is important not to assume, as many in and outside Algeria would come to believe, that the *janviéristes* were either a single, closely united interest group, or that this group was simply the instrument of a diabolical, neo-colonial plot. Some of them, particularly those close to the influential power broker Belkheir, could certainly be identified with a *hizb fransa* in terms of their own personal, political and commercial connections with elements of the French political establishment, business elite and security services. But they were not a unified bloc, and if they acted in the service of their own lucrative connections to foreign interests, they did so, too, in concert with a vision of the Algerian state, and in particular of the role of the army, that they shared with others of quite different backgrounds. Nezzar would insist on the custodial role of the ANP, established since 1962, as 'safeguarding independence and national sovereignty'. While duly removing its officers from the FLN's central committee after the 1989 constitutional changes, the army, he declared, could not remain 'neutral' in the face of what its commanders saw as threats to 'the destiny of the nation'.[25] He was joined on the HCE by Ali Kafi, whose nationalist background could not be more impeccable – he had been in the PPA before joining *wilaya* 2, where he was Zighout's adjutant, participating in the August 1955 offensive and the Soummam Congress, and from 1957 to 1959 was Zighout's successor – and Ali Haroun, the lawyer and wartime FFFLN veteran, who had worked with Abbane on *El Moudjahid* in 1957 before retiring from politics after participating in the first Constituent Assembly in 1963 and re-emerging in the human rights movement in the mid-1980s.

Others agreed with them as to what was to be done in January 1992. Ali Kafi held the presidency of the National Organisation of Mujahidin (ONM), a powerful mechanism for distributing and leveraging influence through networks of ALN veterans (or those claiming to be such). In 1993, a new movement, the National Organisation of the Children of

Mujahidin (ONEM), was set up to transmit the same system to a new generation, modelled on the existing National Organisation of the Children of Martyrs (ONEC). In the years after independence, a tiny pension was all the state had accorded to the widows and orphans of the revolution – and sons and daughters of *shuhada* ('martyrs' to independence) experienced their status as such as a personal, familial matter, as a private grief as well as the sense of dignity that loved ones had 'done their duty'. 'He was dead; it was done with': some at least, probably many, were revolted by the notion that it should be a source of lifetime rent.[26] Now, such inheritances of the revolution were politically mobilised through the ONM, ONEC and ONEM, which would be called the 'revolutionary family', to rally anti-Islamist social forces and bolster the regime.

Another veteran revolutionary, Redha Malek, the Évian negotiator and contributor to the Tripoli program, became the president of the HCE's rubber-stamp 'parliament', the National Consultative Council (CNC), and later joined the HCE itself. Malek saw Islamism as an anti-modern 'regression', an undoing of the revolution that threatened the life's work of his generation, and considered that political figures like himself who backed the military intervention had 'done [their] duty': 'we assumed our responsibilities.'[27] Mostefa Lacheraf, the more liberal intellectual and pre-war PPA veteran who had been Malek's colleague on the Tripoli program, agreed.[28] In April 1995 these two would be the principal founders, with Ali Haroun, of a 'modernist' political party, the National Republican Alliance (ANR), which would have no electoral significance but was nonetheless several times awarded a ministerial portfolio.[29] As Prime Minister in March 1994, Malek famously declared at the funeral of the murdered playwright Abdelkader Alloula in Oran that 'It's time fear changed sides' (*La peur doit changer de camp*). Fifteen years later, he was unrepentant at the phrase, which, he said, was intended 'to give courage to the population' that was 'wavering', and to counter 'defeatists, accomplices, and opportunists' whose 'misinformation' and 'conspiracy-obsession' (*complotite*) expressed the anti-Algerian *Schadenfreude* of a 'colonial *revanche*'.[30] At the time, his declaration announced an escalation and generalisation of hostilities.

The *janviéristes'* coup was thus supported by a broad coalition of actively mobilised interests, as well as by more diffuse anti-Islamist opinion, while being rejected by others, especially the FFS and FLN, which for a short period became an opposition party. Questions of the coup's 'constitutionality' – which Nezzar and others defended, referring to their 'Novembrist' action in defence of the integrity of the revolution, while others decried its blatant illegality – were largely beside the point, since the one consistent feature of Algeria's politics had long been its lack of law-bound government. This formal problem, however, was underlain by a more serious, deeper one, revealed in the widespread adoption both by establishment figures outside the army's core elite and among the opposition, including 'democrats' on the left, of the view that the crisis was a security matter that should be 'managed' by the army, not a political problem requiring resolution through a political process, debate and compromise.[31] Once again, the military took, and was largely granted, precedence over the political.

The HCE, presiding over a dramatic political crisis, was nonetheless opposed by the three parties (FIS, FFS and FLN) that had garnered most votes in December 1991, and although it had some real support within Algeria – from the PAGS and the RCD, the powerful UGTA, intellectuals and cultural figures mobilised to 'safeguard Algeria' – and the backing of the French establishment, it lacked any broader international legitimacy. Redha Malek, who had served as an intermediary during the US embassy hostage crisis in Tehran in 1980, flew to Washington where he pressed for support of the regime against potential Islamist takeovers across the region.[32] But the HCE, having resurrected the old principle of collegial leadership and assumed the powers of the Presidency, nonetheless needed a credible face. After some hesitation, they agreed to invite Mohamed Boudiaf out of exile in Morocco to become president of the Council. The 73-year-old veteran revolutionary, untouched by compromise or corruption since 1962, would represent 'honesty'. For those who thought like Redha Malek, the austere Boudiaf, in 'suit and tie, clean-shaven', would incarnate 'modernity' in contrast to the Islamists' gowns, beards and 'regression'.[33]

A few months earlier, Boudiaf had been interviewed by an Algerian journalist who had found him at his very modest brickworks at Kenitra, on the Moroccan coast north of Rabat, preparing clay for moulding himself, with his sleeves and trousers rolled up.[34] Suddenly called back to politics after thirty years in opposition and exile, he took a similarly direct approach to the task at hand in Algeria: he certainly was not content to be a front for the *décideurs*. He arrived in Algiers on January 16. While pursuing the repression of armed Islamism, he also had thousands of detained FIS sympathisers who, he said, were no more than 'stone-throwers', released.[35] Above all, he ordered major investigations into corruption, and reached out directly to younger Algerians, to whom he promised a re-foundation of the state. Completely unknown to the younger generation when he arrived, he took the initiative of addressing them directly, in particular by speaking Algerian dialect in speeches and interviews: as one, 14 years old in 1992, would remember, 'he spoke the

Figure 7.1 Mohamed Boudiaf, photographed on his return to Algeria from exile, 16 January 1992 (AP).

language of the people. You felt the Algerian in him . . . You felt you could trust this man – he was like us.'[36] There was a feeling, among many who had opposed both the FIS and the generals' coup, that Algeria might yet be saved from plunging into the abyss. Then, on 29 June 1992, Boudiaf was shot dead by one of his bodyguards while addressing a televised meeting in Annaba.

## The Terror

The escalation of violence, already begun, now proceeded headlong. The FIS had been banned in March; in April the municipal and regional councils (APCs and APWs) that since June 1990 had been run by FIS-majority administrations were dissolved and replaced by appointed 'Executive Municipal Delegations' (DECs). On 15 July, the principal

FIS leaders Abassi and Benhadj were sentenced to twelve years' imprisonment by a military court at Blida. In the six months of Boudiaf's Presidency, thousands of FIS militants had already been interned in detention camps in the Sahara. Others, radicalising the violence already practised by the movement in the 1980s, took to the maquis and launched an armed insurgency.

Islamists had occasionally physically attacked their political opponents before the elections. Tiny splinter groups calling themselves 'Algerian Hizballah' or *Takfir wa'l-hijra*, borrowing the name invented by the Egyptian government for the *gama'a islamiyya* of the 1980s, already existed on the margins of the movement, and an armed attack at Guemmar, north of El Oued near the Tunisian border in November 1991, involved militants associated with the FIS-affiliated Islamist trade union, the SIT. In early 1992 armed militants engaged in sporadic clashes with soldiers and the police.[37] In late 1990, veterans of Mustafa Bouyali's mid-1980s insurgency, led by an ex-soldier, 'General' Abdelkader Chebouti, constituted guerilla groups in the Atlas south of Blida and resurrected the MIA. While, by agreement with the FIS, abstaining from obstructing the electoral process which they opposed in principle, Chebouti's militia gained considerable prestige among FIS sympathisers for their more uncompromising posture. After the coup they emerged as the principal armed Islamist opposition movement, thought to number 2,000 fighters already in 1992, and engaged in low-level attacks on regime targets and security forces. An alternative strategy was followed by another group, FIS founder member and Afghanistan veteran Saïd Mekhloufi's MEI (*Mouvement pour l'état islamique*). Mekhloufi had been head of security for the FIS before being removed from the party's leadership 'consultative council' (*majlis al-shura*) at its emergency conference in Batna in July 1991. Declaring that 'injustice arises and endures mainly because of the docility and silence of the majority', he called for civil disobedience and hoped to create a 'popular Islamist army' – failing which, the MEI began to turn its violence on 'recalcitrants' among the people, hoping to provoke the radicalisation and inspire the loyalty that the ALN had achieved during the war of independence.[38]

These groups inherited a stock of ideas and images, a diffuse political imagination, from the war of independence, and a sense of continuity with the radicalism of earlier Islamist activism that had espoused violence as both justified and efficacious in the 1970s and 1980s.[39] Among peri-urban populations that had moved from the countryside during the war or since independence, they also tapped into the long-standing mythology of the social bandit, the avenging outcast of the mountains, that had persisted through the colonial period and was still celebrated in popular culture – by the mid-1980s, among other media, on TV and in cartoon strip books that retold stories like that of Mas'ud Ben Zelmat for a new generation, as well as in oral storytelling. Many FIS activists previously committed, whether on principle or by calculation, to constitutional politics, but who were now faced with the 'theft' of their electoral victory, undoubtedly gravitated towards armed struggle. At the same time, some of those who in previous decades had been student radicals, involved in violence against 'apostate' professors or 'immodest' women and committed to a radical vision of an Islamic state, had stood aside from the FIS, and now opted to pursue social and political regeneration without recourse to arms. Abdallah Djaballah, who had been a militant law student at the University of Constantine in the mid-1970s and by 1992 had become one of the most followed preachers in the Constantinois, in 1990 created a *Harakat al-nahda 'l-islamiyya* (Islamic Renaissance Movement, MNI) which preached 'reconciliation' instead of armed struggle and opted to work within the scope allowed by the system.[40]

These groups were not motivated by any unified, atavistic 'imaginary' (let alone the libidinal 'violent pulsions' that, recycling colonial-era psychology, some commentary on the war would evoke[41]). Rather, international circumstances and experiences or inspiration from elsewhere – most notably, the anti-Soviet jihad in Afghanistan – as well as the domestic situation and the internal diversity of the Islamist movement itself directed different individuals and groups into different avenues of action. The regime's careful opening of managed, oppositional political space for some groups and co-optation of others, combined with ruthless repression and covert 'management by violence' of both the jihadist fringe and the broader social base that had propelled the FIS towards power, did the rest. Djaballah's Nahda and Mahfoud Nahnah's HAMAS, a political party created on the basis of his *irshad wa 'l-islah* society, were less populist, more cautious than the FIS, although sharing most of its views and its aspiration to create a 'truly Islamic' society and state. Electorally marginalised in the FIS's brief high tide, they survived the subsequent crash and became part of the re-institutionalised political landscape.

While largely retaining the same rhetoric, HAMAS (which tellingly amended its name in 1997, without needing to change its acronym, from 'Movement for an Islamic Society' to 'Movement of Society for Peace') would opt for an entryist strategy, working in coalition with the recuperated FLN and regime party the RND in the late 1990s, while Djaballah's various parties would maintain a more oppositional stance.

The more intellectually inclined, non-violent Islamic reformism of the PRA (Party for Algerian Renewal), founded by disciples of Bennabi, sought to revive and apply his ideas. Rejecting the salafist notion that society must be 're-Islamised', and drawing on Max Weber as well as Bennabi, they saw the challenge instead as being to revive Islamic 'authenticity' as a total social ethic that would become socially and economically 'efficacious'. The party, under its founder Noureddine Boukrouh, faded into obscurity and compromise with the system, but some of its original adherents – who, while referring to communists, for example, as 'those who had gone out of the community', nonetheless rejected the label 'Islamist' and were sometimes themselves vigorously opposed to the FIS – continued to re-publish Bennabi's works and to work quietly to disseminate their views.[42]

While these more quietist trends took different paths, the militant edge of the Islamist movement escalated its jihad against *taghut*, the 'tyranni-cal' regime, and those who supported it – and the regime escalated its violence too. On the night of 9–10 February 1992, as the state of emer-gency came into force, six young policemen (all were between 26 and 31 years old), most of whom were fathers of young children, were gunned down on the rue Bouzrina in the Casbah, signalling the beginning of terrorist action.[43] The first major attack on civilians, a bomb blast at Algiers airport on 26 August 1992, killed nine people and injured 128. Condemned by an FIS publication, it was then attributed to a group of FIS militants, who for their part claimed that their confessions had been forced from them under torture.[44] Attacks on infrastructure, security forces and state targets like members of the DECs, but also on journalists, academics and intellectuals, foreigners (including Algerians' foreign spouses), working women and 'immodest' girls in public places, multi-plied in 1993 and especially from the beginning of 1994. During the worst period of assassinations against writers and cultural figures, one Algiers journalist did not leave his apartment for three months; his wife had to 'take care of everything' and his children were told to tell everyone that they had not seen their father, and did not know where he had gone. Another journalist told his spouse and children never to show any sign that they recognised him if they saw him out of doors.[45] In 1994, while attempting to reintroduce some degree of a 'culture of dialogue' into Algerian life and remind people what Algerian culture was capable of – notably by bringing the celebrated singer Warda al-Jaza'iriyya from Egypt to perform in the country that claimed her – as Minister of Culture Slimane Chikh, the son of national poet Mufdi Zakarya, 'spent [his] time accompanying friends to the cemetery.'[46] The wave of murders of prominent writers and artists forced many of Algeria's cultural producers into exile in France, Europe or North America; ironically, while at home Algerians felt cut off and left to their fate by the rest of the world, these same years saw the beginning of a new global recognition of Algerian culture, especially in music and literature.

But international attention was focused mostly on the increasingly dark drama of the war. In the summer of 1992, a nebulous organisation calling itself the *Jama'a al-islamiyya 'l-musallaha* (Islamic Armed Group, GIA), allegedly an umbrella organisation of Islamist guerilla units, emerged. 'The' GIA was not one group, but many. Pretending to hegemony over the insurgency and ostensibly espousing a more radical line on both the overthrow of the state – rather than simply re-instituting the FIS as a legal political force, which seemed to have become the ostensible short-term war aim of the MIA – and on the forcible Islamisation of society as a whole, the GIA was also a supple and decentralised organisation. Its label, look ('Afghan' style, with beards, shaved heads, turbans and loose-fitting clothing instead of the MIA and MEI's stolen army uniforms) and style of unbridled, extreme and demonstrative violence could be 'franchised' by any local leader with a following. Paradoxically, the avowedly uncompromising aims announced by the GIA facilitated the adoption of its name and style by a plethora of new 'military entrepreneurs' who had much more limited and local objectives.[47] Without any identifiable, concrete political agenda or real overall command structure to follow, pursuit of 'total' war against the local embodiment of *taghut* – policemen and their families, local authorities, existing networks of influence and property – became means of seizing control over local revenue and commerce and of establishing social precedence in particular districts that became the fiefs of (often short-lived) 'emirs'. Ambitious local actors could reinvent both their 'moral' profile and their material fortune in the vacuum left by the removal of the FIS's local government and the withdrawal of the state.

In the economically ravaged and roiling housing estates of the Algiers suburbs, especially, unemployed young men whose occupation, with wry Algerian humour, was said to be that of *hittistes*, 'the men who hold up the walls' (by leaning against them all day long for lack of anything else to do), often saw either the ostensible higher cause or, perhaps more often, the economic opportunities combined with the dark glamour of the GIA maquisards as irresistibly appealing.[48] Local gangsters like Amar Yacine, known as 'Napoli' (supposedly from his desire to make enough money to go live there), in the upper Casbah, Beaufraisier, Eucalyptus, Baraki and other districts of Algiers, ran autonomous armed groups in which 'jihad' against the police was indistinguishable from a racketeering spree. In many places, local logics and interests, and a 'privatisation' as well as a generalisation of violence, were undoubtedly more immediately relevant causal factors of the spread and entrenchment of the war than either Islamist utopia or regime repression alone. If jihadi Islamism and anti-Islamist 'patriotism' often provided languages for expressing such interests, the regime also facilitated this degeneration into violence. In many districts where the FIS had enjoyed strong popular support in 1990–91, an apparent strategy of deliberate neglect of law and order enforcement by the authorities tacitly encouraged generalised insecurity. 'There are thieves everywhere', said an unemployed young graduate of his Algiers suburb in 1993, ' ... it's *normal* now, there are no more police officers, you have to fend for yourself, the thieves are getting rich ... The government, they did this on purpose, I promise you.'[49] This picture of life in Algeria after 1992 – thieves getting rich everywhere, generalised insecurity, a state the population cannot trust and which acts 'on purpose' against them, the need for everyone to fend for themselves – would come to be very widely shared, and would persist over the following decade. In Algerian vernacular, the very word *normal* (used in French whatever language is being spoken) came to designate, with unsurprised, cynical irony, the perfect banality of life in a permanent state of crisis and collapse.

The fluidity and multiplicity of the GIA made the group especially hard to pin down and suppress, as did the frequent succession of its commanding 'emirs': Mohammed Allal ('Moh Léveilley'), the leader of the rue Bouzrina attack who was killed in August 1992; Abdelhak Layada, arrested in Morocco in June 1993 and released from prison in 2006; Djaafar 'el-Afghani', killed in February 1994; Chérif Gousmi, killed in September 1994; Djamel 'Zitouni', killed in July 1996; Antar Zouabri, killed in February 2002; and Hassan Hattab, who left the organisation in 1996 to found a splinter group, the GSPC, and disappeared, having apparently surrendered to the authorities, after 2007. But conversely, the same characteristics also suggested its malleability and liability to manipulation. The GIA was very soon suspected by some of being, if not a network of 'pseudo-gangs' or counter-guerillas directly organised by the DRS, at least heavily infiltrated and manipulated by them to split the insurgency and sow confusion in its ranks, taking the counter-insurgency into the maquis to provoke war between Islamist factions – which by the summer of 1994 the GIA had largely done – and more generally discredit the cause of other 'true *mujahidin*' and terrorise the population by spectacular atrocities against civilians. Thus began the vexing question of *qui tue?*

The emergence of the GIA, its escalation of violence and high media profile and its rapid eclipse of the earlier movements, MEI and MIA, were countered to some degree by the appearance in July 1994 of an Islamic Salvation Army (*Armée islamique du salut*, AIS), which under a 'national emir', Madani Mezrag, declared its loyalty to the imprisoned FIS leadership. Political figures claiming continuity with the FIS had already radicalised their own tone so as not to be outflanked. A 19 March 1993 FIS communiqué signed by Abderrezak Redjam, the FIS's underground communications chief inside Algeria, affirmed that 'what is occurring is not terrorism, but a blessed jihad whose legitimacy arises from the obligation to create an Islamic state, and [in response to] the coup d'état against the choice of the people ... The criminal junta must stand down so that Algeria can devote itself to rebuilding what they have destroyed by theft, despotism and Westernisation.'[50] Anwar Haddam, a nuclear engineer elected to parliament for the FIS from Tlemcen in December 1991 and now in asylum in the United States, where he styled himself the head of a FIS 'Parliamentary Delegation' in Europe and the USA, described the assassination of psychiatry professor Mahfoudh Boucebci, outside his hospital in June 1993, as 'not a crime but a sentence carried out by the mujahidin.'[51] When a massive car bomb claimed by the GIA exploded on 30 January 1995 near the central police station on the boulevard Amirouche in downtown Algiers, as a packed bus was passing, killing 42 people and injuring 286, Haddam justified the attack, describing the death toll as an 'unfortunate' accident of timing.[52]

Rivalries, personal or political or both, between the factions spread, and Islamist leaders and others involved in attempts at brokering negotiations with them were assassinated – Kasdi Merbah in August 1993, Abdelkader Hachani in November 1999. Accusations that assassinations and atrocities officially imputed to the GIA were in fact carried out by disguised army units, or directed by security operatives in the maquis, multiplied in the media, particularly in France and the wider Algerian diaspora, and circulated widely on the internet. Within Algeria, such uncertainty, and a generalised climate of suspicion and insecurity, only added to the fear stoked by 'false roadblocks' set up by guerillas in military uniform, where travellers were racketed or murdered, indiscriminate attacks on trains and buses, car bombs and attacks on individual civilians in towns, and the abduction and rape of young women in the countryside. Uncertainty about who 'the terrorists' really were was expressed in divergent ways: among young conscripts within the army, it was apparently said (repeating a long-standing trope of Islamic martyrology) that the corpses of *mujahidin* found in the mountains did not decay and smelled of musk.[53] At the same time, more prosaically, the word *tango* came to be a widespread derogatory term for Islamists, apparently referring to the radio moniker in use in the police ('T' for *terroristes*): later, the term acquired a delicious irony appreciated by drinkers when *Tango*, manufactured in Rouiba, near Algiers, by the millionaire businessman Djilali Mehri, became Algeria's leading brand of beer.

If martyrology and cynical humour both helped Algerians to put the horror escalating around them into more manageable terms, both the extent of the horror and the stakes involved in accounting for it reached a peak between 1996 and 1998. On the night of 26–27 March 1996, seven Cistercian monks, all French nationals, were abducted from the monastery of Notre Dame de l'Atlas at Tibhirine, high in the mountains just outside Medéa. The monks' long-standing medical mission to the local population was combined with a deep personal and institutional commitment to remaining in Algeria, a commitment they shared with many other clergymen and – women of the Catholic church who had come since independence both to minister to the small remaining European population and to sustain a dialogue of prayer and spiritual exchange with Muslim interlocutors. They had repeatedly refused to leave.[54] On 30 May, their heads were found, without their bodies, near Medéa. The brothers' kidnapping had been claimed in a GIA communiqué on 26 April, and another, dated 23 May, announced that they had been killed, their throats slit, two days earlier. But doubts emerged almost at once: the authorities ineptly attempted to conceal the absence of the monks' bodies, which were never found, and it appeared that the victims had been decapitated post-mortem, disguising the cause of death. Claims abounded that the 'GIA' operation attributed to Djamel Zitouni was in fact a deliberate manipulation by the DRS to implicate the Islamists in an act of 'barbarity', remove the monks (whose determined presence in a highly insecure zone and, worse, their readiness to provide medical care to all comers, including guerillas, was irritating) and shock French opinion into firmer support for the regime. An alternative scenario, published in the Italian daily *La Stampa* in 2008, later suggested that the monks had been inadvertently killed by machine-gun fire from army helicopters attacking the Islamist camp where they were being held.[55] The truth remained inaccessible after twenty years of speculation and occasional pressure on the Algerian authorities: the only clear outcome was the horror of the act, the only indubitable fact the unaccountability of those behind it.

Both the most spectacular and the most bitterly disputed acts of violence were yet to come. In the early hours of 29 August 1997, a massacre of civilians at Raïs, a neighbourhood on the eastern edge of Sidi Moussa in the Mitidja twenty kilometres southeast of Algiers, killed at least 98, and perhaps as many as 300 people: men, women and children were all killed, often with knives and axes, or burned to death. In a carnage that (no doubt deliberately) both recalled and exceeded the worst terror of the war of independence, bodies were mutilated, eviscerated and displayed in the street, heads left on doorsteps. Several young women were abducted by the attackers. The Raïs murders were followed by a spate of mass killings in the Beni Messous district on the outskirts of Algiers to the north, and in the Mitidja again, at Bentalha, near Baraki, a few kilometres north of Sidi Moussa, on 23 September, in which perhaps 250 people were killed. Subsequent massacres, especially in the west of the country in villages around Tiaret and Relizane between December 1997 and April 1998, were thought to have taken up to 400 or 500 lives in single episodes. At the end of 1997, in the first two weeks of Ramadan alone, over 1,000 people were killed in Algeria.[56]

The several hours' duration of these massacres, the non-intervention of nearby army and police forces – or even their alleged complicity in sealing off areas under attack – and the apparently 'false beards' of the attackers, cast doubts on official claims that the atrocities were perpetrated solely by Islamist militia attempting to destabilise the state. Combined with the geography and timing of the violence, which struck especially at former FIS strongholds that had provided material aid to guerillas, and occurred as legislative, local and senatorial elections were being held (in June, October and December 1997), such doubts suggested that, whether committed by 'real' GIA militia that had been infiltrated and instrumentalised by the DRS or by covert army death squads only masquerading as Islamists, the massacres were outward effects of factional conflict within the regime.[57] Others insisted that the bloodbaths were more simply the desperate acts of Islamist extremists whose expected victory over the regime had not materialised, and who found themselves increasingly under pressure from the army, without a realisable war aim, losing support among the population and vengeful against those who, having formerly aided them, had recently stopped supporting their struggle. Whatever the truth, whether intended by elements of the regime to demonstrate that Islamism was beyond the pale and had to be 'eradicated', or by Islamists to demonstrate the lengths to which they would go if pushed, or both, the latter turned to its own purposes by the former, the massacres were clearly intended as an obscenely exemplary spectacle, a theatre of cruelty that horrified ordinary Algerians and played to all the worst imaginings of international opinion and the global media.

The butchery à l'arme blanche, especially the murders and mutilations of mothers and children, recalled and exorbitantly magnified, in entirely incomparable circumstances, the ritualistic peasant violence of anti-colonial insurrection. The open perpetration of atrocity and the elements of display – bodies, or heads, exhibited in the street or on doorsteps – recalled the colonial practice of leaving the bodies of ALN *junud* or suspected sympathisers in village squares and roadways. The particular, grisly details narrated after the fact – such as the claim that attackers at Bentalha had made bets among themselves on the gender of unborn babies before disembowelling pregnant women – directly echoed tropes of the 'increasingly explicit violence' that had characterised commemorative narratives of the war of liberation since the early 1980s, in contrast to the relative circumspection of earlier publicly aired accounts of the war.[58] Such acts were less evidence of an unconscious 'return of the repressed' in a traumatised 'national psyche' than calculated *mises en scène*, a surely deliberate and targeted staging of well-known scripts that had been fed into society and socialisation over the previous fifteen years. As optimism about the revolution's prospects faded, such narratives had increasingly shaped a culture of national memory that emphasised both the glorification of armed struggle and the dehumanising extremes of victimhood.[59]

Commentators, especially in France, where in the mid-1990s debates about the war of independence were resurfacing in both academic and political life, began to refer to the violence as a 'second Algerian war', sometimes with the implication that this new violence had arisen from the 'unhealed wounds' of the older struggle. Within Algeria, language and imagery drawing on the war of 1954–62 was indeed used by all sides to claim credentials and to deny legitimacy to others, and in some areas the conflict must have been structured around local social and generational tensions, as it had been during the war of independence. Citizen militia officially called 'self-defence groups' (*groupes de légitime défense*, GLDs) were thus universally known as *patriotes* and, in many rural areas, were first constituted by the older generation of ALN veterans, supported by the National Organisation of Mujahidin (ONM). At the same time, the Islamist guerillas claimed the mantle of 'true' *mujahidin* for themselves, and while they denounced their enemies as *hizb fransa*, they were themselves accused of being 'the sons of *harkis*'.[60] Whether or not some insurgents were in fact the offspring of formerly caïdal or *harki* families, seeking to regain the property or redeem the social status lost since independence, was in this respect beside the point, since it was the moral charge, not the material accusation, that really mattered, although in some cases the latter might also have been true. Again, rather than simply, compulsively re-enacting the revolution, these narratives were both a means of conflict, staking claims in a 'moral economy' that was effective because shared throughout society, and a means of rationalising and recounting what was otherwise fast becoming, not – by any means –

something 'innate' to all Algerians, but on the contrary horribly foreign and incomprehensible to the vast majority of them.

Whoever was responsible for the wave of massacres that engulfed Algeria in 1997–98 before subsiding into smaller and less frequent, though still persistent, incidents of violence in the following years, there could be no doubt at all that elsewhere, state terror was in full swing. In the escalating struggle to suppress the insurgency and terrorise, in turn, its civilian supporters, from 1992 onwards thousands of suspects 'disappeared' into undocumented detention, where torture by the security services was once again both routine and extreme. Many people – the number, inevitably, being impossible to calculate – never re-emerged. Ever since the war of independence, the torture of suspects had been part of the secret services' regular functions: used against actual or suspected opponents under Ben Bella and Boumediene, and against detainees in October 1988, it was now once more employed on a massive scale – with beatings, electricity, water, electric irons, drills, and soldering tools, blowtorches, rape – in police stations and DRS holding centres across the country.[61] In early 1992, Mohamed Lamari took charge of a combined, multi-service counter-terrorist operation involving the army, gendarmerie and police. His counterpart, the other (unrelated) Lamari, General 'Smaïn' of the DRS, from his office in the Directorate of Counter-Intelligence and Internal Security, took charge of more covert aspects of the counter-guerilla. Among the regular arms of the security services, many police officers saw themselves simply as combating a terrorist threat to their country. Regular policemen accustomed to walking the beat or doing traffic duty volunteered for the new, special anti-terrorist police, the BMPJ; dressed in black, armed with Kalashnikovs and wearing balaclavas during operations, they resembled they army's special intervention units, and like them became known as 'ninjas'. Some, appalled by what they were told to do and later seeking asylum in Europe, would tell horrific stories of torture and of DRS collusion in assassinations and massacres. Others, either uninvolved in the violence of interrogation and intimidation or judging it justified in the struggle against the terrorism that was killing their comrades and relatives, drew satisfaction from their role in winning the war.[62]

As the violence escalated, it also became diffused, dividing families, urban districts and villages across the country. Relatively inaccessible rural areas, vulnerable country roads and settlements, became virtual no-go zones where the state ceased to have any regular presence: police and soldiers sheltered in heavily fortified barracks, and insurgent bands operated with apparent impunity. In the absence of any more formal rule of law, some of the 'self-defence groups' (GLDs) that the government began to arm in 1994 as counter-insurgent militia would also, like the insurgent armed groups, be accused by human rights observers of carrying out extrajudicial killings, acts of terror and involvement in local vendettas. The privatisation of violence and its multiple local logics became divorced from the ostensible conflict of Islamists *versus* government, and fed on local 'war economies', through which local, private or sectional interests and the local networks of the state, whether in competition or in collusion, came to have greater stakes in the perpetuation of the conflict than in its resolution.

In 1992–93, belief was strong among young Islamist sympathisers in the imminent collapse of the regime and the victory of Chebouti, 'the lion of the mountain' and his avenging army: in the words of a newspaper-seller in the Algiers suburbs, 'It won't last, Chebouti, he'll come down from the mountain with his *mujahidin* and I promise you, he'll kill the lot of them'.[63] But it did last. Boudiaf's murder itself, committed by a lone gunman, Lembarek Boumaarafi – a sub-lieutenant in a police special intervention unit who was known to have Islamist sympathies and who had unaccountably been placed, against protocol, in Boudiaf's bodyguard on the day he was killed – was at once widely, and soon almost universally, seen as having been ordered by the hard men of the *pouvoir* who had quickly regretted their choice of president and had no intention of allowing him to undermine or bypass them.[64] On the surface a shocking sign of the fragility of the state even at its highest level, from this perspective the assassination of Boudiaf already displayed the resilience of the system at the centre of the state, its determination to defend itself and the complete absence of any 'red lines' it might hesitate to cross. In 1992–95, the HCE's regime slowly regained ground against the insurgency, averted what its supporters saw as a threatened 'collapse of the state' after Boudiaf's death and could claim to have 'saved Algeria from the *débâcle*' that faced it in 1992.[65] The HCE's supporters would also point out that, as rarely occurs in such circumstances, it respected the anticipated end of its mandate, dissolving itself at the end of 1994 and appointing General Liamine Zeroual, a 53-year-old ex-maquisard from Batna who in July 1993 had succeeded Nezzar as defence minister, as State President for a three-year 'transitional period'.

While the state may have been close to collapse in the immediate crisis of 1992–94, the regime's hard core had now regained the initiative. The men who removed Chadli were sufficiently determined to fight an all-out, and atrocious, war against the Islamist insurgents, and entrenched enough either to co-opt or to sideline their opponents in the political class. An attempt at a negotiated political solution among the opposition parties, put together during talks brokered by the Catholic community of Sant'Egidio near Rome in November 1994 and announced in a platform 'for a peaceful resolution' to the crisis in January 1995, was rejected outright by the regime. Most of the platform's proponents were ignored: the external leadership of the FIS, whose political re-entry was anathema to the *décideurs*, Ben Bella's MDA and the FFS and al-Nahda, which remained opposition movements. The PT was persuaded back into line. Honest opponents of the Rome initiative judged it 'inopportune', since as they (and many in Algeria, long allergic to 'intrusions' into national sovereignty) saw it, any initiative to reach out to the Islamists and resolve the crisis needed to come from within Algeria, not from outside.[66] For others, the reopening of political dialogue simply had to be sabotaged. Abd al-Hamid Mehri, who signed the Sant'Egidio platform for the FLN, was soon taking calls from his central committee colleagues who, they told him, could no longer support the initiative, having been 'put before difficult, and sometimes extreme, choices'.[67]

It was therefore somewhat surprising when, in February 1995, Zeroual renewed the regime's own attempts to engage a 'national dialogue' that, he said, was the only solution to the crisis and must include 'the participation of the national political and social forces without exception.'[68] Presidential elections in November 1995 confirmed Zeroual in office, and a constitutional revision a year later strengthened the Presidency's powers, particularly by establishing an upper chamber, the Council of the Nation (informally known as the 'senate'), one-third of whose members would be designated by the President, and allowing the President to legislate by decree whenever parliament was not in session. At the same time, an important progressive counterweight was introduced in the limitation of a President's mandates to a maximum of two five-year terms, suggesting both the strengthening of the Presidency and the potential for it to become a more fully 'constitutional' office.[69] New legislative, regional and local elections in June and October 1997 were won overall by Zeroual's newly created party, the RND. Accusations of fraud and ballot-rigging were widespread, but the undoubtedly calculated distribution of *kursis* had the effect of parcelling out representation tolerably across the political spectrum. The 'moderate' Islamist parties, Hamas and al-Nahda, now sat in the national assembly alongside the FLN and representatives of other shades of opinion prepared to accept entry into the system under the regime's rules.[70] A wider political dialogue also seemed possible. As Minister of Defence in Redha Malek's government, Zeroual had already pressed for negotiations with Abbasi and Benhadj: Malek had dismissed the idea as 'a waste of time'.[71] Now, feelers were put out to the imprisoned FIS leaders.

But Zeroual's 'national dialogue', while no doubt intended, among other aims, to marginalise Sant'Egidio, was nonetheless opposed by the 'eradicators' in the regime. His loyal lieutenant and ally, the former DGDS chief General Mohamed Betchine, was systematically undermined and discredited by a vitriolic press campaign that revealed the extent of his suspiciously accumulated private wealth. The ANP moderniser Mustafa Belloucif, who had seemingly made the same wrong enemies some years earlier, had already been thrown to the media as a scapegoat for corruption in April 1992. As under Chadli in the early 1980s, such selective and suspiciously timed corruption investigations served particular political interests much more than public justice and accountability. And just as it seemed that the earlier stage of the insurgency was being brought under control – in January 1996, eleven founder members of the FIS called for a ceasefire, the curfew in urban areas that had confined families to their overcrowded apartments every evening for three years was lifted in February, and government spokesmen began to speak of 'residual' terrorism – the violence suddenly multiplied and intensified. The abduction at Tibhirine came just as Zeroual prepared to meet the signatories to the Sant'Egidio statement; after Abdelkader Hachani and Abbasi Madani were conditionally released from prison in July 1997, the wave of massacres of civilians began in earnest.[72] Where some saw GIA extremists resorting to ever more brutal tactics to stop the return to elections and eliminate the possibility of dialogue with the regime by their rivals of the ex-FIS, others saw a clear campaign by the 'eradicators', through Tewfik and Lamari in the DRS and their agents in the GIA, to undermine Zeroual and force him out. He held on for another year, until 11 September 1998, when in a surprise TV address to the nation barely two years into his term of office, the President announced his intention to cut it short. New presidential elections were to be held in April 1999.

### After the War

Although it would flare sporadically for several years still, the violence began to abate. Without any real political or social resolution of the conflict, after seven years of war the Islamist insurgency was effectively exhausted, and society politically demobilised and desperate for a return to normality. The basic elements of the regime – the army and security services, the factional interests and patronage networks of their bosses, and the institutions of the state around them – were firmly restored to power. Observers abroad debated the nature of the violence and the utility of calling it a 'civil war', often, once again, in ways that mostly annoyed Algerians while adding little to anyone else's understanding of what had been happening to them.

The generalisation of violence, the arming of society between Islamists, GLDs, police and the military, with familial survival strategies often – anecdotally, but no doubt on a large scale – involving one son joining the police and another the *'mujahidin'*, the neighbourhood denunciations and the intimacy of violence in the worst-affected areas, the extent of both popular alienation from the security forces and, elsewhere, of popular resistance to the armed Islamists, certainly made the struggle a civil war in the sense that the armed conflict was not simply between clearly demarcated camps of insurgents and government, but turned society in on and against itself.

At the same time, the 'classic' developments often thought characteristic of civil wars did not materialise: the state's institutions, especially the army and police, did not collapse or split, large areas of national territory were never effectively occupied and fought over for any length of time by rival protagonists, and above all, the general population was not mobilised politically in support of one or another clearly distinguished armed force carrying rival political projects.[73]

Figure 7.2 Children and young men look at the photographer between the guns of a citizens' militia (GLD, self-defence group) at Remika, near Relizane, 5 January 1998. The region was in the throes of some of the 'dark decade's' worst violence (AP).

In fact the reverse was mostly true. The insurgency, while it could only survive by retaining at least some support, relatively quickly lost most of its popular support and its political goal, to the extent that there was one at all, was never more than the superficial rhetoric of a utopian 'Islamic State': its material content, capitalising on opposition to *le pouvoir*, was entirely negative. Territorial contests with regime forces were limited to micro-scale, localised urban guerillas and the maintenance of a state of insecurity in rural areas; while this had been enough for the ALN in the late 1950s, the Islamists had absolutely no political equivalent of the FLN's counter-state or the growing popular support that it came to represent. To prevail, the insurgents needed a decisive military victory that was always illusory, or a political collapse of the regime that, when it was possible in 1992–94, would have been the effect of the financial crisis, not a reflection of Islamist strength. And in fact, in military terms the ferocity of the regime's counter-guerilla proved, if anything, to be capable of inflicting more terror than its opponents' terrorism, while its political strength was visible in its ability to suppress the possibility of any agreement unsanctioned by it, as demonstrated by the fate of the 1995 Rome platform.

And instead of mobilising society into competing political camps, out of which either victory for one side or a negotiated peace might have emerged, the violence instead reduced 'politics' to a display of horror, *de*mobilising the social energies that had been so effusively liberated in 1989, destroying the social movement that had carried Islamism to the edge of power, exacerbating the rift between the people and the political class, and directing social strategies and aspirations away from national-level politics and notions of dramatic change towards more limited, local and sectional means of engagement and bargaining with the state. These, in turn, worked through older, and still resilient, networks and practices that, rather than fading away before 'rational' bureaucracy and impersonal, transparently competitive institutions, became newly relevant. The success of the recomposed political party system from 1997 onwards was, in all likelihood, attributable more to its effective meshing with such informal systems than to anything political science would recognise as institutionalised party politics.[74]

Three circumstances, in addition to its ruthlessness, saved the regime. First, debt rescheduling and financing deals with the IMF and with the foreign creditors represented in the Paris Club in April and June 1994, respectively, staved off the financial crisis and released cash for arms and equipment to fight the war. The economists of Hamrouche's group had resisted earlier pressure, especially from France, to reschedule the country's foreign debt repayments: the constraints for structural adjustment that such a move would bring meant a loss of sovereignty, amounted to 'selling the family silver' and would 'put the country on its knees when it already risked collapse'.[75] They also, perhaps above all, wanted to avoid a new flood of credit into an economy without the capacity productively to absorb it, a transfusion that would simply reanimate corrupt rentierism. They had sought instead to re-profile the debt over the longer term, a strategy that had the support of the Japanese, who held much of Algeria's debt portfolio, but which was opposed in particular by the French. The reformers' lack of support from international financial partners, in fact, combined with their fragility within the regime had proved their undoing. While at home they were attacked for reforms that appeared 'American', for neoliberals abroad their project had insufficient deregulation and private sector–led orthodoxy, insufficient rapidity in the devaluation of the currency. Paris, where their opponents in the regime were well connected, did not know or trust them and was especially hostile; and where there was some support for the reforms, turf wars within the French establishment, including between older and newer French businesses and within the French security services (between the internal intelligence service, the DST, thought to be closely connected to its homologues in the DRS, and its external equivalent the DGSE), made matters worse.[76]

But by 1993, the earlier reformers were all out of the picture. After a brief and disastrous flirtation with a return to a planned 'war economy' under the veteran étatist Belaïd Abdesselam in 1992–93, the regime switched to a liberalisation that could be made to work more in its favour. Ahmed Benbitour, an honest technocrat with a Canadian MBA who had already argued that rescheduling was inevitable when he was an advisor to Khellef and Brahimi in 1986, was brought into Redha Malek's government as Minister of Energy to negotiate with IMF. Once the IMF and Paris Club agreements were in place, the Malek government's job was done: the Prime Minister was dismissed the following day, and while Benbitour remained as Finance Minister in the two successor cabinets, his other proposed reforms, notably in the banking sector, were ignored.[77] IMF support came at a high cost. The policy presided over by the governments of Ahmed Ouyahia, a discreet diplomat and unbending 'eradicator' who came to sudden prominence in January 1996 when he was named Prime Minister, and who subsequently became head of the RND, threw the country into rapid and merciless structural adjustment. There were swingeing cuts in government expenditure on health, education and infrastructure; salary reductions for public servants; shutdowns and closures in industry; and rapidly mounting unemployment. Algerians experienced dramatic reductions in living standards, and the country's industrial capacity, instead of being revitalised, as had been planned at the end of the 1980s, was cut to ribbons instead.

Second, once the war was effectively won on the ground, the return to political business as usual was miraculously facilitated by the world market. High oil prices between 2002 and 2015 flooded the system with new money, returning the political class to the illusions of easy unearned income and unassailable foreign currency reserves. The recovery of foreign exchange revenues created a surplus of 32.5 billion US dollars by 2006. Gross domestic product grew at around 5 per cent, the economic recovery program in place since 2001 reinjected investment into the public sector after its previous throttling by structural adjustment and the public debt was finally paid off in 2006.[78] The liberalisation of foreign commerce and the massive consumer demand of the young population stimulated private sector imports and the local franchises of foreign firms, now uncontrolled by any need for domestic reinvestment and freed of any potential competition from a domestic industrial base. Spending and patronage on a grand scale could begin again. A new generation entering the political elite in 1997–99, whose members might otherwise have been obliged to recognise the need for systemic change, could instead simply graft themselves into the reconstituted system of their elders (and patrons), and reproduce their patterns of behaviour.[79]

Third, the attacks by al-Qa'ida on the United States on 11 September 2001 and the subsequent 'global war on terror' at last ended the regime's international isolation. While the resurgence of 'global jihad', the sense of playing a role in a worldwide struggle for Islam against impiety that stretched from New York to Kabul, was undoubtedly a boost to the morale of Algeria's own embattled and partly demobilised jihadists, the George W. Bush administration's response brought even greater benefits to Algeria's army and security hierarchs. The regime was now seen as offering valuable 'lessons' in combating Islamist terror, and became an 'ally' in a global war that, Algeria's leaders would lose no time in pointing out, they had already fought and won. In the mid-1990s, Algeria's war spilled over into France, with the hijacking in Algiers of an Air France Airbus in December 1994, the murder of three passengers and the dramatic liberation of the other hostages by French gendarmerie commandos at Marseille's Marignane airport; the 11 July 1995 murder in Paris of Abdelbaki Sahraoui, a co-founder of the FIS; and, two weeks later, the bombing of the St-Michel underground (RER) station in Paris that killed eight and injured 117. By 2001, these events were widely seen within the *qui tue* dispute, as alleged 'black operations' to provoke French opinion against the Islamists and strengthen material support for the regime. After September 11, they could be seen as premonitory warnings of the reach of globalised jihad. At the same time, as the war within Algeria wound down and most Algerians talked of a return to 'normality', in January 2007 a successor group to the GIA, the so-called Salafist Group for Preaching and Combat (GSPC), declared its adherence to the cause of Osama Bin Laden and re-branded itself as 'al-Qa'ida in the Islamic Maghrib'. A wave of attacks claimed by the GSPC or AQIM between October 2006 and December 2007 marked an uptick of 'residual' terrorism: co-ordinated bomb blasts on 11 April 2007 struck the *qasr al-hukuma*, the former government general building in central Algiers, and the police headquarters in the suburb of Bab Ezzouar; a suicide bombing killed twenty and injured 107 at Batna on 6 September; car bombs targeted the Constitutional Court and destroyed the United Nations Development Program offices in Algiers on 11 December.

In April 1999, Abdelaziz Bouteflika had been brought to the Presidency in succession to Zeroual, as the *décideurs'* 'consensus candidate', promising peace. The presence of Larbi Belkheir as director of the president's office was a strong indicator of where real power still lay; the six other candidates who had put themselves forward to run for the Presidency withdrew on the eve of the election, in a gesture of protest at the imminent fraud that went ahead anyway. As a reminder of the 'good old days' of Boumediene and unalloyed by involvement in the past decade, Bouteflika enjoyed a measure of real popularity. His diplomatic profile and good connections both in the Gulf and elsewhere made him the logical choice to put Algeria back on the international map, and his first term was largely spent in energetic travelling. Buoyed by the rising oil price, long-abandoned *grands projets* were recommenced and joined by new ones: Algiers' underground rail system and international airport terminal, an east–west highway, a million new housing units. Some long-overdue progressive measures were also passed, especially, in 2005, a family law reform that limited the role of a woman's *wali* (guardian) at marriage to a representative rather than a tutor, improved parental rights for divorced women and removed the necessity for the husband or father's authorisation for women and children to leave the country.[80] Bouteflika was re-elected in 2004 with a – perhaps not excessively overinflated – 85 per cent of the vote. But as would soon be apparent, the system's long-established blend of authoritarianism, patrimonialism, rentierism and corruption was reaching a new peak.

The showpieces of Bouteflika's first term were two measures intended to 'turn the page' on the war. The 'civil concord', submitted to a September 1999 referendum, was generally supported as an effort to end the violence and induce insurgents to lay down their arms, which some had already done under a 'clemency' (*rahma*) initiative by Zeroual in 1995, and which more did now. Having announced a ceasefire in September 1997, the AIS ended its insurgency in January 2000. Approved with much reduced popular support in a second referendum in September 2005 and enacted in February 2006, the expanded law on 'national reconciliation' consolidated the 'peace' without resolving the conflict. Much contested by civil society groups, especially the families of the 'disappeared' and families of victims of terrorism, as well as by 'eradicators' who criticised Bouteflika's position as encouraging recidivism among diehard Islamists, the 2006 law legislated sweeping amnesties (supposedly excluding those guilty of murder or rape, but in effect extending to all parties) and made juridical attribution of responsibility for the events of the war – 'the national tragedy', as it was now officially termed – impossible.[81]

The only certainty was that the truth about the thousands of people killed, kidnapped by insurgents or 'disappeared' by the security services, would not be known, justice for them or those who survived them not done and public debate on the whole 'national tragedy' silenced. 'For me,

Figure 7.3 *Familles des disparus*: Women holding placards at a demonstration demanding truth and justice for the 'disappeared' in Algiers, 10 August 1999 (AP).

my problem wasn't the state, it was the terrorist, the Islamist who was my neighbour, to whom I never did any harm and who did harm to me,' said Ali Merabet, spokesman for the Somoud ('Steadfast') group that represented the families of victims of terrorism, and whose two brothers were kidnapped and killed by a local armed group in 1995: 'But we realised that [with the law on national reconciliation] they'd got together; they'd done a deal between themselves ... If the person responsible for murdering my brothers is protected by the state, who is the real aggressor?'[82] Protests like this from Algeria's combative civil society, however, added up to so many voices in the wilderness.

By 2007, with an estimated quarter of the population living below the poverty line, and unemployment officially at around 12 per cent but possibly 40 per cent and anecdotally higher among young people under 30 (who accounted for over half of the total population), the reopening of Algeria to the neoliberal global economy had sharpened an already highly unequal distribution of benefits. The school-age (5- to 14-year-old) population was 25.3 per cent of the total, and after the ravages of the war and budgetary austerity, the school system struggled to equip the rising generation for success in a brave new competitive world. Prospects for most of the country's youth, who had grown up amidst violent upheaval and looked anxiously for something better in the near future, remained very limited. Family connections and patronage were surer recommendations than education and training, and private employers, according to some young job seekers and those advising them, could be even less meritocratic than the public sector. While ostentatious villas mushroomed in some districts, so did the precarious shantytowns on their unclaimed edges, and the entrepreneurial energy of the long-standing urban poor, the recently unemployed and the war's million or more internal refugees from the countryside had to find outlets wherever it could, especially in the informal import and retail world of *trabendo* (from French *contrebande*, 'smuggling') and highly insecure, occasional employment.

At the other end of the spectrum, the vision of possibilities unleashed by unrestrained private enterprise ran to surreal extremes. The tale of Rafic 'Moumen' Khalifa, the young man from Algiers who reportedly began with 1,500 euros and a modest family pharmacy and ten years later owned a bank, a TV station and an airline in a business empire clearing 200 million euros in annual profit, was 'obviously too beautiful to be true.'[83] Khalifa, the son of senior MALG officer Laroussi Khalifa, incarnated the impossible excesses now open to the *tchi-tchi* elite. The Khalifa group collapsed in 2003 with 45 million dollars missing from its flagship private bank. While Khalifa himself had long since fled to London, fifteen of his executives and others implicated in the bank's collapse were sentenced to prison terms in March 2007. While the primary victims of Khalifa's spectacular corporate fraud and personal incompetence were the group's employees and small private investors – ordinary Algerians drawn in by the hope that 'finally, we can have the good life, too'[84] – some public servants who ended up in prison had invested public money in the group's enterprises, apparently on untraceable instructions from above.[85]

At the same time as the Khalifa collapse exposed the country's most spectacular private business empire as a flimsy and inept artifice, international observers and experts shook their heads at the lack of progress actually made in opening up more sectors to foreign investment and privatising the country's state-owned enterprises. The avenues open to private investment in fact remained limited, while the remaining public industries, running constant deficits that were once again being bailed out by the soaring hydrocarbon surplus, could be neither efficiently retained nor advantageously sold, and the regime appeared indifferent to their fate. Foreign direct investment in Algeria in 2002–06 remained at only 2.6 per cent of GDP.[86] An estimated 25–35 per cent of money in the economy circulated outside official banking circuits, and the informal economy accounted for a commercial sector at least as large.

Against this background, deep-running grievances and the alienation of great swathes of society from the reconstituted political system found new outlets. When the outspoken, rebellious singer Matoub Lounès was assassinated in 1998, crowds in Kabylia had chanted *pouvoir assassin* ('murdering *pouvoir*'), a slogan that later became the refrain of a song and Tizi Ouzou football anthem by another militant Kabyle musician, Oulahlou, which openly denounced the SM and compared Boumediene to Pinochet. Public opinion in Kabylia largely espoused a well-worn image of Kabyle resistance to the regime, and saw the past decade in the light of the region's history of patriotic martyrdom and betrayal. While there had certainly been Kabyle Islamists too, the regime itself was widely credited with having deliberately implanted the Islamist maquisards, whose insurgency was now largely confined to a few mountainous areas including parts of Kabylia, to keep the region insecure. On 18 April 2001, an 18-year-old high school student, Massinissa Guermah, was shot and killed while in custody in a gendarmerie post at Beni Douala, in the central Djurdjura just south of Tizi Ouzou. Several months of angry confrontations between Kabyle youths and the security forces, especially the gendarmerie, followed. In what became known as the 'Black Spring' (*printemps noir*) at least several dozen protestors were killed. Mass demonstrations, culminating in a massive march on Algiers on 14 June in which hundreds of thousands took part and which degenerated into violence when protestors tried to reach the presidential palace, expressed a groundswell of dissent against the regime's violence and unaccountability, summed up in the sense that citizens were subject to nothing but *hogra*, the 'contempt' of those who ruled them. For over a year, the confrontations continued: in spring 2002, FFS and RCD party offices as well as symbols of the state were attacked, and unrest rumbled on and flared sporadically across the region for the next several years.

With the region's main political parties incapable of channelling the protests – the RCD's Saïd Sadi was in government, Hocine Aït Ahmed was still in his Swiss exile – in May 2001 a grassroots organisation, the 'Coordination of *aaruch*, daïras and communes' (CADC), emerged to lead what became known interchangeably – and instructively – both as the *mouvement des aaruch*, that is, of the 'tribes' (*la'arash*), and as the *mouvement citoyen*: a movement that expressed the desire for meaningful citizenship, mobilised through the ancient structures of adult, male village assemblies that became the organising bodies of the revolt. On 11 June 2001, the CADC put together a platform of fifteen demands at El Kseur, in the Soummam valley west of Bejaïa. These combined the immediate and particular (cessation of 'punitive expeditions against the population', withdrawal of criminal charges against protestors, withdrawal of the gendarmerie and police reinforcements) with the general and far-reaching: for 'a state guaranteeing all socio-economic rights and democratic liberties', against 'the policies of under-development, pauperisation and impoverishment of the Algerian people'; that 'all the executive functions of the state and its security forces shall be placed under the effective authority of democratically elected bodies', and more simply 'against *hogra*.'[87]

As these demands suggested, combined with those that claimed the 'status of martyr' for victims of the repression and immediate state welfare measures for their families, the movement's demand was for more effective inclusion in a more responsible and accountable state, according to perceptions widely held throughout Algeria as to what that state should be, rather than any rejection of the state. Only two articles of the El Kseur platform made regionally particular stipulations: the demand that Tamazight should be declared a 'national and official' language, and that there should be 'an emergency socio-economic plan' for Kabylia. But the regime's portrayal of the protests as specifically Kabyle and 'Berberist' was largely successful, containing the revolt as an expression of 'identity politics' and regionalism which the rest of the country could (and, largely, did) ignore. At the fringes of the Berberist movement, calls for Kabyle autonomy within a federal Algeria were developing, led by the singer Ferhat Mehenni's Movement for the Autonomy of Kabylia

(MAK), founded at the height of the Black Spring in June 2001, but support for the MAK came mainly from the Kabyle diaspora and such sentiments were vanishingly rare in Kabylia itself.[88] Ahmed Ouyahia, once again Prime Minister, opened negotiations with representatives of the *aaruch* on the more limited terms of the platform. The 1996 constitution had included recognition of the Amazigh as well as the Arab and Islamic aspects of the 'personality' of Algeria but offered nothing concrete on the language question; a 2002 amendment addressed this on the symbolic level, recognising Tamazight as a 'national' language. It would at last be made an official language, its use permitted in official documents, in a further constitutional revision in January 2016.

The 'citizens' movement' was thus effectively circumscribed as a cultural one; the country's other principal idiom of identity politics, militarily defeated, was now dispersed and re-integrated into the system in different ways. Abassi and Benhaj were released at last in July 2003. Some attention was paid to them, and especially to their endorsement of Bouteflika's 'reconciliation' platform, but they had become all but irrelevant. Their constituency had been destroyed, either physically eliminated or – with the regime's refusal to sanction the creation of the Wafa' (Fidelity) party by Taleb Ibrahimi, which was seen as a potential revival of the FIS – reabsorbed either into the parties of Nahnah and Djaballah, or, increasingly, into the Islamist-inclined wing of the FLN led by Abdelaziz Belkhadem, who rose under Bouteflika's patronage to be Foreign Minister in 2000, FLN Secretary General in 2005 and Prime Minister in 2006.

Outside the formal political field, a specifically Algerian Islam was cultivated by a newfound state interest in the *tariqa*s and their *zawiya*s, seen as both a useful counterweight to an 'imported' Islamism and, above all, as a reservoir of political mobilisation. Attacked by the reformists since the 1920s and largely delegitimised since the revolution, the brotherhoods had nonetheless never gone away. They even experienced a modest revival in the 1980s, at the same time as the broader 'Islamic revival' was taking a more reductive turn to orthopraxy and social moralisation, partly thanks to Chadli's family connections (through his second marriage into a Mostaghanem family), but also through the resilience of the *zawaya* networks themselves, which still commanded followings of thousands. The old Rahmaniyya *zawiya* of Tolga, on the edge of the Sahara west of Biskra, was demolished after independence, but only so that new buildings could be erected, beginning in the mid-1960s, to house its well-maintained library and its students. Magnificent new *zawiya* complexes, ostentatiously patronised by local politicians, like that of Sidi Muhammed Belkaid near Oran, were built in the early

2000s.[89] A National Association of Zawaya was created in the early 1990s, and the brotherhoods proved instrumental as part of Bouteflika's coalition in successive presidential elections up to 2009. The revival of the *zawiya*s and of the religious education dispensed there, however, was not merely a political expedient. For some, including disenchanted former FIS sympathisers and militants, the brotherhoods' spirituality and inner discipline was becoming an important alternative avenue in their search for 'serenity', for personal as well as social peace, in religion, at a time when public piety was widespread but seemed more superficial than ever. As one put it, the result of the war had been that 'mosques have never been so full, nor hearts so empty'.[90]

### Autumn in Springtime

As Algeria celebrated fifty years of independence in 2012, the wave of protest and change engulfing the Arab world from Tunisia to Syria ironically seemed to have bypassed the region's most iconically revolutionary nation. In December 2010 and January 2011, at the same time as the first protests began against the Ben Ali regime in Tunisia after the self-immolation of the young street trader Mohamed Bouazizi, similar protests erupted in Algeria, and for similar reasons. A police crackdown on unlicensed pavement trading in Bab el Oued, and the lifting of subsidies that caused a spike in the prices of essential commodities, provoked what became known as the *zzit wa sukkar* ('oil and sugar') riots. Such popular protests had been common in the assertive public spaces of Algeria – unlike its more tightly compressed neighbour – for a decade already. And, in terrible counterpoint to the capacity for collective action in some instances, dozens of Algerians, whose names would go mostly unnoticed by the outside world, had similarly burned themselves, sometimes to death, in desperate, isolated protest outside local offices of the state. More would do so in the first months of 2011, in a wave of dramatic protests that would continue sporadically for the next three years.[91]

But by November 2011, while Egyptians were protesting against the post-Mubarak military authorities' attempt to maintain the unaccountability of the army relative to the new civilian government that was expected to emerge from the elections that were about to begin, while Tunisia witnessed the swearing-in of a new constitutional assembly and Islamists and leftists entered a coalition government, and while elections in Morocco following that country's constitutional revision saw the emergence of the Islamist PJD as the largest party, which prepared to take up the office of Prime Minister and form a government, in Algeria, life carried on as normal: In Tizi Ouzou, a demonstration by the National

Federation of Retired Workers brought pensioners from villages all over Kabylia to stage a sit-in at the regional government office, with placards reading 'We want our rights' and 'No to poverty'. In Sidi Bel Abbès, residents of the Sidi Amar shantytown put up roadblocks and stopped the traffic for several hours, demanding that the state take action to rehouse them. In Boumerdès, university students went on unlimited strike against the expulsion of their activist peers. In Mostaghanem, a young man shot by police lay in a coma, and other young men rioted in protest. Elsewhere, and all that month, other roads were closed by inhabitants of other under-served peripheral housing projects, other students protested in other universities, other workers went on hunger strike, other young people confronted other policemen and rioted in other towns.[92] In the context of the 'Arab Spring', a decade after Kabylia's 'Black' one, Algeria seemed to have been left in the shade – and as the Spring withered and turned sour, with counter-revolution and civil war overwhelming democratic aspiration in Bahrain, Egypt, Libya, Yemen and Syria, Algerians increasingly agreed with regime spokesmen that they were best spared the tumult.

To be sure, demonstrators in Algiers in January and February 2011 echoed the spirit of others in Tunis and Cairo with the slogan *Boutef dégage* ('Boutef get out'). Bouteflika, though he had been in power for a much shorter time than Ben Ali in Tunisia, let alone Libya's Gaddafi or Egypt's Mubarak, was at least physically not unlike the other ageing presidential incumbents in the region whose departure had suddenly become the focus of regional aspirations for social and political change. At 74 years of age and suffering for years from illness that visibly (when he was, occasionally, visible) verged on incapacitation, Bouteflika's long and tenacious decline was also that of the revolutionary generation as a whole. He had been hospitalised in November 2005, apparently for a gastric ulcer, but rumours of stomach cancer abounded as he was repeatedly absent, sometimes for extended periods, for treatment in France; in April 2013 he suffered a minor stroke. His clinging to power, however, was evidence less of his own wilful tenacity than of the general impasse at the summit of the state, the resilience of *le pouvoir* in the wake of the civil war but also its incapacity to imagine the resolution of an unavoidable, impending generational change. As Algerian political sociologist Nacer Djabi observed, it was the whole '*tab jnanou* generation', the generation whose time was done, in Bouteflika's own words, not just Bouteflika himself, that needed 'to organise its departure', but seemed incapable of doing so.[93]

Bouteflika's entrenchment in the Presidency was the most obvious sign of this incapacity to chart a course to a managed transition: a constitutional amendment in November 2008 had allowed him a third mandate, reversing the provision of the 1996 constitution that had fixed a two-term limit to the office. The two subsequent electoral campaigns, in 2009 and 2014, were notable only for the political class's failure to use them as opportunities to address the country's systemic malaise.[94] In place of open, public politics Algerians had only the unedifying theatre, played out via the press and online, of the internal tussle within the regime. This, it was widely thought, was not simply a matter of the DRS versus the regular military and partisans of Bouteflika, as was sometimes reported, but also a function of splits within the DRS, between factions among generals, and their respective business interests and party-political allies or mouthpieces: corruption scandals, imprisonments and cabinet reshuffles were all decoded for evidence of the changing configuration of influence. This had been the case at least since 2004, when former Prime Minister Ali Benflis, Bouteflika's 1999 campaign manager and the FLN's secretary general since 2001, ran for President against his former patron with support from Mohamed Lamari and others. The campaign was especially acrimonious, and led to a hard-fought split in the FLN, which by 2009 was brought back into the fold and to support for Bouteflika under the gradually imposed leadership of a 'corrective' faction (the so-called *mouvement de redressement*) led by the Islamist-leaning Belkhadem. Other notable incidents indicated serious squabbles within the regime. On 25 February 2010, Ali Tounsi, the country's chief police officer, was shot dead at his office in the Algiers police headquarters (DGSN) by one of his colleagues, Chouaib Oultache. Oultache would be jailed in November 2011 in a corruption case along with several other DGSN cadres, having not yet faced trial for the murder. In May 2010, the long-serving and powerful SM veteran Noureddine 'Yezid' Zerhouni was removed from the post of Interior Minister that he had occupied since 1999. Four months earlier, a spectacular corruption scandal had broken at SONATRACH; the investigation would eventually bring down Chekib Khelil, the former World Bank petroleum expert who had been SONATRACH president from 2001 to 2003 and Energy Minister from 1999 to 2010.

If by 2010 *le pouvoir* had become a fragmented, polycentric system, this was, in part, because of an at least limited generational shift. The broader political elite – in parliament, in the bureaucracy and especially in the private sector, into which the children of generals and apparatchiks had flocked on returning from higher education – had been very largely replaced since the mid-1990s.[95] Even the core of the regime was no longer under the sway of the *janviéristes*, who, with the exception, as yet, of 'Tewfik' Mediène, were now all out of power, or relatively tamed and on their way out. Khaled Nezzar had already opted for retirement in 1994 and, although regularly consulted through the later 1990s, was now principally notable for occasional defensive sorties in the media. Mohamed Lamari was pushed out in July 2004 and died in February 2012. Benabbès Gheziel, who officially retired in 1997 but remained active on 'counter-terrorism' policy from an office in the Ministry of Defence, died in July 2014. Larbi Belkheir himself was sent into ambassadorial exile in Morocco in August 2005, and died in January 2010. The especially opaque 'Smaïn' Lamari died in August 2007. In 2011, aside from Tewfik, only two strongmen *décideurs* remained, both by negotiation with the President: Abdelmalek Guenaïzia, who had gone as ambassador to Switzerland in 1993, had returned at Bouteflika's behest in 2005 to the post of Minister-Delegate for Defence (in effect heading the defence ministry, the defence portfolio itself being held once more by the President), which he occupied until 2013. Mohamed 'El-Mokh' Touati had first retired in August 2005, and returned in 2011 as presidential advisor for security affairs, but would finally be removed in July 2014. Bouteflika, it seemed, had done away with all the men who had brought him to power at the end of the war.[96] But their war, and the re-composition through it of a formalised party-political system as the expression of their own, and the broader political class's, factional interests, had put nothing new in place to replace them; and nor, apparently, had Bouteflika any viable notion of how to replace himself.

In the face of this impasse, Algeria's 2011 protests were relatively muted. According to the Interior Ministry, protests and rioting between 5 and 10 January left five dead and perhaps 800 injured; 1,000 arrests were made.[97] In late January, the *Coordination nationale pour le changement et la démocratie* (CNCD), a coalition of political parties and some civil society groups, emerged to organise opposition to the regime, hoping to capitalise on this wave of protest, and demonstrations were held in Algiers in February and April. But after the first weeks of January, in contrast to events elsewhere in the Arab world, Algeria's protests did not coalesce into a mass movement for regime change. In part, this was due to effective management by the regime, which quickly made symbolic gestures to buy time: the state of emergency, in force since 9 February 1992, was lifted on 24 February. A 'reform process' was announced in March, and a commission headed by the President of the Senate, Abdelkader Bensalah, held a flurry of highly publicised meetings with prominent personalities in May and June. But its report, submitted in July, was never published; draft laws on the press, elections and the regulation of political parties and civic associations, published that August, indicated, if anything, a regression of public liberties. There was also, inevitably, repression: while the state of emergency was lifted, a ban on public demonstrations in Algiers was declared instead, and the attempted marches in the capital on 22 January, 12 and 19 February, and in particular the students' demonstration of 12 April, which almost succeeded in reaching the vicinity of the Presidential palace at El Mouradia, were met with overwhelming numbers of police.[98]

At the same time, more significantly, the regime stepped up the strategy that had been followed since Bouteflika was met with endemic protests against economic conditions during the 2004 presidential campaign and throughout his second term: *l'arrosage*, 'spraying' money from the state's deep foreign currency reserves to buy acquiescence. At least while hydrocarbon prices remained high, the regime could afford to revert, after the 1990s straitjacket of indebtedness and structural adjustment had been removed, to the old ruling bargain of redistribution, albeit in a stripped-down, episodic, crisis-management mode, without thereby implying any more genuine inclusion of participatory politics in the government of the country. In 2011, as in 2001, Algerians were engaging not in frontal opposition to the state but in the demand *for* a state, and for the public goods the state was supposed to deliver; in the short term, such demands could be met. In 2005, a development plan for the south amounting to some 3.4 billion US dollars had been announced in areas where the 2004 re-election campaign had been especially hit by local rioting. In 2011, public sector salary hikes varied between 30 and 100 per cent.[99] The price rises in the costs of basic commodities – oil and sugar – were reversed. These responses effectively stifled the immediate dynamics of protest which, in other countries, were at the same time gaining momentum.

But this was not the whole story. The CNCD lacked popular traction, found no echo among the general population. Its few demonstrations were almost comically divided between inimical factions: during a rally at the highly symbolic Place du 1er mai, where in the 1930s communists and trade unionists had united against fascism, and which Algiers bus drivers still called *chamaneuf* (for the pre-1962 *champ de maneouvres*), the fiercely secularist Saïd Sadi, head of the RCD, found himself awkwardly in company with the former FIS firebrand Ali Benhaj. While supporters of the latter chanted *Ya Ali, ya Abbas, al-jabha rahi la bas!* ('Ali [Benhaj], Abbasi [Madani], the Front's still going strong'), other demonstrators shouted *Boulahya barra!* ('"Beardies" [Islamists] out!').[100] Algerians across the country were protesting, demonstrating, rioting and striking on an almost weekly basis, and had been doing so for years. But no broader, coalescing movement of opposition emerged from these many, sporadic, fragmentary but at the same time endemic and constant local protests. Partly this was due to the CNCD's own lack of credibility, especially the prominence within it of Sadi and the RCD, a party long seen as having been partly created in collusion with the security services, and which had sacrificed much of its support by remaining in Bouteflika's 'presidential coalition' government for some time after the beginning of the 'Black Spring' in Kabylia a decade earlier. More important were basic differences between Algeria and its neighbours, both in the structure of the public sphere and its management by the regime, and in the nature of the opposition and of social protest.

Unlike Tunisia, Egypt, Libya and Syria, Algeria's Presidency had perhaps become an office for life, but not a family business.[101] Bouteflika, for all his longevity, was not seen by most Algerians as the embodiment of the system in the same way that Ben Ali or Mubarak were by Tunisians and Egyptians. Algerians well knew that there were multiple centres of power within the regime. Oppositional energy was thus some-what dispersed for lack of a single focus, a dispersal accentuated by the considerable space within the system for the absorption of stress. Unlike the tightly controlled, indeed virtually asphyxiated, public sphere in Tunisia, Algeria's rulers since the mid-1990s had taken care to create plenty of 'free' space for the channelling of social and political energy: the political parties and the proliferation of privately owned newspapers, in French and Arabic, expressing every shade of opinion, provided no end of avenues for the dissipation and cooling and social energies. When demon-strations did occur, care was again taken to give no focus to popular anger – unlike in 2001, and unlike in Tunisia, there were to be no funerals of martyrs. The police hardly needed to use relative restraint, given the balance of forces on the street, in which an estimated 30,000 policemen faced perhaps 2,000 protestors. Several hundred protestors were arrested on 12 February, but all were reportedly released soon afterwards, in some cases within less than an hour.

But more crucial even than the regime's management of the protests was the fragmentation of the opposition and the fact that it existed, not in a simple face-off with *le pouvoir* as a bloc, but as a disjointed series of separate protests that in fact worked within, not against, the logic of the *régime* – in the more technical sense of the political economy of state–society relations. Not only did the political landscape encourage disunity, and not only did the CNCD and especially the RCD suffer from a lack of credibility. The organisation of protest by professional groups, unions and neighbourhoods meant that each could be repressed or bought off as the particular situation demanded, or as local political interests dictated.[102]

As had been true throughout the long colonial period and through the convulsions of the war of independence, the tumultuous surface events and the consistently intractable underlying logics of political life at the summit of the state made up only one, and perhaps not the most significant, layer of Algerian history. Below *le pouvoir* on the heights of Algiers lay a society that was still robust and resilient, and a system of functional, if episodic and informal, engagement between society and the more local instances of the state – the provincial governorates (*wilaya*s), the municipal assemblies (APCs), even the local political parties (*kasma*s) of the FLN and the RND – and informal mechanisms of influence and arbitration still, in some places, embodied in very old forms of local consultation: councils of *la'arash* in Kabylia, sometimes remodelled as 'patrimonial associations' but preserving the function of the ancient male, adult consultative assembly; meetings of 'tribal' heads of families in Tebessa or Timimoun; the *halqa*s of scholars and community leaders in the Mzab who had mediated episodic conflict there since 2008. At these, local and pragmatic levels of political life, Algeria's authoritarianism was not, in fact, as calcified as it might seem; it too was flexible, resilient, capable – as long as it had money to distribute – of a selective responsiveness to popular demands, assertions of sectional interest or bargains of patronage and clientelism.[103]

This was how the political economy of riot had operated throughout the country throughout the past decade. There was no connection between protests across national political space because each riot, sit-in or demonstration, whatever it shared with others, was for both protestors and authorities a local protest over primarily local issues, resolved or kept in deadlock by local mediation and the local deployment of the state's resources: electricity, housing and salaries, or batons, bullets and tear gas. It was only when there was no network of such collective action available, and – of course – no political traction to be gained from the bureaucracy by the law-based demands of the individual citizen, that this informal but relatively functional system broke down: it was in these circumstances that Algerians set themselves on fire. But there was no risk of a wider conflagration, not because Algerians were collectively 'traumatised' by the experiences of the 1990s (and many of the young people protesting could themselves have little or no conscious memory of the war[104]), but because fears of a return to violence, however severe, were outweighed by generalised popular political demobilisation. Rather than being afraid to speak out – which in fact they did, vocally, and all the time – Algerians were for the most part, more simply, as they regularly put it, *dégoûtés*, disgusted, with the thoroughly distasteful, compromised business of politics. If there was no linkage between endemic social protest and anaemic political opposition, this was partly because there was simply no interest in the latter among those, very many, people involved in the former.

This was above all, perhaps, visible in the differences between the social protests of January 2011 – what in the popular quarters of Algiers, Bab el Oued and Belouizdad (Belcourt) became known as *zzit wa sukkar* – and the attempted mobilisation for 'change' in February. The organised political rallies were largely boycotted by those who had been involved in the spontaneous popular protests only weeks earlier. As the apparently 'pro-Bouteflika' youths, who briefly formed a counter-demonstration at *chamaneuf* on 12 February, but who were anything but 'pro-regime' protestors, explained:

> We're just fed up, that's all, they can go have their fights somewhere else, this is our patch (*quartier/houma*), our homeland (*patrie*). Us, when we demonstrate, they call us scum, thugs (*racaille . . . voyous*) . . . So why do they come and have a go at us? Us, when we go out on the streets for two days, at least we get the price of oil and sugar down. And them, what do they want? These parties just use us to climb up to positions of power.[105]

As one taxi-driver in Oran put it, again drawing a clear line between attempted political mobilisation and the past winter's local social protests, 'Us, we know them. They're doing that for themselves, not for us. There'll be nothing happening in our neighbourhoods, 'cos that lot, they did nothing for us in the riots.'[106]

Endemic social protest thus combined with what Algerians called *dégoûtage* for all things *bulitiq*. The war had not only crushed but also effectively delegitimised utopian Islamism as a revolutionary solution capable of 're-enacting' the revolutionary dynamic of the war of independence, as some FIS and MIA militants in 1989–93 had understood themselves to be doing. It had fragmented the Islamist constituency, isolating, manipulating and undermining its most radical factions while co-opting and taming others. Ferociously re-establishing its position, and the status quo ante, against the threats both of Islamism and of a more genuine democratisation through the 1990s, the regime had by 2015 left itself fragile, hollow and with little idea of what to do next save accelerate its rapaciousness. As FLN veteran Abd al-Hamid Mehri put it in 2007, 'the current system contents itself with a democratic facade and a single-party reality [which] can maintain itself, but not solve the problems [that it faces]'.[107]

'The people', the revolutionary FLN's 'sole hero', had long since spilled out of the unified, homogeneous, heroic mould into which the new nation-state had tried to press them, asserting their differences, sometimes to a horrifically violent degree, against each other, but also demonstrating their plurality, their belonging to a shared universe of references – linguistic, religious, cultural – different interpretations of which provided the grounds of their contests among themselves. But the system that governed them had retained of its distributive function only the capacity to buy short-term acquiescence, of its guarantees of law and order only the ability to repress, and of the revolutionary counter-state only the secretive, factional habits of what was now a gerontocracy, whose privileges could be exploited by those who had grown up in its charmed circles. The promise of 1 November, of the establishment of a democratic state by and for its people, integrated into a fraternally united Maghrib, remained the unfulfilled requirement for the solution of the country's pressing social, economic, environmental and political challenges. In Mehri's words, 'to return to the origin of the FLN is [in this sense] also to respond to the reality of the present moment.'[108] But it was the factional politics of the nationalist past, not its project for the future as imagined at the outset of the revolution, that remained hooked in power sixty years later. The generational shift that had produced Algeria's population of 2012 and their aspirations for change thus confronted the maintenance of a status quo untenable in the longer term but capable of reproducing itself apparently indefinitely for the time being. Algeria, which as ever had its share of dramatic events in and after 2011–12, was less in the shade of its neighbours' springtime than in the autumnal shadow of its own revolutions. It was from their shadows that Algeria's contemporary history was, and ordinary Algerians were, still struggling to emerge.

# Afterword
In the Shadow of Revolution (2016)

On 13 September 2015, the man widely believed to be the real centre of power in Algeria left office. General Mohamed 'Tewfik' Mediène, sometimes nicknamed *rabb dzair,* 'the Lord of Algeria', the 76-year-old head of the DRS, had retired, 'relieved of his functions' in the terse formulation of a presidential communiqué. Never seen in public, rarely glimpsed in unverified photographs, the face of the faceless *pouvoir* was suddenly all over newspaper front pages. Whether he left the office he had occupied unchallenged for twenty-five years of his own choosing or under pressure from the coterie around Bouteflika was unclear – and relatively unimportant.

The move could have been significant. 'Tewfik', the architect of the DRS, the iron core of the 'deep' state that had waged its merciless war on and of terror through the 1990s, had become indispensable, untouchable, all but un-nameable, known to every Algerian and answerable to no one. Observers of Algeria and human rights activists both in the country and abroad had long recognised that any meaningful move towards more democratic, accountable and law-bound government must necessarily pass through the removal of the DRS from the centre of the state and its subordination to legal oversight. Doubtless for their own, factional, reasons as well as or rather than on principle, Algerian political party leaders too regularly demanded the dismantling, or at least the thorough 'restructuring', of the political police.[1] In 2015, and for several years before, the rumour mill of the Algerian media was regularly fed with accounts of the ongoing tussle between the Presidency and the DRS, and in the course of the summer the agency did indeed see its prerogatives reduced, transferred to elements of the army, in what some saw as a significant clipping of the secret services' sharp-clawed wings. In the context of a long-deferred 'transition' away from Algeria's authoritarianism, the retirement of Tewfik might indeed have signalled a real departure, 'the end of an epoch', 'an earthquake in the nation's political life'.[2]

But there was no such transition. The appointment of Tewfik's successor was a strong signal of continuity. Major General (retd.)

Athmane 'Bachir' Tartag, a career soldier who had been recruited into the Boumediene-era *sécurité militaire* and trained by the Russians in the 1970s, had been 'number two' in the DRS and most recently, since his earlier retirement from the military, in a holding position as a counsellor to the Presidency. During the 1990s, he commanded the notorious Principal Military Investigation Centre (CPMI) at Ben Aknoun in the south-western suburbs of Algiers. A detention centre nominally charged with combating Islamist influence in the army, by most accounts this was one of the DRS's main centres of torture and extrajudicial killing, where civilian suspects as well as soldiers were held, interrogated and murdered.[3] What distinguished Tartag from Tewfik was simply the fact that he was a decade or so younger, a child during the struggle for independence and a student in the early 1970s when he responded to Boumediene's appeal for graduates to enlist in the army. Like Tewfik, Tartag rose through the ranks in the mid-1980s and found himself in a critical position of power in 1990.[4] Like Tewfik, he would be a relentless 'eradicator' and a leading practitioner of the policy of 'the management of society by violence'. Hardly signalling a generational transition, even less did this suggest an institutional change or even a modification of policy. But the change from Tewfik to Tartag was another small instance of the slow, inexorable passing away of the generation born in the late 1930s, the generation of the revolution, of the youthful, forward-looking men of fifty years ago, of whom Bouteflika himself now remained the last, visibly fading, representative, clinging to power as to life, by his fingertips.

The disarmingly insignificant removal of Tewfik, and his replacement by a man whom Bouteflika, on first assuming the Presidency in 1999, had himself pushed into retirement as having played an especially brutal role in the 'dirty war', who had more recently shown himself less than adroit in handling the hostage crisis at the In Amenas gas facility in the Sahara in January 2013, and who had been returned to office by the factional manoeuvres of the president's brother, was also, however, a sign of other changes.[5] It illustrated the continuity of the 'fierce' dimension of the state, the degree to which Boumediene's desire in 1965 to create 'institutions capable of outliving personalities' had been realised, at least in respect of the secret services and the informal powers around the Presidency that since Boumediene's time had been at the core of the state. But it also illustrated their state of disintegration, their ageing, along with the men who ran them, and their reduction, at the very centre of power, from instruments intended to serve the construction of a strong state that would make its people strong to bickering fiefdoms, instruments of cliques and coteries serving to divide the spoils of the state among themselves.[6] *Le pouvoir* had collapsed into a black hole, sucking resources, opportunities and the very future of the country into itself. American diplomats in 2007 characterised the regime as 'fragile in ways it has not been before, plagued by a lack of vision, unprecedented levels of corruption and rumblings of division in the military … a government drifting and groping for a way forward'. In 2009 they wrote of the system as 'a series of largely incompetent institutions … spinning their wheels independently, with nothing to connect the dots'.[7] By 2015, even the terrible, omnipotent DRS had seemingly become a frayed, thinning institution.[8]

At the centre of *le pouvoir* as throughout the political system, with its ramifying party-clientelism, its proliferation of independent local candidates and their local means of patronage, and throughout the day-to-day economy by which many, perhaps most, Algerians earned their livelihood, it was the 'informal sector' rather than ostensible institutions that now held sway. And while, again ever since the wartime FLN, the 'informal', personal and factional, interior realities of the state had always had primacy over its formal, impersonal and constitutional external appearance, that informality now worked less through the institutionalised forms of the 'shadow cabinet', the departments of the Presidency and the DRS than in personal cliques divorced from any real arm of the state, no more law-bound than the old primacy of informal politics had been, but without their stability and capacity for self-perpetuation. And this, at a time of regional turmoil, with civil war on the country's borders, an ailing president, an interminable, insoluble succession crisis and suddenly falling oil and gas prices.

On 23 December, slightly more than three months after the official departure of 'Tewfik', Hocine Aït Ahmed, since Ben Bella's death in 2012 the last survivor of the FLN's nine historic leaders, passed away, still in exile in Lausanne. He was buried on 1 January 2016, not alongside his former comrades, grouped around the austere tomb of the amir Abd al-Qadir in the martyrs' square at al-Alia cemetery east of Algiers, but high in the Djurdjura, in the village of Aït Ahmed where he was born, near the mausoleum of the Kabyle sage and poet Si Mohand Ou Lhocine. A vast crowd, tens of thousands strong, chanted the *shahada* (*la ilaha illa'llah, Muhammad rasul allah*, the Muslim profession of faith) alongside *Assa, azzeka, Dda Lhocine yella!* ('Today, tomorrow, Father Hocine still lives'), *Corrigez l'histoire, l'Algérie n'est pas arabe!* ('Get your history straight, Algeria is not Arab') and, most insistently, *Pouvoir assassin!*[9] Prime Minister Abdelmalek Sellal's car was spat at, rocks were thrown and the official delegation was obliged to make an undignified withdrawal. The war that tore Algeria apart in the last ten years of the twentieth century had been over for more than a decade. Algeria was as far from the resolution of its conflicts as it had ever been.

Figure A.1 Mohamed Issiakhem's 'sarcophagus' over the 1928 war memorial in central Algiers (the former Government General building in the background) (Author's photograph).

For some time, the concrete shell covering the colonial-era war memorial outside the old Government General building in Algiers had been falling apart. Artist Amina Menia captured the fissures through which the art déco *spahis* and their medievalised horses had begun to peek in a series of photographs, *Enclosed #0*, made in 2013. The 1928 *monument aux morts*, before which Algiers' Europeans had humiliated Guy Mollet in 1956, had been encased after independence by the painter and sculptor Mohamed Issiakhem in a 'sarcophagus', which was now opening up, revealing, as Menia wrote, 'another relation to time and history'.[10] The monument, and Issiakhem's enclosure of it, could be taken to stand for something broader. As the *spahis* bearing aloft the unknown soldier sat still within the minimalist concrete case, out of which Issiakhem moulded two hands breaking their chains, so Algeria's colonial past sat within the crumbling shell of the revolutionary nation-state. Concealed and disavowed, it could not be simply swept away, removed and dispensed with, because it was itself constitutive of the revolution, and of the society and the nation it had sought to liberate. Colonialism and its state were the substructure of independence and the nation-state, as surely as the *qasr al-hukuma* inhabits the former offices of the *gouvernement général*, on whose balcony de Gaulle appeared in 1958, to look down over the *monument aux morts* and the seething crowd in the 'forum' below.

Such evidence is still there, physically present everywhere in Algeria's urban fabric. In the little coastal town of Cherchell, the memorial garden to the martyrs of independence occupies what was once the garden, in which stood a bust of de Gaulle's predecessor General Cavaignac, of the adjoining porticoed church, whose stubby bell tower was built up after independence into an elegant, foursquare minaret. In the Place d'Armes outside the town hall in Oran, the amir Abd al-Qadir's sculpted face, with the inscription *wa ma al-nasru illa min 'indi allahi inna 'llaha azizun hakimun* ('And there is no victory but from God, truly God is mighty, wise'[11]), sits chiselled into each face of the obelisk that was erected in 1898 in memory of the 'heroes of Sidi Brahim', the celebrated stand of an outnumbered force of *chasseurs* against Abd al-Qadir's forces in 1845, atop which the bronze winged victory still stands.[12] Like Issiakhem's sarcophagus over the war memorial in Algiers, and like Menia's later photographs, the victory column in Oran provides a striking instance of an Algerian artist engaging with the past, in recognition, in a kind of dialogue, knowingly, self-knowingly, less triumphant than discreetly, gently admonishing.

This does not mean that Algeria has never been decolonised, that it is somehow still inhabited by a secret trauma. It means, more simply, that Algeria's relationship to its history is not as pathological as has often been supposed. Anyone believing that Algerians have long been animated by powerful 'hatred' of France and everything that France in Algeria entailed, a 'hatred' subsequently turned in on themselves and still today unexpiated, might wonder why, in Oran, where the summer of 1962 was especially bloody and murderous, pedestrians have walked every day for fifty years past a statue to the 1848 constitution that made Algeria part of France, without feeling the need to remove it, or even being concerned about what it is; or why the women of Oran still climb up to the church the settlers built at the very end of the colonial period, in 1959, at Santa Cruz, to light candles to *lalla Maryam*, the Virgin whose statue still looks benignly over their city from the mountaintop.[13] It is not because of a misplaced colonial nostalgia. It is because these things do not matter as signs of colonialism and conflict, the war and fury that outsiders so often see as solely constitutive of Algerian history. They are simply parts of the landscape that Algerians inhabit, have always inhabited, and have re-appropriated for themselves, less, in the

Figure A.2  Oran, 2007: The Place d'Armes and Sidi Brahim
monument, with Abd al-Qadir's portrait added to the base
(Author's photograph).

end, through the sound and fury of war and revolution than through the
quiet endurance of a resilient society, one whose ancestral inheritance
'today, tomorrow, still lives', and with which, above all, its people want
to live at peace.

# Notes

## Introduction

1. Field notes, July–August 2005, May–June 2007.
2. Boyer, *La vie quotidienne à Alger*, summed up colonial stereotypes in a study published immediately after Algerian independence; Davis, *Christian slaves, Muslim masters*, rediscovered the subject for a new audience forty years later.
3. Alistair Horne's *A savage war of peace* remains by far the best-known English-language work on Algeria.
4. Cambon, a relatively liberal official, saw this situation as the result of French misgovernment, which he regretted as having deprived France of 'authorised intermediaries' between the colonial state and its indigenous subjects. Ageron, *Algériens musulmans* vol. 1, 518–19.

## 1  Ecologies, Societies, Cultures and the State, 1516–1830

1. Temimi, 'Lettre de la population algéroise', 98, 100, 101.
2. De Grammont, *Histoire d'Alger*, 29–37; Merouche, *La course*, ch. 1. On the antecedents to Spanish and Ottoman intervention in the Maghrib, see Abun-Nasr, *History of the Maghrib*, 102–51.
3. Merouche, *La course*, 49.
4. De Haëdo, *Histoire des rois*, 35–36; De Grammont, *Histoire d'Alger*, 42; Abun-Nasr, *History of the Maghrib*, 149; Merouche, *La course*, 38.
5. De Grammont, *Histoire d'Alger*, 44; Merouche, *La course*, 38–39.
6. For incomplete 'evolution' towards national integration, see Ruedy, *Modern Algeria* 42–44; for glorious resistance, al-Madani, *Ḥarb thalāthami'at sana*. For a critical view of rival interpretations, Merouche, *La course*, 12–17.
7. Julien, *Histoire de l'Algérie contemporaine* vol. 1, 19–20.
8. Mohsen Toumi, quoted in Grangaud, *La ville imprenable*, 11 n.1
9. Gramaye, *Diarium rerum Argelae gestarum*, in Ben Mansur, *Alger*, 286–87, Morgan, *Complete history of Algiers* vol. 1, 211.
10. On the history, ecology and human geography of the Sahara, and the recent tendency to urbanisation, see Bisson, *Mythes et réalités d'un désert convoité*.
11. This section draws especially on Bellil, *Les oasis du Gourara*.
12. A Moroccan claim to sovereignty over the area would be revived against the extension of French incursions into the Sahara at the end of the nineteenth century.

344     Notes to pages 16–23

13. Bisson, *Mythes et réalités*, 53–55.
14. Valensi, *Eve of colonialism*, 31.
15. Shaw, *Travels or observations*, 253.
16. Nouschi, *Enquête sur le niveau de vie*, 9.
17. Peyssonnel, *Voyage*, 193–94.
18. Nouschi, *Enquête*, 30–31. The likely size of Algeria's population before 1830 has been subject to prolonged and inconclusive debate. The estimate of 3 million has been frequently cited since the 1954 work of Yacono, 'Peut-on évaluer la population de l'Algérie vers 1830?' (e.g. Ruedy, *Modern Algeria*, 20–21); Sari, 'Problèmes de la démographie', 168–71, presents the case for the higher figure. Kateb, *Européens, 'indigènes' et juifs*, 15–16, notes that no estimate can escape from its political implications (the higher the pre-colonial total, the greater the conquest's death toll), and while suggesting 4 million as likely on the grounds of population density, concludes that the real population level might have lain anywhere between 3 and 5 million.
19. The terms '*arsh* and *milk* are used here for practicality, following the literature, to designate these broad types of property regime, but it should be noted that their use, institutionalised in the course of the nineteenth century, is a result of often specious colonial legal usage. Before the 1850s, Algerians would not have used them with the meanings they came to carry. The classification of Algerian landholdings as either 'melk' (=private) or 'arch' (=collective) under the Senatus-Consulte of 1863 (see Chapter 3) was often incomprehensible to the populations subsequently despoiled of the land that their labour had traditionally fructified. See Ageron, *Algériens musulmans* vol. 1, 69–75; Guignard, 'Les inventeurs de la tradition "melk" et "arch" en Algérie'.
20. Warnier, report on '*azel el beylik*, Constantine, 15 February 1841 (30pp.), FR/ANOM/F80/522/1, pp. 3, 7, Nouschi, *Enquête*, 80–81.
21. Warnier (n.20), p. 11.
22. Nouschi, *Enquête*, 81.
23. Ibid., 82–87.
24. Ibid., 91–93.
25. Hanoteaux and Letourneux, *La Kabylie*; Bourdieu, *Outline*. Intensively studied since the mid-nineteenth century, Kabylia holds a remarkable place in ethnographic and sociological literature, from Durkheim to Bourdieu. See Scheele, *Village matters*; Roberts, *Berber government*; Goodman and Silverstein, *Bourdieu in Algeria*.
26. A neat statement of the colonial myth of the 'pestilential Mitidja', 'uncultivated for twelve centuries', is provided in Gautier, *Un siècle de colonisation*, 21–27.
27. Shaler, *Sketches of Algiers*, 83.
28. Report from the Maréchal du Camp to the Duc des Cars, in camp near Fort l'Empereur, 11 July 1830 (3pp.), FR/SHD/1H/4/3.
29. Shaw, *Travels*, 81–82; Saidouni, 'La vie rurale' vol. 1, 151ff., for discussion of conflicting views of the Ottoman Mitidja.
30. Shaw, *Travels*, 253, 258–59, 267; Saidouni, 'La vie rurale' vol. 1, 74, 136.
31. Saidouni, 'La vie rurale' vol. 1, 61.

32. Nouschi, *Enquête*, 153–54.
33. De Grammont, *Histoire d'Alger*, 175.
34. Serious famines struck in 1604, 1660–65, 1700–03, 1712–18, 1722–24, 1739–42, 1762–64, 1777–79, 1803–07 and 1814–17. De Grammont, *Histoire d'Alger*, Merouche, *Monnaies, prix et revenus*.
35. FR/CADN/Alg/Cons/23–25 (2Mi980). French consul's *Journal d'Alger*, no.71, entry for 26 March 1756. The second half of the seventeenth century seems to have been marked by several crises, but the sources for the 1500s and 1600s do not allow for greater precision. Better-attested crises in the eighteenth century may have been, in general, less severe. De Grammont's *événémentiel* chronicle of plague, earthquake, famine and rebellion disguises a long-term agrarian prosperity in the eighteenth century.
36. Valensi, *Eve of colonialism*, 30–31.
37. Ibid., 36. These were also small cities on a regional scale: Fez may have had just under 100,000 inhabitants, Tunis 120,000.
38. For critiques of this model, see Abu-Lughod, 'The Islamic city', Raymond, 'The traditional Arab city'.
39. I borrow the term (*idéologie citadine*) from Grandguillaume, *Nédroma*, though without his structuralist analysis.
40. For a sophisticated consideration of urban settlements in Mediterranean history, see Horden and Purcell, *The corrupting sea*, ch. 4.
41. Mahé, *Histoire de la Grande Kabylie*, 24–25.
42. Valensi, *Eve of colonialism*, 36–37.
43. On Constantine, see Grangaud, *La ville imprenable* and Guechi, *Qsanṭīna fī ʿahd Ṣālaḥ Bey*.
44. The Spanish held Oran from 1509 to 1708, then recaptured it in 1732.
45. Nouschi, *Enquête*, 150–52. The Muqrani family held property estimated at 26,000 hectares, in addition to herds, flocks, mills, orchards and houses. Their fortune was reckoned between 1 and 2 million francs in 1848.
46. Quoted in Sari, *Les villes précoloniales*, 35.
47. Ibid., 47.
48. Grandguillaume, *Nédroma*, 31, 48–71.
49. On Tahert and the antecedents to settlement in the Mzab, see Abun-Nasr, *History of the Maghrib*, 37–49.
50. Holsinger, 'Migration, commerce and community', 63.
51. The main doctrinal and ritual distinctions concerned the visibility of God in paradise, the eternity of hell and the created nature of the Qur'an and the position of the arms in prayer; more significant was the doctrine of the equality of all Muslims, such that any believer might be properly invested as caliph, or imam, of the community.
52. Oussedik, *Relire les itiffiqat*, 94–115.
53. Merouche, *Monnaies*, 206–07.
54. On converts to Islam in the early modern Mediterranean, see Benassar and Benassar, *Les chrétiens d'Allah*.
55. Merouche, *Monnaies*, 205.
56. Ibid., 228.

57. De Haëdo, *Histoire des rois*, 110–16, 118–21; De Grammont, *Histoire d'Alger*, 85–87; Merouche, *La course*, 93.

58. De Haëdo, *Histoire de rois*, 147–63; Merouche, *La course*, 58–59.

59. The judicial system was headed by one mufti for each of the two *madhhab*s (schools of jurisprudence) represented in the Regency. The majority of the population followed the Maliki school, while the Ottoman ruling elite identified with the Hanafi rite that became the 'official' school in Anatolia and in the empire. Major towns had both Hanafi and Maliki mosques; the Ibadi community had their own mosques and, especially, cemeteries. The dual Hanafi/Maliki system was maintained under the French colonial regime.

60. Merouche, *Monnaies*, 204–05.

61. For another view of regional interactions in this period from the eastern Mediterranean, see Greene, *A shared world*.

62. Values are given in Spanish, or Seville, silver eight-réal piasters (SP), the most stable contemporary currency, against which exchanges are most easily measured. The gold coin of Algiers, the *sultani* ('sequin' in European sources), struck from 1516, held a stable value of ca. 2 SP from the late seventeenth century; from 1685, Algiers' primary money of account was the pataque (or 'pataque chique' in French sources), which in the eighteenth century held a relatively stable value at 4, then 4.5 to the SP (8–9 pataques to the sultani) until the economic crises of 1803–07 and 1816–17. The figures here reflect the effect of these crises, with the pataque valued at 7.5 to the SP.

63. Merouche, *Monnaies*, 201.

64. Benassar and Benassar, *Chrétiens d'Allah*, 290–91.

65. Horden and Purcell, *Corrupting sea*, 383–91.

66. *Journal d'Alger* (n.35), no. 69, entries for 26 March and 9 January 1756; Machault, Versailles, to Lemaire, Algiers, 8 September 1756, FR/CADN/ Alg/Cons/3, ff. 132–33, 135; Ambassador to the Two Sicilies, Naples, to Lemaire, Algiers, 23 September 1756, FR/CADN/Alg/Cons/3, ff. 144–45; De Sartine, Versailles to De La Vallée, Algiers, 3 June 1776 and De Sartine, Fontainebleau to De La Valée, Algiers, 21 October 1776, FR/CADN/Alg/ Cons/7, ff. 20–23.

67. Benassar and Benassar, *Chrétiens d'Allah*, 244–45, 252. See also Clancy-Smith, 'The Maghrib and the Mediterranean world in the nineteenth century'.

68. FR/CADN/Alg/Cons/7 f.74.

69. Anon., 'The Algier slaves releasment: or, The unchangeable Boat-Swain' (London, dated ca. 1680). Bodleian Library, Oxford, Douce Ballads 1 (3b).

70. Account (1595) by Richard Haselton (sold in Algiers in 1582, enslaved on both Algerian and Genoese galleys and imprisoned by the Inquisition) quoted in Nabil Matar, Introduction to Vitkus (ed.), *Piracy, slavery and redemption*, 76, 95.

71. June, 1675 report from English state papers, quoted in Matar (n.70), 18.

72. *Journal d'Alger* (n.35), entry for 25 December 1755.

73. Account of an incident involving 'Constantino', a Roman barber and wigmaker serving at the French consul's house, *Journal d'Alger* (n.35), entry for 6 January 1756.

74. Shaler, *Sketches*, 76–77.
75. *Journal d'Alger* (n.35), entry for 10 December 1755.
76. Wright, *Trans-Saharan slave trade*, chs. 1, 4; Lovejoy (ed.), *Slavery on the frontiers of Islam* ch. 8; Loualich, 'Esclaves noirs à Alger', 518–22.
77. Merouche, *Monnaies*, 211–15. On 'white' slavery, see Friedman, 'Christian captives', *Spanish captives in North Africa*; Weiss, 'Barbary captivity', *Captives and corsairs*.
78. Merouche, *Monnaies*, 226, 237.
79. *Habus* (known as *waqf*, plural *awqaf*, further east) were properties whose revenues were assigned in perpetuity to the benefit of a family or, often, a religious institution. Taken out of circulation by their 'consecration' to a pious benefaction, such properties were technically inalienable and safe from confiscation; *habus* foundations were therefore a common means of preserving at least part of the revenues from estates in the founder's family after his or her death.
80. Merouche, *Monnaies*, 240.
81. Contemporary observers often assimilated preponderance in a particular occupation with a *de jure* monopoly, but Algiers' market regulations specifically forbade corporations dominated by particular groups from excluding others from their sector (Merouche, *Monnaies*, 238).
82. Transliterations follow Algerian pronunciation; the term is often transcribed 'couloughlis' or 'kouloghlis', from Turkish *kuloğlu*, pl. *kuloğulları*, 'son of the slave [of the sultan]'.
83. Shuval, *La ville d'Alger* and 'The Ottoman Algerian élite', points to a deliberately maintained ideology of 'Turkishness' especially in the janissary corps, an ideology disguising the real situation (*kuluglis* were not excluded from high office, as contemporary observers and their informants, and subsequent scholarship reliant upon them, claimed). This ideological distinction also disguised the decreasing significance of foreign origin in the distribution of wealth. Merouche, analysing familial *habus* acts (which indicate the preservation of accumulated wealth) by category, shows that in 1630–80, 43 per cent (of 313 cases) are listed as Turks, 28 per cent Andalusis, undifferentiated 'others' 17 per cent and *beldis* only 8 per cent. In 1688–1785 (1081 cases), Turks remain ahead (41 per cent) followed by ascendant 'others' (31 per cent) and *beldis* (23 per cent), with *'uluj* – only 6 cases – and Andalusis – only 5 per cent – effectively disappearing as distinct groups. By 1785–1830 (276 cases), the undifferentiated class of 'others', indistinguishable by origin and now incorporating the descendants of Andalusis and converts, takes the lead, with 49 per cent, ahead of still distinctly visible Turks (33 per cent) and identifiable *beldi* lineages (18 per cent). Although the figures rely on the accidents of those documents that survive, and cannot be absolutely conclusive, they suggest that together, by the end of the Regency, the non-'Turkish' elite accounted for the greatest share of the city's accumulated family capital (Merouche, *Monnaies*, 206–07). In the more pronounced case of Constantine, Grangaud has demonstrated the integrative capacity of local society, whose existing elite was sufficiently powerful that 'to accede to the status of notable … "new

men" [incoming Turkish elites] … are obliged to forget, or at least, may not lay claim to, their origins; from Turks, they must become Constantinois and Constantinois only' (*La ville imprenable*, 229).

84. Shuval, *La ville d'Alger*, 63.
85. Merouche, *Monnaies*, 279–80.
86. Literary clichés about the instability of Algiers politics, originating in the actual tumult of particular periods (notably 1659–71, when each ruling agha of the janissaries was assassinated in turn) are summed up in the myth, originating with the eighteenth-century writer Laugier de Tassy, of seven pashas murdered in one day. Ruedy points out the progressive stabilisation of the regime from the turn of the eighteenth century: in 1683–1700, eight successive deys held office, in 1700–50, ten and in 1750–1800, four (De Grammont, *Histoire d'Alger*, 192; Ruedy, *Modern Algeria*, 19).
87. Bilingual manuscript copy in papers taken from dey's cabinet, FR/SHD/1H/4/2/2.
88. Shuval, 'The Ottoman Algerian élite'.
89. Merouche, *Monnaies*, 52, 12.
90. Head of the families of *sharifs* (plural *ashraf* or *shurafa*) claiming descent from the Prophet.
91. i.e. the Janina ('little garden') palace in the centre of the lower town of Algiers.
92. Sharif al-Zahhar, *Mudhakkirāt*, 23.
93. Bellil, *Les oasis du Gourara* vol. 1, 125–26.
94. Venture de Paradis, *Grammaire et dictionnaire*, xxi.
95. Roberts, *Berber government*, 165–210.
96. e.g. Shaler, *Sketches*, 78.
97. Merouche, *Monnaies*, 67.
98. Ibid., 121.
99. Interview with Sadek Hadjerès, Malakoff, June 2009 (recalling trips into the mountains south of Blida as a boy in the mid-1940s).
100. Grangaud, *La ville imprenable*, ch. 4, Guechi, *Qsantina*.
101. Nacib, *Cultures oasiennes*, chs. 6, 7. For the Banu Hilal, see Brett, 'Ibn Khaldun and the Arabisation of North Africa'; on the epic, Nacib, *Une geste en fragments* (Algerian version), Saada, *La geste hilalienne* (Tunisian version) and Slyomovics, *The merchant of art* (Egyptian version).
102. Bellil, *Les oasis du Gourara* vol. 1, ch. 3, Moussaoui, *Espace et sacré*.
103. Literally, 'those who are bound', i.e. to God, away from the world; originating in the medieval period and generalised from the sixteenth century, in North Africa the institution of the *ribat* was originally both a fortified defensive position and a spiritual retreat from which *murabitun* carried forward the faith as missionaries, and defended it as warriors. Later, local religious specialists as well as the lineages of celebrated saintly individuals were known as *mrabtin*.
104. Sidi Hawari (d. 1439?), scholar from the region of Mostaghanem and adopted patron of Oran, one of whose oldest mosques, and the old quarter of the town, is named after him; Abu Madyan Shu'ayb al-Ansari, *al-ghawth* ('the Nurturer') (d.1198), 'the most influential figure' in early

Maghribi Sufism (Cornell, *Way of Abu Madyan*, 2), buried just outside Tlemcen; Sidi Abd al-Rahman al-Tha'alibi (d. 1468/9), a Qur'anic exegete, writer on Prophetic dreams and hero of miraculous folktales, whose mausoleum outside the walls of Ottoman Algiers was a major religious monument.

105. Al-Wartilani, *Nuzhat al-anẓār*, 4, 7.
106. On forms of Islamic learning, see especially Touati, *Entre dieu et les hommes*.
107. On Sufism, 'maraboutism' and the orders, see Trimingham, *Sufi orders in Islam*, Gilsenan, *Recognising Islam*, chs. 4, 7, Eickelman, *Moroccan Islam*, Clancy-Smith, *Rebel and saint*, ch.2.
108. Grandguillaume, *Nedroma*, 157–58.
109. Haldon, *State and the tributary mode*; cf. Valensi, *Eve of colonialism*, 71–77, 118–20.
110. Panzac, *Corsaires barbaresques*, 111. In the richest years (1798–99) of the brief resurgence during the Napoleonic wars, the state's share of corsair prizes may have risen to just over a quarter of its total revenue. See also Merouche, *La course*, part 3.
111. Christian privateering, especially by the Order of the Knights of St John of Malta, was also a persistent feature of Mediterranean trade and warfare until the suppression of the Order by Napoleon Bonaparte, on his way to invade Egypt, in 1798.
112. On corsairing as regime ideology, see Merouche, *Monnaies*, 216–17. On Algerian relations with Britain, see Fisher, *Barbary legend*; for the Netherlands, van Krieken, *Corsaires et marchands*.
113. De Sartine, Versailles, to De La Valée, Algiers, 21 June 1776 (on retrieval of goods seized by a Spanish vessel from a French ship carrying Algiers' *wakil kharij* with presents from Istanbul to Algiers); 'Etat des batimens françois entrés [...] la rade d'Alger pendant l'année 1776'; Memorandum on Spanish attack on the French ship *Saint-Victor* (carrying 183 Algerian pilgrims to Alexandria in August 1777), 19 December 1777. FR/CADN/Alg/Cons/7, ff. 24–31, 73–76, 143–47.
114. Letter and supporting documents from De Sartine, Versailles, to consul at Algiers, 8 December 1777, FR/CADN/Alg/Cons/7, ff. 125–39.
115. A dry measure (*sa'*) of sixty litres cost three and three-quarter pataques in 1803, thirty-five pataques in March 1805. Merouche, *Monnaies*, 115–17, 273–74.
116. Merouche, *Monnaies*, 117, De Grammont, *Histoire d'Alger*, 284. Contemporary sources suggest between fifty and two hundred killed in anti-Jewish rioting; Eisenbeth, 'Les juifs en Algérie', 376–77, mentions estimates of 200 or 500 dead, while local sources then available to him (as Algiers' Chief Rabbi) mention fourteen Jews killed leaving the synagogue and a total of forty-two killed in the three hours before the dey called a halt to the pillage. These figures are the most conservative estimates available.
117. Quotes from Sharif al-Zahhar, *Mudhakkirāt*, 131–37. See also De Grammont, *Histoire d'Alger*, 297.
118. Sharif al-Zahhar, *Mudhakkirāt*, 141.
119. Laroui, *History of the Maghrib*, 295

## 2     Conquest, Resistance and Accommodation, 1830–1911

1. G. Mercier, 'Les raisons morales de la célébration du Centenaire de l'Afrique française', *Le centenaire de l'Algérie* vol. 1, 20–21.
2. Julien, *Histoire de l'Algérie contemporaine* vol. 1, 21.
3. Zahhar, *Mudhakkirāt*, 178.
4. Song on the fall of Algiers attributed to Si Abd al-Qadir, a mid-nineteenth-century *meddah* (folksinger and storyteller), Heggoy, *French conquest of Algiers*, 20, 22.
5. On 'extermination', see Le Cour Grandmaison, *Coloniser, exterminer*, and critiques by Gilbert Meynier and Pierre Vidal-Naquet, *Esprit* (December 2005), 162–77, and Emmanuelle Saada, *Critique internationale* vol. 32 (July–September 2006), 211–16. Gallois, *A history of violence*, 'Genocide', restates the argument; for a corrective, see Brower, 'Les violences de la conquête', 60–63.
6. 'Les origines de la révolution algérienne', *El Moudjahid*, 13 June 1958, quoted in Chikh, *L'Algérie en armes*, 23.
7. Husayn Dey to Sultan Mahmud II, 30 Jumada-I 1243 (19 December 1827) repr. with tr. in Kuran, 'La lettre du dernier dey d'Alger', 190; Husayn Dey to [French] Minister of Foreign Affairs, 10 September 1824, 29 October 1826 (copies of letters in papers from the dey's cabinet), FR/SHD/1H/4/2/2; Julien, *Histoire de l'Algérie contemporaine* vol. 1, 24.
8. Ultimatum from Admiral Collet, aboard the *Provence*, 14 June 1827, FR/SHD/1H/4/2/2. The dey's dignified reply (preserved among the same papers), and his report to the Sultan, considered that 'any person of talent should laugh at such expressions'.
9. Details of shipments in report, Baron Denniée (the army's Intendant, himself spectacularly enriched after the conquest) to Minister of Finance, 10 August 1830, FR/SHD/1H/4/2/1; Julien, *Histoire de l'Algérie contemporaine* vol. 1, 57–58.
10. Dispatches from a battalion commander at Sidi Fredj, 14, 19 June 1830, FR/SHD/1H/3/8.
11. Julien, *Histoire de l'Algérie contemporaine* vol. 1, 55.
12. Petition from members of the Jewish community of Algiers, 12 June 1831; Letter from Hamdan Ben Amin Seca [*sic*], 20 June 1834; Ministry of War's copy of Bu Darba's proposals, 12 March 1831. FR/ANOM/GGA/1H/1.
13. Hamdan Khoja, *Le Miroir*, ii, 426.
14. Letter from Ahmad Bu Darba in Marseille, 6 May 1840; report to the Minister of War on arrests and expulsions, December 1836; letter from Hamdan Khoja in Istanbul, 10 Safar 1252 (26 May 1836). FR/ANOM/GGA/1H/1.
15. MS letter from the people of Bu Agab (dated October 1832 in margin). FR/ANOM/GGA/1H/2.
16. Letter from Bu Darba, Marseille, 6 May 1840 (n.14).
17. Julien, *Histoire de l'Algérie contemporaine* vol. 1, 90.
18. Pellissier de Reynaud, *Annales algériennes* vol. 1, 247.
19. Letter from Hamdan Khoja, 26 May 1836 (n.14).
20. Julien, *Histoire de l'Algérie contemporaine* vol. 1, 83.

21. Extract from report by Lieutenant-Colonel Lemercier, interim director of fortifications, Algiers, July 1833. FR/ANOM/FM/F80/1670B.
22. 'Instructions pour la Commission d'Afrique', Ministry of War, Paris, July 1833. FR/ANOM/FM/F80/1670B.
23. *Procès-verbaux et rapports de la commission nommée par le Roi le 7 juillet 1833 pour aller recueillir en Afrique tous les faits propres à éclairer le gouvernement sur l'état du pays et sur les mesures que réclame son avenir* and *Procès-verbaux et rapports de la commission d'Afrique instituée par ordonnance du roi du 12 décembre 1833* (Paris, Imprimerie royale, 1834).
24. *Procès-verbaux et rapports de la commission nommée par le Roi le 7 juillet 1833 [. . .]*, quoted in Julien, *Histoire de l'Algérie contemporaine* vol. 1, 110.
25. Ibid.
26. The relativisation of 1830 as an 'external shock' to the more significant internal social and political history of Algeria is owed to Marcel Emerit (*L'Algérie à l'époque d'Abd el-Kader*, 26–27; see also René Gallissot's introduction to the re-edition of this classic text). The following account draws on Emerit's original insight in this respect, although his characterisation of a 'struggle between races' succeeded by a 'French peace' could not be sustained today. For a similar characterisation of post-1830 Algeria as a 'contest state' (in Michael Adas' terms) in which many groups practised 'bet hedging', see Clancy-Smith, *Rebel and saint*, ch. 3.
27. Emerit, *L'Algérie à l'époque d'Abd el-Kader*, 27–35.
28. Emerit, 'Mémoires d'Ahmed, dernier bey de Constantine', 77–88.
29. Sources disagree marginally on the details of Abd al-Qadir's family; Bellemare, *Abd-El-Kader*, 9, has Abd al-Qadir as Muhyi al-Din's third son, cf. the various sources assembled by Danziger, *Abd al-Qadir and the Algerians*, 54, 65 n.15. Muhyi al-Din's dream was said to have reiterated a prophecy made to him in Baghdad during his pilgrimage; the validation of Abd al-Qadir's 'prophetic' investiture was also strengthened by the claimed family connection to the descendants of Abd al-Qadir al-Jilani, as well as their regional leadership of the *tariqa* named after him. Bellemare, *Abd-El-Kader*, 11, 15, 22; Danziger, *Abd al-Qadir and the Algerians*, 57, 71. Bennison, *Jihad and its interpretations*, 77, suggests that investing the younger son with a political role, while preserving Qadiri spiritual succession in the elder, was a deliberate 'division of labour [. . .] which would insulate the lineage and its zawiya from the effects of a possible defeat in the political sphere'.
30. Danziger, *Abd al-Qadir*, 74–78; Bennison, *Jihad*, 81, on the basis of a letter of the sultan dated April 1833.
31. Muhammad ibn Abd al-Salam al-Muqrani, the established chief in the Medjana, allied himself with Abd al-Qadir after the fall of Constantine in 1837; in the south of the province, where Ahmad Bey continued to assert his authority after the fall of the eastern beylik, familial and *tariqa*-affiliated opponents of the bey and his local allies attempted to advance their own cause by seeking investiture as regional deputies of the *amir*. Emerit (ed.), 'Mémoires d'Ahmed', 112; Danziger, *Abd al-Qadir*, 185–86; Clancy-Smith, *Rebel and Saint*, 75–77; Bellemare, *Abd-El-Kader*, 109–10.

32. Muhammad ibn Abd al-Qadir al-Jaza'iri, *Tuḥfat al-zā'ir*, 158; cf. Bellemare, *Abd-El-Kader*, 26–27. The representation of Abd al-Qadir in the *Tuḥfa*, composed much later by his son, is very clearly a careful ideological construction on the basis of canonical, Prophetic and caliphal, models; on the basis of the original texts (the authenticity of which has generally been accepted) preserved within the *Tuḥfa*, however, as well as the other available sources, there is every reason to suppose that the son's ideological position closely mirrors that of his father, rather than in any sense misrepresenting it.

33. Declaration of the *majlis al-'ulama* at Mascara, dated 3 Rajab 1246 [26 November 1832], in Muhammad ibn Abd al-Qadir, *Tuḥfa*, 161–62; see also the partial translation in Danziger, *Abd al-Qadir*, 72.

34. Letter dated 2 April 1833, quoted in Danziger, *Abd al-Qadir*, 79.

35. The principal accusation levelled against Abd al-Qadir by his main Algerian opponents (Ahmad Bey and his in-law allies the Banu Ghana in Constantine, Sidi Muhammad al-Tijani at Aïn Madhi, Mustafa ben Isma'il of the old Oranais *makhzen*) would also, correlatively, be that he undermined 'natural' pre-existing hierarchies and was himself not legitimate in assuming the role of sultan.

36. Danziger, *Abd al-Qadir*, 212, and for the latter argument, *idem*, 76–77 and 186–87; for the former argument, Emerit, *L'Algérie à l'époque d'Abd-El-Kader*, 27; Bellemare, *Abd-El-Kader*, 118 (citing an account attributed to Abd al-Qadir and apparently dictated by him to Daumas, to whose papers Bellemare had access); Ruedy, *Modern Algeria*, 61–62; more subtly, Vatin, *L'Algérie politique*, 138. For an account that takes the sharifian component of Abd al-Qadir's politics seriously as well as critically, see Bennison, *Jihad and its interpretations*.

37. On Abd al-Qadir as objectively nationalist, see Ruedy, *Modern Algeria*, 66; for the 'fanatic' label, Azan, *L'émir Abd el Kader*; on religious sincerity vs. statecraft, Danziger, *Abd al-Qadir, passim*. As Bennison observes, the significance of Abd al-Qadir's enterprise lay in its creation of an indigenous, 'centralising sharifian jihad state' (Bennison, *Jihad*, 79), better likened to the earlier and contemporaneous jihad states of West Africa than to a 'proto-national' state. This is borne out by Abd al-Qadir's own self-image, which seems to have centred on his personal, ethical role as guarantor of properly legitimate rule, exemplified in particular in his claim never to have used the public treasury for his own benefit except *in extremis* (Bellemare, *Abd-el-Kader*, 124).

38. Bennison, *Jihad*, ch. 2; Berque, *Intérieur du Maghreb*, 53.

39. The names of these groups, derived from Arabic words for a circumscription or encampment rather than from the more usual patronymics, both indicate their function as 'state tribes' and suggest the extent to which, more generally, tribal affiliations were often strategic or political rather than simply organic and genealogical, let alone necessarily opposed to state formation per se. See Berque, 'Qu'est-ce qu'une "tribu"?' and for Moroccan examples, El Mansour, *Morocco in the reign of Mawlay Sulayman*, 5–9. The *makhzen* properties in Mascara are enumerated in a (possibly self-interested) report

from Qa'id Ibrahim, repr. in Emerit, *L'Algérie à l'époque d'Abd-El-Kader*, 96–98.

40. For Abd al-Qadir's intention, nonetheless, to spare Ahmad ben Tahar from execution, which was carried out in the amir's absence, see Bellemare, *Abd-El-Kader*, 29–30.

41. Quoted in Bellemare, *Abd-El-Kader*, 40.

42. Bellemare, *Abd-El-Kader*, 38.

43. Abd al-Qadir's later celebrity as saviour of the Christians in Damascus during the 1860 riots and massacre there was thus in no respect as incongruous with his much earlier behaviour as it would appear to have been to nineteenth-century French writers.

44. Reproduction, with translations, of the French and Arabic texts of the treaty and secret addendum in Danziger, *Abd al-Qadir*, 241–47.

45. Desmichels may have believed that the articles undeclared to his superiors represented a preliminary negotiating position on Abd al-Qadir's part. For details of the negotiations and the controversy over the agreement, see Danziger, *Abd al-Qadir*, 89–94; Bellemare, *Abd-El-Kader*, 35–43.

46. Bellemare, *Abd-El-Kader*, 47–48; Danziger, *Abd al-Qadir*, 96–97; Bennison, *Jihad*, 82–85.

47. Julien, *Histoire de l'Algérie contemporaine* vol. 1, 136, 147.

48. Ibid.

49. Emerit, *L'Algérie à l'époque d'Abd-El-Kader*, 130, 138.

50. Letters from Abd al-Qadir to Bugeaud, n.d. [prior to 30 May 1837], translations reproduced in Emerit, *L'Algérie à l'époque d'Abd-El-Kader*, 141–42.

51. Emerit, *L'Algérie à l'époque d'Abd-El-Kader*, 127–28; cf. Danziger, *Abd al-Qadir*, 143–44. French and Arabic texts of the treaty reproduced in Danziger, *Abd al-Qadir*, 248–55.

52. Danziger, *Abd al-Qadir*, 147; Bennison, *Jihad*, 92–93; *Tuhfa*, 320–29, quote at 326. Abd al-Qadir subsequently wrote to the *qadi* of Fez, Abd al-Hadi al-Alawi, seeking stronger condemnation of Muslims who remained under French rule and supplied or served with French forces (*Tuhfa*, 384–86; Bennison, *Jihad*, 96–97). His own excursus on the necessity for Muslims to perform *hijra* from French territory is also preserved in *Tuhfa*, 411–23.

53. Julien, *Histoire de l'Algérie contemporaine* vol. 1, 158.

54. Quoted in Danziger, *Abd al-Qadir*, 165; Julien, *Histoire de l'Algérie contemporaine* vol. 1, 146.

55. Julien, *Histoire de l'Algérie contemporaine* vol. 1, 147, 152.

56. Quoted in *idem*, 157.

57. Letter dated 2 March 1839, repr. in translation in Emerit, *L'Algérie à l'époque d'Abd-El-Kader*, 153–54.

58. Speech to the chamber of deputies, 8 June 1838, in Azan (ed.), *Par l'épée*, 60.

59. Quoted in Julien, *Histoire de l'Algérie contemporaine* vol. 1, 171.

60. Speech to the chamber of deputies, 15 January 1840, in Azan (ed.), *Par l'épée*, 65–66.

61. 'Travail sur l'Algérie' (1841), publ. in de Tocqueville, *De la colonie en Algérie*, 57, 77–78.

62. Speech to the chamber of deputies, 24 January 1845, in Azan (ed.), *Par l'épée*, 193.
63. Saint-Arnaud, *Lettres* vol. 1, 381, 392, 474, 481. (Letters dated 7 April, 5 June 1842; 8 February, 1 March 1843.)
64. Quoted in Bennison, *Jihad*, 136–37.
65. Bennison, *Jihad*, 141.
66. *Al-sīra al-dhātiyya* (tr. Benmansour), 117. This text is a short narrative of Abd al-Qadir's pilgrimage and campaigns, composed for French interlocutors in prison, probably in late 1848.
67. Manuscript copies (in French) of letters between Abd al-Qadir and Lamoricière, 12 Muharram 1264 (20 December 1847), FR/ANOM/GGA/12X/63.
68. In September, 1838, Ahmad concluded a letter to Valée: 'As for your word, that you will bring me back to Algiers, that I cannot endure a tent and heat and harsh living; I can endure much more than that, and will not leave my country (*waṭanī*), and that is all I have to say.' FR/ANOM/GGA/10X/fol.128 (Féraud mss collection, vol. 1).
69. Von Sivers, 'Realm of justice'; Clancy-Smith, *Rebel and saint*, 'Saints, mahdis and arms'.
70. This observation is owed to Clancy-Smith, *Rebel and saint, passim* and esp. 258.
71. Richard, *Etude sur l'insurrection du Dhara*, 5.
72. Idem, 65.
73. Julien, *Histoire de l'Algérie contemporaine* vol. 1, 201–02, 319–20.
74. Clancy-Smith, *Rebel and saint*, ch.4 and esp. 116–17; Julien, *Histoire de l'Algérie contemporaine* vol. 1, 320, 384–85.
75. Quoted in Julien, *Histoire de l'Algérie contemporaine* vol. 1, 386.
76. Ibid., 392.
77. The particular autonomy of the Ibadi community was thus preserved for a while; after 1882, when French troops occupied the Mzab and annexed the area, this was diminished but not eliminated. On the colonial occupation of the Mzab, see Brower, *A desert named peace*, ch. 9, and for the region's later relationship to Algerian nationalism and the nation-state, Jomier, '*Iṣlāḥ* ibadite'.
78. Clancy-Smith, *Rebel and saint*, ch. 6.
79. Von Sivers, 'Rural uprisings as political movements'.
80. The worst of the crisis unfolded from autumn 1867 through the summer of 1868. The official death toll of 217,000, published by the colonial government in June 1868, is certainly an underestimate; Julien wrote in 1964 that a figure of 300,000 would risk being 'inadequate to reality' (*Histoire de l'Algérie contemporaine* vol. 1, 439); Sari, 'Problèmes de la démographie', 157–68, calculates 820,000 deaths as a *minimum* total; Rey-Goldzeiguer, *Le Royaume arabe*, 459, points out that the impact varied by region, but estimates that at least one-fifth and possibly one-third of the total population died; Kateb, *Européens, 'indigènes' et juifs*, 63–65, assesses the cause and scale of the calamity but offers no independent calculation of the mortality rate. Algeria's indigenous population numbered 2,652,072 according to the 1866 census.
81. Sari, 'Problèmes de la démographie', 166–68.

82. The administration's own figures, while barely able to apprehend what was taking place in the wider countryside, clearly show this is in the careful differentiation of the civil territories' Algerian population from those coming into the settled zone from the military territories. For the single month of June 1867, 1,763 Algerian inhabitants of the communes and 451 Algerians from elsewhere were listed as having died within the civil territory of the *département* of Algiers; for June 1868 the figures were 3,502 and 5,641, respectively. For the month of February 1868, one report reckoned the total deaths among Algerians of the civil territories at 399, of which only twenty-eight were said to be due to starvation; among refugees, the total was 939, of whom 851 had starved to death. 'Etat complémentaire des décès survenus dans la population indigène' (June 1867, June 1868), Algiers, September 1868; 'Etat comparatif des décès survenus dans la population indigène' (February 1868), Algiers, April 1868. FR/ANOM/Alger/1I/15.

83. 'Etat nominatif des vagabonds indigènes arrêtés sur le territoire de la commune', Koléa, 1868. FR/ANOM/Alger/F21/11.

84. Sub-Prefect, Miliana to Prefect, Algiers, 13 March 1867 [sic – read 1868?]. FR/ANOM/Alger/F21/11.

85. Mayor, Mouzaiaville, to Prefect, Algiers, 10 February, 6 March 1868. FR/ANOM/Alger/F21/11.

86. Police reports and correspondence, Algiers, April–May 1868. FR/ANOM/Alger/F21/11. On the role of *dépôts de mendicité* in propagating the epidemic, see Kateb, *Européens, 'indigènes' et juifs*, 65.

87. Sub-Prefect, Miliana to Prefect, Algiers (n.84).

88. Prefect, Algiers, to Mayors of Algiers and Blida, 12 March 1868; minutes of the Algiers municipal council, 14 March 1868; Prefect, Algiers, to Mayor of Algiers, 23 March 1868. FR/ANOM/Alger/F21/11.

89. 'Renseignements sur les dépenses d'hospitalisation de 1859 à 1873', Prefect, Algiers, to Governor General, 7 July 1874 no. 5164, DZ/CANA/IBA/ASP/034 (1962), detailing costs borne for the hospitalisation of 'the indigent sick supported by the *département*'. Total expenses for 1866 were reported as 613,628.24 francs; for 1867, 672,355.90; for 1868, 898,010.45, a figure not matched thereafter.

90. Kateb, *Européens, 'indigènes' et juifs*, 63.

91. Julien, *Histoire de l'Algérie contemporaine* vol. 1, 477–84; Ageron, *Algériens musulmans* vol. 1, ch.1; Von Sivers, 'Rural uprisings', 48–52.

92. Ageron, *Algériens musulmans* vol. 1, 9.

93. Quoted in *ibid.*

94. Julien, *Histoire de l'Algérie contemporaine* vol. 1, 491–93.

95. Sari, *A la recherche*, 19, *La dépossession des fellahs*, ch. 3.

96. Mammeri, *Isefra*, 15–18, 132–33, 138–39.

97. Kateb, 'Le bilan démographique', 83–85; Frémeaux, *De quoi fut fait l'empire*, 458.

98. cf. Hobsbawm, 'Peasants and politics', 157, on the peasantry's capacity for '"working the system" to its advantage – or rather to its minimum disadvantage'.

99. Quoted in Desparmet, *Coutumes, institutions, croyances* vol. 2, 'La vie religieuse'; see also McDougall, *History and the culture of nationalism*, 99–103; for Constantine, Grangaud, *La ville imprenable*, 321–33; for a contemporary account of the conquest as willed by 'the council of the saints' (recounted to the Mauritanian pilgrim Ahmad ibn Tuwayr al-Janna), Norris, *Pilgrimage of Ahmad*.
100. Prefect, Constantine, to Minister of War, 22 December 1855. FR/ANOM/GGA/3H/1. The fact that Algerians in French uniform had been defending Ottoman sovereignty against Russia may not have been irrelevant here.
101. Clancy-Smith, *Rebel and saint*, ch.7, Grangaud, *La ville imprenable*, 321–31.
102. List of 'subsidies and temporary relief to native servants', n.d. [1890s?], FR/ANOM/GGA/8H/33/1.
103. 'Notice sur les chefs indigènes et personnages importants, province d'Alger', 5 June 1879, FR/ANOM/GGA/5H3-4; Gouvion and Gouvion, *Kitab aayane*, 6–16, 63–64, 176–81.
104. Note on subdivision of Miliana (n.d.), FR/ANOM/GGA/5H/3-4.
105. See Chapter 4.
106. Von Sivers, 'Indigenous administrators', 116; see also Von Sivers, 'Algerian landownership', 'Insurrection and accommodation', and McDougall, 'The secular state's Islamic empire'.
107. Summaries of deliberations (*mushawwarat*) of douar *jama'as* in the Batna district, January 1869, CAOM/GGA/8H/13/2; MacMaster, 'Roots of insurrection', 429–32; Guignard, 'L'affaire Beni Urjin'.
108. Report, Commissariat spécial dc la police des chemins de fer et des ports, Algiers, 20 April 1897, Note, Bureau des affaires indigènes, 'Cheikh Ali, moqaddem des Rahmania à Alger', 22 April 1897, Note for the Chef de service, Affaires indigènes, 3 June 1897; Prefect, Algiers to Governor General, 25 May 1897, Secretary General, Algiers, to Chef de service, Affaires indigènes, 2 June 1897; Letter from Ben Halima to head of the Oran bureau arabe, June 1897, Prefect, Oran to Governor General, 4 June 1897, Gen. Boitard, commanding the Oran division, to Governor General, 9, 23 July 1897. FR/ANOM/GGA/1H/86/1.
109. Report, Chef du bureau arabe, Tebessa, n.d. [January 1898], FR/ANOM/GGA/1H/86/6.
110. Reports on Margueritte, 7, 13 May 1901, FR/ANOM/FM/F80/1690; Ageron, *Algériens musulmans* vol. 1, 606–08, vol. 2, 965–74.
111. Interviews by the Senatorial Commission at Adelia (7 May 1892). Pensa, *L'Algérie, organisation politique et administrative . . .*, 169.
112. Ageron, 'L'émigration' and *Algériens musulmans* vol. 2, 1083–92.
113. Benhabylès, *L'Algérie française*, 117–21. See Chapter 4.

## 3     The Means of Domination, 1830–1944

1. Quoted in Colonna, Preface to Masqueray, *Formation des cités*, iii.
2. On Saint-Simon and his ideas, see Pétré-Grenouilleau, *Saint-Simon*; on the Saint-Simonians in Algeria, Urbain, *L'Algérie pour les Algériens* and *L'Algérie*

*française*; Levallois, *Ismaÿl Urbain*; Rey-Goldzeiguer, *Le royaume arabe*; Abi Mershed, *Apostles of modernity*.

3. Quoted in Ageron, *Algériens musulmans* vol. 1, 606. The deputy, Charles Marchal, was an anti-Semitic rabble-rouser, but the views he expressed were widespread.
4. The European population who would call themselves 'Algerians' in the 1880s–90s, and who would be called 'néo-Français' in the early 1900s, became commonly called 'pieds-noirs' only at the end of the colonial period (this term, whose etymology is obscure, is attested in Algiers ca. 1901, but was widely used only from the mid-1950s). For simplicity, I use 'Europeans' here consistently.
5. See Chapter 5.
6. Images of a 'fraternal Algeria', especially that of European and Algerian children sitting together in school, supposed to testify to a social peace enjoyed before 1954 and ruined by *les événements*, 'the events' of the war of independence, have become a leitmotif of the memorial literature known in France as *nostalgérie* (nostalgia for French Algeria) and expressing the childhood memories of *pieds noirs* 'repatriated' to France in 1960–62. The genuineness (and, for *pied noir* social memory, importance) of the memory notwithstanding, it is a very misleading image of the colonial period as a whole, and of the background to the revolution in particular.
7. On pre-colonial European migration to North Africa, see Clancy-Smith, *Mediterraneans*.
8. *TEFA*, 1839; Sessions, *Sword and Plow*, 217; Ageron, *Algérie contemporaine* vol. 2, 118–19, 127–28; Larcher and Rechtenwald, *Traité élémentaire* vol. 1, 68; Ruedy, *Modern Algeria*, 94. On 'explosive' settlement colonisation elsewhere in the second half of the nineteenth century, see Belich, *Replenishing the Earth*. In the first sixty years of settlement, as Sessions (*Sword and plow*, 290) points out, the colonial populations of Australia and Algeria grew at very comparable rates, but in Australia, the European population thereafter expanded exponentially, from 405,356 in 1850 to 1,145,585 in 1860, 2,231,531 in 1880 and 4,425,083 by 1910 (Australian Bureau of Statistics, *Australian historical population statistics, 2014*, at www.abs.gov.au/AUSSTATS/abs@.nsf/DetailsPage/3105.0.65 .0012014?OpenDocument).
9. See, for example, Lapasset to Lacroix (1847, 1858), repr. in Frémeaux, *Bureaux arabes*, 303–05.
10. The official figure in 1936 was 180,677 Europeans (compared to almost 4.2 million Algerians). 'Matériaux pour les tableaux de l'économie algérienne', Table 15, 'Population agricole', 1936. FR/CAOM/GGA/12H/ 13. See also Ruedy, *Modern Algeria*, 121.
11. *TEFA* (1838), 389.
12. Sessions, *Sword and plow*, 216, 232–40, and 'Les colons', 66.
13. *TEFA* (1840), 91.
14. Note on expenditure, 'Dispensaire', Algiers, n.d. [1838], 'Notice sur le dispensaire de la ville d'Alger', Intendance civile, 27 January 1838, 'Etat: Dispensaire', 1 April 1831–31 December 1837, 'Etat récapitulatif des femmes publiques traitées au dispensaire de la ville d'Alger', 1836 and

1837, 'Etat de situation des filles publiques', 17 November 1845, Secretary-General of the Government (Paschalski) to Governor General, 2 June 1857. FR/CAOM/FM/F80/668. The dispensary's figures specify patients by 'nation': *mauresques* and/or *arabes*, Jews, *négresses* (all three implying Algerian origin); French, Spaniards, Italians, Germans and sometimes English and Swiss. Respective totals are 343 Algerian women against 93 Europeans treated in 1836; 285 against 148 in 1837. In 1946, a report on venereal medicine would point out that 'until very recently' the same policy, established in the 1830s and reorganised in 1883, had remained in place: 'a matter, above all, of policing, in which the doctor intervenes only as the auxiliary of the *service des moeurs*'. Raynaud, Colonieu, and Hadida, 'Le problème de la lutte antivénérienne en Algérie', 1946, 61pp., quote at 4. FR/CAOM/GGA/8X/198. On the dispensaries, and the segregated treatment there of European and Maghribi women, see Taraud, *La prostitution*, 245–63.

15. On erotic imagery, see Alloula, *Colonial harem* and Taraud, *La prostitution*, 297–317; on the trope of 'Ouled Naïl' prostitution, Ferhati, 'La danseuse'. A detailed inquiry into 'Ouled Naïl' prostitution was carried out in the Algerian south by the sociologist Emile Dermenghem, in the midst of the war, in 1955–59 (papers in FR/CAOM/GGA/8X/202).

16. Sessions, *Sword and plow*, 265–67, 274, 301, 304–06; 'Colonisation de l'Algérie', notice announcing decree of 19 September 1848, O. Douchet to the Minister of War, Amiens, 20 October 1848, 'Les colons de Cuvilly' to the National Assembly, 20 January 1849. FR/CAOM/FM/F80/1397.

17. 'L'Algérie: Des moyens de conserver et d'utiliser cette conquête' (1842), in Azan, *Par l'épée*, 129, 130; Julien, *Algérie contemporaine* vol. 1, 231–39.

18. Enfantin, *Colonisation*, 282–86; Julien, *Algérie contemporaine* vol. 1, 231–32, 256–58; Abi-Mershed, *Apostles of modernity*.

19. Marcel Calvelli, 'Etat de la propriété rurale en Algérie' (doctoral diss. in law, Algiers, 1935), quoted in Sari, *Dépossession*, 43; Ageron, *Algérie contemporaine* vol. 2, 91.

20. Grangaud, 'Masking and unmasking', 192, and 'Le droit colonial au service des spoliations'.

21. A Comité des Domaines had been created as early as 17 July. Ruedy, *Land policy*, 15.

22. A total of 16,258 hectares (compared to 158,721 ha of *beylik* land). A further 10,000 hectares of *habus* had been registered but not yet released for settlement. Ruedy, *Land policy*, 34–35, 67, 78–79.

23. For the complex subsequent history of family (as opposed to public) endowments, and a comparison with British India, see Powers, 'Orientalism, colonialism, and legal history'.

24. The 1852 total comprises 44 per cent and 31 per cent *beylik* and *cantonnement/* 'vacant' land, respectively; sequestered properties constituted a further 14 per cent. Ruedy, *Land policy*, 86–99, 100–01; Sari, *Dépossession*, 15. Legal texts in Ménerville, *Dictionnaire de la législation algérienne* vol. 1, 578–93.

25. Colson, chef d'escadron d'état major, 'Note sur le cantonnement', Algiers, 19 February 1859, FR/CAOM/GGA/8H/16.

26. Sari, *Dépossession*, 14, 20–21.
27. Letter of Napoleon III to the governor general, 6 February 1863, and text of the Sénatus-Consulte (borrowing from Roman terminology, a decree approved by the Senate of the Empire), 22 April 1863, in Ménerville, *Dictionnaire* vol. 2, 186–87 and 186–94.
28. Sari, *Dépossession*, 23–24; Guignard, 'Le Sénatus-Consulte', 80.
29. That is, property to which multiple co-proprietors (sometimes listed in the hundreds) held title: having obtained a part-share, the buyer could force sale of the entirety of the property at auction, the legal fees payable by co-proprietors to block such a sale being prohibitive – often much more than the value of the property.
30. The law of 17 July 1874, intended to prevent the forest fires that sometimes spread from summer brush-clearing, classified such incidents as 'insurrectionary', and stipulated penalties of sequestration and collective punishment to repress them. The French *code forestier* of 1827 was taken to apply in Algeria, although not promulgated there until 1883; although in a quite different environment, the law had also impacted heavily on traditional practices in rural France, provoking the 'war of the demoiselles' in Ariège (on which, see Sahlins, *Forest rites*). *Bulletin officiel du gouvernement général de l'Algérie*, 553 (1874), 450–54; Sari, *Dépossession*, 61–72; Ageron, *Algérie contemporaine* vol. 2, 206–10.
31. Ageron, *Algérie contemporaine* vol. 2, 96–97.
32. Julien, *Algérie contemporaine* vol. 1, 230; Ageron, *Algérie contemporaine* vol. 2, 210. Algerians and Europeans were subject to separate taxation systems until November 1918.
33. For example, in 1881 the Beni Bou Slimane, in the Aurès, possessed 11 horses, 283 mules, 16 cows, 606 sheep and 3,673 goats; they produced 95 quintals of wool and 2,150 of fruit, 1,030 hectolitres of wheat and 1,250 of barley. In 1875, the respective figures had been 82 horses, 1,163 mules, 198 cows, 13,250 sheep, and 32,080 goats; 3,100 quintals (wool), 8,500 quintals (fruit) 2,380 hectolitres (wheat) and 3,250 hectolitres (barley). Subdivision de Batna, 'Tableau comparatif des richesses des indigènes ... ', 22 September 1881. FR/CAOM/GGA/14H/37/3. (The Beni Bou Slimane also suffered significant land sequestration and loss of livestock after the 1879 Aurès insurrection, but the figures in this document, which shows similar losses for other groups in the region not involved in the 1879 rising, appear to predate the effect of these additional losses.) On these years, see also Ageron, *Algérie contemporaine* vol. 2, 211.
34. Most of the increase after the First World War occurred between 1920 and 1934, when another 352,892 hectares were added to colonial holdings. Between 1950 and 1962, privately European-owned rural property decreased, probably mostly to the benefit of individual Algerian buyers, by some 400,000 hectares. Sari, *Dépossession*, 52, 79, 82; Ageron, *Algérie contemporaine* vol. 2, 203–04; Nouschi, 'La dépossession foncière', 189, 193; 'Matériaux pour les tableaux de l'économie algérienne: Propriété agricole' (1944), FR/CAOM/GGA/12H/13.
35. 'Matériaux ... ' (1944) (n.34), FR/CAOM/GGA/12H/13.

36. 'Matériaux . . . ' (data for 1936 and 1944) (n.34), FR/CAOM/GGA/12H/13.
37. Extract of response to questionnaire, n.d. [1937], CM Souk Ahras, in Guernut commission papers, FR/CAOM/FM/Commission Guernut/40(BXV).
38. Abbas, *Nuit coloniale*, 18; Vatin, *L'Algérie politique*, 152–54.
39. Report on social and economic situation, CM Telagh, n.d. [1919]; Administrator, CM Djendel, Lavigerie, to Prefect, Algiers, 18 December 1920; Administrator, CM Aïn el-Ksar, El Madher, to Prefect, Constantine, 3 February 1921; 'Compte rendu mensuel des secours', Mairie, *Lambèse*, 4 February 1921; Wage tables for public works, commune of St-Arnaud (Sétif), January–March 1921. FR/CAOM/GGA/14H/7; Prefect, Algiers, to Governor General, 26 July 1929 (wage tables for women workers attached) and G. Laloe, *Enquête sur le travail des femmes indigènes à Alger* Algiers, Jourdan, 1910, 5–9, in FR/CAOM/GGA/14H/32/1; Ageron, *Algérie contemporaine* vol. 2, 513, 515–16; Nouschi, 'La dépossession', 193.
40. Ageron, *Algérie contemporaine* vol. 2, 98.
41. Ibid., 132.
42. Baroli, *La vie quotidienne*, 44–45.
43. Camus, *Le premier homme*, 313.
44. Thus the Délégations financières, Algiers' colonial 'parliament', comprised *colons* and *non-colons* sections for the representation of the European population.
45. Enfantin, *Colonisation*, 37.
46. Cavaignac, *La Régence d'Alger*, 91.
47. Rey-Goldzeiguer, *Royaume arabe*, 519. The involvement of Cavaignac and Mac Mahon, like that of Bugeaud in the 'massacre of the rue Transnonain' in 1834, in putting down these workers' uprisings ought not, however, to be taken to imply a specifically colonial genealogy of repressive violence in the metropole. The common factor is, rather, that the army and its 'African' generals saw themselves as 'the guarantors of a certain conception of order', to be upheld in the streets of Paris as much as in the colonies. Other experiences of urban and guerilla warfare (notably, in the case of Bugeaud, the Peninsula War in 1807–14) were at least as relevant as Algeria. See Joly, 'Les généraux', 128–30.
48. Tocqueville, *De la colonie* 114, 109, 121.
49. 'Les colons algériens à leur concitoyens en France' (signed by Baron de Vialar et al.), Algiers, 30 October 1846, 'A Messieurs les pairs de France et à Messieurs les députés', 5 March 1847. FR/CAOM/GGA/12X/20. De Vialar, a legitimist aristocrat and refugee in Algeria from the 1830 revolution, was an early enthusiast for colonisation in the Mitidja.
50. Betts, *Assimilation and association*; Rivet, *Le Maghreb*; Burke, *Ethnographic state*; Abi-Mershed, *Apostles*.
51. On 1848 in Algeria, Emérit et al., *La révolution*.
52. Municipal councils, of which there were only six in 1847, were initially appointed; the electoral franchise first granted in 1848 was removed in 1854, and only between 1866 and 1868 did the *commune de plein exercice* take its full shape, with new *centres de colonisation* run by appointed civil commissioners being gradually accorded municipal status. Mayors

remained appointed, and councils elected with no more than one third of their members representing Muslims, Jews and non-French Europeans; the 1884 metropolitan law on municipal government, applied to Algeria, introduced elected mayors, for whom only French citizen council members could vote. Collot, *Institutions*, 83–85, 93–99; Ageron, *Algérie contemporaine* vol. 2, 23, 28–29.

53. A decree of February 1871 provided for two deputies from Algeria as a whole; this was raised to one for each *département* in 1875. Parliamentary representation had been previously accorded to the settlers by the constitution of the Second Republic in 1848, but suppressed in January 1852.

54. Ageron, *Algérie contemporaine* vol. 2, 89. Biographical details from www .assemblee-nationale.fr/sycomore/index.asp. Thomson remains the longest-serving French parliamentarian.

55. Civilian Prefects gained jurisdiction over military-ruled territory in northern Algeria in November 1870; residual military areas in the north were abolished in 1923 (Ageron, *Algériens musulmans* vol. 1, 144; Collot, *Institutions*, 45).

56. Bouveresse, *Un parlement colonial?* vol. 1, 246–79, 587–627.

57. On the 1947 Statute and the Assembly, see Chapter 5.

58. Quoted in Ageron, *Algérie contemporaine* vol. 2, 131–32.

59. Baroli, *La vie quotidienne*, 213.

60. Vermeren, 'Les migrations'; Ageron, *Algérie contemporaine* vol. 2, 119–20.

61. The extent to which 'Muslim' became a racial classification is most apparent in the fact that it was applied to Algerian converts to Christianity, who could be perplexingly labelled *Chrétiens musulmans*, 'Muslim Christians'.

62. Dessoliers, *L'Algérie libre*, 218–23; Ageron, *Algérie contemporaine* vol. 2, 58–59.

63. Ageron, *Algérie contemporaine* vol. 2, 60–67; Guignard, 'Les crises'.

64. 'Chansons antijuives', *L'Antijuif algérien*, 20 January 1898, 3A-B. BnF: http:// gallica.bnf.fr/ark:/12148/bpt6k955213h/f3.image.

65. Quoted in Ageron, *Algérie contemporaine* vol. 2, 64. (The *cahiers de doléances* were petitions of complaint submitted to the Estates General at the outset of the French revolution of 1789.)

66. For a full exploration of colonial 'scandals' and the politics of the 1890s, see Guignard, *L'abus de pouvoir*.

67. For example, advertisements in *Cagayous à la course* (4 May 1905), *Cagayous au miracle* (14 May 1905).

68. Quoted in Siblot, 'Cagayous antijuif', 62.

69. Colonna, *Instituteurs*, 50. By 1938, only 4.4 per cent of European conscripts into the army were illiterate, against 78.4 per cent of Algerians. The law of 16 June 1881 made public primary schooling free of charge; the subsequent law of 28 March 1882 made attendance obligatory for boys and girls aged between 6 and 13.

70. Siblot, 'Cagayous antijuif', 67–71; Prochaska, 'History as literature'; Baroli, *La vie quotidienne*, 219–20. A compilation of Cagayous' 'best stories' was published in Paris in 1931; other tales were still being reprinted in 1949–50. On 'Algérianiste' literature, see Lorcin, *Imperial identities*, Dunwoodie, *Writing French Algeria*.

Notes to pages 113–121

71. Field notes, July–August 2005. On urban society, see Prochaska, *Making Algeria French*, Lespès, *Alger*, Çelik, *Urban forms*.
72. Schreier, *Arabs of the Jewish faith*, 38–40, and 'Mediterranean merchant', 645.
73. Slyomovics and Stein, 'Jews and French colonialism', Schreier, *Arabs of the Jewish faith*, Introduction; for case studies, see Gottreich and Schroeter (eds.), *Jewish culture and society*; for a review of the broader literature, Stein, 'The field of in between'.
74. Schreier, *Arabs of the Jewish faith*, quotes at 76, 143–44 (translation amended), 175; see also, especially, Friedman, *Colonialism and after*; Stein, *Saharan Jews*. Text of the Crémieux decree in Ménerville, *Dictionnaire* vol. 3, 228.
75. Stein, *Saharan Jews*.
76. Election notice, Comité central radical, Algiers, 1871. FR/CAOM/GGA/ 12X/42. Crémieux, aged 76 in 1872, had previously been elected from the Indre-et-Loire, then the Seine; this was his last mandate. He became a Senator in 1875.
77. Sivan, 'Stéréotypes antijuifs', 165, 169 (emphasis added), and 'Colonialism and popular culture'; Schreier, *Arabs of the Jewish faith*, 8.
78. Cole, 'Constantine before the riots', 'Anti-Semitism and the colonial situation'.
79. Peyrouton, a civil servant who had previously been Secretary General of the Government in Algiers, played a leading role in enacting Vichy's *statut des juifs*. In March 1943, with Peyrouton now governor general, the Crémieux decree was abrogated a second time by the Free French General Giraud, at the same time as the Peyrouton law, along with other Vichy legislation, was struck down; Crémieux's measure was re-established seven months later, on 22 October 1943. Cantier, *L'Algérie*; Abitbol, *Les juifs*.
80. Quoted in Ageron, *Algérie contemporaine* vol. 2, 549.
81. Akoun, *Né à Oran*, 41.
82. Eberhardt, *Dans l'ombre chaude*, and *Pages d'Islam*; Kobak, *Isabelle*; Kabbani (ed.), *The passionate nomad*.
83. Aurélie's life was novelised in Roger Frison-Roche, *Djebel Amour* (1978).
84. Colonna, *Le meunier*.
85. Ibid., 12–15.
86. Bahloul, *Architecture of memory*.
87. Abbas, *Autopsie d'une guerre*, 15.
88. Stora, *Histoire de l'Algérie coloniale*, 47, 95; Ageron, *Algérie contemporaine* vol. 2, 495.
89. Quoted in Ageron, *Algérie contemporaine* vol. 2, 32.
90. Ménerville, *Dictionnaire* vol. 1, Preface.
91. 'L'Algérie', in Azan, *Par l'épée* (n.17), 133; General Circular, September– October 1844, in Ménerville, *Dictionnaire* vol. 1, 65 (repr. Frémeaux, *Bureaux arabes*, 290–93); Julien, *Algérie contemporaine* vol. 1, 223–24.
92. General Circular, 5–20 July 1845, in Ménerville, *Dictionnaire* vol. 1, 68; Frémeaux, *Bureaux arabes*, 294–95.
93. Frémeaux, *Bureaux arabes*.

94. Ibid., 58–59.
95. Establet, *Être caïd*; Von Sivers, 'Indigenous administrators', 'Insurrection and accommodation'.
96. 'Renseignements individuels' (Bensalem Aomar Ben Mohamed and Bensalem Dris Ben Mohamed), CM Aïn Bessem, n.d. [1910]. FR/ CAOM/Alger/2I/28.
97. The transition from military to communal government had in fact begun in 1868, with the reorganisation of rural administration and the abolition of the departmental *bureaux arabes*; civil authority was gradually put in place from 1868 to 1872. The former *bureaux arabes* became the *service des affaires indigènes* (Native Affairs department); in the 1870s, especially in eastern Algeria, many existing Arab bureau officers remained in post as 'civil' administrators.
98. *Exposé des motifs* and text of the Sénatus-Consulte in Ménerville, *Dictionnaire* vol. 2, 151–59; see also Brett, 'Legislating for inequality'; Blévis, 'L'invention de l' "indigène"'.
99. On the origins of the *Sénatus Consulte*, see Blévis, 'L'invention de l' "indigène"', 'Les avatars de la citoyenneté', and Surkis, 'Propriété, polygamie et statut personnel'. On colonial understandings of 'Islamic law', see Henry and Balique, *La doctrine colonial du droit musulman*, Christelow, *Muslim law courts*, Powers, 'Orientalism, colonialism, and legal history'; on 'Jewish law', Stein, *Saharan Jews*, ch. 2.
100. See Blévis, 'Quelle citoyenneté . . . ?', Idem, 'Sociologie d'un droit colonial: Citoyenneté et nationalité en Algérie', Weil, *Qu'est-ce qu'un Français?*, Shepard, *Invention of decolonization*; for Senegal, Coquery-Vidrovitch, 'Nationalité et citoyenneté'; for later developments in West Africa, Cooper, *Citizenship between empire and nation*. See also Chapters 4 and 5.
101. The governor general was already empowered to order internment, exile, fines or sequestration of property without legal process. On the *indigénat* more generally, see Merle, 'Le régime de l'indigénat', Thénault, *Violences ordinaires*, Mann, 'What was the indigénat?'
102. The list of punishable 'infractions particular to the *indigénat*' would be repeatedly reduced, the reforms of 1919 (see Chapter 4) took half a million Algerian men out of its jurisdiction, and in 1927 administrators lost their powers under the statute, which were transferred to justices of the peace (who had already exercised them continuously since 1874 in *communes de plein exercice*), but as many as 5,000 sentences were still handed down under the *indigénat* in 1937 and 1938. Frémeaux, *Bureaux arabes*, 56–59, 229–33; Ageron, *Algériens musulmans* vol. 1, 165–76, 206–09, 228–47 and *Algérie contemporaine* vol. 2, 23–25, 198–200; Collot, *Institutions*, 190–200; Thénault, 'Le "code de l'indigénat"' and *Violence ordinaire*.
103. A right of appeal to the Sub-Prefect or Prefect was added by the law of 15 July 1914, one of the periodic re-institutions of the *indigénat*, but this seems to have remained a dead letter. The governor general noted in 1921, apparently without irony, that 'delinquents' sentenced by administrators 'feel themselves to be so justly punished that they appear entirely

uninterested in the right of appeal, to which they practically never have recourse'. Governor General to Minister of the Interior, 25 June 1921, FR/CAOM/GGA/12H/9.

104. The exact figures for fines and imprisonment for 1882–92 are 1,663,468 francs and 701,954 days, respectively. 'Etat général des condamnations prononcées pour infractions à l'indigénat ... ', 1882–1907, FR/CAOM/GGA/12H/7/1; Thénault, 'Le "code de l'indigénat"', 205; Governor General, Algiers, to Minister of the Interior, 6 August 1914, FR/CAOM/AGGA/12H/7/2. In 1914–19, administrators' sentences fell from around 7,000 to around 5,000, then fell again to around 2,000 judgments annually in the early 1920s. In 1927, the last year in which administrators exercised disciplinary powers, 1,222 judgments were recorded (down from 1,457 in 1926 and 1,572 in 1925). Governor General to Minister of the Interior, 'Pouvoirs disciplinaires des administrateurs de commune mixte, compte-rendu annuel', 1928 and 1926; Direction des affaires indigènes, 'Pouvoirs disciplinaires des administrateurs de commune mixte', 1927, FR/CAOM/GGA/12H/8.

105. Ageron noted that sentencing under the *indigénat* in 1881–87, at between a minimum of 12.1 (1886) and a maximum of 16.85 (1883) judgments per 1,000 of the Algerian population in the *communes mixtes*, represented 'a rate of penalisation *fifty to eighty times* more frequent than criminal sentences' (*Algériens musulmans* vol. 1, 240, emphasis added). Ageron gives no explanation for the comparison, but this figure is only possible if criminal convictions in the assize courts alone (where 'major' crimes such as murder, assault, rape, abortion, larceny, fraud, arson, etc. were tried by jury) are considered as 'criminal sentences'. Such crimes, though, were by nature relatively infrequent, and so the comparison is misleading: of course far more Algerians were likely to be sanctioned for 'disrespect' than convicted of murder. If the much more numerous convictions for the inevitably greater number of offences treated as 'middling' and 'petty' crime, such as public order offences, which were tried by *tribunaux correctionnels* or *tribunaux de simple police* and punished by fines or imprisonment, and which are more readily comparable to the 'infractions' criminalised by the *indigénat* statutes, are considered, the rate of sentencing under the latter looks less excessive, but gives a better point of comparison, particularly relative to 'minor', socially disciplinary prosecutions in the metropole. When petty crimes tried before the *tribunaux de simple police*, which in 1883 handed down no fewer than 56,595 convictions in Algeria (and 450,640 for metropolitan France), are included, the relative frequency with which Algerians found themselves condemned becomes clearer: Twelve convictions for *petite criminalité* per thousand of the population in France (compared to a total of 5.1 per thousand in the *tribunaux correctionnels* and *cours d'assises* combined) in 1883, compared to approximately twenty-one convictions per thousand of the population by the police courts in Algeria *in addition* to almost seventeen convictions per thousand under the *indigénat* in the *communes mixtes* alone. Statistics from *Compte général de l'administration de la justice criminelle en France et en Algérie pendant l'année 1883* (Paris,

Imprimerie nationale, 1885), and the 1881 census. The total conviction rate for Algerians in the higher courts was in fact, in the same year, slightly lower than the metropolitan figure, at 3.5 per thousand. The government attributed the higher number of acquittals in Algeria largely to the unreliability of 'native' witnesses. Figures for Algerians convicted are estimates, since the published figures for Algeria categorise the number of defendants, but not acquittals or convictions, by community. I have had to assume that verdicts fell in the same proportion as the numbers of French, Algerian or foreign defendants, and that proportions of defendants before the police courts, which are not specified, were comparable to those brought before higher courts. (In 1883, Algerians accounted for 90 per cent of defendants in the *cours d'assises*, 71 per cent of those before the *tribunaux correctionnels*.) In both respects, this probably gives a lower-limit estimate for convictions of Algerians.

106. Arrêté, CM Tablat, 13 January 1892, and Administrator, CM Tablat to Governor General, 20 April 1904 (public laundry); Arrêté, CM Renault, 23 December 1893 (residence permits: in this case, a higher official has noted in the margin the fact that 'these dispositions are illegal' – there was, indeed, no legal basis for requiring Algerians to obtain permits to live within colonial settlements), FR/CAOM/GGA/12H/9; Administrator, CM Azzefoun, Port-Gueydon, to Prefect, Algiers, 8 August 1901, FR/CAOM/ Alger/F21/5.

## 4    The Politics of Loyalty and Dissent, 1912–1942

1. Benhabylès, *L'Algérie française*, 112.
2. Camus, 'Misère de Kabylie: La Grèce en haillons', *Alger républicain*, 5 June 1939.
3. For the colonial 'public sphere', see Jansen, *Erobern und erinnern*.
4. Rey-Goldzeiguer, *Aux origines*, 76; see Blanchard and Thénault, 'Quel "monde du contact"?'
5. A leitmotif in the film *Pieds noirs, histoires d'une blessure* (dir. Gilles Perez), 2007, shown on FR3 TV in March 2007.
6. Akoun, *Né à Oran*, 39, 40, 27.
7. Conversation with the author, Algiers, 2001.
8. Meynier, *L'Algérie révélée*, 197–98.
9. Prefecture, Algiers, 'Le problème des "bidonvilles": Commission du 13 mars 1941', Municipal council, Algiers, Extract of minutes of meeting, 4 April 1941, 'Recensement des bidonvilles', March 1941, FR/ANOM/Alger/10I/ 10/2; Çelik, *Urban forms*; 'Rabah Serradj' [Sadek Hajerès], 'Bidonvilles, cités de la faim: Le quartier Mahieddine, rendez-vous des exilés', *Liberté* no.370, 13 July 1950, retrieved from www.socialgerie.net/spip.php?article1136#nb1 (accessed 29 May 2015). Thanks to Jim House for rediscovering this account.
10. Jomier, 'Un réformisme'; Merad, *Le réformisme*, 192–98; McDougall, 'Dream of exile', 254–60; Pervillé, *Les étudiants*.

11. Meynier, *L'Algérie révélée*, 398, 400, 405; Stora, *Histoire de l'Algérie coloniale*, 51–52, 123.
12. Ageron, *Algérie contemporaine* vol. 2, 526–29; for difficulties of estimating numbers, Blanchard, *La police parisienne*, 231–35. On Algerians in France in this period, see MacMaster, *Colonial migrants*, Stora, *Ils venaient de l'Algérie*, Rosenberg, *Policing Paris*.
13. Meynier, *L'Algérie révélée*, 454–56.
14. Grandguillaume, 'M'hamed Ben Rahal', and *Nedroma*, 177–86; Bouveresse, *Parlement colonial*, 859–61, 865; Cheurfi, *Classe politique*, 95–96, 302–03.
15. Gouvion and Gouvion, *Kitab aayane*, 55–64; Christelow, *Muslim law courts*, 183–87, 233–34; Bouveresse, *Parlement colonial*, 707–09; McDougall, 'Ibn Badis, ʿAbd al-Ḥamīd'; Merad, *Réformisme musulman*, 79–85.
16. Fromage, 'Innovation politique' vol. 1, 416–19.
17. McDougall, 'A world no longer shared'; Meynier, *L'Algérie révélée*, 198–207.
18. Daoud and Stora, *Ferhat Abbas*, 95; Ageron, *Algérie contemporaine* vol. 2, 536.
19. Roberts, 'Political development in Algeria', and 'The FLN'; Bennoune, *El Akbia*; Mahé, *Histoire de la Grande Kabylie*; Rahem, *Le sillage de la tribu*; MacMaster, 'The roots of insurrection'.
20. Reports on Beni Chougrane insurrection, October 1914, FR/ANOM/9H/16.
21. Meynier, *L'Algérie révélée*, 578–86; Ageron, *Algériens musulmans* vol. 2, 1150–57.
22. Renseignement individuel (request for internment order), 'Kezzouli, Omar ben Saïd', (n.p., n.d.), and Gendarmerie nationale, Report, Lt. Balley, Tizi Ouzou, 14 July 1915, FR/ANOM/Alger/F33/1 and F33/2; for insecurity more generally, Meynier, *L'Algérie révélée*, 560–65.
23. Popular *shawi* song quoted in Déjeux, 'Un bandit d'honneur dans l'Aurès', and Déjeux's papers in FR/ANOM/87APOM/59; Colonna, *Le meunier*, 49–56, 69–72.
24. *Enquête sur la propriété indigène. Procès-verbaux des séances de la Commission instituée par arrêté du Gouverneur général du 28 juin 1898*, Algiers, Imprimerie administrative Victor Heintz, 1904, 3. FR/ANOM/GGA/9X/116.
25. Nouschi, 'La dépossession foncière', 192; Sari, *Dépossession*; Von Sivers, 'Algerian landownership', 61; Meynier, *L'Algérie révélée*, 643; Ageron, *Algérie contemporaine* vol. 2, 508–09; Galissot, 'L'économie coloniale', 366–67; Peyroulou, '1919–1944: L'essor de l'Algérie algérienne', 328.
26. Omar Carlier, 'Les traminots algérois', 'Le café maure', 'Medina and modernity'.
27. Roth, *Le théâtre algérien*; Bachetarzi, *Mémoires*; decree of Governor General Le Beau, Algiers, 2 November 1937 (prohibiting sale and distribution of the *Receuil de chansons Mahieddine 1937*), FR/ANOM/GGA/9H/37/2.
28. Glasser, 'Edmond Yafil and Andalusi musical revival', idem *Lost Paradise*; Merdaci, *Dictionnaire des musiques*; Marouf, *Chant arabo-andalou*; Bougherara, *Voyage sentimental*.
29. Report to the chief of the Sûreté départementale, Algiers, 17 November 1937 no.7839. FR/ANOM/Alger/2I/32/2.
30. 'Bulletin de renseignements des questions musulmanes: Le cinéma en Afrique du nord' (15 November 1937), Police Commissioner, Ténès, to

Prefect, Algiers, 28 February 1938, Administrator, CM Marnia to Sub-
Prefect, Tlemcen, 15 December 1938, Note 'Réactions provoquées par
certaines représentations cinématographiques', CIE, Algiers, 14 May 1938.
FR/ANOM/GGA/9H/37/1.

31. 'Ghādat umm al-qurā' is reprinted in Huhu, *Al-a'māl al-kāmila* vol. 1, 11–43.
32. Reports, correspondence, publicity materials and summaries of performances
    relating to Mahieddine tours, 1936–40. FR/ANOM/GGA/9H/37/2.
33. For schoolteachers, see Colonna, *Instituteurs indigènes*, for medical
    auxiliaries, Clark, 'Doctoring the *bled*'. For other spaces of interaction and
    mobilisation, see Fromage, 'Innovation politique', Marynower, 'Être
    socialiste', Lacroix, 'Une histoire sociale et spatiale', Courreye, 'L'Association
    des oulémas'.
34. Seferdjeli, 'La politique coloniale', 361.
35. Ageron, *Algériens musulmans* vol. 2, 950 and *Algérie contemporaine* vol. 2, 534–
    35; Ruedy, *Modern Algeria*, 126. Until 1949, up to three-quarters of Algerian
    children were taught in separate schools, or in *classes indigènes* attached to
    *écoles communales*, where (according to the official figures) there could be as
    many as eighty or ninety children per class.
36. Meynier, *Algérie révélée*, 733, 580.
37. Hamet, *Les musulmans français*, 12–13.
38. Quoted in Ageron, *Algérie contemporaine*, 235.
39. Ageron, 'Le mouvement "jeune Algérien"', idem, *Algérie contemporaine* vol.
    2, 232–36; Meynier, *L'Algérie révélée*, 212–17; Fromage, 'L'expérience des
    "Jeunes Algériens"'; Ruedy, 'Chérif Benhabylès'; Chalabi, 'Un juriste en
    quête de modernité'; Benhabylès, *L'Algérie française*.
40. Ageron, *Algériens musulmans* vol. 2, 1056–78; Meynier, *L'Algérie révélée*,
    89–104.
41. In 1930, for example, the totality of expenses for 'affairs concerning the
    *indigènes*' amounted to only 4.2 per cent of the Algerian budget. (Ageron,
    *Algérie contemporaine* vol. 2, 534.)
42. Ageron, *Algériens musulmans* vol. 2, 1037–45; 'Note sur les mesure
    demandées par les Musulmans Français de l'Algérie ... ', in Benhabylès,
    *Algérie française*, 117–21, and Collot and Henry (eds.), *Mouvement national*,
    23–24. It remains unclear whether the text originally specified that such
    'naturalisation' should be possible without renunciation of Muslim
    personal status (Ageron, *Algériens musulmans* vol. 2, 1042 n.3).
43. Quoted in Meynier, *L'Algérie révélée*, 216.
44. *La Voix indigène*, 20, 27 December 1935, paraphrased in CIE, Algiers,
    'Analyse de la presse', December 1935, FR/ANOM/15H/1.
45. Dirèche-Slimani, *Chrétiens de Kabylie*, 61–82, 11–12; Amrouche, *Histoire de
    ma vie*, 203.
46. Hearings of 4, 6 May 1892. Pensa, *L'Algérie, organisation politique et
    administrative* ..., 152, 153, 155. Bouderba adduced the example of
    Circassian Muslims within the Russian empire in analogy. By 1904, however,
    he was advocating a single civil law without '*en masse* naturalisation' into
    citizenship, as a step towards 'definitive fusion' in equality without legal
    difference (Bouderba, 'La justice civile musulmane', report discussed at the

Algiers Société d'études politiques et sociales, 10, 24 March 1904, text and transcription in *Société d'études politiques et sociales: Assimilation progressive de l'Algérie à la France. Bulletin trimestriel* 1903–4, Algiers, Secrétariat de la Société, 7 rue Michelet, 84ff). Thanks to Christian Phéline for discussion of this point.

47. The dispositions of both the 1865 Sénatus-Consulte and the law of 4 February 1919 were applied to Algerian women by the law of 18 August 1929. *JORF* 21 August 1929, 9786; Kateb, *Européens, 'indigènes' et juifs*, 344.

48. Ageron, *Algérie contemporaine* vol. 2, 274–75; Collot, *Institutions*, 56–57, 126–28, 277–78; 'Loi sur l'accession des indigènes de l'Algérie aux droits politiques', *JORF*, 6 February 1919, 1358–59.

49. Technically this was illegal, since non-citizens could not hold a rank above lieutenant; Khaled was thus a captain *à titre indigène*, obliged to take orders from 'equal'-ranking French colleagues.

50. Quoted in Koulakssis and Meynier, *L'Emir Khaled*, 340–42. The letter was long lost, and the subject of some controversy in the 1920s and later, before its rediscovery and publication in 1980.

51. Ageron, *Algérie contemporaine* vol. 2, 279–93; Koulakssis and Meynier, *L'Emir Khaled*; Kaddache, *La vie politique à Alger*, and *L'émir Khaled*.

52. Abbas, *Jeune Algérien*, 112.

53. Quoted in Daoud and Stora, *Ferhat Abbas*, 39. He would repeat the same point years later (Preface [1981] to Abbas, *Jeune Algérien*, 27). See also Abbas, *Jeune Algérien*, esp. 89–100, 145–50. The term *pays réel* was coined by the rightist, 'integral' nationalist Charles Maurras, to refer to the 'deep' France of village and parish, distinguished from the abstract *pays légal* of (post-revolutionary, Republican) national institutions.

54. Abbas, *Jeune Algérien*, 30.

55. Ibid., 165–66.

56. Léon Blum's cabinet fell on 21 June 1937, replaced by that of Camille Chautemps; Bendjelloul's move was meant to demonstrate support for Blum's Algerian reform bill, which Chautemps opposed. (On the Blum-Viollette bill, see below.) Fromage, 'Innovation politique' vol. 1, 31, 520–23.

57. Fromage, 'Innovation politique' vol. 1, 415, 427–31, vol. 2, 234.

58. For Algerians' investment in colonial commemorative politics more generally, see Jansen, *Erobern und errinern*.

59. Fromage, 'Innovation politique' vol. 1, 523, 534, 389. Collot, 'L'Union populaire', does not mention these demonstrations. The party's full name clearly expressed its manifesto: *Union populaire algérienne pour la conquête des droits de l'homme et du citoyen*.

60. Abbas, 'En marge du nationalisme: La France c'est moi!' *L'Entente franco-musulmane*, 27 February 1936, reprinted in *La Défense*, 28 February 1936.

61. 'Fi shimāl Ifrīqiya: Kalima ṣarīḥa', *Al-Shihab*, April 1936, 42–45.

62. Ahmad Taleb Ibrahimi recalls how his teacher at primary school, where Ben Badis convinced his father to enrol him, 'eventually taught me to love both school and the French language'. *Mémoires* vol. 1, 29.

63. Abbas, *Jeune Algérien*, 152; Ben Badis in *Al-Shihab*, February 1937, 504–06, quoted in Merad, *Réformisme*, 397.

64. Christelow, *Muslim law courts*, 234, 241; Siari Tengour, 'Constantine, 1887'.
65. Christelow, *Muslim law courts*; Balique and Henry, *La doctrine coloniale*; Collot, *Institutions*, 178–90.
66. Vatin, *L'Algérie politique*, 195 n.114; shaykh al-'Uqbi was equally severe (*Al-Basa'ir* 30 July 1937, quoted in Report, Algiers, 6 August 1937, FR/ANOM/Alger/2I/39/4).
67. Berque, 'Ça et là dans les débuts du réformisme'; Merad, 'L'enseignement politique'; Christelow, 'Algerian Islam'; Chachoua, *L'Islam kabyle*.
68. Jomier, 'Un réformisme islamique' vol. 1, 120.
69. See e.g. McDougall, *History and the culture of nationalism*, 130–35; Jomier, 'Un réformisme islamique' vol. 1, 509; for a comparative case from Egypt, Mayeur-Jaouen, 'Le corps entre sacré et profane'.
70. Ben Badis, 'Da'wat al-'ulamā' al-muslimīn a-jazā'iriyyīn wa uṣūluhā', *Al-Shihab* June 1937, 176–79, tr. as 'Bases fondamentales de la doctrine de l'Association des Oulamas', repr. *Le jeune musulman*, 6 June 1952, and in Collot and Henry, *Mouvement national*, 95–100. For an *islah*ist account of 'maraboutism', Merad, *Réformisme*, 58–76; cf. Andezian, *Expériences du divin*.
71. McDougall, 'The secular state's Islamic empire'.
72. Colonna, *Versets*, 333.
73. McDougall, 'Secular state's Islamic empire'; Achour, 'Entre tradition et réforme' vol. 1, 188–207, 234–45; Jomier, 'Un réformisme islamique', ch.7.
74. McDougall, 'Secular state's Islamic empire', 573–75.
75. Jomier, 'Un réformisme islamique' vol. 1, 286–92.
76. McDougall, *History and the culture of nationalism*, 120–22; Djerbal, 'La guerre d'Algérie au miroir', 542, citing Lakhdar Bentobbal, a future ALN colonel who, born in Mila in 1923, witnessed the social tensions around reformism in his youth.
77. 'Khitatna', *Al-Muntaqid*, 2 July 1925; cf. partial translation in Merad, *Réformisme*, 443–46.
78. Speech at the Majestic cinema, Algiers (Report, Sûreté départementale, Algiers, 25 September 1937, 6559); printed 'Appel au peuple algérien et à ses élus' (Commissaire central adjoint to Prefecture, Algiers, 27 August 1937, 917RS). FR/ANOM/Alger/2I/39/3.
79. McDougall, *History and the culture of nationalism*, 136.
80. The ENA, formally constituted on 26 June 1926, was dissolved for a first time on 20 November 1929 by the courts in the *département* of the Seine for 'threatening the integrity of national territory'; relaunched in May 1933, it was dissolved again on 26 January 1937 by the Popular Front government.
81. Messali, *Mémoires*, 96–98, 104–05, 111–12, 115–20.
82. Lamine Lamoudi (speaking to the *nadi al-tahdhib* in September 1937) quoted in McDougall, 'Secular state's Islamic empire', 577; Lacheraf (recalling events in Paris in 1946), *Des noms et des lieux*, 114–15, 123.
83. Collot and Henry, *Mouvement national*, 39, 48–53; Kaddache, *Histoire du naitonalisme* vol. 2, 907–09; Stora, *Messali*, 69–71; Messali, *Mémoires*, 156–58.
84. Collot and Henry, *Mouvement national*, 25–29; McDougall, *History and the culture of nationalism*, 43–49.
85. Messali, *Mémoires*, 146.

86. Stora, *Messali*, 78–79, 82. Carlier, 'La première Etoile Nord-Africaine'.
87. Marynower, 'Être socialiste', 177–244.
88. Jansen, *Erobern*, 210–13; Marynower, 'Être socialiste'.
89. *L'Entente*, 23 December 1937, quoted in Daoud and Stora, *Ferhat Abbas*, 102 n.50.
90. Marynower, 'Être socialiste', 677–78; Carlier, 'Medina', 77.
91. Jansen, *Erobern*, 208.
92. Messali, *Le problème algérien: Appel aux Nations Unies*, February 1949, FR/ANOM/Alger/4I/178/6.
93. Viollette, *L'Algérie vivra-t-elle?*
94. Collot and Henry, *Mouvement national*, 72–73.
95. Resolution of the Second Algerian Muslim Congress (9–11 July 1937), in Collot and Henry, *Mouvement naitonal*, 102.
96. Ageron, *Algérie contemporaine* vol. 2, 374–75.
97. Report, Chef de la Sûreté départementale to Prefect, Algiers, 20 July 1936, 4670, FR/ANOM/Alger/2I/32/3.
98. Messali, *Mémoires*, 177, 221–22; *El-Ouma*, May–June 1936, quoted in Stora, *Messali*, 144.
99. Text from *El-Ouma*, 26 August 1936 repr. in Kaddache, *Histoire du nationalisme*, 930–32 (annexe 21), and *El-Ouma*, September–October 1936, repr. in Collot and Henry, *Mouvement national*, 82–85. It is not clear how closely the published texts reproduce what Messali actually said; by his own account the speech was improvised (Messali, *Mémoires*, 229).
100. Messali, *Mémoires*, 230; *Le Cri du peuple algérien* (n.d.), quoted in Stora, *Messali*, 149; Kaddache, *Nationalisme* vol. 1, 471.
101. Collot, 'Le Parti du Peuple algérien', 145–46.
102. Jansen, *Erobern*, 227–28; Kaddache, *Nationalisme* vol. 2, 532–33.
103. Kaddache, *Nationalisme* vol. 2, 534, 539–41; Collot, 'Le Parti', 162–63, 166. Ironically, the second-placed candidate, Mahieddine Zerrouk, to whom the Prefecture subsequently attempted to award the election, had as a younger 'Young Algerian' been the unsuccessful candidate supported by Khaled, against the administration's then-favoured *bachagha* Ben Siam, in 1913.
104. Kaddache, *Nationalisme* vol. 2, 537; Cheurfi, *Classe politique*, 216.
105. Collot, 'Le Parti', 172.
106. Ibid., 148–49; Stora, *Messali*, 164–65.
107. Ageron, *Algérie contemporaine* vol. 2, 356–57.
108. Collot, 'Le Parti', 170.
109. On 'lost opportunities', see Julien, *L'Afrique du nord en marche*, 343–53; for a critique, Marynower, 'Être socialiste', 825–29.
110. See Colonna, *Instituteurs*, esp. 169–70.
111. *Receuil des chansons Mahieddine 1937*, FR/ANOM/GGA/9H/37/2.

## 5    Revolution and Civil War, 1942–1962

1. Messali was released from Lambèse after the fall of the Vichy regime in North Africa, but re-imprisoned in December 1943. On 19 April 1945, he attempted

to escape house arrest, but the plan misfired; he was arrested again, and deported four days later. He would remain at Brazzaville until October 1946.

2. Today, these streets are respectively the avenue du 8 mai and rue Ahmed Aggoun.

3. Some 5,400 North Africans may have been killed in the 1939–40 campaign; another 11,193 Muslims were reported killed and 39,645 wounded when France re-entered the war in 1943–45. The latter figures presumably include West Africans, of whom Echenberg estimates up to 25,000 may have died overall. An adequate account would also have to include POWs who died in detention (or who, as the Senegalese at Chasselay, were massacred). Recham, 'Les militaires nord-africains'; Echenberg, '"Morts pour la France"'.

4. 10è Région militaire, État-major 2ème bureau, 'Les troubles du 8 mai 1945 en Algérie', FR/CADN/Alger/Ambassade/51/1; Chenntouf, 'Un document inédit sur le 8 mai 1945' (Tubert report, 1945); Aïned-Tabet, 'Le 8 mai 1945: Jacquerie ou revendication agraire', and *Le mouvement du 8 mai 1945*; Kaddache, *Histoire du nationalisme* vol. 2, 695–718; Ageron, 'Les troubles'; Rey-Goldzeiguer, *Aux origines*; Planche, *Sétif 1945*; Peyroulou, *Guelma, 1945*; Benot, *Massacres*; Thomas, 'Colonial violence'. Estimates of the death toll vary widely; the administration's official maximal figure of 1,500 has always been dismissed as absurdly low, the official Algerian nationalist claim, first of 30,000–35,000, then 45,000, has equally been thought much too high. The sober estimate of 8,000 was advanced initially by Charles-André Julien, *L'Afrique du nord en marche*, 263; see also Ageron, 'Les troubles', 36–37, Peyroulou, *Guelma, 1945*, 197–202, Meynier, *Histoire intérieure*, 67.

5. Ageron, 'Un manuscrit inédit de Ferhat Abbas', 186; 'Face au crime colonial … Appel à la jeunesse algérienne française et musulmane' (1 May 1946), in Collot and Henry, *Mouvement national*, 219–23.

6. 'Kateb Yacine, écrivain public', RTF TV documentary, 21 November 1971, at www.ina.fr/video/CPF86655626/yacine-kateb-ecrivain-public-video.html.

7. Mechati, *Parcours*, 37; Mohamed Mechati, interview, Algiers, 21 March 2007.

8. Abbas, *Autopsie*.

9. Yacine, *Abdelkader et l'indépendance algérienne* (lecture delivered in Paris, 24 May 1947, first published in Algiers later that year), 34–35, 37.

10. Mechati interview (n.7).

11. Kaddache, *Nationalisme* vol. 2, 963.

12. The 'Mandouze declaration' was published in the dissident periodical *Consciences algériennes* (relaunched in 1954 as *Consciences maghribines*) in December 1950. Collot and Henry, *Mouvement national*, 282–86.

13. Ageron, 'Les troubles', 31.

14. The term was first used with reference to Setif in an MTLD brochure published in 1951, *Le génocide de mai 1945*.

15. Aïned-Tabet, 'Le 8 mai 1945', 1009, 1014–16.

16. Mechati interview (n.7).

17. Ageron, 'Ferhat Abbas et l'évolution politique'; Collot and Henry, *Mouvement national*, 155–65.

18. Kaddache, *Histoire du nationalisme* vol. 2, 696–97.
19. Peyroulou, *Guelma*.
20. De Gaulle, *Discours et messages* vol. 1, 351–54.
21. McDougall, 'Rule of experts?'
22. Quoted in Ageron, *Algérie contemporaine* vol. 2, 564.
23. Crevaux, *Yves Chataigneau, fossoyeur général de l'Algérie* (Algiers, 1948); Crevaux, a journalist at *L'Echo d'Alger*, was a member of the Algerian Assembly and from 1953 Mayor of Philippeville. On Chataigneau, see Julien, *L'Afrique du nord en marche*, 261, 266.
24. Collot and Henry, *Mouvement national*, 177–85; Julien, *L'Afrique du nord en marche*, 257; Ageron, *Algérie contemporaine* vol. 2, 565–67.
25. The term is Malika Rahal's. Rahal, 'L'Union démocratique du manifeste algérien', 458.
26. Collot and Henry, *Mouvement national*, 188–91.
27. Rahal, 'L'Union démocratique', 61.
28. Meynier, *Histoire intérieure*, 76–78; Harbi, *Aux origines*, and *Le FLN*, chs. 2, 6.
29. Kaddache, *Histoire du nationalisme* vol. 2, 755–56, 841–53.
30. Abdelhamid Benzine (later an FLN political officer and member of the Communist Party), quoted in Hadjères, *Quand une nation*, 292.
31. Rahal, 'A local approach', 86.
32. Sari, 'Role of the medinas', 76; Brahim Zeddour, interview, Oran, 5 June 2007.
33. Cheurfi, *Classe politique*, 127–28; Rahal, *Ali Boumendjel*.
34. Mouloud Hamrouche, interview, Algiers, 27 May 2009; Cheurfi, *Classe politique*, 193–94. On UDMA-AUMA relations in Constantine, Rahal, 'Prendre parti' and 'L'Union démocratique'.
35. *Dictionnaire des parlementaires français*, at www.assemblee-nationale.fr/syco more/fiche.asp?num_dept=5500.
36. Droz and Lever, *Histoire de la guerre*, 46; Kaddache, *Histoire du nationalisme* vol. 2, 792–98, 865–70.
37. *Liberté*, 2 August 1951.
38. Collot, 'Le Front algérien … ', 381.
39. Julien, *L'Afrique du nord en marche*, 266; Ageron, *Algérie contemporaine* vol. 2, 496–506.
40. Rahal, 'A local approach'.
41. Hadjères, *Quand une nation*, 294–99.
42. Mechati interview (n.7); Sadek Hadjères, interview, Malakoff, 4 June 2009.
43. On the 'Kabyle myth', see Daumas, *La Kabylie*, Hanoteau and Letourneux, *La Kabylie* vol. 1, 305–14, Masqueray, *Formation des cités*; Ageron, *Algérie contemporaine* vol. 2, 137–51, Mahé, *Histoire*, 147–57, Lorcin, *Imperial identities*, McDougall, 'Heresy and salvation'. On schools, Turin, *Affrontements*, Colonna, *Instituteurs*.
44. Harbi, *Le FLN*, 18, 60–61.
45. This text became known under the title *L'Algérie libre vivra* ('Free Algeria will live'), a riposte to Viollette's earlier pamphlet, *L'Algérie vivra-t-elle?*
46. 'Idir el-Wattani', *Vive l'Algérie*.
47. *Le problème algérien: Appel aux nations unies* (Paris, 1949).

48. Harbi, *Le FLN*, 63, 405 n.11.
49. Carlier, 'Note sur la "crise berbériste"'; Harbi, *Aux origines*, 37–39, and *Le FLN*, 59–67; Meynier, *Histoire intérieure*, 94–96; Hadjerès interview (n.41).
50. Jansen, *Erobern*, 453–54.
51. Kaddache, *Histoire du nationalisme* vol. 2, 854–60, 971–72; Harbi, *Le FLN*, 69–77; Mechati interview (n.7).
52. Mechati interview (n.7).
53. Abd al-Hamid Mehri, interview, Algiers, 25 March 2007.
54. Harbi, *Le FLN*, 93–94.
55. Harbi, *Les origines* and *Le FLN*; Meynier, *Histoire intérieure*, 110–26; Mechati interview (n.7).
56. Speech in Oran, 17 October 1954, quoted in Harbi, *Aux origines*, 59.
57. Ageron, 'Un manuscrit … ', 187.
58. Twenty-two former OS militants were invited; twenty-one attended. Mechati, *Parcours*, 78–85; Harbi, *Le FLN*, 102–04.
59. The phrase is Mechati's interview (n.7), and Mechati, *Parcours*, 79.
60. The central and eastern Algerian Sahara was later organised as *wilaya* 6.
61. *L'Echo d'Alger*, *Le Parisien libéré*, *L'Union*, *La dépeche quotidienne*, 2 November 1954. In fact, almost seventy attacks were mounted in some thirty localities. Meynier, *Histoire intérieure*, 275; Harbi, *1954*, 19–25.
62. Mechati interview (n.7).
63. Ibid.; Hocine Zehouane, interview, Algiers, 4 July 2008.
64. Hamrouche interview (n.34).
65. Mehri interview (n.53).
66. 'Proclamation du Front de Libération Nationale', 1 November 1954. Harbi, *Archives*, 101–03.
67. Harbi, *1954*, 21–23; cf. Horne, *Savage war*, 88, 91–93.
68. Meynier, *Histoire intérieure*, 154.
69. Harbi, *Le FLN*, 127.
70. Hadjerès interview (n.41); Meynier, *Histoire intérieure*, 181.
71. Meynier, *Histoire intérieure*, 187; Rahal, 'A local approach', 88–90.
72. Meynier, *Histoire intérieure*, 189; McDougall, 'S'écrire un destin' and *History and the culture of nationalism*, 137–43.
73. Quoted in Ageron, "L'insurrection du 20 août', 29.
74. *Alger républicain*, 28 April 1955. A companion article by Messali, from the Vendée where he was now interned, repeated the old PPA call for a sovereign Algerian constituent assembly.
75. Ageron, 'L'insurrection du 20 août', 28–29.
76. Meynier, *Histoire intérieure*, 280–82; Thénault, *Histoire*, 47–50; Ageron, 'L'insurrection du 20 août'; Mauss-Copeaux, *Algérie, 20 août 1955*, and cf. Vétillard, *20 août 1955*.
77. Hamrouche interview (n.34).
78. 'Motion de politique générale', 26 September 1955. Harbi and Meynier, *FLN, documents*, 220–21.
79. Abbane, Algiers, to External delegation, Cairo, 15 March 1956. Belhocine, *Le courrier*, 163.

80. Algerian supporters were periodically informed of Ibrahimi's diplomacy – in Egypt, Iraq, Pakistan, Kuwait – by the 'second generation' AUMA journal, *Le jeune musulman* (e.g. articles in *Le jeune musulman*, 6 June, 20 June, 26 September 1952; 13 March 1953; 12 February, 26 March 1954). On AUMA relations with the FLN, see Meynier, *Histoire intérieure*, 189; Harbi, *Le FLN*, 136–37.

81. Harbi, *Le FLN*, 159. Generational shifts were sometimes important: while Abdelmalek Benhabylès (b. 1921), an MTLD central committee member in 1954, would serve in the FLN's diplomatic missions, his uncle Chérif, since 1951 a Senator of the Fourth Republic, would be assassinated by the Front at Vichy in 1959. In the 1930s, the *bashagha* Muhammad Ben Siam was one of the administration's principal interlocutors in 'Muslim affairs' in Algiers; in 1957, the family provided a refuge and 'post box' for FLN leaders in the city (Ben M'hidi was arrested there, entirely by chance, during a search).

82. Khider to CCE, 19 October 1955. Belhocine, *Le courrier*, 99–103.

83. Soustelle, *Aimée et souffrante*, 118–25.

84. Quoted in Ageron, 'L'insurrection du 20 août', 47.

85. Thénault, *Histoire*, 57–68, 124–25; Evans, *Algeria*, 143–59.

86. Elsenhans, *La guerre*, 452; Thénault, *Histoire*, 59.

87. Meynier, *Histoire intérieure*, 549–615; Connelly, *Diplomatic revolution*; Byrne, *Mecca of revolution*; Johnson, *Battle for Algeria*.

88. E.g. Kafi, *Du militant politique*, 82.

89. Abbane to External delegation, Cairo, 15 March 1956. Belhocine, *Le courrier*, 161–67.

90. Tract, June 1955, publ. *Consciences maghribines* December 1955. Harbi and Meynier, *FLN, documents*, 219–20; Meynier, *Histoire intérieure*, 176–77.

91. Respectively, the *Union générale des étudiants musulmans algériens* (July 1955), *Union générale des travailleurs algériens* (February 1956), *Union générale des commerçants algériens* (September 1956).

92. Abbane to External delegation, Cairo, 4 November 1955, 15 March 1956. Belhocine, *Le courrier*, 108–10, 161–67.

93. 'Procès-verbal du congrès de la Soummam', 20 August 1956. Harbi and Meynier, *FLN, documents*, 241–45; Meynier, *Histoire intérieure*, 191–95; Harbi, *Archives*, 160–67 and *Le FLN*, 172–86; Quandt, *Revolution*, 99–107.

94. Ben Bella to the CCE, n.d. [autumn 1956]. Harbi, *Archives*, 168.

95. Ben M'hidi's death was announced as 'suicide', which fooled no-one at the time; the truth, that he was hanged in his cell by a death squad under Commandant Paul Aussaresses, with the complicity of the higher command and the French government, would be established later. Abbane's death was announced in *El Moudjahid* (29 May 1958), which claimed he had been killed in action the previous month, an official fiction long maintained in Algeria. (In July 2007, Abbane's portrait in the lobby of the official *Centre de recherches et d'études sur le mouvement national et la révolution du 1er novembre* at the Parc des Pins, El Biar, still carried the inscription 'killed on the field of action in April 1958'.) Krim, Abbane's supporter at the Soummam but thereafter increasingly alienated from him, insisted that he and his fellow Colonels had sentenced Abbane only to imprisonment, and that his death was entirely Boussouf's responsibility (Krim

to former militants, n.d. [1970], publ. Harbi, *Archives*, 177–79). Rumours were spread within the maquis that Abbane, already suspected of 'reformism', had opened separate channels to negotiate with the French, or that he planned his own military coup against his rivals (Kafi, *Du militant*, 82, 133–34). More probably, the increasingly powerful military leadership saw in Abbane a tempestuous rival trespassing on their prerogatives (Harbi, *Le FLN*, 203–05; Meynier, *Histoire intérieure*, 345–49).

96. 'Procès-verbal de la réunion du CNRA', 28 August 1957. Harbi, *Archives*, 175–76.
97. Harbi, *Le FLN*, 182, 204.
98. MacMaster, 'Roots of insurrection'; Meynier, *Histoire intérieure*.
99. Harbi and Meynier, *FLN, documents*, 284–88.
100. Meynier, *Histoire intérieure*, 205.
101. Mohammed Harbi, interview in *Sou'al* 7 (September 1987), 8–9.
102. The students' strike in secondary and higher education, begun in May 1956, was very effective, with many students subsequently joining the FLN; the general school boycott announced for the *rentrée* of 1 October was initially widely followed, but collapsed in February 1957. FLN tract calling for school boycott, September 1957. Harbi and Meynier, *FLN, documents*, 147–48; Elsenhans, *La guerre*, 442–44.
103. Meynier, *Histoire intérieure*, 217.
104. Feraoun, *Journal*, 128–29, 192 (entries for 12, 13 June 1956, 24 January 1957).
105. Inhabitants of *douar* Ihadjadjen to Abdelmadjid Ourabah, 25 February 1956. Harbi and Meynier, *FLN, documents*, 193–94.
106. Meynier, *Histoire intérieure*, 447.
107. Feraoun, *Journal*, 286 (entry for 9 December 1958).
108. 'Y' (former member of SAS self-defence militia, Champlain, Algérois). MMSH/Phonothèque/Récits de vie de harkis (Mathias archive). Interview D662.
109. Named *Sections administrtives urbaines* (SAU) in urban areas.
110. Ageron, 'Les supplétifs'; Chauvin, 'Des appelés'; Elsenhans, *La guerre*, 565; Pervillé, 'Guerre d'Algérie: L'abandon', 304–05, and 'Histoire de l'Algérie et mythes politiques', 330; Jordi and Hamoumou, *Les harkis*; Hamoumou, 'L'histoire des harkis'; Crapanzano, *The harkis*.
111. E.g. the film *180 000*, produced by the Army Cinematographic Service in 1959. ECPAD.
112. Boualem, *Les harkis*; Fabbiano, '"Pour moi, l'Algérie … "', 'Les harkis du Bachagha Boualam'.
113. Anon (former *harki* sergeant). MMSH/Phonothèque/Récits de vie de harkis. Interview D624.
114. Branche, *L'embuscade*.
115. Branche, *La torture*, 33.
116. Quoted in Branche, 'La torture pendant la guerre d'Algérie', 391.
117. Vidal-Nacquet, *La torture;* Branche, *La torture*; Halimi and De Beauvoir, *Djamila Boupacha*; Rahal, *Ali Boumendjel*. The building where Boumendjel

was murdered and where Alleg, Audin, Boupacha and others were tortured is today 92, avenue Ali Khodja. Rahal, 'La terrasse'.

118. Vidal-Nacquet, *L'affaire Audin*; Alleg, *La question*; Evans, *Algeria*, 224, 280–81.

119. Péju, *Les harkis à Paris*; Blanchard, *La police*; Macmaster, *Colonial migrants*.

120. House and MacMaster, *Paris 1961*.

121. Blanchard, *La police*, 377–91; House and MacMaster, *Paris 1961* (on the death toll, see esp. 161–67).

122. *Bulletin de la Caisse d'équipement pour le développement de l'Algérie (CEDA)* 3 (February 1961), 1–2; de Gaulle, *Discours et messages* vol. 4, 48–51.

123. De Gaulle, *Discours et messages* vol. 3, 15–16. On reform and development policy, Elsenhans, *La guerre*, 591–747; McDougall, 'The impossible Republic'.

124. 'Les mille villages', *Bulletin de la CEDA* no. 6 (May 1961), 17–27; De Planhol, *Nouveaux villages*, 25; Cornaton, *Les regroupements*; Bourdieu and Sayad, *Le déracinement*.

125. Letter to a Parisian newspaper from inhabitants of El Afiss, 15 April 1956. Kessel and Pirelli, *Le peuple algérien*, 38–39.

126. *Képi bleu* (Service cinématographique des Armées, 1957), ECPAD; Pinoteau, 'Propaganda cinématographique'; Soustelle, *Aimée et souffrante*; Massu, *La vraie bataille*.

127. GPRA, *Enfants d'Algérie*; Brace and Brace, *Algerian voices*; Darbois and Vigneau, *Les Algériens en guerre*; Kessel and Pirelli, *Le peuple algérien*.

128. *Enfants d'Algérie*, 29 (a largely unedited collection of children's narratives and drawings, produced by the GPRA's Information Ministry but published by Maspéro in October 1962). The reference to the mother being 'put . . . in another room' almost certainly refers to her rape.

129. Jacques Carret, 'La femme musulmane', *Bulletin de Liaison et de documentation*, 57–10 and 58–15 (60pp.), Délégation-Générale du Gouvernement en Algérie, Service de l'action administrative et économique, May 1958. FR/ANOM/GGA/9X/299.

130. Seferdjeli, 'French "reforms"'; MacMaster, *Burning the Veil*.

131. Fanon, 'L'Algérie se dévoile' [1959], 46.

132. Rahal, *Ali Boumendjel*, 64–65.

133. Feraoun, *Journal*, 269, 292 (entries for 3 April 1958, 26 April 1959).

134. E.g. Feraoun, *Journal*, 289–90; Meynier, *Histoire intérieure*, 226–28.

135. *Renaissance algérienne* 1 (internal journal, W3) n.d. [1957]. Harbi and Meynier, *Le FLN*, documents 607–08 (emphasis added).

136. ALN Order, n.d. [1957?], *mintaqa* 55, *wilaya* 5. Harbi and Meynier, *Le FLN*, documents, 607.

137. Extract from ALN directives, *mintaqa* 2, *wilaya* 2, 15 December 1958. Harbi and Meynier, *Le FLN*, documents, 614–15.

138. Extract of ALN leaflet, *wilaya* 4, [summer 1961]. Harbi and Meynier, *Le FLN*, documents, 617–18; Meynier, *Histoire intérieure*, 223–31; Amrane-Minne, *Des femmes*; Gadant, *Le nationalisme*; Vince, *Fighting sisters*.

139. Meynier, *Histoire intérieure*, 423–24; Zehaoune interview (n.63).

140. Colonel Mohamed Lamouri, an MTLD veteran and one of the original 1 November maquisards in the Aurès, led a conspiracy of W1 officers disaffected by what they saw as anti-*shawi* Kabyle arrogance and the misdirection of the revolution by the 'exterior' politicians. Partisans of an Arab nationalism, they found backing in Nasser's secret services, which themselves hoped to curb the FLN's independence. Arrested, tortured and judged by a military tribunal presided over by Boumediene, Lamouri and three other principal conspirators were shot, several others imprisoned; some of the latter would later be 'recuperated' by Boumediene and went on to political careers after independence. Meynier, *Histoire intérieure*, 417–25; Harbi, 'Le complot'.

141. Chikh, *L'Algérie en armes*, 290.

142. Cabinet du Ministre de l'Algérie, *1957 Algérie*, 136–37.

143. Meynier, *Histoire intérieure*, 452–53.

144. Zehouane interview (n. 63).

145. Mechati interview (n.7); Meynier, *Histoire intérieure*, 445–59; Harbi, *Le FLN*, 143–62; Stora, *Messali* and 'L'Union des syndicats'; Ageron, 'Une troisième force'; Sidi-Moussa, 'Devenirs Messalistes'.

146. Ageron, 'Complots'; Meynier, *Histoire intérieure*, 430–45.

147. Abbas, *Autopsie d'une guerre*, 212.

148. De Sérigny, *La révolution*, 157, 131.

149. Droz and Lever, *Histoire de la guerre*, 200.

150. Between 1960 and 1965, there would be seventeen such tests, including four atmospheric (above-ground) tests, at Reggane and In Ekker.

151. Jackson, 'De Gaulle et l'Algérie'.

152. The result was: registered voters, 6,549,736; votes cast, 6,017,680; blank or spoiled ballots, 25,565; 'no', 16,534; 'yes', 5,975,581. *AAN* 1962, 705.

153. The un-rebuilt site of the rue de Thèbes bombing remains visible today.

154. The four putschist generals were among France's most senior soldiers: Marie-André Zeller, aged 63 and retired in 1961, had been chief of the army general staff; Edmond Jouhaud, aged 56, born at Bou Sfer near Oran, was in the wartime Resistance, had commanded the air force in Indochina and then in Algeria, retired in 1960 and was involved in a dissident soldiers' plot against de Gaulle that December before joining the putsch. Challe, the same age as Jouhaud and also an air force general, was part of the French delegation that agreed the Sèvres protocol (the secret agreement with Britain and Israel that launched the 1956 Suez war), was commander in chief in Algeria from December 1958 to April 1960, then NATO Commander in Chief-Central (CINC CENT), the post he left to join the putsch. Salan was France's most highly decorated soldier. Aged 63 in 1961, he had fought in the last months of the First World War, and was commander in chief in Indochina and then Algeria.

155. Susini, *Histoire*, 11.

156. 'Objectifs pour la phase finale de la lutte' ('Passodoble Plan'), [March 1962]. *OAS parle*, 225–26.

157. CNR, 'Historique et objectifs stratégiques et tactiques', 14 June 1962, and 'Déclaration de M. G. Bidault au nom du CNR', 9 April 1962. *OAS parle*, 269–74.
158. Favrod, *La révolution algérienne*, 203 (23 July 1957 interview).
159. Circular addressed to Algérois Jews, n.d. [April-May 1961?], model letter to Jewish civilians, 1961. Harbi and Meynier (eds.), *FLN, documents*, 594–96, 601–02; GPRA, *Tous Algériens* (Tunis, March 1961, 111pp.).
160. Pervillé, 'Guerre d'Algérie: L'abandon ... '; Jordi and Hamoumou, *Les harkis*.
161. 'A.' (engaged in *harka* July 1959, imprisoned in Kabylia 1962–65). MMSH/ Phonothèque/Récits de vie de harkis. Interview D627.
162. French army casualties were 24,614 killed (of whom almost 8,000 were victims of accidents, and 1,144 of disease, leaving 15,583 combat deaths), 64,985 wounded and almost a thousand missing, prisoners or deserted. Horne, *Savage war*, 538; Yacono, 'Les pertes'; Ageron, 'Les pertes humaines'; Ageron (ed.), *L'Algérie des Français*, 275–76; Thénault, *Histoire*, 266–68; Kateb, *Européens*, 307–13; Meynier, *Histoire intérieure*, 287–90; Pervillé, 'La guerre d'Algérie; Combien de morts?'
163. Fanon, 'Décolonisation et indépendance' [April 1958], 122–23, and *Les damnés* 88–89.

## 6    The Unfinished Revolution, 1962–1992

1. *Jeune Afrique*, 93 (16–22 July 1962), 8.
2. Song texts collected by Jean Déjeux; Chénée, 'La guerre d'après quelques chants de bidonville' (typescript, March 1963; part of her dissertation on Bu B'sila); clipping from *Alger républicain* 15 March 1965. FR/ANOM/ 87APOM/59.
3. Harbi, *Le FLN*, 378.
4. Various versions of such rationalisations of Algeria's history since 1962 exist. Commonly encountered in Algeria and among Algerians abroad, and multiplied online, they are in themselves an important element of Algeria's recent political history, especially to the extent that they reflect tensions over cultural and regional politics; and while historically unverifiable, they are usually based on at least some elements of probable fact. One often-repeated theme (proceeding from the assassination of Abbane to the claim that Amirouche too was deliberately 'sold out' and Ben Bella installed by the will of de Gaulle) was published as early as 1963 by the *wilaya* 3 veteran Mohand-Aarav Bessaoud (Bessaoud, *Heureux les martyrs*).
5. Though the label 'Boussouf's Boys' affixed to them before the end of the war would be disputed as denigrating their patriotism (Lemkami, *Les hommes*, 247, 263, 266), the few accounts by MALG veterans demonstrate Boussouf's personal centrality in their organisation, and his importance in their accounts of their place in the revolution. Lemkami, *Les hommes*, and especially Berrouane, *Aux origines*.
6. Abderrahmane Berrouane (who as 'Si Safar' was head of the DVCR, the MALG's 'vigilance' division) writes that the training received was

elementary and not as significant as has usually been supposed. *Aux origines*, 235–37.

7. Berrouane, *Aux origines*, 146–48.
8. Mémoire de l'État Major Général de l'ALN (15 July 1961). Harbi, *Archives*, 322.
9. Harbi, *Le FLN*, 341.
10. Tripoli program (June 1962), *AAN* 1962, 683–704; Lacheraf, 'Colonialisme et féodalités indigènes'; Mostefa Lacheraf, interview, Algiers, August 2001; Redha Malek, interview, Sidi Fredj, May 2009; Harbi, *Le FLN*, 330–37.
11. 'Motion adoptée par la comité inter-wilayas', 25 June 1962, 'Mesures d'urgence prises en comité inter-wilayas', 25 June 1962, 'Rapport présenté par le comité inter-wilayas au GPRA et à Ben Bella', 7 July 1962. Harbi, *Archives*, 344, 346–50.
12. Hocine Zehouane, interview, Algiers, 4 July 2008.
13. Harbi, *Le FLN*, 339–76; Quandt, *Revolution*, 164–73; Haroun, *L'été de la discorde*.
14. Quandt, *Revolution*, 178–79.
15. Tripoli program (n.10), 695; FLN, *Charte d'Alger*; Constitution (10 September 1963), *AAN* 1963, 852–59, Preamble, arts. 23–26; Le Tourneau, 'Le congrès du FLN'; Quandt, *Revolution*, 175–95; Harbi, *Le FLN*, 335; Leca and Vatin, *L'Algérie politique*, 13–45.
16. Quandt, 183, 185–86.
17. Le Tourneau, 'Le congrès du FLN', 22; Harbi, *Le FLN*, 380.
18. Quandt, *Revolution*, 219.
19. Ibid., 215.
20. The official version (reproduced e.g. in Ottaway and Ottaway, *Algeria*, 75 n.16), denied by the family, was that the assassin, Mohamed Zenadi, was a rejected former suitor of Khemisti's wife, Fatima Méchiche, herself a member of the Assembly and the widow of the *wilaya* 5 hero Colonel Lotfi. According to Harbi (*Une vie debout*, 381), Khemisti's brother had been assassinated in Morocco in 1957 by Boussouf's agents. Figures within the regime as well as outside it would continue to meet suspicious and, to some at least, inadequately explained deaths: Saïd Abid, a former *wilaya* 1 officer, member of the Council of the Revolution after the 1965 coup and commander of the first military region (the Algérois, headquartered in Blida), 'committed suicide' after failing to oppose Tahar Zbiri's coup in December 1967; Boumediene's close aide Abdelkader Chabou, in de facto charge of the Ministry of Defence, died in a helicopter crash in 1970 in the midst of negotiations on military contacts with both the USA and the USSR; Interior Minister Ahmed Medeghri, who opposed Boumediene's flagship agrarian revolution after 1971, was shot 'accidentally' at his home in 1974; Mohammed Seddik Benyahia, a lawyer, Ferhat Abbas's *chef de cabinet* in the GPRA and an FLN diplomat in the peace talks with France, Ben Bella's ambassador to Moscow and several times minister under Boumediene, was killed in 1982 during a good offices mission between Iran and Iraq when his aeroplane was shot down by a missile. While Abid *might* have committed suicide rather than being murdered on Boumediene's orders

(cf. Zbiri, *Un demi-siècle*, 267–69), and Chabou *may* have died accidentally rather than being eliminated by rivals (cf. Nezzar, *Mémoires*, 266–67), the accumulation of such deaths over the years helped give rise in each case to suspicions of conspiracy.

21. Aït Ahmed, October 1963 interview by French TV (clip in 1978 interview at www.ina.fr/video/CAB7801826201/historique-ait-ahmed-interview-video .html); Aït Ahmed, *La guerre et l'après-guerre*, 186, 194 (June 1963 interview).
22. Quoted in Vince, *Our fighting sisters*, 39.
23. Taleb Ibrahimi, *Mémoires* vol. 1, 191–205.
24. Byrne, 'The pilot nation', 341.
25. Taleb Ibrahimi, *Mémoires*, 181; Quandt, *Revolution*, 224.
26. Zehouane interview (n.12).
27. Leca and Vatin, *L'Algérie politique*, 68–70.
28. Zbiri, *Un demi-siècle*, 119–20.
29. Proclamation du conseil de la révolution, 19 June 1965. *AAN* 1965, 627–29.
30. *AAN* 1965, 630–34.
31. The phrase 'televisual government' is Omar Carlier's.
32. Zehouane interview (n.12); Sadek Hadjerès, interview, Malakoff, 4 June 2009.
33. Zbiri, *Un demi-siècle*, 142–43.
34. Hadj Ali, *L'arbitraire*, 23, 12–13.
35. Hadjerès interview (n.32); on French views, see Chaliand, *L'Algérie est-elle socialiste?* (1964), cf. Martens, *Le modèle algérien* (1973).
36. Memo, Country Director, Office of Northern Africa Affairs (Root), Washington, to Deputy Assistant Secretary of State (Moore), 3 October 1968. *FRUS* 1964–68 vol. XXIV (Africa), doc. 39; Ghettas, 'Friendly foes', 47–48. Boumediene's confidant Messaoud Zghar apparently told the Swiss ambassador that Boumediene himself had denied any involvement in Krim's murder, which Zghar put down to business 'between arms traffickers' (Ghettas, 'Friendly foes', 80). To Ahmed Taleb, Boumediene later said only 'laconically' that the deaths of Khider and Krim had 'settled scores' (Taleb Ibrahimi, *Mémoires* vol. 2, 434).
37. The UGTA, created in 1956, was re-founded in 1963. Other organisations were the Union nationale des femmes algériennes (UNFA, 1963), Union nationale des paysans algériens (UNPA, 1973) and Union nationale de la jeunesse algérienne (UNJA, 1975).
38. 19 June proclamation (n.29), 628.
39. Bennoune, *Making of contemporary Algeria*, 90.
40. Tlemcani, *State and revolution*, 139–43; World Bank, Report no. 3018AL *Algeria: Recent economic developments and prospects* (3 October 1980), iii, 10–12, 17–18, 20–21.
41. Bennoune, *Making of contemporary Algeria*, 147, 194, 198–99; Ruedy, *Modern Algeria*, 219.
42. Bennoune, *Making of contemporary Algeria*, 216.
43. *AAN* 1980, 683.
44. World Bank, *Algeria: Recent economic developments* (n.40), 16.
45. Blanchard, *La police*, 234; Stora, *Ils venaient*, 143, 401–02.

46. Bennoune, *Making of contemporary Algeria*, 220, 224–27.
47. Knauss, 'Algeria's "Agrarian Revolution"'.
48. Bennoune, *Making of contemporary Algeria*, 141.
49. Account and extracts of Boumediene's speech, 19 June 1970, in *AAN* 1970, 252–53.
50. *Algérie Actualité*, 14–20 November 1965.
51. Address to the nation, 1 November 1972, quoted in *AAN* 1972, 744–47.
52. FLN, *Charte nationale*, 63–64.
53. Taleb Ibrahimi, *de la décolonisation à la révolution culturelle*, 26.
54. McDougall, *History and the culture of nationalism*.
55. Sanson, *Laïcité islamique*, Deheuvels, *Islam et pensée contemporaine*.
56. Hadjerès interview (n.32).
57. Slimane Chikh, interview, Bordj el Kiffan, July 2008.
58. Deheuvels, *Islam et pensée*, 239–40.
59. Hachemi Tidjani, *Humanisme musulman*, 4 (April 1965), 53. Tidjani was commenting on lectures by Roger Garaudy and Maxime Rodinson in Algiers, but the group also denounced the presence of foreign technical advisors.
60. Mokhtar Aniba, 'L'Algérie musulmane', *Humanisme musulman*, 5 (May 1965), 45.
61. For 'fundamentalism' in this period, see Deheuvels, *Islam et pensée contemporaine en Algérie*, 81–88. On *al-Qiyam*, see Hachemi Tidjani, 'L'Association al-Qiyam'. For relations between religion and state more generally, Courreye, 'L'Association des Oulémas', part 2.
62. Deheuvels, *Islam et pensée contemporaine*, 237.
63. *AAN* 1974, 391, *AAN* 1979, 676.
64. *AAN* 1972, 388.
65. Schade-Poulsen, *Men and popular music*; Daoudi and Miliani, *L'aventure du raï*; McMurray and Swedenburg, 'Raï tide rising'.
66. Aniba, 'L'Algérie musulmane', (n.60), 47–49.
67. Quoted in *AAN* 1970, 360.
68. Qasim, 'Al-inniyya wa'l-aṣāla', 4–5 (French)/11–12 (Arabic).
69. Quoted in *AAN* 1978, 459.
70. Summary of the affair in *AAN* 1978, 550–51. Dalila would eventually, three years later, be allowed to return to Montreal, where she declined to press charges against her kidnappers. *Montreal Gazette* 3 March 1981.
71. *AAN* 1981, 719; Pruvost, *Femmes d'Algérie*.
72. Qasim, 'Al-inniyya wa 'l-aṣāla' (n.68), 5–6 (French)/14 (Arabic).
73. Quoted (as 'Ounissi Zemmour'; probably Zhor Ounissi, a schoolteacher associated with the reformist *'ulama*) in *AAN* 1976, 361.
74. *AAN* 1970, 353–54.
75. Ibid., 349.
76. Taleb Ibrahimi, *De la décolonisation*, 19.
77. By the beginning of the 1973–74 school year, primary school teaching posts in French were fully 'Algerianised', that is, the remaining French *coopérants* were replaced with Algerian francophone teachers. By 1977, with the expansion of primary education, in which Arabisation had also proceeded furthest, there were 49,128 arabophone and 21,370 francophone teachers;

382 Notes to pages 267-272

1,316 arabophones were still hired from abroad, compared to only 264 francophone *coopérants*, only 34 of whom were non-Arabs (only 27 were French). Less Arabised, secondary education at the same time employed 22,605 teachers, 11,226 of whom were teaching in Arabic, 11,379 in French. Of the foreign secondary school personnel, 4,080 were reportedly arabophones and 2,795 francophones. *AAN* 1973, 479; *AAN* 1977, 634–35.

78. I owe these observations to Mustafa Haddab. Conversation in Algiers, July 2005.
79. See Goodman, *Berber culture*.
80. Quoted in *AAN* 1973, 483.
81. Taleb-Ibrahimi, *Les Algériens*, 233, 235.
82. Quoted in *AAN* 1978, 546.
83. *AAN* 1977, 635–39. On language policy, see Grandguillaume, *Arabisation*, Benrabah, *Langue et pouvoir* and *Language conflict*.
84. Chikh interview (n.57).
85. *AAN* 1979, 665, 667. Arabisation moved ahead again in 1981 with the introduction of the new, Arabised primary school, the *école fondamentale*; while based on the best current pedagogical thinking, the implementation of this system would be much criticised.
86. Quoted in *AAN* 1980, 679.
87. Quoted in *AAN* 1981, 710.
88. Boumediene's sudden illness and death from a rare blood cancer, diagnosed as Waldenström's disease, has never subsequently ceased to provoke conspiracy theories. Ahmed Taleb, himself a haematologist who was with Boumediene on his final trips to Damascus and Moscow, is ambivalent but inclines to the thesis of poisoning by Mossad (Taleb Ibrahimi, *Mémoires* vol. 2, 445–46). Other versions insist he was poisoned in Algeria by internal enemies.
89. Bennoune, 216, 253.
90. Taleb Ibrahimi, *Mémoires* vol. 2, 179. On social memory of the 1970s as experienced in the 2000s, see McAllister, 'Yesterday's tomorrow', 'Reimagining the *belle époque*'.
91. For scholarly arguments in this vein, see Bennoune, *Making of contemporary Algeria;* Roberts, *The Battlefield*.
92. Interview with a former official in the Boumediene and Chadli Presidencies, Algiers, May 2009.
93. Interview with a former official in Boumediene's Presidency, Algiers, May 2009.
94. It has been generally believed that Chadli joined the ALN after serving as a sergeant in the French army; in his memoirs, he denies having done so, while giving only a very vague account of the years in question (1952–55) (Bendjedid, *Mémoires* vol. 1, 65–73). At any rate, such early and riskier *ralliements* – Chadli joined the north Constantinois maquis in late 1955, as the post-August repression was raging – ought not to be confused with the much later, post-1958 defections, often from France or Germany to Tunisia or Morocco, of those ALN officers later identified as 'DAF' (*déserteurs de l'armée française*).

95. Bendjedid, *Mémoires* vol. 1, 170.
96. 'Algeria taking the slow road to change', *Financial Times* 1 August 1980, 3.
97. Taleb Ibrahimi, *Mémoires* vol. 2, 434–35.
98. Interviews with a former SOE director and a former Ministry of Planning official, Algiers, July 2007, May 2009.
99. *AAN* 1980, 686; *AAN* 1981, 719–20; Pruvost, *Femmes d'Algérie*; on opposition, Vince, *Fighting sisters*, 197–201.
100. Quoted in *AAN* 1982, 508.
101. Quoted in *AAN* 1972, 386; Taleb Ibrahimi, *De la décolonisation à le révolution culturelle*, 17.
102. *AAN* 1980, 687–89.
103. *AAN* 1981, 718.
104. 'L'appel du 12 novembre 1982', al-Ahnaf et al., *L'Algérie par ses islamistes*, 45–48.
105. Soltani, *Al-mazdakiyya hiya aṣl al-ishtirākiyya*.
106. Interview with a former SOE director, July 2007.
107. Interview with a former Ministry of Planning official, Algiers, May 2009.
108. Interview with a former SOE director, July 2007.
109. Ibid.; 'Algeria taking the slow road' (n.96).
110. Ghettas, 'Friendly foes'.
111. The subsequent abandonment, in straitened circumstances, of Chadli's big projects (especially the Algiers metro, which would not open until 2011), and the corruption associated with the Transmed project, later revealed by Italian *mani pulite* investigations, would add to Chadli's disrepute. At the time, however, economists considered the switch of focus from LNG to pipeline to be good sense, especially once Algeria's efforts in 1979–81 to align gas prices with those of oil (and thus, in 1979 prices, double them) led to years of tough negotiations ('Algeria's long, hard fight over gas prices', *Financial Times* 17 November 1982, 14). The Medgaz pipeline from Beni Saf to Almería would eventually open, also, in 2011.
112. Interview with a former Ministry of Planning official, Algiers, May 2009.
113. Interviews with a former SOE director and a former Ministry of Planning official, Algiers, July 2007, May 2009.
114. World Bank, *Algeria: Recent economic developments* (n.40), 21, 31.
115. Ghilès, 'La dette extérieure', 'L'armée'; *AAN* 1988, 576; World Bank report PIC3006, *Algeria: Structural adjustment loan* (December 1995); Lowi, *Oil wealth*; Abderrahmane Hadj Nacer (personal communication).
116. Mouloud Hamrouche, interview, Algiers, May 2009.
117. Interview with a member of the reform working group, Algiers, May 2009.
118. Hamrouche interview (n.116); Interview with a member of the reform working group, Algiers, May 2009.
119. Hadj Nacer, *Cahiers de la réforme*, no. 1, 27.
120. Ibid., 12.
121. Hadj Nacer, *Cahiers* no.1, 19–20, 36–7, no. 4, 87–103; interviews with Abderrahmane Hadj Nacer, May 2009, and other members of the reform working group, Algiers, June 2007, May 2009.
122. Interview with a member of the reform working group, Algiers, May 2009.

123. Hidouci, *Libération inachevée*, 130–32.
124. Interview with a member of the reform working group, Algiers, May 2009.
125. Ibid.
126. The official death toll was 169; other estimates vary between 150 and 500.
127. The latter explanation was insisted upon to the author by a former senior SM officer. Interview, 2016.
128. Abd al-Hamid Mehri, interview, Algiers, March 2007.
129. Charef, *Algérie*, 21–27.
130. Chikh interview (n.57).
131. Interview with a minister in the Hamrouche government, June 2007. This, and the following account, draws especially on interviews and informal conversations in Algeria (August 2001, July–August 2005, March–April and June 2007, May 2009); also Charef, *Algérie*, Hidouci, *Libération inachevée*, Hadj Nacer, *La martingale*, Dahmani, *L'Algérie à l'épreuve*, Lowi, *Oil wealth*.
132. Mehri interview (n.128), Hamrouche interview (n.116), Hadj Nacer interview (n.121), and interview with a member of the reform working group, Algiers, June 2007.
133. On the timing and significance of the FIS's legal recognition, see Chapter 7.
134. Abderrahmane Benamara, interview, El Biar, March 2007. (Benamara was the opposition '7+1' group's emissary to Abassi. The '7+1' was a projected anti-FLN alliance of seven smaller parties, plus Kasdi Merbah.)
135. Conversation with a former minister, Algiers, August 2001; interview with a former government official, Algiers, June 2007. See also Willis, *Islamist challenge*, 158–62, 173–79. For Nezzar's account, which instead paints a picture of an 'insurrectionary' strike poised to topple the regime, see Nezzar, *Mémoires*, 210–14.
136. Interview with a former member of the Hamrouche government, Algiers, June 2007.
137. Henni Benali, local government minister in the Hamrouche government, quoted in Charef, *Algérie*, 292.
138. Of 13.3 million registered voters, 41 per cent abstained from the polls and 7 per cent returned spoiled or blank ballots. Of the remaining 52 per cent (6.9 million voters), 3.26 million, 47.2 per cent of valid votes and 24.5 per cent of the total electorate, voted for the FIS (Fontaine, 'Les élections législatives').
139. Interview with a former member of the Hamrouche government, Algiers, June 2007.

7    The Fragile and Resilient Country, 1992–2012

1. Djaout, *Le dernier été*, 68, 120.
2. On the violence and controversies over accountability, see e.g. Martinez, *La guerre civile*, Moussaoui, *De la violence*, Lloyd, 'From taboo to transnational', Willis, *Islamist challenge*, Roberts, *Battlefield*, parts II, IV, Schatz, 'Algeria's ashes', Silverstein, 'An excess of truth', Souaïdia, *La sale guerre* and *Le procès*, Samraoui, *Chronique*, Haroun and Nezzar, *Algérie: échec*, Nezzar and Maarfia, *Le procès de*

*Paris*, Sisli, 'The western media and the Algerian crisis', Quandt, *Between ballots and bullets*, Pierre and Quandt, *The Algerian crisis*, Amnesty International report, 'Algeria: Civilian population caught in a spiral of violence', 18 November 1997, at www.amnesty.org/en/documents/mde28/023/1997/en/, and the websites of Algeria-Watch, www.algeria-watch.org/index_en.htm, and the dissident 'Algerian Free Officers' Movement', www.anp.org/index.html.

3. Interviews with ex-*Algérie Actualité* journalists, Algiers, and with several academics, Oran and Constantine, July–August 2005; Slimane Chikh, interview, Bordj el Kiffan, July 2008. For similar views expressed by one of Djaout's close friends and colleagues on *Ruptures*, see Arezki Metref, 'Suis-je vraiment Charlie?' *Le Soir d'Algérie* 11 January 2015, www .lesoirdalgerie.com/articles/2015/01/11/article.php?sid=173207&cid=8. For an Algerian Marxist analysis of the FIS as a fascist movement (and a critique of more superficial uses of that term), see Belalloufi, *La démocratie en Algérie*, 173–206.

4. For example, in October 1997 a group of Algerian intellectuals, including several prominent figures living in exile, signed a call for an international commission of inquiry into the violence in Algeria; this was repeated in February 2001 by a 'declaration of concerned scholars', signed by Pierre Bourdieu, Pierre Vidal-Naquet, and others, shortly before French Foreign Minister Hubert Védrine was due to visit Algeria. (*Le Monde*, 8 February 2001). This statement was opposed by a counter-declaration, 'Appel des intellectuels algériens contre la confusion et le défaitisme', published in Algerian dailies *Le Matin* and *La Tribune*, 22 March 2001. Conversations with signatories to the latter in Algeria, 2005, 2010, and with one of the signatories to the 1997 appeal, in France, 2006.

5. I owe this phrase to Judith Scheele.

6. Ordonnance 06–01, 'Charter for peace and national reconciliation', 28 Muharram 1427/27 February 2006, Art. 46. *JORA* 45/11, 28 February 2006.

7. Anthropologist Abderrahmane Moussaoui points out that 'the intensity of discourses on the violence has often corresponded to the levels of intensity of the violence itself' (Moussaoui, *De la violence*, 19). See especially Moussaoui, *De la violence*, 17–20; Silverstein, 'An excess of truth'.

8. I owe this phrase to Kamel Chachoua.

9. For this point in relation to 'conflict science' and the 'new wars' literature, see Mundy, *Imaginative geographies*. On political and economic transition, Werenfels, *Managing instability*, McDougall, 'After the war'.

10. At first, 'the black decade' was a term of opprobrium for the corruption and economic crisis of the 1980s (e.g. Bouamama, *Algérie, les racines de l'intégrisme*; Martinez, *La guerre civile*, 16–20). One early account of the 1990s referred to the latter decade as a 'red' decade (Aslaoui, *Les années rouges*). From around 2002, the term *la décennie noire* became attached to the 1990s, marking a first sense of the closure of a period as levels of violence reduced.

11. Belalloufi, *La démocratie*, 128.

12. Ali Benhadj in *El Munqidh* 23, quoted in Al-Ahnaf et al. (eds.), *L'Algérie par ses islamistes*, 87.

13. On the FIS and its antecedents, see Rouadjia, *Les frères*, Burgat, *L'islamisme*, Labat, *Les islamistes*, Al-Ahnaf et al. (eds.), *L'Algérie par ses islamistes*, Martinez, *Guerre civile*, ch.2, Bellaloufi, *La démocratie*, part 2, Willis, *Islamist challenge*, Roberts, *Battlefield*.

14. Conversations with former members and sympathisers of the FIS (aged in their early twenties in 1992), Oran and Tlemcen, 2007.

15. For a deeper analysis of these social divisions over time, see Rahal, 'Fused together and torn apart'.

16. Roberts, *Battlefield*, 82–104, 133–34, Willis, *Islamist challenge*, 120 and idem, *Politics and power*, 251. A variant of this reading is also advanced by the leading *janviériste* Khaled Nezzar (Nezzar, *Mémoires*, 173–78). For alternative accounts, Ghilès, 'L'armée', Aggoun and Rivoire, *Françalgérie*, ch.6. On the FIS' economic positions, see Al-Ahnaf et al. (eds.), *L'Algérie par ses islamistes*, 155–203.

17. Interview, Algiers, May 2009.

18. Aït Aoudia, 'La naissance du Front islamique du salut', 140–41.

19. The FIS's recognition is usually dated to September 6 (Aït Aoudia, 'Naissance', 129, Bellaloufi, *La démocratie*, 224, Aggoun and Rivoire, *Françalgérie*, 151, Samraoui, *Chronique*, 36), but alternatively, without a firm source in either case, to September 14 (Roberts, *Battlefield*, 368) or 16 (Willis, *Islamist challenge*, 119). Hamrouche was named head of government by decree on 9 September, and his ministers were named on 16 (Presidential decrees 89–171, 9 September 1989, 89–178, 16 September 1989. *JORA* no.28/40, 20 September 1989). The government's official bulletin, the *JORA*, began publishing announcements of the Interior Ministry's receipt of dossiers for the constitution of political associations only in August 1989 (*JORA* no.28/34, 16 August 1989), and announcements of *agréments* (authorisations) by the Interior Ministry often appeared several months after their signature, but neither the formal statement of the constitution of the FIS nor its *agrément* appeared in *JORA* between March 1989 and June 1990. Belkaïd, a former oppositionist linked to both the PRS and the FFS in the 1960s, was imprisoned in 1964 but recuperated into the bureaucracy after 1965 and in 1992 was a member of the group behind the creation of the HCE. Both Merbah and Belkaïd were subsequently assassinated, Merbah in August 1993, Belkaïd in September 1995.

20. Conversation in Oran, July 2005.

21. It bears repeating that the FIS' 'landslide' endorsement at the December 1992 polls, which would have given the party 81 per cent of the seats won in the first round from 47.2 per cent of valid votes cast, represented 24.5 per cent of the registered electorate, or 3.26 million voters, in a population of 27.5 million.

22. Of this group, only Gheziel, and the least well known of all, General 'Smaïn' Lamari, are said to have fought in the maquis during the revolution (in *wilaya*s 1 and 4, respectively).

23. Lakhal-Ayat was dismissed after October 1988; whether this was intended to pin blame on him for the uprising (by implying complicity between him and

Messaadia), or to punish his having failed to prevent it, can only be guessed
at. It does seem likely, as Aggoun and Rivoire suggest, that the effect, if not
the intention, served 'also – and especially – the consolidation of Larbi
Belkheir's hold on the real centre of power' (*Françalgérie*, 142). At the same
time, to add to the confusion, the DGPS was renamed DGDS, *Délégation
générale à la documentation et la sécurité*.

24. Interview with a former senior SM officer.
25. Nezzar, *Mémoires*, 218.
26. Rahmouna Carlier (a *fille de chahid*), interview, Paris, March 2008.
27. Redha Malek, interview, Sidi Frej, May 2009.
28. Mostefa Lacheraf, interview, Algiers, August 2001.
29. Its minister, in several cabinets in the mid-late 1990s, was Selim Saadi,
    another ANR founder who was an ALN veteran, career army officer after
    independence and Minister of Agriculture briefly in 1979.
30. Malek interview (n.27).
31. Abd al-Hamid Mehri, interview, Algiers, 25 March 2007 (Mehri was very
    critical of this view, which he opposed at the time); conversation with
    a former RCD militant, Tizi Ouzou, May 2007 (vigorously defending this
    view).
32. Malek interview (n.27).
33. Ibid.
34. Conversation with Salah Chekirou (the journalist in question), Algiers,
    August 2005.
35. Willis, *Islamist challenge*, 261–62.
36. Conversation in Oran, June 2007.
37. Willis, *Islamist challenge*, 227–28, 268–79.
38. Martinez, *La guerre civile*, 304–06, 314–16; Roberts, *Battlefield*, 153–54. For
    claims that the MIA (though not the MEI) was already in 1990 in the hands of
    the DRS – a notion lent credibility by the circumstantial evidence of the
    timing of the release of Chebouti and others from prison in mid–late 1990 –
    see Samraoui, *Chronique*, 76–95; 'Les généraux et le GIA', www.anp.org/fr/
    LesGenerauxEtLeGIA/LesGenerauxEtLeGIA3.html.
39. For different arguments on the (often much over-emphasised) *imaginaire* of
    war, see e.g. Martinez, *La guerre civile*, 23–32, Moussaoui, 'La guerre
    rejouée', Carlier, 'D'une guerre à l'autre', Stora, 'Algérie: Absence et
    surabondance', Remaoun, 'La question de l'histoire'.
40. The subsequent history of Djaballah and MNI would be instructive. Evinced
    from the party in 1998 by opponents who pressed for alliance with the RND,
    he founded a new party, the National Reform Movement (MRN) or *harakat
    al-islah*. Without him, Nahda became just another tiny faction. Then, during
    the 2007 legislative election campaign, Djaballah was ousted from Islah in
    a split that saw the party plummet at the polls from 43 seats to 3; Islah too
    then became irrelevant. In 2011, Djaballah announced yet another party, the
    Justice and Development Front (*jabhat al-'adala wa'l-tanmiya*).
41. On 'Algiers school' psychology, see Keller, *Colonial madness*.

42. Abderrahmane Benamara, interview, El Biar, March 2007. A 'Fondation Malek Bennabi' was registered with the authorities in 2005, but in 2007 had not received recognition.

43. Charef, *Algérie*, 293.

44. Ibid., 446–50.

45. Interviews with journalists, Algiers, July–August 2005.

46. Chikh interview (n.3). Warda, who made her career in Egypt where she gained a status alongside the greatest Arab singers, Umm Kulthum and Fayrouz, was born to an Algerian father and Lebanese mother in the Paris suburbs near Nanterre in 1939. She died in Cairo in 2012.

47. Martinez, *Guerre civile*, 154–59.

48. Ibid., 159–62, 214–28.

49. Quoted in Ibid., 122 (emphasis added).

50. FIS communiqué 39, quoted in Charef, *Algérie*, 386.

51. See e.g. Karima Bennoune, 'Algérie vingt ans plus tard: Les mots ne meurent pas', *openDemocracy* 24 June 2013 www.opendemocracy.net/5050/karima-bennoune/alg%C3%A9rie-vingt-ans-plus-tard-les-mots-ne-meurent-pas. Willis, *Islamist challenge*, 287, attributes the phrase to a reaction to the murder, seven days later, of Mohamed Boukhobza. In only one example of the local and familial divisions sown by the crisis, Anwar Haddam, from a large clerical family in Tlemcen, was the nephew of Tijani Haddam, Rector of the Paris Mosque and a member of the HCE.

52. In an October 2012 online interview, he repeated his original position, referring to the attack as a *facheux incident* (http://dzactiviste.info/entretien-exclusif-avec-a-haddam/).

53. Conversation with a former soldier who did military service in the Ouarsenis in the mid-1990s, Algiers, 2007.

54. The monastery had been founded in 1938 and the community maintained its presence throughout and after the war of independence. Prior Christian de Chergé, who had been in Algeria since the early 1970s, founded a spiritual circle, the *ribat al-salam*, to foster Muslim–Christian dialogue at Tibhirine in 1979.

55. Valerio Pellizzari, 'I monaci in Algeria uccisi dai militari', *La Stampa*, 6 July 2008; cf. Rivoire, *Le crime de Tibhirine*, and for an account of the official version, Balhi, *Tibhirine*. According to a source close to Smaïn Lamari (personal communication), Lamari admitted in private that the *La Stampa* version was closest to the truth: the monks were killed in a botched covert operation of which counter-insurgency forces in the same area were uninformed, and which was subsequently crudely covered up. The French anti-terror judge charged with an investigation in 2007, Marc Trévidic, was finally allowed into Algeria in October 2014; the monks' heads were exhumed and examined, but Trévidic's forensic experts were not allowed to transport their evidence to France for further examination, a move which the lawyer for the victims' families declared to be 'a kind of avowal of responsibility' by the Algerian authorities (*La Croix*, 23 October 2014, www.la-croix.com/Actualite/France/Moines-de-Tibehirine-les-familles-denoncent-une-confiscation-des-preuves-par-Alger-2014-10-23-1225765).

56. Mundy, *Imaginative geographies*, 1–5, 93–94.
57. See e.g. Souaïdia, *La sale guerre*, Yous, *Qui a tué à Bentalha?*, Bedjaoui et al., *Inquiry*, Fisk, *Great war*, 701–04, Rachid Khiari, '"Guerillas" with walkie-talkies herded Algerians to slaughter', *The Observer*, 4 January 1998. A former senior DRS officer (personal communication) insisted to the author that while the former hypothesis was undoubtedly correct – the GIA at this time were certainly manipulated, in some cases even led, by covert operations officers – the latter, that the massacres had been committed directly by 'disguised' DRS or special forces units, was certainly not. The same source asserted that much of this violence had been organised by factional networks, operating in their own interests, which, while having some leverage within the security services, also and especially operated outside the institutions of the state. None of this information, of course, can be attributed or verified.
58. Vince, *Fighting sisters*, 218; Mundy, *Imaginative geographies*, 3. The Bentalha story in this instance echoes 'the example of Tassadit', graphically recounted in an *El Moudjahid* article of 8 March 1982: the victim in the original story was the pregnant wife of a maquisard tortured and killed by *harkis* in Kabylia.
59. The parameters of this narrative in both these respects were especially visible in the museography of the *mathaf al-mujahid*, the museum devoted to the war of independence attached to the *maqam shahid* at Riyad al-Fath in Algiers, its cult of weaponry, of masculine 'popular [armed] resistance' and of degraded feminine victimhood (Fieldnotes, July–August 2005).
60. These narratives tropes were put to especially effective literary use by former army officer-turned-novelist Yasmina Khadra (the pen-name of Mohamed Moulessehoul) in his fictional accounts of the war that were especially well received in France and gained him an international reputation; see in particular Khadra, *Les agneaux du seigneur*.
61. By the mid-1990s, accounts of such tortures were becoming known outside the country through the press. In Britain, *The Observer*'s John Sweeney published especially harrowing accounts, e.g. 'Surviving Algeria', *The Observer*, 29 June 1997. See also Fisk, *Great war*, 683–85, 704–19.
62. Conversation with a former BMPJ officer, Algiers, June 2007. For a dramatising portrait of the BMPJ, see the photographs produced by Swiss photojournalist Michael von Graffenried, *Algérie, photographies*; for dissidents' testimonies, e.g. François Sergent, 'Un ninja dénonce la torture en Algérie', *Libération* 17 November 1997, John Sweeney, 'Atrocities in Algeria: We were the murderers who killed for the state', *The Observer*, 11 January 1998.
63. Quoted in Martinez, *Guerre civile*, 113.
64. On Boudiaf's assassination and the subsequent inquiry, see Charef, *Algérie*, 356–66.
65. Chikh interview (n.3).
66. Ibid.; Lacheraf interview (n.28).
67. Mehri interview (n.31).
68. Quoted in Willis, *Islamist challenge*, 312.
69. Mahiou, 'Note sur la constitution'.
70. On these elections, see Roberts, *Battlefield*, 191–99.
71. Malek interview (n.27).

72. Abbasi was re-arrested in September after writing to UN Secretary General Kofi Annan declaring his readiness to call for an end to hostilities and join a 'serious dialogue'.
73. For discussion see e.g. Martinez, *Guerre civile*, 11–16, cf. Roberts, *Battlefield*, 250–60.
74. For depoliticisation among former FIS supporters, see Martinez, *Guerre civile*, 337–45; after 2002 this was more generally visible throughout society (McDougall, 'After the war'; McAllister, 'Immunity').
75. Hadj Nacer, interview, Algiers, May 2009
76. Francis Ghilès (*Financial Times* North Africa correspondent, 1981–95), interview (telephone), January 2016.
77. Ahmed Benbitour, interview, Dély Ibrahim, May 2009. Benbitour resigned in 1996 and refused solicitations to stand for the RND in the 1997 elections; a supporter of Zeroual's institution-building, however, he agreed to be named to the Senate, where he presided over the finance commission.
78. McDougall, 'After the war'.
79. For generational change within the political elite, Werenfels, *Managing instability*.
80. In practice, paternal *autorisation de sortie* was still being enforced by policemen at Algiers airport in 2007–09.
81. See International Crisis Group, 'The civil concord: A peace initiative wasted'; Eric Goldstein, 'Algeria's amnesia decree', *OpenDemocracy.net* (10 April 2006).
82. Quoted in Dridi, *Alger*, 82.
83. A member of Khalifa's Paris social set quoted in *Time*, 14 September 2003.
84. Ibid.
85. Fieldnotes and conversations in Algiers, 2007.
86. Economist Intelligence Unit, July 23, 2007.
87. El Kseur platform, 11 June 2001, www.kabyle.com, updated 23 September 2001.
88. In 2013, the MAK became the Movement for Self-determination in Kabylia, promoting a more far-reaching goal of independence for a Kabyle state against the 'colonial power' in Algiers.
89. Fieldnotes, Oran, June 2007, Tolga, June 2008.
90. Conversation with former FIS militants and sympathisers, Oran, June 2007.
91. Self-immolations in Algeria were reported as early as May 2004. A list compiled on Wikipedia collected forty-five cases reported in the press between January and October 2011. See e.g. '2011 Algerian self-immolations', https://en.wikipedia.org/wiki/2011_Algerian_self-immolations (last modified 10 May 2015); 'Voyage dans l'Algérie des immolés', *El Watan*, 29 January 2012, retrieved from www.algeria-watch.org/fr/article/eco/soc/voyage_algerie_im moles.htm; 'Un homme d'une trentaine d'années s'est immolé jeudi à Chlef', *Le Matin Algérie*, 7 February 2014, www.lematindz.net/news/13571-un-homme-dune-trentaine-dannees-sest-immole-jeudi-a-chlef.html; 'Chômeurs, enseignants: L'immolation par le feu n'épargne personne en Algérie', *Algérie-Focus.com*, 24 February 2014, www.algerie-focus.com/2014/10/chomeurs-enseignants-limmolation-par-le-feu-nepargne-personne-en-algerie/.

92. 'Tizi Ouzou: Des milliers de retraités ont marché hier … ', *Liberté*, 29 November 2011; 'Violentes émeutes à Mostaganem', and 'Boumerdès : Les étudiants de l'UMBB en grève illimitée', *El Watan*, 29 November 2011; 'Des travailleurs poursuivent leur grève de la faim', 'Draa el Mizan: Les résidants du lotissement nord protestent', and 'Boumerdès: La RN24 fermée par les habitants de Boukerroucha', *El Watan*, 10 November 2011.

93. 'Nacer Djabi: "'La génération de novembre doit passer le relais"'', *El Watan*, 21 June 2011; 'Si la génération "tab j'nanou" refuse d'organiser son départ … ', *El Watan*, 8 June 2012, at www.algeria-watch.org/fr/article/tribune/djabi_generation_tab_jnanou.htm; Djabi, *Li-madha ta'akhkhara al-rabiʿ al-jaza'iri?* The expression *tab jnanou*, literally 'its garden has ripened', refers to something having passed its time. Bouteflika used the phrase in a widely commented speech in Setif on 8 May 2012, when he said, to general surprise, *Jili tab jnanu, tab jnanu, tab jnanu* ('The time of my generation is done, done, done').

94. Presidential elections were held in September 1999, April 2004, April 2009 and April 2014.

95. Werenfels, *Managing instability*, 69, 79–118.

96. US diplomats noted as much in 2009, during Belkheir's prolonged illness. 'Biology favors Bouteflika on election eve', Daughton, Algiers, to Secretary of State, 23 March 2009, 09ALGIERS278_a, at https://wikileaks.org/plusd/cables/09ALGIERS278_a.html.

97. 'Apaisement en Algérie après les émeutes contre la hausse des prix', *Le Point* (Reuters) 10 January 2011, at www.lepoint.fr/monde/apaisement-en-algerie-apres-les-emeutes-contre-la-hausse-des-prix-10-01-2011-128578_24.php.

98. 'Les étudiants forcent le passage', *El Watan* 13 April 2011.

99. 'Malgré les augmentations consenties, la fonction publique reste en ébullition', *Liberté* 10 November 2011.

100. 'Un premier pas pour le changement', *El Watan* 13 February 2011.

101. While Bouteflika's younger brother Saïd was widely thought to be preparing for the succession, this was not at this stage thought likely to happen, and seemed to have met firm opposition within the system.

102. I am especially grateful to Bob Parks and Mohamed Hachemaoui for discussion of this point. See e.g. Roberts, 'Moral polity', Goodman, 'The man behind the curtain', Hachemaoui, 'Y-at-il des tribus?', Parks, 'Public goods and service provision'.

103. Hachemaoui, *Clientélisme et patronage*.

104. By 2010, 20.8 per cent of the population was aged between 15 and 24, i.e. born between 1986 and 1995; another 27.1 per cent of the population, aged under 15, had been born mostly since the peak of the conflict in the mid-1990s. 'Demographic profile of Algeria', UN-ESCWA data, at www.escwa.un.org/popin/members/algeria.pdf.

105. Mouffok, 'La révolution de onze heures à midi', circulated by email, 16 February 2011, publ. at www.ism-france.org/analyses/La-revolution-de-onze-heures-a-midi-article-15115, 18 February 2011.

106. Quoted in personal communication, 14 February 2011; Parks, 'Algeria and the Arab Uprisings', 115.
107. Mehri interview (n.31).
108. Ibid.

## Afterword: In the Shadow of Revolution (2016)

1. This was particularly the case of Amar Saïdani, secretary general of the FLN since 2013, whose sorties against the DRS were widely seen as reactions to the agency's own (no doubt equally opportunistic) widely mediatised investigations into corruption involving some of those close to Bouteflika, especially the President's younger brother Saïd, a close ally and patron of Saïdani.
2. *El Watan*, 14 September 2015.
3. 'Algérie: La machine de mort, 3: Les centres de détention secrète ...', October 2003, at www.algeria-watch.org/fr/mrv/mrvtort/machine_mort/machine_mort_rapport_3.htm.
4. 'Athmane Tartag, l'oeil d'El-Mouradia', *Jeune Afrique* 9 October 2014; 'Athmane Tartag: Un "bombardier" à la tête du DRS', *El Watan* 14 September 2015.
5. 'Algerian hostage crisis could weaken veteran spymaster', *The Guardian*, 25 January 2015, at www.theguardian.com/world/2013/jan/25/algerian-hostage-crisis-tewfik-mediene. On In Amenas, see www.theguardian.com/world/interactive/2013/jan/25/algeria-hostage-crisis-full-story (25 January 2013). Having been formerly Tewfik's 'right-hand man', in the drawn-out succession struggle from 2011 onwards he appears to have returned to favour, to a post at the Presidency and then to the direction of the DRS, through Saïd Bouteflika's attempt to counter the DRS and shore up his own position at the head of the 'presidential clan'.
6. The great exception to this pattern, the Algerian Foreign Ministry and its diplomatic corps, which despite the protracted impasse in domestic politics was able, in 2011–14, to reposition Algeria as once again a major arbiter in the region, between the collapse of Libya, the near-collapse of Mali and the troubled transition in Tunisia, is all the more remarkable in this context. Since the wartime establishment of the FLN's foreign relations, indeed, skilled diplomacy abroad has been as consistent a characteristic of Algeria's political class as has factional sclerosis at home.
7. 'An ailing and fragile Algerian regime drifts into 2008.' Ford, Algiers, to Secretary of State, 19 December 2007, 07ALGIERS1806_a, at https://wikileaks.org/plusd/cables/07ALGIERS1806_a.html; 'Boutflika's army: Civilian control at what price?' Pearce, Algiers, to Secretary of State, 13 January 2009, 09ALGIERS35_a, at https://wikileaks.org/plusd/cables/09ALGIERS35_a.html. I owe the image of *le pouvoir* as a 'black hole' to an Algerian colleague. Conversation in Algiers, May 2009.
8. 'La police politique: Mirage et réalité', *El Watan*, 14 September 2015. The various press sorties, sometimes mutually vituperative, of former DRS officers Hichem Aboud and Mohamed Samraoui, both authors in

2002 and 2003 of books denouncing the state's complicity in violence attributed to the GIA, and both, from 2012, involved in factional politics once back in Algeria (with Aboud campaigning against Saïd Bouteflika, Samraoui allegedly – an allegation he denied – having been 'recuperated' by Bouteflika's faction), illustrated the extent to which the service's most prominent former dissidents, neither of whom denied that they subsequently remained in touch with their former colleagues, had become part of the game around the succession crisis, something inconceivable a decade earlier, though both were then already at odds over their respective credentials.

9. Videos quickly circulated online. See e.g. the YouTube channel ath hamdoune.fr.
10. Exhibition notes, 'Intervening Space', Mosaic Rooms, London, May–June 2014.
11. Qur'an 8.10.
12. The bronze figure of *La France*, kneeling with the colours in her hand, originally placed at the base of the Sidi Brahim monument, was removed to the village of Périssac in south-western France in 1966, shortly before the statuary of Oran's 1914–18 war memorial was transferred to Lyon.
13. The allegorical statue of law, a monument to the 1848 constitution set up in 1850, still stands near the courthouse. The first chapel of Our Lady of Salvation was built below Santa Cruz in 1850, after the 1849 cholera epidemic; the present tower and basilica were built on the same site in the midst of the war, between 1956 and 1959.

# Bibliography

## Interviews

*Only those interviewees cited by name in endnotes are listed.*

Abderrahmane Benamara. b. 1952. Student of Malek Bennabi. Co-founder, PRA 1990. El Biar, 18 March 2007.

Ahmed Benbitour. b. 1946. Treasury Minister 1992, Energy Minister 1993, Finance Minister 1994–97, Prime Minister 1999–2000. Dely Ibrahim, 25 May 2009.

Rahmouna Carlier. b. 1949. Schoolteacher in Oran 1960s–80s, daughter of an FLN militant killed in custody in 1957. Paris, 29 March 2008.

Slimane Chikh. b. 1930. Rector, University of Algiers 1982–84, Minister of Education 1988–89, 1996, Minister of Culture 1994, Member, Conseil de la Nation 1997. Bordj el Kiffan, 6 July 2008.

Abderrahmane Hadj Nacer. b. 1951. Governor of the Central Bank of Algeria 1989–92. Algiers, 25, 29 May 2009.

Sadek Hadjerès. b. 1928. PPA militant, AEMAN President 1949, PCA central committee member 1952, principal clandestine leader, PAGS 1966–89. Malakoff, 4 June 2009.

Mouloud Hamrouche. b. 1943. ALN (W2) 1958, detached to protocol office at Presidency, 1968, Director of protocol 1979, FLN central committee member, Secretary General of the government 1984, Secretary General at Presidency 1986, Prime Minister 1989–91. Algiers, 27 May 2009.

Mostefa Lacheraf. b. 1917. PPA, FLN militant, hijacked with FLN external leadership 1956, member of the preparatory commissions, Tripoli program 1962, National Charter 1976, Ambassador to Argentina, Education Minister 1977, Ambassador to Mexico, Peru, member, CNC 1992, co-founder, ANR 1995. Algiers, 11 August 2001.

Redha Malek. b. 1931. FLN militant, founder member UGEMA 1955, editor of *El Moudjahid* 1957–62, spokesman for the Algerian delegation at Évian 1961–62, member of the preparatory commissions, Tripoli program 1962, National Charter 1976, Ambassador to Yugoslavia, France, USSR, Minister of Information and Culture 1977, Ambassador to USA, UK, President of the CNC, member of the HCE 1992, Foreign Minister 1993, Prime Minister 1993–94, co-founder ANR 1995. Sidi Fredj, 26 May 2009.

Mohamed Mechati. b. 1921. PPA militant, OS zone commander 1945–50, member of the 'committee of 21' 1954. FFFLN organiser 1955, imprisoned in France 1956–61. Algiers, 21 March 2007.

Abdelhamid Mehri. b. 1926. PPA militant, student liaison with Neo-Destour in Tunis 1948, MTLD central committee member 1953, arrested November 1954, FLN representative in Damascus 1955, CNRA member 1956, CCE member 1957, Minister of Arab Maghrib Affairs in 1st GPRA 1958, Minister of Social and Cultural Affairs in 2nd GPRA 1960–61, Secretary General of the Education Ministry 1970–77, FLN central committee member, Minister of Information and Culture 1979, Ambassador to France, Morocco, FLN Secretary General 1988–96. Algiers, 25 March 2007.

Muhammad Brahim Zeddour. b. 1923. UDMA militant. Son of shaykh Tayyib al-Mehadji, brother of a PPA militant killed in custody, November 1954. Oran, 5 June 2007.

Hocine Zehouane. b. 1939. MTLD militant, imprisoned 1955–57, ALN (W3) 1957–60, ALN in Tunisia 1960–62, FLN Greater Algiers Federation 1962, member of the preparatory commission of the Algiers Charter and the FLN political bureau 1964, co-founder ORP 1965. Imprisoned 1965–71, under house arrest 1971–73, exile in France 1973–81, lawyer, Vice-President, President LADDH. Algiers, 4 June 2008.

## Published Primary and Secondary Sources

Ferhat Abbas *La nuit coloniale* Paris, Julliard, 1962

*Autopsie d'une guerre: L'aurore* Paris, Garnier, 1980

*De la colonie vers la province: Le jeune Algérien* Paris, Garnier, 1981 [1931]

*L'indépendance confisquée* Paris, Flammarion, 1984

Osama Abi Mershed *Apostles of modernity: Saint-Simonians and the civilizing mission in Algeria* Stanford, CA, Stanford University Press, 2010

Michel Abitbol *Les juifs d'Afrique du nord sous Vichy* (2nd ed.), Paris, CNRS, 2008

Janet L. Abu-Lughod 'The Islamic city – Historic myth, Islamic essence, and contemporary relevance', *International Journal of Middle East Studies* 19, 2 (May 1987), 155–76

Jamil M. Abun-Nasr *A history of the Maghrib in the Islamic period* Cambridge, Cambridge University Press, 1987

Nadjib Achour 'Entre tradition et réforme: L'expérience de l'Association des Oulémas dans le département de Constantine (1940–1954)', 2 vols., doctoral diss., Université de Paris-VII (Jussieu), 2014

Charles-Robert Ageron 'Le mouvement "Jeune Algérien" de 1900 à 1923', pp. 217–43 in Jacques Berque et al, *Études maghrébines: Mélanges Charles-André Julien* Paris, PUF, 1964

'L'Emir Khaled, petit-fils d'Abdelkader, fut-il le premier nationaliste algérien?' *Revue de l'Occident musulman et de la Méditerranée* 2 (1966), 9–49

'L'émigration des musulmans algériens et l'exode de Tlemcen (1830–1911)', *Annales ESC* 22, 3 (1967), 1047–66

*Les Algériens musulmans et la France, 1871–1919* (2 vols.), Paris, PUF, 1968

'Ferhat 'Abbâs et l'évolution politique de l'Algérie musulmane pendant la deuxième guerre mondiale', *Revue d'histoire maghrébine* 4 (July 1975), 125–44

*Histoire de l'Algérie contemporaine (vol. 2): de l'insurrection de 1871 au déclenchement de la guerre de libération (1954)* Paris, PUF, 1979

'Les troubles du nord-constantinois en mai 1945: Une tentative insurrectionnelle?' *Vingtième siècle: Revue d'histoire* 4 (October 1984), 23–38

'Les pertes humaines de la guerre d'Algérie', *La France en guerre d'Algérie*, Paris, Musée d'histoire conemporaine/BDIC, 1992

'Un manuscrit inédit de Ferhat Abbas: "Mon testament politique"', *Revue française d'histoire d'Outre Mer* 303 (1994), 181–97

'Les supplétifs algériens dans l'armée française pendant la guerre d'Algérie', *Vingtième Siècle: Revue d'histoire* 48 (October–December 1995), 3–20

'L'insurrection du 20 août 1955 dans le Nord-Constantinois: De la résistance armée à la guerre du peuple', pp. 27–50 in Ch-R. Ageron (ed), *La guerre d'Algérie et les Algériens, 1954–1962* Paris, Armand Colin, 1997

'Complots et purges dans l'armée de libération algérienne (1958–1961)', *Vingtième siècle: Revue d'histoire* 59 (July–September 1998), 15–27

'Une troisième force combattante pendant la guerre d'Algérie. L'armée nationale du peuple algérien et son chef le "général" Bellounis, mai 1957–juillet 1958', *Revue française d'histoire d'outre-mer* 321 (1998), 65–76

Charles-Robert Ageron (ed), *L'Algérie des Français* Paris, Le Seuil/L'Histoire, 1993

Lounis Aggoune and Jean-Baptiste Rivoire *Françalgérie: Crimes et mensonges d'États: Histoire secrète, de la guerre d'indépendance à la 'troisième guerre' d'Algérie* Paris, La Découverte, 2004

Hocine Aït Ahmed *La guerre et l'après-guerre* Paris, Éditions de Minuit, 1964

Myriam Aït Aoudia 'La naissance du Front islamique du salut: Une politisation conflictuelle (1988–1989)', *Critique internationale* 30 (2006), 129–44

Mustafa al-Ahnaf, Bernard Botiveau, and Franck Frégosi *L'Algérie par ses islamistes* Paris, Karthala, 1991

André Akoun *Né à Oran: Autobiographie en troisième personne* Paris, Bouchene, 2004

Algeria. FLN *La charte d'Alger: Ensemble des textes adoptés par le 1er congrès du parti du Front de Libération Nationale* Algiers, Imprimerie Nationale Algérienne, 1964

*Charte nationale 1976* Algiers, Éditions populaires de l'armée, 1976

Algeria. Provisional Government (GPRA) *Tous Algériens* Tunis, 1961

*Les enfants d'Algérie: Témoignages et dessins d'enfants réfugiés en Tunisie, en Libye et au Maroc* Paris, Maspéro, 1962

Henri Alleg *La question* Paris, Éditions de Minuit, 1961

Malek Alloula *The colonial harem* Manchester, Manchester University Press, 1987

Redouane Aïned-Tabet 'Le 8 mai 1945: Jacquerie ou revendication agraire', *Revue algérienne des sciences juridiques, économiques et politiques* 9, 4 (December 1972), 1000–16

*Le mouvement du 8 mai 1945 en Algérie* (2nd rev. ed.), Algiers, OPU, 1987

Fadhma Aïth Mansour Amrouche *Histoire de ma vie* Paris, La Découverte, 2000 [1968]
Djamila Amrane-Minne *Des femmes dans la guerre d'Algérie: Entretiens* Paris, Karthala, 1994
Sossie Andezian 'Mysticisme extatique dans le champ religieux algérien contemporain', pp. 323–28 in Sophie Ferchiou (ed), *L'Islam pluriel au Maghreb* Paris, CNRS, 1996
*Expériences du divin dans l'Algérie contemporaine: Adeptes des saints dans la région de Tlemcen* Paris, CNRS, 2001
Leila Aslaoui *Les années rouges* Algiers, Casbah, 2000
Paul Aussaresses *Services spéciaux, Algérie 1955–57* Paris, Perrin, 2001
Paul Azan *L'émir Abd el Kader, 1808–1883: Du fanatisme musulman au patriotisme français* Paris, Hachette, 1925
(ed), *Par l'épée et par la charrue: Écrits et discours de Bugeaud* Paris, PUF, 1948
Mahieddine Bachetarzi *Mémoires 1919–1939: Suivi de 'Étude sur le théâtre dans les pays islamiques'* Algiers, SNED, 1968
Joëlle Bahloul *The architecture of memory: A Jewish-Muslim household in colonial Algeria, 1937–1962* Cambridge, Cambridge University Press, 1996
Mohamed Balhi *Tibhirine, the kidnapping of the monks* Beirut, Dar al-Farabi, 2002
Marc Baroli *La vie quotidienne des Français en Algérie, 1830–1914* Paris, Hachette, 1967
Youcef Bedjaoui, Abbas Aroua, and Méziane Aït-Larbi (eds), *An inquiry into the Algerian massacres* Geneva, Hoggar, 1999
Mabrouk Belhocine *Le courrier Alger-le Caire, 1954–1956: Le congrès de la soummam dans la révolution* Algiers, Casbah, 2000
James Belich *Replenishing the earth: The settler revolution and the rise of the Anglo-world, 1783–1939* Oxford, Oxford University Press, 2009
Hocine Bellaloufi *La démocratie en Algérie, réforme ou révolution? Sur la crise algérienne et les moyens d'en sortir* Algiers, APIC, 2012
Alexandre Bellemare *Abd-el-Kader, sa vie politique et militaire* Paris, Bouchene, 2003 [1863]
Rachid Bellil *Les oasis du Gourara, Sahara algérien* (3 vols.) Louvain, Peeters, 1999–2000
Abd el-Hadi Ben Mansour *Alger, XVIè-XVIIè siècle: Journal de Jean-Baptiste Gramaye, 'évêque d'Afrique'* Paris, Les Éditions du Cerf, 1998
Bartolomé Bennassar and Lucile Bennassar *Les chrétiens d'Allah: L'histoire extraordinaire des renégats, XVIe et XVIIe siècles* Paris, Perrin, 1989
Chérif Benhabylès *L'Algérie française vue par un indigène* Algiers, Imprimerie orientale Fontana, 1914
Chadli Benjedid *Mémoires, t.1: 1929–1979* Algiers, Casbah, 2012
Amira K. Bennison *Jihad and its interpretations in pre-colonial Morocco: State-society relations during the French conquest of Algeria* London, Routledge, 2002
Mahfoud Bennoune *El-Akbia: Un siècle d'histoire algérienne, 1857–1975* Algiers, OPU, 1986
*The making of contemporary Algeria, 1830–1987: Colonial upheavals and post-independence development* Cambridge, Cambridge University Press, 1988

Yves Benot *Massacres coloniaux, 1944–1950: La IVème République et la mise au pas des colonies françaises* Paris, La Découverte, 2005

Mohamed Benrabah *Langue et pouvoir en Algerie: histoire d'un traumatisme linguistique* Paris, Séguier, 1999

*Language conflict in Algeria: From colonialism to post-independence* Bristol, Multiligual Matters, 2013

Jacques Berque 'Ça et là dans les débuts du réformisme religieux au Maghreb', pp. 471–94 in Jacques Berque et al (eds), *Études d'orientalisme dédiées à la mémoire de Lévi-Provençal* (2 vols.), Paris, Maisonneuve et Larose, 1962

'Qu'est-ce qu'une "tribu" nord-africaine?' pp. 22–34 in Jacques Berque, *Maghreb, histoire et sociétés* Algiers, SNED, 1974

*L'intérieur du Maghreb, XV^ème – XIX^ème siècles* Paris, Gallimard, 1978

*Le Maghreb entre deux guerres* (3rd rev. ed.), Paris, Seuil, 1979 [1962]

Abderrahmane Berrouane *Aux origines du MALG: Témoignage d'un compagnon de Boussouf* Algiers, Barzakh, 2015

Mohand-Aarav Bessaoud *Heureux les martyrs qui n'ont rien vu* Paris, Éditions Berbères, 1991 [1963]

Raymond Betts *Assimilation and association in French colonial theory, 1890–1914* New York, NY, Columbia University Press, 1961

Jean Bisson *Mythes et réalités d'un désert convoité: Le Sahara* Paris, L'Harmattan, 2003

Emmanuel Blanchard *La police parisienne et les Algériens, 1944–1962* Paris, Nouveau monde, 2011

Emmanuel Blanchard and Sylvie Thénault 'Quel "monde du contact" ? Pour une histoire sociale de l'Algérie pendant la période coloniale', *Le mouvement social* 236 (2011), 3–7

Laure Blévis 'Les avatars de la citoyenneté en Algérie coloniale ou les paradoxes d'une catégorisation', *Droit et société* 48 (2001/2), 557–81

'Sociologie d'un droit colonial. Citoyenneté et nationalité en Algérie (1865–1947), une exception républicaine?' doctoral diss., Institut d'Etudes Politiques, Aix-en-Provence, 2004

'L'invention de l'"indigène", Français non citoyen', pp. 212–18 in Bouchène et al (eds), *Histoire de l'Algérie à la période coloniale*

'Quelle citoyenneté pour les Algériens?', pp. 352–58 in Bouchène et al (eds), *Histoire de l'Algérie à la période coloniale*

Saïd Bouamama *Algérie, les racines de l'intégrisme* Brussels, EPO, 2000

Abderrahmane Bouchène, Jean-Pierre Peyroulou, Ounassa Siari Tengour, and Sylvie Thénault (eds), *Histoire de l'Algérie à la période coloniale (1830–1962)* Paris, La Découverte/Algiers, Barzakh, 2012

Saïd Boualam *Les harkis au service de la France* Paris, Éditions France-Empire, 1963

Hadri Bougherara *Voyage sentimental en musique arabo-andalouse* Paris, Edif, 2000

Kamel Bouguessa *Aux sources du nationalisme algérien: Les pionniers du populisme révolutionnaire en marche* Algiers, Casbah, 2000

Pierre Bourdieu *Sociologie de l'Algérie* Paris, PUF, 1958

*Outline of a theory of practice* Cambridge, Cambridge University Press, 1977

Pierre Bourdieu and Abdelmalek Sayad *Le déracinement: La crise de l'agriculture traditionnelle en Algérie* Paris, Éditions de Minuit, 1964

Jacques Bouveresse *Un parlement colonial? Les délégations financières algériennes, 1898–1945* (2 vols.), Mont-Saint-Aignan, Publications des universités de Rouen et du Havre, 2008–10

Pierre Boyer *La vie quotidienne à Alger à la veille de l'intervention française* Paris, Hachette, 1963

Joan Brace and Richard Brace *Algerian voices* Princeton, NJ, Van Nostrand, 1965

Raphaëlle Branche *La torture et l'armée dans la guerre d'Algérie, 1954–62* Paris, Gallimard, 2001

'La torture pendant la guerre d'Algérie', pp. 381–401 in Mohammed Harbi and Benjamin Stora (eds), *La guerre d'Algérie, 1954–2004: La fin de l'amnésie* Paris, Robert Laffont, 2004

*L'embuscade de Palestro: L'Algérie 1956* Paris, Armand Colin, 2010

Michael Brett 'Ibn Khaldun and the Arabisation of North Africa', *The Maghreb Review* 4, 1 (January–February 1979), 9–16

'Legislating for inequality in Algeria: The Senatus-Consulte of 14 July 1865', *Bulletin of the School of Oriental and African Studies* 51 (1988), 440–61

Benjamin C. Brower *A desert named peace: The violence of France's empire in the Algerian Sahara, 1844–1902* New York, NY, Columbia University Press, 2009

'Les violences de la conquête', pp. 58–63 in Bouchène et al (eds), *Histoire de l'Algérie à la période coloniale*

François Burgat *L'islamisme au Maghreb: La voix du Sud (Tunisie, Algérie, Libye, Maroc)* Paris, Karthala, 1988

Edmund Burke III *The ethnographic state: France and the invention of Moroccan Islam* Berkeley, CA, University of California Press, 2014

Jeffrey James Byrne 'The pilot nation: An international history of revolutionary Algeria, 1958–1965', PhD diss., London School of Economics, 2010

*Mecca of revolution: Algeria, decolonization, and the Third World order* Oxford, Oxford University Press, 2015

Albert Camus *Le premier homme* Paris, Gallimard, 1994

Jacques Cantier *L'Algérie sous le régime de Vichy* Paris, Jacob, 2002

Jean-Louis (Omar) Carlier 'La première Étoile Nord-Africaine (1926–1929)', *Revue algérienne des sciences juridiques, économiques et politiques* 9, 4 (December 1972), 907–66

Omar Carlier 'La production sociale de l'image de soi: Note sur la "crise berbériste" de 1949', *AAN* 23 (1984), 347–71

'Les traminots algérois des années 1930: Un groupe social médiateur et novateur', *Le mouvement social* 146 (January–March 1989), 61–89

'Le café maure: Sociabilité masculine et effervescence citoyenne (Algérie XVIIè–XXè siècles)', *Annales ESC* 45, 4 (1990), 975–1001

*Entre nation et jihad: Histoire sociale des radicalismes algériens* Paris, FNSP, 1995

'D'une guerre à l'autre: le redéploiement de la violence entre soi', *Confluences Méditerranée* 25 (Spring 1998), 123–37

'Medina and modernity: The emergence of muslim civil society in Algiers between the two world wars', ch. 2 in Zeynep Çelik, Julia Clancy-Smith, and Frances Terpak (eds), *Walls of Algiers: Narratives of the City through text and image*, Seattle, WA, Washington University Press, 2009

Eugène Cavaignac *De la Régence d'Alger (Notes sur l'occupation)* Paris, Victor Magen, 1839

Zaynep Çelik *Urban forms and colonial confrontations: Algiers under French rule* Berkeley, CA, University of California Press, 1997

Kamel Chachoua *L'Islam kabyle: Religion, état et société en Algérie* Paris, Maisonneuve et Larose, 2001

El Hadi Chalabi 'Un juriste en quête de modernité: Benali Fekar', *Naqd* 11 (1998), 41–58

Gérard Chaliand *L'Algérie est-elle socialiste?* Paris, Maspéro, 1964

Abed Charef *Algérie, le grand dérapage* Paris, Éditions de l'Aube, 1994

Stéphanie Chauvin 'Des appelés pas comme les autres? Les conscrits "français de souche nord-africaine" pendant la guerre d'Algérie', *Vingtième Siècle: Revue d'histoire* 48 (October–December 1995), 21–30

Tayyeb Chenntouf 'Un document indédit sur le 8 mai 1945 dans le Constantinois: Le rapport du Général Tubert', *Revue algérienne des sciences juridiques, économiques et politiques* 11, 4 (December 1974), 289–16

Achour Cheurfi *La classe politique algérienne de 1900 à nos jours: Dictionnaire biographique* Algiers, Casbah, 2001

Slimane Chikh *L'Algérie en armes, ou le temps des certitudes* (2nd rev. ed.), Algiers, Casbah, 2005

Allan Christelow 'Algerian Islam in a time of transition, c.1890–c.1930', *The Maghreb Review* 8, 5–6 (1983), 124–29

*Muslim Law Courts and the French Colonial State in Algeria* Princeton, NJ, Princeton University Press, 1985

Julia A. Clancy-Smith 'Saints, mahdis and arms: Religion and resistance in nineteenth-century North Africa', ch. 4 in Edmund Burke III and Ira Lapidus (eds), *Islam, politics and social movements* Berkeley, CA, University of California Press, 1988

*Rebel and saint: Muslim notables, populist protest, colonial encounters (Algeria and Tunisia, 1800–1904)* Berkeley, CA, University of California Press, 1994

'The Maghrib and the Mediterranean world in the nineteenth century: Illicit exchanges, migrants, and social marginals', pp. 222–39 in Michel Le Gall and Kenneth Perkins (eds), *The Maghrib in question: Essays in history and historiography*, Austin, TX, University of Texas Press, 1997

*Mediterraneans: North Africa and Europe in an age of migration, c.1800–1900* Berkeley, CA, University of California Press, 2011

Hannah-Louise Clark 'Doctoring the *bled*: Medical auxiliaries and the administration of rural life in colonial Algeria 1904–54', PhD diss., Princeton University, 2014

Joshua Cole 'Anti-Semitism and the colonial situation in interwar Algeria: Anti-Jewish riots in Constantine (August 1934)', *Vingtième siècle: Revue d'histoire* 108, 4 (2010), 3–23

'Constantine before the riots of August 1934: Civil status, anti-Semitism, and the politics of assimilation in interwar French Algeria', *Journal of North African Studies* 17, 5 (2012), 839–61

Claude Collot 'Le régime juridique de la presse musulmane algérienne (1881–1962)', *Revue algérienne des sciences juridiques, économiques et politiques* 6, 2 (June 1969), 343–405

'Le Parti du peuple algérien (mars 1937–février 1947)', *Revue algérienne des sciences juridiques, économiques et politiques* 8, 1 (March 1971), 133–204

'L'Union populaire algérienne (1937–39)', *Revue algérienne des sciences juridiques, économiques et politiques* 9, 4 (December 1972), 967–1005

'Le Front algérien pour la défense et le respect de la liberté', *Revue algérienne des sciences juridiques, économiques et politiques* 14, 3 (1977), 355–41

Claude Collot *Les institutions de l'Algérie durant la Période coloniale (1830–1962)* ed., intro. Jean-Robert Henry and Ahmad Mahiou, Paris, CNRS/Algiers, OPU, 1987

Claude Collot and Jean-Robert Henry (eds), *Le mouvement national algérien, Textes 1912–1954* Paris, L'Harmattan, 1978

Fanny Colonna *Instituteurs algériens, 1883–1939* Paris, FNSP, 1975

*Les versets de l'invincibilité: Permanence et changements religieux dans l'Algérie contemporaine* Paris, FSNP, 1995

*Le meunier, les moines et le bandit: Des vies quotidiennes dans l'Aurès (Algérie) du XXè siècle. Récits* Paris, Sindbad, 2010

Matthew Connelly *A diplomatic revolution: Algeria's fight for independence and the origins of the post-Cold War era* Oxford, Oxford University Press, 2002

Frederick Cooper *Citizenship between empire and nation: Remaking France and French Africa, 1945–1960* Princeton, NJ, Princeton University Press, 2014

Catherine Coquery-Vidrovitch 'Nationalité et citoyenneté en Afrique occidentale française: Originaires et citoyens dans le Sénégal colonial', *Journal of African History* 42, 2 (July 2001), 285–305

Michel Cornaton *Les regroupements de la décolonisation en Algérie* Paris, Éditions ouvrières, 1967

Vincent J. Cornell *The way of Abu Madyan: Doctrinal and poetic works of Abū Madyan Shuʿayb ibn al-Ḥusayn al-Anṣārī (c. 509/1115–16–594/1198)* Cambridge, Islamic Texts Society, 1996

Charlotte Courreye 'L'Association des Oulémas Musulmans Algériens et la construction de l'État algérien indépendant: fondation, héritages, appropriations et antagonismes (1931-1991)', doctoral diss., INALCO, 2016

Vincent Crapanzano *The harkis: The wound that never heals* Chicago, IL, University of Chicago Press, 2011

Ahmed Dahmani *L'Algérie à l'épreuve: Économie politique des réformes, 1980–1997* Paris, L'Harmattan, 1999

Raphael Danziger *Abd al Qadir and the Algerians: Resistance to the French and internal consolidation* New York, NY, Holmes & Meier, 1977

Zakya Daoud and Benjamin Stora *Ferhat Abbas: Une utopie algérienne* Paris, Denoël, 1995

Bouziane Daoudi and Hadj Miliani *L'aventure du raï: Musique et société* Paris, Le Seuil, 1997

Dominique Darbois and Philippe Vigneau *Les Algériens en guerre* Milan, Feltrinelli, 1961

Eugène Daumas *La Kabylie* Paris, Jean-Paul Rocher, 2001 [1856]

Robert C. Davis *Christian slaves, Muslim masters: White slavery in the Mediterranean, the Barbary Coast, and Italy, 1500–1800* London, Palgrave, 2003

Simone de Beauvoir and Gisèle Halimi *Djamila Boupacha* Paris, Gallimard, 1962

Henri-Delmas de Grammont *Histoire d'Alger sous la domination turque, 1515–1830* Paris, Bouchene, 2002 [1st ed. Algiers, 1887]

Charles de Gaulle *Discours et messages* (5 vols.), Paris, Plon, 1970–71

Diego de Haëdo [Antonio de Sosa] *Histoire des rois d'Alger* (tr. and notes by H-D. de Grammont, Intro. Jocelyne Dakhlia), Paris, Bouchene, 1998 [1st ed. Algiers, 1881]

Xavier de Planhol *Nouveaux villages algérois (Atlas Blidéen, Chenoua, Mitidja occidentale)* Paris, PUF, 1961

Alain de Sérigny *La révolution du 13 mai* Paris, Plon, 1958

Alexis de Tocqueville *De la colonie en Algérie* ed. T. Todorov, Brussels, Complexe, 1988

Luc-Willy Deheuvels *Islam et pensée contemporaine en Algérie: La revue al-Açâla, 1971–1981* Paris, CNRS, 1991

Jean Déjeux 'Un bandit d'honneur dans l'Aurès de 1917 à 1921', *Revue de l'Occident musulman et de la Méditerranée* 26, 1 (1978), 35–54

Émile Dermenghem *Le culte des saints dans l'Islam maghrébin* Paris, Gallimard, 1954

Félix Dessoliers *L'Algérie libre: Étude économique sur l'Algérie* Algiers, Gojosso, 1895

Joseph Desparmet *Coutumes, institutions, croyances des indigènes de l'Algérie*, vol. 1, *L'Enfance, le marriage et la famille*, vol. 2, *La vie religieuse* Algiers, Typo-Litho/Carbonel, 1939

Karima Dirèche-Slimani *Chrétiens de Kabylie, 1873–1954: Une action missionnaire dans l'Algérie coloniale* Paris, Bouchene, 2004

Nacer Djabi *Li-mādhā ta'akhkhara al-rabī' al-jazā'irī?* Algiers, Chihab, 2012

Tahar Djaout *Le dernier été de la raison* Paris, Le Seuil, 1999

Daho Djerbal 'La guerre d'Algérie au miroir des écritures: Texte écrit et texte oral', pp. 529–42 in Daniel Rivet et al (eds), *La guerre d'Algérie au miroir des décolonisations françaises: Actes du colloque en l'honneur de Ch-R. Ageron* Paris, SFHOM, 2000

Daikha Dridi *Alger, blessée et lumineuse* Paris, Autrement, 2005

Bernard Droz and Évelyne Lever *Histoire de la guerre d'Algérie, 1954–1962* (2nd rev. ed.), Paris, Le Seuil, 1991

Peter Dunwoodie *Writing French Algeria* Oxford, Clarendon Press, 1998

Isabelle Eberhardt *Dans l'ombre chaude de l'Islam* ed. Victor Barrucand, Paris, Charpentier et Fasquelle, 1926

*Pages d'Islam* ed. Victor Barrucand, Paris, Fasquelle, 1932

Myron Echenberg '"Morts pour la France": The African soldier in France during the Second World War', *Journal of African History* 26, 4 (1985), 363–80

Dale F. Eickelman *Moroccan Islam: Tradition and society in a pilgrimage center*, Austin, TX, University of Texas Press, 1976

Maurice Eisenbeth 'Les juifs en Algérie et en Tunisie à l'époque turque, 1516–1830', *Revue africaine* 96 (1952), 114–87, 343–84

Hartmut Elsenhans *La Guerre d'Algérie, 1954–1962: La transition d'une France à une autre: Le passage de la IVe à la Ve République* Paris, Publisud, 1999

Marcel Émerit 'Les mémoires d'Ahmed, dernier bey de Constantine', *Revue africaine* 90 (1949), 65–125

*L'Algérie à l'époque d'Abd-el-Kader* Paris, Bouchene, 2002 [1951]

Marcel Émerit (ed), *La révolution de 1848 en Algérie: Mélanges d'histoire* Paris, Larose, 1949

Prosper Enfantin *Colonisation d'Algérie* Paris, P. Bertrand, 1843

John P. Entelis *Algeria: The revolution institutionalised* Boulder, CO, Westview, 1986

Colette Establet *Être caïd dans l'Algérie coloniale* Paris, CNRS, 1991

Bruno Étienne *L'Algérie, Cultures et Révolution* Paris, Seuil, 1976

Martin Evans *Algeria: France's undeclared war* Oxford, Oxford University Press, 2012

Giulia Fabbiano '"Pour moi, l'Algérie, c'est les Béni-Boudouane, le reste j'en sais rien" Construction, narrations et représentations coloniales en Algérie française', *Le Mouvement Social* 236 (2011), 47–60

'Les harkis du bachaga Boualam', pp. 633–37 in Bouchène et al (eds), *Histoire de l'Algérie à la période coloniale*

Frantz Fanon 'Décolonisation et indépendance' [April 1958], repr. ch. 8 in Frantz Fanon, *Pour la révolution africaine* Paris, La Découverte, 2001 [1964]

'L'Algérie se dévoile', ch. 1 in Frantz Fanon, *L'An V de la révolution algérienne* Paris, La Découverte, 2001 [1959]

*Les damnés de la terre* Paris, Gallimard, 1961

Charles-Henri Favrod (ed) *La révolution algérienne* Paris, Plon, 1959

Mouloud Feraoun *Journal, 1955–1962* Paris, Le Seuil, 1962

Barkahoum Ferhati 'La danseuse prostituée dite "Ouled Naïl", entre mythe et réalité (1830–1962): Des rapports sociaux et des pratiques concrètes', *Clio: Femmes, genre, histoire* 17 (2003), 101–13

Godfrey Fisher *Barbary legend: War, trade, and piracy in North Africa, 1415–1830* Oxford, Clarendon Press, 1957

Robert Fisk *The great war for civilisation: The conquest of the Middle East* London, Fourth Estate, 2005

Jacques Fontaine 'Les élections législatives algériennes: Résultats du premier tour', *Monde arabe: Maghreb-Machrek* 135 (January–March 1992), 155–65

France. Cabinet du Ministre de l'Algérie *1957 Algérie* Algiers, Service d'information du Gouvernement général de l'Algérie, 1957

Jacques Frémeaux *Les bureaux arabes dans l'Algérie de la conquête* Paris, Denoël, 1993

*De quoi fut fait l'empire: Les guerres coloniales au XIXè siècle* Paris, CNRS, 2014

Elizabeth D. Friedman *Colonialism and after: An Algerian Jewish community* South Hadley, MA, Bergin and Garvey, 1988

Ellen G. Friedman 'Christian captives at "hard labor" in Algiers, 16th–18th centuries', *International Journal of African Historical Studies* 13, 4 (1980), 616–32

*Spanish captives in North Africa in the early modern age* Madison, WI, University of Wisconsin Press, 1983

Julien Fromage 'Innovation politique et mobilisation de masse en "situation coloniale": un "printemps algérien" des années 1930? L'expérience de la Fédération des Élus Musulmans du Département de Constantine', (2 vols.), doctoral diss., EHESS, 2012

'L'expérience des "Jeunes Algériens" et l'émergence du militantisme moderne en Algérie (1880–1919)', pp. 238–44 in Bouchène et al (eds), *Histoire de l'Algérie à la période coloniale*

Monique Gadant *Le nationalisme algérien et les femmes* Paris, L'Harmattan, 1995

René Gallissot 'L'économie coloniale dans l'entre-deux-guerres', pp. 363–68 in Bouchène et al (eds), *Histoire de l'Algérie à la période coloniale*

William Gallois 'Genocide in nineteenth century Algeria', *Journal of Genocide Research* 15, 1 (January 2013), 69–88

*A history of violence in the early Algerian colony* Basingstoke, Palgrave, 2013

Émile-Félix Gautier *Un siècle de colonisation: Etudes au microscope* Paris, F. Alcan, 1930

*Le passé de l'Afrique du Nord: Les siècles obscurs* Paris, Payot, 1937

Lakhdar Ghettas 'Friendly foes: An international history of U.S.-Algerian relations, 1969–1978' PhD diss., London School of Economics, 2012

Francis Ghilès 'La dette extérieure algérienne: Situation et perspectives', *AAN* 28 (1989), 419–20

'L'armée a-t-elle une politique économique?' *Pouvoirs* 86 (1998), 85–106

Michael Gilsenan *Recognizing Islam: Religion and society in the modern Middle East*, (new ed.) London, I. B. Tauris, 2000 [1982]

Jonathan Glasser 'Edmond Yafil and Andalusi musical revival in early 20th-century Algeria', *International Journal of Middle East Studies* 44, 4 (November 2012), 671–92

*The lost paradise: Andalusi music in urban North Africa* Chicago, IL, Chicago University Press, 2016

Jane Goodman *Berber culture on the world stage: From village to video* Bloomington, IN, Indiana University Press, 2005

'The man behind the curtain: Theatrics of the state in Algeria', *Journal of North African Studies* 18, 5 (2013), 779–95

Jane Goodman and Paul Silverstein (eds), *Bourdieu in Algeria: Colonial politics, ethnographic practices, theoretical developments* Lincoln, NE, University of Nebraska Press, 2009

Emily Benichou Gottreich and Daniel J. Schroeter (eds), *Jewish culture and society in North Africa* Bloomington, IN, Indiana University Press, 2011

Marthe Gouvion and Edmond Gouvion *Kitab aâyane el-marhariba [The Book of Maghribi Notables]* Algiers, Imprimerie orientale Fontana, 1920

Isabelle Grangaud *La ville imprenable: Une histoire sociale de Constantine au 18$^{ème}$ siècle* Paris, EHESS, 2002

'Masking and unmasking the historic quarters of Algiers: The reassessment of an archive', ch. 6 in Zeynep Çelik, Julia Clancy-Smith, and Frances Terpak (eds), *Walls of Algiers: Narratives of the city through text and image* Seattle, WA, Washington University Press, 2009

'Le droit colonial au service des spoliations à Alger dans les années 1830', pp. 70–76 in Bouchène et al (eds), *Histoire de l'Algérie à la période coloniale*

Gilbert Grandguillaume *Nédroma, l'évolution d'une médina* Leiden, Brill, 1976

*Arabisation et politique linguistique au Maghreb* Paris, Maisonneuve et Larose, 1983

et al *Les Violences en Algérie* Paris, Odile Jacob, 1998

'M'hamed Ben Rahal, entre modernité et tradition', pp. 299–302 in Bouchène et al (eds), *Histoire de l'Algérie à la période coloniale*

Molly Greene *A shared world: Christians and Muslims in the early modern Mediterranean* Princeton, NJ, Princeton University Press, 2000

Fatma Zohra Guechi *Qsanṭīna fī 'ahd Ṣālaḥ Bay al-Bayāt* Constantine, Media-Plus, 2005

Didier Guignard 'L'affaire Beni Urjin: un cas de résistance à la mainmise foncière en Algérie coloniale', *Insaniyat* 25–26 (2004), 101–22

*L'abus de pouvoir dans l'Algérie coloniale (1880–1914)* Nanterre, Presses universitaires de Paris Ouest, 2010

'Le sénatus-consulte de 1863: La dislocation programmée de la société rurale algérienne', pp. 76–81 in Bouchène et al (eds), *Histoire de l'Algérie à la période coloniale*

'Les crises en trompe l'oeil de l'Algérie française des années 1890', pp. 218–23 in Bouchène et al (eds), *Histoire de l'Algérie à la période coloniale*

'Les inventeurs de la tradition "melk" et "arch" en Algérie', ch. 2 in Vanessa Gueno and Didier Guignard (eds), *Les acteurs des transformations foncières autour de la Méditerranée au XIXe siècle*, Paris, Karthala, 2013

Mohamed Hachemaoui 'Y-a-t-il des tribus dans l'urne? Sociologie d'une énigme électorale (Algérie)', *Cahiers d'études africaines* 205 (2012), 103–63

*Clientélisme et patronage dans l'Algérie contemporaine* Paris, Karthala, 2013

Mustafa Haddab 'Les intellectuels et le statut des langues en Algérie' (2 vols.), doctoral diss., Université Paris-VII (Jussieu), 1993

Bachir Hadj Ali *L'arbitraire* Paris, Éditions de Minuit, 1966

Abderrahmane Hadj Nacer *La martingale algérienne: Réflexions sur une crise* Algiers, Barzakh, 2011

Abderrahmane Hadj Nacer (ed), *Les cahiers de la réforme* (4 vols.), Algiers, ENAG, 1989

Sadek Hadjerès *Quand une nation s'éveille: Mémoires, t. 1, 1928–1949* Algiers, INAS, 2014

John Haldon *The state and the tributary mode of production* London, Verso, 1993

Ismaël Hamet *Les Musulmans français du Nord de l'Afrique* Paris, Armand Colin, 1906

Mohand Hamoumou 'L'histoire des harkis et Français musulmans: La fin d'un tabou?' pp. 317–44 in Mohammed Harbi and Benjamin Stora (eds), *La guerre d'Algérie, 1954–2004: La fin de l'amnésie* Paris, Robert Laffont, 2004

Mohand Hamoumou and Jean-Jacques Jordi, *Les harkis, une mémoire enfouie* Paris, Autrement, 1999

Adolphe Hanoteau and Aristide Letourneux *La Kabylie et les coutumes kabyles* (3 vols.), Paris, Bouchene, 2003 [1872–73]

Mohamed Harbi *Aux origines du FLN: le populisme révolutionnaire en Algérie* Paris, Bourgois, 1975

*Le FLN: mirage et réalité, des origines à la prise du pouvoir (1945 – 1962)* Paris, Jeune Afrique, 1980

(ed), *Les archives de la révolution algérienne* Paris, Jeune Afrique, 1981

*1954, la guerre commence en Algérie* Brussels, Complexe, 1984

'Le complot Lamouri', pp. 151–79 in Ch-R. Ageron (ed), *La guerre d'Algérie et les Algériens, 1954–1962* Paris, Armand Colin, 1997

*Une vie debout: Mémoires politiques. t.1: 1945–1962* Paris, la Découverte, 2001

Mohamed Harbi and Gilbert Meynier (eds), *Le FLN, documents et histoire* Paris, Fayard, 2004

Ali Haroun *L'été de la discorde: Algérie 1962* Algiers, Casbah, 2000

and Khaled Nezzar *Algérie: Échec à une regression programme* Paris, Publisud, 2001

Alf Andrew Heggoy *The French conquest of Algiers, 1803: An Algerian oral tradition* Athens, OH, Ohio University Center for International Studies, 1986

Jean-Robert Henry and François Balique *La doctrine coloniale du droit musulman algérien* Paris, CNRS, 1979

Ghazi Hidouci *Algérie: La libération inachevée* Paris, La Découverte, 1995

Eric Hobsbawm 'Peasants and politics', *Journal of Peasant Studies* 1 (1973–74), 3–22

Donald C. Holsinger 'Migration, commerce and community: The Mizabis in eighteenth and nineteenth century Algeria', *Journal of African History* 21, 1 (1980), 61–74

Peregrine Hordern and Nicholas Purcell *The corrupting sea: A study of Mediterranean history* Oxford, Blackwell, 2000

Alistair Horne *A Savage war of peace: Algeria 1954–1962* (rev. ed.), London, Macmillan, 1996 [1977]

Jim House and Neil MacMaster *Paris 1961: Algerians, state terror, and memory* Oxford, Oxford University Press, 2006

Ahmed Reda Huhu *Al-a'māl al-kāmila vol. 1, al-Qiṣaṣ* Algiers, Rabitat Kitab al-Ikhtilaf, 2001

International Crisis Group 'The civil concord: A peace initiative wasted' (Africa Report 31, 9 July 2001) Brussels, ICG, 2001

Julian Jackson 'De Gaulle et l'Algérie: Grand dessein ou adaptation empirique?' paper presented to the colloquium 'Pour une histoire critique et citoyenne: Le cas de l'histoire franco-algérienne', Ecole normale supérieure, Lyon, 21 June 2006. http://ens-web3.ens-lsh.fr/colloques/france-algerie/communication.php3?id_article=240

Jan C. Jansen *Erobern und erinnern: Symbolpolitik, öffentlicher Raum und französischer Kolonialismus in Algerien 1830–1950* Munich, Oldenbourg, 2014

Muhammad b. Abd al-Qadir al-Jaza'iri *Tuḥfat al-zā'ir fi ta'rīkh al-Jazā'ir wa'l-amīr 'Abd al-Qādir* (2 vols.), Beirut, Dar al-Yaqza 'l-'Arabiyya, 1964

Jennifer Johnson *The battle for Algeria: Sovereignty, health care, and humanitarianism* Philadelphia, PA, University of Pennsylvania Press, 2015

Vincent Joly 'Les généraux d'Afrique et la répression des troubles révolutionnaires de 1848', pp. 127–30 in Bouchène et al (eds), *Histoire de l'Algérie à la période coloniale*

Augustin Jomier 'Iṣlāḥ ibadite et intégration nationale: Vers une communauté mozabite? (1925–64)', *Revue des mondes musulmans et de la Mediterranée* 132 (December 2012), 175–95

'Un réformisme islamique dans l'Algérie coloniale. Oulémas ibadites et société du Mzab (c.1880–c.1970)' (2 vols.), doctoral diss., Université du Maine-Le Mans, 2015

Charles-André Julien *Histoire de l'Algérie contemporaine (vol. 1): La conquête et les débuts de la colonisation* Paris, PUF, 1964

*L'Afrique du nord en marche: nationalismes musulmans et souveraineté française* (3rd ed.), Paris, Julliard, 1972 [1952]

Rana Kabbani (ed), *The passionate nomad: The diary of Isabelle Eberhardt* London, Virago, 1987

Mahfoud Kaddache *La vie politique à Alger de 1919 à 1939* Algiers, SNED, 1970

*L'Émir Khaled: Documents et témoignages pour servir à l'étude du nationalisme en Algérie* Algiers, OPU, n.d. [1987]

*Histoire du nationalisme algérien: Question nationale et politique algérienne, 1919 – 1951* (2 vols., 2nd ed.), Algiers, ENAL, 1993

Ali Kafi *Du militant politique au dirigeant militaire: Mémoires (1946–1962)* Algiers, Casbah, 2002

Kamal Kateb 'Le bilan démographique de la conquête de l'Algérie (1830–1880)', pp. 82–88 in Bouchène et al (eds), *Histoire de l'Algérie à la période coloniale*

*Européens, 'indigènes' et juifs en Algérie (1830–1962): Représentations et réalités des populations* Paris, INED, 2001

Richard C. Keller *Colonial madness: Psychiatry in French North Africa* Chicago, IL, University of Chicago Press, 2007

Patrick Kessel and Giovanni Pirelli *Le peuple algérien et la guerre: Lettres et témoignages d'Algériens, 1954–1962* Paris, Maspéro, 1963

Yasmina Khadra [Mohamed Moulessouhoul] *Les agneaux du Seigneur* Paris, Julliard, 1998

Hamdan b. Uthman Khodja *Aperçu historique et statistique sur la Régence d'Alger, intitulé en arabe Le Miroir, traduit de l'arabe par H . . . D . . .*, *oriental* Paris, De Goetschy, 1833

Peter Knauss 'Algeria's "Agrarian revolution": Peasant control or control of peasants?' *African Studies Review* 20, 3 (December 1977), 65–78

Annette Kobak *Isabelle: The life of Isabelle Eberhardt* London, Chatto and Windus, 1988

Ahmed Koulakssis and Gilbert Meynier *L'Émir Khaled, premier za'im? Identité algérienne et colonialisme français* Paris, L'Harmattan, 1987

Ercüment Kuran 'La lettre du dernier dey d'Alger au Grand Vizir de l'empire ottoman', *Revue africaine* 96 (1952), 188–95

Séverine Labat *Les islamistes algériens: Entre les urnes et le maquis* Paris, Le Seuil, 1995

Mostefa Lacheraf 'Colonialisme et féodalités indigènes en Algérie', *Esprit* 213 (April 1954), 523–42

'Le patriotisme rural en Algérie', *Esprit* 224 (March 1955), 376–91

*Des noms et des lieux: Mémoires d'une Algérie oubliée* Algiers, Casbah, 1998

Annick Lacroix 'Une histoire sociale et spatiale de l'État dans l'Algérie colonisée: L'administration des postes, télégraphes et téléphones du milieu du XIXè siècle à la seconde guerre mondiale', doctoral diss., (2 vols.), ENS Cachan, 2014

Émile Larcher and Georges Rechtenwald *Traité élémentaire de législation algérienne* (3 vols., 3rd ed.), Paris, Arthur Rousseau, 1923

Abdallah Laroui *The history of the Maghrib: An interpretive essay* Princeton, NJ, Princeton University Press, 1977

Olivier Le Cour Grandmaison *Coloniser, exterminer: Sur la guerre et l'état colonial* Paris, Fayard, 2005

Roger Le Tourneau 'Le congrès du FLN (Alger, 16–21 avril 196[4]) et la charte d'Alger', *AAN* 2 (1963), 9–26

Jean Leca and Jean-Claude Vatin *L'Algérie politique: Institutions et régime* Paris, FNSP, 1975

Mohamed Lemkami *Les hommes de l'ombre: Mémoires d'un officier du MALG* Algiers, ANEP, 2004

René Lespès *Alger: esquisse de géographie urbaine* Algiers, J. Carbonel, 1925

Michel Levallois *Ismaÿl Urbain, 1812–1884: Une autre conquête de l'Algérie* Paris, Maisonneuve et Larose, 2001

Cathie Lloyd 'From taboo to transnational political issue: Violence against women in Algeria', *Women's Studies International Forum* 29 (2006), 453–62

Patricia M.E. Lorcin *Imperial identities: Stereotyping, prejudice and race in colonial Algeria* London, I.B. Tauris, 1995

Fatiha Loualich 'Les esclaves noirs à Alger (fin du XVIIIè – début du XIXè siècles): De l'esclave à l'affranchi, vers une relation d'allégéance', *Mélanges de l'école française de Rome* 115, 1 (2003), 515–22

Paul Lovejoy (ed), *Slavery on the frontiers of Islam* Princeton, NJ, Markus Wiener, 2004

Miriam R. Lowi *Oil wealth and the poverty of politics: Algeria compared* Cambridge, Cambridge University Press, 2009

Neil MacMaster *Colonial migrants and racism: Algerians in France, 1900–62* New York, NY, St Martin's, 1997

*Burning the veil: The Algerian war and the 'emancipation' of Muslim women, 1954–62* Manchester, Manchester University Press, 2009

'The roots of insurrection: The role of the Algerian village assembly (djemâa) in peasant resistance, 1863–1962', *Comparative Studies in Society and History* 55, 2 (April 2013), 419–47

Ahmad Tawfiq al-Madani *Kitāb al-Jazā'ir* Algiers, al-Matba'a 'l-'arabiyya fi 'l-jaza'ir, 1932

*Ḥarb al-thalāthami'at sana bayna 'l-jazā'ir wa-isbānyā, 1492–1792* Algiers, SNED, n.d. (1972?)

Alain Mahé *Histoire de la grande Kabylie, XIXè – XXè siècles* Paris, Bouchene, 2001

Ahmed Mahiou 'Note sur la constitution algérienne du 28 novembre 1996', *AAN* 35 (1996), 479–90

Réda Malek *Tradition et révolution: Le véritable enjeu* Algiers, Bouchène, 1991

Mouloud Mammeri (ed), *Les isefra de Si Mohand-ou-Mhand* Paris, Maspéro, 1982
    (ed), *Inna-yas Ccix Muḥend/Cheikh Mohand a dit* (2 vols.) Algiers, CNRPAH,
    2005
Gregory Mann 'What was the indigénat? The "empire of law" in French West
    Africa', *Journal of African History* 50, 3 (November 2009), 331–53
Mohamed el-Mansour *Morocco in the reign of Mawlay Sulayman* Wisbech, UK,
    MENAS Press, 1988
Nadir Marouf *Le chant arabo-andalou* Paris, L'Harmattan, 1995
Jean-Claude Martens *Le modèle algérien de développement: Bilan d'une décennie,
    1962–1972* Algiers, SNED, 1973
Luis Martinez *La guerre civile en Algérie, 1992 – 1998* Paris, Karthala, 1998
Claire Marynower 'Être socialiste dans l'Algérie coloniale: Pratiques, cultures et
    identités d'un milieu partisan dans le département d'Oran, 1919–1939',
    doctoral diss., Institut d'Études Politiques, Paris, 2013
Émile Masqueray *Formation des cités chez les populations sédentaires de l'Algérie:
    Kabyles du Djurdjura, Chaouïa de l'Aourâs, Beni Mezâb* Aix-en-Provence,
    Edisud, 1983
Jacques Massu *La vraie bataille d'Alger* Paris, Plon, 1971
Claire Mauss-Copeaux *Algérie, 20 août 1955: Insurrection, répression, massacres*
    Paris, Payot, 2011
Catherine Mayeur-Jaouen 'Le corps entre sacré et profane: La réforme des
    pratiques pèlerines en Égypte (XIXè-XXè siècles)', *Revue des mondes musul-
    mans et de la Méditerranée* 113–14 (2006), 301–25
Edward McAllister 'Immunity to the Arab Spring? Fear, fatigue and fragmenta-
    tion in Algeria', *New Middle Eastern Studies* 3 (2013), www.brismes.ac.uk/n
    mes/archives/1048
    'Reimagining the belle époque: Remembering nation-building in an Algiers
    neighbourhood', *Jadaliyya*, 4 November 2013, www.jadaliyya.com/pages/i
    ndex/14888/reimagining-the-belle-epoque_remembering-nation-bu
    'Yesterday's tomorrow is not today: Memory and place in an Algiers neigh-
    bourhood' DPhil diss., University of Oxford, 2014
James McDougall 'S'écrire un destin: L'association des 'ulama dans la révolution
    algérienne', *Bulletin de l'Institut d'histoire du temps présent* 83 (June 2004), 38–52
    *History and the culture of nationalism in Algeria* Cambridge, Cambridge University
    Press, 2006
    'After the war: Algeria's transition to uncertainty', *Middle East Report* 245
    (Winter 2007), 35–41
    'The secular state's Islamic empire: Muslim spaces and subjects of jurisdiction
    in Paris and Algiers, 1905–57', *Comparative Studies in Society and History* 52,
    3 (July 2010), 553–80
    'Histories of heresy and salvation: Arabs, Berbers, community and the state',
    ch. 1 in Katherine Hoffman and Susan Gilson Miller (eds), *Berbers and others:
    Beyond tribe and nation in North Africa* Bloomington, IN, Indiana University
    Press, 2010
    'Dream of exile, promise of home: Language, education, and Arabism in
    Algeria', *International Journal of Middle East Studies* 43, 2 (April 2011), 251–70
    'Ibn Bādīs, ʿAbd al-Ḥamīd', *Encyclopedia of Islam* (3rd ed.), Leiden, Brill, 2016

'A world no longer shared: Losing the *droit de cité* in nineteenth century Algiers', *Journal of the Economic and Social History of the Orient*, 60, 1 (February 2017), 18–49

'Rule of experts? Governing modernisation in late colonial French Africa', in Ed Naylor (ed), *France's modernising mission: Citizenship, welfare, and the ends of empire* Basingstoke, Palgrave, forthcoming

'The impossible Republic: The reconquest of Algeria and the decolonization of France, 1945–62', *Journal of Modern History*, forthcoming

David McMurray and Ted Swedenburg 'Rai tide rising', *Middle East Report* 169 (March–April 1991), 39–42

Mohamed Mechati *Parcours d'un militant* Algiers, Chihab, 2009

Ali Merad 'L'enseignement politique de Muhammad Abduh aux Algériens (1903)', *Confluent* 42–43 (1964), 643–89

*Le réformisme musulman en Algérie, 1925 – 1940: Essai d'histoire sociale et religieuse* Paris and the Hague, Mouton, 1967

Gustave Mercier *Le centenaire de l'Algérie, exposé d'ensemble* (2 vols.), Algiers, Soubiron, 1931

Abdelmadjid Merdaci *Dictionnaire des musiques et des musiciens de Constantine* Constantine, Simoun, 2002

Isabelle Merle 'De la "légalisation" de la violence en contexte colonial: Le régime de l'indigénat en question', *Politix* 66 (2004), 137–62

Lemnouar Merouche *Monnaies, prix et revenus, 1520–1830 (Recherches sur l'Algérie à l'époque ottomane t.1)* Paris, Bouchene, 2002

*La course, mythes et réalité (Recherches sur l'Algérie à l'époque ottomane t.2)* Paris, Bouchene, 2007

Messali Hadj (Ahmad Mesli) *Les mémoires de Messali Hadj, 1898–1938* Algiers, ANEP, 2005

Gilbert Meynier *L'Algérie révélée: la Guerre de 1914 – 1918 et le premier quart du XX^e Siècle* (2nd ed.), Paris, Bouchene, 2015 [1981]

*Histoire intérieure du FLN, 1954–1962* Paris, Fayard, 2002

Joseph Morgan *A complete history of Algiers* (2 vols.), London, 1728–29

Abderrahmane Moussaoui *Espace et sacré au Sahara: Ksour et oasis du sud-ouest algérien* Paris, CNRS, 2002

*De la violence en Algérie: les lois du chaos* Paris, Actes Sud, 2006

'Algérie, la guerre rejouée', *La pensée du midi* 3 (2003), 28–37

Jacob Mundy *Imaginative geographies of Algerian violence: Conflict science, conflict management, antipolitics* Stanford, CA, Stanford University Press, 2015

Youssef Nacib *Cultures oasiennes: Essai d'histoire sociale de l'oasis de Bou-Saâda* Paris, Publisud, 1986

*Une geste en fragments: Contribution à l'étude de la légende hilalienne des Hauts-Plateaux algériens* Paris, Publisud, 1994

Khaled Nezzar *Mémoires du Général Khaled Nezzar* Algiers, Chihab, 1999

Khaled Nezzar and Mohamed Maarfia *Le procès de Paris: L'armée algérienne face à la désinformation* Paris, Médiane, 2003

H. T. Norris *The pilgrimage of Ahmad, son of the little bird of paradise: An account of a 19th century pilgrimage from Mauretania to Mecca* Warminster, Aris and Philips, 1977

Andre Nouschi *Enquête sur le niveau de vie des populations rurales constantinoises, de la conquête jusqu'en 1919: Essai d'histoire économique et sociale* Paris, Presses universitaires de France, 1961

*La naissance du nationalisme algérien* Paris, Minuit, 1962

'La dépossession foncière et la paupérisation de la paysannerie algérienne', pp. 189–93 in Bouchène et al (eds), *Histoire de l'Algérie à la période coloniale*

Organisation de l'Armée secrète *OAS parle* Paris, Julliard, 1964

David Ottaway and Marina Ottaway *Algeria: The politics of a socialist revolution* Berkeley, CA, California University Press, 1970

Fatma Oussedik *Relire les ittifaqat: Essai d'interprétation sociologique* Algiers, ENAG, 2007

Daniel Panzac *Les corsaires barbaresques: La fin d'une épopée, 1800–1820* Paris, CNRS, 1999

Robert P. Parks 'Local-national relations and the politics of property rights in Algeria and Tunisia' PhD diss., University of Texas at Austin, 2011

'Algeria and the Arab uprisings', pp. 101–26 in Clement Henry and Ji-Hyang Jang (eds), *The Arab Spring: Will it lead to democratic transitions?* New York, NY, Palgrave Macmillan, 2013

'Public goods and service provision in Algeria: Subnational supply and demand', unpubl. working paper presented at the Middle East Centre, London School of Economics and Political Science, 2015

Paulette Péju *Les harkis à Paris* Paris, Maspéro, 1961

Henri Pellissier de Reynaud *Annales algériennes* (3 vols.), Paris, 1857

Henri Pensa *L'Algérie: Organisation politique et administrative – Justice - Sécurité – Instruction publique – Travaux publics … Voyage de la délégation de la commission sénatoriale d'études des questions algériennes présidée par Jules Ferry* Paris, Rothschild, 1894

Guy Pervillé *Les étudiants algériens de l'université française, 1880–1962* Paris, CNRS, 1984

'Guerre d'Algérie: L'abandon des harkis', pp. 303–12 in Charles-Robert Ageron (ed), *L'Algérie des Français* Paris, Le Seuil/L'Histoire, 1993

'Histoire de l'Algérie et mythes politiques algériens: Du "parti de la France" aux "anciens et nouveaux harkis"', pp. 323–31 in Ch-R. Ageron (ed), *La guerre d'Algérie et les Algériens, 1954–1962* Paris, Armand Colin, 1997

'La guerre d'Algérie: Combien de morts?' pp. 477–93 in Mohammed Harbi and Benjamin Stora (eds), *La guerre d'Algérie, 1954–2004: La fin de l'amnésie* Paris, Robert Laffont, 2004

Olivier Pétré-Grenouilleau *Saint-Simon: L'utopie ou la raison en actes* Paris, Payot, 2001

Jean-Pierre Peyroulou *Guelma, 1945: Une subversion française dans l'Algérie coloniale* Paris, La Découverte, 2009

'1919–1944: L'essor de l'Algérie algérienne', pp. 319–46 in Bouchène et al (eds), *Histoire de l'Algérie à la période coloniale*

Jean-André Peyssonnel *Voyage dans les régences de Tunis et d'Alger* (Intro., notes by Lucette Valensi), Paris, La Découverte, 1987

Andrew J. Pierre and William B. Quandt *The Algerian crisis: Policy options for the West* Washington, DC, Carnegie Endowment, 1996

Pascal Pinoteau 'Propagande cinématographique et décolonisation: L'exemple français (1949–1958)', *Vingtième siècle: Revue d'histoire* 80 (2003), 55–69

Charles-Louis Pinson de Ménerville, *Dictionnaire de législation algérienne: Code annoté et manuel raisonné* (3 vols., 2nd ed.), Algiers, Bastide, 1867–72

Jean-Louis Planche *Sétif 1945: Chronique d'un massacre annoncé* Paris, Perrin, 2010

David S. Powers 'Orientalism, colonialism, and legal history: The attack on Muslim family endowments in Algeria and India', *Comparative Studies in Society and History* 31, 3 (July 1993), 535–71

David Prochaska *Making Algeria French: Colonialism in Bône, 1870–1920* Cambridge, Cambridge University Press, 1990
    'History as literature, literature as history: Cagayous of Algiers', *American Historical Review* 101, 3 (June 1996), 670–711

Lucie Pruvost *Femmes d'Algérie: Société, famille et citoyenneté* Algiers, Casbah, 2002

Mouloud Qasim 'Al-inniya wa'l-aṣāla/Identité et authenticité', opening address delivered to the 4th Seminar of Islamic Thought, Constantine, 10 August 1970, *al-Aṣāla* 1 (March 1971), 3–8 (French tr.), 6–20 (Arabic text)

William B. Quandt *Revolution and political leadership: Algeria, 1954–68* Cambridge, MA, MIT Press, 1969
    *Between ballots and bullets: Algeria's transition from authoritarianism* Washington, DC, Brookings Institution, 1998

Malika Rahal 'L'Union démocratique du manifeste algérien (1946–1956): Histoire d'un parti politique. L'autre nationalisme algérien' (2 vols.), doctoral diss., INALCO, Paris, 2007
    'Prendre parti à Constantine: L'UDMA de 1946 à 1956', *Insaniyat: Revue algérienne d'anthropologie et de sciences sociales* 35–36 (2007), 63–77
    *Ali Boumendjel (1919–1957): Une affaire française, une histoire algérienne* Paris, Les Belles Lettres, 2010
    'Fused together and torn apart: Stories and violence in contemporary Algeria', *History and Memory* 24, 1 (2012), 118–51
    'A local approach to the UDMA: Local-level politics during the decade of political parties, 1946–56', *Journal of North African Studies* 18, 5 (December 2013), 703–24
    'La terrasse: Retour sur une histoire du temps présent', *Textures du temps*, 16 August 2015. http://texturesdutemps.hypotheses.org/1108

Karim Rahem *Le sillage de la tribu: Imaginaires politiques et histoire en Algérie, 1843–1993* Paris, Riveneuve, 2008

André Raymond 'The traditional Arab city', ch. 11 in Youssef Choueiri (ed), *A companion to the history of the Middle East* Malden, MA, Blackwell, 2005

Bekacem Recham 'Les militaires nord-africains pendant la seconde guerre mondiale', paper presented to the colloquium *Pour une histoire critique et citoyenne: Le cas de l'histoire franco-algérienne*, ENS, Lyon, June 2006. http://colloque-algerie.ens-lsh.fr/communication.php3?id_article=262#appel10

Hassan Remaoun 'La question de l'histoire dans le débat sur la violence en Algérie', *Insaniyat: Revue algérienne d'anthropologie et de sciences sociales* 10 (January–April 2000), 31–43

Annie Rey-Goldzeiguer *Le royaume arabe: la politique algérienne de Napoléon III, 1861–1870* Algiers, SNED, 1977

*Aux origines de la guerre d'Algérie, 1940–1945: De Mers-El-Kébir aux massacres du nord-constantinois* Paris, La Découverte, 2002

Charles Richard *Étude sur l'insurrection du Dhara: (1845–1846)* Algiers, Besancenez, 1846

Daniel Rivet *Le Maghreb à l'épreuve de la colonisation* Paris, Hachette, 2002

Jean-Baptiste Rivoire *Le crime de Tibhirine: Révélations sur les responsables* Paris, La Découverte, 2011

Hugh Roberts 'Political development in Algeria: The region of Greater Kabylia', DPhil diss., University of Oxford, 1980

'The FLN: French conceptions, Algerian realities', ch.8 in George Joffé (ed), *North Africa: Nation, State and Region*, London, Routledge, 1989

'Moral economy or moral polity? The political anthropology of Algerian riots' Crisis States Research Centre working papers series 1, 17 (2002). Crisis States Research Centre, London School of Economics and Political Science. http://eprints.lse.ac.uk/28292/

*The Battlefield. Algeria, 1988–2002: Studies in a broken polity* London, Verso, 2003

*Berber government: The Kabyle polity in pre-colonial Algeria* London, I.B. Tauris, 2014

Clifford Rosenberg *Policing Paris: The origins of modern immigration control between the wars* Ithaca, NY, Cornell University Press, 2006

Arlette Roth *Le théâtre algérien de langue dialectale, 1926–1964* Paris, Maspero, 1967

Ahmed Rouadjia *Les Frères et la mosquée: Enquête sur le mouvement islamiste en Algérie* Paris, Karthala, 1990

John Ruedy *Land policy in colonial Algeria: The origins of the rural public domain* Berkeley, CA, University of California Press, 1967

*Modern Algeria: The origins and development of a nation* Bloomington, IN, Indiana University Press, 1992

'Chérif Benhabylès and the young Algerians', pp. 345–69 in L. Carl Brown and Matthew S. Gordon (eds), *Franco-Arab encounters: Studies in memory of David C. Gordon* Beirut, AUB Press, 1996

Lucienne Saada *La geste hilalienne: Version de Bou Thadi (Tunisie)* Paris, Gallimard, 1985

Peter Sahlins *Forest rites: The war of the Demoiselles in nineteenth-century France* Cambridge, MA, Harvard University Press, 1994

Nacereddine Saidouni 'La vie rurale dans l'Algérois de 1791 à 1830', doctoral diss. (2 vols.), Université d'Aix-en-Provence, 1988

Mohammed Samraoui *Chronique des années de sang* Paris, Denoël, 2003

Henri Sanson *Laïcité islamique en Algérie* Paris, CNRS, 1983

Djilali Sari *Les villes précoloniales de l'Algérie occidentale: Nédroma, Mazouna, Kalâa* Algiers, SNED, 1970

*La dépossession des fellahs, 1830–1962* Algiers, SNED, 1975

*Le désastre démographique de 1867–68 en Algérie* Algiers, SNED, 1982

'Problèmes de la démographie contemporaine', ch. 5 in Djilali Sari, *A la recherche de notre histoire* Algiers, Casbah, 2003

'The role of the medinas in the reconstruction of Algerian culture and identity', pp. 69–80 in Susan Slyomovics (ed), *The walled Arab city in literature, architecture and history: The living medina in the Maghrib* London, Frank Cass, 2000

Marc Schade-Poulsen *Men and popular music in Algeria: The social significance of raï* Austin, TX, University of Texas Press, 1999

Adam Schatz 'Algeria's ashes', *New York Review of Books* 50, 11 (3 July 2003)

Judith Scheele *Village matters: Knowledge, politics and community in Kabylia, Algeria* Woodbridge, James Currey, 2009

Joshua Schreier *Arabs of the Jewish faith: The civilizing mission in colonial Algeria* New Brunswick, NJ, Rutgers University Press, 2010

'From Mediterranean merchant to French civilizer: Jacob Lasry and the economy of conquest in early colonial Algeria', *International Journal of Middle East Studies* 44, 4 (November 2012), 631–49

Ryme Seferdjeli 'French "reforms" and Muslim women's emancipation during the Algerian war', *Journal of North African Studies* 9, 4 (December 2004), 19–61

'La politique coloniale à l'égard des femmes "musulmanes"', pp. 359–63 in Bouchène et al (eds), *Histoire de l'Algérie à la période coloniale*

Jennifer Sessions *By sword and plow: France and the conquest of Algeria* Ithaca, NY, Cornell University Press, 2011

'Les colons avant la IIIè République: Peupler et mettre en valeur l'Algérie', pp. 64–70 in Bouchène et al (eds), *Histoire de l'Algérie à la période coloniale*

William Shaler *Sketches of Algiers, political, historical and civil* Boston, MA, Cummings, Hilliard and Co., 1826

Thomas Shaw *Travels, or observations relating to several parts of Barbary and the Levant* Oxford, Printed at the Theatre, 1738

Todd Shepard *The invention of decolonization: The Algerian war and the remaking of France* Ithaca, NY, Cornell University Press, 2006

Tal Shuval 'The Ottoman Algerian élite and its ideology', *International Journal of Middle East Studies* 32, 3 (August 2000), 323–44

*La ville d'Alger vers la fin du XVIIIè siècle: Population et cadre urbain* Paris, CNRS, 2002

Ounassa Siari Tengour 'Constantine, 1887: Des notables contre la "naturalisation"', pp. 235–38 in Bouchène et al (ed), *Histoire de l'Algérie à la période coloniale*

Paul Siblot '"Cagayous antijuif": Un discours colonial en proie à la racisation', *Mots* 15 (October 1987), 59–75

Nedjib Sidi Moussa 'Devenirs Messalistes (1925–2013): Sociologie historique d'une aristocratie révolutionnaire', doctoral diss., Université de Paris I, Panthéon-Sorbonne, 2013

Paul Silverstein 'An excess of truth: Violence, conspiracy theorizing, and the Algerian civil war', *Anthropological Quarterly* 75, 4 (Fall 2002), 643–74

*Algeria in France: Transpolitics, race and nation* Bloomington, IN, Indiana University Press, 2004

Fouzi Sisli 'The western media and the Algerian crisis', *Race and Class* 41, 3 (2000), 43–57

Susan Slyomovics *The merchant of art: An Egyptian Hilali oral epic poet in performance* Berkeley, CA, California University Press, 1987

Susan Slyomovics and Sarah Abrevaya Stein 'Jews and French colonialism in Algeria: An introduction', *Journal of North African Studies* 17, 5 (December 2012), 749–55

Abd al-Latif b. Ali al-Soltani *Al-mazdakiyya hiya aṣl al-ishtirākiyya* Casablanca, Muṭābi'at Dār al-Kitāb, 1974

Habib Souaïdia *La sale guerre* Paris, La Découverte, 2001

*Le procès de 'La sale guerre'* Paris, La Decouverte, 2002

Fouad Soufi 'La fabrication d'une mémoire: les médias algériens (1963 – 1995) et la guerre d'Algérie', pp. 289–303 in Ch-R. Ageron (ed), *La guerre d'Algérie et les Algériens, 1954–1962*

Jacques Soustelle *Aimée et souffrante Algérie* Paris, Plon, 1956

Sarah Abrevaya Stein 'The field of in between', *International Journal of Middle East Studies* 46, 3 (August 2014), 581–84

*Saharan Jews and the fate of French Algeria* Chicago, IL, University of Chicago Press, 2014

Benjamin Stora 'L'union des syndicats des travailleurs algériens USTA: La brève existence du syndicat messaliste (1956–1959)', *Le Mouvement social* 116 (July–September 1981), 95–122

*Messali Hadj, pionnier du nationalisme algérien (1898 – 1974)* Paris, L'Harmattan, 1986

*Les sources du nationalisme algérien: parcours idéologiques, origines des acteurs* Paris, L'Harmattan, 1988

*Histoire de l'Algérie coloniale, 1830 – 1954* Paris, La Découverte, 1991

*Ils venaient d'Algérie: Histoire de l'immigration algérienne en France, 1912–1992* Paris, Fayard, 1992

'Algérie: Absence et surabondance de mémoire', pp. 145–54 in Gilbert Grandguillaume et al (eds), *Les Violences en Algérie*, Paris, Odile Jacob, 1998

Judith Surkis 'Propriété, polygamie et statut personnel en Algérie coloniale, 1830–1873', *Revue d'histoire du XIXè siècle* 41 (2010), 27–48

Jean-Jacques Susini *Histoire de l'OAS* Paris, Table ronde, 1963

Ahmed Taleb Ibrahimi *De la décolonisation à la révolution culturelle, 1962 – 1972* Algiers, SNED, 1973

*Mémoires d'un Algérien (vol. 1), Rêves et épreuves (1932–1965), (vol. 2), La passion de bâtir (1965–1978)* Algiers, Casbah, 2006–8

Khaoula Taleb-Ibrahimi *Les Algériens et leur(s) langue(s): Éléments pour une approche sociolinguistique de la société algérienne* (2nd ed.), Algiers, Éditions El Hikma, 1997

Christelle Taraud *La prostitution coloniale: Algérie, Tunisie, Maroc, 1830–1962* Paris, Payot, 2003

Abdeljalil Temimi 'Lettre de la population algéroise au sultan Selim 1er en 1519', *Revue d'histoire maghrébine* 6 (1976), 95–101

Sylvie Thénault *Une drôle de justice: Les magistrats dans la guerre d'Algérie* Paris, La Découverte, 2001

*Histoire de la guerre d'indépendance algérienne* Paris, Flammarion, 2005

*Violence ordinaire dans l'Algérie coloniale: Camps, internements, assignations à résidence* Paris, Odile Jacob, 2011

'Le "code de l'indigénat"', pp. 200–06 in Bouchène et al (eds), *Histoire de l'Algérie à la période coloniale*

Martin Thomas 'Colonial violence in Algeria and the distorted logic of state retribution: The Sétif uprising of 1945', *Journal of Military History* 75, 1 (2011), 125–58

Al-Hachemi Tidjani, 'L'Association al-Qiyam et les valeurs islamiques', *Confluent* (1964), 609–35.

Rachid Tlemcani *State and revolution in Algeria* Boulder, CO, Westview, 1986

Houari Touati *Entre dieu et les hommes: Lettrés, saints et sorciers au Maghreb (17è siècle)* Paris, EHESS, 1994

John S. Trimingham *The Sufi orders in Islam* Oxford, Clarendon Press, 1971

Yvonne Turin *Affrontements culturels dans l'Algérie coloniale: Écoles, médecines, religion, 1830–1880* Paris, Maspero, 1971

Ismaël Urbain *L'Algérie pour les Algériens* Paris, Michel Lévy, 1861

*L'Algérie française, indigènes et immigrants* Paris, Challamel, 1862

Lucette Valensi *On the Eve of Colonialism: North Africa before the French conquest* New York, NY, Africana, 1977

Gérard van Krieken *Corsaires et marchands: Les relations entre Alger et les Pays-Bas, 1604–1830* Paris, Bouchene, 2002

Jean-Claude Vatin 'Popular puritanism versus state reformism: Islam in Algeria', ch.6 in James P. Piscatori (ed), *Islam in the political process*, Cambridge, Cambridge University Press, 1983

*L'Algérie politique: Histoire et société* (2nd ed.), Paris, FNSP, 1983, [1974]

Jean-Michel Venture de Paradis *Grammaire et dictionnaire abrégés de la langue berbère* Paris, Société de Géographie, 1844

*Tunis et Alger au XVIIIème siècle* (ed) Joseph Cuoq, Paris, Sindbad, 1983

Hugo Vermeren 'Les migrations françaises et européennes vers l'Algérie au début de la IIIè République', pp. 194–200 in Bouchène et al (eds), *Histoire de l'Algérie à la période coloniale*

Roger Vétillard *20 Août 1955 dans le nord-constantinois: Un tournant dans la guerre d'Algérie?* Paris, Riveneuve, 2012

Pierre Vidal-Nacquet *L'affaire Audin* Paris, Éditions de Minuit, 1958

*La torture dans la République: essai d'histoire et de politique contemporaines (1954–1962)* Paris, Éditions de Minuit, 1972

Natalya Vince *Our fighting sisters: Nation, memory and gender in Algeria, 1954–2012* Manchester, Manchester University Press, 2015

Daniel J. Vitkus (ed), *Piracy, slavery, and redemption: Barbary captivity narratives from early modern England* New York, NY, Columbia University Press, 2001

Maurice Viollette *L'Algérie vivra-t-elle? Notes d'un ancien Gouverneur-général* Paris, F. Alcan, 1931

Michael von Graffenried *Algérie, photographies d'une guerre sans images* Paris, Hazan, 1998

Peter von Sivers 'The realm of justice: apocalyptic revolts in Algeria (1849–1879)', *Humaniora Islamica* 1 (1973), 47–60
'Insurrection and accommodation: indigenous leadership in eastern Algeria, 1840–1900', *International Journal of Middle East Studies* 6, 3 (July 1975), 259–75
'Algerian landownership and rural leadership, 1860–1940: A quantitative approach', *The Maghreb Review* 4, 2 (1979), 58–62
'Les plaisirs du collectionneur: Capitalisme fiscal et chefs indigènes en Algérie (1840–1860)', *Annales ESC* 35, 3–4 (May–August 1980), 679–99
'Indigenous administrators in Algeria, 1846–1914: Manipulation and manipulators', *The Maghreb Review* 7, 5–6 (1982), 116–21
'Rural uprisings as political movements in colonial Algeria, 1851–1914', ch. 3 in Edmund Burke III and Ira Lapidus (eds), *Islam, politics and social movements* Berkeley, CA, University of California Press, 1988
Husayn b. Muhammad al-Wartilani *Nuzhat al-anẓār fi faḍl 'ilm al-ta'rīkh wa'l-akhbār* Beirut, Dar al-Kitab al-'Arabi, 1974
Patrick Weil *Qu'est-ce qu'un Français? Histoire de la nationalité française depuis la révolution* Paris, Grasset, 2002
Gillian Weiss 'Barbary captivity and the French idea of freedom', *French Historical Studies* 28, 2 (Spring 2005), 231–64
*Captives and corsairs: France and slavery in the early modern Mediterranean* Stanford, CA, Stanford University Press, 2011
Isabelle Werenfels *Managing instability in Algeria: Elites and political change since 1995* London, Routledge, 2009
Michael Willis *The Islamist challenge in Algeria: A political history* Reading, Ithaca Press, 1996
*Politics and power in the Maghreb: Algeria, Tunisia and Morocco from independence to the Arab Spring* London, Hurst, 2014
John Wright *The trans-Saharan slave trade* London, Routledge, 2007
Kateb Yacine *Abdelkader et l'indépendance algérienne* Algiers, Éditions En-Nahda, 1948
Xavier Yacono 'Peut-on évaluer la population de l'Algérie vers 1830?' *Revue africaine* 98 (1954), 277–307
'Les pertes algériennes de 1954 à 1962', *Revue de l'Occident musulman et de la Méditerranée* 34 (1982), 119–34
Nesroulah Yous with Salima Mellah *Qui a tué à Bentalha? Chronique d'un massacre annoncé* Paris, La Decouverte, 2000
Ahmad Sharif al-Zahhar *Mudhakkirāt al-Ḥājj Aḥmad al-Sharīf al-Zahhār naqīb al-ashrāf al-Jazā'ir 1168–1246/1754–1830* ed. Ahmad T. al-Madani, Algiers, SNED, 1974
Tahar Zbiri *Un demi-siècle de combat: Mémoires d'un chef d'état-major algérien* Algiers, Ech-Chourouk, 2012

# Index

CPSIA information can be obtained
at www.ICGtesting.com
Printed in the USA
LVHW051613271218
601927LV00010B/161/P